W9-DCN-708

Advance Praise for *MySQL Stored Procedure Programming*

"I didn't honestly believe a book could be written on this topic that wouldn't be too dry. But Guy and Steven show the depth of the subject and make the material available to readers. It was a wonderful read."

— Brian Aker, Director of Architecture, MySQL AB

"It was a pleasure to work with Guy and the editor at O'Reilly, doing the tech review of many of the chapters for this book. The authors have an excellent grasp of the subject matter. I found the material easy to read, with lots of code examples. MySQL users should find this book an excellent resource."

— Arjen Lentz, Community Relations Manager, MySQL AB

"Because MySQL usage is growing so rapidly among modern enterprises, developers and DBAs alike are desperately looking for expert help that shows them how to create high-performance stored procedures and other efficient MySQL code. I doubt that anyone will find better guides than Guy Harrison and Steven Feuerstein when it comes to advice on writing the absolutely best MySQL code."

— Robin Schumacher, Director of Product Management, MySQL AB

"This is the first book I've seen that really concentrates on MySQL's stored procedures. I found tips here that I'd never seen before."

— Peter Gulutzan, MySQL Software Architect

"MySQL 5.0 opens up a new world to MySQL users, and this book is a great tour guide."

— Andy Dustman, Author of MySQL Python API

"Guy and Steven have provided MySQL developers with a gem. They not only cover the nuts and bolts of writing stored procedures in MySQL, but also provide sound advice on designing database applications in the real world. In addition, they write with a sense of humor that makes the book a joy to read."

— James Cooper, Technology Consultant, Seattle, WA

MySQL Stored Procedure Programming

Other resources from O'Reilly

Related titles

MySQL in a Nutshell	SQL in a Nutshell
MySQL Cookbook™	SQL Cookbook™
High Performance MySQL	Learning SQL
Web Database Application with PHP and MySQL	SQL Pocket Guide

oreilly.com

oreilly.com is more than a complete catalog of O'Reilly books. You'll also find links to news, events, articles, weblogs, sample chapters, and code examples.

oreillynet.com is the essential portal for developers interested in open and emerging technologies, including new platforms, programming languages, and operating systems.

Conferences

O'Reilly brings diverse innovators together to nurture the ideas that spark revolutionary industries. We specialize in documenting the latest tools and systems, translating the innovator's knowledge into useful skills for those in the trenches. Visit *conferences.oreilly.com* for our upcoming events.

Safari Bookshelf (*safari.oreilly.com*) is the premier online reference library for programmers and IT professionals. Conduct searches across more than 1,000 books. Subscribers can zero in on answers to time-critical questions in a matter of seconds. Read the books on your Bookshelf from cover to cover or simply flip to the page you need. Try it today for free.

MySQL Stored Procedure Programming

Guy Harrison
with *Steven Feuerstein*

O'REILLY®

Beijing · Cambridge · Farnham · Köln · Paris · Sebastopol · Taipei · Tokyo

MySQL Stored Procedure Programming
by Guy Harrison with Steven Feuerstein

Copyright © 2006 O'Reilly Media, Inc. All rights reserved.
Printed in the United States of America.

Published by O'Reilly Media, Inc., 1005 Gravenstein Highway North, Sebastopol, CA 95472.

O'Reilly books may be purchased for educational, business, or sales promotional use. Online editions
are also available for most titles (*safari.oreilly.com*). For more information, contact our
corporate/institutional sales department: (800) 998-9938 or *corporate@oreilly.com*.

Editor: Deborah Russell	**Cover Designer:** Karen Montgomery
Production Editor: Adam Witwer	**Interior Designer:** David Futato
Production Services: Argosy Publishing	**Illustrators:** Robert Romano, Jessamyn Read, and Lesley Borash

Printing History:

March 2006:   First Edition.

 This book uses RepKover,™ a durable and flexible lay-flat binding.

ISBN: 0-596-10089-2
[M]

Table of Contents

Part II.   Stored Program Construction

Part III.   Using MySQL Stored Programs in Applications

Part IV.   Optimizing Stored Programs

Preface

Over the past five years or so, we have seen an explosion in the use of open source software in commercial environments. Linux has almost completely displaced various flavors of Unix as the dominant non-Windows operating system; Apache is by far the most significant web server; Perl and PHP form the foundation for millions of commercial web sites; while JBoss, Hibernate, Spring, and Eclipse are making strong inroads into the Java™ and J2EE development and application server markets. Although the world of relational databases continues to be dominated by the commercial players (Oracle, IBM, and Microsoft), the commercial use of open source databases is growing exponentially. MySQL is the dominant open source database management system: it is being used increasingly to build very significant applications based on the LAMP (Linux-Apache-MySQL-PHP/Perl/Python) and LAMJ (Linux-Apache-MySQL-JBoss) open source stacks, and it is, more and more, being deployed wherever a high-performance, reliable, relational database is required.

In the landmark book *The Innovators Dilemma*,* Clayton Christenmen provided the first widely accepted model of how open source and other "disruptive" technologies displace more traditional "sustaining" technologies.

When a disruptive technology—Linux for example—first appears, its capabilities and performance are typically way below what would be acceptable in the mainstream or high-end market. However, the new technology is highly attractive to those whose requirements or budgets preclude the use of the established commercial alternatives. These very low-end markets are typically associated with low profit margins and low revenues, so the established vendors are more than happy to retreat from these markets and give the disruptive technology this first foothold. As both the sustaining/traditional and disruptive/innovative technologies improve their capabilities, the disruptive technology becomes attractive to a wider segment of the mainstream market, while the established technologies tend to "overshoot" the demands of the average—or even high-end—consumer.

---

* *The Innovator's Dilemma*, Clayton Christensen (New York, 2000), HarperBusiness Essentials.

For the established vendors, the lower ends of the market are always associated with lower profit margins, and the established vendors make a series of apparently sensible business decisions to successively abandon these markets to the newer disruptive technologies. By the time the disruptive technology is seen as a real threat, the established vendors are unable to compete without cannibalizing the revenues from their established products, and in many cases, they become resigned to losing their market dominance.

Open source in general, and MySQL in particular, shows all the characteristics of the disruptive technology model. Five years ago, the capabilities of MySQL were so far behind the requirements of the majority of business users that the use of MySQL in a business environment was almost unheard of. However, MySQL—being free or extremely low cost*—had a definite appeal for users who were unable to afford a commercial relational database. As with most open source technologies, MySQL has experienced rapid technological development—adding transactions, subqueries, and other features normally associated with expensive commercial offerings. By the release of MySQL 4.0, MySQL was being used in a mission-critical manner by an increasing number of high-profile companies, including Yahoo, Google, and Sabre.

Meanwhile, the commercial database companies have been adding features that, although significant for the very high end of the market, have arguably exceeded the requirements of the majority of database users: they are more concerned with performance, manageability, and stability than with advanced features such as composite object data types, embedded Java Virtual Machines, or complex partitioning and clustering capabilities.

With the 5.0 release, MySQL has arguably crossed one of the last remaining capability thresholds for enterprise credibility. The ability to create stored procedures, functions, triggers, and updateable views removes one of the last remaining objections to using MySQL as a mainstream commercial database. For instance, prior to the introduction of stored procedures, MySQL could not claim Java J2EE certification, because the certification tests include stored procedure routines. While the "commercial" databases still include many features not found in MySQL, these features are often superfluous to the needs of mainstream database applications.

We believe that MySQL will continue to grow in significance as the premier open source RDBMS and that stored programs—procedures, functions, and triggers—will play a major part in the ongoing MySQL success story.

---

* MySQL has a dual licensing model that allows for free use in many circumstances but does require a commercial license in some circumstances.

First, a note about this book's title and terminology.

The IT industry, the media, and MySQL AB itself generally use the term *stored procedures* to refer to both stored procedures and stored functions. While this is technically inaccurate (a function is not a procedure), we felt that the title *MySQL Stored Procedure Programming* would most accurately and succinctly describe the purpose and content of this book. We also felt that the title *MySQL Stored Procedure, Function, and Trigger Programming* would just be too much of a mouthful!

To avoid any confusion, we use the general term *stored program* within this book to refer to the set of database routines that includes procedures, functions, and triggers, and to specific types of programs (e.g., stored procedures) when appropriate.

Objectives of This Book

The new capabilities provided by stored procedures, functions, and triggers (we call these, in general, *stored programs*) require new disciplines for MySQL developers, only some of whom will have prior experience in stored program development using other relational databases. Wise use of stored programs will lead to MySQL applications that are more robust, reliable, and efficient. However, inappropriate use of stored programs, or poorly constructed stored programs, can lead to applications that perform poorly, are hard to maintain, or are unreliable.

Thus, we see the need for a book that will help MySQL practitioners realize the full potential of MySQL stored programs. We hope this book will help you to use stored programs appropriately, and to write stored procedures, functions, and triggers that are reliable, correct, efficient, and easy to maintain.

Best practice stored program development relies on four fundamentals:

Appropriate use
> Used appropriately, stored programs can improve the performance, reliability, and maintainability of your MySQL-based application. However, stored programs are not a universal panacea, and they should be used only where appropriate. In this book, we describe where stored programs can be used to good effect, and we outline some significant patterns (and anti-patterns) involving stored programs.

Reliability
> As with any programming language, the MySQL stored program language allows you to write code that will behave predictably and correctly in all possible circumstances, but the language also allows you to write code subject to catastrophic failure or unpredictable behavior when unanticipated scenarios arise.

We outline how to write stored programs that can deal appropriately with error conditions, that fail gracefully and predictably, and that are—to the greatest extent possible—bug free.

Maintainability

We have all had that sinking feeling of having to amend some piece of code—whether written by a colleague or by ourselves—and finding that the intention, logic, and mechanisms of the code are almost impossible to understand. So-called "spaghetti" code can be written in any language, and MySQL stored programs are no exception. We explain how to construct code that is easily maintained through best practice naming conventions, program structure, commenting, and other mechanisms.

Performance

Any nontrivial application has to perform to either implicitly or explicitly stated performance requirements. The performance of the database access code—SQL and stored program code—is often the most significant factor in overall application performance. Furthermore, poorly constructed database code often fails to scale predictably or at all when data or transaction volumes increase. In this book, we show you when to use stored programs to improve application performance and how to write stored program code that delivers the highest possible performance. The SQL within a stored program is often the most performance-critical part of the stored program, so we explain in depth how to write high-performance SQL as well.

Structure of This Book

MySQL Stored Procedure Programming is divided into four major sections:

Part I, *Stored Programming Fundamentals*

This first part of the book introduces the MySQL stored program language and provides a detailed description of the language structure and usage.

- Chapter 1, *Introduction to MySQL Stored Programs,* asks the fundamental questions: Where did the language come from? What is it good for? What are the main features of the language?

- Chapter 2, *MySQL Stored Programming Tutorial,* is a tutorial that is designed to get you started with the language as quickly as possible; it shows you how to create basic stored programs of each type and provides interactive examples of major language functions.

- Chapter 3, *Language Fundamentals,* describes how to work with variables, literals, operators, and expressions.

- Chapter 4, *Blocks, Conditional Statements, and Iterative Programming,* explains how to implement conditional commands (IF and CASE) and looping structures.

- Chapter 5, *Using SQL in Stored Programming*, discusses how SQL can be used within the language.
- Chapter 6, *Error Handling*, provides the details of how errors can be handled.

Part II, *Stored Program Construction*

This part of the book describes how you can use the elements described in Part I to build functional and useful stored programs.

- Chapter 7, *Creating and Maintaining Stored Programs*, outlines the statements available for creating and modifying stored programs and provides some advice on how to manage your stored program source code.
- Chapter 8, *Transaction Management*, explains the fundamentals of transaction handling in stored programs.
- Chapter 9, *MySQL Built-in Functions*, details the built-in functions that can be used in stored programs.
- Chapter 10, *Stored Functions,* describes how you can create and use one particular type of stored program: the stored function.
- Chapter 11, *Triggers*, describes another special type of stored program—the database trigger—which is activated in response to DML (Data Manipulation Language) executed on a database table.

Part III, *Using MySQL Stored Programs in Applications*

Stored programs can be used for a variety of purposes, including the implementation of utility routines for use by MySQL DBAs and developers. However, the most important use of stored programs is within applications, as we describe in this part of the book. Stored programs allow us to move some of our application code into the database server itself; if we do this wisely, we may benefit from an application that will then be more secure, efficient, and maintainable.

- Chapter 12, *Using MySQL Stored Programs in Applications*, considers the merits of and best practices for using stored programs inside modern—typically, web-based—applications. The other chapters in this part of the book show you how to use stored procedures and functions from within the development languages most commonly used in conjunction with MySQL.
- Chapter 13, *Using MySQL Stored Programs with PHP*, describes the use of stored programs from PHP. We primarily discuss the `mysqli` and PDO interfaces—recently bundled by MySQL asConnector/PHP—and their stored program support.
- Chapter 14, *Using MySQL Stored Programs with Java*, describes the use of stored programs from Java and includes the use of stored programs using JDBC, Servlets, Enterprise JavaBeans™, Hibernate, and Spring.
- Chapter 15, *Using MySQL Stored Programs with Perl*, describes the use of stored programs from Perl.

- Chapter 16, *Using MySQL Stored Programs with Python*, describes the use of stored programs from Python.
- Chapter 17, *Using MySQL Stored Programs with .NET*, describes the use of stored programs from .NET languages such as C# and VB.NET.

Part IV, *Optimizing Stored Programs*

This final part of the book hopes to take you from "good" to "great." Getting programs to work correctly is hard enough: any program that works is probably a good program. A great program is one that performs efficiently, is robust and secure, and is easily maintained.

- Chapter 18, *Stored Program Security,* discusses the unique security concerns and opportunities raised by stored procedures and functions.
- Chapter 19, *Tuning Stored Programs and Their SQL.* This chapter, along with Chapters 20 through 22, covers the performance optimization of stored programs. This chapter kicks off with a general discussion of performance tuning tools and techniques.
- Chapter 20, *Basic SQL Tuning.* The performance of your stored programs will be largely dependent on the performance of the SQL inside them, so this chapter provides guidelines for tuning basic SQL.
- Chapter 21, *Advanced SQL Tuning.* This chapter builds on Chapter 20, describing more advanced tuning approaches.
- Chapter 22, *Optimizing Stored Program Code,* covers the performance tuning of the stored program code itself.
- Chapter 23, *Best Practices in MySQL Stored Program Development,* wraps up the book with a look at best practices in stored program development. These guidelines should help you write stored programs that are fast, secure, maintainable, and bug free.

You'll find that a significant proportion of the book includes material that pertains not only to stored program development, but also to development in other languages such as PHP or Java. For instance, we believe that you cannot write a high-performance stored program without tuning the SQL that the program contains; therefore, we have devoted significant coverage to SQL tuning—material that would also be of benefit regardless of the language in which the SQL is embedded. Likewise, some of the discussions around transaction design and security could be applicable in other languages.

What This Book Does Not Cover

This book is not intended to be a complete reference to MySQL. It focuses on the stored program language. The following topics are therefore outside the scope of this book and are not covered, except in an occasional and peripheral fashion:

The SQL language

We assume that you already have a working knowledge of the SQL language, and that you know how to write `SELECT`, `UPDATE`, `INSERT`, and `DELETE` statements.

Administration of MySQL databases

While DBAs can use this book to learn how to write the code needed to build and maintain databases, this book does not explore all the nuances of the DDL (Data Definition Language) of MySQL's SQL.

Conventions Used in This Book

The following conventions are used in this book:

Italic

Used for URLs and for emphasis when introducing a new term.

`Constant width`

Used for MySQL and SQL keywords and for code examples.

`Constant width bold`

In some code examples, highlights the statements being discussed.

`Constant width italic`

In some code examples, indicates an element (e.g., a filename) that you supply.

UPPERCASE

In code examples, generally indicates MySQL keywords.

lowercase

In code examples, generally indicates user-defined items such as variables, parameters, etc.

punctuation

In code examples, enter exactly as shown.

indentation

In code examples, helps to show structure but is not required.

`--`

In code examples, begins a single-line comment that extends to the end of a line.

/* and */

In code examples, delimit a multiline comment that can extend from one line to another.

.   In code examples and related discussions, qualifies a reference by separating an object name from a component name.

[ ] In syntax descriptions, enclose optional items.

{ } In syntax descriptions, enclose a set of items from which you must choose only one.

| In syntax descriptions, separates the items enclosed in curly brackets, as in {TRUE | FALSE}.

... In syntax descriptions, indicates repeating elements. An ellipsis also shows that statements or clauses irrelevant to the discussion were left out.

 Indicates a tip, suggestion, or general note. For example, we'll tell you if a certain setting is version-specific.

 Indicates a warning or caution. For example, we'll tell you if a certain setting has some kind of negative impact on the system.

Which Version?

This book describes the stored program language introduced in MySQL 5.0. At the time the book went to press, MySQL 5.0.18 was the most recently available binary Community edition, although we were working with versions up to 5.1.7 built directly from source code.

Resources Available at the Book's Web Site

We have provided all of the code included in this book on the book's O'Reilly web site. Go to:

http://www.oreilly.com/catalog/mysqlspp

and click on the Examples link to go to the book's web companion.

To find the code for a specific example, look for the file corresponding to the example or figure in which that code appeared. For instance, to obtain the code for Example 3-1, you would access the file *example0301.sql*.

At this web site you will also be able to download a dump file containing the sample database used throughout the book, the source code to some utilities we used during our development of the examples, errata, and addenda to the book's content.

In particular, we will use this web site to keep you posted on the status of any restrictions or problems relating to stored programs in MySQL or other tools. Because the MySQL stored program language is relatively new, MySQL AB will be refining the behavior and capabilities of the language in each new release of the MySQL server. Also, support for stored programs in other languages (PHP, Perl, Python, Hibernate) was sometimes only partially completed as this book went to press; we'll keep you updated with the status of these languages at the web site.

Using Code Examples

This book is here to help you get your job done. In general, you may use the code in this book in your programs and documentation. You do not need to contact us for permission unless you're reproducing a significant portion of the code. For example, writing a program that uses several chunks of code from this book does not require permission. Selling or distributing a CD-ROM of examples from O'Reilly books *does* require permission. Answering a question by citing this book and quoting example code does not require permission. Incorporating a significant amount of example code from this book into your product's documentation *does* require permission.

We appreciate, but do not require, attribution. An attribution usually includes the title, author, publisher, and ISBN. For example: "*MySQL Stored Procedure Programming* by Guy Harrison with Steven Feuerstein. Copyright 2006 O'Reilly Media, Inc., 0-596-10089-2."

If you feel that your use of code examples falls outside fair use or the permission given here, feel free to contact us at *permissions@oreilly.com*.

Safari® Enabled

 When you see a Safari® Enabled icon on the cover of your favorite technology book, that means the book is available online through the O'Reilly Network Safari Bookshelf.

Safari offers a solution that's better than e-books. It's a virtual library that lets you easily search thousands of top tech books, cut and paste code samples, download chapters, and find quick answers when you need the most accurate, current information. Try it for free at *http://safari.oreilly.com*.

How to Contact Us

We have tested and verified the information in this book and in the source code to the best of our ability, but given the amount of text and the rapid evolution of technology, you may find that features have changed or that we have made mistakes. If so, please notify us by writing to:

O'Reilly Media, Inc.
1005 Gravenstein Highway North
Sebastopol, CA 95472
800-998-9938 (in the United States or Canada)
707-829-0515 (international or local)
707-829-0104 (fax)

You can also send messages electronically. To be put on the mailing list or request a catalog, send email to:

info@oreilly.com

To ask technical questions or comment on the book, send email to:

bookquestions@oreilly.com

As mentioned in the earlier section, we have a web site for this book where you can find code, errata (previously reported errors and corrections available for public view), and other book information. You can access this web site at:

http://www.oreilly.com/catalog/mysqlspp

For more information about this book and others, see the O'Reilly web site:

http://www.oreilly.com

Acknowledgments

We'd first like to thank Debby Russell, our editor at O'Reilly Media, for supporting us through this endeavor and for being the organizing force behind the end-to-end project. Many other people at O'Reilly also played a big role in the book's development, including Adam Witwer, the production editor, and Rob Romano, the illustrator; additional production services were provided by Argosy Publishing.

The role of the technical reviewers in the production of this book was absolutely critical. The scope of coverage included not just the MySQL stored program language but also five other development languages and many features of the MySQL 5.0 server itself. Furthermore, the stored program language was evolving as we constructed the book. Without the valuable inputs from our technical reviewers, we would have been unable to achieve any reasonable degree of accuracy and currency across the entire scope. Reviewers included Tim Allwine, Brian Aker, James Cooper, Greg Cottman, Paul DuBois, Andy Dustman, Peter Gulutzan, Mike Hillyer, Arjen Lentz, and Mark Matthews. Thanks guys!

To the open source community in general and to the MySQL development community in particular, we also give thanks. The availability of free (both as in beer and as in speech) software of such quality and innovation is a source of constant amazement and gratification. Many in the MySQL and associated communities contributed to the existence of this in so many ways.

We worked with some of the maintainers of the various open source interfaces to MySQL to ensure that these were able to support some of the new features introduced in MySQL 5.0. Thanks to Wez Furlong, Patrick Galbraith, and Andy Dustman in particular for their help in patching the PHP PDO, Perl DBI, and Python MySQLdb interfaces.

From Guy: On a personal note, I would like to—as always—thank my wife Jenni and children Christopher, Katherine, Michael, and William for putting up with me during this and other writing projects. Thanks with much love. Also—of course—thanks to Steven for working with me on this book.

From Steven: I have spent the last 10 years studying, working with, and writing about the Oracle PL/SQL language. That experience has demonstrated very clearly to me the value and importance of stored programs. I was very excited, therefore, when Guy invited me to work with him on a book about MySQL stored programs. I have no doubt that this new functionality will help extend the reach and usefulness of MySQL, and I thank Guy for the opportunity to help MySQL programmers make the most of this key open source relational database.

Stored Programming Fundamentals

This first part of the book introduces the MySQL stored program language and provides a detailed description of the language structure and usage. Chapter 1 asks the fundamental questions: Where did the language come from? What is it good for? What are the main features of the language? Chapter 2 is a tutorial that is designed to get you started with the language as quickly as possible; it shows you how to create basic stored programs of each type and provides interactive examples of major language functions. Chapters 3 through 6 describe the MySQL stored program language in detail: how to work with variables, how to implement conditional and iterative control structures, how SQL can be used within the language, and how errors can be handled.

## CHAPTER 1

Introduction to MySQL Stored Programs

When MySQL first emerged into the IT world in the mid-1990s, it had few of the characteristics normally associated with commercial relational databases. Features such as transactional support, subqueries, views, and stored procedures were conspicuously absent. Subsequent releases provided most of the missing features, and now—with the introduction of stored procedures, functions, and triggers in MySQL 5 (as well as updateable views and a data dictionary)—the feature gap between MySQL and other relational database systems is narrow indeed.

The introduction of stored programs (our generic term for stored procedures, functions, and triggers) has significance beyond simply winning a features war with competitive database systems. Without stored programs, MySQL cannot claim full compliance with a variety of standards, including ANSI/ISO standards that describe how a DBMS should execute stored programs. Furthermore, judicious use of stored programs can lead to greater database security and integrity and can improve overall application performance and maintainability. We outline these advantages in greater detail later in this chapter.

In short, stored programs—procedures, functions, and triggers—add significantly to the capabilities of MySQL, and a working knowledge of stored programming should be an essential skill for the MySQL professional.

This chapter introduces the MySQL stored program language, its origins, and its capabilities. It also offers a guide to additional resources for MySQL stored program developers and some words of overall development advice.

What Is a Stored Program?

A database *stored program*—sometimes called a *stored module* or a *stored routine*—is a computer program (a series of instructions associated with a *name*) that is stored within, and executes within, the database server. The source code and (sometimes) any compiled version of the stored program are almost always held within the database server's system tables as well. When the program is executed, it is executed within the memory address of a database server process or thread.

There are three major types of MySQL stored programs:

Stored procedures

Stored procedures are the most common type of stored program. A stored procedure is a generic program unit that is executed on request and that can accept multiple input and output parameters.

Stored functions

Stored functions are similar to stored procedures, but their execution results in the return of a single value. Most importantly, a stored function can be used within a standard SQL statement, allowing the programmer to effectively extend the capabilities of the SQL language.

Triggers

Triggers are stored programs that are activated in response to, or are *triggered* by, an activity within the database. Typically, a trigger will be invoked in response to a DML operation (INSERT, UPDATE, DELETE) against a database table. Triggers can be used for data validation or for the automation of denormalization.

 Other databases offer additional types of stored programs, including packages and classes, both of which allow you to define or collect multiple procedures and functions within a single, named context. MySQL does not currently support such structures—in MySQL, each stored program is a standalone entity.

Throughout this book, we are going to use the term *stored programs* to refer to stored procedures, functions, and triggers, and the term *stored program language* to refer to the language used to write these programs. Most of the facilities in the stored program language are applicable across procedures, functions, and triggers; however, both functions and triggers have strict limitations on the language features that may be used with them. Thus, we dedicate a chapter to each of these program types in which we explain these limitations.

Why Use Stored Programs?

Developers have a multitude of programming languages from which to choose. Many of these are not database languages, which means that the code written in these languages does not reside in, nor is it managed by, a database server. Stored programs offer some very important advantages over more general-purpose languages, including:

- The use of stored programs can lead to a more secure database.

- Stored programs offer a mechanism to abstract data access routines, which can improve the maintainability of your code as underlying data structures evolve.

- Stored programs can reduce network traffic, because the program can work on the data from within the server, rather than having to transfer the data across the network.

- Stored programs can be used to implement common routines accessible from multiple applications—possibly using otherwise incompatible frameworks—executed either within or from outside the database server.

- Database-centric logic can be isolated in stored programs and implemented by programmers with more specialized, database experience.

- The use of stored programs can, under some circumstances, improve the portability of your application.

While this is an impressive list of advantages (many of which will be explored in greater detail in this book), we do *not* recommend that you immediately move all your application logic into stored programs. In today's rich and complex world of software technology, you need to understand the strengths *and* weaknesses of each possible element in your software configuration, and figure out how to maximize each element. We spend most of Chapter 12 evaluating how and where to apply MySQL stored programs.

The bottom line is that, used correctly, stored programs—procedures, functions, and triggers—can improve the performance, security, maintainability, and reliability of your applications.

Subsequent chapters will explore how to construct MySQL stored programs and use them to best advantage. Before plunging into the details, however, let's look at how the technology developed and take a quick tour of language capabilities.

A Brief History of MySQL

MySQL has its roots in an in-house (non-SQL) database system called Unireg used by the Swedish company TcX that was first developed in the 1980s and optimized for data warehousing. The author of Unireg, Michael "Monty" Widenius, added a SQL interface to Unireg in 1995, thus creating the first version of MySQL. David Axmark, from Detron HB, approached Monty proposing to release MySQL to the world under a "dual licensing" model that would allow widespread free use, but would still allow for commercial advantage. Together with Allan Larsson, David and Monty became the founders of the MySQL company.

The first widely available version of MySQL was 3.11, which was released in mid-1996. Adoption of MySQL grew rapidly—paralleling the adoption of other related open source technologies. By the year 2005, MySQL could lay claim to over 6 million installations of the MySQL database.

Version 3 of MySQL, while suitable for many types of applications (particularly read-intensive web applications), lacked many of the features normally considered mandatory in a relational database. For instance, transactions, views, and subqueries were not initially supported.

However, the MySQL system was designed to support a particularly extensible data access architecture, in which the SQL layer was decoupled from the underlying data and file access layer. This allowed custom "storage engines" to be employed in place of—or in combination with—the native ISAM (Indexed Sequential Access Method)-based MySQL engine. The Berkeley-DB (BDB) database (from Sleepycat Software) was integrated as an optional storage engine in version 3.23.34 in early 2001. BDB provided MySQL with its initial transaction processing capability. At about the same time, the open source InnoDB storage engine became available and quickly became a natively available option for MySQL users.

The 4.0 release in early 2002 fully incorporated the InnoDB option, making transactions easily available for all MySQL users, and also added improved replication capabilities. The 4.1 release in early 2004 built on the 4.0 release and included—among many other improvements—support for subqueries and Unicode character sets.

With the 5.0 release of MySQL in late 2005, MySQL took an important step closer to functional parity with commercial RDBMS systems; it introduced stored procedures, functions, and triggers, the addition of a data dictionary (the SQL-standard INFORMATION_SCHEMA), and support for updateable views.

The 5.1 release, scheduled for the second half of 2006, will add important factilities such as an internal scheduler, table partitioning, row-based replication, and many other significant enhancements.

MySQL Stored Procedures, Functions, and Triggers

MySQL chose to implement its stored program language within the MySQL server as a subset of the ANSI SQL:2003 SQL/PSM (Persistent Stored Module) specification. What a mouthful! Essentially, MySQL stored programs—procedures, functions, and triggers—comply with the only available open standard for these types of programs —the ANSI standard.

Many MySQL and open source aficionados had been hoping for a stored program language implementation based on an open source language such as PHP or Python. Others anticipated a Java™-based implementation. However, by using the ANSI specification—the same specification adopted within IBM's DB2 database—MySQL has taken advantage of years of work done by the ANSI committee, which included representatives from all of the major RDBMS companies.

The MySQL stored program language is a block-structured language (like Pascal) that includes familiar commands for manipulating variables, implementing conditional execution, performing iterative processing, and handling errors. Users of existing stored program languages, such as Oracle's PL/SQL or SQL Server's Transact-SQL, will find features of the language very familiar. Programmers familiar with other languages, such as PHP or Java, might consider the language somewhat simplistic, but they will find that it is easy to learn and that it is well matched to the common requirements of database programming.

A Quick Tour

Let's look at a few quick examples that demonstrate some key elements of both the structure and the functionality of MySQL's stored program language. For a full tutorial, see Chapter 2.

Integration with SQL

One of the most important aspects of MySQL's stored program language is its tight integration with SQL. You don't need to rely on intermediate software "glue," such as ODBC (Open DataBase Connectivity) or JDBC (Java DataBase Connectivity), to construct and execute SQL statements in your stored program language programs. Instead, you simply write the UPDATE, INSERT, DELETE, and SELECT statements directly into your code, as shown in Example 1-1.

Example 1-1. Embedding SQL in a stored program

```
1   CREATE PROCEDURE example1( )
2   BEGIN
3     DECLARE l_book_count INTEGER;
4
5     SELECT COUNT(*)
6       INTO l_book_count
7       FROM books
8      WHERE author LIKE '%HARRISON,GUY%';
9
10    SELECT CONCAT('Guy has written (or co-written) ',
11           l_book_count ,
12           ' books.');
13
14    -- Oh, and I changed my name, so...
15    UPDATE books
16       SET author = REPLACE (author, 'GUY', 'GUILLERMO')
17     WHERE author LIKE '%HARRISON,GUY%';
18
19  END
```

Let's take a more detailed look at this code in the following table:

Line(s)	Explanation
1	This section, the header of the program, defines the name (example1) and type (PROCEDURE) of our stored program.
2	This BEGIN keyword indicates the beginning of the *program body*, which contains the declarations and executable code that constitutes the procedure. If the program body contains more than one statement (as in this program), the multiple statements are enclosed in a BEGIN-END block.
3	Here we declare an integer variable to hold the results of a database query that we will subsequently execute.
5-8	We run a query to determine the total number of books that Guy has authored or coauthored. Pay special attention to line 6: the INTO clause that appears within the SELECT serves as the "bridge" from the database to the local stored program language variables.
10-12	We use a simple SELECT statement (e.g., one without a FROM clause) to display the number of books. When we issue a SELECT without an INTO clause, the results are returned directly to the calling program. This is a non-ANSI extension that allows stored programs to easily return result sets (a common scenario when working with SQL Server and other RDBMSs).
14	This single-line comment explains the purpose of the UPDATE.
15-17	Guy has decided to change the spelling of his first name to "Guillermo"—he's probably being stalked by fans of his Oracle book—so we issue an UPDATE against the books table. We take advantage of the built-in REPLACE function to locate all instances of "GUY" and replace them with "GUILLERMO".

Control and Conditional Logic

Of course, real-world applications are full of complex conditions and special cases, so you are unlikely to be able to simply execute a series of SQL statements. The stored program language offers a full range of control and conditional statements so that we can control which lines of our programs actually run under a given set of circumstances. These include:

IF and CASE statements
> Both of these statements implement conditional logic with different structures. They allow you to express logic such as "If the page count of a book is greater than 1000, then…".

A full complement of looping and iterative controls
> These include the simple loop, the WHILE loop, and the REPEAT UNTIL loop.

Example 1-2, a procedure that pays out the balance of an account to cover outstanding bills, demonstrates some of the control statements of MySQL.

Example 1-2. Stored procedure with control and conditional logic

```
1  CREATE PROCEDURE pay_out_balance
2       (account_id_in INT)
3
4  BEGIN
5
6  DECLARE l_balance_remaining NUMERIC(10,2);
```

Example 1-2. Stored procedure with control and conditional logic (continued)

```
7
8   payout_loop:LOOP
9     SET l_balance_remaining = account_balance(account_id_in);
10
11    IF l_balance_remaining < 1000 THEN
12      LEAVE payout_loop;
13
14    ELSE
15      CALL apply_balance(account_id_in, l_balance_remaining);
16    END IF;
17
18  END LOOP;
19
20 END
```

Let's take a more detailed look at this code in the following table:

Line(s)	Explanation
1–3	This is the header of our procedure; line 2 contains the parameter list of the procedure, which in this case consists of a single incoming value (the identification number of the account).
6	Declare a variable to hold the remaining balance for an account.
8–18	This simple loop (named so because it is started simply with the keyword LOOP, as opposed to WHILE or REPEAT) iterates until the account balance falls below 1000. In MySQL, we can name the loop (line 8, payout_loop), which then allows us to use the LEAVE statement (see line 12) to terminate that particular loop. After leaving a loop, the MySQL engine will then proceed to the next executable statement following the END LOOP; statement (line 18).
9	Call the account_balance function (which must have been previously defined) to retrieve the balance for this account. MySQL allows you to call a stored program from within another stored program, thus facilitating reuse of code. Since this program is a function, it returns a value and can therefore be called from within a MySQL SET assignment.
11–16	This IF statement causes the loop to terminate if the account balance falls below $1,000. Otherwise (the ELSE clause), it applies the balance to the next charge. You can construct much more complex Boolean expressions with ELSEIF clauses, as well.
15	Call the apply_balance procedure. This is an example of code reuse; rather than repeating the logic of apply_balance in this procedure, we call a common routine.

Stored Functions

A *stored function* is a stored program that returns a single value and that can be used whenever a built-in function can be used—for example, in a SQL statement. Example 1-3 returns the age of a person in years when provided with a date of birth.

Example 1-3. A stored function to calculate age from date of birth

```
1 CREATE FUNCTION f_age (in_dob datetime) returns int
2   NO SQL
3 BEGIN
4   DECLARE l_age INT;
```

Example 1-3. A stored function to calculate age from date of birth (continued)

```
5    IF DATE_FORMAT(NOW( ),'00-%m-%d') >= DATE_FORMAT(in_dob,'00-%m-%d') THEN
6      -- This person has had a birthday this year
7      SET l_age=DATE_FORMAT(NOW( ),'%Y')-DATE_FORMAT(in_dob,'%Y');
8    ELSE
9      -- Yet to have a birthday this year
10     SET l_age=DATE_FORMAT(NOW( ),'%Y')-DATE_FORMAT(in_dob,'%Y')-1;
11   END IF;
12   RETURN(l_age);

END;
```

Let's step through this code in the following table:

Lines(s)	Explanation
1	Define the function: its name, input parameters (a single date), and return value (an integer).
2	This function contains no SQL statements. There's some controversy about the use of this clause —see Chapters 3 and 10 for more discussion.
4	Declare a local variable to hold the results of our age calculation.
5-11	This IF-ELSE-END IF block checks to see if the birth date in question has occurred yet this year.
7	If the birth date has, in fact, passed in the current year, we can calculate the age by simply subtracting the year of birth from the current year.
10	Otherwise (i.e., the birth date is yet to occur this year), we need to subtract an additional year from our age calculation.
12	Return the age as calculated to the calling program.

We can use our stored function wherever a built-in function would be permitted—within another stored program, in a SET statement, or, as shown in Example 1-4, within a SQL statement.

Example 1-4. Using a stored function within a SQL statement

```
mysql> SELECT firstname,surname, date_of_birth, f_age(date_of_birth) AS age
    ->    FROM employees LIMIT 5;
+-----------+---------+---------------------+------+
| firstname | surname | date_of_birth       | age  |
+-----------+---------+---------------------+------+
| LUCAS     | FERRIS  | 1984-04-17 07:04:27 |   21 |
| STAFFORD  | KIPP    | 1953-04-22 06:04:50 |   52 |
| GUTHREY   | HOLMES  | 1974-09-12 08:09:22 |   31 |
| TALIA     | KNOX    | 1966-08-14 11:08:14 |   39 |
| JOHN      | MORALES | 1956-06-22 07:06:14 |   49 |
+-----------+---------+---------------------+------+
```

When Things Go Wrong

Even if our programs have been thoroughly tested and have no bugs, user input can cause errors to occur in our code. The MySQL stored program language offers a powerful mechanism for handling errors. In Example 1-5, we create a procedure that creates new product codes or—if the product code already exists—updates it with a new name. The procedure detects an attempt to insert a duplicate value by using an *exception handler*. If the attempt to insert fails, the error is trapped and an UPDATE is issued in place of the INSERT. Without the exception handler, the stored program execution is stopped, and the exception is passed back unhandled to the calling program.

Example 1-5. Error handling in a stored program

```
1   CREATE PROCEDURE sp_product_code
2       (in_product_code VARCHAR(2),
3        in_product_name VARCHAR(30))
4
5   BEGIN
6
7     DECLARE l_dupkey_indicator INT DEFAULT 0;
8     DECLARE duplicate_key CONDITION FOR 1062;
9     DECLARE CONTINUE HANDLER FOR duplicate_key SET l_dupkey_indicator =1;
10
11    INSERT INTO product_codes (product_code, product_name)
12    VALUES (in_product_code, in_product_name);
13
14    IF l_dupkey_indicator THEN
15      UPDATE product_codes
16         SET product_name=in_product_name
17       WHERE product_code=in_product_code;
18    END IF;
19
20  END
```

Let's take a more detailed look at the error-handling aspects of this code:

Line(s)	Explanation
1-4	This is the header of the stored procedure, accepting two IN parameters: product code and product name.
7	Declare a variable that we will use to detect the occurrence of a duplicate key violation. The variable is initialized with a value of 0 (false); subsequent code will ensure that it gets set to a value of 1 (true) only if a duplicate key violation takes place.
8	Define a named condition, duplicate_key, that is associated with MySQL error 1062. While this step is not strictly necessary, we recommend that you define such conditions to improve the readability of your code (you can now reference the error by name instead of by number).
9	Define an error handler that will trap the duplicate key error and then set the value of the variable l_dupkey_indicator to 1 (true) if a duplicate key violation is encountered anywhere in the subsequent code.
11-12	Insert a new product with the user-provided code and name.
14	Check the value of the l_dupkey_indicator variable. If it is still 0, then the INSERT was successful and we are done. If the value has been changed to 1 (true), we know that there has been a duplicate key violation. We then run the UPDATE statement in lines 15-17 to change the name of the product with the specified code.

Error handling is a critical aspect of writing robust, maintainable MySQL stored programs. Chapter 6 takes you on an extensive tour of the various error-handling mechanisms in MySQL stored programs.

Triggers

A *trigger* is a stored program that is automatically invoked in response to an event within the database. In the MySQL 5 implementation, triggers are invoked only in response to DML activity on a specific table. The trigger can automatically calculate derived or denormalized values. Example 1-6 shows a trigger that maintains such a derived value; whenever an employee salary is changed, the value of the contrib_401K column is automatically set to an appropriate value.

Example 1-6. Trigger to maintain a derived column value

```
1   CREATE TRIGGER employees_trg_bu
2       BEFORE UPDATE ON employees
3       FOR EACH ROW
4    BEGIN
5      IF NEW.salary <50000 THEN
6         SET NEW.contrib_401K=500;
7      ELSE
8         SET NEW.contrib_401K=500+(NEW.salary-50000)*.01;
9      END IF;
10   END
```

The following table explains this fairly simple and short trigger:

Line(s)	Explanation
1	A trigger has a unique name. Typically, you will want to name the trigger so as to reveal its nature. For example, the "bu" in the trigger's name indicates that this is a BEFORE UPDATE trigger.
2	Define the conditions that will cause the trigger to fire. In this case, the trigger code will execute prior to an UPDATE statement on the employees table.
3	FOR EACH ROW indicates that the trigger code will be executed once for each row being affected by the DML statement. This clause is mandatory in the current MySQL 5 trigger implementation.
4-10	This BEGIN-END block defines the code that will run when the trigger is fired.
5-9	Automatically populate the contrib_401K column in the employees table. If the new value for the salary column is less than 50000, the contrib._401K column will be set to 500. Otherwise, the value will be calculated as shown in line 8.

There is, of course, much more that can be said about the MySQL stored program language—which is why you have hundreds more pages of material to study in this book! These initial examples should, however, give you a good feel for the kind of code you will write with the stored program language, some of its most important syntactical elements, and the ease with which you can write—and read—the stored program language code.

Resources for Developers Using Stored Programs

The introduction of stored programs in MySQL 5 is a significant milestone in the evolution of the MySQL language. For any new technology to be absorbed and leveraged fully, users of that technology need lots of support and guidance in how best to utilize it. Our objective is to offer in this book complete and comprehensive coverage of the MySQL stored program language.

We are certain, however, that you will need help in other ways, so in the following sections we describe additional resources that either complement this book (by providing information about other MySQL technologies) or provide community-based support or late-breaking news. In these sections we provide quick summaries of many of these resources. By taking full advantage of these resources, many of which are available either free or at a relatively low cost, you will greatly improve the quality of your MySQL development experience—and your resulting code.

Books

Over the years, the MySQL series from O'Reilly has grown to include quite a long list of books. Here we list some of the books currently available that we feel could be pertinent to the MySQL stored program developer, as well as relevant books from other publishers. Please check out the MySQL area of the O'Reilly OnLAMP web site (*http://www.onlamp.com/onlamp/general/mysql.csp*) for more complete information.

MySQL Stored Procedure Programming, by Guy Harrison with Steven Feuerstein
> This is the book you are holding now (or maybe even viewing online). This book was designed to be a complete and comprehensive guide to the MySQL stored program language. However, this book does not attempt complete coverage of the MySQL server, the SQL language, or other programming languages that you might use with MySQL. Therefore, you might want to complement this book with one or more other topics from the O'Reilly catalog or even—heaven forbid—from another publisher!

MySQL in a Nutshell, by Russell Dyer
> This compact quick-reference manual covers the MySQL SQL language, utility programs, and APIs for Perl, PHP, and C. This book is the ideal companion for any MySQL user (O'Reilly).

Web Database Applications with PHP and MySQL, by Hugh Williams and David Lane
> This is a comprehensive guide to creating web-based applications using PHP and MySQL. It covers PEAR (PHP Extension and Application Repository) and provides a variety of complete case studies (O'Reilly).

MySQL, by Paul DuBois

> This classic reference—now in its third edition—is a comprehensive reference to MySQL development and administration. The third edition includes prerelease coverage of MySQL 5.0, including some information about stored procedures, functions, and triggers (SAMS).

High Performance MySQL, by Jeremy Zawodny and Derek Balling

> This book covers the construction of high-performance MySQL server environments, along with how you can tune applications to take advantage of these environments. The book focuses on optimization, benchmarking, backups, replication, indexing, and load balancing (O'Reilly).

MySQL Cookbook, by Paul DuBois

> This cookbook provides quick and easily applied recipes for common MySQL problems ranging from program setup to table manipulation and transaction management to data import/export and web interaction (O'Reilly).

Pro MySQL, by Michael Krukenberg and Jay Pipes

> This book covers many advanced MySQL topics, including index structure, internal architecture, replication, clustering, and new features in MySQL 5.0. Some coverage of stored procedures, functions, and triggers is included, although much of the discussion is based on early MySQL 5 beta versions (APress).

MySQL *Design and Tuning*, by Robert D. Schneider

> This is a good source of information on advanced development and administration topics, with a focus on performance (MySQL Press).

SQL in a Nutshell, by Kevin Kline, et al.

> MySQL stored procedures, functions, and triggers rely on the SQL language to interact with database tables. This is a reference to the SQL language as implemented in Oracle, SQL Server, DB2, and MySQL (O'Reilly).

Learning SQL, by Alan Beaulieu

> This book provides an excellent entry point for those unfamiliar with SQL. It covers queries, grouping, sets, filtering, subqueries, joins, indexes, and constraints, along with exercises (O'Reilly).

Internet Resources

There are also some excellent web sites available to MySQL programmers, including some areas devoted to stored programming. You should also make sure to look at the web site for this book (described in the Preface) for updates, errata, and other MySQL information.

MySQL

MySQL AB offers the most comprehensive collection of white papers, documentation, and forums on MySQL in general and MySQL stored programming in particular. Start at *http://www.mysql.com*. We outline some specific areas later.

MySQL Developer Zone

http://dev.mysql.com/ is the main entry point for MySQL programmers. From here you can easily access software downloads, online forums, white papers, documentation, and the bug-tracking system.

MySQL online documentation

The MySQL reference manual—including sections on stored procedures, functions, and triggers—is available online at *http://dev.mysql.com/doc/*. You can also download the manual in various formats from here, or you can order various selections in printed book format at *http://dev.mysql.com/books/mysqlpress/index.html*.

MySQL forums

MySQL forums are great places to discuss MySQL features with others in the MySQL community. The MySQL developers are also frequent participants in these forums. The general forum index can be found at *http://forums.mysql.com/*. The stored procedure forum includes discussions of both procedures and functions, and there is a separate forum for triggers.

MySQL blogs

There are many people blogging about MySQL nowadays, and MySQL has consolidated many of the most significant feeds on the Planet MySQL web site at *http://www.planetmysql.org/*.

MySQL stored routines library

Giuseppe Maxia initiated this routine library, which collects general-purpose MySQL 5 stored procedures and functions. The library is still young, but already there are some extremely useful routines available. For example, you will find routines that emulate arrays, automate repetitive tasks, and perform crosstab manipulations. Check it out at *http://savannah.nongnu.org/projects/mysql-sr-lib/*.

O'Reilly's OnLAMP MySQL section

O'Reilly hosts the OnLAMP site, which is dedicated to the LAMP stack (Linux, Apache, MySQL, PHP/Perl/Python) of which MySQL is such an important part. OnLAMP includes numerous MySQL articles, which you can find at *http://www.onlamp.com/onlamp/general/mysql.csp*.

Some Words of Advice for Developers

By definition, everyone is new to the world of MySQL stored program development, because stored programs are themselves new to MySQL. However, Guy and Steven have both had plenty of experience in stored program development within other relational databases. Steven, in particular, has been a key figure in the world of Oracle PL/SQL (Oracle's stored program language) development for more than a decade. We hope that you will find it helpful if we share some advice with you on how you can work more effectively with this powerful MySQL programming language.

Don't Be in Such a Hurry!

We are almost always working under tight deadlines, or playing catch-up from one setback or another. We have no time to waste, and lots of code to write. So let's get right to it—right?

Wrong. If we dive too quickly into the depths of code construction, slavishly converting requirements to hundreds, thousands, or even tens of thousands of lines of code, we will end up with a total mess that is almost impossible to debug and maintain. Don't respond to looming deadlines with panic; you are more likely to meet those deadlines if you do some careful planning.

We strongly encourage you to resist these time pressures and make sure to do the following before you start a new application, or even a specific program in an application:

Construct test cases and test scripts before you write your code. You should determine how you want to verify a successful implementation before you write a single line of a program. By doing this, you are more likely to get the interface of your program correct and be able to thoroughly identify what it is your program needs to do.

Establish clear rules for how developers will write the SQL statements in the application. In general, we recommend that individual developers not write a whole lot of SQL. Instead, those single-row queries and inserts and updates should be "hidden" behind prebuilt and thoroughly tested procedures and functions (this is called *data encapsulation*). These programs can be optimized, tested, and maintained much more effectively than SQL statements (many of them quite similar) scattered throughout your code.

Establish clear rules for how developers will handle exceptions in the application. If you don't set standards, then everyone will handle errors their own way or not at all, creating software chaos. The best approach to take is to centralize your error-handling logic in a small set of procedures, which hide all the details of how an error log is kept, determine how exceptions are raised and propagated up through nested blocks, and more. Make sure that all developers use these programs and do not write their own complicated, time-consuming, and error-prone error-handling code.

Use "stepwise refinement" (a.k.a. top-down design) to limit the complexity of the requirements you must deal with at any given time. We are usually tasked with implementing very complex requirements. If you try to "do it all" in one big stored program, it will rapidly devolve into spaghetti code that even you will not be able to understand later. Break your big challenges into a sequence of smaller challenges, and then tackle those more manageable problems with reasonably sized programs. If you use this approach, you will find that the executable sections of your modules are shorter and easier to understand, which makes your code easier to maintain and enhance over time.

These are just a few of the important things to keep in mind before you start writing all that code. Just remember: in the world of software development, haste not only makes waste, it virtually guarantees a generous offering of bugs and lost weekends.

Don't Be Afraid to Ask for Help

Chances are, if you are a software professional, you are a smart and well-educated individual. You studied hard, you honed your skills, and now you make a darn good living writing code. You can solve almost any problem you are handed, and that makes you proud.

Unfortunately, your success can also make you egotistical, arrogant, and reluctant to seek out help when you are stumped (we think we are supposed to know *all* the answers). This dynamic is one of the most dangerous and destructive aspects of software development.

Software is written by human beings; it is important, therefore, to recognize that human psychology plays a key role in software development. The following is an example.

Joe, the senior developer in a team of six, has a problem with his program. He studies it for hours, with increasing frustration, but cannot figure out the source of the bug. He wouldn't think of asking any of his peers to help because they all have less experience than he does. Finally, though, he is at wits' end and gives up. Sighing, he picks up his phone and touches an extension: "Sandra, could you come over here and take a look at my program? I've got a problem I can't figure out." Sandra stops by and, with the quickest glance at Joe's program, points out what should have been obvious to him long ago. Hurray! The program is fixed, and Joe expresses gratitude, but in fact he is secretly embarrassed.

Thoughts like "Why didn't I see that?" and "If I'd only spent another five minutes doing my own debugging I would have found it" run though Joe's mind. This is understandable but misguided. The bottom line is that we are often unable to identify our own problems because we are too close to our own code. Sometimes, all we need is a fresh perspective, the relatively objective view of someone with nothing at stake. It has nothing to do with seniority, expertise, or competence.

Besides, Sandra isn't going to think poorly of Joe. Instead, by asking her for help, Joe has made her feel better about herself, and so both members of the development team benefit.

We strongly suggest that you establish the following guidelines in your organization:

Reward admissions of ignorance
> Hiding what you don't know about an application or its code is very dangerous. Develop a culture in which it is OK to say "I don't know" and encourages the asking of lots of questions.

Ask for help
> If you cannot figure out the source of a bug in 30 minutes, immediately ask for help. You might even set up a "buddy system," so that everyone is assigned a person who is expected to be asked for assistance. Don't let yourself (or others in your group) go for hours banging your head against the wall in a fruitless search for answers.

Set up a formal peer code review process
> Don't let any code go to QA (Quality Assurance) or production without being read and critiqued (in a positive, constructive manner) by other developers in your group.

Take a Creative, Even Radical Approach

We all tend to fall into ruts, in almost every aspect of our lives. Humans are creatures of habit: you learn to write code in one way; you assume certain limitations about a product; you turn aside possible solutions without serious examination because you just *know* it can't be done. Developers become downright prejudiced about their own programs, and often not in positive ways. They are often overheard saying things like:

- "It can't run any faster than that; it's a pig."
- "I can't make it work the way the user wants; that'll have to wait for the next version."
- "If I were using X or Y or Z product, it would be a breeze. But with this stuff, everything is a struggle."

But the reality is that your program can almost always run a little faster. And the screen can, in fact, function just the way the user wants it to. And although each product has its limitations, strengths, and weaknesses, you should never have to wait for the next version. Isn't it so much more satisfying to be able to tell your therapist that you tackled the problem head-on, accepted no excuses, and crafted a solution?

How do you do this? Break out of the confines of your hardened views and take a fresh look at the world (or maybe just the walls of your cubicle). Reassess the programming habits you've developed. Be creative—step away from the traditional methods, from the often limited and mechanical approaches constantly reinforced in our places of business.

Try something new: experiment with what may seem to be a radical departure from the norm. You will be surprised at how much you will learn and grow as a programmer and problem solver. Over the years, we have surprised ourselves over and over with what is really achievable when we stopped saying "You can't do that!" and instead simply nodded quietly and wondered to ourselves: "Now, if we do it this way, what will happen…?"

Conclusion

In this chapter, we took you on a whirlwind tour of the MySQL relational database and the new MySQL stored program language. We also provided you with some useful resources and added some general words of advice that we hope you find useful.

In the next chapter, we'll provide a more comprehensive tutorial that will really get you started with MySQL stored procedures, functions, and triggers.

## CHAPTER 2

MySQL Stored Programming Tutorial

MySQL stored programming is a complex topic. We offer this chapter to introduce you to the main and common tasks you will need to perform, including:

- How to create a stored program
- How to pass information in and out of the stored program
- How to interact with the database
- How to create procedures, functions, and triggers in the MySQL stored program language

We don't go into detail in this chapter. Our purpose is to get you started and to give you some appreciation of how stored programs work. Later chapters will explore in detail all of the topics touched on in this chapter.

What You Will Need

To follow along with the examples in this tutorial, you will need:

- A MySQL 5 server
- A text editor such as vi, emacs, or Notepad
- The MySQL Query Browser

You can get the MySQL server and MySQL Query Browser from *http://dev.mysql.com*.

Our First Stored Procedure

We'll start by creating a very simple stored procedure. To do this, you need an editing environment in which to write the stored procedure and a tool that can submit the stored procedure code to the MySQL server.

You can use just about any editor to write your code. Options for compiling that code into MySQL include:

- The MySQL command-line client
- The MySQL Query Browser
- A third-party tool such as Toad for MySQL

In this chapter, we won't make any assumptions about what tools you have installed, so we'll start with the good old MySQL command-line client.

Let's connect to the MySQL server on the local host at port 3306 using the root account. We'll use the preinstalled "test" database in Example 2-1.

Example 2-1. Connecting to the MySQL command-line client

```
[gharriso@guyh-rh4-vm2 ~]$ mysql -uroot -psecret -hlocalhost
Welcome to the MySQL monitor.  Commands end with ; or \g.
Your MySQL connection id is 1 to server version: 5.0.16-nightly-20051017-log

Type 'help;' or '\h' for help. Type '\c' to clear the buffer.

mysql>
```

Creating the Procedure

You can create a stored program with the CREATE PROCEDURE, CREATE FUNCTION, or CREATE TRIGGER statement. It is possible to enter these statements directly at the MySQL command line, but this is not practical for stored programs of more than trivial length, so the best thing for us to do is to create a text file containing our stored program text. Then we can submit this file to the database using the command-line client or another tool.

We will use the MySQL Query Browser as a text editor in this example. If you don't have this tool, you can download it from *http://dev.mysql.com/downloads/*. Alternately, you could use an OS text editor such as vi, emacs, or Notepad. We like the MySQL Query Browser because of its built-in help system, syntax highlighting, ability to run SQL statements, and lots of other features.

Follow these steps:

1. Run the MySQL Query browser. On Windows, from the Start menu select Programs → MySQL → MySQL Query Browser. On Linux, type mysql-query-browser from the command line.
2. Select File → New Script tab from the menu to create a blank script window.
3. Enter your stored program command text.

Figure 2-1 shows our first stored procedure.

We then use the File → Save As menu option to save our file so that we can execute it from the mysql client.

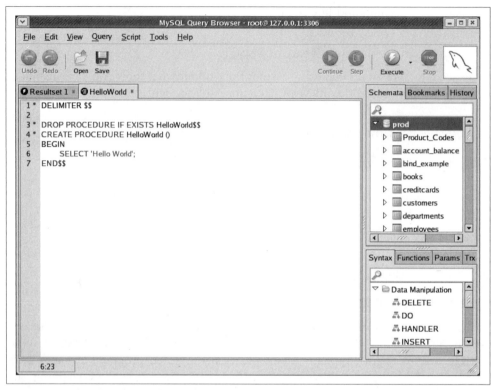

Figure 2-1. A first stored procedure

This first stored procedure is very simple, but let's examine it line by line to make sure you understand it completely:

Line	Explanation
1	Issue the DELIMITER command to set '$$' as the end of a statement. Normally, MySQL regards ";" as the end of a statement, but since stored procedures contain semicolons in the procedure body, we need to use a different delimiter.
3	Issue a DROP PROCEDURE IF EXISTS statement to remove the stored procedure if it already exists. If we don't do this, we will get an error if we then try to re-execute this file with modifications and the stored procedure exists.
4	The CREATE PROCEDURE statement indicates the start of a stored procedure definition. Note that the stored procedure name "HelloWorld" is followed by an empty set of parentheses "( )". If our stored procedure had any parameters, they would be defined within these parentheses. This stored procedure has no parameters, but we need to include the parentheses anyway, or we will get a syntax error.
5	The BEGIN statement indicates the start of the stored procedure program. All stored programs with more than a single statement must have at least one BEGIN and END block that defines the start and end of the stored program.
6	This is the single executable statement in the procedure: a SELECT statement that returns "Hello World" to the calling program. As you will see later, SELECT statements in stored programs can return data to the console or calling program just like SELECT statements entered at the MySQL command line.
7	The END statement terminates the stored procedure definition. Note that we ended the stored procedure definition with $$ so that MySQL knows that we have completed the CREATE PROCEDURE statement.

With our definition stored in a file, we can now use the mysql client to create and then execute the HelloWorld stored procedure, as shown in Example 2-2.

Example 2-2. Creating our first stored procedure

```
$ mysql -uroot -psecret -Dprod
Welcome to the MySQL monitor.  Commands end with ; or \g.
Your MySQL connection id is 16 to server version: 5.0.18-nightly-20051208-log

Type 'help;' or '\h' for help. Type '\c' to clear the buffer.

mysql> SOURCE HelloWorld.sql
Query OK, 0 rows affected, 1 warning (0.01 sec)

Query OK, 0 rows affected (0.00 sec)

mysql> CALL HelloWorld() $$
+-------------+
| Hello World |
+-------------+
| Hello World |
+-------------+
1 row in set (0.01 sec)

Query OK, 0 rows affected (0.01 sec)

mysql>
```

Here is an explanation of the MySQL commands used to get all this to work:

Command	Explanation
SOURCE HelloWorld.sql	Reads commands from the nominated file. In this case, we specify the file we just saved from the MySQL Query Browser. No errors are returned, so the stored procedure appears to have been created successfully.
CALL HelloWorld() $$	Executes the stored procedure. Calling our stored procedure successfully results in "Hello World" being output as a result set. Note that we terminated the CALL command with '$$', since that is still what the DELIMITER is set to.

Creating the Procedure Using the MySQL Query Browser

In this tutorial—and indeed throughout this book—we will mostly create and demonstrate stored programs the old-fashioned way: using the MySQL command-line client to create the stored program. By doing this, you'll always be able to duplicate the examples. However, you do have the option of using a GUI tool to create stored programs: there are a number of good third-party GUI tools for MySQL available, and you always have the option of installing and using the MySQL Query Browser, available from *http://dev.mysql.com/downloads/*.

In this section we offer a brief overview of creating a stored procedure using the MySQL Query Browser. Using the Query Browser is certainly a more user-friendly way of creating stored programs, although it might not be available on all platforms, and you may prefer to use the MySQL command line or the various third-party alternatives.

On Windows, you launch the Query Browser (if installed) from the Start menu option Programs → MySQL → MySQL Query Browser. On Linux, you type `mysql-query-browser`.

When the Query Browser launches, it prompts you for connection details for your MySQL server. Once you have provided these, a blank GUI window appears. From this window, select Script and then Create Stored Procedure. You will be prompted for the name of the stored program to create, after which an empty template for the stored program will be displayed. An example of such a template is shown in Figure 2-2.

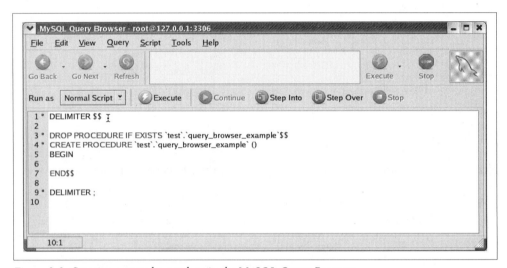

Figure 2-2. Creating a stored procedure in the MySQL Query Browser

You can then enter the text of the stored procedure at the appropriate point (between the BEGIN and END statements—the cursor is handily positioned there automatically). Once you have finished entering our text, simply click the Execute button to create the stored procedure. If an error occurs, the Query Browser highlights the line and displays the error in the lower half of the Query Browser window. Otherwise, you'll see the name of the new stored procedure appear in the Schemata tab to the left of the stored procedure, as shown in Figure 2-3.

To execute the stored procedure, double-click on the name of the procedure within the Schemata tab. An appropriate CALL statement will be pasted into the execution window above the stored procedure. Clicking on the Execute button to the right of the CALL statement executes the stored procedure and displays a results window, as shown in Figure 2-4.

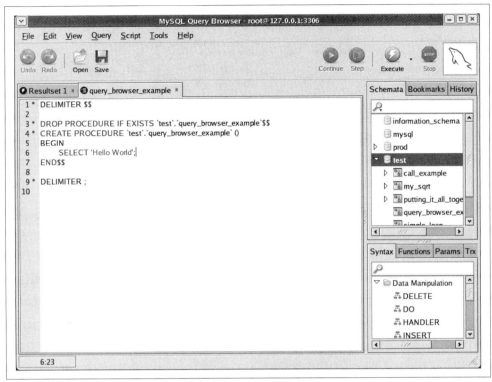

Figure 2-3. Stored procedure is created by clicking the Execute button

We hope this brief example gives you a feel for the general process of creating and executing a stored procedure in the MySQL Query Browser. The Query Browser offers a convenient environment for the development of stored programs, but it is really up to you whether to use the Query Browser, a third-party tool, or simply your favorite editor and the MySQL command-line client.

Variables

Local variables can be declared within stored procedures using the DECLARE statement. Variable names follow the same naming rules as MySQL table column names and can be of any MySQL data type. You can give variables an initial value with the DEFAULT clause and assign them new values using the SET command, as shown in Figure 2-5.

Parameters

Most of the stored programs you write will include one or more parameters. Parameters make stored programs much more flexible and therefore more useful. Next, let's create a stored procedure that accepts parameters.

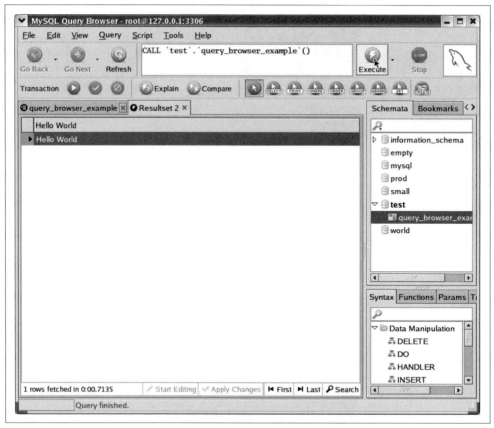

Figure 2-4. Executing the stored procedure in the Query Browser

The stored procedure shown in Figure 2-6 accepts an integer parameter, input_number, and calculates the square root of that number. The resulting number is returned as a result set.

Place parameters within parentheses that are located immediately after the name of the stored procedure. Each parameter has a name, a data type, and, optionally, a mode. Valid modes are IN (read-only), INOUT (read-write), and OUT (write-only). No parameter mode appears in Figure 2-6, because IN is the default and this is an IN parameter.

We'll take a closer look at parameter modes following this example.

In addition to the parameter, this stored procedure introduces two other features of MySQL stored programs:

DECLARE
   A statement used to create local variables for use in the stored program. In this case, we create a floating-point number called l_sqrt.

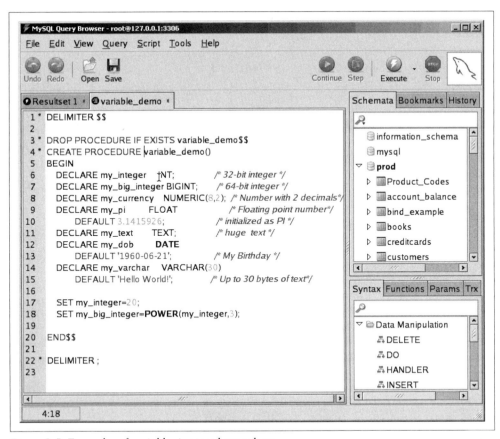

Figure 2-5. Examples of variables in stored procedures

SET

> A statement used to assign a value to a variable. In this case, we assign the square root of our input parameter (using the built-in SQRT function) to the floating-point number we created with the DECLARE command.

We can run this script, and test the resulting stored procedure in the MySQL client, as shown in Example 2-3.

Example 2-3. Creating and executing a stored procedure with a parameter

```
mysql> SOURCE my_sqrt.sql
Query OK, 0 rows affected (0.00 sec)

Query OK, 0 rows affected (0.00 sec)

mysql> CALL my_sqrt(12)$$
+-----------------+
| l_sqrt          |
+-----------------+
```

Example 2-3. Creating and executing a stored procedure with a parameter (continued)

```
| 3.4641016151378 |
+-----------------+
1 row in set (0.12 sec)

Query OK, 0 rows affected (0.12 sec)
```

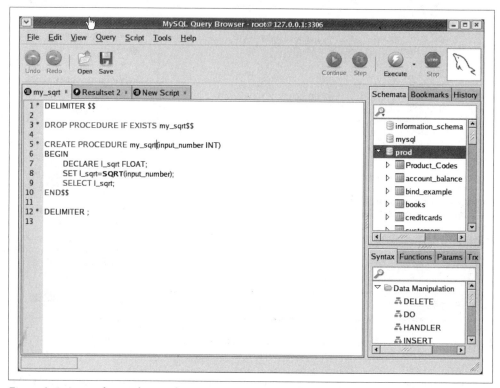

Figure 2-6. A stored procedure with parameters

Parameter Modes

Parameters in MySQL can be defined as IN, OUT, or INOUT:

IN

This mode is the default. It indicates that the parameter can be passed into the stored program but that any modifications are not returned to the calling program.

OUT

This mode means that the stored program can assign a value to the parameter, and that value will be passed back to the calling program.

INOUT

This mode means that the stored program can read the parameter and that the calling program can see any modifications that the stored program may make to that parameter.

You can use all of these parameter modes in stored procedures, but only the IN mode in stored functions (see the later "Stored Functions" section).

Let's change our square root program so that it puts the result of its calculations into an OUT variable, as shown in Figure 2-7.

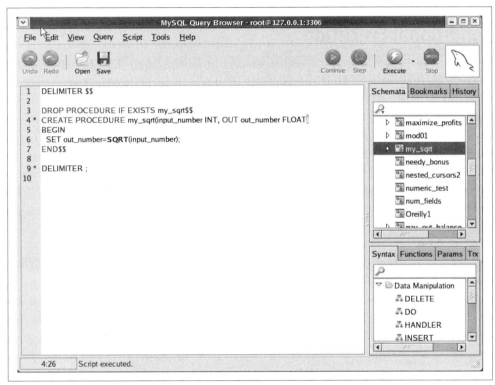

Figure 2-7. Example of using OUT parameter in a stored procedure

In the MySQL client, we now have to provide a variable to hold the value of the OUT parameter. After the stored procedure has finished executing, we can look at that variable to retrieve the output, as shown in Example 2-4.

Example 2-4. Creating and executing a stored procedure with an OUT parameter

```
mysql> SOURCE my_sqrt2.sql
Query OK, 0 rows affected (0.00 sec)

Query OK, 0 rows affected (0.02 sec)
```

Example 2-4. Creating and executing a stored procedure with an OUT parameter (continued)

```
mysql> CALL my_sqrt(12,@out_value) $$
Query OK, 0 rows affected (0.03 sec)

mysql> SELECT @out_value $$
+-----------------+
| @out_value      |
+-----------------+
| 3.4641016151378 |
+-----------------+
1 row in set (0.00 sec)
```

Conditional Execution

You can control the flow of execution in your stored program by using IF or CASE statements. Both have roughly the same functionality; we will demonstrate the use of IF in this tutorial, as it's probably the most familiar of the two constructs.

Figure 2-8 shows a stored program that works out the discounted rate for a purchase based on the size of the purchase, and Example 2-5 shows its execution. Purchases over $500 get a 20% discount, while purchases over $100 get a 10% discount.

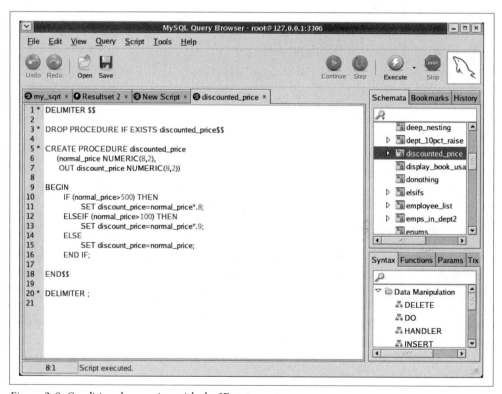

Figure 2-8. Conditional execution with the IF statement

Example 2-5. Creating and executing a stored procedure that contains an IF statement

```
mysql> SOURCE discounted_price.sql
Query OK, 0 rows affected (0.01 sec)

Query OK, 0 rows affected (0.00 sec)

mysql> CALL discounted_price(300,@new_price) $$
Query OK, 0 rows affected (0.00 sec)

mysql> SELECT @new_price$$
+------------+
| @new_price |
+------------+
| 270.0      |
+------------+
1 row in set (0.00 sec)
```

The IF statement allows you to test the truth of an expression such as normal_price > 500 and take appropriate action based on the result of the expression. As with other programming languages, the ELSEIF clause is used for all conditional branches after the initial IF. The ELSE clause is executed if the Boolean expressions in the IF and ELSEIF clauses all evaluate to false.

CASE has very similar functionality, and may be preferable when you are comparing a single expression against a set of possible distinct values. The two conditional statements are explored and contrasted in Chapter 4.

Loops

Loops allow stored programs to execute statements repetitively. The MySQL stored program language offers three types of loops:

- Simple loops using the LOOP and END LOOP clauses
- Loops that continue *while* a condition is true, using the WHILE and END WHILE clauses
- Loops that continue *until* a condition is true, using the REPEAT and UNTIL clauses

With all three loop types, you terminate execution of the loop with the LEAVE statement.

All three types of loops are described in detail in Chapter 4; we'll only demonstrate the LOOP-LEAVE-END LOOP (simple loop) sequence in this tutorial.

Figure 2-9 shows a very simple loop.

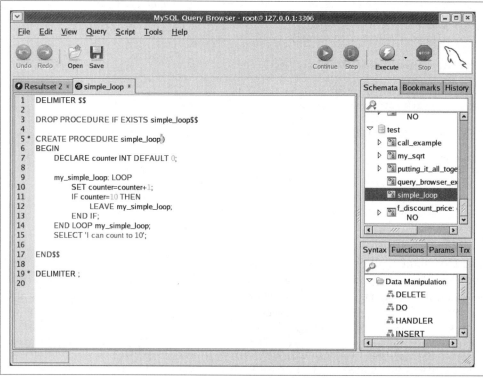

Figure 2-9. A simple loop inside a stored procedure

Here is an explanation of the activity in this stored procedure:

Line(s)	Explanation
7	Declare a simple numeric variable called counter with an initial value of 0.
9-14	The simple loop. All statements between LOOP and END LOOP are repeated until a LEAVE clause is executed.
9	The LOOP statement is prefixed by the my_simple_loop: label. The LEAVE statement requires that the loop be labeled so it knows which loop to exit.
10	Increment the counter variable by one.
11-13	Test for the value of counter. If the value of counter is 10, we execute the LEAVE statement to terminate the loop. Otherwise, we continue with the next iteration of the loop.
15	We proudly announce that we can count to 10!

Dealing with Errors

When an error occurs in a stored program, the default behavior of MySQL is to terminate execution of the program and pass the error out to the calling program. If you need a different kind of response to an error, you create an *error handler* that defines the way in which the stored program should respond to one or more error conditions.

The following are two relatively common scenarios that call for the definition of error handlers:

- If you think that an embedded SQL statement might return no rows, or you need to fetch all the rows from a SELECT statement using a cursor, a NOT FOUND error handler will prevent the stored program from terminating prematurely.

- If you think that a SQL statement might return an error (a constraint violation, for instance), you may need to create a handler to prevent program termination. The handler will, instead, allow you to process the error and continue program execution.

Chapter 6 describes in detail how to use error handlers. An example of using a NOT FOUND error handler with a cursor is shown in the next section.

Interacting with the Database

Most stored programs involve some kind of interaction with database tables. There are four main types of interactions:

- Store the results of a SQL statement that returns a single row into local variables.

- Create a "cursor" that allows the stored program to iterate through the rows returned by a SQL statement.

- Execute a SQL statement, returning the result set(s) to the calling program.

- Embed a SQL statement that does not return a result set, such as INSERT, UPDATE, DELETE, etc.

The following sections look briefly at each type of interaction.

 To run the examples in this section of the chapter, you should install the book's sample database, available at this book's web site (see the Preface for details).

SELECTing INTO Local Variables

Use the SELECT INTO syntax when you are querying information from a single row of data (whether retrieved from a single row, an aggregate of many rows, or a join of multiple tables). In this case, you include an INTO clause "inside" the SELECT statement that tells MySQL where to put the data retrieved by the query.

Figure 2-10 shows a stored procedure that obtains and then displays the total sales for the specified customer ID. Example 2-6 executes the procedure.

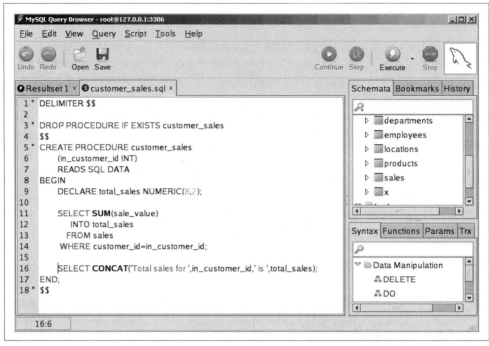

Figure 2-10. A stored procedure with an embedded SELECT INTO statement

Example 2-6. Executing a stored procedure that includes a SELECT INTO statement

```
mysql> CALL customer_sales(2) $$
+----------------------------------------------------------------+
| CONCAT('Total sales for ',in_customer_id,' is ',total_sales) |
+----------------------------------------------------------------+
| Total sales for 2 is 7632237                                   |
+----------------------------------------------------------------+
1 row in set (18.29 sec)

Query OK, 0 rows affected (18.29 sec)
```

Using Cursors

SELECT INTO is fine for single-row queries, but many applications require the querying of multiple rows of data. You will use a *cursor* in MySQL to accomplish this. A cursor lets you fetch one or more rows from a SQL result set into stored program variables, usually with the intention of performing some row-by-row processing on the result set.

The stored procedure in Figure 2-11 uses a cursor to fetch all rows from the employees table.

Here is an explanation of the significant lines in this procedure:

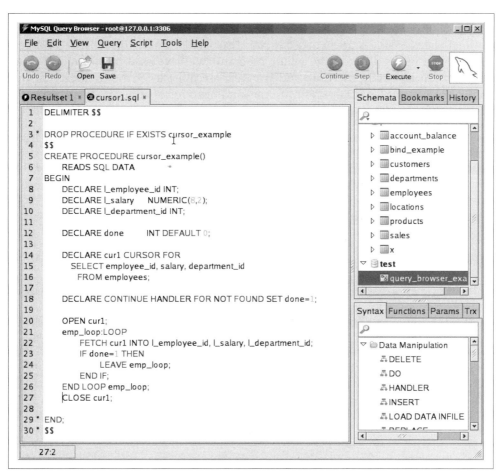

Figure 2-11. Using a cursor in a stored procedure

Line(s)	Explanation
8-12	Declare local variables. The first three are created in order to receive the results of our SELECT statement. The fourth (done) lets us know when all the rows have been retrieved from the result set.
14-16	Define our cursor. This is based on a simple SELECT that will retrieve results from the employees table.
18	Declare a "handler" that defines the actions we will take when no more rows can be retrieved from a SELECT statement. Handlers can be used to catch all kinds of errors, but a simple handler like this is always needed to alert us that no more rows can be retrieved from a result set.
20	Open the cursor.
21-26	The simple loop that fetches all the rows from the cursor.
22	Use the FETCH clause to get a single row from the cursor into our local variables.
23-25	Check the value of the done variable. If it is set to 1, then we have fetched beyond the last row within the cursor, so we execute the LEAVE statement to terminate the loop.

Returning Result Sets from Stored Procedures

An *unbounded* SELECT statement—one not associated with an INTO clause or a cursor—returns its result set to the calling program. We have used this form of interaction between a stored procedure and the database quite a few times already in this book, using simple SELECTs to return some kind of status or result from a stored procedure. So far, we've used only single-row result sets, but we could equally include a complex SQL statement that returns multiple rows within the stored procedure.

If we execute such a stored procedure from the MySQL command line, the results are returned to us in the same way as if we executed a SELECT or SHOW statement. Figure 2-12 shows a stored procedure that contains such an unbounded SELECT statement.

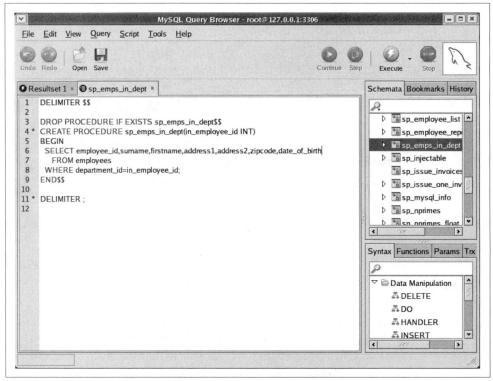

Figure 2-12. An unbounded SELECT statement in a stored procedure

If we execute the stored procedure and supply an appropriate value for the input parameter, the results of the SELECT within the stored procedure are returned. In Figure 2-13 we see the results of the SELECT statement being returned from the stored procedure call from within the MySQL Query Browser.

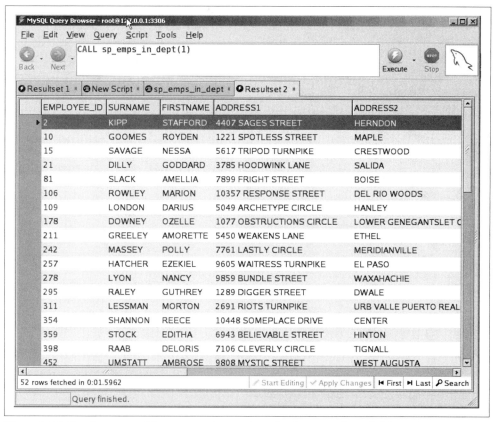

Figure 2-13. Results returned from a stored procedure that has an unbounded SELECT

Note that a stored program call can return more than one result set. This creates special challenges for the calling program, which we discuss—for each specific programming language—in Chapters 13 through 17.

Embedding Non-SELECTs

"Simple" SQL statements that do not return results can also be embedded in your stored programs. These statements include DML statements such as UPDATE, INSERT, and DELETE and may also include certain DDL statements such as CREATE TABLE. Some statements—specifically those that create or manipulate stored programs—are not allowed; these are outlined in Chapter 5.

Figure 2-14 shows a stored procedure that includes an update operation. The UPDATE statement is enclosed in some validation logic that prevents the update from proceeding if the input values are invalid.

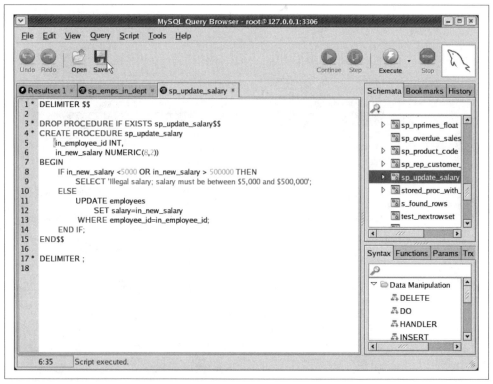

Figure 2-14. Stored procedure with an embedded UPDATE

Calling Stored Programs from Stored Programs

Calling one stored program from another is perfectly simple. You do this with the CALL statement, just as you would from the MySQL command-line client.

Figure 2-15 shows a simple stored procedure that chooses between two stored procedures based on an input parameter. The output of the stored procedure (l_bonus_amount is populated from an OUT parameter) is passed to a third procedure.

Here is an explanation of the significant lines:

Line(s)	Explanation
11	Determine if the employee is a manager. If he is a manager, we call the calc_manager_bonus stored procedure; if he is not a manager, we call the calc_minion_bonus stored procedure.
12 and 14	With both stored procedures, pass in the employee_id and provide a variable—l_bonus_amount—to receive the output of the stored procedure.
16	Call the grant_bonus stored procedure that passes as arguments the employee_id and the bonus amount, as calculated by the stored procedure we called in line 12 or 14.

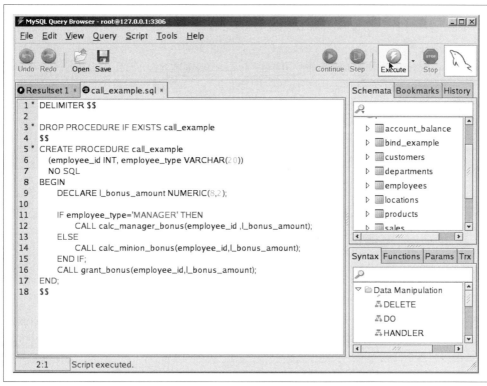

Figure 2-15. Example of calling one stored procedure from another

Putting It All Together

In Example 2-7 we show a stored procedure that uses all the features of the stored program language we have covered so far in this tutorial.

Example 2-7. A more complex stored procedure

```
1   CREATE PROCEDURE putting_it_all_together(in_department_id INT)
2       MODIFIES SQL DATA
3   BEGIN
4       DECLARE l_employee_id INT;
5       DECLARE l_salary      NUMERIC(8,2);
6       DECLARE l_department_id INT;
7       DECLARE l_new_salary  NUMERIC(8,2);
8       DECLARE done          INT DEFAULT 0;
9
10      DECLARE cur1 CURSOR FOR
11            SELECT employee_id, salary, department_id
12              FROM employees
13             WHERE department_id=in_department_id;
14
15
```

Example 2-7. A more complex stored procedure (continued)

```
16    DECLARE CONTINUE HANDLER FOR NOT FOUND SET done=1;
17
18    CREATE TEMPORARY TABLE IF NOT EXISTS emp_raises
19      (employee_id INT, department_id INT, new_salary NUMERIC(8,2));
20
21    OPEN cur1;
22    emp_loop: LOOP
23
24      FETCH cur1 INTO l_employee_id, l_salary, l_department_id;
25
26      IF done=1 THEN         /* No more rows*/
27        LEAVE emp_loop;
28      END IF;
29
30      CALL new_salary(l_employee_id,l_new_salary); /*get new salary*/
31
32      IF (l_new_salary<>l_salary) THEN              /*Salary changed*/
33
34        UPDATE employees
35          SET salary=l_new_salary
36         WHERE employee_id=l_employee_id;
37        /* Keep track of changed salaries*/
38         INSERT INTO emp_raises (employee_id,department_id,new_salary)
39         VALUES (l_employee_id,l_department_id,l_new_salary);
40      END IF;
41
42    END LOOP emp_loop;
43    CLOSE cur1;
44    /* Print out the changed salaries*/
45    SELECT employee_id,department_id,new_salary from emp_raises
46      ORDER BY employee_id;
47 END;
```

This is the most complex procedure we have written so far, so let's go through it line by line:

Line(s)	Explanation
1	Create the procedure. It takes a single parameter—in_department_id. Since we did not specify the OUT or INOUT mode, the parameter is for input only (that is, the calling program cannot read any changes to the parameter made within the procedure).
4-8	Declare local variables for use within the procedure. The final parameter, done, is given an initial value of 0.
10-13	Create a cursor to retrieve rows from the employees table. Only employees from the department passed in as a parameter to the procedure will be retrieved.
16	Create an error handler to deal with "not found" conditions, so that the program will not terminate with an error after the last row is fetched from the cursor. The handler specifies the CONTINUE clause, so the program execution will continue after the "not found" error is raised. The hander also specifies that the variable done will be set to 1 when this occurs.

Line(s)	Explanation
18	Create a temporary table to hold a list of rows affected by this procedure. This table, as well as any other temporary tables created in this session, will be dropped automatically when the session terminates.
21	Open our cursor to prepare it to return rows.
22	Create the loop that will execute once for each row returned by the stored procedure. The loop terminates on line 42.
24	Fetch a new row from the cursor into the local variables that were declared earlier in the procedure.
26-28	Declare an IF condition that will execute the LEAVE statement if the variable done is set to 1 (accomplished through the "not found" handler, which means that all rows were fetched).
30	Call the new_salary procedure to calculate the employee's new salary. It takes as its arguments the employee_id and an OUT variable to accept the new salary (l_new_salary).
32	Compare the new salary calculated by the procedure called on line 30 with the existing salary returned by the cursor defined on line 10. If they are different, execute the block of code between lines 32 and 40.
34-36	Update the employee salary to the new salary as returned by the new_salary procedure.
38 and 39	Insert a row into our temporary table (defined on line 21) to record the salary adjustment.
43	After all of the rows have been processed, close the cursor.
45	Issue an unbounded SELECT (e.g., one without a WHERE clause) against the temporary table, retrieving the list of employees whose salaries have been updated. Because the SELECT statement is not associated with a cursor or an INTO clause, the rows retrieved will be returned as a result set to the calling program.
47	Terminate the stored procedure.

When this stored procedure is executed from the MySQL command line with the parameter of department_id set to 18, a list of updated salaries is printed as shown in Example 2-8.

Example 2-8. Output from the "putting it all together" example

```
mysql> CALL cursor_example2(18) //
+-------------+---------------+------------+
| employee_id | department_id | new_salary |
+-------------+---------------+------------+
|         396 |            18 |   75560.00 |
|         990 |            18 |  118347.00 |
+-------------+---------------+------------+
2 rows in set (0.23 sec)

Query OK, 0 rows affected (0.23 sec)
```

Stored Functions

Stored functions are similar to stored procedures: they are named program units that contain one or more MySQL statements. They differ from procedures in the following ways:

- The parameter list of a function may contain only IN parameters. OUT and INOUT parameters are not allowed. Specifying the IN keyword is neither required nor allowed.

- The function itself must return a single value, whose type is defined in the header of the function.

- Functions can be called from within SQL statements.

- A function may not return a result set.

Generally, you should consider using a stored function rather than a stored procedure when you have a program whose sole purpose is to compute and return a single value or when you want to create a user-defined function for use within SQL statements.

Figure 2-16 shows a function that implements the same functionality found in the discount_price stored procedure we created earlier in this chapter.

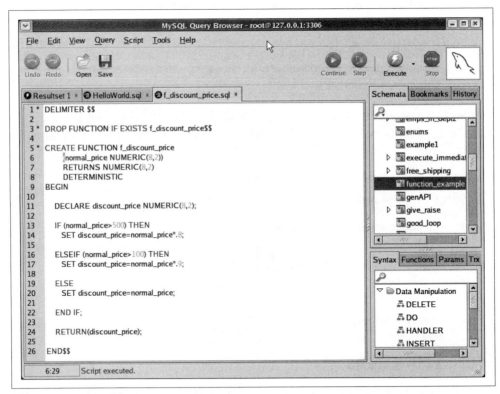

Figure 2-16. A stored function

The following table explains a few things that set apart this function from its stored procedure equivalent:

Line	Explanation
7	Specify a RETURNS clause as part of the function definition. This specifies the type of data that the function will return.
8	MySQL applies stricter rules to stored functions than it does to procedures. A function must either be declared not to modify SQL (using the NO SQL or READS SQL DATA clauses) or be declared to be DETERMINISTIC (if it is to be allowed in servers that have binary logging enabled). This restriction is designed to prevent inconsistencies between replicated databases caused by functions that return an unpredictable value (see Chapter 10 for more details). Our example routine is "deterministic" —we can guarantee that it will return the same result if it is provided with the same input parameter.
21	Use the RETURN statement to pass back the discount price calculated by the IF statement.

Example 2-9 shows calling this function from within a SQL statement.

Example 2-9. Calling a stored function from a SELECT statement

```
mysql> SELECT f_discount_price(300) $$
+-----------------------+
| f_discount_price(300) |
+-----------------------+
|                 270.0 |
+-----------------------+
```

We can also call this function from within another stored program (procedure, function, or trigger), or any place that we could use a built-in MySQL function.

Triggers

A trigger is a special type of stored program that fires when a table is modified by an INSERT, UPDATE, or DELETE (DML) statement. Triggers implement functionality that must take place whenever a certain change occurs to the table. Because triggers are attached directly to the table, application code cannot bypass database triggers.

Typical uses of triggers include the implementation of critical business logic, the denormalization of data for performance reasons, and the auditing of changes made to a table. Triggers can be defined to fire before or after a specific DML statement executes.

In Figure 2 17, we create a trigger that fires before any INSERT statement completes against the sales table. It automatically applies free shipping and discounts to orders of a specified value.

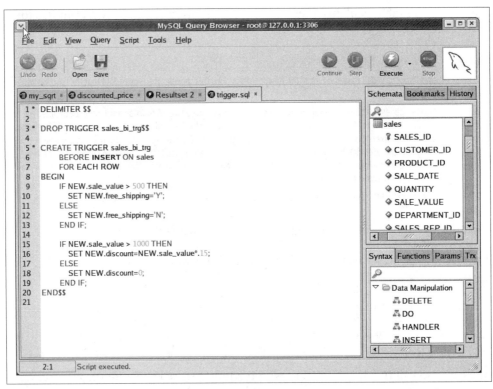

Figure 2-17. A database trigger

Here is an explanation of the trigger definition:

Line(s)	Explanation
5	Specify the trigger name.
6	Specify that the trigger fires before an insert on the sales table.
7	Include the (currently) mandatory FOR EACH ROW clause, indicating that the statements within the trigger will be executed once for every row inserted into the sales table.
8	Use BEGIN to start the block containing statements to be executed by the trigger.
9-13	If the sale_value is greater than $500, set the value of the free_shipping column to 'Y'. Otherwise, set it to 'N'.
15-19	If the sale_value is greater than $1000, calculate a 15% discount and insert that value into the discount column. Otherwise, set the discount to 0.

The effect of the trigger is to automatically set the value of the free_shipping and discount columns. Consider the INSERT statement shown in Example 2-10.

Example 2-10. An INSERT into the sales table

```
INSERT INTO sales
       (customer_id, product_id, sale_date, quantity, sale_value,
        department_id, sales_rep_id)
 VALUES(20,10,now(),20,10034,4,12)
```

The sale is valued at $10,034 and, as such, is eligible for a 15% discount and free shipping. Example 2-11 demonstrates that the trigger correctly set these values.

Example 2-11. A trigger automatically populates the free_shipping and discount columns

```
mysql> SELECT sale_value,free_shipping,discount
    ->   FROM sales
    ->  WHERE sales_id=2500003;
+------------+---------------+----------+
| sale_value | free_shipping | discount |
+------------+---------------+----------+
|      10034 | Y             |     1505 |
+------------+---------------+----------+
1 row in set (0.22 sec)
```

Using a trigger to maintain the free_shipping and discount columns ensures that the columns are correctly maintained regardless of the SQL statements that might be executed from PHP, C#, or Java, or even from the MySQL command-line client.

Calling a Stored Procedure from PHP

We've shown you how to call stored programs from the MySQL command-line client, from the MySQL Query Browser, and from another stored program. In the real world, however, you are more likely to call a stored program from another programming environment, such as PHP, Java, Perl, Python, or .NET. We discuss the details of using stored programs within each of these environments in Chapters 12 through 17.

For now, let's look at how you can call a stored procedure (shown in Figure 2-18) from PHP, which is probably the development environment most commonly used in conjunction with MySQL.

When interacting with MySQL from PHP, we can choose between the database-independent PEAR::DB extension, the mysqli (MySQL "improved") extension, and the more recent PHP Data Objects (PDO) extension. In this example we will use the mysqli extension. Chapter 13 describes the details of these extensions.

Figure 2-19 shows PHP code that connects to the MySQL server and calls the stored procedure. We won't step through the code here, but we hope that it will give you a sense of how stored programs can be used in web and other applications.

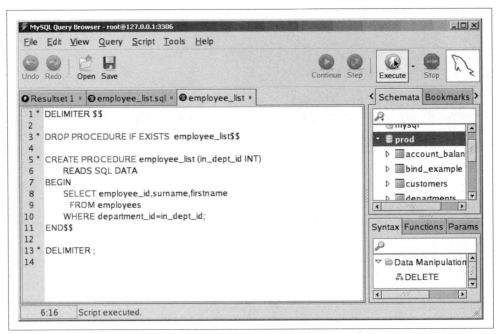

Figure 2-18. Stored procedure to be called from PHP

The PHP program prompts the user to specify a department ID; it then calls the stored procedure employee_list to retrieve a list of employees that belong to that department. Figure 2-20 shows the output displayed by the PHP/stored procedure example.

Conclusion

In this chapter we presented a brief "getting started" tutorial that introduced you to the basics of MySQL stored programs. We showed you how to:

- Create a simple "Hello World" stored procedure.
- Define local variables and procedure parameters.
- Perform conditional execution with the IF statement.
- Perform iterative processing with simple loops.
- Include SQL statements inside stored procedures, including how to perform row-at-a-time processing with cursors.
- Call a stored program from another stored program.
- Create a stored function (and differentiate stored functions from stored procedures).
- Create a trigger on a table to automate denormalization.
- Call a stored procedure from PHP.

Figure 2-19. Sample PHP program calling a stored procedure

You may now be tempted to put down this book and start writing MySQL stored programs. If so, we congratulate you on your enthusiasm. May we suggest, however, that you first spend some time reading more detailed explanations of each of these areas of functionality in the following chapters? That way, you are likely to make fewer mistakes and write higher-quality code.

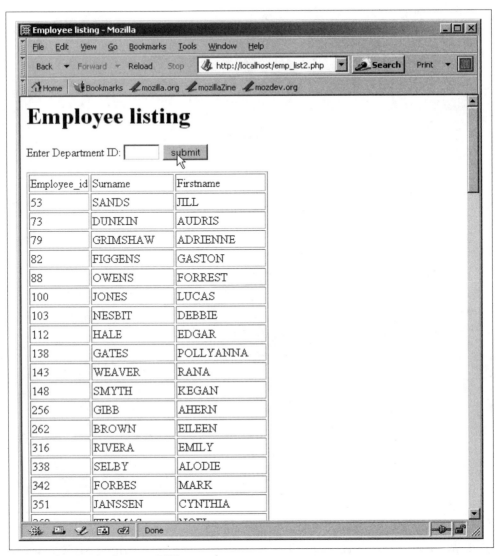

Figure 2-20. Output from our PHP example

## CHAPTER 3

Language Fundamentals

This chapter introduces the MySQL stored program language, a simple, readable but complete programming language based on the ANSI SQL:2003 SQL/PSM (Persistent Stored Module) specification.

The MySQL stored program language is a block-structured language (like Pascal) that includes familiar statements for manipulating variables, implementing conditional execution, performing iterative processing, and handling errors. Users of other stored program languages such as Oracle PL/SQL or Microsoft SQL Server Transact-SQL will find features of the language very familiar. In fact, users of the IBM DB2 SQL Procedural language will find MySQL's stored program language almost identical—both are based on the SQL/PSM specification. Users of other programming languages that are typically used with MySQL—such as PHP, Java, or Perl—might find the stored program language a little verbose, but should have no difficulty at all learning the language.

In this chapter we will look at the fundamental building blocks of the stored program language—variables, literals, parameters, comments, operators, expressions, and data types. We will also discuss MySQL 5 "strict" mode and its implications. In the next chapter we will build on this base by describing the block structure, conditional statements (IF and CASE), and looping capabilities of the language.

Variables, Literals, Parameters, and Comments

Let's start with a review of how we define and use various data items—variables, literals, and parameters—in our stored programs and how we can add comments to document our code.

Variables

The first thing we'll look at is how the MySQL stored program language deals with variables and literals, because without some understanding of these items, we can't create any meaningful examples for any other topics.

A *variable* is a named data item whose value can change during program execution. A *literal* (described in the next section) is an unnamed data item that can be assigned to a variable. Typically, literals are hardcoded into your stored program code and are usually assigned to variables, passed as parameters, or used as arguments to SELECT statements.

The DECLARE statement allows us to create a variable. As we will see a bit later on, it appears within a block of code before any cursor or handler declarations and before any procedural statements. The syntax of the DECLARE statement is:

```
DECLARE variable_name [,variable_name...] datatype [DEFAULT value];
```

Multiple variables may be declared in a single DECLARE statement, and the variable(s) can be assigned a default (or initial) value. If you don't use the DEFAULT clause, then the variable starts off with the NULL value.

Using DEFAULT is a good practice because, unless you initialize a variable, any subsequent operations on that variable—other than a simple assignment—may also return NULL. We'll give an example of this type of error later in the chapter.

The *datatype* may be any of the valid MySQL data types that you can use in a CREATE TABLE statement. We provide detailed descriptions of each data type later in this chapter; Table 3-1 summarizes those most commonly used.

Table 3-1. Commonly used MySQL data types

Data type	Explanation	Examples of corresponding values
INT, INTEGER	A 32-bit integer (whole number). Values can be from approximately -2.1 billion to +2.1 billion. If unsigned, the value can reach about 4.2 billion, but negative numbers are not allowed.	123,345 -2,000,000,000
BIGINT	A 64-bit integer (whole number). Values can be from approximately -9 million trillion to +9 million trillion or from 0 to 18 million trillion if unsigned.	9,000,000,000,000,000,000 -9,000,000,000,000,000,000
FLOAT	A 32-bit floating-point number. Values can range from about -1.7e38 to 1.7e38 for signed numbers or 0 to 3.4e38 if unsigned.	0.00000000000002 17897.890790 -345.8908770 1.7e21
DOUBLE	A 64-bit floating-point number. The value range is close to infinite (1.7e308).	1.765e203 -1.765e100
DECIMAL(precision,scale) NUMERIC(precision,scale)	A fixed-point number. Storage depends on the precision, as do the possible numbers that can be stored. NUMERICs are typically used where the number of decimals is important, such as for currency.	78979.00 -87.50 9.95
DATE	A calendar date, with no specification of time.	'1999-12-31'

Table 3-1. Commonly used MySQL data types (continued)

Data type	Explanation	Examples of corresponding values
DATETIME	A date and time, with resolution to a particular second.	`'1999-12-31 23:59:59'`
CHAR(*length*)	A fixed-length character string. The value will be right-padded up to the length specified. A maximum of 255 bytes can be specified for the length.	`'hello world          '`
VARCHAR(*length*)	A variable-length string up to 64K in length.	`'Hello world'`
BLOB, TEXT	Up to 64K of data, binary in the case of BLOB, or text in the case of TEXT.	Almost anything imaginable
LONGBLOB, LONGTEXT	Longer versions of the BLOB and TEXT types, capable of storing up to 4GB of data.	Almost anything imaginable, but a lot more than you would have imagined for BLOB or TEXT

Some examples of variable declarations for each of the data types are shown in Example 3-1.

Example 3-1. Examples of variable declarations

```
DECLARE l_int1     INT DEFAULT -2000000;
DECLARE l_int2     INT UNSIGNED DEFAULT 4000000;
DECLARE l_bigint1  BIGINT DEFAULT 4000000000000000;
DECLARE l_float    FLOAT DEFAULT 1.8e8;
DECLARE l_double   DOUBLE DEFAULT 2e45;
DECLARE l_numeric  NUMERIC(8,2) DEFAULT 9.95;

DECLARE l_date     DATE DEFAULT '1999-12-31';
DECLARE l_datetime DATETIME DEFAULT '1999-12-31 23:59:59';

DECLARE l_char     CHAR(255) DEFAULT 'This will be padded to 255 chars';
DECLARE l_varchar  VARCHAR(255) DEFAULT 'This will not be padded';

DECLARE l_text     TEXT DEFAULT 'This is a really long string.  In stored programs
                   we can use text columns fairly freely, but in tables there are some
                   limitations regarding indexing and use in various expressions.';
```

Literals

A *literal* is a data value hardcoded into your program. You commonly use literals in variable assignment statements or comparisons (IF, for instance), as arguments to procedures or functions, or within SQL statements.

There are three fundamental types of literals:

Numeric literals

A numeric literal represents a number and can be defined as a raw number (300, 30.45, etc.), as a hexadecimal value, or in scientific notation. Scientific notation is a way of representing very large or very high-precision values. The letter 'e' in what otherwise appears to be a number indicates that the numeric value on the left of the 'e' is multiplied by 10 to the power of the number to the right of the 'e'. So 2.4e is equivalent to 2.4×10^4 or 24,000. You cannot use commas in numeric literals.

Hexadecimal values are represented in the traditional format, by prefixing them with '0x'. So 0xA represents the hexadecimal number 'A', which is 10 in decimal.

Date literals

A date literal is a string in the format 'YYYY-MM-DD' or—for the DATETIME data type—in the format 'YYYY-MM-DD HH24:MI:SS'. So '1999-12-31 23:59:59' represents the last second of the last century (unless you believe that because there was no year 0, the century actually ended on 2000-12-31).

String literals

A string literal is simply any string value surrounded by quotes. If single quotes themselves need to be included within the literal itself delimited by single quotes, they can be represented by two single quotes or prefixed with a backslash (\'). You can also enclose strings in double quotes, and you can use escape sequences for special characters (\t for a tab, \n for a new line, \\ for a backslash, etc.).

If the server is running in ANSI_QUOTES mode (SET sql_mode='ANSI_QUOTES') then only single quotes can be used for literals. Sequences enclosed in double quotes will be interpreted as identifiers (variables or column names, for instance) that contain special characters, in accordance with the ANSI standard.

Rules for Variable Names

MySQL is amazingly flexible when it comes to naming variables. Unlike most other programming languages, MySQL allows variable names to be extremely long (more than 255 characters); they can contain special characters and can commence with numeric characters. However, we recommend that you not take advantage of MySQL's flexibility in this case—use sensible naming conventions and avoid overly long variable names (see Chapter 23 for these and other best practices).

Assigning Values to Variables

You manipulate variable values with the SET statement, which has the following syntax:

```
SET variable_name = expression [,variable_name = expression ...]
```

As you can see, it is possible to perform multiple assignments with a single SET statement.

Most languages do not require a SET statement for variable assignment, and consequently, one of the easiest mistakes to make when getting started is to try to assign a value to a variable without specifying SET, as in Example 3-2.

Example 3-2. Attempting to manipulate a variable without the SET statement

```
mysql> CREATE PROCEDURE no_set_stmt( )
BEGIN
        DECLARE i INTEGER;
        i=1;
END;
$$

ERROR 1064 (42000): You have an error in your SQL syntax; check the manual that
corresponds to your MySQL server version for the right syntax to use near 'procedure no_
set_stmt( )
BEGIN
        DECLARE i INT;
        i=1;
END' at line 1
```

As is often the case with stored program compilation errors, the error message does not directly identify the absence of the SET statement, so when checking your program for strange compilation errors, double check that all variable assignments include SET.

Parameters

Parameters are variables that can be passed into—or out of—the stored program from the calling program. Parameters are defined in the CREATE statement for the function or procedure as follows:

```
CREATE PROCEDURE|FUNCTION(
    [[IN|OUT|INOUT] parameter_name data_type ...])
```

The parameter names follow the same naming rules that apply to variables. The *data_type* can be any of the types available to local variables. Parameters can be associated with an IN, OUT, or INOUT attribute:

IN

> Unless otherwise specified, parameters assume the IN attribute. This means that their value must be specified by the calling program, and any modifications made to the parameter in the stored program cannot be accessed from the calling program.

OUT

> An OUT parameter can be modified by the stored program, and the modified value can be retrieved from the calling program. The calling program must supply a variable to receive the output of the OUT parameter, but the stored program itself has no access to whatever might be initially stored in that variable. When

the stored program commences, the value of any OUT variables appear as NULL, regardless of what value they may have been assigned in the calling program.

INOUT

An INOUT parameter acts both as an IN and as an OUT parameter. That is, the calling program may supply a value, the stored program itself may modify the value of the parameter, and the calling program may access this changed value when the stored program completes.

The IN, OUT, and INOUT keywords apply only to stored procedures and not to stored functions. In stored functions all parameters behave as IN parameters (although you cannot specify the IN keyword).

The next three examples illustrate these principles.

First, although MySQL lets us change the value of an IN parameter in a stored program, the change cannot be seen by the calling program. The stored program in Example 3-3 prints and then modifies the value of the parameter. While modification of the input parameter is allowed within the stored program, the original variable (@p_in) is unchanged.

Example 3-3. Example of an IN parameter

```
mysql> CREATE PROCEDURE sp_demo_in_parameter(IN p_in INT)
BEGIN
    /* We can see the value of the IN parameter */
    SELECT p_in;
    /* We can modify it*/
    SET p_in=2;
    /* show that the modification took effect */
    select p_in;
END;

/* This output shows that the changes made within the stored program cannot be accessed
from the calling program (in this case, the mysql client):*/

mysql> SET @p_in=1

Query OK, 0 rows affected (0.00 sec)

mysql> CALL sp_demo_in_parameter(@p_in)

+------+-------------------------------------------+
| p_in | We can see the value of the IN parameter  |
+------+-------------------------------------------+
|    1 | We can see the value of the IN parameter  |
+------+-------------------------------------------+
1 row in set (0.00 sec)

+------+------------------------------------+
| p_in | IN parameter value has been changed |
+------+------------------------------------+
```

Example 3-3. Example of an IN parameter (continued)

```
|    2 | IN parameter value has been changed |
+------+-------------------------------------+
1 row in set (0.00 sec)

Query OK, 0 rows affected (0.00 sec)

mysql> SELECT @p_in,'We can''t see the changed value from the calling program'

+-------+----------------------------------------------------------+
| @p_in | We can't see the changed value from the calling program |
+-------+----------------------------------------------------------+
| 1     | We can't see the changed value from the calling program |
+-------+----------------------------------------------------------+
1 row in set (0.00 sec)

Query OK, 0 rows affected (0.00 sec)
```

Next, in Example 3-4 we examine the behavior of an OUT parameter. Although the calling program has initialized the OUT parameter with a value, the stored program does not see that value. The calling program, however, sees the changed values when the procedure completes execution.

Example 3-4. Example of an OUT parameter

```
mysql> CREATE PROCEDURE sp_demo_out_parameter(OUT p_out INT)

BEGIN
    /* We can't see the value of the OUT parameter */
    SELECT p_out,'We can''t see the value of the OUT parameter';
    /* We can modify it*/
    SET p_out=2;
    SELECT p_out,'OUT parameter value has been changed';

END;

mysql> SET @p_out=1

Query OK, 0 rows affected (0.00 sec)

mysql> CALL sp_demo_out_parameter(@p_out)

+-------+----------------------------------------------------------------+
| p_out | We can't see the value of the OUT parameter in the stored program |
+-------+----------------------------------------------------------------+
| NULL  | We can't see the value of the OUT parameter in the stored program |
+-------+----------------------------------------------------------------+
1 row in set (0.00 sec)

+-------+--------------------------------------+
| p_out | OUT parameter value has been changed |
+-------+--------------------------------------+
|    2 | OUT parameter value has been changed |
```

Example 3-4. Example of an OUT parameter (continued)

```
+-------+-------------------------------------+
1 row in set (0.00 sec)

Query OK, 0 rows affected (0.00 sec)

mysql> SELECT @p_out,"Calling program can see the value of the changed OUT parameter"

+----------------------------------------------------------------+
| Calling program can see the value of the changed OUT parameter |
+----------------------------------------------------------------+
| 2                                                              |
+----------------------------------------------------------------+
1 row in set (0.00 sec)
```

Finally, Example 3-5 shows that the value of an INOUT parameter can be seen by the stored program, modified, and returned in its modified form to the calling program.

Example 3-5. Example of an INOUT parameter

```
mysql> CREATE PROCEDURE sp_demo_inout_parameter(INOUT p_inout INT)

BEGIN

    SELECT p_inout,'We can see the value of the INOUT parameter in the stored program';

    SET p_inout=2;
    SELECT p_inout,'INOUT parameter value has been changed';

END;
//
Query OK, 0 rows affected (0.00 sec)

SET @p_inout=1
//

Query OK, 0 rows affected (0.00 sec)

CALL sp_demo_inout_parameter(@p_inout) //

+---------+-----------------------------------------------------------------+
| p_inout | We can see the value of the INOUT parameter in the stored program |
+---------+-----------------------------------------------------------------+
|       1 | We can see the value of the INOUT parameter in the stored program |
+---------+-----------------------------------------------------------------+
1 row in set (0.00 sec)

+---------+----------------------------------------+
| p_inout | INOUT parameter value has been changed |
+---------+----------------------------------------+
|       2 | INOUT parameter value has been changed |
+---------+----------------------------------------+
1 row in set (0.00 sec)
```

Example 3-5. Example of an INOUT parameter (continued)

```
Query OK, 0 rows affected (0.00 sec)

SELECT @p_inout ,"Calling program can see the value of the changed INOUT parameter"
//

+----------+----------------------------------------------------------------------+
| @p_inout | Calling program can see the value of the changed INOUT parameter |
+----------+----------------------------------------------------------------------+
| 2        | Calling program can see the value of the changed INOUT parameter |
+----------+----------------------------------------------------------------------+
1 row in set (0.00 sec)
```

User Variables

User variables are special MySQL variables that can be defined and manipulated inside or outside stored programs. They have been available in MySQL since version 3 and are a feature of the MySQL base product, not the stored program language. However, we can make good use of user variables in two ways:

- Since user variables have a scope that is outside of individual stored programs, they can be used to represent variables that should be accessible from any stored program within a session. This approach is similar in principle to the use of global variables in other programming languages.

- User variables can provide an alternative method of passing information to stored programs. Stored programs can access the values of user variables, which can avoid the need to pass in the values as parameters. (See the earlier "Parameters" section for more information on parameters.)

User variables can be created and manipulated from the MySQL command-line client—or from any other program that can issue MySQL statements—using the SET statement. Example 3-6 shows some examples of using SET from the MySQL client.

Example 3-6. Manipulating user variables in the MySQL client

```
mysql> SELECT 'Hello World' into @x ;
Query OK, 1 row affected (0.00 sec)

mysql> SELECT @x;
+-------------+
| @x          |
+-------------+
| Hello World |
+-------------+
1 row in set (0.03 sec)

mysql> SET @y='Goodbye Cruel World';
Query OK, 0 rows affected (0.00 sec)

mysql> SELECT @y;
```

Example 3-6. Manipulating user variables in the MySQL client (continued)

```
+---------------------+
| @y                  |
+---------------------+
| Goodbye Cruel World |
+---------------------+
1 row in set (0.00 sec)

mysql> SET @z=1+2+3;
Query OK, 0 rows affected (0.00 sec)

mysql> SELECT @z;
+------+
| @z   |
+------+
| 6    |
+------+
1 row in set (0.00 sec)
```

You can access any user variable defined in the current session (e.g., connection) from within a stored program. For instance, Example 3-7 shows how to pass information to a stored procedure without using a procedure parameter.

Example 3-7. Using user variables to pass information from the calling program to the stored procedure

```
mysql> CREATE PROCEDURE GreetWorld( )
    ->   SELECT CONCAT(@greeting,' World');
Query OK, 0 rows affected (0.00 sec)

mysql> SET @greeting='Hello';
Query OK, 0 rows affected (0.00 sec)

mysql> CALL GreetWorld( );
+--------------------------+
| CONCAT(@greeting,' World') |
+--------------------------+
| Hello World              |
+--------------------------+
1 row in set (0.00 sec)

Query OK, 0 rows affected (0.00 sec)
```

We can also create a user variable within a stored program. It will then be available from all other stored programs, acting like a global variable would in a language such as PHP. For instance, in Example 3-8, procedure p1( ) creates the user variable, which is visible within procedure p2( ).

Example 3-8. Using a user variable as a "global variable" across stored programs

```
mysql> CREATE PROCEDURE p1( )
    ->   SET @last_procedure='p1';
Query OK, 0 rows affected (0.00 sec)

mysql> CREATE PROCEDURE p2( )
    ->   SELECT CONCAT('Last procedure was ',@last_procedure);
Query OK, 0 rows affected (0.00 sec)

mysql> CALL p1( );
Query OK, 0 rows affected (0.00 sec)

mysql> CALL p2( );
+-----------------------------------------------+
| CONCAT('Last procedure was ',@last_procedure) |
+-----------------------------------------------+
| Last procedure was p1                         |
+-----------------------------------------------+
1 row in set (0.00 sec)
```

A user variable is a variant data type—it can store a string, date, or numeric value. Data type conversions are performed automatically. User variables remain in existence for the duration of a MySQL session and can be accessed by any program or statement running within that session. They cannot, however, be accessed by other sessions.

In some programming languages (such as PHP), variables whose scope extends beyond a single function are identified by the global keyword. In other languages the syntax for defining these variables may differ, but they are often still referred to as "global" variables. In MySQL, the global clause of the SET statement allows you to set the server-wide value of system variables, not to create the equivalent of a PHP global variable. For this reason, referring to user variables as "global" in scope can lead to confusion and probably should be avoided. Note that you cannot use the global clause of the SET statement to create your own variables.

Using user variables to implement variables that are available across multiple stored programs can be useful on occasion. However, you should definitely use this technique sparingly. As in all programming languages, overuse of global variables that scope beyond a single program can lead to code that is hard to understand and maintain. Routines that share such variables become tightly coupled and hence hard to maintain, test, or even understand in isolation.

 Use "user" variables sparingly in your stored programs. Excessive use of variables that scope beyond a single program leads to code that is nonmodular and hard to maintain.

Comments

Two styles of comments are supported in MySQL stored programs:

- Two dashes -- followed by a space create a comment that continues until the end of the current line. We'll call these *single-line comments*.

- C-style comments commence with /* and terminate with */. We'll call these *multiline comments*.

Single-line comments are useful for documenting variable declarations and simple single-line statements. Multiline comments are more useful for creating larger comment chunks, such as a standard comment header that accompanies each stored program definition.

The chunk of code in Example 3-9 illustrates both types of comments.

Example 3-9. Example of stored program comments

```
CREATE PROCEDURE comment_demo
    (IN p_input_parameter INT  -- Dummy parameter to illustrate styles
    )
/*
|    Program: comment_demo
|    Purpose: demonstrate comment styles
|    Author:  Guy Harrison
|    Change History:
|        2005-09-21 - Initial
|
*/
```

Operators

MySQL operators include the familiar operators common to most programming languages, although C-style operators (++, --, +=, etc.) are not supported.

Operators are typically used within the SET statement to change the value of a variable, within comparison statements such as IF or CASE, and in loop control expressions. Example 3-10 shows a few simple examples of using operators within stored programs.

Example 3-10. Examples of operators in a stored program

```
CREATE PROCEDURE operators()
BEGIN
        DECLARE a int default 2;
        DECLARE b int default 3;
        DECLARE c FLOAT;

        SET c=a+b; select 'a+b=',c;
        SET c=a/b; select 'a/b=',c;
        SET c=a*b; Select 'a*b=',c;
```

Example 3-10. Examples of operators in a stored program (continued)

```
        IF (a<b) THEN
                SELECT 'a is less than b';
        END IF;
        IF NOT (a=b) THEN
                SELECT 'a is not equal to b';
        END IF;
end;
```

The various types of operators (mathematical, comparison, logical, and bitwise) are described in the following subsections.

Mathematical Operators

MySQL supports the basic mathematical operators you learned about in elementary school (pay attention class!): addition (+), subtraction (-), multiplication (*), and division (/).

In addition, MySQL supports two additional operators related to division: the DIV operator returns only the integer portion of division, while the modulus operator (%) returns only the remainder from a division. Table 3-2 lists, describes, and provides an example of the MySQL mathematical operators.

Table 3-2. MySQL mathematical operators

Operator	Description	Example
+	Addition	SET var1=2+2; → 4
-	Subtraction	SET var2=3-2; → 1
*	Multiplication	SET var3=3*2; → 6
/	Division	SET var4=10/3; → 3.3333
DIV	Integer division	SET var5=10 DIV 3; → 3
%	Modulus	SET var6=10%3 ; → 1

Comparison Operators

Comparison operators compare values and return TRUE, FALSE, or UNKNOWN (usually if one of the values being compared is NULL or UNKNOWN). They are typically used within expressions in IF, CASE, and loop control statements.

Table 3-3 summarizes the MySQL comparison operators.

Table 3-3. Comparison operators

Operator	Description	Example	Example result
>	Is greater than	1>2	FALSE
<	Is less than	2<1	FALSE
<=	Is less than or equal to	2<=2	TRUE
>=	Is greater than or equal to	3>=2	TRUE
BETWEEN	Value is between two values	5 BETWEEN 1 AND 10	TRUE
NOT BETWEEN	Value is not between two values	5 NOT BETWEEN 1 AND 10	FALSE
IN	Value is in a list	5 IN (1,2,3,4)	FALSE
NOT IN	Value is not in a list	5 NOT IN (1,2,3,4)	TRUE
=	Is equal to	2=3	FALSE
<>, !=	Is not equal to	2<>3	FALSE
<=>	Null safe equal (returns TRUE if both arguments are NULL)	NULL<=>NULL	TRUE
LIKE	Matches a simple pattern	"Guy Harrison" LIKE "Guy%"	TRUE
REGEXP	Matches an extended regular expression	"Guy Harrison" REGEXP "[Gg]reg"	FALSE
IS NULL	Value is NULL	0 IS NULL	FALSE
IS NOT NULL	Value is not NULL	0 IS NOT NULL	TRUE

Logical Operators

Logical operators operate on the three-valued logic values TRUE, FALSE, and NULL and return a like value. These operators are typically used with comparison operators to create more complex expressions.

For many of the logical operations, if any of the values being compared is NULL, then the result is also NULL. It is extremely important to remember this simple fact when creating logical expressions since, otherwise, subtle bugs can arise in your code.

The AND operator compares two Boolean expressions and returns TRUE only if both of the expressions are true. Table 3-4 shows the possible values generated by the AND function.

Table 3-4. Truth table for AND operator

AND	TRUE	FALSE	NULL
TRUE	TRUE	FALSE	NULL
FALSE	FALSE	FALSE	NULL
NULL	NULL	NULL	NULL

The OR operator compares two Boolean expressions and returns TRUE if either of the expressions provided is TRUE (Table 3-5).

Table 3-5. Truth table for the OR operator

OR	TRUE	FALSE	NULL
TRUE	TRUE	TRUE	TRUE
FALSE	TRUE	FALSE	NULL
NULL	TRUE	NULL	NULL

The XOR operator returns TRUE if either—but not both—of the values is TRUE. Table 3-6 shows the possible values for an XOR expression.

Table 3-6. Truth table for the XOR operator

XOR	TRUE	FALSE	NULL
TRUE	FALSE	TRUE	NULL
FALSE	TRUE	FALSE	NULL
NULL	NULL	NULL	NULL

Example 3-11 shows the use of the AND operator to combine multiple comparisons.

Example 3-11. Example of logical operators in practice

```
CREATE FUNCTION f_title(in_gender CHAR(1),
                        in_age INT, in_marital_status VARCHAR(7))
  RETURNS VARCHAR(6)
BEGIN
  DECLARE title VARCHAR(6);
  IF in_gender='F' AND in_age<16 THEN
     SET title='Miss';
  ELSEIF in_gender='F' AND in_age>=16 AND in_marital_status='Married' THEN
     SET title='Mrs';
  ELSEIF in_gender='F' AND in_age>=16 AND in_marital_status='Single' THEN
     SET title='Ms';
  ELSEIF in_gender='M' AND in_age<16 THEN
     SET title='Master';
  ELSEIF in_gender='M' AND in_age>=16 THEN
     SET title='Mr';
  END IF;
  RETURN(title);
END;
```

Bitwise Operators

Bitwise operators perform operations on the underlying binary representation of a variable. Table 3-7 lists the bitwise operators.

Table 3-7. Bitwise operators

Operator	Use
|	OR
&	AND
<<	Shift bits to left
>>	Shift bits to right
~	NOT or invert bits

Bitwise operators are similar to logical operators, except that they perform their operations on each bit within a variable.

For instance, consider the integers 5 (binary 101) and 4 (binary 010). The OR operator sets each bit if either of the bits is set in the inputs; so 5|2=7, because 101|010=111, which is 7 in decimal.

The bitwise AND operator sets a bit only if both the bits are true in the input. So 5&6=7, because 101&110=111, which equals 4.

Expressions

An *expression* is a combination of literals, variables, and operators that resolves to some value. Conditional execution and flow-control statements usually depend on the value of an expression to determine loop continuation or code branching.

Example 3-12 shows a variety of expressions.

Example 3-12. Examples of expressions

```
Myvariable_name
Myvariable_name+1
ABS(Myvariable_name)
3.14159
IF(Myvariable='M','Male','Female')
(2+4)/12
```

Built-in Functions

You can use most of the functions that MySQL makes available for use in SQL statements within stored programs. These are fully documented in the MySQL reference manual, and we provide details and examples for most of these functions in Chapter 9. We'll also talk about how you can create your own "stored" functions in the MySQL stored program language in Chapter 10.

The functions that may be used in SQL but not in stored programs are those involved in group (multiple-row) operators. These include functions such as SUM,

`COUNT`, `MIN`, `MAX`, and `AVG`. MySQL accepts these functions within expressions, but they will return NULL as shown in Example 3-13.

Example 3-13. Aggregate functions in stored procedures return NULL

```
mysql> CREATE PROCEDURE functions()
BEGIN
        DECLARE a int default 2;
        DECLARE b int default 3;
        DECLARE c FLOAT;

        SET c=SUM(a); select c;

END;

Query OK, 0 rows affected (0.00 sec)

mysql> CALL functions();

+------+
| c    |
+------+
| NULL |
+------+
1 row in set (0.00 sec)
```

MySQL functions fall into the following categories:

String functions

These functions perform operations on string variables. For example, you can concatenate strings, find characters within strings, obtain a substring, and perform other common operations.

Mathematical functions

These functions perform operations on numbers. For example, you can perform exponentiation (raise to a power), trigonometric functions (sine, cosine, etc.), random number functions, logarithms, and so on.

Date and time functions

These functions perform operations on dates and times. For example, you can get the current date, add or subtract time intervals from dates, find the difference between two dates, and extract certain portions of a date (e.g., get the time of day from a date-time).

Miscellaneous functions

These functions include everything not easily categorized in the above three groupings. They include cast functions, flow control functions (e.g., `CASE`), informational functions (e.g., server version), and encryption functions.

Table 3-8 summarizes some of the most frequently used functions; see Chapter 9 for a more complete coverage of function syntax and examples.

Table 3-8. Commonly used MySQL functions

Function	Description
ABS(*number*)	Returns the absolute value of the number supplied. For instance, ABS(-2.3)=2.3.
CEILING(*number*)	Returns the next highest integer. For instance, CEILING(2.3)=3.
CONCAT(*string1*[,*string2*,*string3*,...])	Returns a string comprised of all the supplied strings joined (concatenated) together.
CURDATE	Returns the current date (without the time portion).
DATE_ADD(*date*,INTERVAL *amount_type*)	Adds the specified interval to the specified date and returns a new date. Valid types include SECOND, MINUTE, HOUR, DAY, MONTH, and YEAR.
DATE_SUB(*date*,INTERVAL *interval_type*)	Subtracts the specified interval from the specified date and returns a new date. Valid types include SECOND, MINUTE, HOUR, DAY, MONTH, and YEAR.
FORMAT(*number*,*decimals*)	Returns a number with a specified number of decimal places and with 1000 separators (usually ",").
GREATEST(*num1*,*num2*[,*num3*, ...])	Returns the greatest number from all the numbers supplied as arguments.
IF(*test*, *value1*,*value2*)	Tests a logical condition. If TRUE, returns *value1*; otherwise, returns *value2*.
IFNULL(*value*,*value2*)	Returns the value of the first argument, unless that argument is NULL; in that case, it returns the value of the second argument.
INSERT(*string*,*position*,*length*,*new*)	Inserts a string into the middle of another string.
INSTR(*string*,*substring*)	Finds the location of a substring within a string.
ISNULL(*expression*)	Returns 1 if the argument is NULL, 0 otherwise.
LEAST(*num1*,*num2*[,*num3*, ...])	Returns the smallest number from the list of arguments.
LEFT(*string*,*length*)	Returns the leftmost portion of a string.
LENGTH(*string*)	Returns the length of a string in bytes. CHAR_LENGTH can be used if you want to return the number of characters (which could be different if you are using a multibyte character set).
LOCATE(*substring*,*string*[,*number*])	Returns the location of the substring within the string, optionally starting the search at the position given by the third argument.
LOWER(*string*)	Translates the given string into lowercase.
LPAD(*string*,*length*,*padding*)	Left-pads the string to the given length, using the third argument as the pad character.
LTRIM(*string*)	Removes all leading whitespace from a string.
MOD(*num1*,*num2*)	Returns the modulo (remainder) returned by the division of the first number by the second number.
NOW	Returns the current date and time.
POWER(*num1*,*num2*)	Raises *num1* to the power *num2*.

Table 3-8. Commonly used MySQL functions (continued)

Function	Description
RAND([seed])	Returns a random number. The seed may be used to initialize the random number generator.
REPEAT(string,number)	Returns a string consisting of number repetitions of the given string.
REPLACE(string,old,new)	Replaces all occurrences of old with new in the given string.
ROUND(number[,decimal])	Rounds a numeric value to the specified number of decimal places.
RPAD(string,length,padding)	Right-pads string to the specified length using the specified padding character.
RTRIM(string)	Removes all trailing blanks from string.
SIGN(number)	Returns -1 if the number is less than 0, 1 if the number is greater than 0, or 0 if the number is equal to 0.
SQRT(number)	Returns the square root of the given number.
STRCMP(string1,string2)	Returns 0 if the two strings are identical, -1 if the first string would sort earlier than the second string, or 1 otherwise.
SUBSTRING(string,position,length)	Extracts length characters from string starting at the specified position.
UPPER(string)	Returns the specified string converted to uppercase.
VERSION	Returns a string containing version information for the current MySQL server.

Functions can be used in any statement that accepts an expression—for example, in SET statements, conditional statements (IF, CASE), and loop control clauses. Example 3-14 shows some examples that use functions in SET and IF clauses.

Example 3-14. Examples of functions in SET and IF clauses

```
CREATE PROCEDURE function_example()
BEGIN

  DECLARE TwentyYearsAgoToday DATE;
  DECLARE mystring VARCHAR(250);

  SET TwentyYearsAgoToday=date_sub(curdate(), interval 20 year);

  SET mystring=concat('It was ',TwentyYearsAgoToday,
      ' Sgt Pepper taught the band to play...');

  SELECT mystring;

  IF (CAST(SUBSTR(version(),1,3) AS DECIMAL(2,1)) <5.0) THEN
    SELECT 'MySQL versions earlier than 5.0 cannot run stored programs - you
          must be hallucinating';
  ELSE
```

Example 3-14. Examples of functions in SET and IF clauses (continued)

```
    SELECT 'Thank goodness you are running 5.0 or higher!';
  END IF;

END$$

CALL function_example( )$$

+-----------------------------------------------------------+
| mystring                                                  |
+-----------------------------------------------------------+
| It was 1985-11-22 Sgt Pepper taught the band to play... |
+-----------------------------------------------------------+
1 row in set (0.03 sec)

+-----------------------------------------------+
| Thank goodness you are running 5.0 or higher! |
+-----------------------------------------------+
| Thank goodness you are running 5.0 or higher! |
+-----------------------------------------------+
1 row in set (0.03 sec)
```

Data Types

Variables in MySQL stored programs can be assigned any of the data types available to columns in MySQL tables. We previewed most of the data types earlier, in Table 3-1.

All variables in MySQL stored programs are *scalars*, which is to say variables that store only a single item. There are no equivalents to arrays, records, or structures such as you can find in some other programming languages.

String Data Types

MySQL supports two basic string data types: CHAR and VARCHAR. CHAR stores fixed-length strings, while VARCHAR stores variable-length strings. If a CHAR variable is assigned a value shorter than its declared length, it will be blank-padded out to the declared length. This does not occur with VARCHAR variables.

When used in MySQL tables, the choice of CHAR or VARCHAR can be significant because it can affect the amount of disk storage needed. However, in stored programs, the additional memory requirements will be minimal and, use CHARs and VARCHARs can be used interchangeably in all expressions, there is little advantage to either data type. We generally use VARCHARs because they are capable of storing longer strings.

The CHAR data type can store a maximum of 255 bytes, and the VARCHAR a maximum of 65,532 bytes.

The ENUM data type

The ENUM data type is used to store one of a set of permissible values. These values can be accessed as their string value or as their indexed position in the set of possibilities. If you attempt to assign a value into an ENUM that does not appear in the list, MySQL will either issue a warning and insert a NULL or—if the sql_mode includes one of the "strict" values (see the later section "MySQL 5 "Strict" Mode")—issue an error.

Example 3-15 illustrates the use of ENUMs in stored programs.

Example 3-15. Using ENUMs in stored programs

```
CREATE PROCEDURE sp_enums(in_option ENUM('Yes','No','Maybe'))
BEGIN
  DECLARE position INTEGER;
  SET position=in_option;
  SELECT in_option,position;
END
--------------

Query OK, 0 rows affected (0.01 sec)

--------------
CALL sp_enums('Maybe')
--------------

+-----------+----------+
| in_option | position |
+-----------+----------+
| Maybe     |        3 |
+-----------+----------+
1 row in set (0.00 sec)

Query OK, 0 rows affected (0.00 sec)

--------------
CALL sp_enums(2)
--------------

+-----------+----------+
| in_option | position |
+-----------+----------+
| No        |        2 |
+-----------+----------+
1 row in set (0.00 sec)

Query OK, 0 rows affected (0.00 sec)

--------------
CALL sp_enums('What?')
--------------

ERROR 1265 (01000): Data truncated for column 'in_option' at row 1
```

The SET data type

The SET type is similar to the ENUM type, except that multiple values from the list of allowable values can occur in the variables (see Example 3-16). As with the ENUM type, an attempt to assign a value not in the list will generate an error in "strict" mode, and a warning otherwise.

Example 3-16. Behavior of SET variables in stored programs

```
CREATE PROCEDURE sp_set(in_option SET('Yes','No','Maybe'))
BEGIN

  SELECT in_option;
END
--------------

Query OK, 0 rows affected (0.00 sec)

--------------
CALL sp_set('Yes')
--------------

+-----------+
| in_option |
+-----------+
| Yes       |
+-----------+
1 row in set (0.01 sec)

Query OK, 0 rows affected (0.01 sec)

--------------
CALL sp_set('Yes,No,Maybe')
--------------

+--------------+
| in_option    |
+--------------+
| Yes,No,Maybe |
+--------------+
1 row in set (0.00 sec)

Query OK, 0 rows affected (0.00 sec)

--------------
CALL sp_set('Yes,No,Go away')
--------------

ERROR 1265 (01000): Data truncated for column 'in_option' at row 1
```

Numeric Data Types

MySQL supports two families of numeric types:

- Exact numeric types such as the INT and DECIMAL types
- Approximate numeric types such as FLOAT

Accurate numeric types store an exact value for a number. The various INT types (INT, BIGINT, TINYINT) differ in that they use different amounts of storage, which therefore restricts the magnitude of the numbers that they can store. Each type can be signed (capable of storing positive or negative numbers) or unsigned, which further restricts the maximum values that the type may store (allowing a variable to be unsigned doubles the maximum possible number that can be stored). Table 3-9 shows the limits for the various integer types.

Table 3-9. Limits for the various integer data types

Data type	Storage (bits)	Signed maximum	Unsigned maximum
TINYINT	8	127	255
SMALLINT	16	32767	65535
MEDIUMINT	24	8388607	16777215
INT	32	2147483647	4294967295
BIGINT	64	9223372036854775807	9223372036854775807

Floating-point data types (FLOAT, DOUBLE, REAL) store numbers of variable size and precision. In MySQL tables, FLOAT types use 32 bits of storage by default, while DOUBLE uses 64 bits of storage.

Be aware, however, that the floating-point data types store approximate representations of numbers. Most of the time this is unimportant, but in some circumstances you will want to use the precision data types, such as DECIMAL or NUMERIC, to avoid rounding errors that can occur when performing mathematical operations on floating-point numbers.

Date and Time Data Types

MySQL stores date-times with a precision down to one second. In MySQL tables, columns of the DATE data type can store the date part of a date-time only, while the DATETIME can store both a date and a time.

TEXT and BLOB Data Types

In MySQL tables, the TEXT data type can store up to 64K of data, and LONGTEXT can store up to 4,294,967,295 characters. BLOB and LONGBLOB data types can store similar amounts of data, but are able to store binary as well as character data.

MySQL 5 "Strict" Mode

MySQL 5 "strict" mode applies when either STRICT_TRANS_TABLES or STRICT_ALL_TABLES is included in the list of options supplied to the sql_mode configuration variable. STRICT_ALL_TABLES will cause any attempt to set a column to an invalid value to fail with an error. STRICT_TRANS_TABLES has the same effect, but only if the table is transactional.

If neither of these settings is in effect, MySQL will either accept the update or do a "best fit" of the invalid value into a legal column value. For instance, if you try to assign a string value into an integer column, MySQL may set the value of the column to 0. A warning will be generated whenever such a "truncation" occurs.

Strict mode will also cause errors to occur for missing columns in an INSERT statement, unless that column has an associated DEFAULT clause.

STRICT_ALL_TABLES can have some dubious side effects when you are performing multirow updates or inserts into nontransactional tables. Because there is no rollback capability for a nontransactional table, the error may occur after a certain number of valid row updates have occurred. This means that in the event of a strict-mode error on a nontransactional table, the SQL statement may partially succeed. This is rarely desirable behavior, and for this reason the default setting in MySQL 5.0 is STRICT_TRANS_TABLES.

You can change your strict mode at any time with a SET statement:

```
SET sql_mode='STRICT_ALL_TABLES'
```

The strict mode also determines how stored programs deal with attempts to assign invalid values to variables. If either of the strict modes is in effect, then an error will be generated whenever an attempt to assign an invalid value to a variable occurs. If no strict modes are in effect, then only warnings are generated.

Note that this behavior is controlled by the sql_mode settings that are in effect when the program is created, not when it is run. So once a strict stored program is created, it remains strict, even if the sql_mode settings are relaxed later on. In the same way, programs that are created when none of the strict modes are in effect will continue to generate warnings rather than errors when invalid data is assigned, regardless of the sql_mode that is in effect when the program runs.

Stored Program Behavior and Strict Mode

All variables in a MySQL stored program must be declared before use—with the exception of "user" variables, which are prefixed by the @ symbol and may be defined outside of the stored program. Furthermore, variables in MySQL stored programs must be assigned an explicit data type, and this data type cannot change during program execution. In this respect, the MySQL stored program language resembles "strongly typed" languages such as C, Java, and C# rather than dynamically typed languages such as Perl and PHP.

When created in strict mode, as explained in the previous section, stored programs will reject with an error any attempt to assign an invalid or inappropriate value to a variable. Such rejected assignments will include attempts to assign strings to numeric data or attempts to assign values that exceed the storage limitations declared for the variable.

However, when a stored program is created in non-strict mode, MySQL will perform a best attempt to convert invalid data and will generate a warning rather than an error. This allows you to—for instance—assign a string value to a variable defined as an integer. This non-strict behavior can lead to unexpected results or subtle bugs if you do not carefully ensure that you always use variables in ways that are appropriate for their data type. For these reasons it is usually best to create stored programs in strict mode and generate an error that you cannot possibly fail to notice during program testing or execution.

Program Examples

We'll illustrate these differences with an example that compares the behavior of the MySQL stored program in non-strict mode with several other programming languages.

Example 3-17 shows a Java program that intends to concatenate an integer value to a string value with the intention of printing the string "99 bottles of beer on the wall". Unfortunately for the beer, the programmer accidentally declared variable c as an int, rather than as a String. The Java compiler detects this error during compile time when it detects an attempt to assign a string expression to an integer variable, and the program fails to compile—no harm done.

Example 3-17. Type checking in a Java program

```
$cat simplejava.java
package simplejava;

public class SimpleJava {

        public static void main(String[] args) {
                String b;
                int a;
                int c;
                a=99;
                b="Bottles of beer on the wall";
                c=a+" "+c;

                System.out.println(c);
```

Example 3-17. Type checking in a Java program (continued)

```
        }
}

$javac simplejava.java
simplejava.java:11: incompatible types
found   : java.lang.String
required: int
                c=a+" "+c;
                   ^

1 error
```

Now let's look at an equivalent example (in a dynamically typed language—in this case, PHP). In PHP and Perl, variable data types change on the fly as required. In Example 3-18, the variable c started as a number, but when subjected to a string assignment, the data type dynamically changed to a string. The program therefore works as required.

Example 3-18. Dynamic variable typing in PHP

```
$cat simplephp.php
<?php
                $a=99;
                $b="Bottles of beer on the wall";
                $c=0;           #c is a number
                $c=$a." ".$b;   #c is now a string

                print $c."\n";
?>

$php simplephp.php
99 Bottles of beer on the wall
```

Now let's look at the equivalent non-strict MySQL stored program version of this logic, as shown in Example 3-19. This procedure has the same data type error as in the previous examples—the variable c should be defined as a VARCHAR, but it is instead declared as an INT.

Example 3-19. MySQL stored program non-strict type checking

```
CREATE PROCEDURE strict_test( )
BEGIN

  DECLARE a INT;
  DECLARE b VARCHAR(20);
  DECLARE c INT;

  SET a=99;
  SET b="Bottles of beer on the wall";
  SET c=CONCAT(a," ",b);
  SELECT c;
END
```

Example 3-19. MySQL stored program non-strict type checking (continued)

```
--------------

Query OK, 0 rows affected (0.01 sec)

mysql> CALL strict_test();
+------+
| C    |
+------+
|   99 |
+------+
1 row in set (0.00 sec)

Query OK, 0 rows affected, 2 warnings (0.00 sec)

mysql> SHOW WARNINGS;
+---------+------+---------------------------------------+
| Level   | Code | Message                               |
+---------+------+---------------------------------------+
| Warning | 1265 | Data truncated for column 'b' at row 1 |
| Warning | 1265 | Data truncated for column 'c' at row 1 |
+---------+------+---------------------------------------+
2 rows in set (0.01 sec)
```

Without the strict mode, MySQL does not generate an error when the attempt to supply a string to an integer value occurs, nor does it dynamically convert the data type of the integer variables. Instead, it assigns only the numeric part of the string expression to the integer—leading to an unexpected and erroneous result. However, if we had created the procedure when in strict mode, we would have generated a runtime error, as shown in Example 3-20.

Example 3-20. Stored program type checking in strict mode

```
mysql> CALL strict_test();
ERROR 1406 (22001): Data too long for column 'b' at row 1
```

It's almost always preferable for your programs to operate in strict mode. While a non-strict program will sometimes be able to continue where a strict program would fail with an error, the risk that the non-strict program will exhibit unexpected and inappropriate behaviors is usually too high. Remember that the behavior of a stored program depends on the setting of the variable sql_mode *when the program is created,* not when the program is run.

> Stored programs should almost always operate in strict mode to avoid unpredictable behavior when invalid data assignments occur. The strict mode for a stored program is determined by the setting of the sql_mode variable in effect when the program is created, not when the program is run.

As always, the onus is on the programmer to ensure that data types are used appropriately. As Bruce Eckel noted in his article "Strong Typing vs. Strong Testing" (*http://www.mindview.net/WebLog/log-0025*), strong *typing* in computer languages only provides an illusion of safety—true validation of correct behavior can only be obtained through strong *testing*. You should not assume that by declaring a variable as being of a certain type you are implicitly performing validation of the data being applied to that variable.

Conclusion

In this chapter we provided an overview of the building blocks of the MySQL stored program language. The MySQL stored program language—based on the ANSI SQL: 2003 PSM specification—is a block-structured language that supports all the programming fundamentals that you would expect from a procedural language. The major aspects of the stored program language with which you should be familiar at this point are:

- The DECLARE statement, which allows you to define and initialize program variables.
- Stored program parameters, which allow you to pass information into or—in the case of stored procedures—out of a stored program.
- The SET statement, which allows you to change the value of a program variable.
- MySQL functions, operators, and data types—the MySQL stored program language utilizes most of the equivalents available in the MySQL SQL language.

Stored program type checking is very dependent on the setting of the sql_mode configuration variable. If a program is created when the sql_mode variable includes one of the strict settings (STRICT_TRANS_TABLES or STRICT_ALL_TABLES), then the program will reject invalid variable assignments with an error. If neither of the strict modes is in effect, then the stored program will generate an error when invalid data assignments occur, but will continue execution. Non-strict stored program behavior can lead to unexpected and subtle bugs, and we recommend that you usually use the strict mode when creating your stored programs.

## CHAPTER 4

Blocks, Conditional Statements, and Iterative Programming

This chapter describes the constructs in the MySQL language that control the scope and flow of execution.

In MySQL, as in all block-structured languages, groups of statements may be grouped together into *blocks*. A block can normally occur whenever a single statement would be permitted, and the block may contain its own distinct variable, cursor, and handler declarations.

The MySQL stored program language supports two types of stored program control statements: conditional control statements and iteration (looping) statements. Almost every piece of code you write requires conditional control, which is the ability to direct the flow of execution through your program based on a condition. You do this with IF-THEN-ELSE and CASE statements.

Iterative control structures—otherwise known as *loops*—let you execute the same code repeatedly. MySQL provides three different kinds of loop constructs:

Simple loop
>   Continues until you issue a LEAVE statement to terminate the loop

REPEAT UNTIL *loop*
>   Continues until an expression evaluates as true

WHILE *loop*
>   Continues as long as an expression evaluates as true

Block Structure of Stored Programs

Most MySQL stored programs consist of one or more blocks (the only exception is when a stored program contains only a single executable statement). Each block commences with a BEGIN statement and is terminated by an END statement. So in the simplest case, a stored program consists of a program definition statement (CREATE

PROCEDURE, CREATE FUNCTION, or CREATE TRIGGER) followed by a single block that contains the program code to be executed:

```
CREATE {PROCEDURE|FUNCTION|TRIGGER} program_name
BEGIN
    program_statements
END;
```

The purpose of a block is twofold:

To logically group related code segments

For instance, a handler declaration (see Chapter 6 for an explanation of error handlers) can include a block definition allowing it to execute multiple commands. All of the statements within the block will be executed if the handler is invoked.

To control the scope of variables and other objects

You can define a variable within a block that is not visible outside the block. Furthermore, you can declare a variable within a block that overrides the definition of a variable with the same name declared outside of the block.

A compound statement consists of a BEGIN-END block, which encloses one or more stored program commands.

Structure of a Block

A block consists of various types of declarations (e.g., variables, cursors, handlers) and program code (e.g., assignments, conditional statements, loops). The order in which these can occur is as follows:

1. Variable and condition declarations. Variables were discussed earlier in Chapter 3, and condition declarations are discussed in Chapter 6.

2. Cursor declarations, discussed in Chapter 5.

3. Handler declarations, discussed in Chapter 6.

4. Program code.

If you violate this order—for instance, by issuing a DECLARE statement after a SET statement—MySQL will generate an error message when you try to create your stored program code. The error messages do not always clearly indicate that you have used statements in the wrong order, so it's important to develop the habit of declaring things in the correct order.

The order of statements in a block must be Variables and conditions, followed by Cursors, then Exception handlers, and finally Other statements. We remember this order using the following mnemonic: "Very Carefully Establish Order" in your stored programs.

You can also name a block with a *label*. The label can occur both before the BEGIN statement and after the END statement. Labeling a block has the following advantages:

- It improves code readability—for instance, by allowing you to quickly match the BEGIN statement with its associated END statement.
- It allows you to terminate block execution with the LEAVE statement (see the section describing this statement later in this chapter).

So a simplified representation of the structure of a block is:

```
[label:] BEGIN
    variable and condition declarations
    cursor declarations
    handler declarations

    program code

END [label];
```

Nested Blocks

If all stored programs contained only a single block, the block structure would be hardly worth mentioning. However, many programs include blocks that are defined within an enclosing block—at least within the main block that encloses all the stored program code. As suggested earlier, variables declared *within* a block are not available *outside* the block, but may be visible to blocks that are declared within the block. You can override an "outer" variable with a new definition within the block, and you can manipulate this variable without affecting the value of the "outer" variable.

Let's illustrate some of these principles with some examples.

In Example 4-1, we create a variable within a block. The variable is not available in the outer block, so this example generates an error.

Example 4-1. Declarations within a block are not visible outside the block

```
mysql> CREATE PROCEDURE nested_blocks1( )
BEGIN
        DECLARE outer_variable VARCHAR(20);
        BEGIN
                DECLARE inner_variable VARCHAR(20);
                SET inner_variable='This is my private data';
        END;
        SELECT inner_variable,' This statement causes an error ';
END;
$$

Query OK, 0 rows affected (0.00 sec)

mysql> CALL nested_blocks1( )
--------------

ERROR 1054 (42S22): Unknown column 'inner_variable' in 'field list'
```

In Example 4-2, we modify a variable declared in the "outer" block inside of an "inner" block. The changes made are visible outside of the inner block.

Example 4-2. Variables within a block can override variables defined outside the block

```
mysql> CREATE PROCEDURE nested_blocks2( )
BEGIN
        DECLARE my_variable varchar(20);
        SET my_variable='This value was set in the outer block';
        BEGIN
                SET my_variable='This value was set in the inner block';
        END;
        SELECT my_variable, 'Changes in the inner block are visible in the outer block';
END;
$$

Query OK, 0 rows affected (0.00 sec)


mysql> CALL nested_blocks2( )
//

+--------------------+----------------------------------------------------------+
| my_variable        | Changes in the inner block are visible in the outer block |
+--------------------+----------------------------------------------------------+
| This value was set |                                                          |
|  in the inner block | Changes in the inner block are visible in the outer block |
+--------------------+----------------------------------------------------------+
1 row in set (0.00 sec)

Query OK, 0 rows affected (0.01 sec)
```

In Example 4-3, we create a variable in the inner block with the same name as one in the outer block. When we change the value within the inner block, the changes are not reflected in the outer block—that's because although the two variables have the same name, they are really two separate variables. Overriding a variable name inside of a block in this way can be fairly confusing, reducing code readability and possibly encouraging bugs. In general, don't override variable definitions in this way unless you have a very compelling reason.

Example 4-3. Changes made to an overloaded variable in an inner block are not visible outside the block

```
mysql> CREATE PROCEDURE nested_blocks3( )
BEGIN
        DECLARE my_variable varchar(20);
        SET my_variable='This value was set in the outer block';
        BEGIN
                DECLARE my_variable VARCHAR(20);
```

Example 4-3. Changes made to an overloaded variable in an inner block are not visible outside the block (continued)

```
                SET my_variable='This value was set in the inner block';
        END;
        SELECT my_variable, 'Can''t see changes made in the inner block';
END;
//

Query OK, 0 rows affected (0.00 sec)

mysql> CALL nested_blocks3( )
$$


+--------------------------+-------------------------------------------+
| my_variable              | Can't see changes made in the inner block |
+--------------------------+-------------------------------------------+
| This value was set in the |                                          |
|   outer block            | Can't see changes made in the inner block |
+--------------------------+-------------------------------------------+
1 row in set (0.00 sec)

Query OK, 0 rows affected (0.00 sec)
```

 Avoid overriding a variable declared within an outer block inside an inner block.

In our final nested blocks example (Example 4-4), we use a block label and the LEAVE statement to terminate block execution. We discuss the use of the LEAVE statement later in this chapter, but for now it's enough to point out that you can terminate execution of a block with a LEAVE statement at any time, providing that the block is labeled.

Example 4-4. Example of using a LEAVE statement to exit a labeled block

```
mysql> CREATE PROCEDURE nested_blocks5( )
 outer_block: BEGIN
        DECLARE l_status int;
        SET l_status=1;
        inner_block: BEGIN
                IF (l_status=1) THEN
                        LEAVE inner_block;
                END IF;
                SELECT 'This statement will never be executed';
        END inner_block;
        SELECT 'End of program';
END outer_block$$

Query OK, 0 rows affected (0.00 sec)
```

Example 4-4. Example of using a LEAVE statement to exit a labeled block (continued)

```
mysql> CALL nested_blocks5( )$$

+----------------+
| End of program |
+----------------+
| End of program |
+----------------+
1 row in set (0.00 sec)

Query OK, 0 rows affected (0.00 sec)
```

Conditional Control

Conditional control—or "flow of control"—statements allow you to execute code based on the value of some expression. As we said earlier, an expression can be any combination of MySQL literals, variables, operators, and functions that returns a value. Conditional control statements allow you to take different actions depending on the value of such an expression, which could refer to parameters to the stored program, to data in the database, or to other variable data (such as the day of the week or the time of the day).

The MySQL stored program language supports two conditional control statements: IF and CASE. Both IF and CASE perform very similar functions, and there is always a way to rewrite an IF statement as a CASE statement or vice versa. Usually, choosing between IF and CASE is a matter of personal preference or programming standards. However, there are circumstances in which one type of statement is more readable or efficient than the other.

The following subsections describe the syntax of both statements, provide usage examples, and, finally, compare the pros and cons of each.

The IF Statement

All programmers will be familiar with some variation of the IF statement, and MySQL's implementation of the IF statement contains no surprises. The syntax of IF in stored programs is:

```
IF expression THEN commands
    [ELSEIF expression THEN commands ....]
    [ELSE commands]
END IF;
```

TRUE or FALSE (or neither)?

The commands associated with IF or ELSEIF statements will only be executed if the associated *expression* evaluates to TRUE. Expressions such as 1=1 or 2>1 will evaluate to TRUE. Expressions such as 1>3 will evaluate to FALSE.

However, if you are performing an operation on one or more variables, and one of the variables has a NULL value, then the result of the expression can be NULL—neither TRUE nor FALSE. This can lead to some erroneous conclusions if your code assumes that expressions that are not TRUE are necessarily FALSE, or vice versa. So, for instance, in Example 4-5, if we can't find 'alpha' or 'beta' in the version string, we assume that the release is production. However, if l_version is NULL, then the ELSE condition will always fire, although we actually have no basis for making any such assertion.

Example 4-5. Incorrectly assuming that NOT TRUE = FALSE

```
IF (INSTR(l_version_string,'alpha')>0) THEN
     SELECT 'Alpha release of MySQL';
 ELSEIF (INSTR(l_version_string,'beta')>0) THEN
     SELECT 'Beta release of MySQL';
 ELSE
     SELECT 'Production release of MySQL';
 END IF;
```

 Don't assume that the result of an expression is either TRUE or FALSE. It could also evaluate to NULL (UNKNOWN) if any of the participating variables is NULL.

Also note that any expressions that return numeric values—or strings that look like numbers—may evaluate to TRUE, FALSE, or NULL. The rules are:

- If the absolute value of a numeric expression is 1 or greater, then it will be evaluated to TRUE by the IF or ELSEIF statement. Note that the term "absolute value" means that both 1 and –1 will evaluate to TRUE.
- If the value of the numeric expression is 0, then it will evaluate to FALSE.

Simple IF-THEN combinations

In its simplest form, IF can be used to specify a set of statements that executes only if a condition evaluates to TRUE. The syntax for this type of IF statement is as follows:

```
IF expression THEN
    statements
END IF;
```

Example 4-6 shows a simple IF statement.

Example 4-6. Example of simple IF statement

```
IF sale_value > 200 THEN
    CALL apply_free_shipping(sale_id);
END IF;
```

We can include multiple statements between the THEN and END IF clauses, as in Example 4-7.

Example 4-7. Multistatement IF statement

```
IF sale_value > 200 THEN
    CALL apply_free_shipping(sale_id);
    CALL apply_discount(sale_id,10);
END IF;
```

As shown in Example 4-8, we can also include any other executable statement inside the IF statement, such as looping constructs, SET statements, and other IF statements (although, as we will see later, it's often best to avoid nesting IF statements in this manner if possible).

Example 4-8. Nested IF statements

```
IF sale_value > 200 THEN
    CALL apply_free_shipping(sale_id);
    IF sale_value > 500 THEN
        CALL apply_discount(sale_id,20);
    END IF;
END IF;
```

It is not necessary to break the IF statement across multiple lines; all of the IF statements in Example 4-9 are treated identically by MySQL.

Example 4-9. Alternate formatting for IF statements

```
IF sale_value > 200 THEN CALL apply_free_shipping(sale_id); END IF;

IF sale_value > 200
THEN
    CALL apply_free_shipping(sale_id);
END IF;

IF sale_value > 200 THEN
    CALL apply_free_shipping(sale_id);
END IF;
```

It's probably OK to put a very simple IF statement on a single line, but it is definitely not a good practice to do this for complex or nested IF structures. For instance, which is easier to read, understand, and maintain? This:

```
IF sale_value > 200 THEN
    CALL apply_free_shipping(sale_id);
    IF sale_value > 500 THEN
        CALL apply_discount(sale_id,20);
    END IF;
END IF;
```

Or this:

```
IF sale_value > 200 THEN CALL apply_free_shipping(sale_id); IF sale_value > 500 THEN
CALL apply_discount(sale_id,20);END IF;END IF;
```

Some programmers like to place the THEN clause on a separate line, as follows:

```
IF sale_value > 200
THEN
    CALL apply_free_shipping(sale_id);
END IF;
```

But this is really a matter of personal preference and/or programming standards.

 For any nontrivial IF statement, use indenting and formatting to ensure that the logic of your IF statement is easily understood.

IF-THEN-ELSE statements

Adding an ELSE condition to your IF statements allows you to specify statements that will execute if the IF condition is NOT TRUE. We'll emphasize again—because it is important—that NOT TRUE does not always mean FALSE. If the IF statement condition evaluates to NULL, then the ELSE statements will still be executed; this can lead to subtle bugs if you don't protect against NULL variables in your IF conditions.

An `IF-THEN-ELSE` block has the following syntax:

```
IF expression THEN
    statements that execute if the expression is TRUE
ELSE
    statements that execute if the expression is FALSE or NULL
END IF;
```

So in Example 4-10, we apply shipping to an order if it is less than $200; otherwise, we apply a discount (and don't charge shipping).

Example 4-10. Simple IF-THEN ELSE example

```
IF sale_value <200 THEN
    CALL apply_shipping(sale_id);
ELSE
    CALL apply_discount(sale_id);
END IF;
```

IF-THEN-ELSEIF-ELSE statements

The full syntax of the `IF` statements allows for multiple conditions to be defined. The first condition that evaluates to TRUE will execute. If none of the statements evaluates to TRUE, then the `ELSE` clause (if present) will execute. The syntax for an `IF-THEN-ELSEIF-ELSE IF` statement looks like this:

```
IF expression THEN
    statements that execute if the expression is TRUE
ELSEIF expression THEN
    statements that execute if expression1 is TRUE
ELSE
    statements that execute if all the preceding expressions are FALSE or NULL
END IF;
```

You can have as many `ELSEIF` conditions as you like.

The conditions do not need to be mutually exclusive. That is, more than one of the conditions can evaluate to TRUE. The first condition that evaluates to TRUE is the one that executes. Creating overlapping conditions like this can be useful, but you have to be very careful when ordering the conditions. For instance, consider the `IF-ELSEIF` statement shown in Example 4-11.

Example 4-11. Example of an IF-ELSEIF block with overlapping conditions

```
IF (sale_value>200) THEN
    CALL free_shipping(sale_id);
ELSEIF (sale_value >200 and customer_status='PREFERRED') THEN
    CALL free_shipping(sale_id);
    CALL apply_discount(sale_id,20);
END IF;
```

The intention of this code fragment is clear: apply free shipping to all orders over $200, and add a 20% discount for preferred customers. However, because the first condition will evaluate to TRUE for all orders over $200, the `ELSEIF` condition will not be evaluated for any orders over $200, and our preferred customers will not get their discount. No discount for preferred customers means no end-of-year bonus for our stored procedure programmer!

There are a number of better ways to craft this statement: for one thing, we could move the `ELSEIF` condition into the `IF` clause to ensure that it gets evaluated first; alternately, we could nest an `IF` statement within the `sale_value>200` `IF` clause to test the customer status, as shown in Example 4-12.

Example 4-12. Two ways of correcting the logic error in the previous example

```
/* Reordering the IF conditions */
IF (sale_value >200 and customer_status='PREFERED') THEN
        CALL free_shipping(sale_id);
        CALL apply_discount(sale_id,20);
ELSEIF (sale_value>200) THEN
        CALL free_shipping(sale_id);

END IF;

/* Nesting the IF conditions */

IF (sale_value >200) THEN
    CALL free_shipping(sale_id);
    IF (customer_satus='PREFERRED') THEN
      CALL apply_discount(sale_id,20);
    END IF;
END IF:
```

Both of the alternatives shown in Example 4-12 are perfectly valid. Generally we want to avoid nesting `IF` statements where possible, but if there are a lot of additional evaluations that we need to conduct when the `sale_value` is greater than $200, then it might make sense to perform the `sale_value` test once, and then individually test for all the other conditions. So let's say our business rules state that for orders over $200 we give free shipping, along with a variable discount based on the customer's status in our loyalty program. The logic in a single `IF-ELSEIF` block might look like that shown in Example 4-13.

Example 4-13. IF block with many redundant conditions

```
IF (sale_value >200 and customer_status='PLATINUM') THEN
    CALL free_shipping(sale_id);       /* Free shipping*/
    CALL apply_discount(sale_id,20);  /* 20% discount */

ELSEIF (sale_value >200 and customer_status='GOLD') THEN
    CALL free_shipping(sale_id);       /* Free shipping*/
    CALL apply_discount(sale_id,15); /* 15% discount */
```

Example 4-13. IF block with many redundant conditions (continued)

```
ELSEIF (sale_value >200 and customer_status='SILVER') THEN
    CALL free_shipping(sale_id);     /* Free shipping*/
    CALL apply_discount(sale_id,10); /* 10% discount */

ELSEIF (sale_value >200 and customer_status='BRONZE') THEN
    CALL free_shipping(sale_id);     /* Free shipping*/
    CALL apply_discount(sale_id,5); /* 5% discount*/

ELSEIF (sale_value>200) THEN
    CALL free_shipping(sale_id);     /* Free shipping*/

END IF;
```

In this case, the constant repetition of the sale_value condition and the free_ shipping call actually undermines the readability of our logic—as well as imposing a performance overhead (see Chapter 22). It might be better to use a nested IF structure that makes it clear that everyone gets free shipping for orders over $200, and that discounts are then applied based on the customer loyalty status only. Example 4-14 shows the nested IF implementation.

Example 4-14. Using nested IF to avoid redundant evaluations

```
IF (sale_value > 200) THEN
    CALL free_shipping(sale_id);     /*Free shipping*/

    IF (customer_status='PLATINUM') THEN
        CALL apply_discount(sale_id,20); /* 20% discount */

    ELSEIF (customer_status='GOLD') THEN
        CALL apply_discount(sale_id,15); /* 15% discount */

    ELSEIF (customer_status='SILVER') THEN
        CALL apply_discount(sale_id,10); /* 10% discount */

    ELSEIF (customer_status='BRONZE') THEN
        CALL apply_discount(sale_id,5); /* 5% discount*/
    END IF;

END IF;
```

The CASE Statement

The CASE statement is an alternative conditional execution or flow control statement. Anything that can be done with CASE statements can be done with IF statements (and vice versa), but CASE statements are often more readable and efficient when multiple conditions need to be evaluated, especially when the conditions all compare the output from a single expression.

Simple CASE statement

CASE statements can take two forms. The first—sometimes referred to as a *simple CASE statement*—compares the output of an expression with multiple conditions:

```
CASE expression
    WHEN value THEN
        statements
    [WHEN value THEN
        statements ...]
    [ELSE
        statements]
END CASE;
```

This syntax is useful when we are checking the output of some expression against a set of distinct values. For instance, we could check the customer loyalty status from our previous example using the simple CASE statement shown in Example 4-15.

Example 4-15. Example of a simple CASE statement

```
CASE customer_status
    WHEN 'PLATINUM'  THEN
        CALL apply_discount(sale_id,20); /* 20% discount */

    WHEN 'GOLD' THEN
        CALL apply_discount(sale_id,15); /* 15% discount */

    WHEN 'SILVER' THEN
        CALL apply_discount(sale_id,10); /* 10% discount */

    WHEN 'BRONZE' THEN
        CALL apply_discount(sale_id,5); /* 5% discount*/
END CASE;
```

As with the IF command, you can specify multiple WHEN statements and you can specify an ELSE clause that executes if none of the other conditions apply.

However, it is critical to realize that a CASE statement will raise an exception if none of the conditions apply. This means that in Example 4-15 if the customer_status was not one of 'PLATINUM', 'GOLD', 'SILVER', or 'BRONZE' then the following runtime exception would occur:

```
ERROR 1339 (20000): Case not found for CASE statement
```

We could create an exception handler to cause this error to be ignored (as described in Chapter 6), but it is probably better practice to code an ELSE clause to ensure that all possible conditions are handled. So, we should probably adapt the previous example to include an ELSE clause that applies a zero discount to a customer who meets none of the preceding conditions.

If none of the CASE statements matches the input condition, CASE will raise MySQL error 1339. You should either construct an error handler to ignore this error, or ensure that the exception never occurs by including an ELSE clause in your CASE statement.

The simple CASE statement is useful when comparing the value of an expression to a series of specific values. However, the simple CASE statement cannot easily or naturally match ranges, or handle more complex conditions involving multiple expressions. For these more complex "cases" we can use a "searched" CASE statement, described in the next section.

"Searched" CASE statement

The *searched* CASE statement is functionally equivalent to an IF-ELSEIF-ELSE-END IF block. The searched CASE statement has the following syntax:

```
CASE
    WHEN condition THEN
        statements
    [WHEN condition THEN
        statements...]
    [ELSE
        statements]
END CASE;
```

Using the searched CASE structure, we can implement the free shipping and discount logic that we implemented earlier using IF. A direct translation of our sales discount and free shipping logic using a searched CASE statement is shown in Example 4-16.

Example 4-16. Example of a searched CASE statement

```
CASE
    WHEN (sale_value >200 AND customer_status='PLATINUM') THEN
        CALL free_shipping(sale_id);     /* Free shipping*/
        CALL apply_discount(sale_id,20); /* 20% discount */

    WHEN (sale_value >200 AND customer_status='GOLD') THEN
        CALL free_shipping(sale_id);     /* Free shipping*/
        CALL apply_discount(sale_id,15); /* 15% discount */

    WHEN (sale_value >200 AND customer_status='SILVER') THEN
        CALL free_shipping(sale_id);     /* Free shipping*/
        CALL apply_discount(sale_id,10); /* 10% discount */

    WHEN (sale_value >200 AND customer_status='BRONZE') THEN
        CALL free_shipping(sale_id);     /* Free shipping*/
        CALL apply_discount(sale_id,5); /* 5% discount*/

    WHEN (sale_value>200)     THEN
```

Example 4-16. Example of a searched CASE statement (continued)

```
        CALL free_shipping(sale_id);      /* Free shipping*/


END CASE;
```

However, remember that if none of the WHERE clauses is matched, a 1339 error will occur. Therefore, this code will cause a fatal error if the order is less than $200 or the customer is not in our loyalty program—not a happy outcome. So we should protect our code—and our job security—by including an ELSE clause as shown in Example 4-17.

Example 4-17. Adding a dummy ELSE clause to our searched CASE example

```
CASE
    WHEN (sale_value >200 AND customer_status='PLATINUM') THEN
         CALL free_shipping(sale_id);      /* Free shipping*/
         CALL apply_discount(sale_id,20); /* 20% discount */

    WHEN (sale_value >200 AND customer_status='GOLD') THEN
         CALL free_shipping(sale_id);      /* Free shipping*/
         CALL apply_discount(sale_id,15); /* 15% discount */

    WHEN (sale_value >200 AND customer_status='SILVER') THEN
         CALL free_shipping(sale_id);      /* Free shipping*/
         CALL apply_discount(sale_id,10); /* 10% discount */

    WHEN (sale_value >200 AND customer_status='BRONZE') THEN
         CALL free_shipping(sale_id);      /* Free shipping*/
         CALL apply_discount(sale_id,5); /* 5% discount*/

    WHEN (sale_value>200) THEN
         CALL free_shipping(sale_id);      /* Free shipping*/
    ELSE
         SET dummy=dummy;

END CASE;
```

Note that because MySQL lacks a NULL (do nothing) statement in the stored program language, we had to add a dummy statement—but this statement has negligible overhead.

As with our IF implementation of this logic, we could also use nested CASE statements to perform the same logic with arguably greater clarity. In Example 4-18 we combine simple and searched CASE statements, and also include a "not found" handler to avoid having to include ELSE statements. We enclose the entire thing in a block so that our handler does not inadvertently influence other statements within the stored program.

Example 4-18. Using nested CASE statements and a block-scoped "not found" handler

```
BEGIN
    DECLARE not_found INT DEFAULT 0;
    DECLARE CONTINUE HANDLER FOR 1339 SET not_found=1;

    CASE
        WHEN (sale_value>200) THEN
            CALL free_shipping(sale_id);
            CASE customer_status
                WHEN 'PLATINUM' THEN
                    CALL apply_discount(sale_id,20);
                WHEN 'GOLD' THEN
                    CALL apply_discount(sale_id,15);
                WHEN 'SILVER' THEN
                    CALL apply_discount(sale_id,10);
                WHEN 'BRONZE' THEN
                    CALL apply_discount(sale_id,5);
            END CASE;
    END CASE;

END;
```

IF Versus CASE

We've seen that both IF and CASE statements can implement the same flow control functionality. So which is best? To a large extent, choosing between IF and CASE is more a matter of personal preference and programming standards than of any implicit advantages offered by either of the two statements. However, when deciding between CASE and IF, consider the following:

- Consistency in style is probably more important than any slight advantages either approach might have in a particular circumstance. We therefore suggest that you choose between CASE and IF consistently, and not randomly switch between the two depending on your mood, the weather, or your horoscope!
- CASE is slightly more readable when you are comparing a single expression against a range of distinct values (using a "simple" CASE statement).
- IF is probably a more familiar and easily understood construct when you are evaluating ranges or complex expressions based on multiple variables.
- If you choose CASE, you need to ensure that at least one of the CASE conditions is matched, or define an error handler to catch the error that will occur if no CASE condition is satisfied. IF has no such restriction.

Remember—whichever construct you use—that:

- Once any condition in the CASE or IF structure is satisfied, no more conditions will be evaluated. This means that if your conditions overlap in any way, the order of evaluation is critical.

- The MySQL stored program language uses three-valued logic; just because a statement is NOT TRUE does not mean that it is necessary FALSE—it could be NULL.

- You should think carefully about the readability of your statements—sometimes a nested set of IF or CASE statements will be more readable and possibly more efficient. However, more often it is better to avoid nesting, especially if the statements become deeply nested (say three or more levels).

Iterative Processing with Loops

In this section we examine the statements that the MySQL stored program language provides for iteratively (repeatedly) processing commands. There are many reasons why a program may need to iterate:

- A program that supports a user interface may run a main loop that waits for, and then processes, user keystrokes (this doesn't apply to stored programs, however).

- Many mathematical algorithms can be implemented only by loops in computer programs.

- When processing a file, a program may loop through each record in the file and perform computations.

- A database program may loop through the rows returned by a SELECT statement.

It's fairly obvious that it is the last case—processing rows returned by a SELECT statement—that will be the most common reason for looping in MySQL stored programs, and we will give this topic a great deal of consideration in Chapter 5. In this chapter, we consider the looping commands in their general form.

LOOP Statement

The simplest possible looping construct is the LOOP statement. The syntax for this statement is as follows:

```
[label:] LOOP
    statements
END LOOP [label];
```

The statements between the LOOP and END LOOP statements will be repeated indefinitely, until the LOOP is terminated. You can terminate the LOOP using the LEAVE statement, which we will describe shortly.

You can supply labels to the loop, which have the same syntax as those we can add to BEGIN-END blocks. Labels can help you identify the END LOOP statement that corresponds to a particular LOOP statement. Equally important, labels can be used to control execution flow, as we will see in subsequent sections.

Example 4-19 shows a very simple (and very dangerous) loop. It will continue forever, or at least until you manage to somehow terminate it. Because stored programs run inside of the database server, using Ctrl-C or other forms of keyboard interrupts will be ineffective—you will only be able to terminate this loop by issuing a KILL command against the MySQL session, or by shutting down the database server. In the meantime, the loop will consume as much CPU as it can, so we don't recommend that you run this example on your mission-critical production systems.

Example 4-19. Infinite loop (don't try this at home!)

```
Infinite_loop: LOOP
    SELECT 'Welcome to my infinite loop from hell!!';
END LOOP inifinite_loop;
```

Obviously we almost never want to program an infinite loop, and therefore we need some way to terminate the loop. We can do this with the LEAVE statement, so let's move on to this statement without delay....

LEAVE Statement

The LEAVE statement allows us to terminate a loop. The general syntax for the LEAVE statement is:

```
LEAVE label;
```

LEAVE causes the current loop to be terminated. The label matches the loop to be terminated, so if a loop is enclosed within another loop, we can break out of both loops with a single statement.

In the simplest case, we simply execute LEAVE when we are ready to exit from the LOOP, as shown in Example 4-20.

Example 4-20. Using LEAVE to terminate a loop

```
SET i=1;
myloop: LOOP
    SET i=i+1;
    IF i=10 then
            LEAVE myloop;
    END IF;
END LOOP myloop;
SELECT 'I can count to 10';
```

LEAVE can be used to exit from any of the alternative looping structures, as we'll examine in upcoming sections. In fact, you can also use LEAVE if you want to break out of a named BEGIN-END block (introduced earlier in this chapter).

ITERATE Statement

The ITERATE statement is used to restart execution at the beginning of a loop, without executing any of the remaining statements in the loop. ITERATE has the following syntax:

```
ITERATE label;
```

When MySQL encounters the ITERATE statement, it recommences execution at the start of the nominated loop. In Example 4-21, we print all odd numbers less than 10. ITERATE is used to repeat the loop if the number we have is not odd. LEAVE is used to terminate the loop once we reach 10.

Example 4-21. Using ITERATE to return to the start of a loop

```
SET i=0;
loop1: LOOP
    SET i=i+1;
    IF i>=10 THEN          /*Last number - exit loop*/
        LEAVE loop1;
    ELSEIF MOD(i,2)=0 THEN /*Even number - try again*/
        ITERATE loop1;
    END IF;

    SELECT CONCAT(i," is an odd number");

END LOOP loop1;
```

While this loop is useful to illustrate the use of LEAVE and ITERATE to control a loop, it is a rather poorly constructed algorithm. We could easily have halved the number of loop iterations by incrementing the loop variable i by two rather than by one.

ITERATE causes the execution of the loop to restart at the top of the loop. If you are using a REPEAT loop (see the next section), this means that the loop will re-execute unconditionally, bypassing the UNTIL condition that would otherwise terminate the loop. This may result in unexpected behavior. In a WHILE loop, ITERATE will result in the WHILE condition being re-evaluated before the next iteration of the loop.

We can construct just about any conceivable form of loop using the LOOP, LEAVE, and ITERATE statements. However, in practice these "manual" loops are awkward when compared to some of the alternatives we are about to consider. The WHILE and REPEAT statements described in the following sections allow us to create loops that are easier to write, read, and maintain.

REPEAT ... UNTIL Loop

The REPEAT and UNTIL statements can be used to create a loop that continues until some logical condition is met. The syntax for REPEAT...UNTIL is:

```
[label:] REPEAT
    statements
```

```
UNTIL expression
END REPEAT [label]
```

A REPEAT loop continues until the expression defined in the UNTIL clause evaluates to TRUE. In essence, a REPEAT loop is logically equivalent to a LOOP-LEAVE-END LOOP block like this one:

```
some_label:LOOP
    statements
    IF expression THEN LEAVE some_label; END IF;
END LOOP;
```

The REPEAT loop is somewhat easier to maintain because it is more obvious which conditions will cause the loop to terminate. The LEAVE statement in a simple loop could be anywhere, while the UNTIL statement is always associated with the END REPEAT clause at the very end of the loop. Furthermore, we don't need to specify a label for the REPEAT loop since the UNTIL condition is always specific to the current loop. However, we still recommend using labels with REPEAT loops to improve readability, especially if the loops are nested.

Example 4-22 shows using REPEAT to print out odd numbers less than 10. Compare this syntax with that of our previous example using the LOOP and LEAVE statements.

Example 4-22. Example of a REPEAT loop

```
SET i=0;
loop1: REPEAT
    SET i=i+1;
    IF MOD(i,2)<>0 THEN /*Even number - try again*/
        Select concat(i," is an odd number");
    END IF;
UNTIL i >= 10
END REPEAT;
```

There are a few things worth noting about the REPEAT loop:

- A REPEAT loop is always guaranteed to run at least once—that is, the UNTIL condition is first evaluated after the first execution of the loop. For loops that should not run even once unless some condition is satisfied, use WHILE (see the next section).

- Using ITERATE in a REPEAT loop can lead to unexpected outcomes, since doing so bypasses the UNTIL test and may result in the loop executing even though the UNTIL condition is no longer satisfied. Therefore, you will probably not want to use ITERATE in a REPEAT loop.

WHILE Loop

A WHILE loop executes as long as a condition is true. If the condition is not true to begin with, then the loop will never execute—unlike the REPEAT loop, which is guaranteed to execute at least once.

The WHILE loop has the following syntax:

```
[label:] WHILE expression DO
    statements
END WHILE [label]
```

A WHILE loop is functionally equivalent to a simple LOOP-LEAVE-END LOOP construction that has a LEAVE clause as its very first statement, as described in the "LEAVE Statement" section. Example 4-23 demonstrates the LOOP-LEAVE-END-LOOP.

Example 4-23. LOOP-END LOOP that implements same functionality as WHILE loop

```
myloop: LOOP
    IF expression THEN LEAVE myloop; END IF;
    other statements;
END LOOP myloop;
```

Example 4-24 shows our odd-numbers-less-than-10 loop implemented using WHILE.

Example 4-24. Odd numbers less than 10 implemented as a WHILE loop

```
SET i=1;
loop1: WHILE i<=10 DO
    IF MOD(i,2)<>0 THEN /*Even number - try again*/
        SELECT CONCAT(i," is an odd number");
    END IF;
    SET i=i+1;
END WHILE loop1;
```

Nested Loops

We often want to nest loops. In the simple code in Example 4-25, we print out the elementary "times table" using a nested LOOP-LEAVE-END LOOP structure.

Example 4-25. Example of nesting loops

```
DECLARE i,j INT DEFAULT 1;
outer_loop: LOOP
    SET j=1;
    inner_loop: LOOP
        SELECT concat(i," times ", j," is ",i*j);
        SET j=j+1;
        IF j>12 THEN
            LEAVE inner_loop;
        END IF;
    END LOOP inner_loop;
    SET i=i+1;
    IF i>12 THEN
        LEAVE outer_loop;
    END IF;
END LOOP outer_loop;
```

When nesting loops, it is particularly useful to label the start and the end of the loop so as to clearly associate the start of each loop with its end. Of course, if we need to use LEAVE, we must label the loop.

Parting Comments on Loops

We've now seen three simple and identical looping algorithms implemented using the three looping constructs available within the MySQL stored program language. Each of the three loop constructs is capable of implementing virtually any loop logic that you might need to implement.

The example loops given in this chapter are fairly simplistic and have little real-world relevance. We did this partially for the sake of clarity, but also because the reality is that in stored programming, almost all your looping constructs will involve iterating through the rows returned by a SELECT statement, which is the subject of the next chapter.

Conclusion

In this chapter we looked at conditional and iterative control structures in the MySQL stored program language. Almost any nontrivial program will need to make some kind of decision based on input data, and these decisions will usually be expressed as IF or CASE statements.

Looping is another extremely common programming task—especially common in stored programs that need to iterate through the outputs from some SQL statement. MySQL provides a number of alternative ways to format a loop, including a simple loop terminated by a LEAVE statement, a REPEAT UNTIL loop, and a WHILE loop.

## CHAPTER 5

Using SQL in Stored Programming

While we can use the MySQL stored program language to perform traditional programming tasks, in reality almost all stored programs will engage in an interaction with the database through the execution of SQL statements. This chapter focuses on how you can use SQL within your stored programs.

In this chapter we'll look at the various ways in which you can use SQL inside of stored programs:

- Simple (non-SELECT) SQL statements that do not return a result set can be freely embedded within stored procedures and functions.

- A SELECT statement that returns only a single row can pass its result INTO local variables.

- A SELECT statement that returns multiple rows can form the basis for a cursor that allows you to loop through each row, taking whatever action you deem appropriate for that row.

- Any SELECT statement can be included in a stored procedure (but not in a stored function) "unbound" by an INTO clause or a CURSOR statement. The result set from such a SQL statement will be returned to the calling program (but not, alas, to a calling stored procedure).

- SQL statements can be prepared dynamically using MySQL server-side prepared statements (in stored procedures only).

Using Non-SELECT SQL in Stored Programs

When we include a SQL statement that does not return a result set—such as an UPDATE, INSERT, or SET statement—within a stored program, it will execute exactly as it would if it were executed in some other context (such as if it were called from PHP or issued from the MySQL command line).

SQL statements within stored programs follow the same syntax as they would outside of the stored program. The SQL statements have full access to any stored program variables, which can be used wherever a literal or expression would normally be provided to the SQL.

You can use all the major categories of SQL statements inside stored programs. DML, DDL, and utility statements can be used without restriction.

Example 5-1 uses a combination of DDL and DML to create and manipulate the data in a table.

Example 5-1. Embedding non-SELECT statements in stored programs

```
CREATE PROCEDURE simple_sqls()
BEGIN
    DECLARE i INT DEFAULT 1;

    /* Example of a utility statement */
    SET autocommit=0;

    /* Example of DDL statements */
    DROP TABLE IF EXISTS test_table ;
    CREATE TABLE test_table
        (id         INT PRIMARY KEY,
          some_data VARCHAR(30))
      ENGINE=innodb;

    /* Example of an INSERT using a procedure variable */
    WHILE (i<=10) DO
        INSERT INTO TEST_TABLE VALUES(i,CONCAT("record ",i));
        SET i=i+1;
    END WHILE;

    /* Example of an UPDATE using procedure variables*/
    SET i=5;
    UPDATE test_table
      SET some_data=CONCAT("I updated row ",i)
     WHERE id=i;

    /* DELETE with a procedure variable */
    DELETE FROM test_table
     WHERE id>i;

END;
```

Using SELECT Statements with an INTO Clause

If you have a SELECT statement that returns only a single row, you can return that row into stored program variables by using the INTO statement within the SELECT statement. The format for such a SELECT is:

```
SELECT expression1 [, expression2 ....]
  INTO variable1 [, variable2 ...]
  other SELECT statement clauses
```

Example 5-2 shows how we can retrieve details from a single customer. The customer ID is passed in as a parameter.

Example 5-2. Using a SELECT-INTO statement

```
CREATE PROCEDURE get_customer_details(in_customer_id INT)
BEGIN
    DECLARE l_customer_name     VARCHAR(30);
    DECLARE l_contact_surname   VARCHAR(30);
    DECLARE l_contact_firstname VARCHAR(30);

    SELECT customer_name, contact_surname,contact_firstname
      INTO l_customer_name,l_contact_surname,l_contact_firstname
      FROM customers
     WHERE customer_id=in_customer_id;

    /* Do something with the customer record */

END;
```

If the SQL statement returns more than one row, a runtime error will result. For instance, if we omitted the WHERE clause in Example 5-2, the following error would result when we tried to run the stored procedure:

```
mysql> CALL get_customer_details(2) ;
ERROR 1172 (42000): Result consisted of more than one row
```

Creating and Using Cursors

To handle a SELECT statement that returns more than one row, we must create and then manipulate a *cursor*. A cursor is an object that provides programmatic access to the result set returned by your SELECT statement. Use a cursor to iterate through the rows in the result set and take action for each row individually.

Currently, MySQL only allows us to fetch each row in the result set from first to last as determined by the SELECT statement. We cannot fetch from the last to first row, and cannot jump directly to a specific row in the result set.

Defining a Cursor

Define a cursor with the DECLARE statement, which has the following syntax:

```
DECLARE cursor_name CURSOR FOR SELECT_statement;
```

As we mentioned in Chapter 3, cursor declarations must occur after all of our variable declarations. Declaring a cursor before declaring our variables generates error 1337, as shown in Example 5-3.

Example 5-3. Declaring a cursor before a variable generates a 1337 error

```
mysql> CREATE PROCEDURE bad_cursor( )
BEGIN
        DECLARE c CURSOR FOR SELECT * from departments;
        DECLARE i INT;
END;

ERROR 1337 (42000): Variable or condition declaration after cursor or handler declaration
```

A cursor is always associated with a SELECT statement; Example 5-4 shows a simple cursor declaration that retrieves certain columns from the customers table.

Example 5-4. Simple cursor declaration

```
DECLARE cursor1 CURSOR FOR
        SELECT customer_name, contact_surname,contact_firstname
            FROM customers;
```

A cursor can reference stored program variables within the WHERE clause or (less frequently) the column list. In Example 5-5, the cursor includes a reference to a stored procedure parameter, both in the WHERE clause and in the SELECT list. When the cursor is opened, it will use the value of the parameter variable to determine which rows to return.

Example 5-5. Cursor definition including a stored procedure variable

```
CREATE PROCEDURE cursor_demo (in_customer_id INT)
BEGIN
  DECLARE v_customer_id    INT;
  DECLARE v_customer_name VARCHAR(30);
  DECLARE c1 CURSOR FOR
      SELECT in_customer_id,customer_name
        FROM customers
        WHERE customer_id=in_customer_id;
```

Cursor Statements

The MySQL stored program language supports three statements for performing operations on cursors:

OPEN
> Initializes the result set for the cursor. We must open a cursor before fetching any rows from that cursor. The syntax for the OPEN statement is very simple:
>
> ```
> OPEN cursor_name;
> ```

FETCH
> Retrieves the next row from the cursor and moves the cursor "pointer" to the following row in the result set. It has the following syntax:
>
> ```
> FETCH cursor_name INTO variable list;
> ```

The variable list must contain one variable of a compatible data type for each column returned by the SELECT statement contained in the cursor declaration. We'll discuss FETCH in more detail later in this chapter.

CLOSE

Deactivates the cursor and releases the memory associated with that cursor. The syntax for this statement is:

```
CLOSE cursor_name;
```

We should close a cursor when we have finished fetching from it, or when we need to open that cursor again after changing a variable that affects the cursor's result set.

In the following sections, we will see many examples of these statements in action.

Fetching a Single Row from a Cursor

This is the most basic use of a cursor: we open a cursor, fetch a single row, and then close the result set, as shown in Example 5-6 (opening the cursor defined in Example 5-4). This is logically equivalent to a simple SELECT with an INTO clause.

Example 5-6. Fetching a single row from a cursor

```
OPEN cursor1;
FETCH cursor1 INTO l_customer_name,l_contact_surname,l_contact_firstname;
CLOSE cursor1;
```

Fetching an Entire Result Set

The most common way that cursors are processed is to fetch each row identified by the cursor's SELECT statement, perform one or more operations on the data retrieved, and then close the cursor after the last row has been retrieved.

Example 5-7 shows how we can declare and open a cursor, then fetch rows from the cursor in a loop, and finally close the cursor.

Example 5-7. Simple (flawed) cursor loop

```
DECLARE c_dept CURSOR FOR
        SELECT department_id
          FROM departments;

OPEN c_dept;
dept_cursor: LOOP
    FETCH c_dept INTO l_dept_id;
END LOOP dept_cursor;
CLOSE c_dept;
```

While this code might seem sensible and complete, there is a problem: if we attempt to fetch a row after the last row in the cursor has been fetched, MySQL will raise the "no data to fetch" error (MySQL error 1329; SQLSTATE 02000). So the code in Example 5-7 will abort as shown here:

```
mysql> call simple_cursor_loop();
ERROR 1329 (02000): No data to FETCH
```

To avoid this error, we declare an error handler that will catch "no data to fetch" and set a flag (implemented as a local variable). We then interrogate that variable to determine if the last row has been fetched. Using this technique, we can terminate our loop and close the cursor with intuitive, easy-to-understand code.

We discuss error handlers in detail in Chapter 6. However, in this situation, we will add the following statement to our code:

```
DECLARE CONTINUE HANDLER FOR NOT FOUND SET l_last_row_fetched=1;
```

This handler instructs MySQL to do two things when the "no data to fetch" scenario occurs:

1. Set the value of the "last row variable" (l_last_row_fetched) to 1.

2. Allow the program to continue executing.

Our program can now check the value of l_last_row_fetched. If it is set to 1, then we know that the last row has been fetched, and we can terminate the loop and close the cursor.

It is very important that we reset the "end of result set" indicator after the cursor has been closed. Otherwise, the next time we try to fetch from this cursor, the program will immediately terminate the loop, thinking that we are done.

Example 5-8 shows all of these steps: declare the CONTINUE handler, loop through the rows of the result set, leave the loop if the variable has been set, and then clean up.

 Almost all cursor loops require a NOT FOUND handler to avoid raising a fatal "no data to fetch" condition.

Example 5-8. Simple cursor loop

```
DECLARE CONTINUE HANDLER FOR NOT FOUND SET l_last_row_fetched=1;

SET l_last_row_fetched=0;
OPEN cursor1;
cursor_loop:LOOP
    FETCH cursor1 INTO l_customer_name,l_contact_surname,l_contact_firstname;
    IF l_last_row_fetched=1 THEN
        LEAVE cursor_loop;
    END IF;
    /*Do something with the row fetched*/
END LOOP cursor_loop;
CLOSE cursor1;
SET l_last_row_fetched=0;
```

Note that we don't *have* to process all the rows in the result set; we can issue the LEAVE statement at any time to terminate the cursor loop if we have processed all the data we need.

Types of Cursor Loops

We can use any of the three looping constructs (simple loop, WHILE loop, and REPEAT UNTIL loop) to iterate through the rows returned by a cursor. In each case, we need to construct the loop so that the loop will terminate when the "last row variable" is set by the NOT FOUND handler.

Consider the cursor and the NOT FOUND handler shown in Example 5-9.

Example 5-9. Cursor declaration with associated handler

```
DECLARE dept_csr CURSOR FOR
    SELECT department_id,department_name, location
      FROM departments;
DECLARE CONTINUE HANDLER FOR NOT FOUND SET no_more_departments=1;
```

The simplest construct is the LOOP-LEAVE-END LOOP sequence. In this case, our cursor loop would look like that shown in Example 5-10.

Example 5-10. A LOOP-LEAVE-END LOOP cursor loop

```
OPEN dept_csr;
dept_loop1:LOOP
    FETCH dept_csr INTO l_department_id,l_department_name,l_location;
    IF no_more_departments=1 THEN
        LEAVE dept_loop1;
    END IF;
    SET l_department_count=l_department_count+1;
END LOOP;
CLOSE dept_csr;
SET no_more_departments=0;
```

The logic of Example 5-10 is simple: we open the cursor and then iteratively fetch the rows. If we try to fetch beyond the end of the result set, the handler sets no_more_departments to 1 and we call the LEAVE statement to terminate the loop. Finally, we close the cursor and reset the no_more_departments variable.

The WHILE loop is very familiar to programmers and might therefore seem like a natural choice for constructing a cursor loop. In fact, however, you will very likely find that the REPEAT UNTIL loop is a more appropriate construct for a cursor loop. The REPEAT always executes its body at least once before evaluating the continuation expression. In the context of cursor processing, we usually will want to fetch at least once before checking to see if we are done processing the cursor's result set. Hence, using the REPEAT UNTIL loop can produce more readable code, as shown in Example 5-11.

Example 5-11. Cursor loop with REPEAT UNTIL loop

```
DECLARE dept_csr CURSOR FOR
    SELECT department_id,department_name, location
      FROM departments;

DECLARE CONTINUE HANDLER FOR NOT FOUND SET no_more_departments=1;

SET no_more_departments=0;
OPEN dept_csr;
REPEAT
    FETCH dept_csr INTO l_department_id,l_department_name,l_location;
UNTIL no_more_departments
END REPEAT;
CLOSE dept_csr;
SET no_more_departments=0;
```

However, this loop only works because we did nothing with each row fetched by the cursor. Fetching rows from a cursor just for the heck of it is very unusual—it is far more common to do something with the rows returned. For instance, in our first LOOP-LEAVE-END LOOP example, we at least counted the rows returned by the cursor. However, since the final fetch returns no rows, we need a way to avoid processing after that final fetch. So in fact, even if we use the REPEAT UNTIL loop, we still need a LEAVE statement to avoid processing the nonexistent row returned (or rather, not returned) by the final fetch. Thus, if we want to count the number of rows returned by the cursor (or do anything else with the results) we will need to include loop labels and a LEAVE statement, as in the amended version of our previous example, shown in Example 5-12.

Example 5-12. Most REPEAT UNTIL loops also need a LEAVE statement

```
DECLARE dept_csr CURSOR FOR
    SELECT department_id,department_name, location
      FROM departments;

DECLARE CONTINUE HANDLER FOR NOT FOUND SET no_more_departments=1;

SET no_more_departments=0;
OPEN dept_csr;
dept_loop:REPEAT
    FETCH dept_csr INTO l_department_id,l_department_name,l_location;
        IF no_more_departments THEN
            LEAVE dept_loop;
        END IF;
        SET l_department_count=l_department_count+1;
UNTIL no_more_departments
END REPEAT dept_loop;
CLOSE dept_csr;
SET no_more_departments=0;
```

The necessity of including a LEAVE statement in almost every REPEAT UNTIL loop makes the presence of the UNTIL clause redundant—although it arguably improves readability and protects you against the possibility of an infinite loop if your LEAVE statement fails to execute (perhaps you miscoded the IF clause). In the end, valid cursor loops can be established in either fashion, and there is no compelling case to recommend one style over the other. All we can say is that your code as a whole will be more readable if you use a consistent style for all of your cursor loops.

An alternative to a LEAVE statement would be an IF statement that executes whatever post-processing occurs once we determine that the FETCH has reached the end of the result set. Example 5-13 shows how we could construct this loop for our example. In this case, an IF statement is added that performs row processing only if the no_more_ departments variable has not been set.

Example 5-13. Using an IF block as an alternative to a LEAVE statement in a REPEAT UNTIL cursor loop

```
DECLARE dept_csr CURSOR FOR
    SELECT department_id,department_name, location
      FROM departments;

DECLARE CONTINUE HANDLER FOR NOT FOUND SET no_more_departments=1;

SET no_more_departments=0;
OPEN dept_csr;
dept_loop:REPEAT
    FETCH dept_csr INTO l_department_id,l_department_name,l_location;
        IF no_more_departments=0 THEN
            SET l_department_count=l_department_count+1;
        END IF;
UNTIL no_more_departments
END REPEAT dept_loop;
CLOSE dept_csr;
SET no_more_departments=0;
```

The third style of cursor loop involves the WHILE-END WHILE loop. WHILE evaluates its condition before the first execution of the loop, so it is a less logical choice than REPEAT-UNTIL or LOOP-END LOOP, since logically we cannot know if we have reached the end of the cursor until we have fetched at least one row. On the other hand, WHILE is probably the looping construct used in the widest variety of other programming languages, so it might confer a clearer understanding of the program's intentions to those who are not familiar with the MySQL stored program language.

In any case, the WHILE loop also requires a LEAVE statement if there is any processing of the cursor results attempted within the loop, so the code in Example 5-14 looks very similar to our previous examples.

Example 5-14. A cursor WHILE loop

```
DECLARE dept_csr CURSOR FOR
    SELECT department_id,department_name, location
      FROM departments;

DECLARE CONTINUE HANDLER FOR NOT FOUND SET no_more_departments=1;

SET no_more_departments=0;
OPEN dept_csr;
dept_loop:WHILE(no_more_departments=0) DO
    FETCH dept_csr INTO l_department_id,l_department_name,l_location;
    IF no_more_departments=1 THEN
        LEAVE dept_loop;
    END IF;
    SET l_department_count=l_department_count+1;
END WHILE dept_loop;
CLOSE dept_csr;
SET no_more_departments=0;
```

Nested Cursor Loops

It is not uncommon to nest cursor loops. For instance, one loop might retrieve a list of interesting customers, while an inner loop retrieves all the orders for those customers. The most significant issue relating to this sort of nesting is that the NOT FOUND handler variable will be set whenever either cursor completes—so you are going to need to be very careful to ensure that a NOT FOUND condition does not cause both cursors to be closed.

For instance, consider the nested cursor loops shown in Example 5-15.

Example 5-15. A (flawed) nested cursor loop

```
CREATE PROCEDURE bad_nested_cursors()
  READS SQL DATA
BEGIN

  DECLARE l_department_id INT;
  DECLARE l_employee_id   INT;
  DECLARE l_emp_count      INT DEFAULT 0 ;
  DECLARE l_done          INT DEFAULT  0;

  DECLARE dept_csr cursor  FOR
    SELECT department_id FROM departments;

  DECLARE emp_csr cursor  FOR
    SELECT employee_id FROM employees
     WHERE department_id=l_department_id;

  DECLARE CONTINUE HANDLER FOR NOT FOUND SET l_done=1;

  OPEN dept_csr;
  dept_loop: LOOP   -- Loop through departments
```

Example 5-15. A (flawed) nested cursor loop (continued)

```
    FETCH dept_csr into l_department_id;

    IF l_done=1 THEN
        LEAVE dept_loop;
    END IF;

    OPEN emp_csr;
    SET l_emp_count=0;
    emp_loop: LOOP        -- Loop through employee in dept.
      FETCH emp_csr INTO l_employee_id;

      IF l_done=1 THEN
          LEAVE emp_loop;
      END IF;
      SET l_emp_count=l_emp_count+1;
    END LOOP;
    CLOSE emp_csr;

    SELECT CONCAT('Department ',l_department_id,' has ',
          l_emp_count,' employees');

  END LOOP dept_loop;
  CLOSE dept_csr;

END;
```

This stored procedure contains a subtle bug. When the first "inner" loop through the emp_csr cursor completes, the value of l_done is set to 1. Consequently, at the next iteration through the "outer" loop through the dept_csr, the value of l_done is still set to 1 and the outer loop is inadvertently terminated. As a result, we only ever process a single department. There are two possible solutions to this problem: the easier of the two is simply to reset the "not found" variable at the end of each loop, as in Example 5-16.

Example 5-16. A correct nested cursor example

```
CREATE PROCEDURE good_nested_cursors1( )
   READS SQL DATA
BEGIN

  DECLARE l_department_id INT;
  DECLARE l_employee_id   INT;
  DECLARE l_emp_count      INT DEFAULT 0 ;
  DECLARE l_done           INT DEFAULT  0;

  DECLARE dept_csr cursor  FOR
    SELECT department_id FROM departments;
  DECLARE emp_csr cursor   FOR
    SELECT employee_id FROM employees
     WHERE department_id=l_department_id;
```

Example 5-16. A correct nested cursor example (continued)

```
DECLARE CONTINUE HANDLER FOR NOT FOUND SET l_done=1;

OPEN dept_csr;
dept_loop: LOOP    -- Loop through departments
  FETCH dept_csr into l_department_id;

  IF l_done=1 THEN
     LEAVE dept_loop;
  END IF;

  OPEN emp_csr;
  SET l_emp_count=0;
  emp_loop: LOOP        -- Loop through employee in dept.
    FETCH emp_csr INTO l_employee_id;

    IF l_done=1 THEN
       LEAVE emp_loop;
    END IF;
    SET l_emp_count=l_emp_count+1;
  END LOOP;
  CLOSE emp_csr;
  SET l_done=0;

  SELECT CONCAT('Department ',l_department_id,' has ',
          l_emp_count,' employees');

END LOOP dept_loop;
CLOSE dept_csr;

END;
```

It is always good practice to reset the value of a "not found" variable once it has been used so that subsequent cursor iterations are not affected.

 Always reset the "not found" variable set by a NOT FOUND handler after you terminate a cursor loop. Failure to do this may cause subsequent or nested cursor loops to terminate prematurely.

A slightly more complex—but arguably more robust solution—is to give each cursor its own handler. Because you can only have one NOT FOUND handler active within any particular block, this can only be done by enclosing each cursor in its own block. For instance, we could place the sales cursor in its own block with its own NOT FOUND handler, as in Example 5-17.

Example 5-17. Nested cursors using nested blocks

```
DECLARE CONTINUE HANDLER FOR NOT FOUND SET l_last_customer=1;

SET l_last_customer=0;
OPEN customer_csr;
```

Example 5-17. Nested cursors using nested blocks (continued)

```
cust_loop:LOOP        /* Loop through overdue customers*/

    FETCH customer_csr INTO l_customer_id;
    IF l_last_customer=1 THEN LEAVE cust_loop; END IF; /*no more rows*/
    SET l_customer_count=l_customer_count+1;

    sales_block: BEGIN
        DECLARE l_last_sale INT DEFAULT 0;
        DECLARE CONTINUE HANDLER FOR NOT FOUND SET l_last_sale=1;
        OPEN  sales_csr;
        sales_loop:LOOP     /* Get all sales for the customer */

            FETCH sales_csr INTO l_sales_id;
            IF l_last_sale=1 THEN LEAVE sales_loop; END IF; /*no more rows*/

            CALL check_sale(l_sales_id);  /* Check the sale status */
            SET l_sales_count=l_sales_count+1;

        END LOOP sales_loop;
        SET l_last_sale=0;
        CLOSE sales_csr;
    END sales_block;

END LOOP cust_loop;
SET l_last_customer=0;
CLOSE customer_csr;
```

Note that we now have a separate "not found" variable for each cursor, and we have eliminated any possibility that the closing of one cursor could affect the status of another. However, also note that we still reset the "not found" variables after we completed each cursor loop—this remains highly recommended since you may still wish to reopen a cursor within the same block.

Exiting the Cursor Loop Prematurely

Don't assume that you can only exit the cursor loop when the last row has been retrieved—you can issue a LEAVE statement at any time that you think that your processing has been completed. You may be looking for only one or a limited number of candidate records in the result set, or you may have detected some other condition suggesting that further processing is unnecessary.

Cursor Error Conditions

Cursor statements must occur in the sequence OPEN-FETCH-CLOSE. Any variation on this sequence will result in runtime errors.

For instance, if you try to CLOSE or FETCH from a cursor that is not open, you will encounter a Cursor is not open error, as shown in Example 5-18.

Example 5-18. Cursor is not open error

```
mysql> CREATE PROCEDURE csr_error2( )
BEGIN
        DECLARE x INT DEFAULT 0;
        DECLARE c cursor for select 1 from departments;
        CLOSE c;

END;

Query OK, 0 rows affected (0.00 sec)
mysql> CALL csr_error2( );
```

ERROR 1326 (24000): Cursor is not open

Attempting to open a cursor that is already open results in a Cursor is already open error, as shown in Example 5-19.

Example 5-19. Cursor is already open error

```
mysql> CREATE PROCEDURE csr_error3( )
BEGIN
        DECLARE x INT DEFAULT 0;
        DECLARE c cursor for select 1 from departments;
        OPEN c;
        OPEN c;

END;
//

Query OK, 0 rows affected (0.00 sec)
mysql> CALL csr_error3( );
```

ERROR 1325 (24000): Cursor is already open

Using Unbounded SELECT Statements

MySQL stored procedures (but not functions) can return result sets to the calling program (though not, unfortunately, directly to another stored procedure). A result set is returned from a stored procedure whenever a SQL statement that returns a result set is not associated with either an INTO clause or a cursor. We call these SQL statements *unbounded*. Such SQL statements will usually be SELECT statements, although other statements that return result sets—SHOW, EXPLAIN, DESC, and so on—can also be included within the stored procedure.

We have used unbounded SELECT statements throughout many of our examples in order to return information about stored procedure execution. You'll most likely do the same either for debugging purposes or to return some useful status information to the user or calling program. Example 5-20 shows an example of a stored procedure that uses this feature to return a list of employees within a specific department.

Example 5-20. Using unbounded SELECTs to return data to the calling program

```
CREATE PROCEDURE emps_in_dept(in_department_id INT)
BEGIN
    SELECT department_name, location
      FROM departments
     WHERE department_id=in_department_id;

    SELECT employee_id,surname,firstname
      FROM employees
     WHERE department_id=in_department_id;
END;
```

When run, the stored procedure from Example 5-20 produces the following output:

```
mysql> CALL emps_in_dept(31) //
+-------------------+----------+
| department_name   | location |
+-------------------+----------+
| ADVANCED RESEARCH | PAYSON   |
+-------------------+----------+
1 row in set (0.00 sec)


+-------------+----------+-----------+
| employee_id | surname  | firstname |
+-------------+----------+-----------+
|         149 | EPPLING  | LAUREL    |
|         298 | CHARRON  | NEWLIN    |
|         447 | RAMBO    | ROSWALD   |
|         596 | GRESSETT | STANFORD  |
|         745 | KANE     | CARLIN    |
|         894 | ABELL    | JAMIE     |
|        1043 | BROOKS   | LYNN      |
|        1192 | WENSEL   | ZENAS     |
|        1341 | ZANIS    | ALDA      |
|        1490 | PUGH     | ALICE     |
|        1639 | KUEHLER  | SIZA      |
|        1788 | RUST     | PAINE     |
|        1937 | BARRY    | LEO       |
+-------------+----------+-----------+
13 rows in set (0.00 sec)
```

In some respects, using stored procedures to return result sets in this way provides similar functionality to creating a view to support specific queries. Like a view, the stored procedure can encapsulate complex SQL operations, thus making it easier for a user to retrieve data without necessarily having to understand the complexities of the schema design. Encapsulating SQL inside a stored procedure can also improve security, because you can perform complex validation checks or even encryption/decryption before returning the result set.

Unlike a view, a stored procedure can return multiple result sets, as shown in Example 5-20. Returning multiple result sets can be a convenient way to encapsulate all of the logic required to produce multiple sets of application data in a single call to the database.

Retrieving the Result Sets in the Calling Program

It is relatively easy to retrieve a result set from a stored procedure. Provided that the stored procedure returns only a single result set, it can be handled in the same way as a normal SQL call. Example 5-21 shows a PHP program using the `mysqli` interface that retrieves a single result set from a stored procedure call.

Example 5-21. Retrieving a stored procedure result set from PHP

```
1   <h1>Department listing</h1>
2   <table border="1" width="90%">
3     <tr> <td><b>Department ID</b></td>
4          <td><b>Department Name</b></td>
5   <?php
6       $hostname="localhost";
7       $username="root";
8       $password="secret";
9       $database="sqltune";
10
11      $p1="";
12      $p2="";
13
14
15      $dbh = new mysqli($hostname, $username, $password, $database);
16
17      /* check connection */
18      if (mysqli_connect_errno()) {
19          printf("Connect failed: %s\n", mysqli_connect_error());
20          exit();
21      }
22
23      if ($result_set = $dbh->query("call department_list()"))
24      {
25          printf('');
26          while($row=$result_set->fetch_object())
27          {
28              printf("<tr><td>%s</td><td>%s</td></tr>\n",
29                      $row->department_id, $row->department_name);
30          }
31      }
32      else // Query failed - show error
33      {
34          printf("<p>Error retrieving stored procedure result set:%d (%s) %s\n",
35                  mysqli_errno($dbh),mysqli_sqlstate($dbh),mysqli_error($dbh));
36          $dbh->close();
37          exit();
38      }
39      /* free result set */
40      $result_set->close();
41      $dbh->close();
42
43  ?>
```

```
44   </table>
45   </body>
46   </html>
```

The significant lines of code from Example 5-21 include:

Line(s)	Explanation
23	Call the `department_list` stored procedure, which will return a result set containing a list of departments. The `$result_set` object represents the result set that is returned.
26	Iteratively call the `fetch_object` method, which returns an object representing a single row.
28 and 29	Extract individual columns from the `$row` object, by using the `department_id` and `department_name` properties, which contain the values for the corresponding columns.

The output of the PHP program is shown in Figure 5-1.

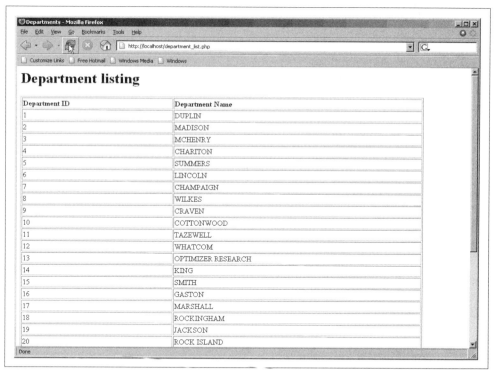

Figure 5-1. Output of a PHP program that retrieves a stored procedure result set

The ability to return multiple result sets from a stored procedure can be either a blessing or a curse, depending on your perspective. The multiple result set feature can allow you to return multiple logically related sets of data in a single operation.

For instance, all the result sets necessary to populate a multilevel master-detail report can be requested from the database in one operation. This could result in a greater level of separation between presentation (often web) logic and data access (database) logic.

However, handling multiple result sets may require unfamiliar processing requirements in our client-side programming. Some third-party report-generating tools may be unprepared for the possibility of multiple result sets being sent out by a single database call. In fact, some of these third-party tools may be unable to cope with a stored procedure sending out a result set at all.

Luckily, the major programming interfaces we use with MySQL—PHP, Java, Perl, Python, and .NET C# and VB.NET—are all capable of handling multiple result sets. In Chapters 13 through 17, we explore in detail how to process result sets and perform other operations on MySQL stored procedures in these languages. To give you a preview of the general process, Example 5-22 shows how we retrieve multiple results sets from a MySQL stored procedure in Java.

Example 5-22. Retrieving multiple result sets from a stored procedure in Java

```
1    private void empsInDept(Connection myConnect, int deptId) throws SQLException {
2
3        CallableStatement cStmt = myConnect
4                    .prepareCall("{CALL sp_emps_in_dept(?)}");
5        cStmt.setInt(1, deptId);
6        cStmt.execute();
7        ResultSet rs1 = cStmt.getResultSet();
8        while (rs1.next()) {
9            System.out.println(rs1.getString("department_name") + " "
10                    + rs1.getString("location"));
11        }
12        rs1.close();
13
14        /* process second result set */
15        if (cStmt.getMoreResults()) {
16            ResultSet rs2 = cStmt.getResultSet();
17            while (rs2.next()) {
18                System.out.println(rs2.getInt(1) + " " + rs2.getString(2) + " "
19                    + rs2.getString(3));
20            }
21            rs2.close();
22        }
23        cStmt.close();
24    }
```

Let's step through the important parts of Example 5-22:

Line(s)	Explanation
3	Create a `CallableStatement` object corresponding to the stored procedure from Example 5-20.
5	Provide the parameter (`department_id`) to the stored procedure.
6	Execute the stored procedure.
7	Create a `ResultSet` object corresponding to the first result set.
8-11	Loop through the rows in that result set and print the results to the console.
15	Use the `getMoreResults` method to move to the next result set.
16	Create a `ResultSet` object for the second result set.
17-20	Retrieve the rows from the result set and print them to the console.

Returning Result Sets to Another Stored Procedure

We know that we can return result sets to a calling program (such as PHP)—but is there a way to return the result set to another stored procedure?

Unfortunately, the only way to pass a result set from one stored procedure to another is to pass the results via a temporary table. This is an awkward solution, and—because the temporary table has scope throughout the entire session—it creates many of the same maintainability issues raised by the use of global variables. But if one stored program needs to supply another stored program with results, then a temporary table can be the best solution.

Let's look at an example. In Example 5-23, we have a stored procedure that is responsible for creating a temporary table that contains all overdue sales. Although this SQL is simple enough that we could replicate the SQL in every stored procedure that needs to process overdue orders, our performance is improved if we create this list only once during our batch run, and modularity and maintainability are improved if we define this query in only one place.

Example 5-23. Stored procedure that creates a temporary table

```
CREATE PROCEDURE sp_overdue_sales ()

BEGIN
  DROP TEMPORARY TABLE IF EXISTS overdue_sales_tmp;
  CREATE TEMPORARY TABLE overdue_sales_tmp AS
  SELECT sales_id,customer_id,sale_date,quantity,sale_value
    FROM sales
   WHERE sale_status='0';

END;
```

In Example 5-24 we see a stored procedure that calls the previous stored procedure and consumes the rows placed in the temporary table. In practice, this is pretty much equivalent to passing the result set from one stored procedure to another.

Example 5-24. Stored procedure that consumes data from a temporary table

```
CREATE PROCEDURE sp_issue_invoices()

BEGIN
  DECLARE l_sale_id INT;
  DECLARE l_last_sale INT DEFAULT 0;

  DECLARE sale_csr CURSOR FOR
    SELECT sales_id
      FROM overdue_sales_tmp;

  DECLARE CONTINUE HANDLER FOR NOT FOUND SET l_last_sale=1;

  CALL sp_overdue_sales();

  OPEN sale_csr;
  sale_loop:LOOP
    FETCH sale_csr INTO l_sale_id;
    IF l_last_sale THEN
      LEAVE sale_loop;
    END IF;
    CALL sp_issue_one_invoice(l_sale_id);
  END LOOP sale_loop;
  CLOSE sale_csr;

END;
```

Note that in MySQL, temporary tables have scope only within the specific session that creates the table, and they are automatically de-allocated when that session completes. So we don't have to worry about cleaning up the temporary table or be concerned that the table could be simultaneously updated by another session.

Performing Dynamic SQL with Prepared Statements

MySQL supports a facility known as *server-side prepared statements*, which provides an API-independent way of preparing a SQL statement for repeated execution efficiently and securely. Prepared statements are interesting from a stored programming perspective because they allow us to create dynamic SQL calls.

We create a prepared statement with the PREPARE statement:

```
PREPARE statement_name FROM sql_text
```

The SQL text may contain placeholders for data values that must be supplied when the SQL is executed. These placeholders are represented by ? characters.

The prepared statement is executed with the, EXECUTE statement:

```
EXECUTE statement_name [USING variable [,variable...]]
```

The USING clause can be used to specify values for the placeholders specified in the PREPARE statement. These must be supplied as user variables (prefixed with the @ character), which we described in Chapter 3.

Finally, we can drop the prepared statement with the DEALLOCATE statement:

```
DEALLOCATE PREPARE statement_name
```

An example of using prepared statements within the MySQL command-line client is shown in Example 5-25.

Example 5-25. Using prepared statements

```
mysql> PREPARE prod_insert_stmt FROM "INSERT INTO product_codes VALUES(?,?)";
Query OK, 0 rows affected (0.00 sec)
Statement prepared

mysql>
mysql> SET @code='QB';
Query OK, 0 rows affected (0.00 sec)

mysql> SET @name='MySQL Query Browser';
Query OK, 0 rows affected (0.00 sec)

mysql> EXECUTE prod_insert_stmt USING @code,@name;
Query OK, 1 row affected (0.00 sec)

mysql> SET @code='AD';
Query OK, 0 rows affected (0.00 sec)

mysql> SET @name='MySQL Administrator';
Query OK, 0 rows affected (0.02 sec)

mysql> EXECUTE prod_insert_stmt USING @code,@name;
Query OK, 1 row affected (0.00 sec)

mysql> DEALLOCATE PREPARE prod_insert_stmt;
Query OK, 0 rows affected (0.00 sec)
```

Now, the idea of prepared statements is to reduce the overhead of re-parsing (preparing) a SQL statement for execution if all that has changed is a few data values, and to enhance security by allowing SQL statement parameters to be supplied in a way that prevents SQL injection (for more about SQL injection, see Chapter 18). Stored procedures don't need prepared statements for these reasons, since the SQL statements in stored procedures are already "prepared" for execution. Moreover, SQL injection is not really a threat in stored programs (ironically enough, *unless* you use prepared statements!).

However, prepared statements come in handy in stored programs, because they allow you to execute *dynamic SQL* from within a procedure (but not from within a trigger or function). A SQL statement is dynamic if it is constructed at runtime (whereas a static SQL statement is one that is constructed at the time of compilation of the program unit). You will generally rely on dynamic SQL only when you don't have all the information you need at compile time to complete your statement. This usually occurs because you need input from a user or from some other data source.

The stored procedure in Example 5-26 offers a demonstration of running dynamic SQL as a prepared statement; it will, in fact, execute *any* SQL that is passed in as an argument.

Example 5-26. Stored procedure with dynamic SQL

```
CREATE PROCEDURE execute_immediate(in_sql VARCHAR(4000))
BEGIN

   SET @tmp_sql=in_sql;
   PREPARE s1 FROM @tmp_sql;
   EXECUTE s1;
   DEALLOCATE PREPARE s1;

END;
```

SQL executed as a prepared statement within a stored procedure acts pretty much the same way as a static SQL statement that is embedded inside the stored procedure. However, the EXECUTE statement does not support an INTO clause, nor is it possible to define a cursor from a prepared statement. Therefore, any results from a prepared statement will be returned to the calling program and cannot be trapped in the stored procedure. To catch the rows returned by a dynamic SQL call, store them in a temporary table, as outlined in the section "Returning Result Sets to Another Stored Procedure," earlier in this chapter.

You should rely on dynamic SQL only when needed. It is more complex and less efficient than static SQL, but it does allow you to implement otherwise impossible tasks and create useful, generic utility routines. For instance, the stored procedure in Example 5-27 accepts a table name, column name, WHERE clause, and value; the procedure uses these parameters to build up an UPDATE statement that can update any table column value.

Example 5-27. Stored procedure that can update any column in any table

```
CREATE PROCEDURE set_col_value
        (in_table     VARCHAR(128),
         in_column    VARCHAR(128),
         in_new_value VARCHAR(1000),
         in_where     VARCHAR(4000))

BEGIN
   DECLARE l_sql VARCHAR(4000);
   SET l_sql=CONCAT_ws(' ',
             'UPDATE',in_table,
               'SET',in_column,'=',in_new_value,
             ' WHERE',in_where);
```

```
   SET @sql=l_sql;
   PREPARE s1 FROM @sql;
   EXECUTE s1;
   DEALLOCATE PREPARE s1;
END;
```

We could call this program to zero-out the salary of employee ID 1 (eat this, CEO!) by invoking the procedure as follows:

```
   mysql> CALL set_col_value('employees','salary','0','employee_id=1')
```

Another common application of dynamic SQL is to build up conditional WHERE clauses. Often, we construct user interfaces in which the user may specify multiple search criteria. Handling the "missing" conditions without dynamic SQL can lead to complex and awkward SQL, which can be difficult for MySQL to optimize. Example 5-28 shows a simple example of a search procedure that allows the user to specify any combination of customer name, contact name, or phone number.

Example 5-28. Search procedure without dynamic SQL

```
CREATE PROCEDURE sp_customer_search
   (in_customer_name VARCHAR(30),
    in_contact_surname VARCHAR(30),
    in_contact_firstname VARCHAR(30),
    in_phoneno VARCHAR(10))

BEGIN
  SELECT *
    FROM customers
   WHERE (customer_name LIKE in_customer_name
          OR in_customer_name IS NULL)
     AND (contact_surname LIKE in_contact_surname
          OR in_contact_surname IS NULL)
     AND (contact_firstname LIKE in_contact_firstname
          OR in_contact_firstname IS NULL)
     AND (phoneno LIKE in_phoneno
          OR in_phoneno IS NULL) ;

END;
```

The SQL in Example 5-28 is not yet *unbearably* complex, but as the number of candidate search columns increases, the maintainability of this statement will rapidly diminish. Even with this statement, however, we may be legitimately concerned that the SQL is not correctly optimized for the specific search criteria supplied by the end user. We may therefore wish to build up a more customized search query. Example 5-29 shows a procedure in which we construct the WHERE clause dynamically to match the search criteria supplied by the user and call that SQL dynamically using prepared statements.

Example 5-29. Search procedure with dynamic SQL

```
CREATE PROCEDURE sp_customer_search_dyn
    (in_customer_name VARCHAR(30),
     in_contact_surname VARCHAR(30),
     in_contact_firstname VARCHAR(30),
     in_phoneno VARCHAR(10))

BEGIN
  DECLARE l_where_clause VARCHAR(1000) DEFAULT 'WHERE';

  IF in_customer_name IS NOT NULL THEN
      SET l_where_clause=CONCAT(l_where_clause,
          ' customer_name="',in_customer_name,'"');
  END IF;

  IF in_contact_surname IS NOT NULL THEN
     IF l_where_clause<>'WHERE' THEN
        SET l_where_clause=CONCAT(l_where_clause,' AND ');
     END IF;
     SET l_where_clause=CONCAT(l_where_clause,
         ' contact_surname="',in_contact_surname,'"');
  END IF;

  IF in_contact_firstname IS NOT NULL THEN
     IF l_where_clause<>'WHERE' THEN
        SET l_where_clause=CONCAT(l_where_clause,' AND ');
     END IF;
     SET l_where_clause=CONCAT(l_where_clause,
         ' contact_firstname="',in_contact_firstname,'"');
  END IF;

  IF in_phoneno IS NOT NULL THEN
     IF l_where_clause<>'WHERE' THEN
        SET l_where_clause=CONCAT(l_where_clause,' AND ');
     END IF;
     SET l_where_clause=CONCAT(l_where_clause,
         ' phoneno="',in_phoneno,'"');
  END IF;

  SET @sql=CONCAT('SELECT * FROM customers ',
                  l_where_clause);


  PREPARE s1 FROM @sql;
  EXECUTE s1;
  DEALLOCATE PREPARE s1;

END;
```

Although the procedure in Example 5-29 is longer and more complicated than the static example shown in Example 5-28, it may execute faster because we have eliminated redundant WHERE clauses from the SQL that is finally executed. In that way, we give MySQL better data on which to base its decisions regarding indexes and other optimizations.

You will probably not need to use dynamic SQL and prepared statements very often, but they can certainly save the day when you are faced with the need to construct a SQL statement based on user input or stored program parameters. However, a final word of caution: when you construct SQL based on user input, you allow for the security attack known as *SQL injection* to occur, and SQL injection in stored procedures can pose a particularly high risk because of the unique execution context of stored procedures. We discuss SQL injection in stored programs in detail within Chapter 18.

Handling SQL Errors: A Preview

Error handling in MySQL stored programs is such an important and complex topic that we have dedicated an entire chapter—Chapter 6—to this topic. However, let's provide a quick summary here.

By default, if a SQL statement within a stored program generates an error, the stored program will cease execution and the error will be returned to the calling program. If you don't want this to happen, you must specify an *error handler* using the following syntax:

```
DECLARE {CONTINUE | EXIT} HANDLER FOR
    {SQLSTATE sqlstate_code| MySQL error code| condition_name}
    stored_program_statement
```

The handler nominates an error condition—using a MySQL error code, an ANSI-standard SQLSTATE, or a named condition—and describes what is to happen if the error is encountered. The handler can do one of two things:

- Allow execution to CONTINUE.
- Immediately exit the block or stored program containing the handler.

The handler specifies stored program statements that will be executed when the handler is activated. These statements often set a status variable that could be checked within the main line of the program but that could also specify a BEGIN-END block containing many lines of code.

We have already looked at the use of handlers in determining when a cursor has returned the last row of its result set (see "Fetching an Entire Result Set" earlier in this chapter).

We discuss handlers in depth in the next chapter.

Conclusion

In this chapter we reviewed the facilities MySQL provides for including SQL within stored programs. The following types of SQL statements can appear in stored programs:

- Simple embedded non-SELECT statements, including DML statements (INSERT, DELETE, UPDATE) and DDL statements (CREATE, DROP, ALTER, etc.) can be included within stored programs without any particular restrictions.

- SELECT statements that return only one row may include an INTO clause that stores the results of the SELECT statement into stored program variables.

- SELECT statements allow you to iterate through the rows returned by a multirow SELECT statement by using a cursor. Cursors involve a bit more programming effort, including a looping structure and a condition handler to prevent "no data to fetch" errors when all rows from the cursor have been retrieved. Nevertheless, cursors will probably be your main mechanism for performing complex data processing in stored programs.

- "Unbounded" SELECT statements—those without an INTO clause or a CURSOR statement—can be included within stored procedures (but not within stored functions). The output from these SELECT statements will be returned to the calling program (but not to a calling stored procedure). You will need to employ special code in your calling program to handle result sets from stored procedures, especially if more than a single result set is returned.

SQL statements can also be prepared dynamically using MySQL server-side prepared statements.

If your SQL statements generate an error, your stored program will terminate and return control to the calling program unless you create an *error handler* that "catches" the error and takes appropriate action. We saw a simple example of an error handler in this chapter and looked at NOT FOUND handlers that handle the end of a cursor result set. In the next chapter we'll cover the topic of error handlers in greater detail.

## CHAPTER 6

Error Handling

The perfect programmer, living in a perfect world, would always write programs that anticipate every possible circumstance. Those programs would either always work correctly, or fail "gracefully" by providing comprehensive diagnostic information to the support team and very readable messages to the user.

For a certain class of applications—software supporting life support systems or the space shuttle, for instance—this level of perfection is actually a part of the requirements, because any unexpected failure of the software would be catastrophic. However, in the world of business applications, we usually make certain assumptions about our execution environment—we assume the MySQL server will be running, that our tables have not been dropped, that the host machine is not on fire, and so on. If any of these conditions occurs, then we accept that our application will fail. In many other circumstances, we can and should anticipate potential failures and write code to manage those situations. This is where exception handling comes into play.

When a stored program encounters an error condition, execution ceases and an error is returned to the calling application. That's the default behavior. What if we need a different kind of behavior? What if, for example, we want to trap that error, log it, or report on it, and then continue execution of our application? For that kind of control, we need to define exception handlers in our programs.

When developing MySQL stored programs, a very common scenario—fetching to the end of a result set—also requires that we define an *exception handler*.

In this chapter we explain how to create various types of exception handlers and how to improve the readability of error handling by using "named" conditions. We also identify several gaps in exception-handling functionality in MySQL 5, and explore ways of compensating for these omissions.

Introduction to Error Handling

Let's begin by looking at several examples of stored program error handling.

A Simple First Example

Consider a simple stored procedure that creates a location record, as shown in Example 6-1.

Example 6-1. Simple stored procedure without error handling

```
CREATE PROCEDURE sp_add_location
        (in_location    VARCHAR(30),
         in_address1    VARCHAR(30),
         in_address2    VARCHAR(30),
         zipcode        VARCHAR(10))
    MODIFIES SQL DATA
BEGIN
    INSERT INTO locations
      (location,address1,address2,zipcode)
    VALUES
      (in_location,in_address1,in_address2,zipcode);
END$$
```

This procedure works fine when the location does not already exist, as shown in the following output:

```
mysql> CALL sp_add_location('Guys place','30 Blakely Drv',
                            'Irvine CA','92618-20');

Query OK, 1 row affected, 1 warning (0.44 sec)
```

However, if we try to insert a department that already exists, MySQL raises an error:

```
mysql> CALL sp_add_location('Guys place','30 Blakely Drv',
                            'Irvine CA','92618-20');

ERROR 1062 (23000): Duplicate entry 'Guys place' for key 1
```

If the stored procedure is called by an external program such as PHP, we could *probably* get away with leaving this program "as is." PHP, and other external programs, can detect such error conditions and then take appropriate action. If the stored procedure is called from another stored procedure, however, we risk causing the entire procedure call stack to abort. That may not be what we want.

Since we can anticipate that MySQL error 1062 could be raised by this procedure, we can write code to handle that specific error code. Example 6-2 demonstrates this technique. Rather than allow the exception to propagate out of the procedure unhandled (causing failures in the calling program), the stored procedure traps the exception, sets a status flag, and returns that status information to the calling program.

The calling program can then decide if this failure warrants termination or if it should continue execution.

Example 6-2. Simple stored procedure with error handling

```
CREATE PROCEDURE sp_add_location
        (in_location    VARCHAR(30),
         in_address1    VARCHAR(30),
         in_address2    VARCHAR(30),
         zipcode        VARCHAR(10),
         OUT out_status VARCHAR(30))
   MODIFIES SQL DATA
BEGIN
   DECLARE CONTINUE HANDLER FOR 1062
     SET out_status='Duplicate Entry';

   SET out_status='OK';
   INSERT INTO locations
     (location,address1,address2,zipcode)
     VALUES
     (in_location,in_address1,in_address2,zipcode);
END;
```

We'll review in detail the syntax of the HANDLER clause later in this chapter. For now, it is enough to understand that the DECLARE CONTINUE HANDLER statement tells MySQL that "if you encounter MySQL error 1062 (duplicate entry for key), then *continue* execution but set the variable p_status to 'Duplicate Entry'."

As expected, this implementation does not return an error to the calling program, and we can examine the status variable to see if the stored procedure execution was successful. In Example 6-3 we show a stored procedure that creates new department records. This procedure calls our previous procedure to add a new location. If the location already exists, the stored procedure generates a warning and continues. Without the exception handling in sp_add_location, this procedure would terminate when the unhandled exception is raised.

Example 6-3. Calling a stored procedure that has an error handler

```
CREATE PROCEDURE sp_add_department
      (in_department_name VARCHAR(30),
       in_manager_id      INT,
       in_location        VARCHAR(30),
       in_address1        VARCHAR(30),
       in_address2        VARCHAR(30),
       in_zipcode         VARCHAR(10)
       )
   MODIFIES SQL DATA
BEGIN
   DECLARE l_status VARCHAR(20);

   CALL sp_add_location(in_location,in_address1,in_address2,
                        in_zipcode, l_status);
     IF l_status='Duplicate Entry' THEN
         SELECT CONCAT('Warning: using existing definition for location ',
                  in_location) AS warning;
```

Example 6-3. Calling a stored procedure that has an error handler (continued)

```
    END IF;

    INSERT INTO departments (manager_id,department_name,location)
    VALUES(in_manager_id,in_department_name,in_location);

END;
```

Handling Last Row Conditions

One of the most common operations in a MySQL stored program involves fetching one or more rows of data. You can do this in a stored program through the use of a cursor (explained in Chapter 5). However, MySQL (and the ANSI standard) considers an attempt to fetch past the last row of the cursor an error. Therefore, you almost always need to catch that particular error when looping through the results from a cursor.

Consider the simple cursor loop shown in Example 6-4. At first glance, you might worry that we might inadvertently have created an infinite loop, since we have not coded any way to leave the dept_loop loop.

Example 6-4. Cursor loop without a NOT FOUND handler

```
CREATE PROCEDURE sp_fetch_forever( )
   READS SQL DATA
BEGIN
    DECLARE l_dept_id  INT;
    DECLARE c_dept CURSOR FOR
            SELECT department_id
              FROM departments;

    OPEN c_dept;
    dept_cursor: LOOP
        FETCH c_dept INTO l_dept_id;
    END LOOP dept_cursor;
    CLOSE c_dept;
END
```

Bravely, we run this program and find that the seemingly infinite loop fails as soon as we attempt to fetch beyond the final row in the result set:

```
mysql> CALL sp_fetch_forever( );
ERROR 1329 (02000): No data to FETCH
```

Since we likely want to do something with the data after we've fetched it, we cannot let this exception propagate out of the procedure unhandled. So we will add a declaration for a CONTINUE HANDLER in the procedure, setting a flag to indicate that the last row has been fetched. This technique is shown in Example 6-5.

Example 6-5. Cursor loop with a NOT FOUND handler

```
1  CREATE PROCEDURE sp_not_found( )
2      READS SQL DATA
3  BEGIN
4      DECLARE l_last_row INT DEFAULT 0;
5      DECLARE l_dept_id  INT;
6      DECLARE c_dept CURSOR FOR
7            SELECT department_id
8              FROM departments;
9      /* handler to set l_last_row=1 if a cursor returns no more rows */
10     DECLARE CONTINUE HANDLER FOR NOT FOUND SET l_last_row=1;
11
12     OPEN c_dept;
13     dept_cursor: LOOP
14         FETCH c_dept INTO l_dept_id;
15         IF (l_last_row=1) THEN
16             LEAVE dept_cursor;
17         END IF;
18         /* Do something with the data*/
19
20     END LOOP dept_cursor;
21     CLOSE c_dept;
22
23  END;
```

In plain English, the handler on line 10 says "When a fetch from a cursor returns no more rows, continue execution, but set the variable l_last_row to 1." After retrieving each row, we check the l_last_row variable and exit from the cursor loop if the last row is returned. Without this handler, our cursor loop will fetch too many times and raise an exception.

Now that you have seen two simple examples of declaring handlers for error situations that you can anticipate, let's explore this functionality in more detail.

Condition Handlers

A *condition handler* defines the actions that the stored program is to take when a specified event—such as a warning or an error—occurs.

Here is the syntax of the DECLARE HANDLER command:

```
DECLARE {CONTINUE | EXIT} HANDLER FOR
    {SQLSTATE sqlstate_code| MySQL error code| condition_name}
    handler_actions
```

Note that handlers must be defined after any variable or cursor declarations, which makes sense, since the handlers frequently access local variables or perform actions on cursors (such as closing them). They must also be declared before any executable statements. Chapter 4 includes more details on the rules governing the positioning of statements within a block.

The hander declaration has three main clauses;

- Handler type (CONTINUE, EXIT)
- Handler condition (SQLSTATE, MySQL error code, named condition)
- Hander actions

Let's look at each of these clauses in turn.

Types of Handlers

Condition handlers can be one of two types:

EXIT

> When an EXIT handler fires, the currently executing block is terminated. If this block is the main block for the stored program, the procedure terminates, and control is returned to the procedure or external program that invoked the procedure. If the block is enclosed within an outer block inside of the same stored program, control is returned to that outer block.

CONTINUE

> With a CONTINUE handler, execution continues with the statement following the one that caused the error to occur.

In either case, any statements defined within the hander (the *handler actions*) are run before either the EXIT or CONTINUE takes place.

Let's look at examples of both types of handlers. Example 6-6 shows a stored procedure that creates a department record and attempts to gracefully handle the situation in which the specified department already exists.

Example 6-6. Example of an EXIT handler

```
1   CREATE PROCEDURE add_department
2        (in_dept_name VARCHAR(30),
3         in_location VARCHAR(30),
4         in_manager_id INT)
5      MODIFIES SQL DATA
6   BEGIN
7      DECLARE duplicate_key INT DEFAULT 0;
8      BEGIN
9         DECLARE EXIT HANDLER FOR 1062 /* Duplicate key*/ SET duplicate_key=1;
10
11        INSERT INTO departments (department_name,location,manager_id)
12        VALUES(in_dept_name,in_location,in_manager_id);
13
14        SELECT CONCAT('Department ',in_dept_name,' created') as "Result";
15     END;
16
17     IF duplicate_key=1 THEN
18        SELECT CONCAT('Failed to insert ',in_dept_name,
```

Example 6-6. Example of an EXIT handler (continued)

```
19                          ': duplicate key') as "Result";
20      END IF;
21 END$$
```

Let's examine the logic for Example 6-6:

Lines(s)	Explanation
7	Declare a status variable that will record the status of our insert attempt.
8-15	This BEGIN-END block encloses the INSERT statement that will attempt to create the department row. The block includes the EXIT handler that will terminate the block if a 1062 error occurs.
11	Attempt to insert our row—if we get a duplicate key error, the handler will set the variable and terminate the block.
14	This line executes only if the EXIT handler did not fire, and reports success to the user. If the handler fired, then the block was terminated and this line would never be executed.
17	Execution will then continue on this line, where we check the value of the variable and—if the hander has fired—advise the user that the insert was unsuccessful.

Following is the output from this stored procedure for both unsuccessful and successful execution:

```
MySQL> CALL add_department('OPTIMIZER RESEARCH','SEATTLE',4) //

+------------------------------------------------------+
| Result                                               |
+------------------------------------------------------+
| Failed to insert OPTIMIZER RESEARCH: duplicate key   |
+------------------------------------------------------+
1 row in set (0.02 sec)

MySQL> CALL add_department('CUSTOMER SATISFACTION','DAVIS',4);

+-----------------------------------------+
| Result                                  |
+-----------------------------------------+
| Department CUSTOMER SATISFACTION created |
+-----------------------------------------+
1 row in set (0.00 sec)
```

Example 6-7 provides an example of the same functionality implemented with a CONTINUE handler. In this example, when the handler fires, execution continues with the statement immediately following the INSERT statement. This IF statement checks to see if the handler has fired, and if it has, it displays the failure message. Otherwise, the success message is displayed.

Example 6-7. Example of a CONTINUE handler

```
CREATE PROCEDURE add_department
      (in_dept_name VARCHAR(30),
       in_location VARCHAR(30),
```

Example 6-7. Example of a CONTINUE handler (continued)

```
         in_manager_id INT)
  MODIFIES SQL DATA
BEGIN
    DECLARE duplicate_key INT DEFAULT 0;

    DECLARE CONTINUE HANDLER FOR 1062 /* Duplicate key*/
          SET duplicate_key=1;

    INSERT INTO departments (department_name,location,manager_id)
    VALUES(in_dept_name,in_location,in_manager_id);

    IF duplicate_key=1 THEN
        SELECT CONCAT('Failed to insert ',in_dept_name,
                          ': duplicate key') as "Result";
    ELSE
            SELECT CONCAT('Department ',in_dept_name,' created') as "Result";
    END IF;
END$$
```

EXIT or CONTINUE?

The choice between creating an EXIT handler and creating a CONTINUE handler is based primarily on program flow-of-control considerations.

An EXIT handler will exit from the block in which it is declared, which precludes the possibility that any other statements in the block (or the entire procedure) might be executed. This type of handler is most suitable for catastrophic errors that do not allow for any form of continued processing.

A CONTINUE handler allows subsequent statements to be executed. Generally, you will detect that the handler has fired (through some form of status variable set in the handler) and determine the most appropriate course of action. This type of handler is most suitable when you have some alternative processing that you will execute if the exception occurs.

Handler Conditions

The handler condition defines the circumstances under which the handler will be invoked. The circumstance is always associated with an error condition, but you have three choices as to how you define that error:

- As a MySQL error code.
- As an ANSI-standard SQLSTATE code.
- As a named condition. You may define your own named conditions (described in the later section "Named Conditions") or use one of the built-in conditions SQLEXCEPTION, SQLWARNING, and NOT FOUND.

MySQL has its own set of error codes that are unique to the MySQL server. A handler condition that refers to a numeric code without qualification is referring to a MySQL error code. For instance, the following handler will fire when MySQL error code 1062 (duplicate key value) is encountered:

```
DECLARE CONTINUE HANDLER FOR 1062 SET duplicate_key=1;
```

SQLSTATE error codes are defined by the ANSI standard and are database-independent, meaning that they will have the same value regardless of the underlying database. So, for instance, Oracle, SQL Server, DB2, and MySQL will always report the same SQLSTATE value (23000) when a duplicate key value error is encountered. Every MySQL error code has an associated SQLSTATE code, but the relationship is not one-to-one; some SQLSTATE codes are associated with many MySQL codes; HY000 is a general-purpose SQLSTATE code that is raised for MySQL codes that have no specific associated SQLSTATE code.

The following handler will fire when SQLSTATE 23000 (duplicate key value) is encountered:

```
DECLARE CONTINUE HANDLER FOR SQLSTATE '23000' SET duplicate_key=1;
```

SQLSTATE or MySQL Error Code?

In theory, using the SQLSTATE codes will make your code more portable to other database platforms and might therefore seem to be the best choice. However, there are a number of reasons to use MySQL error codes rather than SQLSTATE codes when writing MySQL stored programs:

- In reality, it is unlikely that you will move your stored programs to another RDBMS. The Oracle and SQL Server stored program languages are totally incompatible with MySQL. The DB2 stored program language is somewhat compatible (both are based on the SQL:2003 standard). It is very likely, however, that you will use MySQL-specific syntax as you write your application, which will prevent your stored code from being portable.

- Not all MySQL error codes have SQLSTATE equivalents. Although every MySQL error code is associated with some SQLSTATE error code, often it will be a general-purpose SQLSTATE that is not specific (such as HY000). Therefore, you will almost certainly have to code some handlers that refer directly to MySQL error codes. You'll probably find that the advantages of using a consistent handler format will outweigh the theoretical portability advantage of SQLSTATE error codes.

We will, for the most part, use MySQL error codes in this book.

When the MySQL client encounters an error, it will report both the MySQL error code and the associated SQLSTATE code, as in the following output:

```
mysql> CALL nosuch_sp();

ERROR 1305 (42000): PROCEDURE sqltune.nosuch_sp does not exist
```

In this case, the MySQL error code is 1305 and the SQLSTATE code is 42000.

Table 6-1 lists some of the error codes you might expect to encounter in a MySQL stored program together with their SQLSTATE equivalents. Note, again, that many MySQL error codes map to the same SQLSTATE code (many map to HY000, for instance), which is why you may wish to sacrifice portability and use MySQL error codes— rather than SQLSTATE codes—in your error handlers.

Table 6-1. Some common MySQL error codes and SQLSTATE codes

MySQL error code	SQLSTATE code	Error message
1011	HY000	Error on delete of '%s' (errno: %d)
1021	HY000	Disk full (%s); waiting for someone to free some space…
1022	23000	Can't write; duplicate key in table '%s'
1027	HY000	'%s' is locked against change
1036	HY000	Table '%s' is read only
1048	23000	Column '%s' cannot be null
1062	23000	Duplicate entry '%s' for key %d
1099	HY000	Table '%s' was locked with a READ lock and can't be updated
1100	HY000	Table '%s' was not locked with LOCK TABLES
1104	42000	The SELECT would examine more than MAX_JOIN_SIZE rows; check your WHERE and use SET SQL_BIG_SELECTS=1 or SET SQL_MAX_JOIN_SIZE=# if the SELECT is okay
1106	42000	Incorrect parameters to procedure '%s'
1114	HY000	The table '%s' is full
1150	HY000	Delayed insert thread couldn't get requested lock for table %s
1165	HY000	INSERT DELAYED can't be used with table '%s' because it is locked with LOCK TABLES
1242	21000	Subquery returns more than 1 row
1263	22004	Column set to default value; NULL supplied to NOT NULL column '%s' at row %ld
1264	22003	Out of range value adjusted for column '%s' at row %ld
1265	1000	Data truncated for column '%s' at row %ld
1312	0A000	SELECT in a stored program must have INTO
1317	70100	Query execution was interrupted
1319	42000	Undefined CONDITION: %s
1325	24000	Cursor is already open

Table 6-1. *Some common MySQL error codes and SQLSTATE codes (continued)*

MySQL error code	SQLSTATE code	Error message
1326	24000	Cursor is not open
1328	HY000	Incorrect number of FETCH variables
1329	2000	No data to FETCH
1336	42000	USE is not allowed in a stored program
1337	42000	Variable or condition declaration after cursor or handler declaration
1338	42000	Cursor declaration after handler declaration
1339	20000	Case not found for CASE statement
1348	HY000	Column '%s' is not updatable
1357	HY000	Can't drop a %s from within another stored routine
1358	HY000	GOTO is not allowed in a stored program handler
1362	HY000	Updating of %s row is not allowed in %s trigger
1363	HY000	There is no %s row in %s trigger

You can find a complete and up-to-date list of error codes in Appendix B of the MySQL reference manual, available online at *http://dev.mysql.com/doc/*.

Handler Examples

Here are some examples of handler declarations:

- If any error condition arises (other than a NOT FOUND), continue execution after setting l_error=1:

```
DECLARE CONTINUE HANDLER FOR SQLEXCEPTION
    SET l_error=1;
```

- If any error condition arises (other than a NOT FOUND), exit the current block or stored program after issuing a ROLLBACK statement and issuing an error message:

```
DECLARE EXIT HANDLER FOR SQLEXCEPTION
BEGIN
    ROLLBACK;
    SELECT 'Error occurred - terminating';
END;
```

- If MySQL error 1062 (duplicate key value) is encountered, continue execution after executing the SELECT statement (which generates a message for the calling program):

```
DECLARE CONTINUE HANDER FOR 1062
    SELECT 'Duplicate key in index';
```

- If SQLSTATE 23000 (duplicate key value) is encountered, continue execution after executing the SELECT statement (which generates a message for the calling program):

```
DECLARE CONTINUE HANDER FOR SQLSTATE '23000'
    SELECT 'Duplicate key in index';
```

- When a cursor fetch or SQL retrieves no values, continue execution after setting `l_done=1`:

```
DECLARE CONTINUE HANDLER FOR NOT FOUND
    SET l_done=1;
```

- Same as the previous example, except specified using a `SQLSTATE` variable rather than a named condition:

```
DECLARE CONTINUE HANDLER FOR SQLSTATE '02000'
    SET l_done=1;
```

- Same as the previous two examples, except specified using a MySQL error code variable rather than a named condition or `SQLSTATE` variable:

```
DECLARE CONTINUE HANDLER FOR 1329
    SET l_done=1;
```

Handler Precedence

As we've described, MySQL lets you define handler conditions in terms of a MySQL error code, a `SQLSTATE` error, or a named condition such as `SQLEXCEPTION`. It is possible, therefore, that you could define several handlers in a stored program that would *all* be eligible to fire when a specific error occurred. Yet only one handler can fire in response to an error, and MySQL has clearly defined rules that determine the precedence of handlers in such a situation.

To understand the problem, consider the code fragment in Example 6-8. We have declared three different handlers, each of which would be eligible to execute if a duplicate key value error occurs. Which handler will execute? The answer is that the *most specific* handler will execute.

Example 6-8. Overlapping condition handlers

```
DECLARE EXIT HANDLER FOR 1062 SELECT 'MySQL error 1062 encountered';
DECLARE EXIT HANDLER FOR SQLEXCEPTION SELECT 'SQLException encountered';
DECLARE EXIT HANDLER FOR SQLSTATE '23000' SELECT 'SQLSTATE 23000';

INSERT INTO departments VALUES (1, 'Department of Fred',22,'House of Fred');
```

Handlers based on MySQL error codes are the most specific type of handler, since an error condition will always correspond to a single MySQL error code. `SQLSTATE` codes can sometimes map to many MySQL error codes, so they are less specific. General conditions such as `SQLEXCEPTION` and `SQLWARNING` are not at all specific. Therefore, a MySQL error code takes precedence over a `SQLSTATE` exception, which, in turn, takes precedence over a `SQLEXCEPTION` condition.

 If multiple exception handlers are eligible to fire upon an error, the most specific handler will be invoked. This means that a MySQL error code handler fires before a `SQLSTATE` handler, which, in turn, fires before a `SQLEXCEPTION` handler.

This strictly defined precedence allows us to define a general-purpose handler for unexpected conditions, while creating a specific handler for those circumstances that we can easily anticipate. So, for instance, in Example 6-9, the first handler will be invoked if something catastrophic happens (perhaps a jealous colleague drops your database tables), while the second will fire in the more likely event that someone tries to create a duplicate row within your database.

Example 6-9. Example of overlapping condition handling

```
DECLARE EXIT HANDLER FOR 1062
    SELECT 'Attempt to create a duplicate entry occurred';
DECLARE EXIT HANDLER FOR SQLEXCEPTION
    SELECT 'Unexpected error occurred -
            make sure Fred did not drop your tables again';
```

Note, however, that we generally don't advise creating SQLEXCEPTION handlers until MySQL implements the SIGNAL statement; see "Missing SQL:2003 Features" later in this chapter.

Scope of Condition Handlers

The *scope* of a handler determines which statements within the stored program are covered by the handler. In essence, the scope of a handler is the same as for a stored program variable: the handler applies to all statements in the block in which it is defined, including any statements in nested blocks. Furthermore, handlers in a stored program also cover statements that execute in any stored program that might be called by the first program, unless that program declares its own handler.

For instance, in Example 6-10 the handler will be invoked when the INSERT statement executes (because it violates a NOT NULL constraint). The handler fires because the INSERT statement is contained within the same block as the handler—even though the INSERT statement is in a nested block.

Example 6-10. Handler scope includes statements within BEGIN-END blocks

```
DECLARE CONTINUE HANDLER FOR 1048 SELECT 'Attempt to insert a null value';
BEGIN
    INSERT INTO departments (department_name,manager_id,location)
    VALUES (NULL,1,'Wouldn''t you like to know?');
END;
```

However, in Example 6-11 the handler will not be invoked—the scope of the handler is limited to the nested block, and the INSERT statement occurs outside that block.

Example 6-11. Handlers within a nested block do not cover statements in enclosing blocks

```
BEGIN
    BEGIN
        DECLARE CONTINUE HANDLER FOR 1216 select
                'Foreign key constraint violated';
    END;
    INSERT INTO departments (department_name,manager_id,location)
        VALUES ('Elbonian HR','Catbert','Catbertia');
END;
```

Handler scope extends to any stored procedures or functions that are invoked within the handler scope. This means that if one stored program calls another, a handler in the calling program can trap errors that occur in the program that has been called. So, for instance, in Example 6-12, the handler in calling_procedure( ) traps the null value exception that occurs in sub_procedure ( ).

Example 6-12. A handler can catch conditions raised in called procedures

```
CREATE PROCEDURE calling_procedure( )
BEGIN
  DECLARE EXIT HANDLER FOR 1048 SELECT 'Attempt to insert a null value';
  CALL sub_procedure( );
END;

Query OK, 0 rows affected (0.00 sec)


--------------
CREATE PROCEDURE sub_procedure( )
BEGIN
  INSERT INTO departments (department_name,manager_id,location)
  VALUES (NULL,1,'Wouldn''t you like to know');
  SELECT 'Row inserted';

END;

Query OK, 0 rows affected (0.00 sec)

CALL calling_procedure( );

+-------------------------------+
| Attempt to insert a null value |
+-------------------------------+
| Attempt to insert a null value |
+-------------------------------+
1 row in set (0.01 sec)

Query OK, 0 rows affected (0.01 sec)
```

Of course, a handler in a procedure will override the scope of a hander that exists in a calling procedure. Only one handler can ever be activated in response to a specific error condition.

Named Conditions

So far, our examples have used conditions based on MySQL error codes, SQLSTATE codes, or predefined named conditions (SQLEXCEPTION, SQLWARNING, NOT FOUND). These handlers do the job required, but they do not result in particularly readable code, since they rely on the hardcoding of literal error numbers. Unless you memorize all or most of the MySQL error codes and SQLSTATE codes (and expect everyone maintaining your code to do the same), you are going to have to refer to a manual to understand exactly what error a handler is trying to catch.

You can improve the readability of your handlers by defining a condition declaration, which associates a MySQL error code or SQLSTATE code with a meaningful name that you can then use in your handler declarations. The syntax for a condition declaration is:

```
DECLARE condition_name CONDITION FOR {SQLSTATE sqlstate_code | MySQL_error_code};
```

Once we have declared our condition name, we can use it in our code instead of a MySQL error code or SQLSTATE code. So instead of the following declaration:

```
DECLARE CONTINUE HANDLER FOR 1216 MySQL_statements;
```

we could use the following more readable declaration:

```
DECLARE foreign_key_error CONDITION FOR 1216;

DECLARE CONTINUE HANDLER FOR foreign_key_error MySQL_statements;
```

 Create named conditions using condition declarations, and use these named conditions in your handlers to improve the readability and maintainability of your stored program code.

Missing SQL:2003 Features

The SQL:2003 specification includes a few useful features that—at the time of writing—are not currently implemented in the MySQL stored program language. The absence of these features certainly limits your ability to handle unexpected conditions, but we expect that they will be implemented in MySQL server 5.2. Specifically:

- There is no way to examine the current MySQL error code or SQLSTATE code. This means that in an exception handler based on a generic condition such as SQLEXCEPTION, you have no way of knowing what error just occurred.

- You cannot raise an exception of your own to indicate an application-specific error or to re-signal an exception after first catching the exception and examining its context.

We'll describe these situations in the following sections and suggest ways to deal with them.

Directly Accessing SQLCODE or SQLSTATE

Implementing a general-purpose exception handler would be a good practice, except that if you cannot reveal the reason why the exception occurred, you make debugging your stored programs difficult or impossible. For instance, consider Example 6-13.

Example 6-13. General-purpose—but mostly useless—condition handler

```
DECLARE CONTINUE HANDLER FOR SQLEXCEPTION
BEGIN
    SET l_status=-1;
    Set l_message='Some sort of error detected somewhere in the application';
END;
```

Receiving an error message like this is not much help—in fact, there is almost nothing more frustrating than receiving such an error message when trying to debug an application. Obscuring the actual cause of the error makes the condition handler worse than useless in most circumstances.

The SQL:2003 specification allows for direct access to the values of SQLCODE (the "vendor"—in this case MySQL—error code) and the SQLSTATE code. If we had access to these codes, we could produce a far more helpful message such as shown in Example 6-14.

Example 6-14. A more useful—but not supported—form of condition handler

```
DECLARE CONTINUE HANDLER FOR SQLEXCEPTION
BEGIN
    SET l_status=-1;
    SET l_message='Error '||sqlcode||' encountered';
END;
```

We can partially emulate the existence of a SQLCODE or SQLSTATE variable by defining a more comprehensive set of condition handlers that create appropriate SQLCODE variables when they are fired. The general approach would look like Example 6-15.

Example 6-15. Using multiple condition handlers to expose the actual error code

```
DECLARE sqlcode INT DEFAULT 0;
DECLARE status_message VARCHAR(50);

DECLARE CONTINUE HANDLER FOR duplicate_key
BEGIN
    SET sqlcode=1052;
    SET status_message='Duplicate key error';
END;

DECLARE CONTINUE HANDLER FOR foreign_key_violated
BEGIN
    SET sqlcode=1216;
```

Example 6-15. Using multiple condition handlers to expose the actual error code (continued)

```
    SET status_message='Foreign key violated';
END;

DECLARE CONTINUE HANDLER FOR NOT FOUND
BEGIN
    SET sqlcode=1329;
    SET status_message='No record found';
END;
```

In most circumstances, it is best not to define a SQLEXCEPTION handler, because without the ability to display the SQLSTATE or SQLSTATE, it is better to let the exception occur and allow the calling application to have full access to the error codes and messages concerned.

 Until MySQL implements a SQLSTATE or SQLSTATE variable, avoid creating a general-purpose SQLEXCEPTION handler. Instead, create handlers for individual error conditions that generate appropriate messages and status codes.

Creating Your Own Exceptions with the SIGNAL Statement

So far in this chapter, we have talked about how you can handle errors raised by MySQL as it executes SQL statements within the stored program. In addition to these system-raised exceptions, however, you will surely have to deal with errors that are specific to an application's domain of requirements and rules. If that rule is violated in your code, you may want to raise your *own* error and communicate this problem back to the user. The SQL:2003 specification provides the SIGNAL statement for this purpose.

The SIGNAL statement allows you to raise your own error conditions. Unfortunately, at the time of writing, the SIGNAL statement is not implemented within the MySQL stored program language (it is currently scheduled for MySQL 5.2).

You can't use the SIGNAL statement in MySQL 5.0, but we are going to describe it here, in case you are using a later version of MySQL in which the statement has been implemented. Visit this book's web site (see the Preface for details) to check on the status of this and other enhancements to the MySQL stored program language.

So let's say that we are creating a stored procedure to process employee date-of-birth changes, as shown in Example 6-16. Our company never employs people under the age of 16, so we put a check in the stored procedure to ensure that the updated date of birth is more than 16 years ago (the curdate( ) function returns the current timestamp).

Example 6-16. Example stored procedure with date-of-birth validation

```
CREATE PROCEDURE sp_update_employee_dob
    (p_employee_id INT, p_dob DATE, OUT p_status varchar(30))
BEGIN
    IF DATE_SUB(curdate( ), INTERVAL 16 YEAR) <p_dob THEN
        SET p_status='Employee must be 16 years or older';
    ELSE
        UPDATE employees
            SET date_of_birth=p_dob
          WHERE employee_id=p_employee_id;
          SET p_status='Ok';
    END IF;
END;
```

This implementation will work, but it has a few disadvantages. The most significant problem is that if the procedure is called from another program, the procedure will return success (at least, it will not raise an error) even if the update was actually rejected. Of course, the calling program could detect this by examining the p_status variable, but there is a good chance that the program will assume that the procedure succeeded since the procedure call itself does not raise an exception.

We have designed the procedure so that it depends on the diligence of the programmer calling the procedure to check the value of the returning status argument. It is all too tempting and easy to assume that everything went fine, since there was no error.

To illustrate, if we try to set an employee's date of birth to the current date from the MySQL command line, everything seems OK:

```
mysql> CALL sp_update_employee_dob(1,now( ),@status);
Query OK, 0 rows affected (0.01 sec)
```

It is only if we examine the status variable that we realize that the update did not complete:

```
mysql> SELECT @status;
+------------------------------------+
| @status                            |
+------------------------------------+
| Employee must be 16 years or older |
+------------------------------------+
1 row in set (0.00 sec)
```

This stored procedure would be more robust, and less likely to allow errors to slip by, if it actually raised an error condition when the date of birth was invalid. The ANSI SQL:2003 SIGNAL statement allows you to do this:

SIGNAL takes the following form:

```
SIGNAL SQLSTATE sqlstate_code|condition_name [SET MESSAGE_TEXT=string_or_variable];
```

You can create your own SQLSTATE codes (there are some rules for the numbers you are allowed to use) or use an existing SQLSTATE code or named condition. When

MySQL implements SIGNAL, you will probably be allowed to use a MySQL error code (within designated ranges) as well.

When the SIGNAL statement is executed, a database error condition is raised that acts in exactly the same way as an error that might be raised by an invalid SQL statement or a constraint violation. This error could be returned to the calling program or could be trapped by a handler in this or another stored program. If SIGNAL were available to us, we might write the employee date-of-birth birth procedure, as shown in Example 6-17.

Example 6-17. Using the SIGNAL statement (expected to be implemented in MySQL 5.2)

```
CREATE PROCEDURE sp_update_employee_dob
    (p_employee_id int, p_dob date)
BEGIN
    DECLARE employee_is_too_young CONDITION FOR SQLSTATE '99001';

    IF DATE_SUB(curdate( ), INTERVAL 16 YEAR) <P_DOB THEN
        SIGNAL employee_is_too_young
            SET MESSAGE_TEST='Employee must be 16 years or older';
    ELSE
        UPDATE employees
            SET date_of_birth=p_dob
        WHERE employee_id=p_employee_id;
    END IF;
END;
```

If we ran this new procedure from the MySQL command line (when MySQL implements SIGNAL), we would expect the following output:

```
mysql> CALL sp_update_employee(1,now( ));
ERROR 90001 (99001): Employee must be 16 years or older
```

Using SIGNAL, we could make it completely obvious to the user or calling program that the stored program execution failed.

Emulating the SIGNAL Statement

The absence of the SIGNAL statement makes some stored program logic awkward, and in some cases demands that calling applications examine OUT variables, rather than SQL return codes, to check the results of some operations.

There is, however, a way to force an error to occur and pass some diagnostic information back to the calling application. You can, in other words, emulate SIGNAL in MySQL 5.0, but we warn you: this solution is not pretty!

Where we would otherwise want to use the SIGNAL statement to return an error to the calling application, we can instead issue a SQL statement that will fail—and fail in such a way that we can embed our error message within the standard error message.

The best way to do this is to issue a SQL statement that attempts to reference a non-existent table or column. The name of the nonexistent column or table can include the error message itself, which will be useful because the name of the column or table is included in the error message.

Example 6-18 shows how we can do this. We try to select a nonexistent column name from a table and we make the nonexistent column name comprise our error message. Note that in order for a string to be interpreted as a column name, it must be enclosed by backquotes (these are the quote characters normally found on your keyboard to the left of the 1 key).

Example 6-18. Using a nonexistent column name to force an error to the calling program

```
CREATE PROCEDURE sp_update_employee_dob2
    (p_employee_id INT, p_dob DATE)
BEGIN

    IF datediff(curdate( ),p_dob)<(16*365) THEN
        UPDATE `Error: employee_is_too_young; Employee must be 16 years or older`
            SET x=1;
    ELSE
        UPDATE employees
            SET date_of_birth=p_dob
        WHERE employee_id=p_dob;
    END IF;
END;
```

If we try to run the stored procedure from the MySQL command line, passing in an invalid date of birth, we get a somewhat informative error message:

```
MySQL> CALL sp_update_employee_dob2(2,now( )) ;

ERROR 1054 (42S22): Unknown column 'Error: employee_is_too_young; Employee must be 16
years or older' in 'field list'
```

The error code is somewhat garbled, and the error code is not in itself accurate, but at least we have managed to signal to the calling application that the procedure did not execute successfully and we have at least provided some helpful information.

We can somewhat improve the reliability of our error handling—and also prepare for a future in which the SIGNAL statement is implemented—by creating a generic procedure to implement our SIGNAL workaround. Example 6-19 shows a procedure that accepts an error message and then constructs dynamic SQL that includes that message within an invalid table name error.

Example 6-19. Standard procedure to emulate SIGNAL

```
CREATE PROCEDURE `my_signal`(in_errortext VARCHAR(255))
BEGIN
    SET @sql=CONCAT('UPDATE `',
            in_errortext,
            '` SET x=1');
```

Example 6-19. Standard procedure to emulate SIGNAL (continued)

```
    PREPARE my_signal_stmt FROM @sql;
    EXECUTE my_signal_stmt;
    DEALLOCATE PREPARE my_signal_stmt;
END$$
```

We could now implement our employee date-of-birth update routine to call this routine, as shown in Example 6-20.

Example 6-20. Using our SIGNAL emulation procedure to raise an error

```
CREATE PROCEDURE sp_update_employee_dob2(p_employee_id INT, p_dob DATE)

BEGIN

    IF datediff(curdate(),p_dob)<(16*365) THEN
        CALL my_signal('Error: employee_is_too_young; Employee must be 16
                        years or older');
    ELSE
        UPDATE employees
           SET date_of_birth=p_dob
         WHERE employee_id=p_employee_id;
    END IF;
END$$
```

Not only does this routine result in cleaner code that is easier to maintain, but when MySQL does implement SIGNAL, we will only need to update our code in a single procedure.

Putting It All Together

We have now covered in detail the error-handling features of MySQL. We'll finish up this discussion by offering an example that puts all of these features together. We will take a simple stored procedure that contains no exception handling and apply the concepts from this chapter to ensure that it will not raise any unhandled exceptions for all problems that we can reasonably anticipate.

The example stored procedure creates a new departments row. It takes the names of the new department, the manager of the department, and the department's location. It retrieves the appropriate employee_id from the employees table using the manager's name. Example 6-21 shows the version of the stored procedure without exception handling.

Example 6-21. Stored procedure without error handling

```
CREATE PROCEDURE sp_add_department
        (p_department_name        VARCHAR(30),
         p_manager_surname        VARCHAR(30),
         p_manager_firstname      VARCHAR(30),
```

Example 6-21. Stored procedure without error handling (continued)

```
        p_location                  VARCHAR(30),
        out p_sqlcode               INT,
        out p_status_message        VARCHAR(100))
  MODIFIES SQL DATA
BEGIN

    DECLARE l_manager_id        INT;
    DECLARE csr_mgr_id cursor for
        SELECT employee_id
          FROM employees
         WHERE surname=UPPER(p_manager_surname)
           AND firstname=UPPER(p_manager_firstname);

    OPEN csr_mgr_id;
    FETCH csr_mgr_id INTO l_manager_id;

    INSERT INTO departments (department_name,manager_id,location)
    VALUES(UPPER(p_department_name),l_manager_id,UPPER(p_location));

    CLOSE csr_mgr_id;
END$$
```

This program reflects the typical development process for many of us: we concentrate on implementing the required functionality (the "positive") and generally pay little attention to (or more likely, want to avoid thinking about) what could possibly go wrong. The end result is a stored program that contains no error handling.

So either before you write the program (ideally) or after the first iteration is done, you should sit down and list out all the errors that might be raised by MySQL when the program is run.

Here are several of the failure points of this stored procedure:

- If the manager's name is incorrect, we will fail to find a matching manager in the employees table. We will then attempt to insert a NULL value for the MANAGER_ID column, which will violate its NOT NULL constraint.

- If the location argument does not match a location in the locations table, the foreign key constraint between the two tables will be violated.

- If we specify a department_name that already exists, we will violate the unique constraint on the department_name.

The code in Example 6-22 demonstrates these failure scenarios.

Example 6-22. Some of the errors generated by a stored procedure without error handling

```
mysql> CALL sp_add_department
    ('Optimizer Research','Yan','Bianca','Berkshire',@p_sqlcode,@p_status_message)

ERROR 1062 (23000): Duplicate entry 'OPTIMIZER RESEARCH' for key 2
```

```
mysql> CALL sp_add_department
    ('Optimizer Research','Yan','Binca','Berkshire',@p_sqlcode,@p_status_message);
```

ERROR 1048 (23000): Column 'MANAGER_ID' cannot be null

```
mysql> CALL sp_add_department('Advanced Research','Yan','Bianca','Bercshire',@p_
sqlcode,@p_status_message)
```

ERROR 1216 (23000): Cannot add or update a child row: a foreign key constraint fails

The good news is that MySQL detects these problems and will not allow bad data to
be placed into the table. If this stored procedure will be called only by the host language, such as PHP or Java, we could declare ourselves done. If, on the other hand,
this program might be called from another MySQL stored program, then we need to
handle the errors and return status information so that the calling stored program
can take appropriate action. Example 6-23 shows a version of the stored procedure
that handles all the errors shown in Example 6-22.

Example 6-23. Stored procedure with error handling

```
1   CREATE PROCEDURE sp_add_department2
2       (p_department_name        VARCHAR(30),
3        p_manager_surname         VARCHAR(30),
4        p_manager_firstname       VARCHAR(30),
5        p_location                VARCHAR(30),
6        OUT p_sqlcode             INT,
7        OUT p_status_message      VARCHAR(100))
8   BEGIN
9
10  /* START Declare Conditions */
11
12    DECLARE duplicate_key CONDITION FOR 1062;
13    DECLARE foreign_key_violated CONDITION FOR 1216;
14
15  /* END Declare Conditions */
16
17  /* START Declare variables and cursors */
18
19    DECLARE l_manager_id       INT;
20
21      DECLARE csr_mgr_id CURSOR FOR
22        SELECT employee_id
23          FROM employees
24         WHERE surname=UPPER(p_manager_surname)
25           AND firstname=UPPER(p_manager_firstname);
26
27    /* END Declare variables and cursors */
28
29    /* START Declare Exception Handlers */
30
31      DECLARE CONTINUE HANDLER FOR duplicate_key
```

Example 6-23. Stored procedure with error handling (continued)

```
32      BEGIN
33        SET p_sqlcode=1052;
34        SET p_status_message='Duplicate key error';
35      END;
36
37   DECLARE CONTINUE HANDLER FOR foreign_key_violated
38     BEGIN
39       SET p_sqlcode=1216;
40       SET p_status_message='Foreign key violated';
41     END;
42
43     DECLARE CONTINUE HANDLER FOR not FOUND
44       BEGIN
45         SET p_sqlcode=1329;
46         SET p_status_message='No record found';
47       END;
48
49  /* END Declare Exception Handlers */
50
51  /* START Execution */
52
53     SET p_sqlcode=0;
54     OPEN csr_mgr_id;
55     FETCH csr_mgr_id INTO l_manager_id;
56
57     IF p_sqlcode<>0 THEN        /* Failed to get manager id*/
58       SET p_status_message=CONCAT(p_status_message,' when fetching manager id');
59     ELSE
60                     /* Got manager id, we can try and insert */
61       INSERT INTO departments (department_name,manager_id,location)
62       VALUES(UPPER(p_department_name),l_manager_id,UPPER(p_location));
63       IF p_sqlcode<>0 THEN/* Failed to insert new department */
64         SET p_status_message=CONCAT(p_status_message,
65                           ' when inserting new department');
66       END IF;
67     END IF;
68
69     CLOSE csr_mgr_id;
70
71  / * END Execution */
72
73  END
```

Let's go through Example 6-23 and review the error-handling code we have added.

Line(s)	Significance
12 and 13	Create condition declarations for duplicate key (1062) and foreign key (1216) errors. As we noted earlier, these declarations are not strictly necessary, but they improve the readability of the condition handlers we will declare later.
31-48	Define handlers for each of the exceptions we think might occur. The condition names match those we defined in lines 10 and 11. We didn't have to create a NOT FOUND condition, since this is a predefined condition name. Each handler sets an appropriate value for the output status variables p_sqlcode and p_status_message.

Line(s)	Significance
57	On this line we check the value of the p_sqlcode variable following our fetch from the cursor that retrieves the manager's employee_id. If p_sqlcode is not 0, then we know that one of our exception handlers has fired. We add some context information to the message—identifying the statement we were executing—and avoid attempting to execute the insert into the departments table.
53	Check the value of the p_sqlcode variable following our insert operation. Again, if the value is nonzero, we know that an error has occurred, and we add some context information to the error message. At line 53, we don't know what error has occurred—it could be either the foreign key or the unique index constraint. The handler itself controls the error message returned to the user, and so we could add handling for more error conditions by adding additional handlers without having to amend this section of code.

Running the stored procedure from the MySQL command line shows us that all the exceptions are now correctly handled. Example 6-24 shows the output generated by various invalid inputs.

Example 6-24. Output from stored procedure with exception handling

```
mysql> CALL sp_add_department2('Optimizer Research','Yan','Bianca','Berkshire',
@p_sqlcode,@p_status_message)

Query OK, 0 rows affected (0.17 sec)

mysql> SELECT @p_sqlcode,@p_status_message


+------------+---------------------------------------------------+
| @p_sqlcode | @p_status_message                                 |
+------------+---------------------------------------------------+
| 1052       | Duplicate key error when inserting new department |
+------------+---------------------------------------------------+
1 row in set (0.00 sec)

mysql> CALL sp_add_department2('Optimizer Research','Yan','Binca','Berkshire',
@p_sqlcode,@p_status_message)

Query OK, 0 rows affected (0.00 sec)

mysql> SELECT @p_sqlcode,@p_status_message


+------------+--------------------------------------+
| @p_sqlcode | @p_status_message                    |
+------------+--------------------------------------+
| 1329       | No record found when fetching manager id |
+------------+--------------------------------------+
1 row in set (0.00 sec)

mysql> call sp_add_department2('Advanced Research','Yan','Bianca','Bercshire',
@p_sqlcode,@p_status_message)

Query OK, 0 rows affected (0.12 sec)

mysql> SELECT @p_sqlcode,@p_status_message
```

```
+------------+--------------------------------------------------------+
| @p_sqlcode | @p_status_message                                      |
+------------+--------------------------------------------------------+
| 1216       | Foreign key violated when inserting new department     |
+------------+--------------------------------------------------------+
1 row in set (0.00 sec)
```

Handling Stored Program Errors in the Calling Application

Throughout this chapter, we've often talked about "returning the error to the calling application." In our examples we have used the MySQL command-line client to represent the calling application since this client is common to all environments and readers, and it allows you (and us) to quickly test out the stored program.

In production environments, however, the calling application will not be the MySQL command-line program, but possibly a web-based application using PHP, Perl, Java, Python, or .NET (C# or Visual Basic) to interface with the MySQL stored program. In Chapters 12 through 17, we look in detail at how to invoke stored programs from a variety of languages. We also cover various techniques for retrieving status and error messages from these languages. However, since we're on the topic of error handling, let's briefly look at how we can process errors generated by a stored program called from each of these languages.

PHP

PHP provides a variety of ways of interacting with MySQL. There are four major interfaces available:

PEAR (PHP Extension and Application Repository)
    The PEAR repository includes a standard, database-independent module called PEAR DB that can be used to interface with almost any relational database.

mysql
    PHP includes a MySQL-specific interface inventively called the mysql extension.

mysqli
    Commencing with PHP 5, a new interface—mysqli—was introduced (according to the developer, the "i" stands for "any one of: improved, interface, ingenious, incompatible, or incomplete"). This interface provides better support for new features of MySQL.

PDO (PHP Data Objects)
    PDO, a new interface with PHP 5.1, provides a PHP 5N compatible, object-oriented, database-independent interface.

The mysqli and PDO interfaces provide the best support for MySQL stored programs and other new features of MySQL 5.0.

In Chapter 13, we show in detail how to use stored programs with each of the major PHP interfaces and provide examples of both procedural and nonprocedural styles. For now, let's look at a simple example showing how to process errors using the object-oriented variant of the mysqli interface.

In Example 6-25, a simple stored procedure—one without OUT parameters or result sets—is executed on line 8. If the method call returns failure, we can examine various properties of the database connection object ($dbh in this example). $dbh->errno contains the MySQL error code, $dbh->error contains the error message, and $dbh->sqlstate contains the SQLSTATE code.

Example 6-25. Error handling in the PHP 5 mysqli interface

```
1  $dbh = new mysqli($hostname, $username, $password, $database);
2  /* check connection */
3  if (mysqli_connect_errno()) {
4      printf("Connect failed: %s\n", mysqli_connect_error());
5      exit();
6  }
7
8  if ($dbh->query("call error_test_proc(1)"))  /*execute stored procedure*/
9  {
10     printf("Stored procedure execution succeded");
11  }
12 else // Stored procedure failed - show error
13 {
14     printf("<p>Stored procedure error: MySQL error %d (SQLSTATE %s)\n %s\n",
15            $dbh->errno,$dbh->sqlstate,$dbh->error);
16 }
```

Perl

The Perl DBI interface provides a consistent interface to various relational databases. The error-handling techniques for Perl are very similar to those of PHP.

DBI objects—such as database and statement handles—include the following properties:

Err
  Contains the database-specific return code (in our case, the MySQL error code).

Errstr
  Contains the full message text.

State
  Contains the SQLSTATE variable. However, the SQLSTATE variable usually includes only a generic success or failure code.

Each of these items can be referenced as a method or a property, so, for instance, you can reference the last MySQL error code for the connect handle $dbh as either $dbh::err or $dbh->err.

Example 6-26 shows a simple Perl code fragment that executes a stored procedure and checks the error status. On line 5 we execute a simple stored procedure (one without parameters or result sets). If the stored procedure call fails, we interrogate the error methods from the database handle.

Example 6-26. Error handling in Perl DBI

```
1    $dbh = DBI->connect("DBI:mysql:$database:$host:$port",
2                     "$user", "$password",
3                     { PrintError => 0}) || die $DBI::errstr;
4
5    if ($dbh->do("call error_test_proc(1)"))
6    {
7        printf("Stored procedure execution succeeded\n");
8    }
9    else
10   {
11       printf("Error executing stored procedure: MySQL error %d (SQLSTATE %s)\n %s\n",
12                     $dbh->err,$dbh->state,$dbh->errstr);
13   }
```

Java/JDBC

MySQL provides a Java JDBC 3.0 driver—MySQL Connector/J—that allows Java programs to interact with a MySQL server.

Like most modern object-oriented languages, Java uses structured exception handling to allow for flexible and efficient interception and handling of runtime errors. Rather than check the error status of every database call, we enclose our JDBC statements within a try block. If any of these statements causes a SQLException error, then the catch handler will be invoked to handle the error.

The catch handler has access to a SQLException object that provides various methods and properties for diagnosing and interpreting the error. Of most interest to us are these three methods:

getErrorCode( )
    Returns the MySQL-specific error code

getSQLState( )
    Returns the ANSI-standard SQLSTATE code

getMessage( )
    Returns the full text of the error message

Example 6-27 shows an example of invoking a simple stored procedure that involves no OUT parameters or result sets. On line 8 we create a statement object, and on line 9 we use the execute method of that object to execute the stored procedure. If an error occurs, the catch block on line 11 is invoked, and the relevant methods of the SQLException object are used to display the details of the error.

Example 6-27. Stored procedure error handling in Java/JDBC

```
1  try {
2      Class.forName("com.mysql.jdbc.Driver").newInstance( );
3
4      String ConnectionString="jdbc:mysql://" + hostname + "/" + database + "?user=" +
5              username + "&password=" + password;
6      System.out.println(ConnectionString);
7      Connection conn = DriverManager.getConnection(ConnectionString);
8      Statement stmt=conn.createStatement( );
9      stmt.execute("call error_test_proc(1)");
10 }
11 catch(SQLException SQLEx) {
12     System.out.println("MySQL error: "+SQLEx.getErrorCode( )+
13             " SQLSTATE:" +SQLEx.getSQLState( ));
14     System.out.println(SQLEx.getMessage( ));
15 }
```

Python

Python can connect to MySQL using the MySQLdb extension. This extension generates Python exceptions if any MySQL errors are raised during execution. We enclose our calls to MySQL in a try block and catch any errors in an except block.

Example 6-28 shows how we can connect to MySQL and execute a stored procedure in Python. Line 1 commences the try block, which contains our calls to MySQL. On line 2 we connect to MySQL. On line 7 we create a cursor (SQL statement handle), and on line 8 we execute a stored procedure call.

Example 6-28. Stored procedure error handling in Python

```
1       try:
2               conn = MySQLdb.connect (host = 'localhost',
3                               user = 'root',
4                               passwd = 'secret',
5                               db = 'prod',
6                               port=3306)
7               cursor1=conn.cursor( )
8               cursor1.execute("CALL error_test_proc( )")
9               cursor1.close( )
10
11      except MySQLdb.Error, e:
12              print "Mysql Error %d: %s" % (e.args[0], e.args[1])
```

If any of these calls generates a MySQL error condition, we jump to the except block on line 11. The MySQLdb.Error object (aliased here as e) contains two elements: element 0 is the MySQL error code, and element 1 is the MySQL error message.

C# .NET

MySQL provides an ADO.NET connector—MySQL Connector/Net—that allows any .NET-compatible language to interact with a MySQL server.

In this chapter we provide a short example of handling stored procedure errors from a C# program. More details are provided in Chapter 17.

As in Java, C# provides an exception-handling model that relieves the developer of the necessity of checking for error conditions after every statement execution. Instead, commands to be executed are included within a try block. If an error occurs for any of these statements, execution switches to the catch block, in which appropriate error handling can be implemented.

Example 6-29 shows an example of error handling for a simple stored procedure (one without output parameters or result sets) in C#. A statement object for the stored procedure is created on line 15, and the statement is executed on line 17. If a MySqlException (essentially any MySQL error) occurs, the error handler defined on line 19 is invoked.

Example 6-29. Error handling in C#/ADO.NET

```
1    MySqlConnection myConnection;
2    myConnection = new MySqlConnection( );
3    myConnection.ConnectionString = "database="+database+";server="+server+
4                             ";user id="+user+";Password="+password;
5    try {
6        myConnection.Open( );
7    }
8    catch (MySqlException MyException)           {
9        Console.WriteLine("Connection error: MySQL code: "+MyException.Number
10                      +" "+ MyException.Message);
11   }
12
13   try {
14
15       MySqlCommand myCommand = new MySqlCommand("call error_test_proc(1)",
16                                       myConnection);
17       myCommand.ExecuteNonQuery( );
18   }
19   catch (MySqlException MyException)           {
20       Console.WriteLine("Stored procedure error: MySQL code: " + MyException.Number
21                      + "   " + MyException.Message);
22   }
```

catch blocks have access to a MySQLException object; this object includes Message and Number properties, which contain the MySQL error message and error number, respectively.

Visual Basic .NET

The process for handling stored program errors in Visual Basic .NET (VB.NET) is practically identical to that of C#.

Example 6-30 shows an example of error handling for a simple stored procedure (one without output parameters or result sets) in VB.NET. A statement object for the stored procedure is created on lines 16 and 17, and the statement is executed on line 18. If a `MySqlException` (essentially any MySQL error) occurs, the error handler defined in lines 20-24 is invoked.

Example 6-30. Stored procedure error handling in VB.NET

```
1    Dim myConnectionString As String = "Database=" & myDatabase & _
2        " ;Data Source=" & myHost & _
3        ";User Id=" & myUserId & ";Password=" & myPassword
4
5    Dim myConnection As New MySqlConnection(myConnectionString)
6
7    Try
8        myConnection.Open( )
9    Catch MyException As MySqlException
10       Console.WriteLine("Connection error: MySQL code: " & MyException.Number & _
11                      " " + MyException.Message)
12   End Try
13
14   Try
15
16       Dim myCommand As New MySqlCommand("call error_test_proc(1)")
17       myCommand.Connection = myConnection
18       myCommand.ExecuteNonQuery( )
19
20   Catch MyException As MySqlException
21       Console.WriteLine("Stored procedure error: MySQL code: " & _
22                   MyException.Number & "  " & _
23                   MyException.Message)
24   End Try
```

Catch blocks have access to a `MySQLException` object; this object includes `Message` and `Number` properties, which contain the MySQL error message and error number, respectively.

Conclusion

In this chapter we examined the MySQL error handlers that allow you to catch error conditions and take appropriate corrective actions. Without error handlers, your stored programs will abort whenever they encounter SQL errors, returning control to the calling program. While this might be acceptable for some simple stored programs, it is more likely that you will want to trap and handle errors within the stored program environment, especially if you plan to call one stored program from another. In addition, you need to declare handlers for cursor loops so that an error is not thrown when the last row is retrieved from the cursor.

Handlers can be constructed to catch all errors, although this is currently not best practice in MySQL, since you do not have access to an error code variable that would allow you to differentiate between possible error conditions or to report an appropriate diagnostic to the calling program. Instead, you should declare individual handlers for error conditions that can reasonably be anticipated. When an unexpected error occurs, it is best to let the stored program abort so that the calling program has access to the error codes and messages.

Handlers can be constructed that catch either ANSI-standard SQLSTATE codes or MySQL-specific error codes. Using the SQLSTATE codes leads to more portable code, but because specific SQLSTATE codes are not available for all MySQL error conditions, you should feel free to construct handlers against MySQL-specific error conditions.

To improve the readability of your code, you will normally want to declare named conditions against the error codes you are handling, so that the intention of your handlers is clear. It is far easier to understand a handler that traps DUPLICATE_KEY_VALUE than one that checks for MySQL error code 1062.

At the time of writing, some critical SQL:2003 error-handling functionality has yet to be implemented in MySQL, most notably the ability to directly access the SQLSTATE or SQLSTATE variables, as well as the ability to raise an error condition using the SIGNAL statement. In the absence of a SQLSTATE or SQLCODE variable, it is good practice for you to define handlers against all error conditions that can reasonably be anticipated that populate a SQLCODE-like variable that you can use within your program code to detect errors and take appropriate action. We expect MySQL to add these "missing" features in version 5.2—you should check to see if they have been implemented in the time since this book was written (see the book's web site for details). Note also that it is currently possible to provide a workaround (though a somewhat awkward one) for the missing SIGNAL statement if you find that it is absolutely necessary in your programs.

## PART II

Stored Program Construction

This part of the book describes how you can use the elements described in Part I to build functional and useful stored programs. In Chapter 7 we outline the commands available for creating and modifying stored programs and provide some advice on how to manage your stored program source code. Chapter 8 outlines transaction handling in stored programs, while Chapter 9 details the built-in functions that can be used in stored programs. Chapters 10 and 11 detail two "special" types of stored programs: Chapter 10 shows how you can create and use stored functions; Chapter 11 describes triggers, which are stored programs that are invoked in response to DML executed on a database table.

## CHAPTER 7

Creating and Maintaining Stored Programs

In this chapter, we'll explain how to create, maintain, and delete stored programs.

By definition, a stored program exists in the database (it wouldn't be *stored* otherwise, right?). So the fundamental process of creating a stored program involves submitting SQL statements to MySQL, just as creating a table involves submitting the CREATE TABLE statement. The basic process of creating and maintaining a stored program is very similar to that of creating any other kind of database object: you write some SQL to create the object and you (hopefully) save that SQL somewhere safe so that you can reuse it later. At some later time you may alter the object (or drop and recreate it), and you may want to find out information about it.

Creating Stored Programs

The CREATE PROCEDURE, CREATE FUNCTION, and CREATE TRIGGER statements allow you to create the various stored program objects: procedures, functions, and triggers.

You are no doubt familiar with the CREATE statements used to create tables, indexes, and other objects. There are some minor differences between the process of creating these objects and the process of creating stored programs. In addition to describing these differences, the following subsections describe the various environments in which you can issue the CREATE PROCEDURE, CREATE FUNCTION, and CREATE TRIGGER statements.

Before we dig into the syntax for creating and maintaining stored programs, let's look at the mechanics of editing the stored program text and submitting it to MySQL. There are three main ways you can edit your stored program code and submit it to MySQL:

- Edit the stored program using a standard editor such as vi, Emacs, or Notepad, and then use the MySQL command-line console to submit the statements.

- Edit and create the stored program inside the MySQL Query Browser.

- Use a third-party graphical tool—such as Quest Software's Toad for MySQL— to create the stored program.

Editing Stored Programs Using a System Editor

It is not a good idea to create a stored program by typing code directly into the MySQL command-line client. Instead, we normally use a GUI program such as the MySQL Query Browser (see the next section, "Using the MySQL Query Browser") or use a text editor or program editor to create the procedure and then load it into the database using the MySQL command-line client.

In Figure 7-1 we demonstrate creating a stored procedure using the Emacs editor on Linux. Emacs allows you to create a "shell" window—shown in the lower half of the Emacs window in Figure 7-1—in which you can execute the MySQL client.

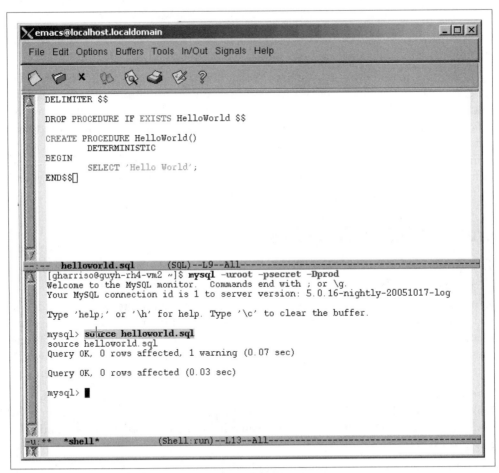

Figure 7-1. Editing a stored program in Linux with Emacs

In the top window in Figure 7-1, we create a text file called helloworld.sql. It contains a DROP PROCEDURE statement—used to delete the procedure in case it already exists—and a CREATE PROCEDURE statement.

In the lower window, we execute the MySQL command-line client and then use the SOURCE statement to execute the commands held in the external file. Our stored procedure is now created.

In Windows, we could use a text or program editor, such as Notepad, and run the MySQL client in a separate window. Figure 7-2 shows how to do that.

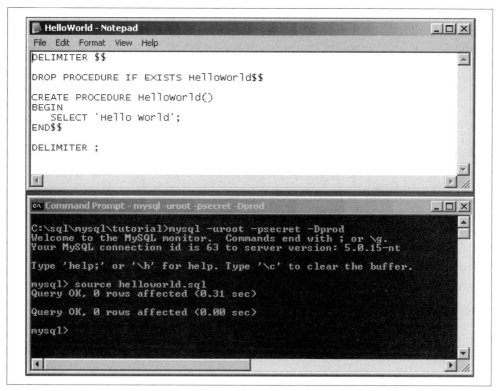

Figure 7-2. Editing a stored program in Windows with Notepad

Using the MySQL Query Browser

Using a text editor and the command-line client to edit and create a stored program is certainly feasible, as shown in the previous section, but it is hardly an efficient or productive process. Your stored program development will probably be faster and more pleasurable if you use a specialized graphical tool to create your program.

MySQL provides a graphical tool—the MySQL Query Browser (introduced in Chapter 1)—to help us edit and create stored programs. The Query Browser also allows us to execute simple SQL statements and perform some basic schema management. Let's walk through the steps required to create a procedure using the Query Browser.

First we invoke the Create Stored Procedure/Function option from the Script menu, as shown in Figure 7-3. This opens the Create Stored Procedure dialog box (see Figure 7-4).

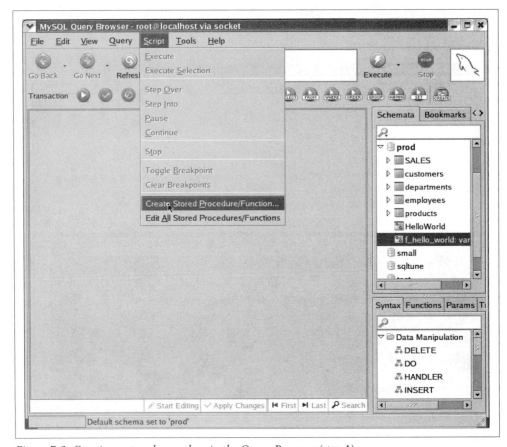

Figure 7-3. Creating a stored procedure in the Query Browser (step 1)

In the dialog box, type the name of the stored program and click the appropriate button to create either a stored procedure or a stored function.

The MySQL Query Browser loads a template file for the stored program. Into this template we can enter the stored program code. In this case, we simply add the SELECT 'Hello World'; text, as shown in Figure 7-5.

Finally, we click the Execute button to execute the script and create our procedure. Make sure that you use the Execute option in the Script menu (middle left of the window) rather than the Execute button (upper right). If we are successful, the procedure name should appear in the Schemata window on the right, as shown in Figure 7-6.

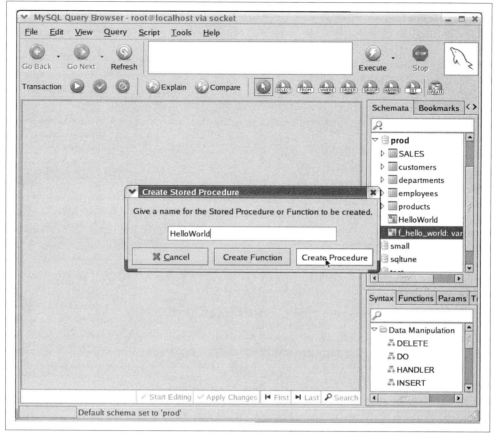

Figure 7-4. Creating a stored procedure in the Query Browser (step 2)

Our stored procedure has now been created.

Using Third-Party Tools

The MySQL Query Browser is a fine tool for creating and maintaining stored programs. However, there are many tools on the market that provide additional features such as code formatting, improved editing features, and more powerful administration and schema management capabilities. Some of these products are also able to work with other RDBMS systems such as Oracle and SQL Server.

Quest Software's Toad for MySQL, illustrated in Figure 7-7, is such an Integrated Development Environment (IDE) product. Toad is a standard in the Oracle community for stored program (PL/SQL) development and is available for Oracle, DB2, and SQL Server as well as for MySQL.

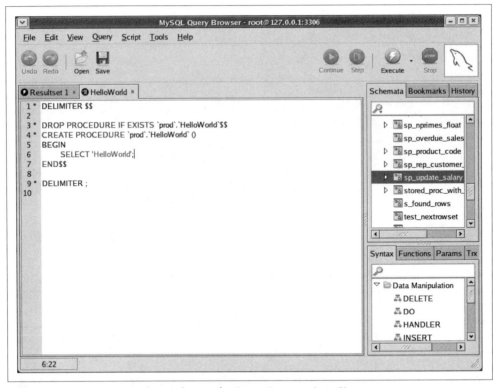

Figure 7-5. Creating a stored procedure in the Query Browser (step 3)

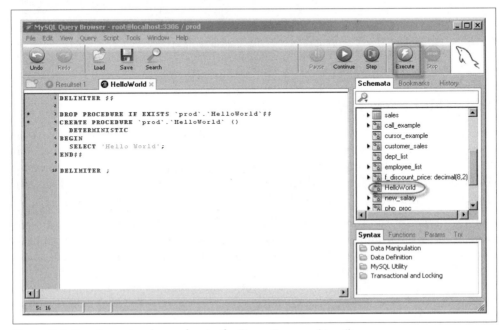

Figure 7-6. Creating a stored procedure in the Query Browser (step 4)

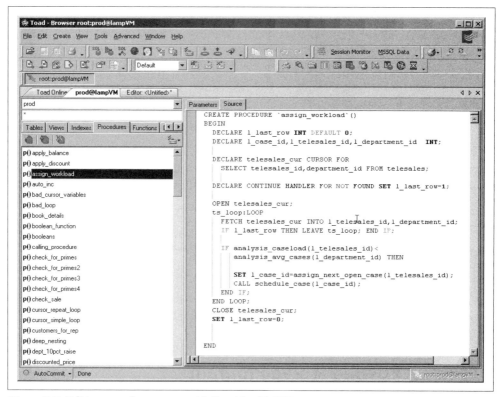

Figure 7-7. Editing stored programs with Toad for MySQL

Handling Semicolons in Stored Program Code

When you type the text of a stored program, you will need to deal with the issue of semicolons in your code.

MySQL uses the semicolon to mark the end of a SQL statement. However, stored programs usually contain semicolons within the program code, and this can cause MySQL to get rather confused. For instance, in Example 7-1, note that while we are typing in the text of a stored procedure, the first semicolon in the stored procedure causes MySQL to try to compile the procedure, causing an error because the stored procedure code is not yet complete.

Example 7-1. Semicolons indicate end of SQL statement, causing an error when creating a stored procedure

```
Welcome to the MySQL monitor.  Commands end with ; or \g.
Your MySQL connection id is 2 to server version: 5.0.16-nightly-20051017-log

Type 'help;' or '\h' for help. Type '\c' to clear the buffer.
```

```
mysql> CREATE PROCEDURE HelloWorld( )
    -> BEGIN
    ->    SELECT 'Hello World';
ERROR 1064 (42000): You have an error in your SQL syntax; check the manual that
corresponds to your MySQL server version for the right syntax to use near 'SELECT 'Hello
World'' at line 3
mysql>
```

To avoid this kind of error, we need to inform MySQL that we are not going to use semicolons to define the end of a statement. In Example 7-2 we use the DELIMITER statement to change the delimiter from ";" to "$$", allowing us to successfully create the procedure.

Example 7-2. Using a nondefault delimiter when creating a stored object

```
mysql> DELIMITER $$

mysql> CREATE PROCEDURE HelloWorld( )
    -> BEGIN
    ->    SELECT 'Hello World';
    -> END$$
Query OK, 0 rows affected (0.00 sec)
```

Editing an Existing Stored Program

There are two approaches to editing the text of existing stored programs. The easiest —though probably not the best—way to edit an existing stored program is to use the MySQL Query Browser to edit the stored program in place. By "in place," we mean that you work directly with the copy of the stored program held in the database. A better way is to edit an external text file that contains the stored procedure code. We describe these approaches in the following subsections.

Editing a Program in Place

Editing a stored program in place is certainly easy, as shown in Figure 7-8. To edit an existing stored program in this way, you simply locate and select the stored program in the MySQL Query Browser's Schemata browser, right-click, and select Edit Procedure (or Edit Function) from the context menu. The relevant stored program code is loaded from the database into the edit window where you can make your changes. Clicking the Execute button runs the modified script and replaces the stored program in the database.

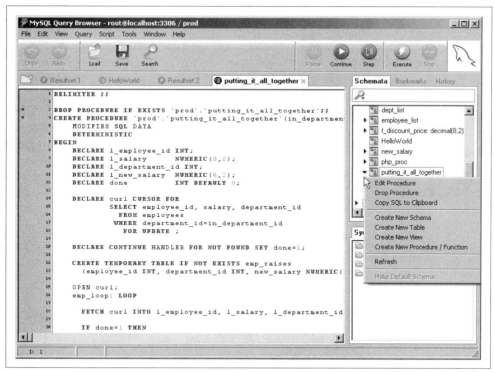

Figure 7-8. Editing a stored program in place with the MySQL Query Browser

Maintaining Stored Programs in External Files

There are a number of reasons why you may not want to edit stored programs in place, as we did in Figure 7-8:

- When you retrieve the text for a stored program from the database (as Query Browser and other similar programs do), you may find that the text of the stored program is slightly different from the version you originally created. In particular, the name of the stored routine may be quoted and the name of the database prepended. This prepending of the database name is a bad idea if you want to migrate stored programs to other databases.

- It is definitely best practice to use a source control system (such as Microsoft SourceSafe, Subversion, or CVS) to store each changed iteration of your stored program. This allows you to roll back changes to a stored program that turn out to be problematic, and allows you to retrieve a specific version of a program when multiple versions are in use.

Some third-party MySQL development tools allow you to load and save your stored program source directly into a version control system such as CVS. For instance, in Toad for MySQL we can check files in and out of CVS or SourceSafe from within our programming environment, as shown in Figure 7-9.

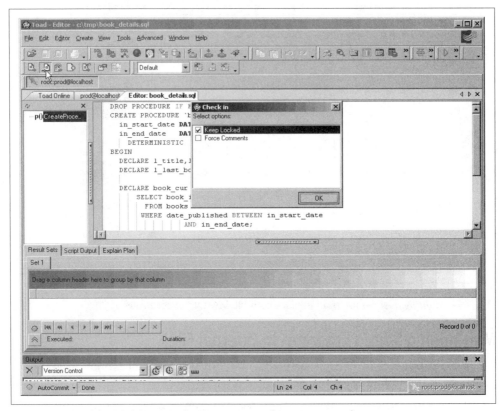

Figure 7-9. Toad for MySQL provides integration with version control systems

Regardless of whether your IDE directly supports integration with a version control system, you should still use version control to maintain stored program code. Rather than extract the stored program code from the database, you will extract it from an external file before editing, and you will save the external file—and check it into your version control system—when it is complete.

Figure 7-10 shows how we can perform these actions on a Linux system using the MySQL Query Browser as our editing environment and RCS as our version control system.

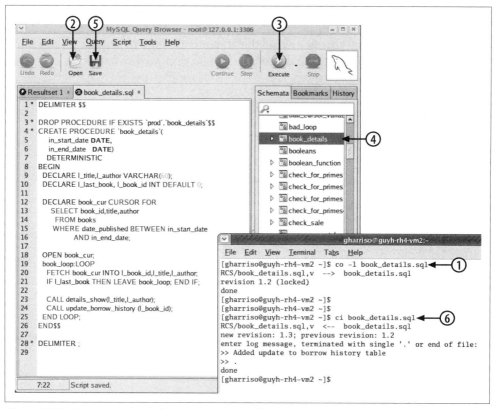

Figure 7-10. Maintaining stored program source code in a source control system

Let's work through the steps highlighted in Figure 7-10:

1. Before we get started, we need to extract the source file from the version control system and lock it for editing. In the RCS system this is done with the co -l command.

2. Now we can load the source file into an edit window in the MySQL Query Browser.

3. After making our edits, we can save our changes to the database by clicking the Execute button.

4. We can perform basic testing of the stored program by running it from within the Query Browser. Double-clicking the stored program name in the Schemata browser is one way to do this.

5. If we are satisfied that our changes are good, we can save them back to the disk file we originally loaded.

6. Now we check the changes back into version control. In RCS this is done with the ci command.

SQL Statements for Managing Stored Programs

This section summarizes the syntax of the statements used to create, modify, and remove stored programs from the database. This section provides only an overview; we'll drill down into many of the details of these statements in other chapters.

CREATE PROCEDURE

The CREATE PROCEDURE statement—you guessed it—creates a stored procedure. The syntax for the statement is:

```
CREATE PROCEDURE procedure_name ([parameter[,...]])
    [LANGUAGE SQL]
    [ [NOT] DETERMINISTIC ]
    [ {CONTAINS SQL|MODIFIES SQL DATA|READS SQL DATA|NO SQL} ]
    [SQL SECURITY {DEFINER|INVOKER} ]
    [COMMENT comment_string]
    procedure_statements
```

The procedure_name follows the normal conventions for the naming of database objects (see Chapter 3).

The parameter list consists of a comma-separated list of arguments that can be provided to the stored procedure. We spent quite a bit of time on parameters in Chapter 3, but to summarize, each parameter is of the form:

```
[{IN|OUT|INOUT} ] parameter_name datatype
```

By default, parameters are of the IN type: this means that their values must be specified by the calling program and that any modifications made to the parameter in the stored program cannot be accessed from the calling program. OUT parameters, on the other hand, can be modified by the stored program, and the modified values can be retrieved from the calling program.

An INOUT parameter acts as both an IN and an OUT parameter: the calling program can supply a value and can see whatever changes are made to the parameter inside the stored procedure.

The following are descriptions of the other keywords you can specify in the CREATE PROCEDURE statement:

LANGUAGE SQL

> Indicates that the stored procedure uses the SQL:PSM standard stored procedure language. Since MySQL currently supports only those stored procedures written in this language, specifying this keyword is unnecessary at present. However, in future versions, MySQL might support stored procedures written in other languages (Java, for instance), and if this occurs, you may need to specify this keyword.

SQL SECURITY {DEFINER|INVOKER}

Determines whether the stored procedure should execute using the permissions of the user who created the stored procedure (DEFINER) or the permissions of the user who is currently executing the stored procedure (INVOKER). The default is DEFINER. We look at the implications of these two security modes in Chapter 18.

[NOT] DETERMINISTIC

Indicates whether the stored procedure will always return the same results if the same inputs are provided. For instance, an SQRT function is deterministic because the square root of a number never changes, while an AGE function is nondeterministic because people are getting older all the time (sigh). By default, MySQL will assume that a stored procedure (or function) is NOT DETERMINISTIC.

In fact, the only time this keyword is critical is when you are creating a stored function (but because the CREATE PROCEDURE syntax allows you to specify it, we mention it here): when binary logging is enabled, you need to specify either DETERMINISTIC or one of NO SQL or READS SQL DATA to create your function. This issue is examined in depth in Chapter 10.

NO SQL|CONTAINS SQL|READS SQL DATA|MODIFIES SQL DATA

Indicates the type of access to database data that the stored procedure will perform. If a program reads data from the database, you may specify the READS SQL DATA keyword. If the program modifies data in the database, you could specify MODIFIES SQL DATA. If the procedure or function performs no database accesses, you may specify NO SQL.*

COMMENT comment_string

Specifies a comment that is stored in the database along with the procedure definition. You can see these comments in the INFORMATION_SCHEMA.ROUTINES table, in the output of SHOW PROCEDURE/FUNCTION STATUS, and in a SHOW CREATE PROCEDURE or SHOW CREATE FUNCTION statement.

The procedure code consists of one or more SQL or stored program language statements. If there is more than one statement—and there almost always will be—then the statements must be enclosed in a BEGIN-END block.

CREATE FUNCTION

The CREATE FUNCTION statement creates a stored function. This statement has a very similar syntax to CREATE PROCEDURE:

---

* A strict interpretation of the ANSI standard suggests that NO SQL is only applicable for non-SQL languages (PHP, Java, etc.). Although NO SQL is arguably only really intended for non-SQL stored procedures, the current behavior of MySQL makes the NO SQL clause the best choice when you must specify a SQL clause for a function that performs no database accesses.

```
CREATE FUNCTION function_name ([parameter[,...]])
      RETURNS datatype
    [LANGUAGE SQL]
    [ [NOT] DETERMINISTIC ]
    [ { CONTAINS SQL|NO SQL|MODIFIES SQL DATA|READS SQL DATA} ]
    [SQL SECURITY {DEFINER|INVOKER} ]
    [COMMENT comment_string]
    function_statements
```

There are only a few fundamental differences between the syntax of CREATE PROCEDURE and that of CREATE FUNCTION:

- CREATE FUNCTION includes a mandatory RETURNS statement that specifies the data type that will be returned from the function call.

- With CREATE FUNCTION, you cannot specify the IN, OUT, or INOUT modifiers to parameters. All parameters are implicitly IN parameters.

- The function body must contain one or more RETURN statements, which terminate function execution and return the specified result to the calling program.

We look at stored functions in detail in Chapter 10.

CREATE TRIGGER

The CREATE TRIGGER statement creates a trigger. Its syntax follows:

```
CREATE [DEFINER = { user|CURRENT_USER }] TRIGGER trigger_name
      {BEFORE|AFTER}
      {UPDATE|INSERT|DELETE}
      ON table_name
      FOR EACH ROW
      trigger_statements
```

As with other stored programs, the trigger name must conform to the general rules for naming objects, as outlined in Chapter 3. There are several differences between this statement syntax and that of CREATE PROCEDURE and CREATE FUNCTION:

DEFINER
> This optional clause specifies the security privileges that the trigger code will assume when it is invoked. The default CURRENT_USER setting results in the trigger executing with the privileges of the account that executes the CREATE TRIGGER statement. Specifying a *user* allows the trigger to execute with the privileges of another account.

BEFORE *or* AFTER
> These clauses control the sequence in which the trigger will fire—either before or after the triggering statement is executed.

UPDATE, INSERT, *or* DELETE
> These clauses specify the type of DML statement that will cause the trigger to be invoked.

trigger_statements

This code can be one or more stored program language statements. If more than one statement is specified, they must all be contained within a `BEGIN-END` block.

Triggers are described in detail in Chapter 11.

ALTER PROCEDURE/FUNCTION

You can use the `ALTER` statement to change the `SQL SECURITY` characteristic of a stored procedure or stored function, or to change the comment associated with the procedure or function. This statement cannot currently be issued for triggers. The syntax of this statement is shown below:

```
ALTER {PROCEDURE|FUNCTION} procedure_or_function_name
    [SQL SECURITY {DEFINER|INVOKER}]
    [COMMENT comment_string ]
```

DROP PROCEDURE/FUNCTION/TRIGGER

You can use the `DROP` statement to remove a stored procedure, function, or trigger from the database:

```
DROP {PROCEDURE|FUNCTION|TRIGGER} [IF EXISTS] program_name
```

`IF EXISTS` is only valid for stored procedures and triggers, not for triggers.

We frequently include a `DROP PROCEDURE IF EXISTS` statement in the same source file as our `CREATE` statement to remove the previous definition of the procedure before creating the new version (see Figure 7-10 for an example of this).

Getting Information About Stored Programs

This section describes ways you can retrieve information about the stored programs that exist in your database.

In releases of MySQL prior to 5.0, extracting information about objects in the database was achieved by issuing `SHOW` statements. MySQL has extended the `SHOW` statement in version 5 to include information about stored programs.

However, in 5.0, MySQL also introduced the `INFORMATION_SCHEMA` database, which contains various tables that provide information about the objects that exist within the server. These tables are typically referred to as the *data dictionary* or as *server metadata*.

If you are a long-time user of the MySQL server, then using `SHOW` statements may seem a more natural approach to obtaining information about stored programs. However, the `INFORMATION_SCHEMA` tables—in addition to being ANSI standard—have the advantage of being amenable to various handy SELECT operations, such as grouping, counting, joining, and advanced filtering operations. You can also use INFORMATION_SCHEMA tables within your stored program code—something that is not practical with SHOW statement output.

SHOW PROCEDURE/FUNCTION STATUS

The SHOW PROCEDURE STATUS and SHOW FUNCTION STATUS statements return information about the stored programs within the server. The syntax of this form of the SHOW statement is:

```
SHOW {PROCEDURE|FUNCTION} STATUS [LIKE pattern]
```

Figure 7-11 provides an example of SHOW PROCEDURE status output.

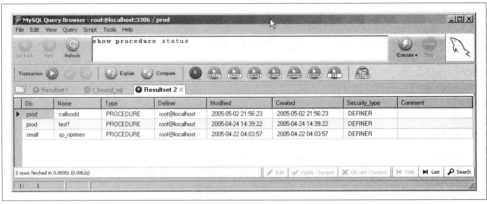

Figure 7-11. SHOW PROCEDURE STATUS

SHOW CREATE PROCEDURE/FUNCTION

The SHOW CREATE PROCEDURE and SHOW CREATE FUNCTION statements return the CREATE statement necessary to re-create a particular stored program. Figure 7-12 shows the output of this version of SHOW. Note that we used the "View Field pop-up editor" right-click option to load the text output returned by this statement into a more readable Field Viewer window.

INFORMATION_SCHEMA.ROUTINES Table

The INFORMATION_SCHEMA.ROUTINES table returns a variety of information about stored procedures and functions. You can use the WHERE clause and column lists within the SELECT statement to format this output in various interesting ways.

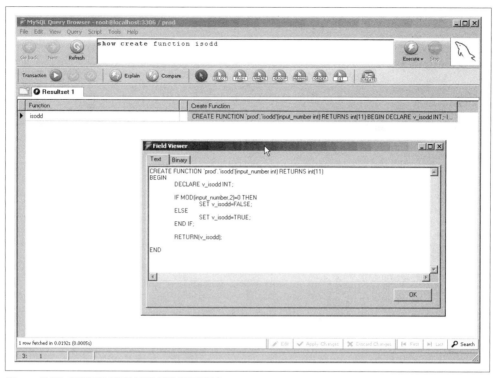

Figure 7-12. SHOW CREATE FUNCTION

This table does not contain information about triggers, but you can retrieve trigger information from the INFORMATION_SCHEMA.TRIGGERS table described in the next section.

Figure 7-13 shows the structure of the INFORMATION_SCHEMA.ROUTINES table.

You can use INFORMATION_SCHEMA.ROUTINES to return any of the data returned by the SHOW PROCEDURE STATUS, SHOW FUNCTION STATUS, SHOW CREATE PROCEDURE, and SHOW CREATE FUNCTION statements. For instance, in Figure 7-14, we produce a report that includes both the procedure/function definitions and other information about these programs.

INFORMATION_SCHEMA.TRIGGERS Table

The INFORMATION_SCHEMA.TRIGGERS table contains details about all of the triggers that are defined on the MySQL server. Figure 7-15 shows the output from a query against this table (using the "View Field pop-up editor" right-click option to view the contents of the action_statement column).

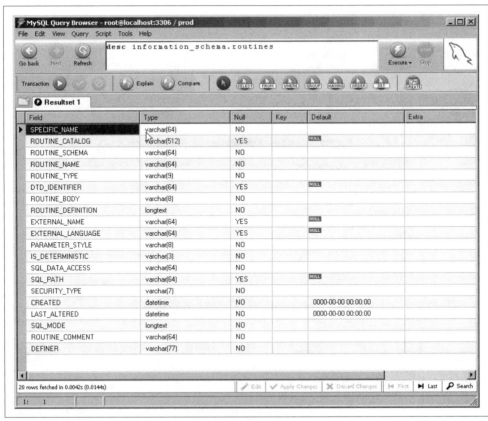

Figure 7-13. Structure of the INFORMATION_SCHEMA.ROUTINES table

Conclusion

In this chapter we looked at the process of creating and managing stored objects (procedures, functions, and triggers). Let's conclude with an outline of what we regard as the best practices for creating and managing stored objects:

- Make sure that the reference (e.g., official) copy of each of your stored programs exists as a file on disk, not as the copy stored in the MySQL server. Stored programs might need to be shared between multiple servers, and you therefore need at least one copy—not on a server—that represents the current version.

- Use a version control system to maintain a copy of any version of a stored program that is deployed to a MySQL server. In other words, subject stored program code to the same discipline that you apply to other program code.

- When you are editing a stored program, check it out of the source control system and load the checked-out copy into the MySQL Query Browser or other tool.

Figure 7-14. Viewing the INFORMATION_SCHEMA.ROUTINES table

- When you are satisfied with your changes, save the stored program code to a disk file and check it into the version control system.

- Deploy the stored program by creating command-line routines using the MySQL client program, and embed these into Make files or other build/deploy scripts that you can use to apply schema changes and other server object changes.

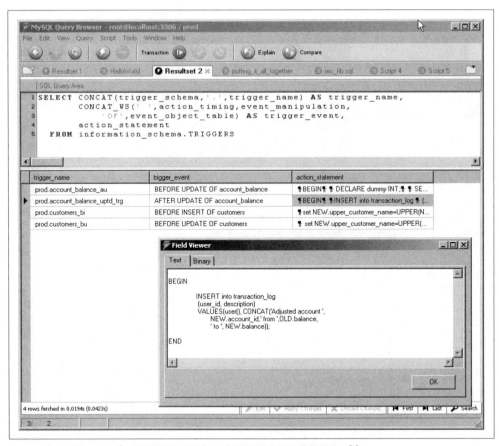

Figure 7-15. Viewing the INFORMATION_SCHEMA.TRIGGERS table

## CHAPTER 8

Transaction Management

A *transaction* is a set of one or more SQL statements that are logically grouped together and that must be either applied to the database in their entirety or not applied at all.

Consider the commonly cited example of a funds transfer from one account to another. In its most simple form, this transfer will involve two UPDATE statements: one to reduce the account balance in the "from" account, and another to increase the account balance in the "to" account. Suppose that the "from" account has been updated, but then the change to the "to" account cannot be completed. We must be sure to undo that first update, or the money that was to be transferred will have, in effect, "disappeared."

We expect database transactions to conform to the *ACID* principle, which means that transactions should be:

Atomic

> The transaction is indivisible—either all the statements in the transaction are applied to the database, or none are.

Consistent

> The database remains in a consistent state before and after transaction execution.

Isolated

> While multiple transactions can be executed by one or more users simultaneously, one transaction should not see the effects of other concurrent transactions.

Durable

> Once a transaction is saved to the database (an action referred to in database programming circles as a *commit*), its changes are expected to *persist*. Even if the user turns off her computer or the database server goes down, the changes will be saved. This usually means that the result of the transaction must be written to a nonvolatile form of storage, such as a hard disk (alternatively, it could be redundantly stored in multiple memory stores, written to battery-backed memory, or written to solid state disk).

Stored programs provide an excellent mechanism for defining, encapsulating, and managing transactions. Without the features available in stored progams, the calling program would need to issue the relevant SQL statements for the transaction and provide the logic to control locking and handle transaction failure. With MySQL stored program support, we can now encapsulate the multiple, interdependent SQL statements of the transaction into a single stored program. The application code, such as a PHP program, calls the stored program and transfers the responsibility for transaction management to the program executing in the database server.

In this chapter we review transactional support in MySQL and show how to create a transaction within a stored program. We also discuss how to deal with common transaction-related issues, such as lock timeouts, deadlocks, and locking strategies. We conclude by providing a general-purpose set of guidelines for transaction design.

Transactional Support in MySQL

MySQL is virtually unique in modern relational databases in that transactions are not mandatory. Under certain circumstances, they are not even possible. In fact, with MySQL, transactional support is a property not of the MySQL server itself, but of the underlying storage engine employed. Currently, the two most popular storage engines used with MySQL are MyISAM and InnoDB, although a small number of users use BerkeleyDB:

MyISAM

> MyISAM does *not* support transactions. Using a nontransactional storage engine is fine for certain applications—in particular those that are overwhelmingly read-only. Certainly, if you do not need to manage transactions, you can improve the performance of some applications by avoiding the overhead associated with transaction management. If, on the other hand, you are building an application with a significant amount of updates and concurrent updates to the database, you will probably want to avoid MyISAM and instead rely on a transactional engine.

InnoDB

> InnoDB is the most popular transaction-safe MySQL storage engine. It supports ACID transactions as well as row-level locking and multiversion concurrency.

Berkeley DB

> This storage engine also supports transactions but is currently less widely used than InnoDB.

In a survey conducted by MySQL AB (*http://dev.mysql.com/tech-resources/quickpolls/storage-engines.html*), about 60% of respondents reported using MyISAM as their primary storage engine, while 37% used InnoDB and about 1% used BerkeleyDB. However, these figures are likely to change over the next few years, as MySQL AB releases additional storage engine types, many of which will be transactional.

This chapter assumes that you are using a transactional storage engine such as InnoDB or BerkeleyDB.

First, we need to discuss the concept of isolation levels and sessions.

Isolation Levels

Before we can talk sensibly about transactions and isolation levels, we need to be clear on the concept of a *session*. A database session is a unique connection to the database that commences when you log on to MySQL and that terminates when you disconnect—either explicitly or when MySQL notices that your client program has "gone away."

Every session has its own memory areas and—more importantly—can hold locks on data or have a unique view of certain data. *Isolation levels* determine the degree to which transactions in one session may affect the data seen or accessed by another session. All isolation levels are compromises between *concurrency*—the ability for multiple sessions to perform operations on the database at the same time—and *consistency*—the degree to which a session sees a logical and correct view of the data regardless of what activities might be going on in other sessions.

The isolation level of a transaction also determines the degree to which that transaction conforms to the ACID properties described at the beginning of this chapter. Each of the four isolation levels represents a different balance between the isolation and concurrency of transactions. At the highest isolation levels, very few transactions will be able to execute concurrently, but the chances of one transaction interfering with another will be minimized. At the lower isolation levels, many transactions will be able to execute concurrently, but the chances of conflicts between transactions will be higher.

The ANSI standard defines four isolation levels, all of which are supported by MySQL when using the InnoDB engine:

READ UNCOMMITTED

> This is the lowest possible isolation level. Sometimes called *dirty read*, this level permits a transaction to read rows that have not yet been committed. Using this isolation level might improve performance, but the idea of one user retrieving data changed by another user, which might not actually be committed, is usually unacceptable.

READ COMMITTED

> At this isolation level, only committed rows can be seen by a transaction. Furthermore, any changes committed after a statement commences execution cannot be seen. For example, if you have a long-running SELECT statement in session

A that queries from the BOOKS table, and session B inserts a row into BOOKS while A's query is still running, that new row will *not* be visible to the SELECT.

REPEATABLE READ

At this isolation level, no changes to the database that are made by other sessions since the transaction commenced can be seen within the transaction, until the transaction is committed or rolled back (cancelled). This means that if you re-execute a SELECT within your transaction, it will always show the same results (other than any updates that occurred in the same transaction).

SERIALIZABLE

At this isolation level, every transaction is completely isolated so that transactions behave as if they had executed serially, one after the other. In order to achieve this, the RDBMS will typically lock every row that is read, so other sessions may not modify that data until the transaction is done with it. The locks are released when you commit or cancel the transaction.

You can change the isolation level in your MySQL session with the SET statement:

```
SET TRANSACTION ISOLATION LEVEL {READ UNCOMMITTED | READ COMMITTED
                                 |REPEATABLE READ | SERIALIZABLE}
```

Under normal circumstances, you should avoid changing the transaction isolation level from the default of REPEATABLE READ. In particular, think carefully before setting the isolation level to READ UNCOMMITTED or SERIALIZABLE. READ UNCOMMITTED can lead to serious problems with the integrity of the data returned by the SELECT statement, while SERIALIZABLE will have a noticeable, negative effect on performance and can also increase the chance of "deadlocks" (described later in this chapter).

Transaction Management Statements

Use the following transaction management statements in MySQL stored programs:

START TRANSACTION

Signifies the commencement of a new transaction. If an existing transaction is already in progress, then START TRANSACTION will issue an implicit COMMIT. When you issue START TRANSACTION, the autocommit property (described in the next section) is effectively and implicitly set to 0 until the transaction ends. We recommend that you explicitly commit or roll back existing transactions before any START TRANSACTION statements, since the implicit COMMIT might not be obvious to someone reading or maintaining your code.

COMMIT

Saves all changes made in the transaction to the database and then terminates a transaction. COMMIT also releases any locks that might be in effect, whether they are explicit locks from FOR UPDATE or LOCK TABLES or implicit locks acquired as a result of executing DML statements.

ROLLBACK

> Undoes any changes to the database made by the transaction and then terminates that transaction. Like COMMIT, ROLLBACK releases any locks held by the transaction.

SAVEPOINT *savepoint_name*

> Creates a named savepoint identifier that can be the target of a ROLLBACK TO SAVEPOINT statement.

ROLLBACK TO SAVEPOINT *savepoint_name*

> Performs a rollback on all statements that have been executed since the specified savepoint was created. In this way, you can roll back only part of a transaction, preserving some subset of your changes to still be saved. You may find savepoints useful when you need to save part of your work after an error has occurred. See the section "Working with Savepoints" later in this chapter for more details.

SET TRANSACTION

> Allows you to change the isolation level of your transaction. See the section "Isolation Levels" earlier in this chapter for more details.

LOCK TABLES

> Allows you to explicitly lock one or more tables. Note that LOCK TABLES implicitly closes any currently open transactions. We recommend that you explicitly commit or roll back your transaction before any LOCK TABLES statements. We rarely want to lock entire tables in the normal course of transaction processing, so we don't usually include LOCK TABLES statements in our transactional code.

Defining a Transaction

The default behavior of MySQL is to perform a COMMIT after the execution of each individual SQL statement, effectively turning every statement into an individual transaction. This approach is inadequate for most complex applications.

To enable transactions, allowing multiple SQL statements to be executed before a COMMIT or ROLLBACK is performed, you must take one of the following two steps:

* Set the MySQL autocommit property or variable to 0. The default setting for AUTOCOMMIT is 1.
* Explicitly initiate a transaction with the START TRANSACTION statement.

Since it is dangerous to assume that the MySQL environment is running with the necessary transaction setting, you should generally include either a SET AUTOCOMMIT=0 or START TRANSACTION statement in any transactional stored program.

The SET autocommit=0 statement simply ensures that MySQL will not implicitly issue a COMMIT after every SQL statement. Note, however, that if you have already initiated a transaction, issuing SET autocommit will have no effect. START TRANSACTION, on the other hand, implicitly commits any currently outstanding changes in your session, terminating the existing transaction and starting a new one.

We recommend that you leave nothing to chance when programming transactions in MySQL stored programs. Therefore, we suggest that you always explicitly commence a transaction with a START TRANSACTION statement and explicitly end your transaction with a COMMIT or ROLLBACK.

 Wherever possible, define explicitly the beginning and end of every transaction with START TRANSACTION and COMMIT/ROLLBACK statements. Place the START TRANSACTION statement at the beginning of your transaction, and terminate it with either COMMIT or ROLLBACK. If your program ends with conditional logic as part of its error handling, you may, in fact, need to use both of these statements—in different branches of your IF or CASE statement.

Example 8-1 shows a transaction implemented in a stored procedure using a SET AUTOCOMMIT statement.

Example 8-1. Commencing a transaction using SET AUTOCOMMIT

```
CREATE PROCEDURE tfer_funds
      (from_account int, to_account int,tfer_amount numeric(10,2))
BEGIN
    SET autocommit=0;

    UPDATE account_balance
       SET balance=balance-tfer_amount
     WHERE account_id=from_account;

    UPDATE account_balance
       SET balance=balance+tfer_amount
     WHERE account_id=to_account;

    COMMIT;
END;
```

Example 8-2 shows an example of defining a transaction using START TRANSACTION.

Example 8-2. Commencing a transaction using START TRANSACTION

```
CREATE PROCEDURE tfer_funds
      (from_account int, to_account int,tfer_amount numeric(10,2))
BEGIN
    START TRANSACTION;

    UPDATE account_balance
       SET balance=balance-tfer_amount
     WHERE account_id=from_account;

    UPDATE account_balance
```

```
        SET balance=balance+tfer_amount
     WHERE account_id=to_account;

    COMMIT;
END;
```

As we've said, transactions normally complete when either a COMMIT or a ROLLBACK statement is executed. However, be aware that some statements—usually Data Definition Language (DDL) statements—can cause *implicit* COMMITs. The statements that implicitly commit, and should therefore be avoided when a transaction is active, include the following:

ALTER FUNCTION	ALTER PROCEDURE	ALTER TABLE
BEGIN	CREATE DATABASE	CREATE FUNCTION
CREATE INDEX	CREATE PROCEDURE	CREATE TABLE
DROP DATABASE	DROP FUNCTION	DROP INDEX
DROP PROCEDURE	DROP TABLE	UNLOCK TABLES
LOAD MASTER DATA	LOCK TABLES	RENAME TABLE
TRUNCATE TABLE	SET AUTOCOMMIT=1	START TRANSACTION

Working with Savepoints

Savepoints allow you to perform a partial rollback of the changes in your transaction. If you issue an unqualified ROLLBACK, any and all changes in your current session are erased. If, however, you place a SAVEPOINT statement in your program, then you can roll back to that point in your program (and your transaction). In other words, any changes made before that statement can still be saved to the database with a COMMIT.

Generally, savepoints are intended to allow you to recover from a statement-level error without having to abort and restart your transaction. In these circumstances, the transaction includes one or more statements that might fail, yet should not force the invalidation of the entire transaction. Usually you will want to roll back to a savepoint, as part of handling the error, and then take the appropriate action, as indicated by the particular error that was raised.

Example 8-3 demonstrates the use of a savepoint with a transaction that creates or updates a location record, and then creates or updates a departments record that resides at that location:

Example 8-3. Example of a transaction that uses a savepoint

```
1  CREATE PROCEDURE savepoint_example(in_department_name VARCHAR(30),
2                                     in_location VARCHAR(30),
3                                     in_address1 VARCHAR(30),
```

Example 8-3. Example of a transaction that uses a savepoint (continued)

```
4                                    in_address2 VARCHAR(30),
5                                    in_zipcode             VARCHAR(10),
6                                    in_manager_id INT)
7  BEGIN
8      DECLARE sp_location_exists INT DEFAULT 0;
9      DECLARE duplicate_dept  INT DEFAULT 0;
10
11
12     START TRANSACTION;
13
14     -- Does the location exist?
15     SELECT COUNT(*)
16       INTO location_exists
17       FROM locations
18      WHERE location=in_location;
19
20     IF location_exists=0 THEN
21
22         INSERT INTO AUDIT_LOG (audit_message)
23                      VALUES (CONCAT('Creating new location',in_location));
24
25         INSERT INTO locations (location,address1,address2,zipcode)
26          VALUES (in_location,in_address1,in_address2,in_zipcode);
27     ELSE
28
29         UPDATE locations set address1=in_address1,
30                      address2=in_address2,
31                      zipcode=in_zipcode
32         WHERE location=in_location;
33
34     END IF;
35
36     SAVEPOINT savepoint_location_exists;
37
38     BEGIN
39         DECLARE DUPLICATE_KEY CONDITION FOR 1062;
40         DECLARE CONTINUE HANDLER FOR DUPLICATE_KEY /*Duplicate key value*/
41             BEGIN
42               SET duplicate_dept=1;
43               ROLLBACK TO SAVEPOINT savepoint_location_exists;
44             END;
45
46       INSERT INTO AUDIT_LOG (audit_message)
47             VALUES (CONCAT('Creating new department',in_department_name));
48
49       INSERT INTO DEPARTMENTS (department_name,location,manager_id)
50                      VALUES (in_department_name,in_location, in_manager_id);
51
52       IF duplicate_dept=1 THEN
53
54           UPDATE departments
55             SET location=in_location,
```

Example 8-3. Example of a transaction that uses a savepoint (continued)

```
56                      manager_id=in_manager_id
57         WHERE department_name=in_department_name;
58      END IF;
59
60   END;
61
62   COMMIT;
63
64 END;
```

Here is an explanation of this complex transaction logic:

Line(s)	Explanation
12	The START TRANSACTION statement denotes the start of the transaction. We can place this statement after our declarations, since they do not participate in any way in the transaction.
15	In this SQL statement we check to see if a matching location exists.
20-26	If the location does not exist (line 20), we insert an audit log record (lines 22-23) and then create the location (lines 25-26).
29-32	If the location already exists, we update it with new detail.
36	Whether or not the location existed in line 20, it definitely exists now, so we establish a savepoint indicating that we have gotten this much work done.
39-44	Define an error handler that will fire in the event of a duplicate key error. If the handler is invoked, it will issue a rollback to our savepoint and then set the duplicate_dept variable so that we can detect that the rollback has occurred. You will find more information about handler logic in Chapter 6.
46-50	Insert an audit record and then insert a new department. If a department already exists with this name, the handler will fire, setting the duplicate_dept variable and rolling back to the savepoint. This partial rollback will undo the audit log entry for the new department, but will preserve the inserts or update executed to ensure that the location existed.
52-58	Check the duplicate_dept variable to see if there was a problem inserting the department. If so, then update the existing DEPARTMENTS record with the new information.

Now that you have seen how to use the SAVEPOINT and ROLLBACK TO statements, we need to point out two undesirable side effects of this approach and then offer a restructuring of the program that renders savepoints unnecessary. These are the side effects:

- The insert into the AUDIT_LOG table on line 46 will, indeed, be rolled back when the department cannot be inserted. However, the overhead of inserting and then rolling back that insert might not be trivial in a high-throughput environment.

- The execution flow of the transaction is unclear. The rollback is defined in the handler on line 43, but actually will be triggered only when the insert fails on line 49. It is hard to tell just by looking at the INSERT statement what will happen, making it difficult to understand the overall logic of the transaction. It is, quite simply, more complicated than necessary.

We can rewrite this program to avoid the use of savepoints altogether (see Example 8-4). A hint of this approach was offered earlier in the procedure (lines 20-34): check to see if the record exists, then issue the INSERT or UPDATE as appropriate. The resulting logic is more straightforward, and actually reduces the number of SQL statements we need to code.

Example 8-4. Alternative to the SAVEPOINT implementation

```
CREATE PROCEDURE nosavepoint_example(in_department_name VARCHAR(30),
                                     in_location VARCHAR(30),
                                     in_address1 VARCHAR(30),
                                     in_address2 VARCHAR(30),
                                     in_zipcode  VARCHAR(10),
                                     in_manager_id INT)
BEGIN
    DECLARE location_exists    INT DEFAULT 0;
    DECLARE department_exists  INT DEFAULT 0;

    START TRANSACTION;

    -- Does the location exist?
    SELECT COUNT(*)
      INTO location_exists
      FROM locations
     WHERE location=in_location;

    IF location_exists=0 THEN

        INSERT INTO AUDIT_LOG (audit_message)
                    VALUES (CONCAT('Creating new location',in_location));

        INSERT INTO locations (location,address1,address2,zipcode)
         VALUES (in_location,in_address1,in_address2,in_zipcode);
    ELSE

        UPDATE locations set address1=in_address1,
                    address2=in_address2,
                    zipcode=in_zipcode
        WHERE location=in_location;

    END IF;

    -- Does the department exists?
    SELECT COUNT(*)
      INTO department_exists
        FROM departments
     WHERE department_name=in_department_name;

    IF department_exists=1 THEN

        UPDATE departments
            SET location=in_location,
                manager_id=in_manager_id
```

Example 8-4. Alternative to the SAVEPOINT implementation (continued)

```
            WHERE department_name=in_department_name;

    ELSE

        INSERT INTO AUDIT_LOG (audit_message)
                VALUES (CONCAT('Creating new department',in_department_name));

        INSERT INTO DEPARTMENTS (department_name,location,manager_id)
                VALUES (in_department_name,in_location, in_manager_id);

    END IF;

    COMMIT;

END;
```

 Savepoints can be used to partially roll back transactions in the event of an error. If you cannot achieve the same effect through the use of exception handlers and conditional logic, then savepoints may be required. Watch out for SAVEPOINT-based implementations, however, that result in unnecessary and unnecessarily complicated code.

One good use of savepoints is to implement "nested" transactions inside of discrete stored programs. You may with to implement a stored program that performs a small transaction, but you don't want a rollback in that program to abort any larger transaction that may be in progress. A savepoint is a good way to do this, since you can easily roll back only the statements that you have issued within the procedure. Example 8-5 shows a stored program that implements this approach.

Example 8-5. Example of a "nested" transaction using a savepoint

```
CREATE PROCEDURE nested_tfer_funds(
  in_from_acct INTEGER,
  in_to_acct   INTEGER,
  in_tfer_amount DECIMAL(8,2))
BEGIN

  DECLARE txn_error INTEGER DEFAULT 0 ;

  DECLARE CONTINUE HANDLER FOR SQLEXCEPTION BEGIN
    SET txn_error=1;
  END;

  SAVEPOINT savepoint_tfer;

  UPDATE account_balance
     SET balance=balance-in_tfer_amount
   WHERE account_id=in_from_acct;
```

```
IF txn_error THEN
  ROLLBACK TO savepoint_tfer;
  SELECT 'Transfer aborted ';
ELSE
  UPDATE account_balance
    SET balance=balance+in_tfer_amount
  WHERE account_id=in_to_acct;

  IF txn_error THEN
    ROLLBACK TO savepoint_tfer;
    SELECT 'Transfer aborted ';
  END IF;
END IF;

END;
```

The program in Example 8-5 creates a savepoint before issuing any DML statements. Should any errors occur, the program issues a rollback to that savepoint to ensure that the DML statements issued by the program—but *only* those statements—are reversed.

Transactions and Locks

The ACID properties of a transaction can only be implemented by restricting simultaneous changes to the database. This is achieved by placing locks on modified data. These locks persist until the transaction issues a COMMIT or ROLLBACK statement.

Without locks, a change made by one transaction could be overwritten by another transaction that executes at the same time. Consider, for example, the scenario shown in Figure 8-1, based on the tfer_funds procedure of Example 8-2. When two different sessions run this program for the same account number, we encounter some obvious difficulties if locks are not in place.

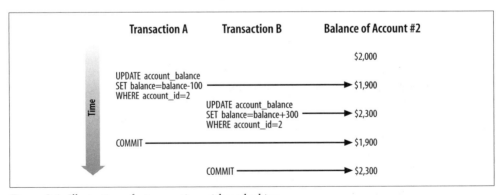

Figure 8-1. Illustration of a transaction without locking

In this scenario, account 2 starts with a balance of $2,000. Transaction A reduces the balance of the account by $100. Before transaction A commits, transaction B increases the account value by $300. Because transaction B cannot see the uncommitted updates made by transaction A, it increases the balance to $2,300. Because we allowed two transactions to simultaneously modify the same row, the database is now in an inconsistent state. The end balance for the account will be the value set by whichever transaction commits last. If transaction B is the last to commit, then the owner of account 2 will have $100 more than she should. On the other hand, if transaction A commits first, the account owner will be $300 out of pocket!

This clearly unacceptable result is completely avoidable when locks are placed on rows that have been changed, as is illustrated in Figure 8-2.

Now, when transaction A updates account 2, the relevant row is locked and cannot be updated by another transaction. Transaction B must wait for transaction A to be committed before its update can proceed. When transaction A commits, transaction B applies its update to the modified account balance, and the integrity of the account balance is maintained.

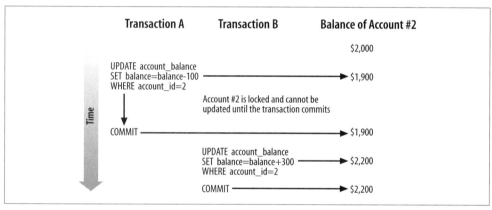

Figure 8-2. Illustration of a transaction with locking

The downside of this locking strategy is that transaction B must wait for transaction A to complete. The more programs you have waiting for locks to clear, the less throughput your transactional system will be able to support.

MySQL/InnoDB minimizes the amount of lock contention by locking at the row level only. In our example, updates to other rows in the ACCOUNT_BALANCE table are able to proceed without restriction. Furthermore, with InnoDB, reads do not normally cause locks to occur, and *readers* do not need to wait for locks to be released before accessing data. Other transactional storage engines—and other RDBMS systems—may behave differently.

You can, however, place locks on rows that have only been read by using the FOR UPDATE or LOCK IN SHARE MODE clause in the SELECT statement, and this is sometimes required to implement a specific locking strategy (see "Optimistic and Pessimistic Locking Strategies," later in this chapter).

In the following subsections we'll look at various types of locking situations, problems, and strategies.

Situations in Which Locks Arise

While it is possible for you to lock rows explicitly, you will generally rely on the storage engine to lock rows (or an entire table) implicitly, which it will do under the following circumstances:

- When an UPDATE statement is executed, all rows modified will be locked.
- An INSERT statement will cause any primary or unique key records to be locked. This will prevent a concurrent insert of a statement with an identical primary key.
- You can lock entire tables with the LOCK TABLES statement. This is not generally recommended, because it not only reduces concurrency, it operates above the storage engine layer, which might mean that any storage engine deadlock resolution mechanisms may be ineffectual.
- If you use the FOR UPDATE or LOCK IN SHARE MODE clauses in a SELECT statement, all of the rows returned by that SELECT statement will be locked.

Locking rows as they are read is an important technique that we'll demonstrate in subsequent examples. To read and simultaneously lock a row, you include the FOR UPDATE or LOCK IN SHARE MODE clause in the SELECT statement, as follows:

```
SELECT SELECT_statement options
       [FOR UPDATE|LOCK IN SHARE MODE]
```

The two locking options differ in the following ways:

FOR UPDATE
    When you use this clause, you acquire an exclusive lock on the row with the same characteristics as an UPDATE on that row. Only one SELECT statement can simultaneously hold a FOR UPDATE lock on a given row; other SELECT statements (or DML statements) will have to wait until the transaction ends.

LOCK IN SHARE MODE
    When you use this clause, it prevents any DML from being applied to the row you have locked. However—unlike FOR UPDATE—any number of SHARE MODE locks can be applied to a single row simultaneously.

Deadlocks

A *deadlock* occurs when two transactions are each waiting for the other to release a lock—they each block each other, and neither can proceed. For instance, consider the situation in which one transaction attempts to transfer $100 from account 2 to account 1. Simultaneously, another transaction attempts to transfer $300 from account 1 to account 2. If the timing of the two transactions is sufficiently unfortunate, then each may end up waiting for the other to release a lock, resulting in a stalemate that will never end. Figure 8-3 shows the sequence of events.

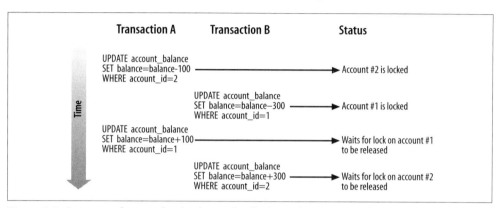

Figure 8-3. Sequence of events that leads to a deadlock condition

When MySQL/InnoDB detects a deadlock situation, it will force one of the transactions to roll back and issue an error message, as shown in Example 8-6. In the case of InnoDB, the transaction thus selected will be the transaction that has done the least work (in terms of rows modified).

Example 8-6. Example of a deadlock error

```
mysql> CALL tfer_funds(1,2,300);
ERROR 1213 (40001): Deadlock found when trying to get lock; try restarting transaction
```

Deadlocks can occur in any database system, but in row-level locking databases like MySQL/InnoDB, the possibility of a deadlock is usually low. You can further reduce the frequency of deadlocks by locking rows or tables in a consistent order, and by keeping your transactions as short as possible.

If you are building (or debugging) an application in which deadlocks seem likely to occur, and you cannot reorganize your transactions to avoid them, you can add logic to your programs to handle deadlocks and retry the transaction.

Example 8-7 shows a modified version of the stored procedure in Example 8-2 that will retry its transaction up to three times in the event of a deadlock.

Example 8-7. Stored procedure with deadlock-handling logic

```
1   CREATE PROCEDURE tfer_funds2
2         (from_account INT, to_account INT,
3          tfer_amount numeric(10,2), OUT out_status INT,
4          OUT out_message VARCHAR(30))
5   BEGIN
6
7       DECLARE deadlock INT DEFAULT 0;
8       DECLARE attempts INT DEFAULT 0;
9
10      tfer_loop:WHILE (attempts<3) DO
11          BEGIN
12              DECLARE deadlock_detected CONDITION FOR 1213;
13              DECLARE EXIT HANDLER FOR deadlock_detected
14                  BEGIN
15                      ROLLBACK;
16                      SET deadlock=1;
17                  END;
18              SET deadlock=0;
19
20              START TRANSACTION;
21
22              UPDATE account_balance
23                  SET balance=balance-tfer_amount
24               WHERE account_id=from_account;
25
26              UPDATE account_balance
27                  SET balance=balance+tfer_amount
28               WHERE account_id=to_account;
29
30              COMMIT;
31
32          END;
33          IF deadlock=0 THEN
34              LEAVE tfer_loop;
35          ELSE
36              SET attempts=attempts+1;
37          END IF;
38      END WHILE tfer_loop;
39
40      IF deadlock=1 THEN
41          SET out_status=-1;
42          SET out_message="Failed with deadlock for 3 attempts";
43
44      ELSE
45          SET out_status=0;
46          SET out_message=CONCAT("OK (",attempts," deadlocks)");
47      END IF;
48
49  END;
```

The error-handling techniques in Example 8-7 rely on statements introduced in Chapter 6. Here is a line-by-line explanation of the code:

Line(s)	Explanation
10	Commence a WHILE loop that will control attempts to execute (and possibly re-execute) the transaction. The WHILE loop condition of (attempts<3) ensures that we will try no more than three times to complete this task.
11	Define an anonymous BEGIN block within the loop to contain the transaction. The END statement for this block appears on line 32. The block allows us to trap an error within the body of the loop, but not exit the loop itself.
12-18	Prepare the block for the execution of the transaction. Define an EXIT handler and associate it with the deadlock error. When a deadlock occurs, the handler will set a variable indicating failure, issue a ROLLBACK, and then terminate the block, while remaining within the loop.
20-30	The SQL statements that make up the transaction for this program.
33-37	Determine if it is time to leave the loop or increment the counter. If a deadlock did not occur, the value of the deadlock variable is 0, so we use the LEAVE statement to terminate the WHILE loop.
	If deadlock equals 1, then the BEGIN-END block has terminated because of a deadlock, so we increment the attempts variable and (provided that attempts has not yet reached 3) allow the loop to re-execute the SQL statements and thereby retry the transaction.
40-47	On these lines we examine the deadlock and attempts variables to determine the final state of the transaction. If deadlock=1, then our most recent attempt to execute the transaction failed with a deadlock, and—since we have tried three times—we terminate with an error. Otherwise, we signal a successful end to the transaction, although we note how many times we encountered a deadlock in the process.

Going to this much effort to handle deadlocks will be overkill for most applications. Unless your application design is particularly vulnerable to deadlocks, you will encounter deadlocks so infrequently that you actually weaken your application by including so much hard-to-maintain deadlock-handling code.

As noted above, there are usually other ways to avoid deadlock scenarios. For instance, in Example 8-8 we lock the rows to be updated in numerical order before issuing any UPDATEs. Because the rows are always locked in the same order, one instance of this transaction should not cause a deadlock if another session runs the same program.

Example 8-8. Locking rows in order to avoid deadlock conditions

```
CREATE PROCEDURE tfer_funds3
    (from_account INT, to_account INT,tfer_amount NUMERIC(10,2))
BEGIN
    DECLARE local_account_id INT;
    DECLARE lock_cursor CURSOR FOR
        SELECT account_id
          FROM account_balance
         WHERE account_id IN (from_account,to_account)
         ORDER BY account_id
           FOR UPDATE;

    START TRANSACTION;
```

Example 8-8. Locking rows in order to avoid deadlock conditions (continued)

```
   OPEN lock_cursor;
   FETCH lock_cursor INTO local_account_id;

   UPDATE account_balance
      SET balance=balance-tfer_amount
    WHERE account_id=from_account;

   UPDATE account_balance
      SET balance=balance+tfer_amount
    WHERE account_id=to_account;

   CLOSE lock_cursor;

   COMMIT;
END;
```

Lock Timeouts

A deadlock is the most severe result of locking. Yet, in many other situations, a program in one session may be unable to read or write a particular row, because it is locked by another session. In this case, the program can and—by default—will wait for a certain period of time for the lock to be released. It will then either acquire the lock or time out. You can set the length of time a session will wait for an InnoDB lock to be released by setting the value of the innodb_lock_wait_timeout configuration value, which has a default of 50 seconds.

When a timeout occurs, MySQL/InnoDB will roll back the transaction and issue an error code 1205, as shown in Example 8-9.

Example 8-9. Lock timeout error

```
mysql> SELECT * FROM account_balance FOR UPDATE;
ERROR 1205 (HY000): Lock wait timeout exceeded; try restarting transaction
```

So if you have very long-running transactions, you may want to increase the value of innodb_lock_wait_timeout or introduce error-handling code to cope with the occasional 1205 error.

In some circumstances—particularly when you mix MySQL/InnoDB and non-InnoDB tables in the same transaction (a practice we do not normally recommend)—MySQL/InnoDB may be unable to detect a deadlock. In such cases, the "lock wait timeout" error will eventually occur. If you are mixing MySQL/InnoDB and non-InnoDB tables, and you are particularly concerned about deadlocks, you may want to implement error-handling logic for lock timeouts similar to that implemented for deadlocks in Example 8-7.

Optimistic and Pessimistic Locking Strategies

If your transaction reads data that subsequently participates in an UPDATE, INSERT, or DELETE, you need to take steps to ensure that the integrity of your transaction is not jeopardized by the possibility of another transaction changing the relevant data between the time you read it and the time you update it.

For instance, consider the transaction in Example 8-10. This variation on our funds transfer transaction makes sure that there are sufficient funds in the "from" account before executing the transaction. It first queries the account balance, and then takes an action depending on that value (the balance must be greater than the transfer amount).

Example 8-10. Funds transfer program without locking strategy

```
CREATE PROCEDURE tfer_funds4
      (from_account int, to_account int,tfer_amount numeric(10,2),
       OUT status int, OUT message VARCHAR(30))
BEGIN
   DECLARE from_account_balance NUMERIC(10,2);

   SELECT balance
     INTO from_account_balance
     FROM account_balance
    WHERE account_id=from_account;

   IF from_account_balance >= tfer_amount THEN

       START TRANSACTION;

       UPDATE account_balance
          SET balance=balance-tfer_amount
        WHERE account_id=from_account;

       UPDATE account_balance
          SET balance=balance+tfer_amount
        WHERE account_id=to_account;
       COMMIT;

       SET status=0;
       SET message='OK';
   ELSE
       SET status=-1;
       SET message='Insufficient funds';
   END IF;
END;
```

Unfortunately, as currently written, this program might under the right circumstances allow the "from" account to become overdrawn. Since some amount of time elapses between the query that establishes the current balance and the update transaction that reduces that balance, it is possible that another transaction could reduce the balance of the account within that period of time with its own UPDATE statement. This program's UPDATE would, then, cause a negative balance in the account.

Figure 8-4 shows the business policy violation that can result from a poor locking strategy. Transaction A determines that account 1 has sufficient funds before executing the transfer, but in the meantime transaction B has reduced the available funds by $300. When transaction A finally executes its update, the result is a negative balance.

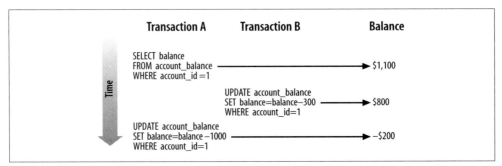

Figure 8-4. Error resulting from a poor locking strategy

There are two typical solutions to this kind of scenario:

The pessimistic locking strategy
> Assume that concurrent updates are quite likely to occur, and write programs to prevent them from happening. Generally, this means you will need to lock rows as they are read. Other transactions that want to update the row must wait until the "pessimistic transaction" ends.

The optimistic locking strategy
> Assume that it is *unlikely* that anyone will update a row between the time we view it and the time we update it. Since we cannot be sure that this assumption is true, we must then, at the last possible moment, make sure that the row has not been updated. If the row has been updated, the transaction cannot be trusted and will have to be aborted.

Pessimistic locking strategy

Let's explore the pessimistic strategy first, with a simple example. We ensure that nobody modifies the balance of the "from" account by locking it with the FOR UPDATE clause as we retrieve the balance. We can now rest assured that when we issue our UPDATE statement, the balance of the account cannot have been altered. Example 8-11 shows how easy this is; all we needed to do was move the SELECT statement inside of the transaction and cause it to lock the rows selected with the FOR UPDATE clause.

Example 8-11. Pessimistic locking strategy

```
CREATE PROCEDURE tfer_funds5
        (from_account INT, to_account INT,tfer_amount NUMERIC(10,2),
        OUT status INT, OUT message VARCHAR(30))
BEGIN
    DECLARE from_account_balance NUMERIC(10,2);

    START TRANSACTION;

    SELECT balance
      INTO from_account_balance
      FROM account_balance
     WHERE account_id=from_account
       FOR UPDATE;

    IF from_account_balance>=tfer_amount THEN

        UPDATE account_balance
           SET balance=balance-tfer_amount
         WHERE account_id=from_account;

        UPDATE account_balance
           SET balance=balance+tfer_amount
         WHERE account_id=to_account;
        COMMIT;

        SET status=0;
        SET message='OK';
    ELSE
        ROLLBACK;
        SET status=-1;
        SET message='Insufficient funds';
    END IF;
END;
```

The pessimistic locking strategy usually results in the simplest and most robust code —code that ensures consistency between SELECT and DML statements within your transaction. The pessimistic strategy can, however, lead to long-held locks that degrade performance (forcing a large number of sessions to wait for the locks to be released). For instance, suppose that after you validate the balance of the transaction, you are required to perform some long-running validation—perhaps you need to check various other databases (credit checking, blocked accounts, online fraud, etc.) before finalizing the transaction. In this case, you may end up locking the account for several minutes—leading to disgruntlement if the customer happens to be trying to withdraw funds at the same time.

Optimistic locking strategy

The optimistic locking strategy assumes that it is unlikely that the row will be updated between the initial SELECT and the end of the transaction, and therefore does not attempt to lock that row. Instead, the optimistic strategy requires that we perform a check *just* before the update to ensure that the row has not been altered.

To detect if a row has been changed, we simply refetch the row—locking the row as we do so—and compare the current values with the previous values.

Example 8-12 demonstrates the optimistic locking strategy. If the account row has changed since the time of the initial balance check, the transaction will be aborted (line 33), although alternatively you could retry the transaction.

Example 8-12. Optimistic locking strategy

```
1    CREATE PROCEDURE tfer_funds6
2            (from_account INT, to_account INT, tfer_amount NUMERIC(10,2),
3             OUT status INT, OUT message VARCHAR(30) )
4
5    BEGIN
6
7        DECLARE from_account_balance     NUMERIC(8,2);
8        DECLARE from_account_balance2    NUMERIC(8,2);
9        DECLARE from_account_timestamp1 TIMESTAMP;
10       DECLARE from_account_timestamp2 TIMESTAMP;
11
12       SELECT account_timestamp,balance
13         INTO from_account_timestamp1,from_account_balance
14         FROM account_balance
15        WHERE account_id=from_account;
16
17       IF (from_account_balance>=tfer_amount) THEN
18
19         -- Here we perform some long running validation that
20         -- might take a few minutes */
21         CALL long_running_validation(from_account);
22
23         START TRANSACTION;
24
25         -- Make sure the account row has not been updated since
26         -- our initial check
27         SELECT account_timestamp, balance
28           INTO from_account_timestamp2,from_account_balance2
29           FROM account_balance
30          WHERE account_id=from_account
31            FOR UPDATE;
32
33         IF (from_account_timestamp1 <> from_account_timestamp2 OR
34             from_account_balance    <> from_account_balance2)  THEN
35           ROLLBACK;
36           SET status=-1;
37           SET message=CONCAT("Transaction cancelled due to concurrent update",
38                             " of account"  ,from_account);
39         ELSE
40            UPDATE account_balance
41               SET balance=balance-tfer_amount
```

Example 8-12. Optimistic locking strategy (continued)

```
42          WHERE account_id=from_account;
43
44       UPDATE account_balance
45          SET balance=balance+tfer_amount
46        WHERE account_id=to_account;
47
48       COMMIT;
49
50       SET status=0;
51       SET message="OK";
52     END IF;
53
54   ELSE
55     ROLLBACK;
56     SET status=-1;
57     SET message="Insufficient funds";
58   END IF;
59 END$$
```

Optimistic locking strategies are often employed by transactions that involve user inter-action, since there is sometimes the chance that a user will "go to lunch," leaving a pes-simistic lock in place for an extended period. Since stored programs do not involve direct user interaction, optimistic strategies in stored programs are not required for this reason. However, an optimistic strategy might still be selected as a means of reducing overall lock duration and improving application throughput—at the cost of occasion-ally having to retry the transaction when the optimism is misplaced.

Choosing between strategies

Don't choose between optimistic and pessimistic strategies based on your personal-ity or disposition. Just because your analyst assures you that you are a fairly fun-lov-ing, optimistic guy or gal, that does not mean you should affirm this by always choosing the optimistic locking strategy!

The choice between the two strategies is based on a trade-off between concurrency and robustness: pessimistic locking is less likely to require transaction retries or fail-ures, while optimistic locking minimizes the duration of locks, thus improving con-currency and transaction throughput. Usually, we choose optimistic locking only if the duration of the locks or the number of rows locked by the pessimistic solution would be unacceptable.

Transaction Design Guidelines

A well-designed transaction should have the following properties:

- The integrity of the database will be maintained at all times.
- The duration and coverage of locks will be minimized. Locks should be applied to as few rows as possible and maintained for the shortest possible duration.

- Rollbacks will be minimal—transactions that eventually issue a rollback have needlessly consumed resources.

- User expectations about the persistence of data will be met. For instance, a user who clicks a Save or Apply button has a reasonable expectation that the data will not disappear if he subsequently clicks Cancel on another page.

To achieve these goals, we recommend the following general guidelines for transaction design:

Keep transactions small
> A transaction should generally include as small a logical unit of work as possible to reduce the duration of locks.

Avoid a transaction design that encourages rollbacks
> For instance, rather than trying an insert and rolling back if there is a "duplicate key" error, check for the existence of the key value before issuing the DML.

Avoid savepoints whenever possible
> The existence of a savepoint may indicate that you have failed to check for success criteria before issuing a DML statement and may indicate a transaction design that encourages rollbacks.

By default, rely on a pessimistic locking strategy
> Lock rows that you SELECT if the results of the SELECT statement affect DML executed later in the transaction. Pessimistic locking is easy to implement and is a robust solution. However, issue SELECTs with FOR UPDATE as late in the transaction as possible to minimize duration of locks.

Consider optimistic locking for throughput-critical transactions
> Optimistic locking requires more coding (to handle failed transactions) and may lead to user frustration if the optimism is misplaced. However, optimistic locking can reduce lock duration and thereby increase throughput for high-volume transactions.

Explicitly commence transactions and avoid leaving transactions "dangling"
> Stored programs that issue transactional statements should generally take responsibility for commencing and terminating the transaction, rather than assuming that some external program is going to handle a COMMIT or ROLLBACK.

While these are reasonable guidelines, there are sometimes trade-offs that you will need to consider:

- Unlike any other MySQL statement, the COMMIT statement always requires a physical write to disk to complete. Therefore, although it is a good idea in general to commit as soon as some logical unit of work is completed, there is a strong performance incentive to commit infrequently when possible. This usually means that for OLTP operations, you commit when the logical transaction is complete, whereas in batch programs and bulk operations, you commit infrequently. We discuss the performance implications of COMMIT in Chapter 21.

- Checking all possible success criteria before issuing a DML statement might be overly expensive in some cases. It might be preferable to let a DML statement fail and then roll back to a savepoint under certain circumstances.

- The trade-offs for the optimistic and pessimistic locking strategies are heavily dependent on the characteristics of your application.

- Modular design considerations may sometimes lead you to write a stored program in such a way that the control of the overall transaction is delegated to a higher-level program.

Conclusion

In this chapter we looked at how to manage transactions in MySQL stored programs, allowing us to group together related database changes, applying them all or aborting them all as a single logical unit. Implementing transactions using stored programs is a fairly natural choice, since a stored program can encapsulate complex transaction logic into a single database call, providing good separation between database and application logic.

To use transactions in MySQL, you will need to create tables using one of the transactional storage engines—such as the InnoDB engine that ships with the MySQL standard distributions.

By default, transactions are disabled in MySQL; to enable them you need to either set AUTOCOMMIT=0 or (recommended) commence a transaction with the START TRANSACTION statement. Transactions are normally terminated with a COMMIT or ROLLBACK statement, though be aware that certain DDL statements can cause implicit COMMITs to occur.

Savepoints can be used to partially roll back transactions in the event of an error. We believe, however, that the reliance on savepoints is justified in only a very few specific circumstances.

Transactional databases use locking mechanisms to prevent data inconsistencies or logical errors when rows are updated, inserted, and deleted. MySQL/InnoDB minimizes the overhead of these locking mechanisms by using an efficient row-level locking mechanism in which readers never block other readers or writers. Even with this row-level locking, though, you should construct your transactions to minimize the duration of any locks taken out as a result of DML statements or SELECTs with the FOR UPDATE or LOCK IN SHARE MODE clause.

In rare circumstances, errors can occur if a lock timeout is exceeded or if an irresolvable lock conflict arises (a deadlock). There are mechanisms for reducing the frequency with which these occur, but you may want to add exception handlers to your stored programs or restructure them to handle these occurrences.

Whenever you SELECT data that is used to construct DML statements later in a transaction, you need to ensure that the data is not changed between the time it is read and the time the read data is used to modify the database. Locking the data as it is read—a pessimistic locking strategy—is usually the simplest and most robust solution. However, an optimistic locking strategy—in which the data is confirmed just prior to the DML being applied—can reduce the duration of locks and improve transaction throughput in some circumstances.

Good transaction design can improve the reliability, integrity, and performance of your application. In general, transactions—and the duration of locks—should be kept as short as possible. However, the overriding consideration is to maintain data integrity and the reliability of transaction processing.

## CHAPTER 9

MySQL Built-in Functions

This chapter provides a reference to the MySQL built-in functions that you can use in your MySQL stored programs. You can use virtually all of the MySQL functions that are available in SQL statements within stored programs, so if you are already familiar with traditional MySQL functions, you can safely skip this chapter. Because this is a reference chapter, we expect you will come back to it from time to time when you need to use a particular function—so don't feel guilty if you decide to skip or only briefly review this chapter.

In general, you can use any of the standard MySQL functions inside stored programs except those functions that work on groups or sets of data. These functions—often used in combination with the GROUP BY clause in a SQL statement—include MAX, MIN, COUNT, AVERAGE, and SUM. These functions are not applicable in stored programs (other than in SQL statements embedded in the programs) because stored program variables are scalar (consist of only a single value).

This chapter looks at the built-in functions that we anticipate you might want to use in stored programs; we describe these in the following categories:

- String functions
- Numeric functions
- Date and time functions
- Other functions

MySQL includes a huge number of built-in functions, however, so we can't cover all of them in depth; for a complete list, refer to the online *MySQL Reference Manual* (*http://dev.mysql.com/doc/*).

String Functions

String functions perform operations on string data types such as VARCHAR, CHAR, and TEXT.

ASCII

> *string1*=**ASCII**(*string2*)

ASCII returns the ASCII character code corresponding to the first character in the provided input string.

Since the ASCII function returns only the ASCII code for the first character, we can create a stored function to extend this capability to allow us to return the ASCII codes corresponding to all of the characters in the string. Example 9-1 shows an implementation of such a stored function. It uses the LENGTH and SUBSTR functions to extract each character in the input string, and then uses the ASCII and CONCAT functions to build up a string consisting of all of the ASCII codes corresponding to the entire input string.

Example 9-1. Using the ASCII function

```
CREATE FUNCTION ascii_string (in_string VARCHAR(80) )
 RETURNS VARCHAR(256)
 DETERMINISTIC
BEGIN
   DECLARE i INT DEFAULT 1;
      DECLARE string_len INT;
      DECLARE out_string VARCHAR(256) DEFAULT '';

      SET string_len=LENGTH(in_string);
      WHILE (i<string_len) DO
         SET out_string=CONCAT(out_string,ASCII(SUBSTR(in_string,i,1)),' ');
         SET i=i+1;
      END WHILE;
      RETURN (out_string);

END
--------------

Query OK, 0 rows affected (0.00 sec)

--------------
SELECT ascii_string('MySQL Rocks!')
--------------

+---------------------------------------+
| ascii_string('MySQL Rocks!')          |
+---------------------------------------+
| 77 121 83 81 76 32 82 111 99 107 115  |
+---------------------------------------+
1 row in set (0.00 sec)
```

CHAR

> *string*=**CHAR**(*ascii code* [,...])

CHAR returns the characters corresponding to one or more ASCII codes provided. Example 9-2 uses the CHAR function to create a temporary table containing the ASCII characters for the first 128 ASCII codes.

Example 9-2. Using the CHAR function to generate an ASCII chart

```
CREATE PROCEDURE ascii_chart()
BEGIN
        DECLARE i INT DEFAULT 1;

        CREATE TEMPORARY TABLE ascii_chart
            (ascii_code INT, ascii_char CHAR(1));

        WHILE (i<=128) DO
                INSERT INTO ascii_chart VALUES(i,CHAR(i));
                SET i=i+1;
        END WHILE;

END
--------------

Query OK, 0 rows affected (0.01 sec)

--------------
CALL ascii_chart()
--------------

Query OK, 1 row affected (5.96 sec)

--------------
SELECT * FROM ascii_chart
--------------

+------------+------------+
| ascii_code | ascii_char |
+------------+------------+
|          1 | ☺          |
|          2 | ☻          |
|          3 | ♥          |
|          4 | ♦          |
|          5 | ♣          |
|          6 | ♠          |
|          7 |            |
|          8 |            |
|          9 |            |
|         10 |            |
|         11 | ♂          |
|         12 | ♀          |
|         13 |            |
|         14 | ♫          |
|         15 | ☼          |
|         16 | ►          |
|         17 | ◄          |
```

```
|    18 |  ↕       |
|    19 |  ‼       |
|    20 |  ¶       |
|    21 |  §       |
|    22 |  ▬       |
|    23 |  ↨       |
|    24 |  ↑       |
|    25 |  ↓       |
|    26 |  →       |
|    27 |  ←       |
```

CHARSET

```
character_set=CHARSET(string)
```

CHARSET returns the character set of the supplied string.

```
SET var1=CHARSET("My name is Guy") ;      →   latin1
```

CONCAT

```
string1=CONCAT(string2 [,...])
```

CONCAT returns a string consisting of the concatenation of all of the supplied input strings. If any of the input strings is NULL, then CONCAT will also return NULL.

Example 9-3 uses the CONCAT function to create a well-formatted name including—if appropriate—title and middle initial. First, we use the ISNULL function to check for NULLs in the input string so as to avoid inadvertently returning a NULL string if one of the inputs is NULL.

Example 9-3. Using CONCAT to concatenate strings

```
CREATE FUNCTION concat_example(in_title VARCHAR(4),
        in_gender         CHAR(1),
        in_firstname      VARCHAR(20),
        in_middle_initial CHAR(1),
        in_surname        VARCHAR(20))

  RETURNS VARCHAR(60)
BEGIN
  DECLARE l_title        VARCHAR(4);
  DECLARE l_name_string  VARCHAR(60);

  IF ISNULL(in_title)  THEN
     IF in_gender='M' THEN
        SET l_title='Mr';
     ELSE
        SET l_title='Ms';
     END IF;
  END IF;
```

Example 9-3. Using CONCAT to concatenate strings (continued)

```
  IF ISNULL(in_middle_initial) THEN
     SET l_name_string=CONCAT(l_title,' ',in_firstname,' ',in_surname);
  ELSE
     SET l_name_string=CONCAT(l_title,' ',in_firstname,' ',
                            in_middle_initial,' ',in_surname);
  END IF;

  RETURN(l_name_string);
END;
--------------

Query OK, 0 rows affected (0.00 sec)

--------------
SELECT concat_example(null,'F','Mary',null,'Smith')
--------------

+-----------------------------------------------+
| concat_example(null,'F','Mary',null,'Smith') |
+-----------------------------------------------+
| Ms Mary Smith                                 |
+-----------------------------------------------+
1 row in set (0.00 sec)
```

If your database is running in ANSI mode (sql_mode='ANSI') or if the sql_mode variable includes the PIPES_AS_CONCAT setting, you can use the || (pipe) characters to concatenate strings. The use of pipe characters to indicate concatenation in stored programs is dependent on the setting of sql_mode when the stored program is created, not when it runs. So you can happily use the || method of concatenating strings provided that you set sql_mode='ANSI' when you create the program. If the program runs when sql_mode is set to some other value, the stored program will still return the correct results.

Example 9-4 illustrates the use of ANSI mode and || characters to perform string concatenation. Note that while sql_mode was set to 'ANSI' when the stored function was created, the stored program still returned the correct results even though the sql_mode had been set to 'TRADITIONAL' at runtime.

Example 9-4. Using || to concatenate when sql_mode=ANSI

```
set sql_mode='ANSI'
--------------

Query OK, 0 rows affected (0.00 sec)
--------------
CREATE FUNCTION concat_example_ansi(
       in_title          VARCHAR(4),
       in_gender         CHAR(1),
       in_firstname      VARCHAR(20),
```

Example 9-4. Using || to concatenate when sql_mode=ANSI (continued)

```
        in_middle_initial CHAR(1),
        in_surname        VARCHAR(20))

  RETURNS VARCHAR(60)
BEGIN
  DECLARE l_title              VARCHAR(4);
  DECLARE l_name_string        VARCHAR(60);

  IF ISNULL(in_title)  THEN
     IF in_gender='M' THEN
        SET l_title='Mr';
     ELSE
        SET l_title='Ms';
     END IF;
  END IF;

  IF ISNULL(in_middle_initial) THEN
     SET l_name_string=l_title||' '||in_firstname||' '||in_surname;
  ELSE
     SET l_name_string=l_title||' '||in_firstname||' '||
                       in_middle_initial||' '||in_surname;
  END IF;

  RETURN(l_name_string);
END;
--------------


Query OK, 0 rows affected (0.00 sec)


--------------
SET sql_mode='TRADITIONAL'
--------------


Query OK, 0 rows affected (0.00 sec)


--------------
SELECT concat_example_ansi(null,'F','Mary',null,'Smith')
--------------


+---------------------------------------------------+
| concat_example_ansi(null,'F','Mary',null,'Smith') |
+---------------------------------------------------+
| Ms Mary Smith                                     |
+---------------------------------------------------+
```

CONCAT_WS

> *string1*=**CONCAT_WS**(*delimiter*,*string2* [,...])

CONCAT_WS acts like the CONCAT function, but it inserts the specified delimiter between each string. Note in Example 9-3 that we manually inserted single space characters between each string, as shown below:

```
    SET l_name_string=CONCAT(l_title,' ',in_firstname,' ',
                        in_middle_initial,' ',in_surname);
```

Using CONCAT_WS, we could simplify this statement as follows:

```
    SET l_name_string=CONCAT_WS(' ',l_title ,in_firstname ,
                        in_middle_initial,in_surname);
```

INSERT

> *string*=**INSERT**(*original_string,position,length,new_string*)

INSERT inserts *new_string* into the *original_string* at the specified *position*, option-ally overwriting up to *length* characters of the original string.

Example 9-5 shows how we might use the INSERT function to emulate the MySQL REPLACE function to implement "search and replace" functionality. We first use the INSTR function to find the location of the "find string" and then replace it with the "replace string." We set *length* to the length of the find string so that the find string is overwritten with the replace string, even if the two strings are of different lengths.

Example 9-5. Using the INSERT function

```
CREATE FUNCTION my_replace
    (in_string      VARCHAR(255),
     in_find_str    VARCHAR(20),
     in_repl_str    VARCHAR(20))

  RETURNS VARCHAR(255)
BEGIN
  DECLARE l_new_string VARCHAR(255);
  DECLARE l_find_pos   INT;

  SET l_find_pos=INSTR(in_string,in_find_str);

  IF (l_find_pos>0) THEN
    SET l_new_string=INSERT(in_string,l_find_pos,LENGTH(in_find_str),in_repl_str);
  ELSE
    SET l_new_string=in_string;
  END IF;
  RETURN(l_new_string);

END
-------------

Query OK, 0 rows affected (0.00 sec)

-------------
SELECT my_replace('We love the Oracle server','Oracle','MySQL')
-------------

+----------------------------------------------------------+
| my_replace('We love the Oracle server','Oracle','MySQL') |
```

Example 9-5. Using the INSERT function (continued)

```
+------------------------------------------------------------+
| We love the MySQL server                                   |
+------------------------------------------------------------+
1 row in set (0.00 sec)
```

INSTR

> *position*=**INSTR**(*string*,*substring*)

INSTR returns the location of the first occurrence of a substring within a string. If no occurrence of the substring is found, INSTR returns 0.

In Example 9-5 we used INSTR to locate the "find string" within a string prior to using INSERT to replace that string with the "replace string."

LCASE

> *string1*=**LCASE**(*string2*)

LCASE returns an input string with any of its uppercase letters translated to lowercase. Nonalphabetic characters are ignored.

Here are some examples of the effect of LCASE:

```
SET a=LCASE('McTavish Jewelers');      →  'mctavish jewelers'
SET b=LCASE('23rd June');              →  '23rd june'
```

LEFT

> *string*=**LEFT**(*string2*,*length*)

LEFT returns the leftmost characters (the number is specified by *length*) in the input string.

```
SET a=LEFT('Hi There',2);  →  'Hi'
```

LENGTH

> *characters*=**LENGTH**(*string*)

LENGTH returns the number of bytes in the input string. For single-byte character sets (e.g., English, Swedish), this is equivalent to the number of characters in the string. However, for multibyte character sets (e.g., Kanji, Klingon), you may be better off using the CHAR_LENGTH function, which returns the number of characters rather than the number of bytes.

```
SET a=LENGTH(null);    →  NULL
SET b=LENGTH('');      →  0
SET c=LENGTH('Guy');   →  3
SET d=LENGTH('Guy ');  →  4
```

LOAD_FILE

> *string=***LOAD_FILE**(*file_name*)

LOAD_FILE loads the contents of the specified file into a variable of a suitable data type—usually BLOB or TEXT. The file has to be accessible to the MySQL server—that is, the file needs to exist on the machine that hosts the MySQL server, and the server needs to have sufficient permissions to read the file.

Example 9-6 shows how we can use the LOAD_FILE function to load the contents of an operating system file and report the number of bytes loaded. Note that on Windows we need to use double-backslash characters, \\, instead of single slashes as directory separators. Thus, in order to specify the file 'c:\tmp\mydata.txt' we specified 'c:\\tmp\\mydata.txt'.

Example 9-6. Using LOAD_FILE to read an OS file

```
CREATE PROCEDURE filesize(in_file_name VARCHAR(128))

BEGIN
  DECLARE mytext TEXT;
  SET mytext=LOAD_FILE(in_file_name);
  SELECT in_file_name||' contains '||length(mytext)||' bytes'
      AS output;
END
--------------

Query OK, 0 rows affected (0.00 sec)

--------------
CALL filesize('c:\\tmp\\mydata.txt')
--------------

+------------------------------------+
| output                             |
+------------------------------------+
| c:\tmp\mydata.txt contains 98 bytes |
+------------------------------------+
1 row in set (0.02 sec)
```

LOCATE

> *position=***LOCATE**(*substring, string* [,*start_position*])

LOCATE is similar to the INSTR function in that it searches for the location of a substring within a string. However, it also allows us to specify a starting position for the search. If the substring is not found, LOCATE returns 0.

In Example 9-7 we use LOCATE to count the number of occurrences of a substring within a string. Once we find an instance of the substring, we set the starting position to just past that string and repeat until all instances of the substring have been found.

Example 9-7. Using LOCATE to find substrings

```
CREATE FUNCTION count_strings
      (in_string VARCHAR(256),in_substr VARCHAR(128))
  RETURNS INT
  DETERMINISTIC
BEGIN
  DECLARE l_count INT DEFAULT 0;
  DECLARE l_start INT DEFAULT 1;
  DECLARE l_pos   INT;

  MainLoop:
  LOOP
    SET l_pos=LOCATE(in_substr,in_string,l_start);
    IF l_pos=0 THEN
       LEAVE MainLoop;
    ELSE
      SET l_count=l_count+1;
      SET l_start=l_pos+1;
    END IF;

  END LOOP;
  RETURN(l_count);
END
--------------

Query OK, 0 rows affected (0.00 sec)

--------------
SELECT count_strings('She sells sea shells by the sea shore','sea') as count
--------------

+-------+
| count |
+-------+
|     2 |
+-------+
1 row in set (0.00 sec)
```

LPAD

> *string1=**LPAD**(string2,length,pad)*

LPAD adds occurrences of the *pad* string to the input string until the output string reaches the specified *length*.

```
SET a=LPAD('Hello',10,'.');  →  '.....Hello'
SET b=lpad('hi',10,'()');    →  '()()()()hi'
```

LTRIM

> *string1=**LTRIM**(string2)*

LTRIM trims any leading spaces from a string.

```
SET a=LTRIM('    Hello');  →  'Hello'
```

REPEAT

> *string1*=**REPEAT**(*string2*,*count*)

REPEAT returns a string in which the input string is repeated *count* times.

    SET a=REPEAT('Dive! ',3);   →   'Dive! Dive! Dive!'

REPLACE

> *string1*=**REPLACE**(*string2*,*search_string*,*replace_string*)

REPLACE returns a string in which all occurrences of the *search_string* are replaced by the *replace_string*.

    SET a=REPLACE('Monty & David','&','and');   →   'Monty and David'

RPAD

> *string1*=**RPAD**(*string2*,*length*,*pad*)

RPAD adds a sequence of *pad* characters to the string up to the specified *length*.

    SET var1=RPAD("MySQL",10,".") ;   →   MySQL.....

RTRIM

> *string1*=**RTRIM**(*string2*)

RTRIM trims any trailing spaces from a string.

    SET a=RTRIM('Guy   '); → 'Guy'

STRCMP

> *position*=**STRCMP**(*string1*,*string2*)

STRCMP compares two strings and determines if the first string is "before" or "after" the second string in the ASCII collation sequence. The function returns -1 if the first string is before the second string, 1 if the first string collates after the second string, and 0 if the two strings are identical.

    SET a=STRCMP('Guy','Guy')   →   0
    SET b=STRCMP('Guy','Steven')   → -1
    SET c=STRCMP('Steven','Guy')   →   1

SUBSTRING

> *string1*=**SUBSTRING**(*string2*, *position* [,*length*])

SUBSTRING returns a portion of the supplied string starting at the specified *position* from the beginning of the string (starting at 1). If a negative position is specified, then the substring commences from the end of the string; for example, -2 indicates the second to last character of the string. If *length* is omitted, SUBSTRING returns all of the remaining portion of the input string.

```
SET a=SUBSTR('MySQL AB',7)     → 'AB'
SET b=SUBSTR('MySQL AB',-2)    → 'AB'
SET c=SUBSTR('MySQL AB',3,3)   → 'SQL'
```

TRIM

> *string1*=TRIM([[BOTH|LEADING|TRAILING] [*padding*] FROM]*string2*)

TRIM strips leading and/or trailing characters from a string. By default, it trims both leading and trailing spaces.

```
SET a=TRIM(LEADING '>' FROM '>>>>>>>>>Fred');          → 'Fred'
SET b=TRIM(BOTH '-' FROM '---------Fred-------');      → 'Fred'
SET c=TRIM(BOTH FROM '        Guy          ')          → 'Guy';
SET d=TRIM('          Guy            ');               → 'Guy'
```

UCASE

> *string1*=**UCASE**(*string2*)

UCASE converts a string to uppercase.

Other String Functions

Table 9-1 lists the string functions not covered in previous sections. Some of these functions are aliases for functions we have already discussed, while others are rarely used in mainstream MySQL programming. You can find out more about these functions by reading the section "Functions and Operators" in the *MySQL Reference Manual*, available online.

Table 9-1. Additional string functions

Function	Syntax	Description
BINARY	*string1*=BINARY(*string2*)	Returns the binary representation of a string. This function can be used to force case-sensitive comparisons when they would otherwise not occur.
BIT_LENGTH	*bits*=BIT_LENGTH(*string*)	Returns the number of bits in a string.
CHAR_LENGTH	*length*=CHAR_LENGTH(*string*)	Returns the number of characters in a string. Like LENGTH, except that it returns the number of characters, rather than the number of bytes, for multibyte character sets.
CHARACTER_LENGTH	*length*=CHARACTER_LENGTH(*string*)	Alias for CHAR_LENGTH.
COMPRESS	*string1*=COMPRESS(*string2*)	Returns a compressed version of a string.

Table 9-1. Additional string functions (continued)

Function	Syntax	Description
DECODE	*string1*=DECODE(*string2*,*password*)	Decrypts a string that has been encrypted with ENCRYPT.
ELT	*string1*=ELT(*number*,*string2*[,...])	Returns one of the elements in a list.
ENCODE	*string1*=ENCODE(*string2*,*password*)	Encrypts a string. The string can be decrypted with DECODE.
ENCRYPT	*string1*=ENCRYPT(*string2*,*seed*)	Encrypts a string. The string cannot be decrypted with DECODE.
EXPORT_SET	*string*=ENCODE_SET(*number*,*on_string*, *off_string*,*seperator*,*no_of_bits*)	Returns the binary representation of a number encoded with strings for on and off bits.
FIELD	*number*=FIELD(*string1*,*string2*[,...])	Searches for a string in a list of strings.
INET_ATON	*number*=INET_ATON(*IPAddress*)	Converts an IP address into a numeric representation.
INET_NTOA	*IPAddress*=INET_NTOA(*number*)	Converts a number into a corresponding IP address.
LOWER	*string1*=LOWER(*string2*)	Synonym for LCASE.
MID	*string1*=MID(*string2*,*start* [,*length*])	Returns a substring. Similar to SUBSTR.
OCTET_LENGTH	*length*=OCTET_LENGTH(*string*)	Alias for LENGTH.
ORD	*position*=ORD(*string*)	Returns the ordinal value of the character in the ASCII character set.
PASSWORD	*string1*=PASSWORD(*string2*)	Encrypts the given string as a MySQL password.
POSITION	*position*=POSITION(*substring* IN *string*)	Returns the position of the substring in the string. Similar to LOCATE.
QUOTE	*string1*=QUOTE(*string2*)	Returns a string with special characters preceded by an escape character.
REVERSE	*string1*=REVERSE(*string2*)	Reverses the order of characters in a string.
RIGHT	*string1*=RIGHT(*string2*,*length*)	Returns the rightmost portion of a string.
SHA	*string1*=SHA(*string2*)	Returns a 160-bit Secure Hash Algorithm (SHA) checksum for the string.
SHA1	*string1*=SHA1(*string2*)	Alias for SHA.
SOUNDEX	*string1*=SOUNDEX(*string2*)	Returns the SOUNDEX for a string. In theory, two strings that "sound alike" will have similar SOUNDEX values.
SPACE	*spaces*=SPACE(*count*)	Returns the specified number of space characters.
SUBSTRING_INDEX	*string1*=SUBSTRING_INDEX(*string2*, *delimiter*,*count*)	Returns a string from a character-delimited set of strings.
UNCOMPRESSED_ LENGTH	*length*=UNCOMPRESSED_ LENGTH(*compressed_string*)	Returns the length of a compressed string as if it were decompressed.

Table 9-1. Additional string functions (continued)

Function	Syntax	Description
UNCOMPRESS	*string1*=UNCOMPRESS(*string2*)	Reverses the effect of COMPRESS.
UNHEX	*character*=UNHEX(*HexNumber*)	Converts a hexadecimal number to its ASCII equivalent.
UPPER	*string1*=UPPER(*string2*)	Converts a string to uppercase. Synonym for UCASE.

Numeric Functions

Numeric functions perform operations on numeric data types such as INT and FLOAT.

ABS

```
number1=ABS(number2)
```

ABS returns the absolute value of a number—that is, the magnitude of the value ignoring any minus sign.

```
SET var1=ABS(2.143);      →   2.143
SET var2=ABS(-10);        →   10
SET var3=ABS(10);         →   10
SET var4=ABS(-2.3);       →   2.3
```

BIN

```
binary_number=BIN(decimal_number)
```

BIN returns the binary (base 2) representation of an integer value.

```
SET var1=BIN(1);     →   1
SET var2=BIN(2);     →   10
SET var3=BIN(3);     →   11
SET var4=BIN(45);    →   101101
```

CEILING

```
number1=CEILING(number2)
```

CEILING returns the next integer number that is higher than the input floating-point number.

```
SET var1=CEILING(3.5);     →   4
SET var2=CEILING(-3.5);    →   -3
```

CONV

```
number1=CONV(number2,from_base,to_base)
```

CONV converts numbers from one base system to another. Although CONV is, in essence, a numeric function, it may return values that you may need to deal with as strings (e.g., hexadecimal numbers).

The following CONV statements convert the number 45 (base 10) into binary (base 2), hexadecimal (base 16), and octal (base 8):

```
SET var1=CONV(45,10,2);     →   101101
SET var2=CONV(45,10,16);    →   2D
SET var3=CONV(45,10,8) ;    →   55
```

These statements convert the number 45 (base 2) into base 10, and converts 45 (base 8) into base 2:

```
SET var4=CONV(101101,2,10);   →   45
SET var5=CONV(55,8,2);        →   101101
```

FLOOR

```
number1=FLOOR(number2)
```

FLOOR returns the largest integer value not greater than *X*.

```
SET var1=FLOOR(3.5);     →   3
SET var2=FLOOR(-3.5);    →   -4
```

FORMAT

```
string=FORMAT(number,decimal_places)
```

FORMAT returns a string representation of a number with comma separators at each thousand and with the specified number of decimal places.

```
SET var1=FORMAT(21321.3424,2);     →   21,321.34
```

HEX

```
HexNumber=HEX(DecimalNumber)
```

HEX returns the hexadecimal representation of a number.

```
SET var1=HEX(9);     →   9
SET var2=HEX(11);    →   B
SET var3=HEX(32);    →   20
```

LEAST

```
number1=LEAST(number, number2 [,..])
```

LEAST returns the number in the input series with the smallest numerical value.

```
SET var1=LEAST(32,432,-2,-1.4);     →   -2
```

MOD

```
remainder=MOD(numerator,denominator)
```

MOD returns the remainder (modulus) when the first number is divided by the second number.

MOD is particularly handy when you want something to happen at regular intervals in a loop. For instance, Example 9-8 purges (deletes) rows from the LOG_ARCHIVE table based on some criteria. As we discuss in Chapter 22, reducing commit frequency is an important optimization for transactional storage engines such as InnoDB. However, we do want to commit at regular intervals; otherwise, we risk losing all the work if the program fails midway through execution.

So Example 9-8 calculates the modulus of the delete count divided by 100. If this modulus is 0—which happens every 100 rows—a COMMIT is issued. The end result is that the program commits the delete operations every 100 rows.

Example 9-8. Using the MOD function to perform periodic COMMITs

```
CREATE PROCEDURE bulk_processing_example( )
  MODIFIES SQL DATA
BEGIN
  DECLARE delete_count INT DEFAULT 0;
  DECLARE last_row     INT DEFAULT 0;
  DECLARE l_rec_id     INT;

  DECLARE c1 CURSOR FOR SELECT rec_id FROM log_archive;

  DECLARE CONTINUE HANDLER FOR NOT FOUND SET last_row=1;

  OPEN c1;
MainLoop:
LOOP
    FETCH c1 INTO l_rec_id;
    IF last_row THEN
      LEAVE MainLoop;
    END IF;
    IF purge_due(l_rec_id) THEN
      DELETE FROM log_archive WHERE rec_id=l_rec_id;
      SET delete_count=delete_count+1;
      IF MOD(delete_count,100)=0 THEN
        COMMIT;
      END IF;
    END IF;
  END LOOP MainLoop;
  CLOSE c1;

END;
```

You can also calculate a modulus using *numerator%denominator* or *numerator* MOD *denominator*. Thus, these three assignments are all equivalent:

```
SET var1=MOD(5,3);      →   2
SET var2=5%3;           →   2
SET var3=5 MOD 3 ;      →   2
```

POWER

*result=**POWER**(number,power)*

POWER returns the result of raising the first number to the power of the second number. You can use POW as a synonym for POWER.

```
SET var1=POWER(3,2);     →   9 (3*3)
SET var2=POWER(2,3);     →   8 (2*2*2)
SET var3=POWER(4,.5);    →   2 (square root of 4)
SET var4=POWER(10,-2);   →   0.01
SET var5=POWER(10,-3);   →   0.001
SET var6=POW(2,2);       →   4
```

RAND

*number=**RAND**([seed])*

RAND returns a random floating-point number between 0 and 1. If *seed* is specified, it is used to initialize the random-number generator, which lets you avoid generating repeatable sequences.

```
SET var1=RAND();     →   0.86494333191304
SET var2=RAND();     →   0.96148952838172
SET var3=RAND(5);    →   0.40613597483014
SET var4=RAND();     →   0.21261767690314
SET var5=RAND(5) ;   →   0.40613597483014
SET var6=RAND();     →   0.17861983010417
```

RAND can be used within stored programs to generate or select random table data. For instance, in Example 9-9, we use the RAND function to randomly select the employee of the week (and you thought we based it on performance!). We first find the maximum employee_id and then generate a random number between 1 and that number. Since RAND returns a floating-point number between 0 and 1, we multiply that number by the maximum employee number, generating a number between 0 and the maximum employee number. Next, we use FLOOR to convert the number to an integer value, and then add 1 to avoid generating an employee_id of 0.

Example 9-9. Using the RAND function to retrieve random rows

```
CREATE PROCEDURE select_winner()
  READS SQL DATA
BEGIN
  DECLARE winner_id INT;
  DECLARE max_employee_id INT;
  DECLARE winner_name VARCHAR(70);

  SELECT MAX(employee_id)
```

Example 9-9. Using the RAND function to retrieve random rows (continued)

```
    INTO max_employee_id
    FROM employees;

  SET winner_id=FLOOR(RAND( )*max_employee_id)+1;

  SELECT CONCAT_WS(' ','Employee of the week is',firstname,surname)
    FROM employees
   WHERE employee_id=winner_id;
END;
```

ROUND

> *integer=*ROUND(*number* [*,decimals*])

ROUND converts a floating-point number to the nearest integer value or—if the second argument is specified—to the specified number of decimal points.

```
SET var1=PI( );            →   3.141593
SET var2=ROUND(PI( ));     →   3
SET var3=ROUND(PI( ),4);   →   3.1416
SET var5=ROUND(4.49);      →   4
SET var6=ROUND(4.51);      →   5
```

SIGN

> *number1=*SIGN(*number2*)

SIGN returns -1 if a number is less than 0, 0 if the number is 0, and 1 if the number is greater than 0.

```
SET var1=SIGN(-5);   →   -1
SET var2=SIGN(0);    →   0
SET var3=SIGN(5);    →   1
```

SQRT

> *number1=*SQRT(*number2*)

SQRT returns the square root of a number. It is equivalent to POWER(*number*,.5).

```
SET var1=SQRT(4);        →   2
SET var2=SQRT(64);       →   8
SET var3=POWER(64,.5);   →   8
```

Other Numeric Functions

Table 9-2 lists additional numeric functions. These functions are rarely used in mainstream MySQL applications; in this category are the trigonometric and logarithmic functions that you probably studied in high school and have never used since!

Table 9-2. Additional numeric functions

Function	Syntax	Description
ACOS	*number1*=ACOS(*number2*)	Arc cosine of a number.
ASIN	*number1*=ASIN(*number2*)	Arc sine of a number.
ATAN	*number1*=ATAN(*number2*)	Arc tangent of a number.
COT	*number1*=COT(*number2*)	Cotangent of a number.
CRC32	*number*=CRC32(*string*)	Cyclic redundancy check value for a string.
DEGREES	*degrees*=DEGREES(*radians*)	Converts radians to degrees.
EXP	*number1*=EXP(*number2*)	Natural logarithm (base *e*) to the power of a number.
LN	*number1*=LN(*number2*)	Natural logarithm of a number.
LOG	*number1*=LOG(*number2*,*base*)	Logarithm of a number in the base specified.
LOG10	*number*=LOG10(*number2*)	Base 10 logarithm of a number.
LOG2	*number1*=LOG2(*number*)	Base 2 logarithm of a number.
PI	*number*=PI( )	Returns the value of PI.
RADIANS	*radians*=RADIANS(*degrees*)	Converts radians to degrees.
SIN	*number1*=SIN(*number2*)	Sine of a number (expressed in radians).
TAN	*number1*=TAN(*number2*)	Tangent of a number expressed in radians.

Date and Time Functions

Date and time functions operate on MySQL date-time data types such as DATE and DATETIME.

ADDTIME

> *date1*=**ADDTIME**(*date2*,*time_interval*)

ADDTIME adds the specified time interval to the date-time provided and returns the amended date. Time intervals are specified in the format *hh:mm:ss.hh*, so you can add any time interval down to one-hundredth of a second.

```
SET var1=NOW( );                          →   2005-07-21 18:56:46
SET var2=ADDTIME(NOW( ),"0:00:01.00");    →   2005-07-21 18:56:47
SET var3=ADDTIME(NOW( ),"0:01:00.00");    →   2005-07-21 18:57:46
SET var4=ADDTIME(NOW( ),"1:00:00.00") ;   →   2005-07-21 19:56:46
```

CONVERT_TZ

> *datetime1*=**CONVERT_TZ**(*datetime2*,*fromTZ*,*toTZ*)

This function converts a date-time value from one time zone to another. The valid time zone values can be found in the table mysql.time_zone_name.

You may have to load the MySQL time zone tables; for instructions, see the MySQL manual section "MySQL Server Time Zone Support."

CURRENT_DATE

date=**CURRENT_DATE**( )

CURRENT_DATE returns the current date. It does not show the time.

```
SET var1=CURRENT_DATE();    →  2005-07-21
```

CURRENT_TIME

time=**CURRENT_TIME**( )

CURRENT_TIME returns the current time. It does not show the date.

```
SET var1=CURRENT_TIME();    →  22:12:21
```

CURRENT_TIMESTAMP

timestamp=**CURRENT_TIMESTAMP**( )

CURRENT_TIMESTAMP returns the current date and time in the format *yyyy-mm-dd hh:mm:ss*.

```
SET var1=CURRENT_TIMESTAMP();    →  2005-07-21 22:15:02
```

DATE

date=**DATE**(*datetime*)

DATE returns the date part of a date-time value.

```
SET var1=NOW();         →  2005-07-23 12:08:52
SET var2=DATE(var1) ;   →  2005-07-23
```

DATE_ADD

date1=**DATE_ADD**(*date2*, INTERVAL *interval_value interval_type*)

DATE_ADD returns the date-time that results from adding the specified interval to the date-time provided. Possible intervals are listed in Table 9-3.

```
SET var1=NOW();                                        →  2005-07-20 22:33:21
SET var2=DATE_ADD(NOW(), INTERVAL 7 DAY);              →  2005-07-27 22:33:21
SET var3=DATE_ADD(NOW(), INTERVAL 0623 DAY_HOUR) ;     →  2005-08-15 21:33:21
SET var4=DATE_ADD(NOW(), INTERVAL 06235959 DAY_SECOND) ; →  2005-10-01 02:46:00
SET var5=DATE_ADD(NOW(), INTERVAL 2 MONTH);            →  2005-09-20 22:33:21
SET var6=DATE_ADD(NOW(), INTERVAL 10 YEAR);            →  2015-07-20 22:33:21
SET var7=DATE_ADD(NOW(), INTERVAL 3600 SECOND);        →  2005-07-20 23:33:21
```

Table 9-3. Date-time formats for DATE_ADD and DATE_SUB

Interval name	Interval format
DAY	*dd*
DAY_HOUR	*ddhh*
DAY_MINUTE	*dd hh:mm*
DAY_SECOND	*dd hh:mm:ss*
HOUR	*hh*
HOUR_MINUTE	*hh:mm*
HOUR_SECOND	*hh:mm:ss*
MINUTE	*mm*
MINUTE_SECOND	*mm:ss*
MONTH	*mm*
SECOND	*ss*
YEAR	*yyyy*

DATE_FORMAT

```
string=DATE_FORMAT(datetime,FormatCodes)
```

DATE_FORMAT accepts a date-time value and returns a string representation of the date in the desired format. Format codes are shown in Table 9-4.

```
SET var1=NOW( );                              →   2005-07-23 13:28:21
SET var2=DATE_FORMAT(NOW( ),"%a %d %b %y");   →   Sat 23 Jul 05
SET var3=DATE_FORMAT(NOW( ),"%W, %D %M %Y");  →   Saturday, 23rd July 2005
SET var4=DATE_FORMAT(NOW( ),"%H:%i:%s") ;     →   13:28:21
SET var5=DATE_FORMAT(NOW( ),"%T");            →   13:28:21
SET var6=DATE_FORMAT(NOW( ),"%r");            →   01:28:22 PM
```

Table 9-4. Format codes for DATE_FORMAT

Code	Explanation
%%	The % sign
%a	Short day of the week (Mon-Sun)
%b	Short month name (Jan-Feb)
%c	Month number (1-12)
%d	Day of the month (1-31)
%D	Day of the month with suffix (1st, 2nd, 3rd, etc.)
%e	Day of the month, numeric (1-31)
%h	12-hour clock hour of the day (1-12)
%H	24-hour clock hour of the day (00-23)

Table 9-4. Format codes for DATE_FORMAT (continued)

Code	Explanation
%i	Minute of the hour (00...59)
%I	12-hour clock hour of the day (1-12)
%j	Day of the year (1-365)
%k	24-hour clock hour of the day (00-23)
%l	12-hour clock hour of the day (1-12)
%m	Month of the year (1-12)
%M	Long month name (January-December)
%p	AM/PM
%r	Hour, minute, and second of the day, 12-hour format (*hh:mm:ss* AM|PM)
%s	Seconds within a minute (0-59)
%S	Seconds within a minute (0-59)
%T	Hour, minute, and second of the day, 24-hour format (*HH:mm:ss*)
%u	Week of the year (0-52) (Monday is the first day of the week)
%U	Week of the year (0-52) (Sunday is the first day of the week)
%v	Week of the year (1-53) (Monday is the first day of the week)
%V	Week of the year (1-53) (Sunday is the first day of the week)
%w	Numeric day of the week (0=Sunday, 6=Saturday)
%W	Long weekday name (Sunday, Saturday)
%y	Year, numeric, 2 digits
%Y	Year, numeric, 4 digits

DATE_SUB

```
date1=DATE_SUB(date2, INTERVAL interval_value interval_type)
```

DATE_SUB returns the date-time resulting from subtracting the specified interval from the date-time provided. Possible intervals are listed in Table 9-3.

Example 9-10 shows a stored procedure that determines if an employee's date of birth indicates an age of greater than 18 years. DATE_SUB is used to create a date 18 years earlier than the current date. This date is compared to the date of birth and, if it is earlier, we can conclude that the employee is less than 18 years old.

Example 9-10. Using DATE_SUB

```
CREATE PROCEDURE validate_age
    (in_dob DATE,
     OUT status_code INT,
     OUT status_message VARCHAR(30))
BEGIN
```

Example 9-10. Using DATE_SUB (continued)

```
  IF DATE_SUB(now( ), INTERVAL 18 YEAR) <in_dob THEN
    SET status_code=-1;
    SET status_message="Error: employee is less than 18 years old";
  ELSE
    SET status_code=0;
    SET status_message="OK";
  END IF;
END;
```

DATEDIFF

> *days=***DATEDIFF***(date1,date2)*

DATEDIFF returns the number of days between two dates. If *date2* is greater than *date1*, then the result will be negative; otherwise, it will be positive.

Example 9-11 uses DATEDIFF to calculate the number of days that have elapsed since a bill due date, and returns appropriate status and messages if the bill is more than 30 or 90 days old.

Example 9-11. Using DATEDIFF

```
CREATE PROCEDURE check_billing_status
    (in_due_date DATE,
     OUT status_code INT,
     OUT status_message VARCHAR(30))
BEGIN
  DECLARE days_past_due INT;

  SET days_past_due=FLOOR(DATEDIFF(now( ),in_due_date));
  IF days_past_due>90 THEN
    SET status_code=-2;
    SET status_message='Bill more than 90 days overdue';
  ELSEIF days_past_due >30 THEN
    SET status_code=-1;
    SET status_message='Bill more than 30 days overdue';
  ELSE
    SET status_code=0;
    SET status_message='OK';

  END IF;
END;
```

DAY

> *day=***DAY***(date)*

DAY returns the day of the month (in numeric format) for the specified date.

```
    SET var1=NOW( );        →   2005-07-23 13:47:13
    SET var2=DAY(NOW( ));    →   23
```

DAYNAME

*day=***DAYNAME**(*date*)

DAYNAME returns the day of the week—as in Sunday, Monday, etc.—for the specified date.

```
SET var1=NOW( );              →  2005-07-23 13:50:02
SET var2=DAYNAME(NOW( ));     →  Saturday
```

DAYOFWEEK

*day=***DAYOFWEEK**(*date*)

DAYOFWEEK returns the day of the week as a number, where 1 returns Sunday.

```
SET var1=NOW( );                            →  2005-07-23 13:53:07
SET var2=DATE_FORMAT(NOW( ),"%W, %D %M %Y"); →  Saturday, 23rd July 2005
SET var3=DAYOFWEEK(NOW( ));                  →  7
```

DAYOFYEAR

*day=***DAYOFYEAR**(*date*)

DAYOFYEAR returns the day of the year as a number, where 1-JAN returns 1 and 31-DEC returns 365 (except in leap years, where it returns 366).

```
SET var1=NOW( );              →  2005-07-23 13:55:57
SET var2=DAYOFYEAR(NOW( ));   →  204
```

EXTRACT

*date_part=***EXTRACT**(*interval_name* FROM *date*)

EXTRACT returns a specified portion of a date-time. The applicable intervals are shown in Table 9-3.

```
SET var1=NOW( );                          →  2005-07-23 14:01:03
SET var2=EXTRACT(HOUR FROM NOW( ));       →  14
SET var3=EXTRACT(YEAR FROM NOW( ));       →  2005
SET var4=EXTRACT(MONTH FROM NOW( ));      →  7
SET var5=EXTRACT(HOUR_SECOND FROM NOW( )); →  140103
SET var6=EXTRACT(DAY_MINUTE FROM NOW( ));  →  231401
```

GET_FORMAT

*format=***GET_FORMAT**(*datetime_type*,*locale*)

GET_FORMAT returns a set of date formatting code—suitable for use with DATE_FORMAT—for various date-time types and locales.

Format type can be one of the following:

- DATE
- TIME
- DATETIME
- TIMESTAMP

Format code can be one of the following:

- INTERNAL
- ISO
- JIS
- USA
- EUR

```
SET var1=GET_FORMAT(DATE,"USA");                        →   %m.%d.%Y
SET var2=GET_FORMAT(DATE,"ISO");                        →   %Y-%m-%d
SET var3=GET_FORMAT(DATETIME,"JIS") ;                   →   %Y-%m-%d %H:%i:%s
SET var4=NOW( );                                        →   2005-07-24 13:27:58
SET var5=DATE_FORMAT(NOW( ),GET_FORMAT(DATE,"USA"));    →   07.24.2005
```

MAKEDATE

date=**MAKEDATE**(*year*,*day*)

MAKEDATE takes the year (YYYY) and day-of-year arguments and converts them to a date value. The day-of-year argument is in the form that would be returned by DAYOFYEAR.

```
SET var1=MAKEDATE(2006,1);      →   2006-01-01
SET var2=MAKEDATE(2006,365);    →   2006-12-31
SET var3=MAKEDATE(2006,200);    →   2006-07-19
```

MAKETIME

time=**MAKETIME**(*hour*,*minute*,*second*)

MAKETIME takes the hour, minute, and second arguments and returns a time value.

```
SET var4=MAKETIME(16,30,25);    →   16:30:25
SET var5=MAKETIME(0,0,0);       →   00:00:00
SET var6=MAKETIME(23,59,59);    →   23:59:59
```

MONTHNAME

monthname=**MONTHNAME**(*date*)

MONTHNAME returns the full name of the month corresponding to the provided date.

```
SET var1=NOW( );                →   2005-07-24 13:44:54
SET var2=MONTHNAME(NOW( ));      →   July
```

NOW

*datetime=*NOW( )

NOW returns the current date and time. We have used this function in many previous examples as input to date and time functions.

SEC_TO_TIME

*time=*SEC_TO_TIME(*seconds*)

SEC_TO_TIME returns a time value for a given number of seconds. The time is shown in hours, minutes, and seconds.

```
SET var1=SEC_TO_TIME(1);              →   00:00:01
SET var2=SEC_TO_TIME(3600);           →   01:00:00
SET var3=SEC_TO_TIME(10*60*60);       →   10:00:00
```

STR_TO_DATE

*date=*STR_TO_DATE(*string,format*)

STR_TO_DATE takes a string representation of a date (as might be returned by DATE_FORMAT) and returns a standard *date* data type in the format specified by the *format* argument. The format string is the same as that used in DATE_FORMAT; possible values are listed in Table 9-4.

```
SET var1=STR_TO_DATE("Sun 24 Jul 05","%a %d %b %y");          →   2005-07-24
SET var2=STR_TO_DATE("Sunday, 24th July 2005","%W, %D %M %Y");  →   2005-07-24
SET var3=STR_TO_DATE("3:53:54","%H:%i:%s");                   →   03:53:54
SET var4=STR_TO_DATE("13:53:54","%T");                        →   13:53:54
SET var5=STR_TO_DATE("01:53:54 PM","%r");                     →   13:53:54
```

TIME_TO_SEC

*seconds=*TIME_TO_SEC(*time*)

TIME_TO_SEC returns the number of seconds in the specified *time* value. If a date-time is provided, TIME_TO_SEC provides the number of seconds in the time part of that date only.

```
SET var1=NOW( );                →   2005-07-24 14:05:21
SET var2=TIME_TO_SEC("00:01:01");  →   61
SET var3=TIME_TO_SEC(NOW( ));    →   50721
```

TIMEDIFF

*time=*TIMEDIFF(*datetime1,datetime2*)

TIMEDIFF returns the time difference between two arguments specified as date-time data types.

```
SET var1=TIMEDIFF("2005-12-31 00:00:01","2005-12-31 23:59:59");    →   -23:59:58
```

TIMESTAMP

datetime=**TIMESTAMP**(*date*,*time*)

TIMESTAMP returns a date-time value from a specified date and time.

```
SET var2=TIMESTAMP("2005-12-31","23:30:01");    →   2005-12-31 23:30:01
```

TIMESTAMPADD

date_time=**TIMESTAMPADD**(*interval_type*,*interval_value*,*date_time*)

TIMESTAMPADD adds the specified *interval_value*, which is of the *interval_type* data type, to the *datetime* provided and returns the resulting date-time.

Possible values for *interval_type* are listed in Table 9-3.

```
SET var1=NOW();                          →   2005-07-31 16:08:18
SET var2=TIMESTAMPADD(YEAR,100,NOW());   →   2105-07-31 16:08:18
SET var3=TIMESTAMPADD(HOUR,24,NOW());    →   2005-08-01 16:08:18
```

TIMESTAMPDIFF

interval_value=**TIMESTAMPDIFF**(*interval_type*,*date_time1*,*date_time2*)

TIMESTAMPDIFF returns the difference between two date-times, expressed in terms of the specified *interval_type*.

```
SET var1=NOW();                                               →   2005-07-31 16:12:30
SET var2=TIMESTAMPDIFF(YEAR,NOW(),"2006-07-31 18:00:00");     →   1
SET var3=TIMESTAMPDIFF(HOUR,NOW(),"2005-08-01 13:00:00");     →   20
```

WEEK

number=**WEEK**(*date_time*[,*start_of_week*])

WEEK returns the number of weeks since the start of the current year. Weeks are considered to start on Sunday unless you specify an alternative start day (1=Monday) in the second argument.

```
SET var1=NOW();           →   2005-07-31 16:20:09
SET var2=WEEK(NOW());     →   31
```

WEEKDAY

number=**WEEKDAY**(*date*)

WEEKDAY returns the number for the current day of the week, with Monday returning a value of 0.

```
SET var1=NOW();              →   2005-07-31 16:22:05
SET var2=DAYNAME(NOW());     →   Sunday
SET var3=WEEKDAY(NOW());     →   6
```

YEAR

> *number*=**YEAR**(*datetime*)

YEAR returns the year portion of the *datetime* argument, which is specified in date-time format.

```
SET var1=NOW( );            →   2005-07-31 16:27:12
SET var2=YEAR(NOW( ));      →   2005
```

YEARWEEK

> *YearAndWeek*=**YEARWEEK**(*datetime*[,*StartOfWeek*])

YEARWEEK returns the year and week of the year for the given date. Weeks are considered to start on Sunday unless you specify an alternative start day (1=Monday) in the second argument.

```
SET var1=NOW( );               →   2005-07-31 16:30:24
SET var2=DAYNAME(NOW( ));      →   Sunday
SET var3=YEARWEEK(NOW( ));     →   200531
SET var4=YEARWEEK(NOW( ),1);   →   200530
```

Other Date and Time Functions

Table 9-5 lists date and time functions not discussed in previous sections. Some of these are synonyms for functions we have discussed above, while others are rarely required in MySQL programming.

Table 9-5. Additional date-time functions

Function	Syntax	Description
ADDDATE	*datetime*=ADDDATE(*date*,*interval_value*, *intervaltype*)	Synonym for DATE_ADD.
CURDATE	*datetime*=CURDATE( )	Alias for NOW.
CURTIME	*time*=CURTIME( )	Current time.
DAYOFMONTH	*day*=DAYOFMONTH(*datetime*)	Day of the month.
FROM_DAYS	*days*=FROM_DAYS(*datetime*)	Number of days since the start of the current calendar.
HOUR	*number*=HOUR(*datetime*)	Hour of the day for the given date.
LAST_DAY	*date*=LAST_DAY(*date*)	Returns the last day of the month for the given date.
LOCALTIME	*datetime*=LOCALTIME( )	Synonym for NOW.
LOCALTIMESTAMP	*datetime*=LOCALTIMESTAMP( )	Synonym for NOW.
MICROSECOND	*microseconds*=MICROSECOND(*datetime*)	Microsecond portion of the provided time.
MINUTE	*minute*=MINUTE(*datetime*)	Minute part of the given time.

Table 9-5. Additional date-time functions (continued)

Function	Syntax	Description
MONTH	*month*=MONTH(*datetime*)	Month part of the given time.
PERIOD_ADD	*date*=PERIOD_ADD(*year_month, months*)	Adds the specified number of months to the provided *year_month* value.
PERIOD_DIFF	*date*=PERIOD_DIFF(*year_month_1,year_month_2*)	Returns the number of months between the two *year_month* values provided.
QUARTER	*quarter*=QUARTER(*datetime*)	Returns the quarter of the given date.
SECOND	*seconds*=SECOND(*datetime*)	Returns the seconds portion of the provided *datetime*.
SUBDATE	*date1*=SUBDATE(*date2, interval_value, interval_type*)	Synonym for DATE_SUB.
SUBTIME	*datetime1*=SUBTIME(*datetime2, time*)	Subtracts the *time* from the *datetime*.
SYSDATE	*datetime*=SYSDATE()	Synonym for NOW.
TO_DAYS	*datetime*=TO_DAYS(*days*)	Adds the *days* argument to the start of the standard calendar.
WEEKOFYEAR	*week*=WEEKOFYEAR(*datetime*)	Synonym for WEEK.

Other Functions

The miscellaneous built-in functions described in the following sections perform operations that do not fall into the categories described in earlier sections.

BENCHMARK

```
zero=BENCHMARK(no_of_repeats, expression)
```

BENCHMARK executes the specified expression repeatedly. It is intended to be used to benchmark MySQL performance. This function has very little applicability in a stored program context, although in theory you could use it to repeatedly execute a stored program.

COALESCE

```
value=COALESCE(value[,...])
```

COALESCE returns the first non-NULL value in the provided list of values.

```
SET var1=1;                         →  1
SET var2=2;                         →  2
SET var3=NULL;                      →
SET var4=COALESCE(var1,var2,var3);  →  1
SET var5=COALESCE(var3,var2,var1) ; →  2
```

CURRENT_USER

*username=*CURRENT_USER( )

CURRENT_USER returns the username and hostname of the current MySQL user. It may report a different value from that returned by USER, since the USER function reports the connection requested by the user, rather than the connection that was actually used.

```
SET var1=CURRENT_USER( );        →   root@%
SET var2=USER( );                →   root@mel601439.quest.com
```

DATABASE

*database_name=*DATABASE( )

DATABASE returns the name of the database currently in use.

```
USE prod;
SET var1=database( );            →   prod
```

GET_LOCK

*return_code=*GET_LOCK(*lock_name,timeout*)

GET_LOCK allows you to define and acquire a user-defined lock. The *lock_name* can be a string of your choice. GET_LOCK will attempt to acquire the lock; then, if no other session holds the lock, it will return 1. If the lock is held by another session, GET_LOCK will wait until *timeout* seconds has elapsed; then, if the lock can still not be acquired, it will return 0.

Only one "user" lock can be held at any time—that is, each invocation of GET_LOCK releases any previous locks.

GET_LOCK can be used to ensure that only one copy of a stored program is executing a particular segment of code at any one time. Note, however, that for most activities that might be performed by a stored program, table locking is preferable.

Example 9-12 provides an example of both the GET_LOCK and RELEASE_LOCK functions.

Example 9-12. Example of GET_LOCK and RELEASE_LOCK

```
CREATE PROCEDURE sp_critical_section( )

 BEGIN
    DECLARE lock_result INT;
    IF get_lock('sp_critical_section_lock',60) THEN
       /* This block can only be run by one user at a time*/
       SELECT 'got lock';
       /* Critical code here */
    SET lock_result=release_lock('sp_critical_section_lock');
    ELSE
       SELECT 'failed to acquire lock';
```

Example 9-12. Example of GET_LOCK and RELEASE_LOCK (continued)

```
      /* Error handling here */
   END IF;
 END;
```

IFNULL

*value1=***IFNULL**(*value2,nullvalue*)

IFNULL returns the value provided as *value2*. If that value is NULL, it returns the value provided in the second argument.

INTERVAL

*position=***INTERVAL**(*search,number, ...*)

INTERVAL returns the position (starting at 0) that the *search* value would take within the specified list of *numbers*. The list must be in ascending order.

```
SET var2=INTERVAL(20,5,10,30,50);     →   2
```

IS_FREE_LOCK

*integer=***IS_FREE_LOCK**(*string*)

IF_FREE_LOCK returns 1 if the specified user-defined lock is available (e.g., not locked) and 0 if the lock is taken. See GET_LOCK.

ISNULL

*integer=***ISNULL**(*value*)

ISNULL returns 1 if the parameter value is NULL and returns 0 otherwise.

NULLIF

*value1=***NULLIF**(*value2,value3*)

NULLIF returns NULL if the two values provided are equal. Otherwise, it returns the first value.

RELEASE_LOCK

*integer=***RELEASE_LOCK**(*string*)

RELEASE_LOCK releases a lock acquired by the GET_LOCK function. See GET_LOCK for more details and an example of usage.

SESSION_USER

Synonym for USER.

SYSTEM_USER

Synonym for USER.

USER

username=**USER**( )

USER returns the username and hostname for the current MySQL connection. This function reports the username and hostname that were used to establish the connection, while the CURRENT_USER function reports the username from the mysql.user table that is actually in use.

```
SET var1=CURRENT_USER( );    →   root@%
SET var2=USER( );            →   root@mel601439.quest.com
```

UUID

string=**UUID**( )

UUID returns a 128-bit Universal Unique Identifier (UUID). Each invocation of UUID returns a unique value. Part of the UUID is generated from your computer name and part from the current date and time. Therefore, you can be quite confident that UUIDs are unique across the world (subject to the very small chance that a computer with your exact configuration generated a UUID at the exact same time).

```
SET var1=UUID( );    →   7a89e3d9-52ea-1028-abea-122ba2ad7d69
SET var2=UUID( );    →   7a9ca65d-52ea-1028-abea-122ba2ad7d69
SET var3=UUID( );    →   7aa78e82-52ea-1028-abea-122ba2ad7d69
```

VERSION

string=**VERSION**( )

VERSION reports the current version of the MySQL server software.

```
SET var1=VERSION( );    →   5.0.18-nightly-20051211-log
```

In Example 9-13 we extract the major version of the version string and print an (impossible) error message if the version does not support stored programs.

Example 9-13. Using the VERSION function

```
CREATE PROCEDURE sp_mysql_version( )

BEGIN
  DECLARE major_version INT;
```

Example 9-13. Using the VERSION function (continued)

```
SET major_version=SUBSTR(version(),1,INSTR(version( ),'.')-1);
IF major_version>=5 THEN
    SELECT 'Good thing you are using version 5 or later';
ELSE
    SELECT 'This version of MySQL does not support stored procedures',
            'you must be dreaming';
END IF;

END;
```

This function returns the MySQL server version. There are no arguments for the function.

Conclusion

In this chapter we took a quick look at the built-in functions that you can use in your stored programs. In general, these are the same functions that you can use in standard MySQL. The only exception is that you cannot use aggregate functions that might be used in SQL statements that include a GROUP_BY clause.

We did not want to bulk up this book with verbose descriptions of every single function supported by MySQL. For functions not listed—or for those that received only cursory treatment in this chapter—refer to the *MySQL Reference Manual* available online (*http://dev.mysql.com/doc/*).

## CHAPTER 10

Stored Functions

A *stored function* is a stored program that returns a value. While stored procedures may return values via OUT or INOUT variables, a function can—and must—return data only via a single RETURN value. Unlike stored procedures, stored functions can be used in expressions wherever you can use a built-in function of the same return data type and can be used inside of SQL statements such as SELECT, UPDATE, DELETE, and INSERT.

In this chapter we will look at how and when to use stored functions.

The use of stored functions can improve the readability and maintainability of stored program code by encapsulating commonly used business rules or formulas. You can also use stored function return values to control the overall program flow.

Using stored functions in standard SQL statements can simplify the syntax of the SQL by hiding complex calculations and avoiding the repetitive coding of these calculations throughout your code. Stored functions can also be used in SQL to implement operations that would otherwise require subqueries or joins, although you need to be careful to avoid possible performance problems that can occur if a function called from a SQL statement itself calls other SQL statements.

Stored functions may not return result sets and may not include dynamic SQL.

Creating Stored Functions

We provided an overview of the CREATE FUNCTION statement in Chapter 7, but we will recap here. You create a stored function using the following syntax:

```
CREATE FUNCTION function_name (parameter[,...])
    RETURNS datatype
    [LANGUAGE SQL]
    [ [NOT] DETERMINISTIC ]
    [ {CONTAINS SQL | NO SQL | MODIFIES SQL DATA | READS SQL DATA} ]
    [ SQL SECURITY {DEFINER|INVOKER} ]
    [ COMMENT comment_string ]
    function_statements
```

Most of the options for the CREATE FUNCTION statement also apply to CREATE PROCEDURE and are documented in Chapter 7. However, the following are unique to stored functions:

- The RETURNS clause is mandatory and defines the data type that the function will return.
- You cannot specify the IN, OUT, or INOUT modifiers to parameters. All parameters are implicitly IN parameters.
- The function body must contain one or more RETURN statements, which terminate function execution and return the specified result to the calling program, as described in the following section.

The RETURN Statement

The RETURN statement terminates stored function execution and returns the specified value to the calling program. You can have as many RETURN statements in your stored function as makes sense. Example 10-1 shows an example of a stored function that has multiple RETURN statements.

Example 10-1. Simple stored function with multiple RETURN statements

```
CREATE FUNCTION cust_status(in_status CHAR(1))
    RETURNS VARCHAR(20)
BEGIN
    IF in_status = 'O' THEN
        RETURN('Overdue');
    ELSEIF in_status = 'U' THEN
        RETURN('Up to date');
    ELSEIF in_status = 'N' THEN
        RETURN('New');
    END IF;
END;
```

However, it is usually regarded as good practice to include only a single RETURN statement ("one way in and one way out"), and to use variable assignments within conditional statements to change the return value. Aside from arguably resulting in more comprehensible program flow, using a single RETURN statement can avoid the situation in which none of the RETURN statements get executed. "Falling out" of a function, rather than exiting cleanly via a RETURN statement, will cause a runtime error, as shown in Example 10-2.

Example 10-2. "Falling out" of a function without executing a RETURN statement

```
mysql> SELECT cust_status('X');
ERROR 1321 (2F005): FUNCTION cust_status ended without RETURN
```

Example 10-3 shows our previous example recoded to include only a single RETURN statement.

Example 10-3. Simple stored function with single RETURN statement

```
CREATE FUNCTION cust_status(in_status CHAR(1))
    RETURNS VARCHAR(20)
BEGIN
    DECLARE long_status VARCHAR(20);

    IF in_status = 'O' THEN
        SET long_status='Overdue';
    ELSEIF in_status = 'U' THEN
        SET long_status='Up to date';
    ELSEIF in_status = 'N' THEN
        SET long_status='New';
    END IF;

    RETURN(long_status);
END;
```

 It is good practice to include only a single RETURN statement—as the last line of executable code—in your stored functions. Avoid any flow control that could allow the stored function to terminate without calling a RETURN statement.

Parameters to Stored Functions

Stored functions can include multiple parameters, but these may only be IN parameters. That is, you can specify neither the OUT nor INOUT clause (nor even the IN clause) when defining your parameters (see Chapter 7 for a more detailed description of OUT and INOUT parameters). So, for instance, the function defined in Example 10-4 will not compile.

Example 10-4. Function will not compile due to the INOUT clause

```
CREATE FUNCTION f_inout(INOUT x INT) RETURNS INT
BEGIN
    SET x=1;
    RETURN(1);
END;
```

 Stored functions cannot include OUT or INOUT parameters; if you need to return multiple variables from your stored program, then a procedure is possibly more appropriate than a function.

The DETERMINISTIC and SQL Clauses

When binary logging is enabled, MySQL needs to know if a stored function that modifies SQL is deterministic—that is, if it always performs the same actions and returns the same results when provided with the same inputs. Since the default for stored programs is NOT DETERMINISTIC CONTAINS SQL, you need to explicitly set the

---

appropriate keywords in order for the function to compile when binary logging is enabled. This requirement relates to the need to ensure that changes made in the stored function can be correctly replicated to another server. If the actions performed by the function are nondeterministic, then correct replication cannot be assured.

A nondeterministic routine is one that can produce different outputs when provided with the same inputs. In this context, "outputs" include not just the return values of the stored program, but also any modifications that may be made to data within the MySQL databases. Currently, MySQL only cares about the determinism of a function or a procedure in the context of replication. In the future, however, the DETERMINISTIC keyword may also be used to perform certain optimizations (such as caching function return values) or to allow a function to be used in an index or partition definition.

If you declare a stored function without one of the SQL mode clauses NO SQL or READS SQL, and if you have not specified the DETERMINISTIC clause, *and* if the binary log is enabled, you may receive the following error:

```
ERROR 1418 (HY000): This function has none of DETERMINISTIC, NO SQL, or READS SQL
DATA in its declaration and binary logging is enabled (you *might* want to use the
less safe log_bin_trust_function_creators variable)
```

To avoid this error, you must do one of the following:

- Specify one or more of the DETERMINISTIC, NO SQL, and/or READS SQL DATA keywords in your stored function definition.
- Set the value of log_bin_trust_routine_creators to 1 (SET GLOBAL log_bin_trust_routine_creators = 1)

Of course, you should not specify that a stored function is DETERMINISTIC if it is not, and you should avoid setting log_bin_trust_routine_creators to 1 unless you are unconcerned about the correctness of data recovery or replication. Therefore, as a general rule, you should avoid creating nondeterministic stored functions that modify data.

The use of the NOW function or any similar time-based functions does not necessarily cause a stored function to become nondeterministic (at least from a replication perspective), since MySQL logs the timestamp in the binary log, resulting in NOW( ) being calculated correctly during replication or recovery. Likewise, a single random number will also not cause the routine to become nondeterministic, since the seed to the random number generator will be identical on the slave and during data recovery. However, multiple calls to RAND( ) will cause a routine to become nondeterministic.

This restriction on nondeterministic routines applied to both stored functions and stored procedures in the initial production release of MySQL 5.0, but from 5.0.16 on it applies only to stored functions.

If your function is nondeterministic, and it reads but does not modify the database, then you may use the clauses NOT DETERMINISTIC READS SQL DATA to allow the function to be created. If the function is nondeterministic and performs no database access at all, then we recommend using NOT DETERMINISTIC NO SQL.

The relevant ANSI standard intended that the NO SQL clause should pertain only to "external" stored programs written in nondatabase languages such as (for instance) Java or PHP. Therefore, the use of NO SQL may not be strictly correct from a standards perspective. However, we think that the alternatives—to specify READS SQL DATA for a function that performs no database access at all or to declare a nondeterministic function as DETERMINISTIC—are clearly unacceptable. Therefore, we recommend that you use NO SQL when required to denote that a stored function performs no database operations.

Issues relating to replication and nondeterministic functions are expected to be resolved in MySQL 5.1 with the introduction of row-level binary logging.

SQL Statements in Stored Functions

You can include SQL statements within stored functions, although you should be very careful about including SQL statements in a stored function that might itself be used inside a SQL statement (more on that later).

However, you cannot return a result set from a stored function: trying to create a stored function that contains a SELECT statement without an INTO clause will result in a 1415 error, as shown in Example 10-5.

Example 10-5. Stored functions cannot return result sets

```
mysql> CREATE FUNCTION test_func( )
    -> RETURNS INT
    -> BEGIN
    -> SELECT 'Hello World';
    -> RETURN 1;
    -> END;$$
ERROR 1415 (0A000): Not allowed to return a result set from a function
```

Calling Stored Functions

A function can be called by specifying its name and parameter list wherever an expression of the appropriate data type may be used. To show how stored functions can be called, we'll use the simple stored function shown in Example 10-6.

Example 10-6. Simple stored function

```
CREATE FUNCTION isodd(input_number int)
        RETURNS int
BEGIN
        DECLARE v_isodd INT;
```

Example 10-6. Simple stored function (continued)

```
        IF MOD(input_number,2)=0 THEN
                SET v_isodd=FALSE;
        ELSE
                SET v_isodd=TRUE;
        END IF;

        RETURN(v_isodd);

END ;
```

From the MySQL command line, we can invoke our simple stored function in a number of ways. Example 10-7 shows how to call the stored function from a SET statement and from a SELECT statement.

Example 10-7. Calling a stored function from the MySQL command line

```
mysql> SET @x=isodd(42);
Query OK, 0 rows affected (0.00 sec)

mysql> SELECT @x;
+------+
| @x   |
+------+
| 0    |
+------+
1 row in set (0.02 sec)

mysql> SELECT isodd(42)
    -> ;
+-----------+
| isodd(42) |
+-----------+
|         0 |
+-----------+
```

From within a stored procedure, we can invoke the function both within a SET clause and within a variety of flow control statements. Example 10-8 shows how to call a stored function from within a SET statement, as well as from an IF statement.

Example 10-8. Calling a stored function from within a stored procedure

```
SET l_isodd=isodd(aNumber);

IF (isodd(aNumber)) THEN
    SELECT CONCAT(aNumber," is odd") as isodd;
ELSE
    SELECT CONCAT(aNumber," is even") AS isodd;
END IF;
```

Programming languages support a variety of methods for calling a stored function. Java and .NET languages (VB.NET and C#) provide methods to call stored functions directly. However, in many of the dynamic languages (PHP, Perl, Python) there is no API for directly accessing a stored function. (We give guidelines for common programming languages in Chapters 12 through 17.)

If a language does not support a method for directly calling a stored function, you should embed the call in a SELECT statement without a FROM clause and retrieve the function result from the subsequent result set. For instance, in PHP, with the mysqli interface, we can retrieve a stored function result as shown in Example 10-9.

Example 10-9. Calling a stored function from PHP

```
$stmt=$my_db->prepare("SELECT isodd(?)") or die($my_db->error);

$stmt->bind_param('i',$aNumber) or die($stmt->error);

$stmt->execute( ) or die($stmt->error);

$stmt->bind_result($isodd);

$stmt->fetch( );

if ($isodd == 1 )
    printf("%d is an odd number\n",$aNumber);
else
    printf("%d is an even number\n",$aNumber);
```

Some languages specifically support calling stored functions. For instance, Java JDBC allows a stored function to be called directly, as shown in Example 10-10.

Example 10-10. JDBC support for stored functions

```
CallableStatement PreparedFunc =
    MyConnect.prepareCall("{ ? = call isodd( ? ) }");
PreparedFunc.registerOutParameter(1, Types.INTEGER);

PreparedFunc.setInt(1, aNumber);
PreparedFunc.execute( );

if (PreparedFunc.getInt(1) == 1)
    System.out.println(aNumber + " is odd");
else
    System.out.println(aNumber + " is even");
```

Using Stored Functions in SQL

So far, we have looked at stored functions as though they were simply a variant on the stored procedure syntax—a special type of stored procedure that can return a value. While this is certainly a valid use for a stored function, stored functions have an additional and significant role to play: as *user-defined functions* (UDFs) within SQL statements.

Consider the SELECT statement shown in Example 10-11: it returns a count of customers by status, with the one-byte status code decoded into a meaningful description. It also sorts by the decoded customer status. Notice that we must repeat the rather awkward CASE statement in both the SELECT list and the ORDER BY clause.

Example 10-11. SQL statement with multiple CASE statements

```
SELECT CASE customer_status
           WHEN 'U' THEN 'Up to Date'
           WHEN 'N' THEN 'New'
           WHEN 'O' THEN 'Overdue'
       END  as Status, count(*) as Count
  FROM customers
 GROUP BY customer_status
 ORDER BY CASE customer_status
           WHEN 'U' THEN 'Up to Date'
           WHEN 'N' THEN 'New'
           WHEN 'O' THEN 'Overdue'
       END
```

Now imagine an application with many similar CASE statements, as well as complex calculations involving business accounting logic, scattered throughout our application. Such statements—often with embedded expressions far more complex than the one shown in Example 10-11—result in code that is difficult to understand and maintain. Whenever the CASE constructs or business calculations need to be modified, it will be necessary to find and then modify a large number of SQL statements, affecting many different modules.

Stored functions can help us minimize this problem, by centralizing the complex code in one program unit, and then deploying that program wherever needed. Example 10-12 shows the result of transferring the logic in the previous query's CASE expression into a stored function.

Example 10-12. Stored function for use in our SQL statement

```
CREATE FUNCTION cust_status(IN in_status CHAR(1))
    RETURNS VARCHAR(20)
BEGIN
    DECLARE long_status VARCHAR(20);

    IF in_status = 'O' THEN
        SET long_status='Overdue';
    ELSEIF in_status = 'U' THEN
        SET long_status='Up to date';
    ELSEIF in_status = 'N' THEN
        SET long_status='New';
    END IF;

    RETURN(long_status);
END;
```

We can now use this function in our SQL statement, as shown in Example 10-13.

Example 10-13. Stored function in a SQL statement

```
SELECT cust_status(customer_status) as Status, count(*) as Count
  FROM customers
 GROUP BY customer_status
 ORDER BY cust_status(customer_status);
```

Notice that the repetition has been removed and the query is also much more readable, since it is hiding the details of the customer status formula. If and when a programmer needs to understand the logic used to determine customer status, she can open up the stored function and take a look.

Using SQL in Stored Functions

You can include SQL statements inside of stored functions that are themselves used within SQL statements as user-defined functions. However, be careful when doing so, since functions calling SQL inside of SQL statements can lead to unpredictable and often poor performance.

For instance, consider the stored function shown in Example 10-14.

Example 10-14. Stored function to return customer count for a sales rep

```
CREATE FUNCTION customers_for_rep(in_rep_id INT)
    RETURNS INT
    READS SQL DATA
BEGIN
    DECLARE customer_count INT;

    SELECT COUNT(*)
      INTO customer_count
      FROM customers
      WHERE sales_rep_id=in_rep_id;

    RETURN(customer_count);

END;
```

This function returns the number of customers assigned to a given sales representative. We might use this function in a stored program when calculating a commission, as shown in Example 10-15.

Example 10-15. Using the sales rep function in a stored program

```
IF customers_for_rep(in_employee_id) > 0 THEN
    CALL calc_sales_rep_bonus(in_employee_id);
ELSE
    CALL calc_nonrep_bonus(in_employee_id);
END IF;
```

If this stored function is called for a single employee, then the use of the stored function is probably appropriate—it improves the clarity of the business logic, and performance would be no worse than it would be with an embedded SQL statement.

However, consider the case where we want to issue a query listing all the sales representatives with more than 10 customers together with their customer counts. In standard SQL, the query might look like that shown in Example 10-16.

Example 10-16. Standard SQL to retrieve sales reps with more than 10 customers

```
SELECT employee_id,COUNT(*)
  FROM employees JOIN customers
    ON (employee_id=sales_rep_id)
 GROUP BY employee_id
 HAVING COUNT(*) > 10
 ORDER BY COUNT(*) desc;
```

Alternately, we can use our stored function, which will—apparently—avoid the join between employees and customers and also avoid a GROUP BY. The stored function version of the query is shown in Example 10-17.

Example 10-17. Function-based query to retrieve sales reps with more than 10 customers

```
SELECT employee_id,customers_for_rep(employee_id)
  FROM employees
 WHERE customers_for_rep(employee_id)>10
 ORDER BY customers_for_rep(employee_id) desc
```

Although the stored function solution looks a lot simpler, it actually takes much longer to run than the standard SQL. For every row retrieved from the employees table, the stored function must be called three times (once for the SELECT, once for the WHERE, and once for the ORDER BY). Furthermore, each invocation of the stored function performs a full table scan of the customers table—resulting in three such full scans for each employee row. In contrast, the standard SQL performs just one scan of the customers table and then joins that to the employees table using the primary key (employee_id).

For our sample data, the standard SQL returned the required results almost instantaneously, while the stored function solution took almost half a minute. Figure 10-1 compares the execution times for the two solutions.

Using a stored function inside of a SQL statement that, in turn, contains SQL will not *always* cause such extreme response time degradation. In general, though, you should think twice about using a function that contains SQL inside of another SQL statement unless the embedded SQL is very efficient—such as a SQL statement that retrieves data via a quick index lookup.

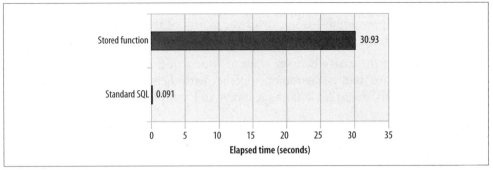

Figure 10-1. Comparison of performance between standard SQL and SQL using a stored function containing embedded SQL

 Be careful using SQL inside of stored functions that are called by other SQL statements. The resulting performance can be very poor unless the stored function is extremely efficient.

Conclusion

A stored function is a special type of stored program that returns a single result. Stored functions can be used in SQL statements or within other stored programs wherever an expression that returns a corresponding data type can be used.

Stored functions have the following limitations when compared to stored procedures:

- They may not include OUT or INOUT parameters.
- They may not return result sets.

A stored function terminates when a RETURN statement is encountered. In general, it is good practice to include a single RETURN statement at the end of the function rather than including multiple RETURN statements inside flow control statements. If a stored function terminates without issuing a RETURN statement, an error will be raised.

You can use stored functions within standard SQL. Doing so can improve the readability and maintainability of the SQL by centralizing the definition of complex calculations, decodes, or other application logic.

Be careful, however, when using stored functions inside SQL statements if those functions embed SQL statements. Stored functions that include SQL can often perform badly when included within standard SQL statements.

## CHAPTER 11

Triggers

Database *triggers* are stored programs that are executed in response to some kind of event that occurs within the database. In the current MySQL implementation of triggers, triggers fire in response to a DML statement (INSERT, UPDATE, DELETE) on a specified table.

Triggers are a powerful mechanism for ensuring the integrity of your data, as well as a useful means of automating certain operations in the database, such as denormalization and audit logging.

Creating Triggers

Triggers are created with the—you guessed it—CREATE TRIGGER statement, which has the following syntax:

```
CREATE [DEFINER={user|CURRENT_USER}] TRIGGER trigger_name
   {BEFORE|AFTER}
   {UPDATE|INSERT|DELETE}
ON table_name
FOR EACH ROW
trigger_statements
```

Let's look at each part of the CREATE TRIGGER statement in turn:

DEFINER={*user* | CURRENT_USER}

Controls the account that will be used to check privileges when the trigger is invoked. The default of CURRENT_USER indicates that the trigger statements will run with the authority of the account that issued the CREATE TRIGGER statement, rather than the account that issued the DML that caused the trigger to fire.

trigger_name

The trigger name follows the normal conventions for MySQL's naming of database objects. While you can call your trigger virtually anything, we recommend that you adopt a predictable naming convention. There can be only one trigger for any combination of BEFORE or AFTER and UPDATE, INSERT, or DELETE (for example, there can be only one BEFORE UPDATE trigger on a table), so a sensible convention might result in triggers being given names such as *table_name*_bu (for a BEFORE UPDATE trigger) or *table_name*_ai (for an AFTER INSERT trigger).

BEFORE|AFTER
:   Specifies whether the trigger fires before or after the DML statement itself has been executed. We'll discuss the implications of this shortly.

UPDATE|INSERT|DELETE
:   Defines the DML statement to which the trigger is associated.

ON *table_name*
:   Associates the trigger with a specific table.

FOR EACH ROW
:   This clause is mandatory in the initial MySQL implementation. It indicates that the trigger will be executed once for every row affected by the DML statement. The ANSI standard also provides for a FOR EACH STATEMENT mode, which might be supported in an upcoming version of MySQL.

trigger_statements
:   Define the statements that will be executed when the trigger is invoked. If there is more than one statement, then the statements need to be enclosed in a BEGIN-END block.

Prior to MySQL 5.1.6, you needed the SUPER privilege to create a trigger. In 5.1.6 and above, the TRIGGER privilege is required.

Referring to Column Values Within the Trigger

Trigger statements can include references to the values of the columns being affected by the trigger. You can access and sometimes modify the values of these columns.

To distinguish between the values of the columns "before" and "after" the relevant DML has fired, you use the NEW and OLD modifiers. For instance, in a BEFORE UPDATE trigger, the value of the column mycolumn before the update is applied is OLD. mycolumn, and the value after modification is NEW.mycolumn.

If the trigger is an INSERT trigger, only the NEW value is available (there is no OLD value). Within a DELETE trigger, only the OLD value is available (there is no NEW value).

Within BEFORE triggers you can modify a NEW value with a SET statement—thus changing the effect of the DML.

Triggering Actions

Triggers will normally execute in response to the DML statements matching their specification—for instance, BEFORE INSERT will always be invoked in response to an INSERT statement.

However, triggers also fire in response to implicit—as well as explicit—DML. Some statements are capable of generating DML as a side effect of their primary activity. For instance, an INSERT statement that contains an ON DUPLICATE KEY UPDATE clause can issue an implicit UPDATE statement causing BEFORE UPDATE or AFTER UPDATE triggers to fire. Likewise, the REPLACE statement can cause both INSERT and DELETE triggers to fire (since, for an existing row, REPLACE issues a DELETE followed by an INSERT).

BEFORE and AFTER Triggers

The BEFORE and AFTER clauses determine when your trigger code executes: either *before* or *after* the DML statement that causes the trigger to be invoked.

The most significant difference between BEFORE and AFTER triggers is that in an AFTER trigger you are not able to modify the values about to be inserted into or updated with the table in question—the DML has executed, and it is too late to try to change what the DML is going to do.

IF you try to modify a NEW value in an AFTER trigger, you will encounter an error, as shown in Example 11-1.

Example 11-1. AFTER triggers cannot modify NEW values

```
mysql> CREATE TRIGGER account_balance_au
 AFTER UPDATE ON account_balance FOR EACH ROW
BEGIN
  DECLARE dummy INT;

  IF NEW.balance<0 THEN
    SET NEW.balance=NULL;
  END IF;

END
$$

ERROR 1362 (HY000): Updating of NEW row is not allowed in after trigger
```

Although you can do pretty much anything you need to do in a BEFORE trigger, you still may wish to use AFTER triggers for activities that logically should occur in a transaction after a DML has successfully executed. Auditing activities, for example, are best executed in an AFTER trigger, since you will first want to make sure that the DML succeeded.

Using Triggers

Triggers can be used to implement a variety of useful requirements, such as automating the maintenance of denormalized or derived data, implementing logging, and validating data.

Maintaining Derived Data

We often need to maintain redundant "denormalized" information in our tables to optimize critical SQL queries. The code to perform this denormalization *could* be placed within the application code, but then you would have to make sure that any and every application module that modifies the table also performs the denormalization. If you want to *guarantee* that this code is run whenever a change is made to the table, you can attach that functionality to the table itself, via a trigger.

Let's take a look at an example of the value of denormalized data in our tables. Suppose that we have a table within our database that contains the total sales for all orders from each customer. This allows us to quickly identify our most significant customers without having to do a costly query on the very large sales table.

Unfortunately, we have a variety of order processing systems, not all of which can be modified to maintain this table. So we need a way of making sure that the table is modified every time an INSERT occurs into the sales table. A trigger is an ideal way of maintaining the values in this summary table.

Example 11-2 shows example triggers that maintain the values in the customer_ sales_totals table whenever there is an UPDATE, INSERT, or DELETE operation on the sales table.

Example 11-2. Using triggers to maintain denormalized data

```
DELIMITER $$

CREATE TRIGGER sales_bi_trg
  BEFORE INSERT ON sales
  FOR EACH ROW
BEGIN
  DECLARE row_count INTEGER;

  SELECT COUNT(*)
    INTO row_count
    FROM customer_sales_totals
   WHERE customer_id=NEW.customer_id;

  IF row_count > 0 THEN
    UPDATE customer_sales_totals
       SET sale_value=sale_value+NEW.sale_value
     WHERE customer_id=NEW.customer_id;
  ELSE
    INSERT INTO customer_sales_totals
      (customer_id,sale_value)
      VALUES(NEW.customer_id,NEW.sale_value);
  END IF;

END$$

CREATE TRIGGER sales_bu_trg
```

Example 11-2. Using triggers to maintain denormalized data (continued)

```
  BEFORE UPDATE ON sales
  FOR EACH ROW
BEGIN

  UPDATE customer_sales_totals
    SET sale_value=sale_value+(NEW.sale_value-OLD.sale_value)
   WHERE customer_id=NEW.customer_id;

END$$

CREATE  TRIGGER sales_bd_trg
  BEFORE DELETE ON sales
  FOR EACH ROW
BEGIN

  UPDATE customer_sales_totals
    SET sale_value=sale_value-OLD.sale_value
   WHERE customer_id=OLD.customer_id;

END$$
```

Implementing Logging

The ability to identify the source and nature of updates to application data is increasingly critical in our security-conscious societies. Indeed, the tracking of database changes is often mandated by government and industry regulations such as Sarbanes-Oxley and HIPAA. Although an application can be designed and implemented such that it performs its own auditing, many organizations require that *any* database updates—including those performed directly against the database using command-line clients or database utilities—also be logged. Triggers are an ideal way of implementing this kind of logging.

Suppose that we are building a financial application, for which we must track all modifications to a user's account balance. In Chapter 8, we implemented such a scheme using a stored procedure that controlled all account balance transactions. However, triggers provide a superior solution since they will also log any transactions performed *outside* of the stored procedure.

Example 11-3 shows a trigger that will perform this type of logging for UPDATE statements. In order to ensure universal logging, we would need to create a similar trigger for INSERT and DELETE statements.

Example 11-3. Using triggers to implement audit logging

```
CREATE TRIGGER account_balance_au
 AFTER UPDATE ON account_balance FOR EACH ROW
 BEGIN
        INSERT into transaction_log
             (user_id, description)
```

Example 11-3. Using triggers to implement audit logging (continued)

```
        VALUES (user( ),
              CONCAT('Adjusted account ',
                 NEW.account_id,' from ',OLD.balance,
                 ' to ', NEW.balance));
END;
```

Validating Data with Triggers

A typical and traditional use of triggers in relational databases is to validate data or implement business rules to ensure that the data in the database is logically consistent and does not violate the rules of the business or the application. These triggers are sometimes referred to as *check constraint triggers*.

Data validation triggers may perform tasks such as:

Implementing checks on allowable values for columns
> For instance, a percentage value must fall between 0 and 100, a date of birth cannot be greater than today's date, and so on.

Performing cross-column or cross-table validations
> For example, an employee cannot be his own manager, a sales person must have an associated quota, and seafood pizzas cannot include anchovies (here the authors must agree to disagree: Guy hates anchovies, while Steven finds them almost a requirement for an enjoyable pizza!).

Performing advanced referential integrity
> Referential constraints are usually best implemented using foreign key constraints; sometimes, however, you may have some advanced referential integrity that can only be implemented using triggers. For instance, a foreign key column may be required to match a primary key in one of a number of tables (an *arc* relationship).

A data validation trigger typically prevents a DML operation from completing if it would result in some kind of validation check failing.

If MySQL 5.0 or 5.1 implemented all ANSI-standard functionality, we would implement such checks in a database trigger by issuing a SIGNAL statement, as shown in Example 11-4.

Example 11-4. ANSI-standard trigger to enforce a business rule

```
CREATE TRIGGER account_balance_bu
    BEFORE UPDATE
    ON account_balance
    FOR EACH ROW
BEGIN
    -- The account balance cannot be set to a negative value.
    IF (NEW.balance < 0) THEN
        -- Warning! Not implemented in MySQL 5.0...
```

```
        SIGNAL SQLSTATE '80000'
            SET MESSAGE_TEXT='Account balance cannot be less than 0';
    END IF;
END;
```

Unfortunately, MySQL 5.0 and 5.1 do not support the SIGNAL statement; we expect it to appear in version 5.2. Consequently, we do not currently have a standard way of aborting a DML statement that violates a business rule.

Luckily, we can use a variation on the workaround we introduced in Chapter 6 to force a trigger to fail in such a way that it prevents the DML statement from completing and provides a marginally acceptable error message.

In Example 6-19, we introduced a stored procedure—my_signal—that used dynamic SQL to create an "Invalid table name" error condition and embedded an error message of our choosing into that error. Unfortunately, we cannot call the my_signal procedure directly, because triggers are forbidden from executing dynamic SQL. However, we can include very similar logic into the trigger that will have the same effect. Example 11-5 shows a trigger that ensures that there will be no negative account balance. If a negative account balance is detected, the trigger attempts to execute a SELECT statement that references a nonexistent column. The name of the column includes the error message that we will report to the calling program.

Example 11-5. MySQL trigger to perform data validation

```
CREATE TRIGGER account_balance_bu
  BEFORE UPDATE
      ON account_balance
    FOR EACH ROW
BEGIN
  DECLARE dummy INT;
  IF NEW.balance<0 THEN
    SELECT `Account balance cannot be less than 0` INTO dummy
      FROM account_balance
     WHERE account_id=NEW.account_id;
  END IF;
END;
```

Example 11-6 shows how the trigger prevents any updates from proceeding if the end result would be to create an account_balance row with a negative value in the balance column. While the error code is not ideal, and the error message is embedded in another error message, we at least have prevented the UPDATE from creating a negative balance, and we have provided an error message that does include the reason why the UPDATE was rejected.

Example 11-6. Behavior of our data validation trigger

```
SELECT * FROM account_balance WHERE account_id=1;

+------------+---------+---------------------+
| account_id | balance | account_timestamp   |
+------------+---------+---------------------+
|          1 |  800.00 | 2005-12-13 22:12:28 |
+------------+---------+---------------------+
1 row in set (0.00 sec)

UPDATE account_balance SET balance=balance-1000 WHERE account_id=1;

ERROR 1054 (42S22): Unknown column 'Account balance cannot be less than 0' in 'field list'

SELECT * FROM account_balance WHERE account_id=1;

+------------+---------+---------------------+
| account_id | balance | account_timestamp   |
+------------+---------+---------------------+
|          1 |  800.00 | 2005-12-13 22:12:28 |
+------------+---------+---------------------+
1 row in set (0.00 sec)

UPDATE account_balance SET balance=500 WHERE account_id=1;

Query OK, 1 row affected (0.15 sec)
Rows matched: 1  Changed: 1  Warnings: 0

SELECT * FROM account_balance WHERE account_id=1;

+------------+---------+---------------------+
| account_id | balance | account_timestamp   |
+------------+---------+---------------------+
|          1 |  500.00 | 2005-12-13 22:12:34 |
+------------+---------+---------------------+
1 row in set (0.00 sec)
```

This trigger can be easily modified to use the SIGNAL statement when it becomes available.

Trigger Overhead

It is important to remember that, by necessity, triggers add overhead to the DML statements to which they apply. The actual amount of overhead will depend upon the nature of the trigger, but—as all MySQL triggers execute FOR EACH ROW—the overhead can rapidly accumulate for statements that process large numbers of rows. You should therefore avoid placing any expensive SQL statements or procedural code in triggers.

We will look at an example of trigger overhead in Chapter 22.

Conclusion

MySQL triggers allow you to execute stored program code whenever a DML statement is issued against a database table. In MySQL 5.0, triggers can be used to automate denormalization or logging.

Implementation of data validation in MySQL triggers is more of a challenge, as in MySQL there is no easy or straightforward way to raise an error condition or abort the transaction when validation fails. This will be remedied when the SIGNAL statement is implemented in MySQL 5.2. In this chapter we presented a workaround that does allow data validation triggers to be created in the interim, although the error text generated is far from ideal.

## PART III

Using MySQL Stored Programs in Applications

Stored programs can be used for a variety of purposes, including the implementation of utility routines for MySQL DBAs and developers. However, the most important use of stored programs is within applications, as we describe in this part of the book. Stored programs allow us to move some of our application code into the database server itself; if we do this wisely, we may benefit from applications that are more secure, efficient, and maintainable. In Chapter 12 we consider the merits of, and best practices for, using stored programs inside modern—typically web-based—applications. In the subsequent chapters, Chapters 13 through 17, we show how to use stored procedures and functions from within the development languages most commonly used in conjunction with MySQL: PHP, Java, Perl, Python, and .NET languages such as C# and VB.NET.

Chapter 12, *Using MySQL Stored Programs in Applications*
Chapter 13, *Using MySQL Stored Programs with PHP*
Chapter 14, *Using MySQL Stored Programs with Java*
Chapter 15, *Using MySQL Stored Programs with Perl*
Chapter 16, *Using MySQL Stored Programs with Python*
Chapter 17, *Using MySQL Stored Programs with .NET*

Using MySQL Stored Programs
in Applications

In the next few chapters we are going to show you how to use stored programs in a variety of external programming environments—PHP, Java, Perl, Python, and .NET. In those chapters we'll describe how to use the MySQL drivers provided with these languages to execute stored programs, retrieve the output of stored programs, and handle any error conditions that may arise during execution. Before we delve into those specific environments, we'll start with a general discussion of using MySQL stored programs in applications.

The purpose of this preliminary chapter is twofold:

- To present the overall benefits of using stored programs in your applications.

- To outline the general principles and program flow considerations that apply when using stored programs from any programming environment. Chapters 13 through 17 will describe the details for specific programming environments.

The Pros and Cons of Stored Programs in Modern Applications

There is a persistent—and often lively—debate in the programming community about the benefits and appropriateness of using stored programs in applications.

Database stored programs first came to prominence in the late 1980s and early 1990s during what might be called the *client/server revolution*. In the client/server environment of that time, stored programs had some obvious advantages (aspects of which persist in *N*-tier and Internet-based architectures):

- Client/server applications typically had to carefully balance processing load between the client PC and the (relatively) more powerful server machine. Using stored programs was one way to reduce the load on the client, which might otherwise be overloaded.

- Network bandwidth was often a serious constraint on client/server applications; execution of multiple server-side operations in a single stored program could reduce network traffic.

- Maintaining correct versions of client software in a client/server environment was often problematic. Centralizing at least some of the processing on the server allowed a greater measure of control over core logic.

- Stored programs offered clear security advantages, because in the client/server paradigm, end users typically connected directly to the database to run the application. By restricting access to stored programs only, users would not be able to perform ad hoc operations against tables and other database structures.

The use of stored programs in client/server applications was, and is, most prevalent in applications that use Microsoft SQL Server (and its technological predecessor, Sybase) and Oracle. The Microsoft SQL Server and Oracle stored program languages (Transact-SQL and PL/SQL, respectively) have substantially different characteristics—especially regarding the ability of a stored program to return a result set. The differences between the two languages have resulted in somewhat different usage patterns:

SQL Server–based applications
> For these applications, the dominant pattern is to encapsulate all database interaction between client and server—including queries—into stored programs. This is cited as providing better security and reduced network traffic.

Oracle-based applications
> For these applications, it was initially impossible to return a result set from a stored program and, although this became possible in later releases, it was never particularly convenient or easy to do so. As a result, Oracle-based applications tended to use stored programs to implement transaction processing, but would use native SQL to retrieve result sets.

With the emergence of three-tier architectures and web applications, many of the incentives to use stored programs from within applications disappeared. Application clients are now often browser-based; security is predominantly handled by a middle tier; and the middle tier possesses the ability to encapsulate business logic. Most of the functions for which stored programs were used in client/server applications can now be implemented in middle-tier code (e.g., in PHP, Java, C#, etc.). Transferring processing to the middle tier can also enhance load balancing and scalability.

Even so, many of the original advantages of stored programs (such as enhanced security and reduction in network traffic) still apply, if to a reduced degree. The use of stored programs is still regarded as a "best practice" by many application developers and architects.

Today, there are three schools of thought regarding the use of stored programs in applications:

All stored programs, all the time
> This segment of the development community continues to believe that stored programs should be used for *all* interaction between the client (now the middle tier) and the database. They argue that this pattern provides more security to the database, and also provides a level of abstraction between the underlying data model and the business logic in the middle tier.

Stored programs only when absolutely necessary
> This segment believes that stored programs should play only a minor role in a modern application development. They argue that stored programs add additional and unnecessary complexity to the application design; that they fragment the logic between the middle tier and the database; and that they get in the way of object-relational mapping schemes such as Java J2EE's CMP and Hibernate.

Use what works
> This segment (probably the quiet majority) is fairly pragmatic—they use stored programs selectively when the use of a stored program seems warranted, but they tend to use native SQL when it is easier and more convenient to do so.

It's up to you to decide which model works best for you and your application. In the next few sections we will try to provide you with as much information as we can to help you make an informed decision. To sum up our personal feelings on the matter, we do think that an application that encapsulates all database interaction within stored programs is employing a valid and effective pattern. In particular, this kind of application can be made virtually immune to SQL injection attacks, and will be much less vulnerable to exploits based on compromised passwords. We also believe in separating data access logic from business logic, and the use of stored programs is a good way to do this. However, stored programs are not a natural choice for all applications; for instance, using stored programs exclusively tends to interfere with object-relational mapping schemes such as J2EE CMP and Hibernate.

In the next few sections, we'll look in some detail at the advantages stored programs offer an application and compare those to possible disadvantages. To summarize here, stored programs offer these advantages:

- Stored programs can improve the security of your database server.
- Stored programs offer a mechanism to abstract data access routines, hiding your implementation behind a procedural interface and making it easier to evolve your data structures over time.
- Stored programs can reduce network traffic.
- Stored programs can be used to implement functionality that is needed—and can be called—from multiple applications, and from multiple places within a single application. This can be handy when applications written in frameworks

that don't interoperate very well (.NET and Java for instance) access the same database.

- Stored programs allow for a convenient division of duties between those whose skills are database-centric and those whose skills are programming-centric.

- You can often improve the portability of your application code by moving logic into stored programs.

Against these possible advantages, consider the following disadvantages:

- Stored programs might be slower—especially for computationally expensive operations—than equivalent middle-tier code.

- The use of stored programs can lead to fragmentation of your application logic—logic may be split between the database and the application server tier, making it difficult to track down design flaws or implementation bugs.

- Stored programs are usually written in a different language from your application server tier, requiring a wider range of skills in your development team.

- Stored programs can be more difficult to debug (depending on the implementation: MySQL does not yet offer an integrated stored program debugger).

- Most object-relational mapping systems (e.g., J2EE CMP and Hibernate) cannot seamlessly exploit stored programs.

- While stored program calls may sometimes be more portable than native SQL, in practice this is not true for all implementations. Of the "big four," only DB2 and MySQL implement the ANSI standard for stored programs. As a result, MySQL stored program calls often look and act substantially different from calls made in Oracle or SQL Server.

Advantages of Stored Programs

Let's look at each of the advantages of stored programs in turn.

They Enhance Database Security

We'll see in Chapter 18 how the default security mode of stored programs (SQL SECURITY DEFINER) permits a stored program to execute SQL statements even if the calling database account lacks the security privileges to execute these statements as native SQL. By granting a database account access to stored programs only—without granting direct permissions on underlying tables—we can ensure that access to the database occurs only in the manner defined by our stored programs. We can also ensure that these SQL statements are surrounded by whatever business rule validation or logging is required. This concept is explained in more detail in Chapter 18.

In the event that an application account is compromised (for instance, the password is "cracked"), the attacker will *still* only be able to execute our stored programs, as opposed to being able to run any ad hoc SQL. While such a situation constitutes a severe security breach, at least we are assured that the hacker will be subject to the same checks and logging as a normal application user. The hacker will also be denied the opportunity to retrieve information about the underlying database schema, which will hinder attempts to perform further malicious activities.

The security advantages of stored programs are a powerful motivation to include stored programs in our applications, especially with today's increasing focus on securing the underlying database. However, the security advantages of stored programs can only be realized if stored programs are used exclusively within an application. This is because, to be fully effective, this strategy requires that the database connection account have no direct access to the underlying database tables; hence, this account must perform operations only through stored programs. One alternative to this approach is to grant read-only access to the underlying tables, and then use stored programs exclusively for update operations. At least then, a malicious user will not be able to make arbitrary changes to the data.

Another security advantage inherent in stored programs is their resistance to SQL injection attacks. As we will see in Chapter 18, a SQL injection attack can occur when a malicious user manages to "inject" SQL code into the SQL code being constructed by the application. Stored programs do not offer the only protection against SQL injection attacks, but applications that rely exclusively on stored programs to interact with the database are virtually immune to this type of attack (provided that those stored programs do not themselves build dynamic SQL strings without fully validating their inputs).

They Provide a Mechanism for Data Abstraction

It is generally a good practice to separate your data access code from your business logic and presentation logic. Data access routines are often used by multiple program modules, and are likely to be maintained by a separate group of developers. A very common scenario requires changes to the underlying data structures, while minimizing the impact on higher-level logic. Data abstraction makes this much easier to accomplish.

The use of stored programs provides a convenient way of implementing a data access layer. By creating a set of stored programs that implement, all of the data access routines required by the application, we are effectively building an API for the application to use for all database interactions.

They Reduce Network Traffic

Stored programs can radically improve application performance by reducing network traffic in certain situations. Several such situations are described in this section.

One scenario involves an application that may need to accept input from the end user, read some data in the database, decide what statement to execute next, retrieve a result, make a decision, execute some SQL, and so on. If the application code is written entirely outside of the database, each of these steps would require a network round trip between the database and the application. The time taken to perform these network trips can easily dominate overall user response time.

Consider a typical interaction between a bank customer and an ATM machine. The user requests a transfer of funds between two accounts. The application must retrieve the balance of each account from the database, check withdrawal limits and possibly other policy information, issue the relevant UPDATE statements, and finally issue a COMMIT—all before advising the customer that the transaction has succeeded. Even for this relatively simple interaction, at least six separate database queries must be issued, each with its own network round trip between the application server and the database. Figure 12-1 shows the sequence of interactions that would be required without a stored program.

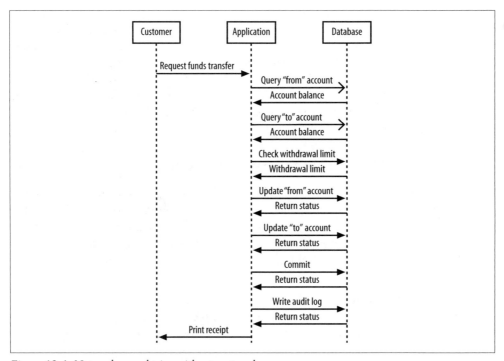

Figure 12-1. Network round trips without a stored program

On the other hand, if a stored program is used to implement the funds transfer logic, only a single database interaction is required. The stored program takes responsibility for checking balances, withdrawal limits, and so on. Figure 12-2 illustrates the reduction in network round trips that occurs as a result.

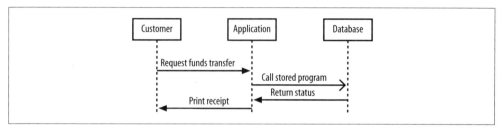

Figure 12-2. Network round trips involving a stored program

Network round trips can also become significant when an application is required to perform some kind of aggregate processing on very large record sets in the database. If the application needs to (for instance) retrieve millions of rows in order to calculate some sort of business metric that cannot easily be computed using native SQL (average time to complete an order, for instance), then a very large number of round trips can result. In such a case, the network delay may again become the dominant factor in application response time. Performing the calculations in a stored program will reduce network overhead, which *might* reduce overall response time—but make sure you take into account the considerations outlined in the section "They Can Be Computationally Inferior" later in this chapter. We provide an example of a stored program reducing network traffic in Chapter 22.

They Allow for Common Routines Across Multiple Application Types

While it is commonplace for a MySQL database to be at the service of a single application, it is not at all uncommon for multiple applications to share a single database. These applications may run on different machines and be written in different languages; it may be hard—or impossible—for these applications to share code. Implementing common code in stored programs may allow these applications to share critical common routines.

For instance, in Chapter 8 we created a procedure called txfer_funds that performed a transactional-safe, logged transfer of funds between two accounts. Some versions of the stored procedure contained code for handling deadlocks and an optimistic locking strategy. Now, in a banking application, a transfer of funds transactions might originate from multiple sources, including a bank teller's console, an Internet browser, an ATM, or a phone banking application. Each of these applications could conceivably have its own database access code written in largely incompatible languages, and, without stored programs, we might have to replicate the transaction logic—including logging, deadlock handling, and optimistic locking strategies—in multiple places in multiple languages.

They Facilitate Division of Duties

It is reasonably commonplace for the responsibility for coding application logic to be held by one set of developers and the responsibility for database design and access routines to be held by a different set of developers. These two groups may have different skill sets, and application development efficiency may be enhanced if the database developers are able to implement the data access routines directly in MySQL using the stored program language.

They May Provide Portability

While all relational databases implement a common set of SQL syntax—typically SQL99 entry-level or similar—each RDBMS offers proprietary extensions to this standard SQL. If you are attempting to write an application that is designed to be independent of the underlying RDBMS vendor, or if you want to avoid RDBMS vendor lock-in, you will probably want to avoid these extensions in your application. However, using these extensions is highly desirable if you want to optimize your use of the underlying database. For instance, in MySQL, you will often want to employ MySQL hints, execute non-ANSI statements such as LOCK TABLES, or use the REPLACE statement.

Using stored programs can help you avoid RDBMS-dependent code in your application layer while allowing you to continue to take advantage of RDBMS-specific optimizations. In theory—but only sometimes in practice—stored program calls against different databases can be made to look and behave identically from the application's perspective. Of course, the underlying stored program code will need to be rewritten for each RDBMS, but at least your application code will be relatively portable.

Unfortunately, not all RDBMSs implement stored programs in a consistent manner. This limits the portability that stored programs can offer. We discuss this in more detail in the section "They Do Not Provide Portability" later in this chapter.

Disadvantages of Stored Programs

So far, we've seen that stored programs can offer some significant advantages. Now let's look at the downside of using stored programs.

They Can Be Computationally Inferior

In Chapter 22 we compare the performance of MySQL stored programs and other languages when performing computationally intensive routines. Our conclusion is that stored programs, in general, and MySQL stored programs, in particular, are slower than languages such as PHP, Java, and Perl when executing "number crunching" algorithms, complex string manipulation, and the like.

Most of the time, stored programs are dominated by database access time—where stored programs have a natural performance advantage over other programming languages because of their lower network overhead. However, if you are writing a number-crunching routine—and you have a choice between implementing it in the stored program language or in another language such as Java—you may wisely decide against using the stored program solution.

They Can Lead to Logic Fragmentation

While it is generally useful to encapsulate data access logic inside stored programs, it is usually inadvisable to "fragment" business and application logic by implementing some of it in stored programs and the rest of it in the middle tier or the application client.

Debugging application errors that involve interactions between stored program code and other application code may be many times more difficult than debugging code that is completely encapsulated in the application layer. For instance, there is currently no debugger that can trace program flow from the application code into the MySQL stored program code.

They Do Not Provide Portability

We said earlier that stored programs could be used to build RDBMS-independent applications by encapsulating RDBMS-dependent SQL in stored program calls. Unfortunately, this is only possible for RDBMS types that support similar semantics for processing parameters and returning result sets.

The stored programs implemented by MySQL, DB2, and Microsoft SQL Server all behave in a very similar way—all can return multiple result sets, and for most languages, the calls for accessing these result sets are compatible.

Unfortunately, Oracle is an exception in this regard; Oracle stored programs can return result sets, but they are returned as references in output parameters, rather than as result sets in their own right. In order to retrieve these result sets, you have to write application code that is highly Oracle specific.

So while applications that use only stored programs are reasonably portable between MySQL and either DB2 or SQL Server, if portability between MySQL and Oracle is your objective, you are probably better advised to use ANSI-standard SQL calls, rather than stored program calls, at least when implementing calls that will return result sets.

Calling Stored Programs from Application Code

Most languages used to build applications that interact with MySQL are able to fully exploit stored programs, although in some languages, support for advanced features such as multiple result sets is a recent addition. In the following chapters we will explain in detail how to use stored programs from within PHP, Java, Perl, Python, and the .NET languages VB.NET and C#. In this section we want to give you an introduction to the general process of calling a stored program from an external programming language.

In general, the techniques for using stored programs differ from those for standard SQL statements in two significant respects:

- While SQL statement calls may take parameters, stored programs can also have OUT or INOUT parameters. This means that you need to understand how to access the value of an OUT or INOUT parameter once the stored program execution completes.

- A SELECT statement can return only one result set, while a stored program can return any number of result sets, and you might not be able to anticipate the number or structure of these result sets.

So, calling a stored program requires a slightly different program flow from standard SQL processing. The overall sequence of events is shown in the UML "retro" diagram (e.g., flowchart) in Figure 12-3.

Here's a brief description of each of these steps. Remember that in the next five chapters, we will be showing you how to follow these steps in various languages.

Preparing a Stored Program Call for Execution

We'll normally want to call a stored program more than once in our application. Typically, we first create a statement handle for the stored program. We then iteratively execute the program, perhaps providing different values for the program's parameters with each execution.

It's usually possible to bypass the preparation stage and execute a stored program directly—at least if the stored program returns no result sets. However, if the stored program takes parameters and you execute the stored program more than once in your program, we recommend that you go to the extra effort of preparing the statement that includes your stored program call.

Registering Parameters

We can pass parameters into stored programs that require them as literals (e.g., concatenate the text of the parameter values into the stored program CALL statement).

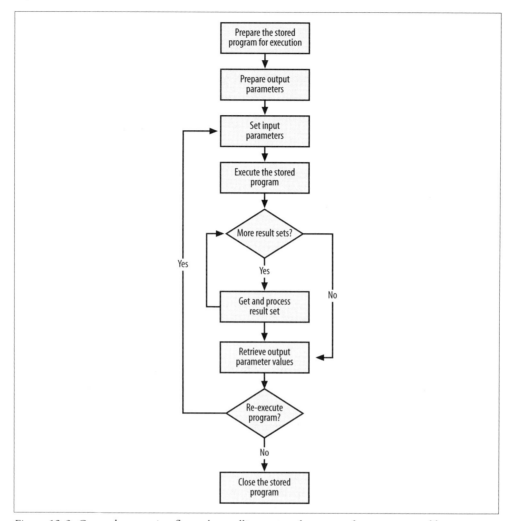

Figure 12-3. General processing flow when calling a stored program from an external language

However, in all of the languages we discuss in subsequent chapters, there are specific parameter-handling methods that allow us to re-execute a stored program with new parameters without having to re-prepare the stored program call. As we said previously, it's best to use these explicit methods if you are going to execute the stored program more than once—both because it is slightly more efficient and because, in some cases, only the prepared statement methods offer full support for bidirectional parameters and multiple result sets.

The methods for passing parameters to stored programs are usually the same as the methods used to pass parameters (or "bind variables") to normal SQL statements.

Setting Output Parameters

Some languages allow us to specifically define and process output parameters. In other languages, we can only access the values of OUT or INOUT parameters by employing "user variables" (variables prefixed with @) to set and retrieve the parameter values.

Both techniques—the direct API calls provided by .NET and JDBC and the session variable solution required by other languages—are documented in the relevant language-specific chapters that follow.

Executing the Stored Program

Once the input parameters are set and—in the case of .NET and Java—once the output parameters are registered, we can execute the stored program. The method for executing a stored program is usually the same as the method for executing a standard SQL statement.

If the stored program returns no result sets, output parameters can immediately be accessed. If the stored program returns one or more result sets, all of those result sets must be processed before the output parameter values can be retrieved.

Retrieving Result Sets

The process of retrieving a single result set from a stored program is identical to the process of retrieving a result set from other SQL statements—such as SELECT or SHOW—that return result sets.

However, unlike SELECT and SHOW statements, a stored program may return multiple result sets, and this requires a different flow of control in our application. To correctly process all of the result sets that may be returned from a stored program, the programming language API must include a method to switch to the "next" result set and possibly a separate method for determining if there are any more result sets to return.

JDBC and ADO.NET languages have included these methods since their earliest incarnations (for use with SQL Server and other RDBMSs that support multiple result sets), and these interfaces have been fully implemented for use with MySQL stored programs. Methods exist to retrieve multiple result sets in PHP, Perl, and Python, but these methods are relatively immature—in some cases, they were implemented only in response to the need to support stored programs in MySQL 5.0.

Retrieving Output Parameters

Once all result sets have been retrieved, we are able to retrieve any stored program output parameters. Not all languages provide methods for directly retrieving the values of output parameters—see the "Setting Output Parameters" section earlier for a description of a language-independent method of retrieving output parameters indirectly through user variables.

JDBC and ADO.NET provide specific calls that allow you to directly retrieve the value of an output parameter.

Closing or Re-Executing the Stored Program

Now that we have retrieved the output parameters, the current stored program execution is complete. If we are sure that we are not going to re-execute the stored program, we should close it using language-specific methods to release all resources associated with the stored program execution. This usually means closing the prepared statement object associated with the stored program call. If we want to re-execute the stored program, we can modify the input parameters and use the language-specific execute method to run the stored program as many times as needed. *Then* you should close the prepared statement and release resources.

Calling Stored Functions

In some languages—JDBC and .NET, in particular—stored functions can be invoked directly, and you have language-specific techniques for obtaining the stored function return value. However, in other languages, you would normally need to embed the stored function in a statement that supports an appropriate expression such as a single-line SELECT statement.

Conclusion

There is no "one-size-fits-all" answer to the question "Should I use stored programs in my application?" There are those who believe that virtually all of an application's database interactions should be made through stored program calls, and those who believe that stored programs should be used only in very special circumstances. You will need to make your own determination as to the value of using MySQL stored programs in your application.

As we've discussed in this chapter, the use of stored programs can provide significant advantages:

- Stored programs can substantially improve the security of your application.
- Stored programs can be used to provide an abstract data access layer that can improve the separation between business logic and data access logic (of course, stored programs are not *required* to do this—they are just one means to do so).
- Stored programs can reduce network traffic.
- Stored programs can be used to implement common routines accessible from multiple applications.

- Stored programs allow for a convenient division of duties between those whose skills are database-centric and those whose skills are programming-centric.
- The use of stored programs can (sometimes) improve application portability.

But you also need to consider the potential disadvantages of using stored programs:

- Stored programs are often slower—especially for computationally expensive operations—than equivalent middle-tier code.
- The use of stored programs can lead to fragmentation of your application logic—logic may be split between the database and application server tier, making it difficult to track down design flaws or implementation bugs.
- The use of stored programs usually results in your application's leveraging more than one programming language, requiring additional skills in your development team.
- Most object-relational mapping systems (e.g., J2EE CMP and Hibernate) do not know how to work with stored programs.
- Although stored program calls may sometimes be more portable than native SQL, in practice this is not true for all implementations. In particular, Oracle stored program calls often look and act substantially different from calls made in MySQL, DB2, or Microsoft SQL Server.

In this chapter we briefly reviewed the general programming logic involved in calling stored programs from external programming languages. In subsequent chapters we will explain the detailed techniques for handling stored program calls in PHP, Java, Perl, Python, C#, and VB.NET.

## CHAPTER 13

Using MySQL Stored Programs with PHP

The combination of PHP and MySQL is one of the most popular and powerful partnerships in open source web development and is a key component of the LAMP (Linux-Apache-MySQL-PHP/Perl/Python) stack. There are reportedly more than 18 million web sites based on PHP technology (according to *http://www.netcraft.com*), and the majority of these are using MySQL as the underlying database.

PHP started off as a simple CGI-based processor for amateur web development in the mid-1990s. It borrowed heavily from the Perl language (at the time, the most popular approach for CGI-based dynamic web development), but was more tightly integrated with HTML and—unlike Perl—was designed specifically for web development.

PHP takes a similar approach to dynamic web content as Microsoft's ASP (Active Server Pages) and J2EE's JSP (Java 2 Enterprise Edition Java Server Pages). All of these technologies involve embedding tags into HTML pages (renamed appropriately as PHP, ASP, or JSP pages, of course) that control the dynamic content of the page. In the case of PHP, the tags contain PHP code. The PHP code is executed by the PHP engine, which is usually deployed within the web server (Apache, IIS, etc.) and typically interacts with a database to provide dynamic, data-driven content.

As a language, PHP delivers much of the flexibility and power of the popular Perl open source scripting language and has a wide variety of interfaces to back-end databases. It is probably fair to characterize PHP as having a shallower learning curve than the ASP.NET or J2EE alternatives. Also, since PHP is open source, software licensing costs are, of course, minimal (although many larger enterprises seek support from Zend Corporation or another commercial entity).

In this chapter we will review the use of PHP with MySQL and show how stored programs can be used within PHP-based applications.

Options for Using MySQL with PHP

PHP currently offers multiple ways of working with MySQL. Some of the more popular methods include:

PEAR (PHP Extension and Application Repository) DB package
> This package offers a database-independent API for communicating with relational databases from PHP. PEAR::DB includes support for MySQL, but provides only rudimentary support for MySQL stored programs.

PHP MySQL extension (ext/mysql)
> This PHP extension provides MySQL-specific support for working with MySQL. However, the mysql extension does not include methods for working with advanced MySQL features introduced in MySQL 4.1 and 5.0 and will probably never provide direct support for stored programs.

mysqli interface (ext/mysqli)
> This PHP extension was introduced to support new features in MySQL 4.1 and 5.0.

PDO (PHP Data Objects)
> PDO is a database-independent interface that will probably become the successor to the PEAR::DB interface. PDO became an officially supported interface only in PHP 5.1, so it is the newest of the PHP database interfaces.

Only the mysqli and PDO extensions provide full support for MySQL stored programs. In this chapter we will show how each can be used to interface with MySQL and how to use MySQL stored programs.

Using PHP with the mysqli Extension

Before we look at how to invoke stored programs using PHP and the mysqli extension, let's look at how we perform operations in PHP involving simple SQL statements. These operations will form the foundation for using stored programs in PHP. If you already feel very familiar with mysqli, you might want to skip forward to "Calling Stored Programs with mysqli," later in this chapter.

Enabling the mysqli Extension

The mysqli extension ships as standard with PHP 5.0 and above, but you may need to enable it. You do this by ensuring that ext_mysqi is listed in the extensions section of your *php.ini* file. The ext_mysqli extension should be included in your default *php.ini* file, but may be commented out. In Windows, it can be found in the Windows extension section. The relevant line will look something like this:

```
extension=php_mysqli.dll
```

On Unix or Linux, the line should look like:

```
extension=mysqli.so
```

Connecting to MySQL

To connect to MySQL we first create an object representing a connection using the mysqli call. The mysqli call takes arguments containing the hostname, username, password, database, and port number. The mysqli_connect_errno( ) call will contain any error code associated with the connection, and mysqi_connect_error( ) will contain the error text.

In Example 13-1 we create an object—$mysqli—representing a MySQL connection, and check for any error condition.

Example 13-1. Creating a mysqli connection

```
# Create a connection
<?php
    $mysqli = new mysqli("localhost", "root", "secret", "test");
    if (mysqli_connect_errno( )) {
        printf("Connect failed: %s\n", mysqli_connect_error( ));
        exit ( );
    } else {
        printf("Connect succeeded\n");
    }
?>
```

Checking for Errors

The mysqli connection object includes properties that reflect any error condition associated with the most recent operation. These properties include:

errno
Contains the MySQL-specific error code

sqlstate
Contains the ANSI SQLSTATE error code

error
Contains the text of the most recent error

When we are using prepared statements (see the section "Using Prepared Statements" later in this chapter), similar properties can be accessed as part of the statement object.

Although PHP 5 supports Java- or C#-style exception handling, the mysqli classes do not currently throw exceptions, so it is usually necessary to check these error codes after every operation.

There are a couple of different common styles for error checking. First, we could check to see if the mysqli call returned TRUE (1) or FALSE (0):

```
if ($mysqli->query($sql) <> TRUE) {
    printf("Statement failed %d: (%s) %s\n"
      ,$mysqli->errno,$mysqli->sqlstate,$mysqli->error);
}
```

If we wanted to make our code very compact, we could do this using an "or" statement, as in this example:

```
$mysqli->query($sql) or printf("Statement failed %d: (%s) %s\n"
      ,$mysqli->errno,$mysqli->sqlstate,$mysqli->error);
```

Unfortunately, this technique is not very reliable, as there are some mysqli methods that return the number of rows affected, rather than TRUE or FALSE. For these calls, you need to explicitly check the value of $mysqli->errno after the calls, as follows:

```
$mysqli->query($sql);
if ($mysqli->errno <> 0 ) {
    printf("Statement failed %d: (%s) %s\n"
      ,$mysqli->errno,$mysqli->sqlstate,$mysqli->error);
}
```

It is probably wiser to explicitly check the value of errno after key method calls so that you can use a consistent style of coding and can avoid introducing bugs that may occur if you misinterpret a method that returns no rows as having encountered an error.

Executing a Simple Non-SELECT Statement

To issue a "one-off" statement that returns no result set, we can use the query method of the mysqli connection object. Example 13-2 provides an example of issuing a simple, one-off statement.

Example 13-2. Issuing a simple statement in mysqli

```
$mysqli->query("CREATE TABLE guy_1 (guys_integers INT)");
if ($mysqli->errno <> 0 ) {
    printf("Statement failed %d: (%s) %s\n"
    ,$mysqli->errno,$mysqli->sqlstate,$mysqli->error);
}
```

Retrieving a Result Set

If the statement issued from the query object returns a result set, we can retrieve the rows using the fetch_object( ) method. This method returns a row object, from which we can retrieve the values of the columns returned. Example 13-3 shows us cycling through the results of a query.

Example 13-3. Retrieving a result set from a simple query

```
$sql="SELECT employee_id, surname, salary
      FROM employees
    WHERE salary>95000
      AND department_id=1
        AND status='G'";

$results=$mysqli->query($sql);
if ($mysqli->errno) { die ($mysqli->errno." ".$mysqli->error); }
while($row=$results->fetch_object())     {
    printf("%d\t%s\t%d\n",$row->employee_id,$row->surname,$row->salary);
}
```

An alternative to the fetch_object( ) method is the fetch_row( ) method, in which columns can be referenced by number rather than name. Example 13-4 illustrates this technique.

Example 13-4. Retrieving a result set using fetch_row

```
$sql="SELECT employee_id, surname, salary
      FROM employees
    WHERE salary>95000
      AND department_id=1
      AND status='G'";

$results=$mysqli->query($sql);
if ($mysqli->errno) { die ($mysqli->errno." ".$mysqli->error); }
while($row=$results->fetch_row()) {
    printf("%d\t%s\t%d\n",$row[0],$row[1],$row[2]);
}
```

The use of fetch_row( ) results in code that is harder to read and maintain and is not generally recommended. However, as we shall soon see, the use of fetch_row( ) is convenient when you don't know what the result set will look like when you are writing your code (for instance, when processing a dynamic SQL statement).

Managing Transactions

As with most of the programmatic interfaces to MySQL, you are always free to manage transactions by executing the usual MySQL statements—for example, SET AUTOCOMMIT, START TRANSACTION, COMMIT, and ROLLBACK. However, instead of using these statements, you may want to take advantage of the native methods available in the mysqli interface. These methods can assist with managing transactions and can be more convenient and result in simpler code. Of course, these statements are only meaningful if you are using a transactional storage engine such as InnoDB.

The following methods of the mysqli object (illustrated in Example 13-5) are transaction-oriented:

autocommit( )
Enables or disables the autocommit setting for the current connection

commit( )
Issues a COMMIT of the transaction

rollback( )
Issues a (you guessed it) rollback of the transaction

Example 13-5. Using mysqli transaction-handling methods

```
$mysqli->autocommit(FALSE);

$mysqli->query("UPDATE account_balance
                   SET balance=balance-$tfer_amount
                 WHERE account_id=$from_account");
if ($mysqli->errno)   {
   printf("transaction aborted: %s\n",$mysqli->error);
   $mysqli->rollback( );
   }
   else   {
   $mysqli->query("UPDATE account_balance
                      SET balance=balance+$tfer_amount
                    WHERE account_id=$to_account");
   if ($mysqli->errno)       {
      printf("transaction aborted: %s\n",$mysqli->error);
      $mysqli->rollback( );
   }
   else    {
      printf("transaction succeeded\n");
      $mysqli->commit( );
   }
}
```

Using Prepared Statements

For SQL statements that may be re-executed, you can use the mysqli prepared statement interfaces. By preparing a statement before execution, you reduce the overhead of re-executing the statement. Furthermore, if a statement contains variable parameters, using the prepare and execute calls is safer than appending these parameters to the SQL and executing, since SQL code cannot be "injected" into prepared statement parameters (see Chapter 18 for a discussion of the security implications of SQL injection).

To create a prepared statement, we use the prepare( ) method of the mysqli interface, which returns a mysqli_stmt object. Any parameters within the prepared statement should be represented by ? characters, which can then be associated with PHP variables through the bind_param( ) method.

Example 13-6 illustrates the process of preparing a statement, binding parameters, and repeatedly executing a SQL statement.

Example 13-6. Preparing and multi-executing a simple SQL statement

```
1   #Preparing the statment
2   $insert_stmt=$mysqli->prepare("INSERT INTO x VALUES(?,?)")
3       or die($mysqli->error);
4   #associate variables with the input parameters
5   $insert_stmt->bind_param("is", $my_number,$my_string); #i=integer
6   #Execute the statement multiple times....
7   for ($my_number = 1; $my_number <= 10; $my_number++) {
8       $my_string="row ".$my_number;
9       $insert_stmt->execute() or die ($insert_stmt->error);
10  }
11  $insert_stmt->close();
```

The relevant sections of this code are shown here:

Line	Explanation
2	Prepare an INSERT statement. The statement has two input parameters, corresponding to the values to be inserted into the table.
5	Use bind_param( ) to associate PHP variables with the SQL parameters. bind_param( ) takes two input values: first a string indicating the data types of the parameters to follow (i=integer, d=double, s=string, b=blob). So the "is" string indicates that the first parameter is to be treated as an integer, and the second as a string. The following arguments to bind_param( ) signify the PHP variables to be associated with the ? placeholders.
7	Create a loop that repeats for each of the numbers 1 to 10.
9	Execute the prepared statement. Each execution will insert the values of the PHP variables $my_number and $my_string into the table.
11	Close the prepared statement, releasing any resources associated with the statement.

Retrieving Result Sets from Prepared Statements

To retrieve a result set from a prepared statement, we must first associate the columns in the result set with the PHP variables that will hold their values. This is done using the bind_result( ) method of the prepared statement object. We then use the fetch( ) method of the prepared statement to retrieve each row. Example 13-7 illustrates this technique.

Example 13-7. Retrieving a result set from a prepared statement

```
$sql="SELECT employee_id,surname,firstname
        FROM employees
       WHERE department_id=?
         AND status=?
       LIMIT 5";
$stmt = $mysqli->prepare($sql);
if ($mysqli->errno<>0) {die($mysqli->errno.": ".$mysqli->error);}
```

```
$stmt->bind_param("is",$input_department_id,$input_status) or die($stmt-error);
$stmt->bind_result( $employee_id,$surname,$firstname ) or die($stmt->error);

$input_department_id=1;
$input_status='G';
$stmt->execute();
if ($mysqli->errno<>0) {die($stmt.errno.": ".$stmt->error) ;}
while ($stmt->fetch()) {
    printf("%s %s %s\n", $employee_id,$surname,$firstname);
}
```

Getting Result Set Metadata

If we don't know in advance the structure of the result set being returned by our query, we can use the result_metadata( ) method of the prepared statement to retrieve the column definitions. This method returns a result object that can be queried to return the names, lengths, and types of the columns to be returned.

Example 13-8 shows us retrieving the structure of a result set from a prepared statement.

Example 13-8. Retrieving metadata from a prepared statement

```
$metadata = $stmt->result_metadata();
$field_cnt = $metadata->field_count;
while ($colinfo = $metadata->fetch_field()) {
    printf("Column:   %s\n",   $colinfo->name);
    printf("max. Len: %d\n",   $colinfo->max_length);
    printf("Type:     %d\n\n", $colinfo->type);
}
```

Processing a Dynamic Result Set

Sometimes we need to process a SQL statement without knowing exactly what the columns in the result set will be. In these cases, we can use the result_metadata( ) interface to determine the composition of the result set and dynamically bind the resulting columns. However, the process is not exactly intuitive. Example 13-9 provides some PHP code that will produce an HTML table based on an arbitrary SELECT statement.

Example 13-9. Processing a dynamic result set

```
1    require_once "HTML/Table.php";
2    $table =new HTML_Table('border=1');
3
4    $stmt=$mysqli->prepare($sql);
5    if ($mysqli->errno) {die($mysqli->errno.": ".$mysqli->error);}
6
7    # Retrieve meta-data and print table headings
```

Example 13-9. Processing a dynamic result set (continued)

```
8   $metadata = $stmt->result_metadata( );
9   $field_cnt = $metadata->field_count;
10  $colnames=array( );
11  while ($colinfo = $metadata->fetch_field( )) {
12      array_push($colnames,$colinfo->name);
13  }
14  $table->addRow($colnames);
15  $table->setRowAttributes(0,array("bgcolor" => "silver"));
16
17
18  # Declare an array to receive column data
19  $stmt_results=array_fill(0,$field_cnt,'');
20  # Set first element of the bind_result parameter as the statement handle
21  $bind_result_parms[0]=$stmt;
22  # Add the references to the column arrays to the parameter list
23  for ($i=0;$i<$field_cnt;$i++)   {
24      array_push($bind_result_parms,  &$stmt_results[$i]);
25  }
26  #Pass the array to the bind_result function
27  call_user_func_array("mysqli_stmt_bind_result", $bind_result_parms);
28  $stmt->execute( );
29  $row=0;
30  while($stmt->fetch( ))   {
31      $row++;
32      for ($i=0;$i<$field_cnt;$i++)   {
33          $table->setCellContents($row,$i,$stmt_results[$i]);
34      }
35  }
36  $stmt->close( );
37  print $table->toHtml( );
```

Let us step through this rather complicated example:

Line(s)	Explanation
1 and 2	Set up the HTML table that will hold our result set. We're using the PEAR Table class to create our HTML table—available at *http://pear.php.net*.
4	Prepare the SQL statement. The text of the SQL statement is contained in the variable $sql: we don't have to know the text of the SQL, since this code will process the output from any SELECT statement.
8	Retrieve the result set metadata.
9	Note the number of columns that will be returned by the query.
10-13	Retrieve the name of each column to be returned into an array.
14 and 15	Create and format a nHTML table row containing our column names.
19	Initialize an array that will contain the column values for each row returned by the SQL statemnet.
21	Create an array variable that we are going to use to pass to the bind_result( ) call. To perform a dynamic bind ,we have to use the procedural version of bind_result( )—mysqli_stmt_bind_result( )—which takes as its first argument the prepared statement object. So the first element of our array is the statement object.

Line(s)	Explanation
23 and 24	Add an element to `$bind_result_parms` for each column to be returned. Because `mysqli_stmt_bind_result( )` expects to have these passed "by reference" rather than "by value," we prefix these array elements with the & symbol.
27	Bind the result variables to the dynamic SQL. The process is complicated—because `bind_result( )` cannot accept an array of result variables, we need to call the PHP function `call_user_func_array( )`, which allows an array to be passed as an argument to a function that normally requires a static set of variables. We also have to use the procedural version of `bind_result( )`, `mysqli_stmt_bind_result( )`. Nevertheless—despite the complexity—we have now successfully bound the elements of `stmt_results` to receive the output of the fetch command.
28-34	Execute the SQL and fetch the results of the SQL. The results for each column will be placed in the `stmt_results` array.
36 and 37	Close the prepared statement and print out the contents of the HTML table that we have built.

The procedure for rendering the results of dynamic SQL in `mysqli` is more complicated than we would like. However, the technique outlined above can be used when we do not know in advance what the SQL is or what result set it will output—and this can be particularly important when dealing with stored procedures, since they may return an unpredictable result set sequence.

Figure 13-1 shows the output produced by Example 13-9 when provided with a simple query against the `departments` table.

Calling Stored Programs with mysqli

All of the `mysqli` methods for calling standard SQL statements can also be used to call stored programs. For instance, in Example 13-10, we call a stored procedure that does not return a result set using the query method.

Example 13-10. Calling a stored procedure without a result set in mysqli

```
$sql = 'call simple_stored_proc( )';
$mysqli->query($sql);
if ($mysqli->errno) {
    die("Execution failed: ".$mysqli->errno.": ".$mysqli->error);
}
else {
    printf("Stored procedure execution succeeded\n");
}
```

If the stored procedure returns a single result set, we can retrieve the result set as for a SELECT statement by using the `fetch_object( )` method. Example 13-11 shows such a simple stored procedure.

department_id	department_name	location
1	DUPLIN	MORENO VALLEY
2	MADISON	BEAVER
3	MCHENRY	OKEECHOBEE
4	CHARITON	TULLYTOWN
5	SUMMERS	OLD CHURCH
6	LINCOLN	SWENGEL
7	CHAMPAIGN	AMF GREENSBORO
8	WILKES	CUSHING
9	CRAVEN	TAHOE PARADISE
10	COTTONWOOD	WICHITA
11	TAZEWELL	KLAWOCK
12	WHATCOM	LAKE MOHEGAN
13	OPTIMIZER RESEARCH	BASTROP
14	KING	KENOSHA
15	SMITH	PAYSON
16	GASTON	OLIVEBRIDGE
17	MARSHALL	URB MELISA
18	ROCKINGHAM	EGGERTSVILLE

Figure 13-1. Sample output from the dynamic SQL PHP routine

Example 13-11. Stored procedure with a single result set

```
CREATE PROCEDURE department_list( )
    READS SQL DATA
    SELECT  department_name,location from departments;
```

Example 13-12 shows how we would retrieve the result set from this stored procedure call using query( ) and fetch_object( ).

Example 13-12. Retrieving a result set from a stored procedure

```
$sql = "call department_list( )";
$results = $mysqli->query($sql);
if ($mysqli->errno) {
    die("Execution failed: ".$mysqli->errno.": ".$mysqli->error);
}
while ($row = $results->fetch_object( )) {
    printf("%s\t%s\n", $row->department_name, $row->location);
}
```

You will often want to execute the same stored procedure multiple times—possibly with varying input parameters—so it is a best practice to use mysqli prepared statements. We can use prepared statements with stored procedure in pretty much the same way as we would for any other SQL statement. For instance, in Example 13-13, we see a stored procedure that accepts an input parameter and generates a result set based on the value of that input parameter.

Example 13-13. Stored procedure with result set and input parameter

```
CREATE PROCEDURE customers_for_rep(in_sales_rep_id INT)
    READS SQL DATA
      SELECT customer_id,customer_name
        FROM customers
          WHERE sales_rep_id=in_sales_rep_id;
```

We can create a prepared statement for this stored procedure and use the bind_param( ) method to associate the stored procedure input parameter with a PHP variable. Example 13-14 illustrates this technique.

Example 13-14. Using a prepared statement to execute a stored procedure with input parameter and result set

```
1    $sql = "CALL customers_for_rep(?)";
2    $stmt = $mysqli->prepare($sql);
3    if ($mysqli->errno) {die($mysqli->errno."::".$mysqli->error);}
4
5    $stmt->bind_param("i", $in_sales_rep_id);
6    $in_sales_rep_id = 1;
7    $stmt->execute( );
8    if ($mysqli->errno) {die($mysqli->errno.": ".$mysqli->error);}
9
10   $stmt->bind_result($customer_id,$customer_name);
11   while ($stmt->fetch( )) {
12       printf("%d %s \n", $customer_id,$customer_name);
13   }
```

Let's look at this example line by line:

Line(s)	Explanation
1-3	Create a prepared statement for the stored procedure call; the ? symbol in the SQL text indicates the presence of an input parameter.
5	Associate a PHP variable ($in_sales_rep_id) with the stored procedure's input parameter.
7-10	Execute the stored procedure and associate PHP variables ($customer_id and $customer_name) with the columns in the output result set.
11-13	Retrieve the result set from the stored procedure call.

Handling Output Parameters

The mysqli extension does not currently include a method for directly retrieving output parameters from a stored program. However, it is relatively easy to work around this limitation by using a user variable to hold the output parameter and then using a simple SQL statement to retrieve that value. Example 13-15 shows a stored procedure that returns the number of customers for a specific sales representative as a stored procedure output variable.

Example 13-15. Stored procedure with an output parameter

```
CREATE PROCEDURE sp_rep_customer_count(
       in_emp_id DECIMAL(8,0),
       OUT out_cust_count INT)
    NOT DETERMINISTIC READS SQL DATA
BEGIN

    SELECT count(*)
      INTO out_cust_count
      FROM customers
     WHERE sales_rep_id=in_emp_id;

END;
```

To retrieve the output parameter from this stored procedure, we specify a user variable (see Chapter 3 for a description of user variables) to hold the value of the output parameter, and then we issue a simple SELECT statement to retrieve the value. Example 13-16 illustrates the technique.

Example 13-16. Retrieving the value of an output parameter in mysqli

```
$sql="CALL sp_rep_customer_count(1,@customer_count)";
$stmt = $mysqli->prepare($sql);
if ($mysqli->errno) {die($mysqli->errno.": ".$mysqli->error);}
$stmt->execute();
if ($mysqli->errno) {die($mysqli->errno.": ".$mysqli->error);}
$stmt->close();

$results = $mysqli->query("SELECT @customer_count AS customer_count");
$row = $results->fetch_object();
printf("Customer count=%d\n",$row->customer_count);
```

Retrieving Multiple Result Sets

If a stored procedure returns more than one result set, then you can use mysqli's multi_query() method to process all the results. The specific coding technique in PHP depends somewhat on whether you know the exact number and structure of the result sets. For instance, in the case of the very simple stored procedure in Example 13-17, we know that two, and only two, result sets will be returned, and we know the exact structure of each.

Example 13-17. Stored procedure that returns two result sets

```
CREATE PROCEDURE stored_proc_with_2_results(in_sales_rep_id INT)
   DETERMINISTIC READS SQL DATA
BEGIN

   SELECT employee_id,surname,firstname
     FROM employees
    WHERE employee_id=in_sales_rep_id;

   SELECT customer_id,customer_name
     FROM customers
    WHERE sales_rep_id=in_sales_rep_id;

END;
```

To process this stored procedure, we first call `multi_query( )` to set up the multiple results, and then we call `store_result( )` to initialize each result set. We can use `fetch_object( )` or `fetch_row( )` to access each row in the result set. Example 13-18 illustrates this technique.

Example 13-18. Fetching two result sets from a stored procedure in mysqli

```
$query  = "call stored_proc_with_2_results( $employee_id )";
if ($mysqli->multi_query($query)) {

    $result = $mysqli->store_result( );
    while ($row = $result->fetch_object( )) {
        printf("%d %s %s\n",$row->employee_id,$row->surname,$row->firstname);
    }
    $mysqli->next_result( );
    $result = $mysqli->store_result( );
    while ($row = $result->fetch_object( )) {
        printf("%d %s \n",$row->customer_id,$row->customer_name);
    }
}
```

Of course, we don't always know exactly how many result sets a stored procedure might return, and each result set can have an unpredictable structure. The next_result( ) method will return TRUE if there is an additional result set, and we can use the field_count property and fetch_field( ) method to retrieve the number of columns as well as their names and other properties, as shown in Example 13-19.

Example 13-19. mysqli code to process a variable number of result sets

```
1   $query  = "call stored_proc_with_2_results( $employee_id )";
2   if ($mysqli->multi_query($query)) {
3   do {
4       if ($result = $mysqli->store_result( )) {
5           while ($finfo = $result->fetch_field( )) {
6               printf("%s\t", $finfo->name);
7           }
```

Example 13-19. mysqli code to process a variable number of result sets (continued)

```
8              printf("\n");
9
10             while ($row = $result->fetch_row()) {
11                 for ($i=0;$i<$result->field_count;$i++) {
12                     printf("%s\t", $row[$i]);
13                 }
14                 printf("\n");
15             }
16             $result->close();
17         }
18     } while ($mysqli->next_result());
```

Let's look at this example line by line:

Line(s)	Explanation
2	Use the `multi_query()` call to invoke the stored procedure.
3-18	Define a loop that will continue so long as `mysqli->next_result()` returns TRUE: the loop will execute at least once, and then will continue as long as there are result sets to process.
4	Use `store_result()` to retrieve the result set into the `$result` object. We can use either `store_result()` or `use_result()`: `store_result()` uses more memory, but allows some additional functionality (such as `seek_result()`).
5-7	Loop through the column in the result set. Each call to `fetch_field()` stores the details of a new column into the `$finfo` object. On line 6 we print the name of the column.
10-15	This loop repeats for each row in the result set. We use `fetch_row()` rather than `fetch_object()`, since it is easier to refer to a column by number when we do not know its name.
11-13	Loop through each column in a particular row. We use the `field_count` property of the result set to control that loop. On line 12 we print the value of a particular column, referring to the column by number.
16	Close the result set.
18	The `while` condition on this line will cause the loop to repeat if there is an additional result set and to terminate otherwise.

Using MySQL with PHP Data Objects

As we outlined earlier in this chapter, PDO is a database-independent object-oriented, interface to relational databases for use in PHP 5.x. PDO was officially released with PHP 5.1, although "experimental" versions were available with the 5.0 release. PDO provides a very powerful and easy-to-use syntax, as well as providing good support for MySQL stored programs.

We'll start with a brief review of PDO basics; if you are already familiar with PDO, you might want to skip forward to the section "Calling Stored Programs with PDO" later in this chapter.

Connecting to MySQL

To create a connection to MySQL, we create a database handle using the PDO constructor method. The constructor takes three arguments:

dsn

The "dsn" string represents the database to be connected; it has the form 'mysql:dbname=*dbname*;host=*hostname*;port=*port_no*'.

user

The username to be used for the connection.

password

The password for the user account specified.

This method will throw an exception if the connection cannot be made, so you will normally enclose it in a try/catch block. The getMessage() method of the PDOException exception will contain details of any problems encountered when establishing the connection.

Example 13-20 shows a connection to MySQL being established.

Example 13-20. Connecting to MySQL using PDO

```php
<?php

$dsn = 'mysql:dbname=prod;host=localhost;port=3305';
$user = 'root';
$password = 'secret';

try {
  $dbh = new PDO($dsn, $user, $password);
}
catch (PDOException $e) {
  die('Connection failed: '.$e->getMessage());
}

print "Connected\n";

?>
```

Executing a Simple Non-SELECT Statement

You can execute a simple one-off statement that does not return a result set (e.g., is not a SELECT, SHOW STATUS, etc.) with the exec() method of the database object, as shown in Example 13-21.

Example 13-21. Executing a non-select with PDO

```php
$sql="CREATE TABLE my_numbers (a_number INT)";
$dbh->exec($sql);
```

The exec( ) method returns the number of rows returned, as opposed to a success or failure status. Example 13-22 shows a code fragment that uses the return value to determine the number of rows inserted.

Example 13-22. Using the return value from the exec() method

```
$rows=$dbh->exec("INSERT INTO my_numbers VALUES (1), (2), (3)");
printf("%d rows inserted\n",$rows);
```

Catching Errors

Some PDO methods return a success or failure status, while others—like $dbh-> exec( )— return the number of rows processed. Therefore, it's usually best to check for an error after each statement has executed. The errorCode( ) method returns the SQLSTATE from the most recent execution, while errorInfo( ) returns a three-element array that contains the SQLSTATE, MySQL error code, and MySQL error message.

Example 13-23 checks the errorCode( ) status from the preceding exec( ) call, and— if the SQLSTATE does not indicate success (00000)—prints the error information from errorInfo( ).

Example 13-23. Using PDO error status methods

```
$sql="CREATE TABLE my_numbers (a_number INT)";
$dbh->exec($sql);
if ($dbh->errorCode( )<>'00000') {
  $error_array=$dbh->errorInfo( );
  printf("SQLSTATE          : %s\n",$error_array[0]);
  printf("MySQL error code  : %s\n",$error_array[1]);
  printf("Message           : %s\n",$error_array[2]);
}
```

The output from Example 13-23 is shown in Example 13-24.

Example 13-24. Output from the errorInfo() method

```
SQLSTATE          : 42S01
MySQL error code  : 1050
Message           : Table 'my_numbers' already exists
```

If you want to produce a more succinct error output, you can use the PHP implode( ) function to join the elements of the errorInfo( ) call into a single string, as shown in Example 13-25.

Example 13-25. Generating a succinct error message

```
$sql="CREATE TABLE my_numbers (a_number INT)";
$dbh->exec($sql);
if ($dbh->errorCode( )<>'00000') {
  die("Error: ".implode(': ',$dbh->errorInfo( ))."\n");
}
```

Managing Transactions

If you are using a transactional storage engine such as InnoDB, then you can control transactions using the standard MySQL statements such as SET AUTOCOMMIT, START TRANSACTION, COMMIT, and ROLLBACK. However, instead of using these statements, you may want to take advantage of the native methods available in the PDO interface, which allow you to directly control transactions. These methods are applied to the database connection object and include beginTransaction( ), commit( ), and rollback( ).

Example 13-26 illustrates the use of these transaction control methods to implement transaction logic in PDO.

Example 13-26. Using PDO transaction control methods

```
$dbh->beginTransaction( );

$dbh->exec("UPDATE account_balance
                SET balance=balance-$tfer_amount
              WHERE account_id=$from_account");

if ($dbh->errorCode( )<>'00000') {
  printf("transaction aborted: %s\n",implode(': ',$dbh->errorInfo( )));
  $dbh->rollback( );
}

else
  {
    $dbh->exec("UPDATE account_balance
                  SET balance=balance+$tfer_amount
                WHERE account_id=$to_account");
    if ($dbh->errorCode( )<>'00000')
    {
        printf("transaction aborted: %s\n",implode(': ',$dbh->errorInfo( )));
        $dbh->rollback( );
    }
    else
    {
        printf("transaction succeeded\n");
        $dbh->commit( );
    }
  }
```

Issuing a One-Off Query

The query( ) method can be used to generate a one-off query. It returns an object containing the result set returned by the query. Individual columns may be accessed either by column name or column number (using column name is recommended to improve readability and maintainability). Example 13-27 shows a query being executed and the results accessed by column name.

Example 13-27. Issuing a simple query in PDO

```
$sql = 'SELECT department_id,department_name FROM departments';
foreach ($dbh->query($sql) as $row) {
  printf("%d \t %s\n",$row['department_id'],$row['department_name']);
}
```

In Example 13-28 we retrieve the column results by column number.

Example 13-28. Accessing query results by column number

```
$sql = 'SELECT department_id,department_name FROM departments';
foreach ($dbh->query($sql) as $row) {
  printf("%d \t %s\n",$row[0],$row[1]);
}
```

Using the query( ) method is a convenient way to quickly execute a query, but it is
not a good way to execute a query that will be re-executed, and it has less functionality than the prepare( ) and execute( ) methods that we are going to discuss next.

Using Prepared Statements

PDO prepared statements should be used whenever you are going to repetitively execute a statement. The prepare( ) and execute( ) methods also allow you to exercise
greater control over statement execution, and they offer some additional capabilities
that are particularly important when executing stored procedures.

The prepare( ) method accepts a SQL statement and returns a PDOStatement object.
The execute( ) method of the statement can then be used to execute the statement.
Example 13-29 shows the use of prepare( ) and execute( ) to execute a simple INSERT
statement.

Example 13-29. Prepared statement without result set

```
$sql = 'INSERT INTO my_numbers VALUES(1),(2),(3)';

$sth = $dbh->prepare($sql);
$sth->execute() or die (implode(':',$sth->errorInfo()));
```

If the SQL statement passed to the statement is a query, then we can use the fetch( )
method of the statement to access the result set. Each call to fetch( ) returns an array
containing the values for that row. As with the query call, we can access the column
values by name or by column number. Example 13-30 shows us accessing the column values by name.

Example 13-30. Retrieving a result set from a prepared statement

```
$sql='SELECT department_id,department_name FROM departments LIMIT 5';

$sth=$dbh->prepare($sql) or die (implode(':',$sth->errorInfo()));
```

```
$sth->execute() or die (implode(':',$sth->errorInfo()));

while($row=$sth->fetch()) {
  printf("%d \t %s \n",$row['department_id'],$row['department_name']);
}
```

Binding Parameters to a Prepared Statement

We usually create prepared statements with the intention of re-executing the statement—often in association with new parameter values.

If you want to re-execute a SQL statement while changing the WHERE clause criteria, DML values, or some other part of the SQL, you will need to include placeholders for substitution variables (sometimes called *SQL parameters* or *bind variables*). These are represented in the SQL text by including variable names prefixed by :, or as ? symbols.

We then use the bindParam() method to associate PHP variables with the placeholders in the SQL text. This must occur after the prepare() method has been called but before the execute() method. bindParam() requires that you specify the data type of the parameter as a PDO constant (such as PDO::PARAM_INT) and—for certain data types such as strings—a length.

Once we have associated PHP variables with a SQL parameter using bindParam(), we are ready to execute our SQL. If we wish to re-execute the SQL, we can simply change the values of the PHP variables and re-issue the execute() call: we do not have to call bindParam() whenever the parameter values change.

Example 13-31 shows how we can bind parameters to a prepared statement.

Example 13-31. Binding parameters to a prepared statement

```
1   $sql='SELECT customer_id,customer_name
2         FROM customers
3         WHERE sales_rep_id=:sales_rep_id
4           AND contact_surname=:surname';
5   $sth = $dbh->prepare($sql);
6   if ($dbh->errorCode()<>'00000') {
7     die("Error: ".implode(': ',$dbh->errorInfo())."\n");
8   }
9
10  $sth->bindParam(':sales_rep_id', $sales_rep_id, PDO::PARAM_INT);
11  $sth->bindParam(':surname',      $surname,      PDO::PARAM_STR, 30);
12
13  $sales_rep_id=41;
14  $surname = 'SMITH';
15  $sth->execute();
16  if ($dbh->errorCode()<>'00000') {
17    die("Error: ".implode(': ',$dbh->errorInfo())."\n");
18  }
```

Example 13-31. Binding parameters to a prepared statement (continued)

```
19  while($row=$sth->fetch()) {
20    printf("%d %s \n",$row['customer_id'],$row['customer_name']);
21  }
```

Let's look at this example line by line:

Line(s)	Explanation
1-5	Prepare a PDO statement for a SELECT statement that will retrieve customer details for a particular customer contact_surname and sales_rep_id. Placeholders are defined in the SQL text to represent the values for those two columns.
10	Call the bindParam( ) method to associate the PHP variable $sales_rep_id with the placeholder :sales_rep_id. The third parameter indicates the data type of the placeholder. A complete list of PDO data types can be found in the PDO documentation (see *http://www.php.net/manual/en/ref.pdo.php*).
11	Call bindParam( ) again to associate a PHP variable with the :surname placeholder. In this case, we also specify a maximum length for the parameter as specified in the fourth parameter.
13-14	Assign values to the PHP variables that have been associated with the prepared statement placeholders. Typically, we would assign new values to these variables before we execute the prepared statement.
15-22	Execute the prepared statement and retrieve rows in the usual fashion.

Getting Result Set Metadata

Sometimes we will need to execute a SQL statement without being sure about the structure of the result set that it might return. This is particularly true of stored programs, which can return multiple result sets in possibly unpredictable ways. We can determine the result set to be returned by a prepared statement by using PDO metadata methods.

The prepared statement object supports a columnCount( ) method, which returns the number of columns to be returned by the prepared statement. getColumnMeta( ) can be called to obtain an array containing details about a specific column such as its name, data type, and length.

Table 13-1 lists the elements contained in the array returned by getColumnMeta( ).

Table 13-1. Elements of the getColumnMeta( ) array

Array element name	Description
native_type	MySQL data type of the column
flags	Any special flags, for the column, such as "not null"
name	Display name for the column
len	Length of the column
precision	Precision for decimal or floating-point numbers
pdo_type	Internal PDO data type used to store the value

In Example 13-32 we use the getColumnMeta( ) function to retrieve and print names, data types, and lengths of columns returned by a query.

Example 13-32. Obtaining column metadata using the getColumnMeta( ) method

```
$sth = $dbh->prepare("SELECT employee_id,surname,date_of_birth
                        FROM employees where employee_id=1");
$sth->execute() or die (implode(':',$sth->errorInfo( )));
$cols=$sth->columnCount( );

for ($i=0; $i<$cols ;$i++) {
  $metadata=$sth->getColumnMeta($i);
  printf("\nDetails for column %d\n",$i+1);
  printf("    Name: %s\n",$metadata["name"]);
  printf(" Datatype: %s\n",$metadata["native_type"]);
  printf("   Length: %d\n",$metadata["len"]);
  printf(" Precision: %d\n",$metadata["precision"]);
}
```

Processing a Dynamic Result Set

Using the columnCount( ) method and (optionally) the getColumnMeta( ) method, we can fairly easily process a result set even if we have no idea what the structure of the result set will be when we code.

Example 13-33 shows a PHP function that will accept any SELECT statement and output an HTML table showing the result set.

Example 13-33. PDO function to generate an HTML table from a SQL statement

```
1   function sql_to_html($dbh,$sql_text) {
2       require_once "HTML/Table.php";
3       $table = new HTML_Table('border=1');
4
5       $sth = $dbh->prepare($sql_text) or die(implode(':', $sth->errorInfo( )));
6       $sth->execute() or die(implode(':', $sth->errorInfo( )));
7       $cols = $sth->columnCount( );
8
9       for ($i = 0; $i < $cols; $i ++) {
10          $metadata = $sth->getColumnMeta($i);
11          $table->setCellContents(0, $i, $metadata["name"]);
12      }
13      $table->setRowAttributes(0, array ("bgcolor" => "silver"));
14
15      $r = 0;
16      while ($row = $sth->fetch( )) {
17          $r ++;
18          for ($i = 0; $i < $cols; $i ++) {
19              $table->setCellContents($r, $i, $row[$i]);
20          }
21      }
22
23      print $table->toHtml( );
24  }
```

Let's step through the code:

Line(s)	Explanation
2 and 3	Initialize the HTML table. We're using the PEAR Table class to create our HTML table (available at *http:// pear.php.net*).
5 and 6	Prepare and execute the SQL in the usual fashion.
7	Retrieve the number of columns in the result set. We'll need to refer to the column count several times, so it's handy to store the results in a local variable.
9-12	Loop through the columns. For each column, we retrieve the column name and add that column name to the header row in our HTML table.
16-21	Loop through the rows from the result set using the fetch( ) method in the usual fashion.
18-20	Loop through the columns returned for a particular row. On line 19 we apply the column value to the appropriate cell of the HTML table.
23	Print the HTML to generate the table.

Figure 13-2 shows the output generated by the PDO routine for a simple SQL statement that prints some columns from the employees table.

Calling Stored Programs with PDO

All of the PDO methods we've examined so far can be used with stored programs. For instance, you can use the exec( ) method to call a simple stored program that doesn't return a result set, as shown in Example 13-34.

Example 13-34. Calling a simple stored procedure in PDO with the exec() method

```
$sql='call simple_stored_proc( )';
$dbh->exec($sql);
if ($dbh->errorCode( )<>'00000') {
  die("Error: ".implode(': ',$dbh->errorInfo( ))."\n");
}
```

If the stored procedure returns a single result set, then you have the same choices as for a SELECT statement or another SQL statement that returns a result set. That is, you can use prepare( ) and execute( ) for the statement, or you can use the query( ) method. Generally we advise that you use prepare( ) and execute( ), since these can be more efficient and have greater flexibility. Example 13-35 shows the use of query( ) to retrieve a single result set from a stored procedure.

Example 13-35. Retrieving a single stored procedure result set using the PDO query() method

```
$sql = 'call stored_proc_with_1_result( )';
foreach ($dbh->query($sql) as $row) {
  printf("%d \t %s\n",$row[0],$row[1]);
}
```

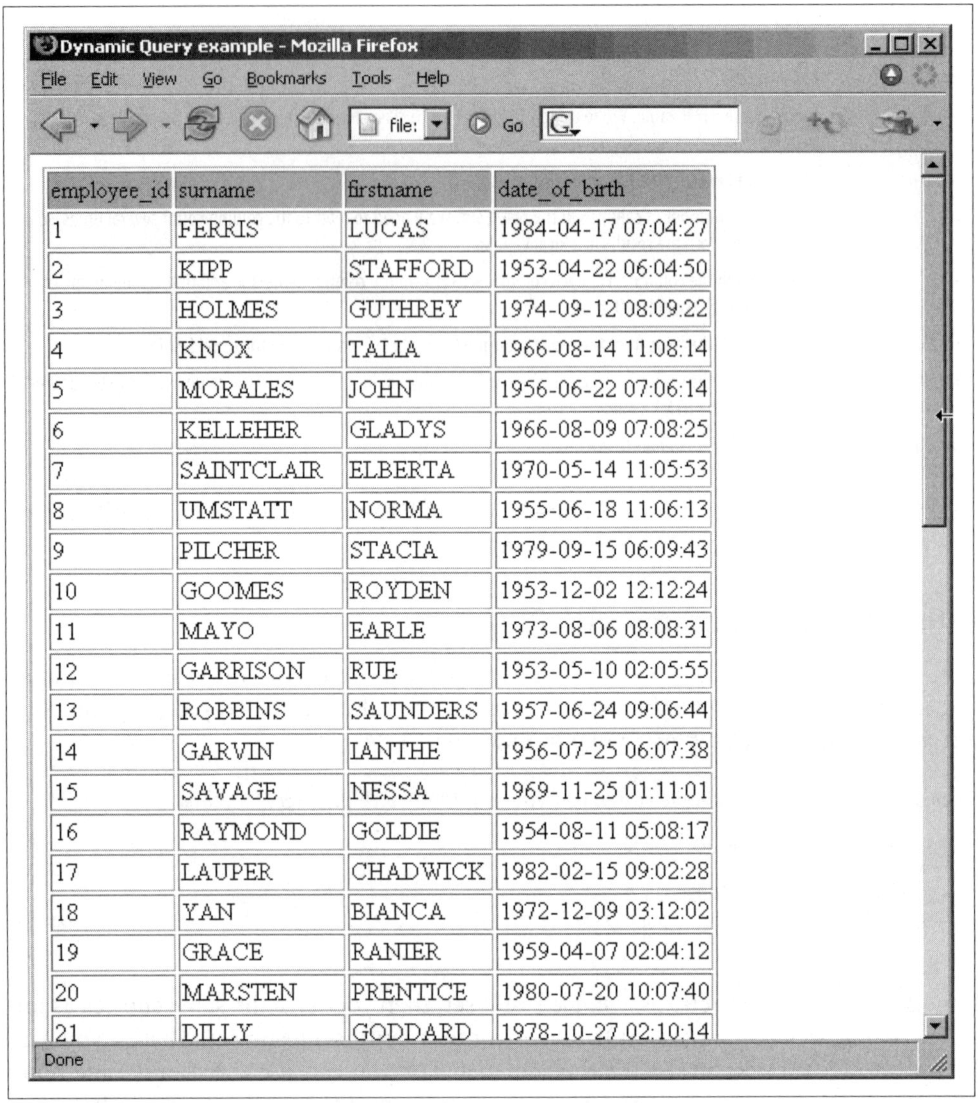

employee_id	surname	firstname	date_of_birth
1	FERRIS	LUCAS	1984-04-17 07:04:27
2	KIPP	STAFFORD	1953-04-22 06:04:50
3	HOLMES	GUTHREY	1974-09-12 08:09:22
4	KNOX	TALIA	1966-08-14 11:08:14
5	MORALES	JOHN	1956-06-22 07:06:14
6	KELLEHER	GLADYS	1966-08-09 07:08:25
7	SAINTCLAIR	ELBERTA	1970-05-14 11:05:53
8	UMSTATT	NORMA	1955-06-18 11:06:13
9	PILCHER	STACIA	1979-09-15 06:09:43
10	GOOMES	ROYDEN	1953-12-02 12:12:24
11	MAYO	EARLE	1973-08-06 08:08:31
12	GARRISON	RUE	1953-05-10 02:05:55
13	ROBBINS	SAUNDERS	1957-06-24 09:06:44
14	GARVIN	IANTHE	1956-07-25 06:07:38
15	SAVAGE	NESSA	1969-11-25 01:11:01
16	RAYMOND	GOLDIE	1954-08-11 05:08:17
17	LAUPER	CHADWICK	1982-02-15 09:02:28
18	YAN	BIANCA	1972-12-09 03:12:02
19	GRACE	RANIER	1959-04-07 02:04:12
20	MARSTEN	PRENTICE	1980-07-20 10:07:40
21	DILLY	GODDARD	1978-10-27 02:10:14

Figure 13-2. Output from PDO dynamic query example

The prepare( ), execute( ), and fetch( ) sequence for retrieving a single result set from a stored procedure is exactly the same as for a SELECT statement. Example 13-36 shows the use of this sequence to retrieve a result set from a stored procedure.

Example 13-36. Retrieving a single stored procedure result set using prepare(), execute(), and fetch()

```
$sql='call stored_proc_with_1_result( )';

$sth=$dbh->prepare($sql) or die (implode(':',$sth->errorInfo( )));
```

```
$sth->execute() or die (implode(':',$sth->errorInfo()));

while($row=$sth->fetch()) {
  printf("%s \t %s \n",$row['department_name'],$row['location']);
}
```

Binding Input Parameters to Stored Programs

If we use prepare( ) to ready our stored procedure for execution, we can bind parameters to the stored procedure using the bindParam( ) call, just as we have done with standard SQL statements, as shown in Example 13-37.

Example 13-37. Binding parameters to stored procedures

```
$sql='CALL customers_for_rep(:sales_rep_id,:surname)';
$sth = $dbh->prepare($sql);
if ($dbh->errorCode()<>'00000') {
  die("Error: ".implode(': ',$dbh->errorInfo())."\n");
}

$sth->bindParam(':sales_rep_id', $sales_rep_id, PDO::PARAM_INT);
$sth->bindParam(':surname',      $surname,      PDO::PARAM_STR, 30);

$sales_rep_id=41;
$surname = 'SMITH';
$sth->execute();
```

Handling Multiple Result Sets

If a stored procedure returns more than one result set, then you can use the nextRowset( ) method to move through each result set in sequence. The specific coding technique in PHP depends somewhat on whether you know the exact number and structure of the result sets. For instance, in the case of the very simple stored procedure in Example 13-38, we know that two, and only two, result sets will be returned, and we know the exact structure of each.

Example 13-38. Stored procedure that returns two result sets

```
CREATE PROCEDURE stored_proc_with_2_results(in_sales_rep_id INT)
    DETERMINISTIC READS SQL DATA
BEGIN

    SELECT employee_id,surname,firstname
      FROM employees
     WHERE employee_id=in_sales_rep_id;

    SELECT customer_id,customer_name
      FROM customers
```

Example 13-38. Stored procedure that returns two result sets (continued)

```
    WHERE sales_rep_id=in_sales_rep_id;

END;
```

To process this stored procedure, we merely need to code fetch( ) loops to retrieve each result set and add a nextRowset( ) call between the first set of fetches and the second. Example 13-39 illustrates this technique.

Example 13-39. Fetching two result sets from a stored procedure in PDO

```php
$sth = $dbh->prepare("call stored_proc_with_2_results( $employee_id )");
$sth->execute() or die (implode(':',$sth->errorInfo( )));

while ($row1=$sth->fetch( )) {
  printf("%d %s %s\n",$row1['employee_id'],$row1['surname'],$row1['firstname']);
}

$sth->nextRowset( );

while ($row2=$sth->fetch( )) {
  printf("%d %s \n",$row2['customer_id'],$row2['customer_name']);
}
```

Of course, we don't always know exactly how many result sets a stored procedure might return, and each result set can have an unpredictable structure. Therefore, we often want to combine the nextRowset( ) method with the getColumnMeta( ) method we saw earlier to dynamically process the result sets that the stored procedure produces. For instance, the stored procedure in Example 13-40 will return different result sets depending on whether the employee is a sales representative or not.

Example 13-40. Stored procedure that returns a variable number of result sets

```sql
CREATE PROCEDURE sp_employee_report(in_emp_id decimal(8,0))
    READS SQL DATA
BEGIN
    DECLARE customer_count INT;

    SELECT surname,firstname,date_of_birth
      FROM employees
     WHERE employee_id=in_emp_id;

    SELECT department_id,department_name
      FROM departments
     WHERE department_id=
           (select department_id
              FROM employees
             WHERE employee_id=in_emp_id);

    SELECT count(*)
      INTO customer_count
      FROM customers
     WHERE sales_rep_id=in_emp_id;
```

```
    IF customer_count=0 THEN
        SELECT 'Employee is not a current sales rep';
    ELSE
        SELECT customer_name,customer_status
          FROM customers
         WHERE sales_rep_id=in_emp_id;

        SELECT customer_name,sum(sale_value)
          FROM sales JOIN customers USING (customer_id)
         WHERE customers.sales_rep_id=in_emp_id
         GROUP BY customer_name;
    END IF;

END;
```

It's relatively simple to handle variable result set types with varying results. First, we construct a loop that will continue as long as nextRowset( ) returns TRUE. Within that loop we use the getColumnMeta( ) call to retrieve the names and types of columns and then fetch the rows using the methods we discussed previously in the section "Getting Result Set Metadata," earlier in this chapter.

Example 13-41 shows some PDO code that will process the multiple, variable result sets output by the stored procedure shown in Example 13-40. In fact, this code is capable of processing the result sets from any stored procedure specified in the $sql variable.

Example 13-41. PDO code to process multiple result sets from a stored procedure

```
1   function many_results($dbh, $sql_text) {
2       $sth = $dbh->prepare($sql_text);
3       $sth->execute() or die(implode(':', $sth->errorInfo( )));
4
5       do {
6           if ($sth->columnCount( ) > 0) { /* Yes, there is a result set */
7
8               #Print off the column names
9               for ($i = 0; $i < $sth->columnCount( ); $i ++) {
10                  $meta = $sth->getColumnMeta($i);
11                  printf("%s\t", $meta["name"]);
12              }
13              printf("\n");
14
15              #Loop through the rows
16              while ($row = $sth->fetch( )) {
17                  #Loop through the columns
18                  for ($i = 0; $i < $sth->columnCount( ); $i ++) {
19                      printf("%s\t", $row[$i]);
20                  }
21                  printf("\n");
22
23              }
```

```
24                printf("------------------\n");
25          }
26      }
27      while ($sth->nextRowset());
28  }
```

Let's walk through this example:

Line(s)	Explanation
2-3	Prepare and execute a stored procedure call in the usual manner.
5-27	This is our main loop. It executes once for each result set returned by the stored procedure—it will continue until `nextRowset()` returns FALSE. Note that this loop will always execute at least once (though it may do nothing if there are no rows returned).
6	Check to make sure that there is a result set. Remember that the loop will execute at least once, so we should check that there is at least one result set.
9-12	Loop through the column names and print them off (as a header row).
16-23	This loop repeats once for each row returned by a result set.
18-20	Loop through each column in the current row and print out its value.
27	Having processed all columns in all the rows for a particular result set, we call `nextRowset()` to move onto the next result. If `nextRowset()` returns FALSE, then we will terminate the loop having processed all of the output.

Handling Output Parameters

As we discussed in Chapter 3, MySQL stored procedures can include input (IN), output (OUT), and input-output (INOUT) parameters. For instance, the stored procedure shown in Example 13-42 contains an output parameter that will contain the number of customers for a specific sales representative.

Example 13-42. Stored procedure with an OUT parameter

```
CREATE PROCEDURE `sp_rep_customer_count`(
        in_emp_id DECIMAL(8,0),
        OUT out_cust_count INT)
    READS SQL DATA
BEGIN

  SELECT count(*) AS cust_count
    INTO out_cust_count
    FROM customers
   WHERE sales_rep_id=in_emp_id;

END ;
```

The PDO specification for the bindParam() method allows you to identify a parameter that might return an output value by associating the PDO::PARAM_INPUT_OUTPUT constant with the parameter. Example 13-43 shows how we would use this method to retrieve the value of an output parameter from this stored procedure.

Example 13-43. Binding an output parameter in PDO (not implemented at time of writing)

```
sql = "call sp_rep_customer_count(?,?)";
$sth = $dbh->prepare($sql)  or die(implode(':', $sth->errorInfo( )));
$sth->bindParam(1,$sales_rep_id,PDO::PARAM_STR,4000);
$sth->bindParam(2,$customer_count, PDO::PARAM_INT|PDO::PARAM_INPUT_OUTPUT);
$sth->execute()  or die(implode(':', $sth->errorInfo( )));
```

Unfortunately, as we write this chapter, the ability to use bindParam( ) to retrieve output parameters is not implemented in the PDO MySQL driver (Bug# 11638 current as of MySQL 5.0.19). There is every chance, however, that the method will have been implemented by the time you read this book, so please visit the book's web site where we will report on the status of the PDO driver.

Even without the bindParam( ) method, we can extract the value of an output parameter. We can do this by using a user variable to retrieve the value of the output parameter, and then retrieve this value using a simple SELECT statement. Example 13-44 shows how to do this. We use the @customer_count variable to hold the value of the output parameter and then, in a subsequent step, fetch the value of @customer_count using a one-line SELECT.

Example 13-44. Getting the value of an output parameter without bindParam

```
$sql="call sp_rep_customer_count(1,@customer_count)";
$sth = $dbh->prepare($sql);
$sth->execute() or die (implode(':',$sth->errorInfo( )));

# Now get the output variable

$sql="SELECT @customer_count";
foreach ($dbh->query($sql) as $row) {
  printf("Customer count=%d\n",$row[0]);
}
```

If the parameter were of type INOUT, we would simply issue a SET statement to set the value before execution and then issue a SELECT statemnet to retrieve the altered value after execution. We showed how to do this with the mysqli driver earlier in this chapter.

A Complete Example

Let's put PDO to use to create a web page that executes a stored procedure and formats the results in HTML. The stored procedure is shown in Example 13-45. This stored procedure generates some useful data about the MySQL server, including the details of currently connected sessions, status variables, and configuration settings for the database. The number and types of result sets varies depending upon the input parameters: if a valid database is provided in the first parameter, a list of objects for that table is returned. The server version is returned in an output parameter.

To help us generate a well-formatted report, the stored procedure outputs a header row for each of the result sets it returns. This header row is issued as a single-row, single-column result set in which the column name is table_header.

Example 13-45. MySQL server status stored procedure

```
CREATE PROCEDURE sp_mysql_info(in_database VARCHAR(60),
       OUT server_version VARCHAR(100))
   READS SQL DATA
BEGIN

  DECLARE db_count INT;

  SELECT @@version
    INTO server_version;

  SELECT 'Current processes active in server' AS table_header;
  SHOW FULL PROCESSLIST;

  SELECT 'Databases in server' AS table_header;

  SHOW DATABASES;

  SELECT 'Configuration variables set in server' AS table_header;
  SHOW GLOBAL VARIABLES;
  SELECT 'Status variables in server' AS table_header;
  SHOW GLOBAL STATUS;

  SELECT COUNT(*)
    INTO db_count
    FROM information_schema.schemata s
   WHERE schema_name=in_database;
  IF (db_count=1) THEN
    SELECT CONCAT('Tables in database ',in_database) AS table_header;
    SELECT table_name
      FROM information_schema.tables
     WHERE table_schema=in_database;
  END IF;

END;
```

Our PDO example prompts the user to provide login details for a MySQL server, connects to that server, and attempts to execute the stored procedure. Each result set is formatted as an HTML table and the "special" heading rows are formatted as HTML headers. The output parameter that contains the MySQL server version is retrieved and displayed at the commencement of the output. Example 13-46 displays the complete PDO example.

Example 13-46. A complete PDO example

```
1   <HTML>
2   <TITLE>MySQL Server Statistics</TITLE>
3   <H1>Enter MySQL Server Details</H1>
4   Enter your database connection details below:
5   <p>
6   <FORM ACTION="<?php echo $_SERVER['PHP_SELF']; ?>" METHOD=POST>
7     <TABLE>
8         <TR><TD>Host:</TD><TD> <input type="text" name="mhost"></TD></TR>
9         <TR><TD>Port:</TD><TD>   <input type="text" name="mport"></TD></TR>
10        <TR><TD>Username:</TD><TD>   <input type="text" name="muser"></TD></TR>
11        <TR><TD>Password:</TD><TD>   <input type="password"  name="mpass"></TD></TR>
12        <TR><TD>Database:</TD><TD>   <input type="test" name="mdb"></TD></TR>
13    </TABLE>
14        <TR><TD><input type="submit" name="Submit" value="Submit">
15  </FORM>
16
17  <?php
18  require_once "HTML/Table.php";
19
20  $html_text = array ();
21
22  if (IsSet ($_POST['Submit'])) {
23      $dsn = 'mysql:dbname='.$_POST['mdb'].';host='.$_POST['mhost'].
24            ';port='.$_POST['mport'];
25      $user = $_POST['muser'];
26      $password = $_POST['mpass'];
27
28      try {
29          $dbh = new PDO($dsn, $user, $password);
30      } catch (PDOException $e) {
31          echo 'Connection failed: '.$e->getMessage();
32      }
33      $sql = 'call sp_mysql_info(:dbname,@server_version)';
34      $sth = $dbh->prepare($sql);
35      $sth->bindParam(':dbname', $_POST['mdb'], PDO::PARAM_STR, 30);
36      $sth->execute() or die(implode(':', $sth->errorInfo()));
37
38      do {
39          if ($sth->columnCount() > 0) { /* Yes, there is a result set */
40              $col0 = $sth->getColumnMeta(0);
41              if ($col0["name"] == "table_header") { /*format this as a heading */
42                  $row = $sth->fetch();
43                  array_push($html_text, "<h2>$row[0]</h2>");
44              }
45              else { /* Format this as a table */
46                  $table = new HTML_Table('border=1');
47                  for ($i = 0; $i < $sth->columnCount(); $i ++) {
48                      $meta = $sth->getColumnMeta($i);
49                      $table->setCellContents(0, $i, $meta["name"]);
50                  }
51                  $table->setRowAttributes(0, array ("bgcolor" => "silver"));
52
```

Example 13-46. A complete PDO example (continued)

```
53                  #Loop through the rows
54                  $r = 0;
55                  while ($row = $sth->fetch()) {
56                      #Loop through the columns in the row
57                      $r ++;
58                      for ($i = 0; $i < $sth->columnCount(); $i ++) {
59                          $table->setCellContents($r, $i, $row[$i]);
60                      }
61                  }
62                  array_push($html_text, $table->toHtml());
63              }
64          }
65      }
66      while ($sth->nextRowset());
67
68      foreach ($dbh->query("SELECT @server_version") as $row) {
69          $mysql_version = $row[0];
70      }
71
72      print "<h1>MySQL Server status and statistics</h1>";
73      printf("<b>Host:</b> %s<br>", $_POST['mhost']);
74      printf("<b>Port:</b> %s<br>", $_POST['mport']);
75      printf("<b>Version:</b> %s<br>", $mysql_version);
76      foreach($html_text as $html) {
77          print $html;
78      }
79  }
80  ?>
81  </html>
```

This code uses most of the techniques we have seen in previous examples, as explained next:

Line(s)	Explanation
1-15	Create the HTML form in which the user enters the server details. This is standard PHP HTML. You can see the resulting input form in Figure 13-3.
18	We are using the PEAR HTML Table module to create our HTML tables. You can obtain this from *http://pear. php.net*.
20	Create an array to store our HTML. We do this because we want to display the MySQL version string *before* the HTML tables, although as a stored procedure output variable we can only retrieve it *after* all result sets have been closed. So we need to store our HTML in a variable rather than print it as we go.
22	This if statement starts the section of code that is executed once the user clicks the Submit button defined on line 14.
23-32	Build up the PDO dsn string from the user input and connect to the MySQL server.

Line(s)	Explanation
33-36	Prepare and execute the stored procedure, binding as an input parameter the database name provided in the HTML form. A user variable—@server_version —is provided to receive the value of the second, output parameter.
38-66	This is the loop that will repeat for each result set returned by the stored procedure. The loop will continue as long as the $sth->nextRowset( ) call on line 66 returns true.
42-46	If the first column in the result set is named table_header, then this result set is a "title" for the subsequent result set, so we format the column value as an HTML header (line 45).
47-48	Otherwise (the result set is not a "title"), create a new table object to contain the result set output.
47-51	Retrieve the column names for the result set and add them to the first row of the HTML table.
54-61	Loop through each row of the output and push the column values into the appropriate cells of the HTML table.
62	Add the HTML for the table to our array variable—we'll print the contents of this array later (after we get the value of the output parameter).
68-70	Now that all result sets have been retrieved, we can get the value of the output parameter, which is now contained in the user variable @server_version.
72-75	Print the major header line, and some server details, including host, port, and MySQL server version.
76-78	Print all of the HTML that we saved in the $html_text variable. This includes the HTML tables and headings.

Figure 13-3 shows the output from this PHP example.

Conclusion

In this chapter we saw how we can use MySQL stored programs within PHP by using either the mysqli or PDO extension. Both interfaces provide all the tools you need to take advantage of MySQL stored procedures and functions from within your PHP application.

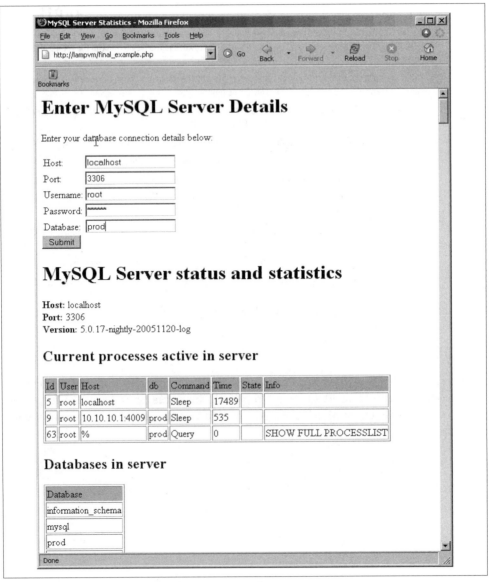

Figure 13-3. Output from our complete PDO example

## CHAPTER 14

Using MySQL Stored Programs with Java

PHP is undoubtedly the most popular language used in combination with MySQL to build commercial applications and—in particular—web applications. However, for applications that aspire to possibly greater scalability and standards compliance, Java offers an attractive alternative. The Java JDBC database-independent API provides robust and mature methods for performing all types of database interaction from within the Java environment and includes very strong support for handling stored programs. The J2EE standard provides a way for Java to be used within commercial and open source web or application servers to construct scalable and efficient web applications that can take advantage of MySQL as a database server, and MySQL stored programs as the interface to the database. There are also alternative Java frameworks such as Hibernate and Spring, which can expedite database access without adding all the overhead and complexity of a J2EE solution, and these can leverage stored programs as well.

In this chapter we will commence with a quick review of how you can use Java JDBC to perform interactions with the database not involving stored programs, including the basic prerequisite functions of installing and registering the JDBC driver and obtaining a connection to a MySQL server. We will also explain how to execute basic SQL from the driver and how to handle database errors.

Next, we'll proceed to examine the JDBC syntax for invoking stored programs, including handling input and output parameters and processing multiple result sets.

Finally, we'll look at how stored programs can be utilized within some of the popular Java frameworks, including servlets or *Enterprise JavaBeans* (EJB) within an application server, from Hibernate, or within the Spring framework.

Review of JDBC Basics

Before examining how we can use stored programs in JDBC, let's look at how JDBC supports database operations that don't include stored programs. These basic operations will serve as the foundation for JDBC that does use stored programs. If you are already familiar with JDBC, you might want to skip forward to "Using Stored Programs in JDBC," later in this chapter.

Installing the Driver and Configuring Your IDE

While the JDBC interface itself is part of native Java, to use JDBC with MySQL we will need to install a MySQL-aware JDBC driver. MySQL provides such a driver, Connector/J, which we can download from *http://dev.mysql.com/downloads/connector/j.html*. Installation is a simple matter of unpacking the contents of a .zip file or a tar archive to a convenient location on our hard drive.

To allow our Java programs to access the Connector/J archive, we need to add the Connector/J JAR (Java Archive) file to our system's CLASSPATH. For instance, if we unpacked the Connector/J files into a directory called *C:\MySQL\ConnectorJ*, then our CLASSPATH might look like this:

```
Set CLASSPATH=C:\MySQL\ConnectorJ\mysql-connector-java-3.1.10-bin.jar;.
```

Most Java IDEs require that we specify any required libraries in either a general or a project-specific dialog box. For example, in Eclipse, we can open the Properties dialog box for the project, select Java Build Path, click Add External JARs, then add the location of the Connector/J JAR file. Figure 14-1 shows the Eclipse dialog box for adding a required library.

Registering the Driver and Connecting to MySQL

Within our Java program we will normally import the java.sql package so that we don't have to fully qualify our references to JDBC classes, as shown in Example 14-1.

Example 14-1. Importing the java.sql package

```
package jdbc_example;

import java.sql.*;
```

Before we can connect to MySQL, we need to initialize the Connector/J driver. This is done with the static Class.forName( ) method, shown in Example 14-2. We can then create a Connection object that represents a specific MySQL connection by using DriverManager.getConnection( ) with an appropriately formatted URL. This also is shown in Example 14-2 .

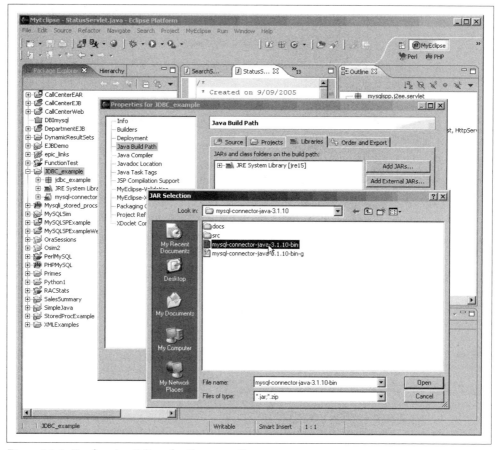

Figure 14-1. Configuring Eclipse for Connector/J

Example 14-2. Connecting to a MySQL instance

```
Class.forName("com.mysql.jdbc.Driver").newInstance( );

Connection myConnection = DriverManager.getConnection(
                "jdbc:mysql://localhost:3306/test?user=root&password=secret");
```

The URL for the getConnection( ) method has the following (simplified) format:

    jdbc:mysql://*host*[:*port*]/[*database*][?*Name1*=*Value1*][&*Name2*=*Value2*]...

The name/value pairs following the ? character typically include user and password together with other optional connection parameters (relating to the use of SSL, time-outs, etc.). You can find a full list of optional connection parameters in the

Connector/J documentation at *http://dev.mysql.com/doc/connector/*. The following are examples of possible URLs:

jdbc:MySQL://localhost/?user=root
> Connect to the MySQL server on the local host at the default port (3306) and connect to root (no password).

jdbc:MySQL://fred:3305/test?user=joe&password=joe1
> Connect to the MySQL server on host fred at port number 3305. Connect as joe/joe1 to database test.

Issuing a Non-SELECT Statement

Now that we have created our connection object, we are ready to issue a SQL statement. The simplest way to execute a SQL statement that does not return a result set (such as INSERT, UPDATE, DELETE, or a DDL statement) is to use the createStatement( ) and executeUpdate( ) methods of the JDBC Connection interface.

The createStatement( ) method creates a reuseable Statement object. The executeUpdate( ) instance method of this Statement object can be used to execute the statement. Example 14-3 shows the use of the createStatement( ) and executeUpdate( ) methods to execute the SET AUTOCOMMIT=0 command.

Example 14-3. Issuing a SQL statement that returns no result set

```
Statement stmt1 = myConnection.createStatement( );
stmt1.executeUpdate("set autocommit=0");
```

In general, it's not a good idea to create statements in this way except for one-off SQL statements. For any statement that may be re-executed (perhaps with different parameters), we should use the PreparedStatement interface (see the "Using Prepared Statements" section later in this chapter).

Issuing a SELECT and Retrieving a Result Set

If our statement is a SELECT statement or another MySQL command that returns a result set, we can call the executeQuery( ) method of a Statement object. This creates a ResultSet object through which we can iterate in much the same way as we would iterate through the rows returned by a stored program cursor. This is, however, quite different programmatically from the way in which the java.util.Iterator interface is normally used to iterate through Java collections.

The next( ) method of the ResultSet object allows us to move to the next row in the result set—the very first call to next( ) will move to the first row—while getInt( ), getString( ), and other similar methods allow us to retrieve specific columns from the current row. Columns can be specified by name or by number. Example 14-4 shows us processing a simple query in JDBC.

Example 14-4. Processing a SELECT in JDBC

```
Statement stmt2 = myConnection.createStatement( );
ResultSet results = stmt2.executeQuery("SELECT department_id, department_name " +
                    "                   FROM departments");
while(results.next( ))
{
    int departmentID = results.getInt("department_id");  // Get column by name
    String departmentName = results.getString(2);        // Got column by number
    System.out.println(departmentID + ":" + departmentName);
}
results.close( );
```

As with non-SELECT statements, we should use the `PreparedStatement` interface rather than `Statement` if there is a chance that we will re-execute the SQL (potentially with different parameters).

Getting Result Set Metadata

If we don't know the exact structure of the result when we write our code (perhaps the SQL is entered by the end user or dynamically generated by some other module), then we can create a `ResultSetMetaData` object that contains information about the structure of the `ResultSet` object. Example 14-5 shows the use of this interface to print a list of column names and data types being returned from a query. Take special note that the first metadata result column has an index of 1 where most Java programmers would assume it to be 0.

Example 14-5. Using the ResultSetMetaData object to get result set structure

```
Statement stmt3 = myConnection.createStatement( );
ResultSet results2 = stmt2.executeQuery("SELECT *" +
                    "                     FROM departments");
ResultSetMetaData meta1 = results2.getMetaData( );

for (int i = 1; i <= meta1.getColumnCount( ); i++)
{
    System.out.println("Column " + i + " "
                    + meta1.getColumnName(i) + " ("
                    + meta1.getColumnTypeName(i) + ")");
}
```

Using Prepared Statements

Most Java applications—particularly those running in a middle tier such as in a J2EE- compliant application server—re-execute SQL statements many times during the life of a database session. While the "parameters" to the statement, such as WHERE clause arguments, might change, the SQL itself is usually executed many times. *Prepared statements* are statement objects that are permanently associated with a particular SQL statement. They can be re-executed with new parameters when required.

Using a prepared statement results in reduced overhead for the MySQL server, since re-executing an existing statement takes less processing time than executing a new SQL statement.

Note that although the MySQL server supports a feature (since 4.1) called *server-side prepared statements*, and although the JDBC implementation of prepared statements may leverage the MySQL implementation, the prepared statements we are discussing here are a JDBC feature, and are not specific to any particular RDBMS or version of MySQL.

The PreparedStatement interface extends the Statement interface and therefore inherits methods from that interface. The primary extensions in the PreparedStatement interface relate to specifying parameters prior to execution so that the PreparedStatement instance can be re-executed in a new context.

To create a prepared statement, we use the prepareStatement() method of the Connection interface, providing a SQL string as the argument. Any variable portions of the SQL string are represented by the ? character. In Example 14-6 we create a prepared statement that includes a single parameter value representing a specific product identifier.

Example 14-6. Creating a prepared statement

```
PreparedStatement prepared1 = myConnection.prepareStatement(
                  "select product_id,product_description,normal_value" +
                  "  from products " +
                  " where product_id=?");
```

Before each execution of the prepared statement, we need to provide values for all the parameters of the statement. The PreparedStatement interface provides setInt( ), setString( ), and other similar methods for doing this. Each method takes the parameter number as the first argument and a value of the appropriate data type as the second argument. For instance, in Example 14-7, we set the value of the product identifier that will be provided to the prepared statement defined in Example 14-6 to a value of 12. Take note again that the index of the first parameter is 1 and not—as we might expect—0.

Example 14-7. Setting a parameter value in a prepared statement

```
prepared1.setInt(1, 12);
```

Now we can execute the prepared statement using its instance method executeQuery( ) if it is expected to return a result set, or executeUpdate( ) otherwise (see Example 14-8).

Example 14-8. Executing a prepared statement

```
ResultSet pstmtResults1 = prepared1.executeQuery( );
```

Example 14-9 shows the prepared statement being declared, the parameter set, and a result set retrieved.

Example 14-9. PreparedStatement example

```
PreparedStatement prepared1 = myConnection.prepareStatement(
                    "select product_id,product_description,normal_value" +
                    "  from products " +
                    " where product_id=?");
prepared1.setInt(1, 12);
ResultSet pstmtResults1 = prepared1.executeQuery( );
while (pstmtResults1.next( ))
{
    System.out.println("Product Description: " + pstmtResults1.getString(2));
}
pstmtResults1.close( );
```

Of course, if we were only going to execute the prepared statement once, this would all be wasted effort. The point is that having created the prepared statement, we can execute it any number of times, feeding different parameters to the prepared statement each time. Example 14-10 illustrates this principle by executing the prepared statement in a loop to print descriptions of the first 10 product IDs.

Example 14-10. Executing a prepared statement repetitively

```
for (int i = 1; i <= 10; i++)
{
    prepared1.setInt(1, i);
    pstmtResults1 = prepared1.executeQuery( );
    pstmtResults1.next( );
    System.out.println("Product ID: " + i +
        "  Product Description: " + pstmtResults1.getString(2));
}
pstmtResults1.close( );
```

Handling Transactions

Although we can issue commands such as COMMIT, ROLLBACK, START TRANSACTION, and SET AUTOCOMMIT using the setUpdate( ) method of Statement or PreparedStatement objects, it is probably easier to perform transaction control using the methods provided by the Connection interface.

The Connection interface supports a setAutocommit( ) method, together with commit( ) and rollback( ) methods, which allow us to disable MySQL autocommit and to perform explicit commit and rollback operations within a connection. So a transaction in JDBC would look like this:

```
myConnection.setAutoCommit(false);
/* transactional statements go in here */
myConnection.commit( );
```

Handling Errors

JDBC methods generally throw a SQLException if the SQL that is being issued results in a database error being generated. Classes that contain JDBC statements should therefore either use a throws clause to indicate that such an exception might be raised, or include the JDBC statements within a try/catch block.

Example 14-11 illustrates the first technique; the createDemoTables( ) method will throw a SQLException if a MySQL error occurs. It is up to the caller to catch that exception; otherwise, the unhandled exception might crash the Java program. This technique is recommended for generic or low-level database code that cannot interpret the exception within the context of the application. Pointless catching and re-throwing of exceptions is one of the cardinal sins of Java programming, because it leads to massive stack traces that just obscure what is actually causing the problem.

Example 14-11. Throwing a SQLException

```
static public void createDemoTables(Connection myConnection)
    throws SQLException
{
    Statement s1 = connection.createStatement( );
    s1.executeUpdate("CREATE TABLE DEMO " +
            "           (MyInt INT, " +
            "            MyString VARCHAR(30))");
}
```

Example 14-12 shows the alternative approach. Here, the JDBC calls are enclosed in a try/catch block that catches the SQLException and reports the error message. Since the exception is caught, the createDemoTables( ) method no longer needs to declare the throws clause. This technique should be used when the catch block is able to adequately deal with the error by logging it or handling it programmatically. The catch block may also re-throw the exception as an application exception that includes valuable context information with regard to what the application was trying to do when the SQL failed.

Example 14-12. Catching a SQLException

```
static public void createDemoTables(Connection connection)
{
    try
    {
        Statement s1 = connection.createStatement( );
        s1.executeUpdate("CREATE TABLE DEMO" +
            "           (MyInt INT," +
            "            MyString VARCHAR(30))");
    }
    catch(SQLException exception)
    {
        System.out.println("Error while creating demo tables: " +
            exception.getErrorCode( ) +
```

Example 14-12. Catching a SQLException (continued)

```
            " SQLSTATE:" + exception.getSQLState( ));
        exception.printStackTrace( );
    }
}
```

The `getErrorCode( )` and `getMessage( )` methods are typically used to report on the specifics of the database error concerned. However, the `SQLException` class inherits a lot of useful diagnostic methods from its super classes `Exception` and `Throwable`. In particular, `printStackTrace( )` will print a stack trace for the exception to standard output, while `getStackTrace( )` allows programmatic access to the trace.

Using Stored Programs in JDBC

So far we have mainly reviewed the JDBC calls that can be used with any database and that don't relate in any way to stored program calls. If you have used JDBC with other RDBMS types or with previous versions of MySQL, you probably haven't learned much. Let's move on to processing stored program calls in JDBC (Figure 14-2).

Stored program calls are very similar to standard JDBC calls. A stored program strongly resembles a prepared statement that executes a query, with the following exceptions:

* A stored program can return more than one result set.
* A stored procedure can be associated with output—as well as input—parameters. This means that we need a way to retrieve the altered values from any stored procedure parameters that are defined as `OUT` or `INOUT`.

In addition to the general sequence of processing involved in creating and executing a prepared statement, when executing a stored program, we may need to retrieve multiple result sets and also—when the stored program execution has completed—retrieve the results of any output variables.

Using the CallableStatement Interface

The `CallableStatement` interface extends the `PreparedStatement` interface. It includes all of the methods of the `PreparedStatement` interface, as well as additional methods specific to stored program calls. You create a `CallableStatement` with the `prepareCall( )` method of a `Connection` object:

```
    CallableStatement statementName = ConnectionName.prepareCall(sql_text);
```

The single argument to the `prepareCall( )` method contains the MySQL statements required to invoke the stored program. Any parameters are indicated by ? characters. The entire call must be enclosed in braces, "{" and "}", which are the standard JDBC escape sequences for indicating database-independent syntax. So to call the

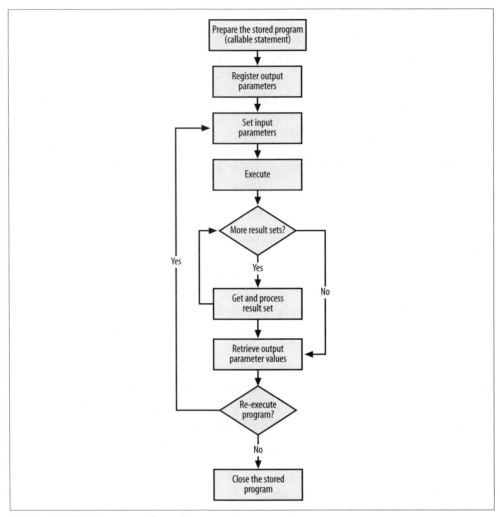

Figure 14-2. JDBC program flow when executing a stored program

stored procedure sp_test_inout_rs2, which has two parameters, we would use the following syntax:

```
CallableStatement callableStmt =
    myConnection.prepareCall("{CALL sp_test_inout_rs2(?,?)}");
```

sp_test_inout_rs2 is a stored procedure that has both an IN and an OUT parameter and that returns two result sets. The stored procedure takes the name of a MySQL schema as an IN argument and returns a list of tables and a list of stored routines owned by that schema. It returns the number of tables in the specified database as an OUT parameter. The text for this stored procedure is shown in Example 14-13.

Example 14-13. Example stored procedure used in Java examples

```
CREATE PROCEDURE sp_test_inout_rs2(IN in_user VARCHAR(30),OUT table_count INT)
BEGIN

  SELECT table_name,table_type
    FROM information_schema.tables
   WHERE upper(table_schema)=upper(in_user);

  SELECT routine_name,routine_type
    FROM information_schema.routines
   WHERE upper(routine_schema)=upper(in_user);

  SELECT COUNT(*)
    INTO table_count
    FROM information_schema.tables
   where upper(table_schema)=upper(in_user);

END ;
```

Registering OUT Variables

If the stored procedure includes any OUT variables, you need to identify these to JDBC. The registerOutParameter( ) instance method of CallableStatement allows you to identify these parameters. This method has the following syntax:

> *callableStatementInstance*.registerOutParameter(*parameter_number*,*data_type*);

Parameters are identified by number, starting with 1 for the first parameter. The data types are those contained in java.sql.Types and include INTEGER, CHAR, NUMERIC, DATE, etc.

In sp_test_inout_rs2, our second parameter is an OUT integer parameter, so we issue the statement to identify the parameter in Example 14-14.

Example 14-14. Registering a stored procedure OUT or INOUT parameter

```
callableStmt.registerOutParameter(2, Types.INTEGER);
```

Supplying Input Parameters

No matter how many times we execute our stored procedure, we only have to create the CallableStatement and register output parameters once. However, most executions of a stored procedure will have different input parameters, so the first step in a new execution is to identify the values of those parameters. The syntax for setting input parameter values is the same as that for a PreparedStatement; we use the setInt( ), setFloat( ), setString( ), setDate( ), or other appropriate methods of the PreparedStatement interface to set each value. In our example stored procedure, we have only a single VARCHAR input parameter, so we set its value as shown in Example 14-15.

Example 14-15. Setting the value of an input parameter

```
callableStmt.setString(1, schemaName);
```

schemaName is a Java String containing the name of the schema for which we want to retrieve information.

Executing the Procedure

Now we are ready to execute the stored procedure, which we do with the execute( ) instance method shown in Example 14-16.

Example 14-16. Executing a stored procedure

```
callableStmt.execute();
```

The execute( ) method returns a Boolean value, which resolves to true if the stored procedure returns at least one result set. So we could call execute( ) as shown in Example 14-17.

Example 14-17. Executing a stored procedure that might return a result set

```
boolean hasResults = callableStmt.execute();
```

If you know that your stored procedure does not return a result set, you can use the executeUpdate( ) method instead, as shown in Example 14-18.

Example 14-18. Executing a stored procedure that does not return a result set

```
CallableStatement noResultStmt = connection.prepareCall("{call sp_noresult()}");
noResultStmt.executeUpdate();
```

Retrieving a Result Set

As we noted earlier, the initial execute( ) call will return true only if the stored procedure returns at least one result set. If this is so, or if you know in advance that the stored procedure has a result set, you can retrieve it in the usual fashion. Example 14-19 shows how to retrieve a single result set from a stored procedure call.

Example 14-19. Retrieving a single result set from a stored procedure call

```
ResultSet rs1 = callableStmt.getResultSet();
while (rs1.next())
    System.out.println(rs1.getString("table_name") + " " +
                       rs1.getString("table_type"));
```

In this case, we knew the names and types of the columns in our result set. If we did not, we could call the getMetaData( ) method to retrieve the result set structure. ResultSetMetaData is described in the section "Getting Result Set Metadata" earlier in this chapter.

Retrieving Multiple Result Sets

If the stored procedure has more than one result set, you can use the getMoreResults( ) method to move to the next set. If there are no more result sets, getMoreResults( ) will return false. So to get a second result set, we can call getMoreResults( ) and then retrieve the result set. Example 14-20 illustrates this technique.

Example 14-20. Obtaining a second result set from the stored procedure call

```
if (callableStmt.getMoreResults( ))
{
    ResultSet rs2 = callableStmt.getResultSet( );
    while (rs2.next( ))
        System.out.println(rs2.getString(1) + " " + rs2.getString(2));
    rs2.close( );
}
```

In this example, we used the column numbers rather than column names to retrieve the results. Using column names (rs2.getString("department_id") for instance) leads to more readable code, but when you are processing dynamic result sets, it may be more convenient to refer to the columns by number.

Dynamically Processing Result Sets

It is possible—but very unusual—that we might call a stored program without knowing the number and types of input and output parameters. However, because we often use unbounded SELECT statements within stored programs to generate debugging or other messages, and because it is relatively easy to conditionally create result sets in our stored program code, we may find that we need to execute a stored program without knowing exactly how many result sets will be returned or what the structure of each result set will look like.

We therefore need to be familiar with the process of dynamically processing result sets. Example 14-21 implements a method that will execute a stored program passed as a parameter and print out all the result sets generated by that stored program.

Example 14-21. JDBC code to dynamically process multiple result sets

```
1    private void executeProcedure(Connection connection, String sqlText)
2            throws SQLException {
3
4        CallableStatement cs = connection.prepareCall("{CALL " + sqlText + "}");
5        boolean moreResultSets = cs.execute( );
6        while (moreResultSets) {
7
8            ResultSet rs = cs.getResultSet( );
9            ResultSetMetaData rsmd = rs.getMetaData( );
10
```

```
11              StringBuffer buffer = new StringBuffer( );
12              for (int i = 1; i <= rsmd.getColumnCount( ); i++)
13                  buffer.append(rsmd.getColumnName(i)).append("\t");
14              System.out.println(buffer.toString( ));
15
16              while (rs.next( )) {
17                  buffer.setLength(0);
18                  for (int i = 1; i <= rsmd.getColumnCount( ); i++)
19                      buffer.append(rs.getString(i)).append("\t");
20                  System.out.println(buffer.toString( ));
21              }
22
23              moreResultSets = cs.getMoreResults( );
24          }
25      }
```

Let's step through Example 14-21:

Line(s)	Explanation
4	Create a `CallableStatement` object that invokes the stored procedure text provided as an argument to the Java procedure.
5	Execute the stored procedure. The `moreResultSets` Boolean value will be `true` if the stored procedure returns any result sets.
6-24	This loop will continue to execute provided that `moreResultSets` is `true`. This means that the code within the loop will execute once for each result set returned by the stored procedure.
8-9	On line 8 we get a `ResultSet` object for the current result set, and on line 9 we retrieve the `ResultSetMetaData` object for that `ResultSet`.
11-14	Print out the column names for the current result set, as retrieved from the `ResultSetMetaData` object.
16-22	Loop through the rows of the current result set. The loop will continue for each row returned by the current result set.
18-21	Loop through each column in the current row. The `getColumnCount( )` method of the `ResultSetMetaData` object tells us how many columns we will need to process, and we use `getString( )` to retrieve the value. `getString( )` will get a string representation of non-string SQL data types such as dates or numeric data.
23	Use the `getMoreResults( )` method of the `CallableStatement` object to determine if there are more result sets. If this call returns `true`, then the `CallableStatement` will move to the next result set and the `while` loop defined on line 6 will continue, allowing us to repeat the above process for the next result set.

Retrieving Output Parameter Values

Once all of the result sets have been retrieved, it is time to retrieve the values of any OUT or INOUT parameters that the procedure may have declared. Remember that in order to do this, we must have used the `registerOutParameter( )` method to set the types of these parameters before we executed the stored procedure.

To get the values of output parameters, we use "get" methods (getInt( ), getFloat( ), getString( ), etc.) that are similar to those used to retrieve column values, but instead of applying the methods to the ResultSet object, we apply them to the CallableStatement object. In the case of our sp_test_inout_rs2 stored procedure, which has a single integer OUT parameter (the second parameter), we can simply retrieve the value of the OUT parameter with the code shown in Example 14-22.

Example 14-22. Retrieving the value of an output parameter
```
System.out.println("Out parameter = " + callableStmt.getInt(2));
```

Stored Programs and J2EE Applications

While it is certainly possible to use JDBC inside Java to construct client/server applications or even Java applets, the most significant interaction between Java programs and a relational database often occurs with a J2EE application server environment, usually within the context of a J2EE-based web application. This application server could be a commercial J2EE implementation such as WebLogic or WebSphere or—perhaps more typically in combination with MySQL—an open source J2EE server such as Tomcat or JBoss.

Modern J2EE applications follow one of two major patterns with respect to database interaction:

Servlet pattern

In the servlet pattern, JDBC code is included within Java programs running within the application server. These programs are known as *servlets*. These servlets are free to communicate directly with the database through embedded JDBC code, although many applications will choose to interact with the database through an object-relational mapping interface such as Hibernate.

EJB pattern

In an Enterprise JavaBeans (EJB) based application, access to database objects is abstracted via entity EJB beans. Each entity bean represents either a table or a common multitable entity, and each instance of the entity bean typically represents a row in that table or result set. The EJB pattern contains methods to retrieve, update, delete, and insert rows within this logical table.

A full tutorial on J2EE database programming is beyond the scope of this book (and probably beyond the expertise of its authors). However, in this section we will take a quick look at how you might use stored programs within a J2EE application.

Using Stored Programs Within Java Servlets

In a servlet-based Java web application, Java code in the application or web server controls the generation of dynamic HTML content based on business logic contained within the Java code and through interaction with back-end databases via JDBC. Servlet technology actually predates J2EE (servlets were introduced in Java 1.1), and there is a wide variety of possible servlet implementation patterns.

In this section, we will use a simple servlet to render the output from a stored procedure that contains multiple and unpredictable result sets and that also contains both input and output parameters. The stored procedure generates a selection of MySQL server status information, takes as an input parameter a specific database within the server, and returns as an output parameter the MySQL version identifier. The stored procedure is shown in Example 14-23.

Example 14-23. Stored procedure to return MySQL server status information

```
CREATE PROCEDURE sp_mysql_info
      (in_database VARCHAR(60),
       OUT server_version VARCHAR(100))
  READS SQL DATA
BEGIN

  DECLARE db_count INT;

  SELECT @@version
    INTO server_version;

  SELECT 'Current processes active in server' as table_header;
  SHOW full processlist;

  SELECT 'Databases in server' as table_header;

  show databases;

  SELECT 'Configuration variables set in server' as table_header;
  SHOW global variables;
  SELECT 'Status variables in server' as table_header;
  SHOW global status;

   /* See if there is a matching database */
  SELECT COUNT(*)
    INTO db_count
    FROM information_schema.schemata s
   WHERE schema_name=in_database;
  IF (db_count=1) THEN
    SELECT CONCAT('Tables in database ',in_database) as table_header;
    SELECT table_name
```

```
    FROM information_schema.tables
  WHERE table_schema=in_database;
END IF;

END;
```

Note that the stored procedure uses a special technique to output "heading" rows for the result sets. When a single row is returned with a column named table_header, that row represents a title or heading for the subsequent result set.

Our example is going to use an HTML page to request the user to enter specific server information, and then use a servlet within the application server to display the output of the stored procedure. The HTML for the input form is very simple and is shown in Example 14-24.

Example 14-24. HTML input form for our servlet example

```
<!DOCTYPE HTML PUBLIC "-//W3C//DTD HTML 4.01 Transitional//EN">
<html>
    <head>
        <TITLE>MySQL Server status</TITLE>
    </head>

<body>
    <H2>Enter MySQL Server details</H2>
    <FORM name="statusForm" method="post" action="mystatus">
        <TABLE>
            <TR><TD>Host:</TD><TD> <input type="text" name="mhost"></TD></TR>
            <TR><TD>Port:</TD><TD>  <input type="text" name="mport"></TD></TR>
            <TR><TD>Username:</TD><TD>
                <input type="text" name="muser"></TD></TR>
            <TR><TD>Password:</TD><TD>
                <input type="password"  name="mpass"></TD></TR>
             <TR><TD>Database:</TD><TD>  <input type="text" name="mdb"></TD></TR>
        </TABLE>
        <INPUT type="submit" value="Submit" />
    </FORM>
</body>
</html>
```

The HTML renders the data entry screen shown in Figure 14-3.

Example 14-25 shows the code for the Java servlet that is invoked when the user clicks the Submit button.

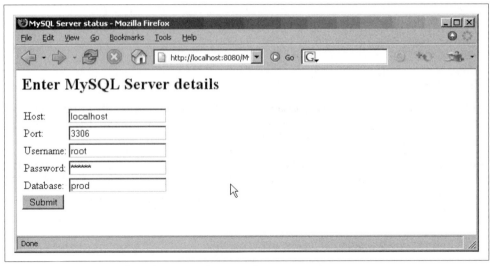

Figure 14-3. Data entry form for our servlet example

Example 14-25. Servlet code that invokes our stored procedure

```
1    public class StatusServlet extends HttpServlet
2    {
3        public void doPost(HttpServletRequest request, HttpServletResponse response)
4            throws ServletException, IOException
5        {
6            String hostname = request.getParameter("mhost");
7            String port = request.getParameter("mport");
8            String username = request.getParameter("muser");
9            String password = request.getParameter("mpass");
10           String database = request.getParameter("mdb");
11           StringBuffer html = new StringBuffer();
12
13           response.setContentType("text/html");
14           PrintWriter out = response.getWriter();
15
16           try {
17               Class.forName("com.mysql.jdbc.Driver").newInstance();
18               String connString = "jdbc:mysql://" + hostname + ":" + port + "/" +
19                   database + "?user=" + username + "&password=" + password;
20               Connection connection = DriverManager.getConnection(connString);
21
22               CallableStatement myproc =
23                   connection.prepareCall("{CALL sp_mysql_info(?,?)}");
24               myproc.registerOutParameter(2, Types.VARCHAR);
25               myproc.setString(1, database);
26
27           boolean moreResultSets = myproc.execute();
28           while (moreResultSets) {
29               ResultSet rs = myproc.getResultSet();
30               ResultSetMetaData rsmd = rs.getMetaData();
```

Example 14-25. Servlet code that invokes our stored procedure (continued)

```
31                      if (rsmd.getColumnName(1).equals("table_header")) {
32                          rs.next( );
33                          html.append("<h2>").append(rs.getString(1))
34                              .append("</h2>");
35                      } else {
36                          makeTable(rs, rsmd, html);
37                      }
38                      moreResultSets = myproc.getMoreResults( );
39                  }
40              String version = myproc.getString(2);
41
42              out.println("<HTML><HEAD><TITLE>MySQL Server status</TITLE></HEAD>");
43              out.println("<H1>MySQL Server status and statistics</H1>");
44              out.println("<b>Server:</b>\t" + hostname + "<br>");
45              out.println("<b>Port:</b>\t" + port + "<br>");
46              out.println("<b>Version:</b>:\t" + version + "<br>");
47              out.println(html.toString( ));
48              out.println("</HTML>");
49          } catch (SQLException e) {
50              out.println(e.getErrorCode() + " " + e.getMessage( ));
51              e.printStackTrace(out);
52          } catch (InstantiationException e) {
53              e.printStackTrace(out);
54          } catch (IllegalAccessException e) {
55              e.printStackTrace(out);
56          } catch (ClassNotFoundException e) {
57              e.printStackTrace(out);
58          } finally {
59              out.flush( );
60              out.close( );
61          }
62      }
63
64      private void makeTable(ResultSet rs, ResultSetMetaData rsmd, StringBuffer html)
65          throws SQLException
66      {
67          html.append("<table border=\"1\"><tr>");
68
69          for (int i = 1; i <= rsmd.getColumnCount( ); i++)
70              html.append("<td bgcolor=\"silver\">").append(rsmd.getColumnName(i))
71                  .append("</td>");
72          html.append("</tr>");
73
74          while (rs.next( )) {
75              html.append("<tr>");
76              for (int i = 1; i <= rsmd.getColumnCount( ); i++)
77                  html.append("<td>").append(rs.getString(i)).append("</td>");
78              html.append("</tr>\n");
79          }
80
81          html.append("</table>\n");
82      }
83 }
```

Let's examine this servlet code:

Line(s)	Explanation
6-10	Retrieve the server connection details as entered by the user on the calling HTML form.
11	Create a `StringBuffer` object for building the HTML text to avoid churning lots of throwaway `String` objects.
13 and 14	Initialize an output stream to return HTML output.
17-20	Create a connection to the MySQL server using the connection details supplied by the user.
22-25	Prepare the stored procedure shown in Example 14-23. On line 24 we register our output parameter, and on line 25 we supply the input parameter—the name of a database within the server—provided by the user in the HTML form.
27	Execute the stored procedure.
28-39	This loop executes once for each result set returned by the stored procedure.
29 and 30	Retrieve a result set and—on line 30—a `ResultSetMetaData` object for that result set.
31-37	If the first column in the result set is called "table_header", then the result set represents a heading row for a subsequent result set, so we create an HTML header tag. Otherwise, we pass the result set to the `makeTable( )` method, which returns an HTML table formatted from the result set (see below for a description of the `makeTable( )` method).
37	Call the `getMoreResults( )` method to see if there are further result sets. If there are, then `moreResultSets` will be set to `true` and the loop will continue. Otherwise, it will be set to `false` and the loop will terminate.
40	Now that all result sets have been processed, retrieve the value of the output parameter, which contains the MySQL version string.
42-48	Write our formatted HTML report to the print stream.
49-57	Catch any exceptions and print a stack trace to the print stream.
58-61	Whether there is an exception or not, we must flush and close the print stream to send our output back to the calling session.
64-82	Define the private `makeTable( )` method that takes `ResultSet` and `ResultSetMetaData` objects and appends an HTML table representation of that result set to the specified `StringBuffer`.
69-72	Loop through the column names for the result set and format HTML to create the heading row for the table.
74-79	Loop through the rows returned by the result set and—in lines 76-77—append the columns in each row. We generate HTML to create an HTML table cell for each row returned in the result set.

Figure 14-4 shows the output generated by the servlet and stored procedure.

Using Stored Programs from EJB

Enterprise JavaBeans (EJB) is a feature of the J2EE specification that provides for distributed server-side Java components intended for enterprise systems development. *Entity EJBs* provide a way to represent persistent data—usually data from an RDBMS—in the EJB component model.

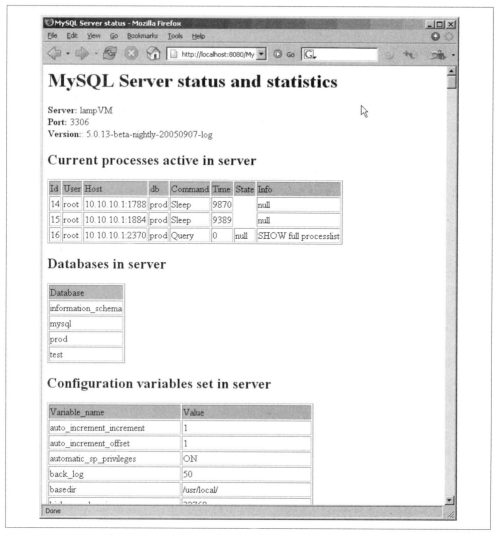

Figure 14-4. Output from our stored procedure/servlet example

In most J2EE applications, EJBs represent a mapping of relational data to Java objects. In a very simple case, an EJB may represent a database table, and each instance of the EJB might represent a row in that table. However, the relationships between EJBs and relational tables can be as complex as the developer chooses, and an EJB may represent a complex business object that is represented across many database tables.

Each EJB includes various methods that allow the application to interact with the underlying data. Some of these methods are listed in Table 14-1.

Table 14-1. Some of the methods of an entity EJB

Method or method type	Description
ejbFind*find_type*	Various "finder" methods allow the application to find a particular instance of an EJB (perhaps a specific row in a table). There will always be at least an `ejbFindByPrimaryKey()` method.
ejbCreate	Creates a new instance of an entity bean. This is roughly equivalent to inserting a row into the database.
ejbStore	Applies the in-memory contents of the entity bean to the database. It usually involves one or more UPDATE statements.
ejbRemove	Permanently removes an instance of an entity bean—usually associated with deleting one or more database rows.
ejbLoad	Loads a particular instance of an EJB. This is equivalent to reading a certain table row into memory.

Entity EJBs in a J2EE application are responsible for representing all persistent data in the application, where *persistent* means that the data will continue to exist when the current thread, process, or application ceases to run. There are two styles of persistence management in entity EJBs:

Bean-Managed Persistence (BMP)
> In this mode, the interaction with the underlying data source is controlled by code that is contained within the EJB. In most cases, this means that the programmer includes JDBC code within the bean to query and update the underlying tables, or uses an abstraction layer such as Hibernate or Spring to generate the JDBC calls.

Container-Managed Persistence (CMP)
> In this mode, the interaction with the underlying data source is controlled by the EJB container itself. The container generates SQL to retrieve and maintain data based on deployment data that defines the relationship between the data represented by the entity bean and the data held in the relational database.

In CMP, the SQL is issued by the EJB container itself and is not under developer control. Consequently it is not really feasible to use stored programs in conjunction with a CMP EJB. It's fair to say that CMP is the recommended method of implementing entity bean persistence, since it reduces the effort involved in implementing the bean and since (somewhat surprisingly) CMP implementations can outperform BMP implementations. Most J2EE experts recommend using BMP only when there is a very complex relationship between beans and the underlying tables or when some special SQL coding is required for performance or security reasons.

Note also that the J2EE specification does not forbid accessing the database from session beans, and the programmer is free to implement JDBC within a session bean framework in order to retrieve and maintain persistent data. In this model, JDBC calls would be embedded in the session bean much as we embedded JDBC within a

Java servlet in the "Using Stored Programs Within Java Servlets" section earlier in this chapter.

However, in the case in which our database logic is contained in a BMP-based entity bean, we can certainly use a stored program implementation if we choose.

For instance, Example 14-26 shows a typical EJB method that we might use to locate an EJB representing a particular customer using the customer's phone number. The bean method accepts the phone number and returns the primary key of the relevant customer (the customer_id). This customer_id would later be used by the ejbLoad() method to load the relevant bean.

Example 14-26. EJB method to find a customer by phone number

```
public int ejbFindByPhoneNo(String phoneNo) throws FinderException
{
    try {
        Connection connection = getConnection( );
        PreparedStatement statement = connection.prepareStatement
            ("SELECT customer_id FROM customers WHERE phoneno=?");
        statement.setString(1, phoneNo);
        ResultSet resultSet = statement.executeQuery( );
        if (!resultSet.next( ))
        {
            statement.close( );
            connection.close( );
            throw new FinderException("Could not find: " + phoneNo);
        }
        statement.close( );
        connection.close( );
        return resultSet.getInt(1);
    }
    catch(SQLException e) {
        throw new EJBException ("Could not find: " + phoneNo, e);
    }
}
```

The SQL within a BMP entity bean can be implemented as a stored program. Example 14-27 shows such a finder method. The finder method calls the stored procedure GetCustomerIdByPhoneno, which returns a customer_id that matches a particular customer name.

Example 14-27. EJB finder method that uses a stored procedure

```
public int ejbFindByPhoneNoSP(String phoneNo) throws FinderException
{
    try {
        Connection connection = getConnection( );
        String sqlText = "{call getcustomeridbyphoneno(?,?,?)}";

        CallableStatement custStmt = connection.prepareCall(sqlText);
        custStmt.registerOutParameter(2, Types.INTEGER);
```

Example 14-27. EJB finder method that uses a stored procedure (continued)

```
            custStmt.registerOutParameter(3, Types.INTEGER);

            custStmt.setString(1, phoneNo);
            custStmt.execute( );
            if (custStmt.getInt(3) == 1) // Not Found indicator
                throw new FinderException("Could not find: " + phoneNo);

            return custStmt.getInt(2);
        }
    catch(SQLException e) {
        throw new EJBException("Could not find: " + phoneNo, e);
    }
}
```

Using Stored Procedures with Hibernate

J2EE provides entity EJBs as a mechanism for mapping Java objects to database tables. In CMP the J2EE system itself generates the SQL necessary to create the EJBs from the database and to update the database to reflect changes made to the EJBs. The generic term for a framework that synchronizes program objects with relational database data in this manner is an *Object-Relational Mapping (ORM) framework*.

J2EE and the EJB model have its supporters as well as its detractors, but almost everyone agrees that it is mainly suitable for large-scale distributed applications. To get the benefits of ORM for non-J2EE applications, programmers typically adopt an alternative ORM framework, the most popular of which is Hibernate (*http://www. hibernate.org*).

Database stored programs and ORM are not necessarily a perfect fit. Gavin King— the creator of Hibernate—was quoted as saying:

> Stored procedures are essentially a nonrelational view of a relational database ... my view, currently, is that the goal of an object-relational mapping tool should be to map between tables and objects, not between objects and "some other stuff."[*]

It's true that programmers who are building applications that make widespread use of stored procedures will get less benefit from Hibernate than those working with native SQL; in particular, Hibernate cannot auto-generate stored procedure calls, so the programmer needs to configure Hibernate with every stored procedure call that might be required.

However, demand for stored procedures in Hibernate has remained high, and their use is now fully supported. This support allows Hibernate to be used with legacy applications that rely on stored procedures and also allows new applications to take advantage of both Hibernate and stored procedures where appropriate.

[*] *http://www.theserverside.com/talks/videos/GavinKing/interview.tss?bandwidth=dsl*

In this section we will provide a brief overview of using Hibernate with MySQL stored procedures. We're going to assume you have some basic familiarity with Hibernate—if you are new to Hibernate, you will find a review of Chapter 2 ("Introduction to Hibernate") of the *Hibernate Reference Documentation* helpful. Our examples in this section are based on the Event class described in that chapter.

Hibernate Support for MySQL Stored Procedures

For every supported RDBMS, Hibernate includes a Dialect definition that defines the capabilities and configurations that the RDBMS supports. At the time of writing, the Hibernate (3.1rc3) MySQLDialect definition did not include a reference to stored procedures and, consequently, Hibernate would generate the following error when configured to use a MySQL stored procedure:

```
[java] Hibernate: { call getEvent(?) }
[java] Exception in thread "main" java.lang.UnsupportedOperationException: org.
hibernate.dialect.MySQLDialect does not support resultsets via stored procedures.
```

Modifying the Hibernate *MySQLDialect.java* file to reflect MySQL 5.0's ability to execute stored procedures is relatively simple, and we have submitted a modified version of this file to the Hibernate team for inclusion in an upcoming release of Hibernate (JIRA key HHH-1244, scheduled for 3.1 production). You can also obtain this file from this book's web site, where we will also include information about the current status of Hibernate support for MySQL stored procedures.

Using a Stored Procedure to Load an Object

The load( ) method of the Hibernate session object allows you to create a Hibernate object using the Hibernate mappings. Under the hood, Hibernate will generate a SELECT statement to extract the appropriate data from the database. Example 14-28 shows us creating and loading an Event object for the event #1.

Example 14-28. Loading a Hibernate object in a Java application

```
Long id = new Long(1);
Event event = (Event) session.load(Event.class, id);
```

We can load the Event object using a stored procedure. A simple stored procedure to retrieve details for a specific event is shown in Example 14-29.

Example 14-29. Stored procedure to load an Event object

```
CREATE PROCEDURE getEvent (in_event_id INTEGER)
BEGIN
  SELECT event_id, title, event_date
    FROM events
   WHERE event_id = in_event_id;

END;
```

To use this stored procedure, we need to create a definition for it in the mapping document and add a loader entry to the class definition. Example 14-30 shows the changes we made to the mapping document (Events.hbm.xml) to enable our stored procedure loader.

Example 14-30. Defining the loader stored procedure in the Hibernate mapping document

```
1   <hibernate-mapping>
2       <class name="Event" table="EVENTS">
3           <id name="id" column="EVENT_ID">
4                 <generator class="increment" />
5           </id>
6           <property name="title" />
7           <property name="date" type="timestamp" column="EVENT_DATE" />
8
9           <loader query-ref="getEventSP"></loader>
10      </class>
11
12      <sql-query name="getEventSP" callable="true">
13          <return alias="event" class="Event">
14              <return-property name="id" column="EVENT_ID" />
15              <return-property name="title" column="TITLE" />
16              <return-property name="date" column="EVENT_DATE" />
17          </return>
18          { call getEvent(?) }
19      </sql-query>
```

Let's look at the important parts of this document:

Line(s)	Explanation
9	The mapping tag loader defines the SQL that will be used when the data for a class is first loaded. query-ref refers to a named query defined elsewhere in the mapping—in this case getEventSP.
12-19	The sql-query section defines a named SQL query that can be used elsewhere in the mapping or from Java code.
12	The name property allows you to provide a meaningful name for the SQL query. The callable property—if set to true— indicates that the SQL query should be executed as a JDBC CallableStatement—i.e., it is a stored procedure or function.
13-17	The return section provides details about the result set that will be returned by the sql-query section.
13	The alias property provides an alias that can be used to prefix column names in the SQL and is not of much interest for a callable SQL. The class property indicates that the SQL will return properties relating to the specified class (in this case the Event class).
18	The SQL code that is executed by this sql-query. For a callable SQL, this should be in the same format used in the prepareCall( ) method of the Connection interface, as described earlier in this chapter.

Once we rebuild our application, all subsequent load( ) calls will use the getEvent( ) stored procedure to retrieve event data from the database.

Hibernate Queries

It is typical for an application to generate lists of matching objects by issuing Hibernate queries. For instance, to create a List object that includes all events, we might include the code shown in Example 14-31 in our application.

Example 14-31. Simple Hibernate query to retrieve all objects

```
List result = session.createQuery("from Event").list();
```

We could retrieve all Events objects raised since yesterday with the Hibernate query shown in Example 14-32.

Example 14-32. Hibernate query with WHERE clause

```
List result =
    session.createQuery("from Event as e where e.date > ?")
        .setDate(0, yesterday).list();
```

Let's implement the query expressed in Example 14-32 through a stored procedure call. A stored procedure to return events raised after a specified date is shown in Example 14-33.

Example 14-33. Stored procedure to support a Hibernate query

```
CREATE PROCEDURE getRecentEvents(in_event_date DATETIME)
BEGIN
  SELECT event_id AS EVENT_ID, title AS EVENT_TITLE, event_date AS EVENT_DATE
    FROM events
   WHERE event_date > in_event_date;
END;
```

As in the previous example, we need to add a definition for the stored procedure call to the mapping file. Example 14-34 shows the mapping for our new stored procedure.

Example 14-34. Mapping for our query stored procedure

```
<sql-query name="getRecentEventsSP" callable="true">
    <return alias="event" class="Event">
        <return-property name="id" column="EVENT_ID" />
        <return-property name="title" column="EVENT_TITLE" />
        <return-property name="date" column="EVENT_DATE" />
    </return>
    { call getRecentEvents(?) }
</sql-query>
```

Now we can use that named query in our Java code. Instead of using the createQuery( ) method, we use the getNamedQuery( ) method, supplying the name we have given our stored procedure call in the mapping file and supplying any necessary parameters. Example 14-35 shows the technique.

Example 14-35. Using a stored procedure to execute a Hibernate query in Java code

```
List result = session.getNamedQuery("getRecentEventsSP")
                .setDate(0,yesterday).list( );
```

Using Stored Procedures for Persistence

By default, Hibernate constructs and issues INSERT, UPDATE, and DELETE statements, as appropriate, to persist the contents of Java objects in the database. However, we can configure Hibernate to use stored procedure calls instead.

For a stored procedure to be used with Hibernate it must accept the same parameters—in the same order—as the SQL that Hibernate would generate by default. For instance, in the case of a stored procedure to replace an INSERT statement, the stored procedure will have to provide parameters representing every column in Hibernate's INSERT statement, and these parameters must appear in the same order as the columns appear in that INSERT statement. The easiest way of determining this sequence is to log the SQL generated by Hibernate before converting it to a stored procedure call.

For UPDATE and DELETE, the stored procedure must return the number of rows affected by the operation as either a function return value or as the first parameter (which will, of course, need to be an OUT parameter).

 The Hibernate documentation implies that a stored function should be used to implement UPDATE and DELETE functionality and that the stored function should return the number of rows affected. Unfortunately, Hibernate treats stored function return values in a way that works for SQL Server but not for MySQL, so for now it is necessary to implement the UPDATE or DELETE through a stored procedure.

Example 14-36 shows stored procedures designed to replace the Hibernate-generated DML statements to maintain Event objects. Note that in the case of the updateEvent and deleteEvent procedures, the first parameter is an OUT parameter that returns the number of rows affected by the DML operation. This parameter is neither required nor permitted for the createEvent procedure.

Example 14-36. Stored procedure to implement a Hibernate update operation

```
CREATE PROCEDURE updateEvent
  (OUT row_count INTEGER, in_event_date DATETIME,
   in_title VARCHAR(60),  in_event_id INTEGER)
BEGIN
  UPDATE events
    SET title = in_title, event_date = in_event_date
   WHERE event_id = in_event_id;

  SET row_count = ROW_COUNT( );
END $$
```

Example 14-36. Stored procedure to implement a Hibernate update operation (continued)

```
CREATE PROCEDURE deleteEvent(OUT row_count INTEGER, in_event_id INTEGER)
BEGIN
  DELETE FROM events
   WHERE event_id = in_event_id;

  SET row_count = ROW_COUNT( );
END$$

CREATE PROCEDURE createEvent
  ( InEventDate DATE, InEventTitle VARCHAR(60), InEventId INT )
BEGIN
  INSERT INTO events (event_date, title, event_id)
   VALUES(InEventDate, CONCAT(InEventId, InEventTitle), InEventId);
END$$
```

To ensure that Hibernate uses these stored procedures in place of its self-generated SQL, we need to add entries in the mapping document to associate the specific operation with the stored procedure call. Example 14-37 shows the entries we added to the Event class definition (in Event.hbm.xml) to enable the stored procedures.

Example 14-37. Configuring Hibernate to use stored procedures for UPDATE, INSERT, and DELETE

```
<sql-insert callable="true">{call createEvent (?, ?, ?)}</sql-insert>
<sql-update callable="true">{call updateEvent(?,?,?,?)}</sql-update>
<sql-delete callable="true">{call deleteEvent(?,?)}</sql-delete>
```

Once we rebuild our application, Hibernate will use these stored procedure calls in place of the INSERT, UPDATE, or DELETE SQL statements that it would normally generate.

We have now completely converted the Event mapping to use stored procedures. Hibernate will now use MySQL stored procedures exclusively when querying, loading or modifying objects of the Event class.

Using Stored Procedures with Spring

Spring (*http://www.springframework.org*) is a popular, lightweight framework for the development of Java applications. Spring offers many facilities that support the development of Java applications, including support for Model-View-Controller design, POJO (Plain Old Java Objects), integration with J2EE objects, Aspect Oriented Programming, integration with other complementary frameworks such as Hibernate, and abstraction layers for transaction management and database access. Spring aims to deliver on many of the promises of the J2EE framework, but in a less invasive and more productive manner.

Spring's JDBC abstraction layer eliminates much of the repetitive coding normally associated with even simple SQL queries. The abstraction layer includes a

StoredProcedure class that can be used to incorporate stored procedure calls into a Spring application. In this section we will provide a brief overview of how to access a MySQL stored procedure from within a Spring application.

Example 14-38 shows the stored procedure we are going to use in our Spring example. It accepts a single input parameter—the department_id—and returns two result sets. The first result set contains a list of employees in that department, and the second contains a list of customers associated with the department. The stored procedure includes an OUT parameter that returns the total value of all sales associated with the department.

Example 14-38. Stored procedure for use with our Spring example

```
CREATE PROCEDURE sp_department_report
  (in_dept_id INTEGER, OUT sales_total DECIMAL(8,2))
BEGIN

  SELECT employee_id, surname, firstname, address1, address2, salary
    FROM employees
   WHERE department_id = in_dept_id;

  SELECT customer_id, customer_name, address1, address2, zipcode
    FROM customers
   WHERE sales_rep_id IN
     (SELECT employee_id FROM employees
       WHERE department_id = in_dept_id);

  SELECT SUM(sale_value)
    INTO sales_total
    FROM sales
   WHERE customer_id IN
       (SELECT customer_id
          FROM customers
         WHERE sales_rep_id IN
             (SELECT employee_id
                 FROM employees
                WHERE department_id = in_dept_id));
END
```

The natural way to represent the customer and employee rows returned by the stored procedure is to create customer and employee Java classes. Example 14-39 shows part of the class that would represent employees. We created a similar class for customers.

Example 14-39. Java class to represent employees

```
public class Employee
{
    private long id;
    private String surname;
    private String firstName;
    private String address1;
    private String address2;
```

Example 14-39. Java class to represent employees (continued)

```java
    private double salary;

    public Employee(long id, String surname, String firstName,
                String address1, String address2, double salary)
    {
        this.id = id;
        this.surname = surname;
        this.firstName = firstName;
        this.address1 = address1;
        this.address2 = address2;
        this.salary = salary;
    }

    public String toString( ) {
        return "Employee : " + employeeId + " " + surname;
    }

    public String getSurname( ) {
        return surname;
    }

    public String getFirstName( ) {
        return firstName;
    }

    /* Other getters and setters would go here */
}
```

To represent the stored procedure, we create a new class that extends the Spring
StoredProcedure class, as shown in Example 14-40.

Example 14-40. Class to represent a stored procedure in Spring

```
1    private class MyStoredProcedure extends StoredProcedure
2    {
3        public MyStoredProcedure(DataSource ds)
4        {
5            setDataSource(ds);
6            setSql("sp_department_report");
7
8            declareParameter(new SqlReturnResultSet("Employees",
9                    new RowMapper( ) {
10                        public Object mapRow(ResultSet rs, int rowNum)
11                                throws SQLException {
12                            Employee e = new Employee(
13                                        rs.getInt("employee_id"),
14                                        rs.getString("surname"),
15                                        rs.getString("firstname"),
16                                        rs.getString("address1"),
17                                        rs.getString("address2"),
18                                        rs.getDouble("salary"));
19                            return e;
```

Example 14-40. Class to represent a stored procedure in Spring (continued)

```
20                                }
21                           }));
22
23              declareParameter(new SqlReturnResultSet("Customers",
24                      new RowMapper() {
25                          public Object mapRow(ResultSet rs, int rowNum)
26                                  throws SQLException {
27              •               Customer c = new Customer(
28                                          rs.getInt("customer_id"),
29                                          rs.getString("customer_name"),
30                                          rs.getString("address1"),
31                                          rs.getString("address2"),
32                                          rs.getString("zipcode"));
33                              return c;
34                      }
35                  }));
36
37              declareParameter(new SqlParameter("department_id", Types.INTEGER));
38
39              declareParameter(new SqlOutParameter("sales_total", Types.DOUBLE));
40
41              compile();
42          }
43
44      }
```

Let's look at the significant lines of this class:

Line(s)	Explanation
3	The constructor method for the class. It takes a single argument that represents the MySQL server connection.
5	Set the data source that was provided as an argument.
6	Set the SQL associated with the stored procedure. The SQL should contain only the stored procedure name — parentheses, the CALL statement, and parameter placeholders are neither required nor allowed.
8-39	The declareParameter( ) method invocations define input and output parameters and also any result sets returned by the stored procedure.
8-21	Specify the definition of the first—employee list—result set. The SqlReturnResultSet class represents a result set.
9	Create an implementation of the RowMapper interface that will map the result set rows.
10	The mapRow( ) method processes a single row in a result set. It returns an object that represents the row.
12-18	Create an Employee object to hold a single employee row from the result set. We create the Employee object using the default constructor with the values of the current row as arguments. We use the normal JDBC syntax to retrieve each column from the row and assign it to the appropriate constructor argument.
19	Return the new Employee object to the RowMapper, which will add it to the Map being constructed for the current result set.
23-35	Repeat the process for the second result set, which is used to create a Map of customer objects.
37	Define our single input parameter—department_id—using the SqlParameter method.
39	Define our single output parameter—sales_total—using the SqlOutParameter method.

Now that we have created a class that knows how to process the inputs and outputs of our stored procedure, we are ready to use the stored procedure within our Java code. The StoredProcedure class takes, as its argument, a Map that includes all of the required parameters to the stored procedure call. The class returns a Map that contains all of the result sets and output parameters. Example 14-41 shows us using the StoredProcedure class in our Java code.

Example 14-41. Using a Spring stored procedure class

```
1       MyStoredProcedure msp = new MyStoredProcedure(datasource);
2       Map inParameters = new HashMap( );
3       inParameters.put("department_id", new Integer(department_id));
4       Map results = msp.execute(inParameters);
5
6       List employees = (List) results.get("Employees");
7       System.out.println("Employees of department " + department_id);
8       for (int i = 0; i < employees.size( ); i++) {
9           Employee e = (Employee) employees.get(i);
10          System.out.println(e.getEmployeeId( ) + "\t" +
11                              e.getFirstname( ) + "\t" + e.getSurname( ));
12      }
13
14      List customers = (List) results.get("Customers");
15      System.out.println("Customers of department " + department_id);
16      for (int i = 0; i < customers.size( ); i++) {
17          Customer c = (Customer) customers.get(i);
18          System.out.println(c.getCustomerId( ) + "\t" + c.getCustomerName( ));
19      }
20
21      Double salesTotal = (Double) results.get("sales_total");
22      System.out.println("Total sales for the department " +
23                          department_id + "=" + salesTotal);
```

Here is an explanation of this code:

Line(s)	Explaination
1	Create a new instance of our MyStoredProcedure class, passing an existing DriverManagerDataSource object (datasource) to represent the MySQL connection.
2	Create a HashMap that will hold the procedure's input parameters.
3	Add name-value pairs to the HashMap for each input parameter. In this case, we have only a single parameter—department_id.
4	Use the execute( ) method of the StoredProcedure object to execute the stored procedure. We pass in the Map containing input parameters, and we retrieve a new Map containing all the outputs of the stored procedure call.
6	Use the get( ) method of the Map to retrieve a List that represents the rows in the first result set (employees).
8	Iterate through each element in the List. This is equivalent to moving through each row in the result set.
9	Cast each list entry to an Employee object representing the current row in the result set.

Line(s)	Explaination
10	Use the methods we created for the Employee class to extract and display the details for the current employee.
14-19	Process the second result set (customers) in the same way as for the employees result set.
21-23	Retrieve and display the value of the single OUT parameter (sales_total).

Conclusion

In this chapter we looked at how to use MySQL stored programs from within Java programs. Java programs access relational databases through the JDBC interfaces supported by the MySQL Connector/J driver.

We first reviewed the fundamentals of using JDBC to process basic SQL—queries, updates, inserts, deletes, DDL, and utility statements. We showed how to use the PreparedStatement interface to execute SQL statements that are repeatedly executed, possibly with variable query parameters or DML inputs. Finally, we looked at JDBC structures for implementing transaction and error handling.

JDBC fully supports stored programs through the CallableStatement interface. Callable statements support multiple result sets, and they support IN, OUT, and INOUT parameters. The ResultSetMetaData interface can be used to determine the structure of result sets returned by stored programs if this is not known in advance.

Stored programs are suitable for use in J2EE applications, and stored procedures can be invoked from within J2EE application servers such as JBoss, WebLogic, and WebSphere. We can use stored programs in J2EE applications wherever we might embed standard SQL calls—from servlets, session EJBs, or Bean Managed Persistence (BMP) EJBs. However, stored programs cannot easily be leveraged from within Container Managed Persistence (CMP) EJBs.

We can use stored procedures in ORM frameworks such as Hibernate, although doing so involves more work than letting Hibernate generate its own native SQL. The Spring framework also provides full support for MySQL stored procedures.

As with other application development environments, the use of stored programs from within Java code offers a number of advantages, including encapsulation of complex transaction logic, abstraction of the underlying schema, and potential performance improvements from reduction in network round trips.

## CHAPTER 15

Using MySQL Stored Programs with Perl

Perl is an open source programming language widely used for system administration tasks, web site development, data manipulation, and reporting. Perl was the brainchild of Larry Wall, who initially developed the language to provide a language for the easy manipulation of text files and the like. Perl rapidly became very popular among the Unix community as a powerful, easy-to-use, general-purpose programming language. During the explosion of the World Wide Web, Perl's ease of use and database connectivity capabilities made it the preferred choice for CGI-based data-driven web sites.

From very early on, Perl was an extensible language and benefited greatly from a wide variety of user-contributed packages allowing it to do everything from handling Unix mail to performing complex statistical analyses. One category of extension showed particularly rapid uptake—extensions that enabled Perl to interact with relational databases, allowing Perl users to manipulate RDBMS data as easily as they could manipulate text files. Initially, these extensions were platform specific—the extension used to access Oracle had little in common with that used to access Sybase, for instance.

Perl's DBI (DataBase Interface) module evolved to provide a common syntax for interacting with relational databases. DBI defines interfaces and utilities common to all databases, while for each specific relational database, we use a DBD (DataBase Driver) module that contains the database-specific implementation of the DBI interface, and may also include database-specific utility routines. The preferred way to use MySQL with Perl is through the DBD::mysql module.

In this chapter we will first provide a general overview of DBD::mysql capabilities and then move on to show how to use DBD::mysql to call MySQL stored programs.

Review of Perl DBD::mysql Basics

Let's start with a review of how to install the DBD::mysql driver, and how to use that driver to perform traditional interactions (i.e., those not using stored programs) with MySQL. These form the building blocks that we can use to work with stored programs. However, if you are already familiar with the Perl DBI, you may wish to skip forward to "Executing Stored Programs with DBD::mysql," later in this chapter.

Installing DBD::mysql

To access MySQL from Perl, you will normally use the DBD::mysql package. DBD::mysql is a Perl package that implements the classes defined by the DBI package that allow Perl to interact with relational databases in a database-independent manner.

The DBI package is probably already included in your Perl distribution. If it is not, you can follow the instructions given in this section.

> Make sure to install the DBI package before installing the DBD::mysql package.

Installing DBD::mysql on Linux or Unix

The easiest way to install DBD::mysql on a Linux/Unix system is to use the CPAN (*Comprehensive Perl Archive Network*) shell. To invoke the CPAN shell, run the following command from a command line (as root):

```
[root@guyh3 root]# perl -MCPAN -e 'shell'
```

This invokes the CPAN command line:

```
[root@guyh3 root]# perl -MCPAN -e 'shell'

cpan shell -- CPAN exploration and modules installation (v1.61)
ReadLine support enabled

cpan>
```

You can then type install DBD::mysql to download, build and install the DBD::mysql driver. It's probably best to specify force install, because otherwise the DBD::mysql driver will not install unless it has passed all the built-in tests. Unfortunately, the tests will probably fail if you have a nonstandard database password, so we generally use force install to ensure that the installation succeeds.

The CPAN install session will look something like this:

```
cpan> force install DBD::mysql
CPAN: Storable loaded ok
Going to read /root/.cpan/Metadata
  Database was generated on Wed, 15 Jun 2005 11:57:49 GMT
```

```
Running install for module DBD::mysql
Running make for R/RU/RUDY/DBD-mysql-2.9008.tar.gz
CPAN: Digest::MD5 loaded ok
Checksum for /root/.cpan/sources/authors/id/R/RU/RUDY/DBD-mysql-2.9008.tar.gz ok
Scanning cache /root/.cpan/build for sizes
DBD-mysql-2.9008/
DBD-mysql-2.9008/t/
DBD-mysql-2.9008/t/60leaks.t
DBD-mysql-2.9008/t/40listfields.t
DBD-mysql-2.9008/t/10dsnlist.t
*** LOTS of other output ***
Failed 16/18 test scripts, 11.11% okay. 725/732 subtests failed, 0.96% okay.
make: *** [test_dynamic] Error 2
  /usr/bin/make test -- NOT OK
Running make install
Installing /usr/lib/perl5/site_perl/5.8.0/i386-linux-thread-multi/auto/DBD/mysql/
mysql.so
Files found in blib/arch: installing files in blib/lib into architecture dependent
library tree
Installing /usr/lib/perl5/site_perl/5.8.0/i386-linux-thread-multi/DBD/mysql.pm
Installing /usr/share/man/man3/DBD::mysql.3pm
Writing /usr/lib/perl5/site_perl/5.8.0/i386-linux-thread-multi/auto/DBD/mysql/.
packlist
Appending installation info to /usr/lib/perl5/5.8.0/i386-linux-thread-multi/
perllocal.pod
  /usr/bin/make install  -- OK
```

Installing DBD::mysql on Windows

If you are using Perl on Windows, you probably are using the ActiveState binary distribution (*http://www.activestate.com*). Activestate Perl includes the Perl Package Manager, which can be used to download binary versions of Perl packages from the ActiveState site. To use PPM you simply type ppm from a Windows command prompt. If you are working through a proxy server, you may need to set appropriate values for HTTP_proxy, HTTP_proxy_user, and HTTP_proxy_pass, as shown below:

```
C:\>set HTTP_proxy=http://something.proxy.com:8080
C:\>set HTTP_proxy_user=myusername
C:\>set HTTP_proxy_pass=mypassword
C:\>ppm
PPM interactive shell (2.1.6) - type 'help' for available commands.
PPM> install DBD::mysql
Install package 'DBD-mysql?' (y/N): y
Installing package 'DBD-mysql'...
Bytes transferred: 597532
Installing C:\Perl\site\lib\auto\DBD\mysql\mysql.bs
Installing C:\Perl\site\lib\auto\DBD\mysql\mysql.dll
Installing C:\Perl\site\lib\auto\DBD\mysql\mysql.exp
Installing C:\Perl\site\lib\auto\DBD\mysql\mysql.lib
Installing C:\Perl\html\site\lib\Mysql.html
Installing C:\Perl\html\site\lib\DBD\mysql.html
Installing C:\Perl\html\site\lib\DBD\mysql\INSTALL.html
Installing C:\Perl\html\site\lib\Bundle\DBD\mysql.html
```

```
Installing C:\Perl\site\lib\Mysql.pm
Installing C:\Perl\site\lib\Mysql\Statement.pm
Installing C:\Perl\site\lib\DBD\mysql.pm
Installing C:\Perl\site\lib\DBD\mysql\GetInfo.pm
Installing C:\Perl\site\lib\DBD\mysql\INSTALL.pod
Installing C:\Perl\site\lib\Bundle\DBD\mysql.pm
Writing C:\Perl\site\lib\auto\DBD\mysql\.packlist
```

Connecting to MySQL

To connect to MySQL from a Perl program, we first need to issue the use DBI clause to load the DBI driver that forms the foundation for the DBD::mysql driver. We then create a database handle using the DBI->connect() method.

The connect method has the following syntax:

```
Database_handle=DBI->connect(DataSourceName,UserName,PassWord,[Attributes]);
```

The resulting database handle is used in all subsequent interactions with the database.

The *DataSourceName* specifies the database details for the connection. The syntax depends on the type of database used, but for MySQL it has the following format:

```
dbi:mysql:database:host:port
```

where *hostname* indicates the hostname or IP address of the machine hosting the MySQL instance, *port* defines the port on which the MySQL server is listening (3306 by default), and *database* specifies the database within the server to which the connection is being made.

Attributes defines some optional attributes for the connection; we'll discuss attributes in the next section.

In Example 15-1 we connect to a database prod on the MySQL server on the local machine localhost at port 3306. We connect as root with the password secret.

Example 15-1. Connecting to a MySQL database from Perl

```
use Strict;
use DBI;
my $dbh = DBI->connect( "DBI:mysql:prod:localhost:3306", "root", "secret" );
```

Connection attributes

DBD:MySQL allows you to specify the following attributes at connection time:

AutoCommit
> Determines whether each SQL statement will automatically commit following execution. This is relevant only for transactional databases such as InnoDB.

PrintError
> Determines whether MySQL errors will be printed as warnings.

```
RaiseError
```
    Determines whether MySQL errors will terminate execution.

These attributes are represented as an associative array within the `connect()` method, and each takes an argument of either 1 (`true`) or 0 (`false`). Example 15-2 shows how to set up a connection in which automatic commits are suppressed and in which any errors encountered are reported without terminating execution.

Example 15-2. Setting database handle attributes on connection

```
my $dbh = DBI->connect( "DBI:mysql:prod:localhost:3306",
    "root", "secret", { AutoCommit => 0, PrintError => 1, RaiseError => 0 } )
```

You can modify any of these database handle attributes during execution, as shown in Example 15-3.

Example 15-3. Enabling autocommit

```
$dbh->{AutoCommit} = 1;    #Enable autocommit
```

Handling Errors

As shown earlier, we can set up some basic error-handling defaults at connection time that will control whether MySQL errors cause immediate termination of a program. However, we will often want to check the error status of a DBD::mysql call immediately after execution and take appropriate action if the call fails.

Usually, a DBI method will return `true` if it is successful, or `false` otherwise, and so we can check that return status to determine whether the call was successful, as shown in Example 15-4. Details about the actual status of execution can be found in the err and errstr properties of the database handle. These properties can be used to determine the root cause of the error or to report the error to the user.

Example 15-4. Checking for errors in a DBI statement

```
my $dbh = DBI->connect( "DBI:mysql:prod:localhost:3306",
    "root", "secret", { AutoCommit => 0, PrintError => 0, RaiseError => 0 } )
  || die "Connection error: ".$DBI::errstr;
```

Issuing a Simple One-off Statement

The DBI do() method allows us to execute a simple statement that returns no result sets and takes no parameters. Example 15-5 shows the use of the do() method to set the value for a user variable.

Example 15-5. Using do( ) to execute a simple SQL

```
$dbh->do('set @myvariable=10')||die $DBI::errstr;
```

Preparing a Statement for Reuse

To execute a statement more than once, or to execute a SQL statement that retrieves a result set, we first need to prepare, and then execute, the statement. Example 15-6 shows the use of prepare() and execute() rather than do() to execute a simple SQL statement.

Example 15-6. Using prepare( ) and execute( )

```
my $sth=$dbh->prepare('set @myvariable=9')||die $DBI::errstr;
$sth->execute||die $DBI::errstr;
```

Using Bind Variables

One of the advantages of using prepared statements is that they can be re-executed with altered parameters without having to be redefined each time. *Bind variables*—also known as *substitution variables*—are indicated within a SQL statement by ? placeholders. Prior to execution, we call the bind_param() method to set the values of these variables.

In Example 15-7 we prepare a statement and then bind and execute() the statement 10 times in a loop. Each execution inserts unique rows into the appropriate table.

Example 15-7. Using bind_param( ) to set placeholder values

```
my $sth=$dbh->prepare('INSERT INTO bind_example(col1,col2) VALUES(?,?)')
    ||die $DBI::errstr;
for (my $i=1; $i<=10;$i++) {
    $sth->bind_param(1,$i);
    $sth->bind_param(2,'Row# '||$i);
    $sth->execute||die $DBI::errstr;
}
$sth->finish;
```

Alternatively, we can specify the bind variables in the execute method, as shown in Example 15-8.

Example 15-8. Specifying bind values in the execute() method

```
my $sth = $dbh->prepare('INSERT INTO bind_example(col1,col2) VALUES(?,?)')
   || die $DBI::errstr;
for ( my $i = 1 ; $i <= 10 ; $i++ ) {
    my $col2_value = 'Row2#' . $i;
    $sth->execute( $i, $col2_value ) || die $DBI::errstr;
}
```

Issuing a Query and Retrieving Results

In line with the core philosophy of Perl—There's More Than One Way To Do It™—Perl DBI and the DBD::mysql driver provide a number of ways to retrieve rows from a query. In Example 15-9, we use the `fetchrow_array` method, which is probably the most commonly used approach.

Example 15-9. Retrieving rows with fetchrow_array

```
my $sql =
   "SELECT customer_id,customer_name FROM customers WHERE sales_rep_id=1";
my $sth = $dbh->prepare($sql) || die $DBI::errstr;
$sth->execute || die $DBI::errstr;
while ( my @row = $sth->fetchrow_array ) {
    print $row[0] ."\t". $row[1] . "\n";
}
$sth->finish;
```

After we have prepared and executed a SQL statement that returns a result set (SELECT, SHOW STATUS, etc.), we can use the `fetchrow_array` method to retrieve each row into a Perl array. We can then refer to the column values as numbered elements in that array (starting with element 0, of course!).

There's More Than One Way To Do It

Perl DBI offers at least five other ways of retrieving rows from a statement handle, described in the following subsections.

fetchrow_arrayref method

The `fetchrow_arrayref` method, shown in Example 15-10, is similar in usage to `fetchrow_array`, and has the advantage of returning a reference to an array, rather than the array itself. This has a small positive impact on performance for each row, since the data is not copied into a new array.

Example 15-10. Retrieving rows with fetchrow_arrayref

```
my $sql =
   "SELECT customer_id,customer_name FROM customers WHERE sales_rep_id=1";
my $sth = $dbh->prepare($sql) || die $DBI::errstr;
$sth->execute || die $DBI::errstr;
while ( my $row_ref = $sth->fetchrow_arrayref ) {
    print $row_ref->[0]."\t".$row_ref->[1]."\n";
}
$sth->finish;
```

fetchrow_hashref method

The `fetchrow_hashref` method, shown in Example 15-11, returns the row as an associative array in which each element of the array is keyed by the column name, rather than the column position. This has the advantage of improving readability, although you have to know the column names that will be returned by the query.

Example 15-11. Retrieving rows with fetchrow_hashref

```
my $sql =
   "SELECT customer_id,customer_name FROM customers WHERE sales_rep_id=1";
my $sth = $dbh->prepare($sql) || die $DBI::errstr;
$sth->execute || die $DBI::errstr;
while ( my $hash_ref = $sth->fetchrow_hashref ) {
    print $hash_ref->{customer_id}   . "\t" .
          $hash_ref->{customer_name} . "\n";
}
$sth->finish;
```

fetchall_arrayref method

The `fetchall_arrayref` method allows you to retrieve an entire result set in a single operation. For noninteractive applications where the result set can fit into available memory, this can be a very efficient way to retrieve a result set. However, it is not necessarily appropriate for interactive applications where the user may wish to view only the first page of data before looking at the rest (for instance, on a web search page you rarely scroll through the entire list of matching sites). If the result set is too large for available memory, this method may degrade overall system performance as memory is swapped out to disk.

There are two main modes for the `fetchall_arrayref` method. In the first and simplest case, shown in Example 15-12, no arguments are provided to the method, and the method passes a reference to an array. Each element in the array contains references to an array containing the column values for a particular row.

Example 15-12. Retrieving rows with fetchall_arrayref

```
my $sql =
   "SELECT customer_id,customer_name FROM customers WHERE sales_rep_id=1";
my $sth = $dbh->prepare($sql) || die $DBI::errstr;
$sth->execute || die $DBI::errstr;
my $table = $sth->fetchall_arrayref||die $DBI::errstr;
for my $i ( 0 .. $#{$table} ) {
    for my $j ( 0 .. $#{ $table->[$i] } ) {
        print "$table->[$i][$j]\t";
    }
    print "\n";
}
```

Providing {} as the argument to `fetchall_arrayref` returns the columns as hashes, indexed by column name. In Example 15-13, we repeat our previous query but access our columns as hash references.

Example 15-13. Using fetchall_arrayref, returning hash references

```
my $sql =
   "SELECT customer_id,customer_name FROM customers WHERE sales_rep_id=1";
my $sth = $dbh->prepare($sql) || die $DBI::errstr;
$sth->execute || die $DBI::errstr;
```

Example 15-13. Using fetchall_arrayref, returning hash references (continued)

```
my $table = $sth->fetchall_arrayref({}) || die $DBI::errstr;
foreach my $row (@$table) {
    print $row->{customer_id} . "\t" . $row->{customer_name} . "\n";
}
```

You can also provide array or hash slice references as an argument to fetchall_ arrayref to restrict the columns returned.

dump_results method

The dump_results method provides a quick-and-dirty way to print the output of a query. By default, dump_results will output all of the rows from a statement handle to standard output, surrounding the values in quotes, separating with commas, terminating each row with a line feed, and truncating columns (if necessary) to a maximum of 35 bytes per value. These default behaviors can be changed by providing arguments to dump_results:

```
my $Rowcount=$statement_handle->dump_results(
    [column_length],[line separator],[column separator],[file handle]);
```

Example 15-14 shows dump_results in action.

Example 15-14. Using dump_results to display a result set

```
my $sql =
    "SELECT customer_id,customer_name FROM customers WHERE sales_rep_id=1";
my $sth = $dbh->prepare($sql) || die $DBI::errstr;
$sth->execute || die $DBI::errstr;
my $row_count = $sth->dump_results;
$sth->finish;
```

The output of dump_results is shown in Example 15-15.

Example 15-15. Output from dump_results

```
'398', 'BELL INDUSTRIES INC.', 'DAHL', 'PHILIPPA'
'2985', 'GEORGIA-PACIFIC CORPORATION', 'OBRIEN', 'DOYLE'
'4776', 'CFC INTERNATIONAL INC', 'KINDRED', 'TOM'
'8756', 'INFODATA SYSTEMS INC', 'WEATHERFORD', 'KRISTIE'
'10746', 'ADTRAN INC.', 'EATON', 'RAYBURN'
```

bind_col and fetch methods

The final method we're going to look at differs from all the preceeding techniques: instead of the fetch( ) method returning an array or a reference to an array, we associate Perl variables ahead of time to each column that will be returned by the query. We perform this association with the bind_col method. Then we call the fetch method, which automatically deposits the values of the columns concerned into the variables nominated earlier. The Perl variables must be passed by reference (preceded by a \ character), which results in a theoretical performance advantage.

Example 15-16 provides an example of using this technique.

Example 15-16. Using bind_col and fetch() to retrieve data from a query

```
my ( $customer_id, $customer_name );
my $sql =
   "SELECT customer_id,customer_name FROM customers WHERE sales_rep_id=1";
my $sth = $dbh->prepare($sql) || die $DBI::errstr;
$sth->execute || die $DBI::errstr;
$sth->bind_col( 1, \$customer_id );
$sth->bind_col( 2, \$customer_name );

while ( $sth->fetch ) {
    print join( "\t", ( $customer_id, $customer_name ) ), "\n";
}
```

Getting Result Set Metadata

We don't necessarily always know the exact structure of the result set that will be returned by a SQL statement: the SQL might have been built up dynamically or even supplied by the user. To allow for this possibility, DBI lets us retrieve details about the result set using attributes of the statement handle. The NUM_OF_FIELDS statement handle attribute returns the number of columns in the result set, while the NAME and TYPE attributes are arrays containing the names and data types of each column.

Example 15-17 shows how we can use these attributes to print out the structure of a result set.

Example 15-17. Retrieving result-set metadata

```
my $sth = $dbh->prepare($sql) || die $DBI::errstr;
$sth->execute || die $DBI::errstr;
foreach my $colno ( 0 .. $sth->{NUM_OF_FIELDS} - 1 ) {
    print "Name= "
       . $sth->{NAME}->[$colno]
       . "\tType="
       . $sth->{TYPE}->[$colno] . "\n";

}
```

These attributes let us write code that can handle dynamically any result set that might be returned. For instance, the code in Example 15-18 will print the result set returned from a SQL statement contained within the $sql variable, without knowing in advance the structure of the result set that SQL might return.

Example 15-18. Handling a dynamic result set

```
1    my $sth = $dbh->prepare($sql) || die $DBI::errstr;
2    $sth->execute || die $DBI::errstr;
3
4    # Print a title row
```

Example 15-18. Handling a dynamic result set (continued)

```
5     print join("\t",@{$sth->{NAME}}),"\n";
6
7     # Print out the values
8     while ( my @row = $sth->fetchrow_array ) {
9         print join("\t",@row),"\n";
10    }
11    $sth->finish;
```

Let's examine this example line by line:

Line(s)	Explanation
5	Print the names of each column in the result set—separated by tab characters—as a header row.
8-10	This loop repeats once for each row in the result set.
9	Print out a tab-separated list of column values for a particular row.

Performing Transaction Management

If you're using a transactional storage engine such as InnoDB, you may want to implement transactional logic within your Perl code. While you can do that by issuing the MySQL START TRANSACTION, ROLLBACK, and COMMIT statements with the DBI do() method, DBI provides some native routines that might be more convenient.

The AutoCommit attribute of the connection handle can be set to 0 to disable automatic commits after each statement, while the rollback() and commit() methods of the connection handle can be used to explicitly roll back or commit transactions.

Example 15-19 uses these methods to control transaction logic in a simple Perl script.

Example 15-19. DBI transaction management commands in action

```
$dbh->{AutoCommit} = 0;

$dbh->do(
    "UPDATE account_balance
       SET balance=balance-$tfer_amount
     WHERE account_id=$from_account"
);
if ($DBI::err) {
    print "transaction aborted: ".$DBI::errstr . "\n";
    $dbh->rollback;
}
else {
    $dbh->do(
        "UPDATE account_balance
           SET balance=balance+$tfer_amount
         WHERE account_id=$to_account"
    );
    if ($DBI::err) {
        print "transaction aborted: ".$DBI::errstr . "\n";
```

Example 15-19. DBI transaction management commands in action (continued)

```
        $dbh->rollback;
    }
    else {
        printf("transaction succeeded\n");
        $dbh->commit;
    }
}
```

Executing Stored Programs with DBD::mysql

We can use the techniques we've discussed in the previous sections for executing stored programs, although there are some circumstances in which you will need to use some additional techniques—specifically, if you need to retrieve multiple result sets or retrieve the value of an output parameter.

To execute a simple, one-off stored procedure that returns no result sets, we can simply invoke it with the do() method of the database handle, as shown in Example 15-20.

Example 15-20. Executing a very simple stored procedure

```
my $sql = 'call simple_stored_proc( )';

$dbh->do($sql)||die $DBI::errstr;
```

Stored procedures that return only a single result set can be treated in the same manner as simple SELECT statements. Example 15-21 shows a stored procedure that returns just one result set.

Example 15-21. Simple stored procedure with a result set

```
CREATE PROCEDURE department_list( )
    SELECT  department_name,location from departments;
```

Example 15-22 shows how we would retrieve that result set in Perl. The approach is exactly the same as the one we would use for a SELECT statement or other SQL that returns a result set.

Example 15-22. Fetching a single result set from a stored procedure

```
my $sth = $dbh->prepare('call department_list()') || die $DBI::errstr;
$sth->execute || die $DBI::errstr;
while ( my @row = $sth->fetchrow_array ) {
    print join("\t",@row),"\n";
}
$sth->finish;
```

Input parameters can be treated in the same way as placeholders in standard SQL. Input parameters are indicated in the prepare statement as ? characters, and the values are set using the bind_param method.

Example 15-23 shows a simple stored procedure that accepts an input parameter.

Example 15-23. Simple stored procedure with an input parameter

```
CREATE PROCEDURE customer_list(in_sales_rep_id INTEGER)
  SELECT customer_id,customer_name
    FROM customers
   WHERE sales_rep_id=in_sales_rep_id;
```

In Example 15-24 we use `bind_param` to set that value before executing the stored procedure and retrieving the result set. The example executes the stored procedure nine times, supplying 1-9 for the `sales_rep_id` parameter.

Example 15-24. Specifying an input parameter

```
    my $sth = $dbh->prepare('call customer_list(?)') || die $DBI::errstr;

    for ( my $sales_rep_id = 1 ; $sales_rep_id < 10 ; $sales_rep_id++ ) {
        print "Customers for sales rep id = " . $sales_rep_id;
        $sth->execute($sales_rep_id) || die $DBI::errstr;
        while ( my @row = $sth->fetchrow_array ) {
            print join( "\t", @row ), "\n";
        }
    }
    $sth->finish;
```

Handling Multiple Result Sets

Since stored procedures may return multiple result sets, DBI provides a method—`more_results`—to move to the next result set in a series. The `DBD::mysql` driver implementation of this method was still experimental at the time of writing (it is available in developer releases 3.0002.4 and above). We'll keep you updated on the status of `DBD::mysql` at this book's web site (see the Preface for details).

Example 15-25 shows a simple stored procedure that returns two result sets.

Example 15-25. Stored procedure with two result sets

```
CREATE PROCEDURE sp_rep_report(in_sales_rep_id int)
BEGIN

   SELECT employee_id,surname,firstname
     FROM employees
    WHERE employee_id=in_sales_rep_id;

   SELECT customer_id,customer_name
     FROM customers
    WHERE sales_rep_id=in_sales_rep_id;

END
```

Because we know in advance the number and structure of the result sets returned by the stored procedure, it is relatively simple to process the results. In Example 15-26, we simply retrieve the first result set as usual, call more_results, and then process the next result set.

Example 15-26. Fetching two result sets from a stored procedure

```
my $sth = $dbh->prepare("CALL sp_rep_report(?)") || die $DBI::errstr;
$sth->execute($sales_rep_id) || die $DBI::errstr;

# first result set: employee_id,surname,firstname
print 'Employee_id' . "\t" . 'Surname' . "\t" . 'Firstname' . "\n";
while ( my $row = $sth->fetchrow_hashref ) {
    print $row->{employee_id} . "\t" .
          $row->{surname}      . "\t" .
          $row->{firstname}    . "\n";
}

$sth->more_results;

# second result set: customer_id,customer_name
print 'Customer_id' . "\t" . 'Customer Name' . "\n";
while ( my $row = $sth->fetchrow_hashref ) {
    print $row->{customer_id} . "\t" . $row->{customer_name} . "\n";
}
$sth->finish;
```

Handling Dynamic Result Sets

A stored program can return a variable number of result sets, and the structure and number of those result sets can be unpredictable. To process the output of such stored programs, we need to combine the more_results method with the DBI attributes that contain result set metadata; these were outlined in the earlier section "Getting Result Set Metadata." The more_results method returns false if there are no further result sets, so we can continue to call more_results until all of the result sets have been processed. Example 15-27 illustrates this technique.

Example 15-27. Dynamically processing multiple result sets

```
1   sub execute_procedure() {
2       my ( $dbh, $stored_procedure_call ) = @_;
3       my $sth = $dbh->prepare($stored_procedure_call)
4           || die $DBI::err . ": " . $DBI::errstr;
5       $sth->execute || die DBI::err . ": " . $DBI::errstr;
6       my $result_set_no = 0;
7
8       do {
9           print "\n", ( '=' x 20 ) . " Result Set # ",
10              ++$result_set_no . ( '=' x 20 ), "\n\n";
11
12          print join( "\t", @{ $sth->{NAME} } ),"\n", ( '-' x 54 ), "\n";
```

Example 15-27. Dynamically processing multiple result sets (continued)

```
13
14                while ( my @row = $sth->fetchrow_array( ) ) {
15                    print join( "\t", @row ), "\n";
16                }
17           }until ( !$sth->more_results );
18     }
```

Let's step through this code:

Lines	Explanation
1-7	Here we define our subroutine, and have it extract a database connection handle ($dbh) and stored procedure call from the parameters passed to the procedure. The stored procedure call is prepared and executed (lines 3-5).
8-17	Specify an until loop that will execute until more_results returns false. This loop will execute at least once.
9 and 10	This statement prints a "divider" line to separate each result set returned by the stored procedure.
12	Print out the column names for the current result set.
14-16	Loop through the rows in the current result set by calling fetchrow_array to retrieve rows until all rows have been processed.
15	Print the column values for the current row and print each column value.
17	Call more_results to move to the next result set. If more_results returns false, then there are no more result sets to be retrieved and the loop will terminate.

Handling Output Variables

A stored procedure may contain OUT or INOUT parameters that can return individual scalar values from the stored procedure call. The DBI specification provides the bind_param_inout method for retrieving the values of such parameters. Unfortunately, this method is not implemented in the DBD::mysql driver as we write this— we'll keep you posted on the status of this method for MySQL at the book's web site.

Luckily, we don't need the bind_param_inout method to retrieve the value of an output parameter. We can pass in a user variable (see Chapter 3) to receive the output parameter value, and then select the value of that variable in a subsequent SELECT. Example 15-28 shows an example of this technique as an alternative to using bind_param_inout.

Example 15-28. Retrieving an output parameter without the bind_param_inout method

```
my $sql =
  'call sp_rep_customer_count(1,@customer_count)';    #watch out for the "@"!
my $sth = $dbh->prepare($sql);
$sth->execute( ) || die $DBI::errstr;
$sth->finish;

# Now get the output variable
```

```
my @result = $dbh->selectrow_array('SELECT @customer_count')
  || die $DBI::errstr;
print "customer_count=", $result[0], "\n";
```

Watch out when creating strings that include user variables in Perl. By default, the @ symbol indicates a Perl array and—if the @ appears in a double-quoted string—Perl will attempt to replace the apparent array with a Perl value. So you should always include these types of strings in single quotes or escape the user variable reference by preceding the @ symbol with "\" (e.g., SELECT \@user_var).

Also, remember that if the stored program includes any result sets, you must process all of these result sets before attempting to retrieve the values of an output parameter.

A Complete Example

In this section we'll put all of the techniques we have described so far into an example procedure that implements a simple web-based MySQL server status display. The example will prompt the user for MySQL server details and return selected status information about that server. The information will be provided by a single stored program that returns multiple result sets and includes both input and output parameters.

The stored procedure is shown in Example 15-29. The stored procedure returns, as result sets, the output of various SHOW statements and—if a valid database name is provided as an input parameter—details about objects in that particular database. The server version is returned as an output parameter.

Example 15-29. Stored procedure that generates an employee report

```
CREATE PROCEDURE sp_mysql_info
       (in_database VARCHAR(60),
        OUT server_version VARCHAR(100))
   READS SQL DATA
BEGIN

  DECLARE db_count INT;

  SELECT @@version
    INTO server_version;

  SELECT 'Current processes active in server' as table_header;
  SHOW full processlist;


  SELECT 'Databases in server' as table_header;

  SHOW databases;

  SELECT 'Configuration variables set in server' as table_header;
  SHOW global variables;
```

```
   SELECT 'Status variables in server' as table_header;
   SHOW global status;

    /* See if there is a matching database */
   SELECT COUNT(*)
     INTO db_count
     FROM information_schema.schemata s
    WHERE schema_name=in_database;
   IF (db_count=1) THEN
     SELECT CONCAT('Tables in database ',in_database) as table_header;
     SELECT table_name
       FROM information_schema.tables
      WHERE table_schema=in_database;
   END IF;
END;
```

To help us generate a well-formatted report, the stored procedure outputs a header row for each of the result sets it returns. This header row is issued as a single-row, single-column result set in which the column name is table_header.

Our Perl example is contained in Example 15-30. This is a Perl CGI script, designed to be run from the "CGI bin" directory of a web server such as Apache or Microsoft IIS. The program generates HTML to prompt for user input, connects to MySQL, runs the stored procedure, and generates the HTML to output the results.

Example 15-30. Perl CGI program to display server status information

```
1    #!/usr/bin/perl
2    use CGI qw(:standard);
3    use HTML::Table;
4    use DBI;
5    use strict;
6    if ( !param( ) ) {
7        my $form_tbl = new HTML::Table( );
8        $form_tbl->addRow( "Hostname:", textfield( 'hostname', 'localhost' ) );
9        $form_tbl->addRow( "Username:", textfield( 'username', 'root' ) );
10       $form_tbl->addRow( "Password:", password_field('password') );
11       $form_tbl->addRow( "Database:", textfield('database') );
12       $form_tbl->addRow( "Port:",     textfield( 'port', 3306 ) );
13       print header, start_html('MySQL Server Status'),
14       h1('Enter MySQL Server details'), start_form, $form_tbl->getTable,
15       submit,end_form, hr;
16   }
17   else {
18       my $hostname = param('hostname');
19       my $username = param('username');
20       my $password = param('password');
21       my $db       = param('database');
22       my $port     = param('port');
23       my @html_body;
24
```

Example 15-30. Perl CGI program to display server status information (continued)

```
25        my $dbh = DBI->connect( "DBI:mysql:$db:$hostname:$port",
26           "$username", "$password", { PrintError => 0 } );
27        if (DBI::err) {
28          print header, start_html("Error"), $DBI::errstr;
29        }
30      else {
31          my $sth = $dbh->prepare('call sp_mysql_info(?,@server_version)')
32            || die $DBI::err . ": " . $DBI::errstr;
33          $sth->bind_param( 1, $db );
34          $sth->execute || die DBI::err . ": " . $DBI::errstr;
35          do {
36              if ($sth->{NAME}->[0] eq "table_header" ) {
37                  my @row = $sth->fetchrow_array( );
38                  push( @html_body, h2( $row[0] ), p );
39              }
40              else {
41                  my $table = new HTML::Table( );
42                  $table->setBorder(1);
43                  foreach my $colno ( 0 .. $sth->{NUM_OF_FIELDS} ) {
44                      $table->setCell( 1, $colno + 1, $sth->{NAME}->[$colno] );
45                      $table->setCellBGColor( 1, $colno + 1, "silver" );
46                  }
47                  my $rowno = 1;
48                  while ( my @row = $sth->fetchrow_array( ) ) {
49                      $rowno++;
50                      foreach my $colno ( 0 .. $#row ) {
51                          $table->setCell( $rowno, $colno + 1, $row[$colno] );
52                      }
53                  }
54                   push( @html_body, $table->getTable );
55              }
56          } until ( !$sth->more_results );
57
58          $sth = $dbh->prepare('SELECT @server_version') || die $DBI::errstr;
59          $sth->execute( ) || die $DBI::errstr;
60          my @row = $sth->fetchrow_array( );
61          my $mysql_version = $row[0];
62
63          print header, start_html('MySQL Server Status'),
64            h1('MySQL Server Status');
65          print "<b>Server: </b>", $hostname, br, "<b>Port: </b>", $port, br,
66            "<b>Database:</b>", $db, br "<b>Version:</b>", $mysql_version, br;
67          for my $html (@html_body) {
68              print $html;
69          }
70          print end_html;
71      }
72  }
```

Let's step through this example:

Line(s)	Explanation
1-4	Define the path to the Perl executable—necessary for CGI programs— and import the Perl packages we are going to use. These packages include the Perl CGI module that assists with HTML formatting, the `HTML::Table` package to assist us with our HTML tables, and— of course—the DBI package to allow database connectivity.
6-16	Create the HTML input form as shown in Figure 15-1. Lines 7-12 create an HTML table that contains our input fields, while lines 13-15 print titles and other HTML. All HTML is generated by the CGI package.
17-72	Executed once the user clicks the Submit button on our HTML form.
18-22	Retrieve the values the user entered on the input form and assign them to Perl variables.
25-29	Using the inputs provided by the user, establish a connection to the MySQL database.
31-34	Prepare the stored procedure call, bind the database name provided by the user as the first parameter, and execute the stored procedure.
35-56	Execute once for each result set returned by the stored procedure.
36-39	If the result set contains a column called `table_header`, then the result set is treated as a title heading for a subsequent result set, and so we generate an H2 heading row. All HTML output is added to the `@html_body` array to be printed once we have retrieved all result sets and the value for the output variable.
41-46	If the result set does not represent a heading, then we initialize an HTML table to display the results. Here we create the heading row for the HTML table. Lines 43-46 loop through the column names in the result set and create a corresponding HTML table heading.
48-53	Loop through the rows in the result set and generate HTML table rows. The loop commencing on line 48 iterates through each row, and the loop commencing on line 50 iterates through each column in each row. Line 51 sets the value for a specific row/column combination.
54	Add the HTML for our table to the `@html_body` array.
56	The `until` clause controls the execution of the loop that commenced on line 35. While the `more_results` call returns `true`, indicating that there are more result sets, the loop will continue to execute.
58-61	Now that all result sets have been processed, we can retrieve the value of the output parameter. When we prepared the stored procedure on line 31, we provided a user variable—`'@server_version'`—to receive the value of the output parameter. Now we issue a `SELECT` statement to get the value of that variable.
63-66	Having retrieved all the result sets and having retrieved the output parameter, we can generate the HTML output. These lines print the heading and server details (including the server version).
67-69	Output the HTML that we have accumulated into the `@html_body` array during our program execution. This includes header rows and HTML tables constructed in our main loop.
70	This completes our HTML output and our Perl example.

This Perl program first generates the HTML input form, as shown in Figure 15-1.

When the user clicks the Submit button, the CGI Perl script generates output, as shown in Figure 15-2.

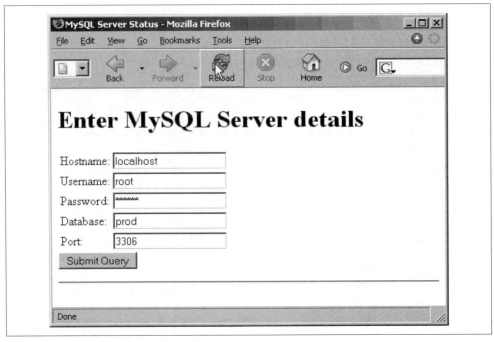

Figure 15-1. Input form for our example

Conclusion

In this chapter we reviewed the Perl DBD::mysql package, which allows Perl to connect to MySQL databases. We also showed how to use DBD::mysql to interact with MySQL stored procedures. Perl provides all of the mechanisms necessary for stored procedure processing, although some of these mechanisms were experimental as we wrote this chapter. We'll keep you updated with the status of these extensions at this book's web site.

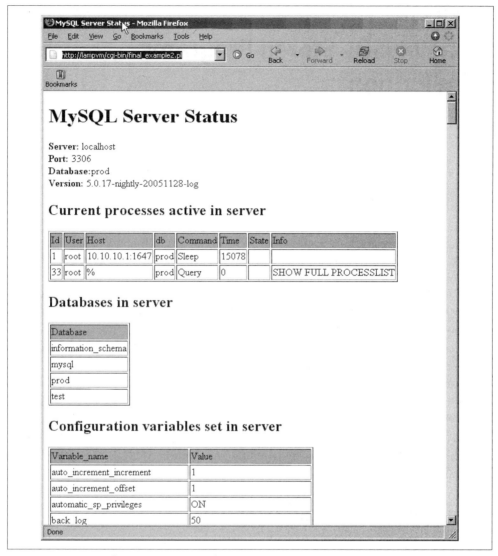

Figure 15-2. Output from our CGI example

## CHAPTER 16

Using MySQL Stored Programs with Python

Python is an open source, object-oriented, cross-platform language commonly used for system administration, application development, and many other purposes. Python is often used in very similar types of applications as Perl. However, Python devotees believe that Python offers many advantages over Perl in that it is natively object oriented, results in more readable and maintainable code, and enables greater programmer productivity, especially for large-scale developments. (Perl devotees have a different opinion, of course!)

The Python language includes a specification for a vendor-independent database-access API, the Python Database API Specification v2.0. You can find the specification for this API at *http://www.python.org/peps/pep-0249.html*. The MySQL implementation of this API is called MySQLdb, and is available at *http://sourceforge.net/projects/mysql-python*.

In this chapter we will review how to interact with a MySQL database using Python and the MySQLdb module, and explain how to exploit MySQL stored programs through this interface.

Installing the MySQLdb Extension

You can obtain the MySQLdb module for Python at *http://sourceforge.net/projects/mysql-python*. For Windows users, the MySQLdb module is packaged as a Windows executable. For Linux or Unix users, the module is packaged as a gzip tar archive; you should download the archive and, after unpacking it, run the following commands in the root directory of the archive (as the root user or using the sudo command):

```
python setup.py build
python setup.py install
```

MySQLdb Basics

In this section we'll review the basic methods provided in the Python MySQLdb extension for establishing a connection to a MySQL server and processing simple SQL statements. These methods provide a foundation that we can use when working with stored programs. If you are already familiar with the MySQLdb extension, then you might like to skip forward to "Using Stored Programs with MySQLdb," later in the chapter.

Creating a Connection

Before we can use MySQLdb, we need to import the module. We can then use the connect() method of the base MySQLdb class to create a connection object. The connect() method takes five arguments—host, user, passwd, db, and port—which identify the MySQL server, account, and database to which we intend to connect. Each of the arguments is optional, with sensible default values (localhost for the hostname, for instance).

Example 16-1 illustrates the basic technique.

Example 16-1. Connecting to MySQL from Python

```
import MySQLdb

conn = MySQLdb.connect (host = "localhost",
                        user = "root",
                        passwd = "secret",
                        db = "mysql",
                        port=3306)
```

Usually we will want to retrieve connection details from the command line. Python includes a powerful and useful command-line option parser that allows us to do this. Example 16-2 shows how to retrieve MySQL connection details from the command line and set up a connection.

Example 16-2. Getting connection details from the command line

```
import MySQLdb
from optparse import OptionParser

parser = OptionParser()
parser.add_option("-u","--username", dest="username",default="root")
parser.add_option("-H","--hostname",default="localhost")
parser.add_option("-p","--password",dest="password",default="")
parser.add_option("-d","--database",dest="database",default="mysql")
parser.add_option("-P","--port",dest="port",type="int",default=3306)
(options, args) = parser.parse_args()

conn = MySQLdb.connect (host = options.hostname,
```

Example 16-2. Getting connection details from the command line (continued)

```
                            user = options.username,
                            passwd = options.password,
                            db = options.database,
                            port=options.port)
```

Another option is to use a defaults file to store your connection details. In Example 16-3 we read our connection details from the file *./mysqldb*, which contains name-value pairs including the host, user, and password options.

Example 16-3. Getting connection details from a defaults file

```
try:
    option_file = ".mysqldb"
    conn = MySQLdb.connect(read_default_file = "././mysqldb")
    print "Connected"
except MySQLdb.Error, e:
    print "Top level Error %d: %s" % (e.args[0], e.args[1])
    sys.exit (1)
```

Older versions of the MySQLdb extension did not enable stored procedure result sets by default. To override the connection flags—and allow stored procedures to return result sets—you add the CLIENT.MULTI_RESULT flag to your connection options. You will also need to import the CLIENT identifer from the MySQLdb.constants module. Example 16-4 illustrates this procedure.

Example 16-4. Enabling procedure result sets in older versions of MySQLdb

```
import MySQLdb
from MySQLdb.constants import CLIENT

conn = MySQLdb.connect(  other connection_options ,
                    client_flag=CLIENT.MULTI_RESULTS)
```

Handling Exceptions

Python employs an exception-handling paradigm for error handling, and this paradigm is fully supported within the MySQLdb module.

Without exception handling, any errors result in program termination and a traceback message being generated. For instance, if our connection details were invalid, we could expect a message such as that shown in Example 16-5.

Example 16-5. Traceback error stack for invalid connection

```
Traceback (most recent call last):
  File "C:\tools\eclipse\workspace\Python1\MySQLexamples1.py", line 16, in ?
    port=options.port)
  File "C:\tools\python\Lib\site-packages\MySQLdb\__init__.py", line 66, in Connect
    return Connection(*args, **kwargs)
```

Example 16-5. Traceback error stack for invalid connection (continued)

```
  File "C:\tools\python\Lib\site-packages\MySQLdb\connections.py", line 134, in __init__
    super(Connection, self).__init__(*args, **kwargs2)
_mysql_exceptions.OperationalError: (1045, "Access denied for user 'root'@'localhost'
(using password: NO)")
```

We can handle the connection failure, or any other MySQL error, by enclosing the commands in a try/except block and catching any MySQLdb.Error that might be raised. If an error is raised by any statement within the try block, control will pass to the except block, which can interrogate the MySQLdb.Error structure to determine the error code (args[0]) and error message (args[1]). Example 16-6 shows this technique.

Example 16-6. Using an exception handler to catch MySQL errors

```
try:
    conn = MySQLdb.connect (host = options.hostname,
                            user = options.username,
                            passwd = options.password,
                            db = options.database,
                            port=options.port)

except MySQLdb.Error, e:
    print "Error connecting %d: %s" % (e.args[0], e.args[1])
```

Executing a Simple Statement

To execute a SQL statement with MySQLdb, we create a cursor object using the cursor() method of the connection object. We can then use the execute() method of the cursor object to execute a statement. The rowcount property of the cursor object will reveal the number of rows affected by the SQL statement. Example 16-7 shows how to execute an UPDATE statement in this manner.

Example 16-7. Executing a simple SQL statement

```
        cursor1=conn.cursor()
        cursor1.execute("UPDATE employees "+
                        "   SET manager_id=28"+
                        " WHERE manager_id=24")
        print "%d rows updated" % cursor1.rowcount
        cursor1.execute("COMMIT")
        cursor1.close()
```

Passing Parameters to a Statement

The execute() method allows for parameters to a statement to be passed as the second parameter to the execute() method. This parameter argument consists of a Python list containing the parameter values. These are substituted into the SQL statement contained in the execute clause. The standard Python string formats (%s) indicate the position of the parameters within the SQL.

In Example 16-8 we submit a SQL statement in a for loop which iterates through a few values of the old_manager parameter. For each employee formally reporting to these managers, we update the employees to report to a new manager.

Example 16-8. Using parameters when executing a SQL statement

```
new_manager=24
cursor1=conn.cursor( )
for old_manager in [28,87,60]:
        cursor1.execute("UPDATE employees "+
                        "    SET manager_id=%s"+
                        " WHERE manager_id=%s",
                        [new_manager,old_manager])
        print "%d employees updated from manager %d to %d" % \
                (cursor1.rowcount,old_manager,new_manager)
cursor1.execute("COMMIT")
cursor1.close( )
```

Retrieving Rows from a Query

The Python DB API gives us a couple of methods for retrieving result sets from a cursor that executes a SELECT statement or another MySQL statement that might return a result set.

The simplest method—fetchone( )—retrieves a single row from the cursor and returns that row as a Python list. To retrieve all rows, we create a loop that calls fetchone() until we encounter a None object. Columns in the row can be accessed by retrieving individual elements in the list. Example 16-9 shows this technique.

Example 16-9. Using fetchone() to retrieve rows from a cursor

```
cursor1=conn.cursor( );
cursor1.execute("SELECT department_id,department_name "+
                "    FROM departments")
while True:
        row = cursor1.fetchone ( )
        if not row:
                break
        print "%6d %-20s" % (row[0], row[1])
cursor1.close( )
```

The fetchall( ) method retrieves all rows in a single operation and returns them as a sequence of sequences (rows of columns).

In Example 16-10 we use fetchall( ) to retrieve all rows into the allrows object, which is a sequence of sequences. We iterate through the allrows sequence, creating row objects, each of which comprises a sequence of values for that row. We then print out each row value.

Example 16-10. Using fetchall( ) to retrieve rows

```
cursor1=conn.cursor( );
cursor1.execute("SELECT department_id,department_name "+
                "  FROM departments")
allrows=cursor1.fetchall( )
for row in allrows:
        print "%6d %-20s" % (row[0],row[1])
cursor1.close( )
```

The fetchmany( ) method is a compromise between fetchone( ) and fetchall( ) in which we retrieve rows in batches. The size of each batch is defined as an argument to fetchmany( ).

In order to retrieve all rows using fetchmany( ), we need to construct two loops: one to retrieve each batch, and an inner loop to retrieve each row in the batch. We terminate the outer loop when we have retrieved an empty set from fetchmany( ).

Example 16-11 shows fetchmany( ) in action.

Example 16-11. Using fetchmany() to retrieve rows

```
1    cursor1=conn.cursor( )
2    cursor1.execute("SELECT department_id,department_name "+ \
3                    "  FROM departments ORDER BY department_id")
4    while True:
5        somerows=cursor1.fetchmany(10)
6        if not somerows :
7            break
8        for row in somerows:
9            print "%6d %-20s" % (row[0],row[1])
10   cursor1.close( )
```

Let's look at this code line by line:

Line(s)	Explanation
4	This is the outer loop in which we loop over batches returned by fetchmany( ). The loop will continue indefinitely, so we need to end it explicitly with a break statement.
5	Call fetchmany(10) to fetch a batch of 10 rows.
6 and 7	If fetchmany( ) returns an empty sequence, we break out of the loop we constructed on line 4, having retrieved all of the rows from the result set.
8 and 9	Iterate through each row in the batch of rows returned by fetchmany( ) and return the row value.

In previous examples, we have retrieved rows as lists of columns. MySQLdb also supports retrieving rows as dictionaries in which each element is indexed by column name rather than by column offset. To retrieve rows as dictionaries, we specify the MySQLdb.cursors.DictCursor type as an argument to the con_cursor() method, as shown in Example 16-12.

Example 16-12. Using DictCursor to retrieve rows as Python dictionaries

```
cursor1 = conn.cursor (MySQLdb.cursors.DictCursor)
cursor1.execute ("SELECT department_id,department_name "+
                 "  FROM departments")
result_set = cursor1.fetchall ()
for row in result_set:
      print "%s, %s" % (row["department_id"], row["department_name"])
```

It is not necessary to use one of the fetch family of methods, at least in recent versions of Python (2.2 and later). Instead, you can access the rows directly from the cursor following a successful execute(). In Example 16-13 we retrieve the column values from the cursor as a sequence.

Example 16-13. . Accessing column values directly from a cursor as a sequence

```
cursor1=conn.cursor();
cursor1.execute("SELECT department_id,department_name "+
                "  FROM departments")
for row in cursor1:
    print "%6d %-20s" % (row[0], row[1])
cursor1.close()
```

We can also retrieve the row directly into appropriately named variables, as shown in Example 16-14.

Example 16-14. Accessing column values directly from a cursor, using named variables

```
cursor1=conn.cursor();
cursor1.execute("SELECT department_id,department_name "+
                "  FROM departments")
for department_id, department_name in cursor1:
    print "%6d %-20s" % (department_id, department_name)
cursor1.close()
```

Managing Transactions

The Python DB API specifies methods to the connection class that can manipulate the autocommit setting and explicitly issue commits and rollbacks. The methods are:

autocommit({True|False})
> Turns autocommit on (True) or off (False). This is equivalent to issuing a SET AUTOCOMMIT= statement.

commit()
> Commit the active transaction in the connection.

rollback()
> Roll back any active transaction in the connection.

Python exception handling is well suited to handling transaction control logic using a try/except/else structure:

---

try

This block contains the statements that constitute the transaction.

except

This block fires if any errors are encountered. It issues a rollback and notifies the user or calling application that the transaction has failed.

else

This block executes if no exceptions have been raised. It is responsible for committing the transaction and advising of successful completion.

Example 16-15 illustrates the use of the try/except/else structure and the connection transaction methods to manage transaction logic.

Example 16-15. Transaction logic in MySQLdb

```
try:
    conn.autocommit(False)
    csr1.execute("UPDATE account_balance "+
                 "  SET balance=balance-%s "+
                 "WHERE account_id=%s",
                 [tfer_amount,from_account])
    csr1.execute("UPDATE account_balance "+
                 "  SET balance=balance+%s "+
                 "WHERE account_id=%s",
                 [tfer_amount,to_account])

except MySQLdb.Error, e:
    conn.rollback()
    print "Transaction aborted:  %d: %s" % (e.args[0], e.args[1])
else:
    conn.commit()
    print "Transaction succeeded"
```

Getting Metadata

If we need to retrieve information about the result set that will be returned by a cursor, we can use the description property of the cursor class. The description property consists of a sequence of sequences. The primary sequence consists of one sequence for each column in the result set. The sequence for each column consists of the following items:

- The name of the column
- A code representing the data type of the column
- The "display size" of the column, which can be used to allocate space in output formats
- The "internal" size of the column
- The precision (for numeric columns)
- The scale (for numeric columns)

You will most often want to access the first and third elements in the sequence so that you can format titles and display lengths for the output of a query. For instance, Example 16-16 uses cursor.description to generate titles for the output of a query.

Example 16-16. Retrieving result set metadata

```
cursor1=conn.cursor( )
cursor1.execute("SELECT *"+
               "  FROM employees")
print "%-20s %8s" % ("Name","Length")
print "----------------------------"
for col_desc in cursor1.description:
        print "%-20s %8d " % \
                (col_desc[0],col_desc[3])
```

Dynamically Processing a Result Set

Using cursor.description, we can handle the output of a query even if we don't know what the SQL will be when we are writing our Python code (such as whether the SQL was dynamically generated or provided by the user).

In Example 16-17, adapted from the *Python Cookbook* by David Ascher, Alex Martelli, and Anna Ravenscroft (O'Reilly, 2005), we define a function that will accept any SQL statement and "pretty print" the output.

Example 16-17. Dynamically processing a result set

```
1   def dynamic_sql(sql):
2           names=[]
3           lengths=[]
4           dividers=[]
5           cursor1=conn.cursor( )
6           cursor1.execute(sql)
7           for col_desc in  cursor1.description:
8                   col_name=col_desc[0]
9                   col_length=col_desc[2]
10                  col_length=max(col_length,len(col_name))
11                  names.append(col_name)
12                  lengths.append(col_length)
13                  dividers.append('-' * col_length)
14          format = " ".join(["%%-%ss" % col_len for col_len in lengths])
15          print format % tuple(names)
16          print format % tuple(dividers)
17          rows=cursor1.fetchall( )
18          for row in rows:
19                  print format % tuple(row)
20          cursor1.close( )
```

Let us step through this example:

Line(s)	Explanation
1	Define the function and its input parameter: a string containing the SQL to be executed.
2-4	These are the empty lists that we will use to store column names, lengths, and divider strings (for our column underlines).
5-6	Create and execute a cursor with the SQL provided as a parameter to the function.
7-13	Loop through the elements (columns) in `cursor1.description`. Lines 8-9 retrieve the column name and display length.
10	Set the column length to be equal either to the display length or to the length of the column name (so that we have room for our titles if the column name is longer than the column data).
11 and 12	Store the column names and lengths in the appropriate list.
13	Append a series of dashes equal to the column length. These will form the column dividers for our output.
14	Create a format string that will be used to format column names, dividers, and column data. The format strings are simply string formats of the appropriate lengths for each column as determined in line 10.
15 and 16	Print the column headings for our formatted output.
17-19	Issue a `fetchall( )` to retrieve all rows from the query and then print each row according to the format we constructed in line 14.
20	All done! So we close the cursor.

If we submit a SQL statement to this function, as shown below:

```
dynamic_sql("SELECT * FROM departments")
```

the function generates a nicely formatted result set:

```
DEPARTMENT_ID DEPARTMENT_NAME MANAGER_ID LOCATION
------------- --------------- ---------- ---------------
1             DUPLIN          33         MORENO VALLEY
2             MADISON         19         BEAVER
3             MCHENRY         5          OKEECHOBEE
4             CHARITON        25         TULLYTOWN
5             SUMMERS         12         OLD CHURCH
6             LINCOLN         20         SWENGEL
7             CHAMPAIGN       37         AMF GREENSBORO
8             WILKES          23         CUSHING
9             CRAVEN          32         TAHOE PARADISE
10            COTTONWOOD      4          WICHITA
11            TAZEWELL        35         KLAWOCK
```

Using Stored Programs with MySQLdb

The techniques for calling stored programs with MySQLdb differ only slightly from those for using traditional SQL statements. That is, we create a cursor, execute the SQL to call the stored program, and iterate through result sets. The two key differences are that we must potentially deal with multiple result sets and that we may have to retrieve output parameters from the stored program call.

If you read the Python DB API specification, you might notice that the specification includes a cursor method for directly calling stored programs—the `callproc` cursor method. The `callproc` method was not implemented in MySQLdb as we went to press, although the maintainer of MySQLdb, Andy Dustman, is working on an implementation that will likely be available by the time you read this. Check out the book's web site (see the Preface) for an update. This method is not implemented in MySQLdb (version 1.2, at least). Luckily, everything you need to call stored programs is available through other methods, so you don't need to wait for `callproc` to use stored programs with Python.

Calling Simple Stored Programs

The procedure for calling a simple stored program—one that returns no result sets and takes no parameters—is the same as for executing any non-SELECT statement. We create a cursor and execute the SQL text, as shown in Example 16-18.

Example 16-18. Executing a simple stored procedure

```
cursor1=conn.cursor()
cursor1.execute("call simple_stored_proc()")
cursor1.close()
```

If the stored procedure takes input parameters, we can supply them using the second argument to the execute( ) method. In Example 16-19, we define a Python function that accepts input parameters and applies them to the sp_apply_discount procedure.

Example 16-19. Supplying input parameters to a stored procedure

```
def apply_discount(p1,p2):

    cursor1=conn.cursor()
    cursor1.execute("call sp_apply_discount(%s,%s)",(p1,p2))
    cursor1.close()
```

Retrieving a Single Stored Program Result Set

Retrieving a single result set from a stored program is exactly the same as retrieving a result set from a SELECT statement. Example 16-20 shows how to retrieve a single result set from a stored procedure.

Example 16-20. Retrieving a single result set from a stored procedure

```
cursor1=conn.cursor(MySQLdb.cursors.DictCursor)
cursor1.execute("CALL sp_emps_in_dept(%s)",(1))
for row in cursor1:
    print "%d %s %s" % \
        (row['employee_id'],row['surname'],row['firstname'])
cursor1.close()
```

If you receive a 1312 error at this point (PROCEDURE X can't return a result set in the given context), then it is an indication that you need to specify the CLIENT.MULTI_RESULTS flag in your connection, as outlined in "Creating a Connection" earlier in this chapter.

Retrieving Multiple Stored Program Result Sets

Unlike other SQL statements, stored programs can return multiple result sets. To access more than one result set, we use the nextset( ) method of the cursor object to move to the next result set.

For instance, suppose that we have a stored procedure that returns two result sets, as shown in Example 16-21.

Example 16-21. Stored procedure that returns two result sets

```
CREATE PROCEDURE sp_rep_report(in_sales_rep_id int)
    READS SQL DATA
BEGIN

    SELECT employee_id,surname,firstname
      FROM employees
     WHERE employee_id=in_sales_rep_id;

    SELECT customer_id,customer_name
      FROM customers
     WHERE sales_rep_id=in_sales_rep_id;

END;
```

To retrieve the two result sets, we fetch the first result set, call nextset( ), then retrieve the second result set. Example 16-22 shows this technique.

Example 16-22. Retrieving two results from a stored procedure

```
cursor=conn.cursor(MySQLdb.cursors.DictCursor)
cursor.execute("CALL sp_rep_report(%s)",(rep_id))
print "Employee details:"
for row in cursor:
    print "%d %s %s" % (row["employee_id"],
                        row["surname"],
                        row["firstname"])
cursor.nextset( )
print "Employees customers:"
for row in cursor:
    print "%d %s" % (row["customer_id"],
                     row["customer_name"])
cursor.close( )
```

Retrieving Dynamic Result Sets

It's not at all uncommon for stored programs to return multiple result sets and for the result set structures to be unpredictable. To process the output of such a stored program, we need to combine the nextset( ) method with the cursor.description property described in the "Getting Metadata" section earlier in this chapter. The nextset( ) method returns a None object if there are no further result sets, so we can keep calling nextset( ) until all of the result sets have been processed. Example 16-23 illustrates this technique.

Example 16-23. Retrieving dynamic result sets from a stored procedure

```
1 def call_multi_rs(sp):
2    rs_id=0;
3    cursor = conn.cursor( )
4    cursor.execute ("CALL "+sp)
5    while True:
6        data = cursor.fetchall( )
7        if cursor.description:   #Make sure there is a result
8            rs_id+=1
9            print "\nResult set %3d" % (rs_id)
10            print "--------------\n"
11            names = []
12            lengths = []
13            rules = []
14            for field_description in cursor.description:
15                field_name = field_description[0]
16                names.append(field_name)
17                field_length = field_description[2] or 12
18                field_length = max(field_length, len(field_name))
19                lengths.append(field_length)
20                rules.append('-' * field_length)
21                format = " ".join(["%%-%ss" % l for l in lengths])
22                result = [ format % tuple(names), format % tuple(rules) ]
23            for row in data:
24                result.append(format % tuple(row))
25            print "\n".join(result)
26        if cursor.nextset( )==None:
27            break
28    print "All rowsets returned"
29    cursor.close( )
```

Example 16-23 implements a Python function that will accept a stored procedure name (together with any arguments to the stored procedure), execute the stored procedure, and retrieve any result sets that might be returned by the stored procedure.

Let's step through this code:

Line(s)	Explanation
2	`rs_id` is a numeric variable that will keep track of our result set sequence.
3-4	Create a cursor and execute the stored procedure call. The `sp` variable contains the stored procedure text and is passed in as an argument to the Python function.
5	Commence the loop that will be used to loop over all of the result sets that the stored procedure call might return.
6	Fetch the result set from the cursor.
7	Ensure that there is a result set from the stored procedure call by checking the value of `cursor.description`. This is a workaround to a minor bug in the `MySQLdb` implementation (version 1.2) in which `nextset()` returns `True` even if there is no next result set, and only returns `False` once an attempt has been made to retrieve that null result. This bug is expected to be resolved in an upcoming version of `MySQLdb`.
11-22	Determine the structure of the result set and create titles and formats to nicely format the output. This is the same formatting logic we introduced in Example 16-17.
23-25	Print out the result set.
26	Check to see if there is another result set. If there is not, `nextset()` returns `None` and we issue a `break` to exit from the loop. If there is another result set, we continue the loop and repeat the process starting at line 6.
28 and 29	Acknowledge the end of all result sets and close the cursor.

Example 16-24 shows a stored procedure with "dynamic" result sets. The number and structure of the result sets to be returned by this stored procedure will vary depending on the status of the employee_id provided to the procedure.

Example 16-24. Stored procedure with dynamic result sets

```
CREATE PROCEDURE sp_employee_report
    (in_emp_id INTEGER,
     OUT out_customer_count INTEGER)
BEGIN

  SELECT employee_id,surname,firstname,date_of_birth
    FROM employees
   WHERE employee_id=in_emp_id;

  SELECT department_id,department_name
    FROM departments
   WHERE department_id=
        (select department_id
           FROM employees
          WHERE employee_id=in_emp_id);

  SELECT COUNT(*)
    INTO out_customer_count
    FROM customers
   WHERE sales_rep_id=in_emp_id;

  IF out_customer_count=0 THEN
    SELECT 'Employee is not a current sales rep';
```

Example 16-24. Stored procedure with dynamic result sets (continued)

```
    ELSE
      SELECT customer_name,customer_status
        FROM customers
       WHERE sales_rep_id=in_emp_id;

      SELECT customer_name,SUM(sale_value) as "TOTAL SALES",
             MAX(sale_value) as "MAX SALE"
        FROM sales JOIN customers USING (customer_id)
       WHERE customers.sales_rep_id=in_emp_id
       GROUP BY customer_name;
    END IF;
END
```

We can use the Python function shown in Example 16-23 to process the output of this stored procedure. We would invoke it with the following command:

```
call_multi_rs("sp_employee_report(1,@out_customer_count)")
```

We pass in 1 to produce a report for employee_id=1; the @out_customer_count variable is included to receive the value of the stored procedure's output parameter (see the next section, "Obtaining Output Parameters"). Partial output from this procedure is shown in Example 16-25.

Example 16-25. Output from a dynamic stored procedure call

```
Result set   1
--------------

employee_id surname firstname date_of_birth
----------- ------- --------- -------------------
1           FERRIS  LUCAS     1960-06-21 00:00:00

Result set   2
--------------

department_id department_name
------------- ---------------
14            KING

Result set   3
--------------

customer_name                   customer_status
------------------------------- ---------------
GRAPHIX ZONE INC DE             None
WASHINGTON M AAAIswAABAAANSjAAS None
```

Obtaining Output Parameters

As you know, stored procedures can include OUT or INOUT parameters, which can pass data back to the calling program. The MySQLdb extension does not provide a method to natively retrieve output parameters, but you can access their values through a simple workaround.

Earlier, in Example 16-24, we showed a stored procedure that returned multiple result sets, but also included an output parameter. We supplied a MySQL user variable (prefixed by the @ symbol) to receive the value of the parameter. All we need to do now, in Example 16-26, is to retrieve the value of that user variable using a simple SELECT.

Example 16-26. Retrieving the value of an output parameter

```
call_multi_rs("sp_employee_report(1,@out_customer_count)")
cursor2=conn.cursor( )
cursor2.execute("SELECT @out_customer_count")
row=cursor2.fetchone( )
print "Customer count=%s" % row[0]
cursor2.close( )
```

What about INOUT parameters? This is a little trickier, although luckily we don't think you'll use INOUT parameters very much (it's usually better practice to use separate IN and OUT parameters). Consider the stored procedure in Example 16-27.

Example 16-27. Stored procedure with an INOUT parameter

```
CREATE PROCEDURE randomizer(INOUT a_number FLOAT)
  NOT DETERMINISTIC NO SQL
  SET a_number=RAND( )*a_number;
```

To handle an INOUT parameter, we first issue a SQL statement to place the value into a user variable, execute the stored procedure, and then retrieve the value of that user parameter. Code that wraps the stored procedure call in a Python function is shown in Example 16-28.

Example 16-28. Handling an INOUT stored procedure parameter

```
def randomizer(python_number):
    cursor1=conn.cursor( )
    cursor1.execute("SET @inoutvar=%s",(python_number))
    cursor1.execute("CALL randomizer(@inoutvar)")
    cursor1.execute("SELECT @inoutvar")
    row=cursor1.fetchone( )
    cursor1.close( )
    return(row[0])
```

A Complete Example

In this section we will present a complete Python program that uses a stored procedure to report on the status and configuration of a MySQL server through a web interface.

The stored procedure we will use is shown in Example 16-29. It takes as an (optional) argument a database name, and reports on the objects within that database as well as a list of users currently connected to the server, server status variables, server configuration variables, and a list of databases contained within the server. It contains one OUT parameter that reports the server version.

Example 16-29. The stored procedure for our complete Python example

```
CREATE PROCEDURE sp_mysql_info
    (in_database VARCHAR(60),
     OUT server_version VARCHAR(100))
    READS SQL DATA
BEGIN

  DECLARE db_count INT;

  SELECT @@version
    INTO server_version;

  SELECT 'Current processes active in server' as table_header;
  SHOW full processlist;

  SELECT 'Databases in server' as table_header;

  SHOW databases;

  SELECT 'Configuration variables set in server' as table_header;
  SHOW global variables;
  SELECT 'Status variables in server' as table_header;
  SHOW global status;

  SELECT COUNT(*)
    INTO db_count
    FROM information_schema.schemata s
   WHERE schema_name=in_database;
  IF (db_count=1) THEN
    SELECT CONCAT('Tables in database ',in_database) as table_header;
    SELECT table_name
      FROM information_schema.tables
     WHERE table_schema=in_database;
  END IF;

END$$
```

The number and type of result sets is unpredictable, since a list of database objects is generated only if a database matching the stored procedure's first parameter is found on the server.

Prior to every major result set, the stored procedure generates a one-row "title" as a result set. This result set is identified by the column title `table_header`.

In this example we are going to use the Apache mod_python module to run Python code from within an Apache web page. mod_python allows the Apache web server to run Python code without having to execute an external Python program. You can find out more about downloading and configuring mod_python at *http://www. modpython.org*.

The HTML part of our web page is shown in Example 16-30. It displays an HTML form that asks for MySQL server connection details, including a database name.

Example 16-30. HTML form for mod_python example

```
<html>
<head>
<title>MySQL Server Statistics</title>
</head>
<h1>Enter MySQL Server Details</h1><b>
    Enter your database connection details below:
  <p>
  <form action="form.py/call_sp" method="POST">
    <table>

      <tr><td>Host:</td>
          <td> <input type="text" name="mhost" value="localhost"></td></tr>
      <tr><td>Port: </td>
          <td><input type="text" name="mport" value="3306"></td></tr>
      <tr><td>Username: </td>
          <td> <input type="text" name="musername" value="root"></td></tr>
      <tr><td>Password: </td>
          <td> <input type="password"  name="mpassword"></td></tr
      <tr><td>Database: </td>
          <td> <input type="test" name="mdatabase" value="prod"></td></tr>
    </table>
    <input type="submit">
  </form>
</html>
```

The most important part of this HTML is the `action="form.py/call_sp"` portion of the FORM tag. This tells Apache that when the form is submitted, the Python program `form.py` should be executed with the function `call_sp()` as the entry point. All of the input values of the form are passed to the Python function as arguments.

Figure 16-1 shows the data entry form created by this HTML.

Example 16-31 shows the Python code that is invoked when the user clicks the Submit Query button.

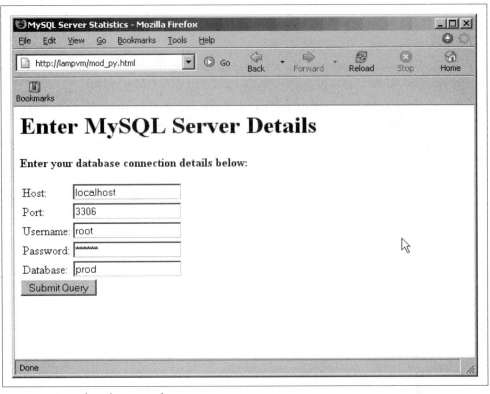

Figure 16-1. mod_python input form

Example 16-31. Python code for our mod_python example

```
1    import MySQLdb
2
3    def call_sp(mhost,musername,mpassword,mdatabase,mport):
4        html_tables=[]
5        html_out=[]
6
7        try:
8            conn = MySQLdb.connect (host = mhost,
9                                    user = musername,
10                                   passwd =mpassword,
11                                   db = mdatabase,
12                                   port=int(mport))
13
14           csr1=conn.cursor();
15           csr1.execute("call sp_mysql_info(%s,@server_version)",(mdatabase))
16           while True:
17               rows=csr1.fetchall()
18               col_desc=csr1.description
19               if col_desc<>None:   #Make sure there is a result
20                  if (col_desc[0][0] == "table_header"):
21                      #This is a special result set that contains a header only
```

Example 16-31. Python code for our mod_python example (continued)

```
22                      html="<h2>%s</h2>" % rows[0][0]
23                  else:
24                      html=html_table(col_desc,rows)
25                  html_tables.append(html)
26              if csr1.nextset( )==None:
27                  break
28          #Get stored procedure output parameter
29          csr1.execute("SELECT @server_version")
30          row=csr1.fetchone( )
31          mysql_version=row[0]
32          csr1.close( )
33
34          #Build up the html output
35          html_out.append("<html><head><title>"+
36                          "MySQL Server status and statistics"+
37                          "</title></head>"+
38                          "<h1>MySQL Server status and statistics</h1>")
39          html_out.append("<b>Host:</b> %s<br>" % mhost)
40          html_out.append("<b>Port:</b> %s<br>" % mport)
41          html_out.append("<b>Version:</b> %s<br>" % mysql_version)
42          html_out.append("".join(html_tables))
43
44          html_out.append("</html>")
45          return "".join(html_out)
46
47      except MySQLdb.Error, e:
48          return "MySQL Error %d: %s" % (e.args[0], e.args[1])
49
50  def html_table(col_desc,rows):
51      # Create HTML table out of cursor.description and cursor.fetchall
52      html_out=[]
53      html_out.append('<table border=1><tr>')
54      for col in col_desc:
55          html_out.append('<td><b>%s</b></td>' % col[0])
56      html_out.append('</tr>')
57      for row in rows:
58          html_out.append('<tr>')
59          for col in row:
60              html_out.append('<td>%s</td>' % col)
61          html_out.append('</tr>')
62      html_out.append('</table>')
63      s='\n'.join(html_out)
64      return s
```

There are two main functions in this Python code:

call_sp()

> Invokes the stored procedure to generate the MySQL server status report. This is the routine referred to in the action clause of the <form> tag within the calling HTML.

html_table()

> A utility function that creates an HTML table from a MySQLdb cursor result set.

Let's start with the call_sp() routine:

Line(s)	Explanation
8-12	Call the MySQLdb.connect( ) method to create the MySQL connection using the parameters specified on the HTML form.
14-15	Create and execute a cursor that invokes the stored procedure.
16	The WHILE loop that commences on this line will iterate through all of the result sets in the stored procedure. The loop ends on line 27.
17-18	On line 17 we use fetchall( ) to retrieve all the rows in the current result set. On line 18 we retrieve the column details for that result set.
20-22	If the title for the first column in the result set is table_header, then this result set contains a heading for a subsequent result set. In that case, we generate an HTML header consisting of the single row and column returned within the result set.
23-24	Otherwise, create an HTML table to represent the result set. This is done using the other function in the file—html_table( )—which we will discuss shortly.
26-27	Request the next result set. If there are no further result sets, we issue break to terminate the loop that commenced on line 16. Otherwise, the loop repeats and we process the next result set.
29-32	Retrieve the value of the OUT parameter.
	On line 29 we issue a SELECT to retrieve the user variable that contains the stored procedure OUT variable. When we called the stored procedure on line 15, we specified @server_version for the second (OUT) parameter. Now we issue a SELECT to retrieve the value of that parameter.
35-45	So far, we have stored HTML that we want to generate into an array called html_tables. Now we construct the final HTML to return to the calling form.
	Lines 35-41 add the initial HTML output into an array html_out. In line 42 we add the HTML generated from the result sets to that HTML. Finally, we return all of the HTML to the calling form on line 45.

The second function—html_table( )—generates an HTML table when passed the results of the cursor.description and cursor.fetchall output. We call this in our main program on line 24 when we encounter a result set that we need to format as a HTML table:

Line(s)	Explanation
50	The routine takes two arguments. The first (col_desc) is a columns.description structure as returned by the description() method of the cursor object. The second is a results structure as would be returned by the fetchall() method.
54-55	Loop through the rows in the col_desc parameter—each row representing a column in the result set—and generate HTML to create a title row for our HTML table.
57-60	Generate the bulk of the HTML table. The loop on line 57 iterates through the rows in the result set. The loop on line 59 iterates through the columns in a specific row. On line 60 we generate the HTML for a specific value (for a particular column in a particular row).
63-64	Consolidate all of the HTML fragments—stored in the html_out array— into a single string, which is returned to the calling function.

Figure 16-2 shows the output from our mod_python example.

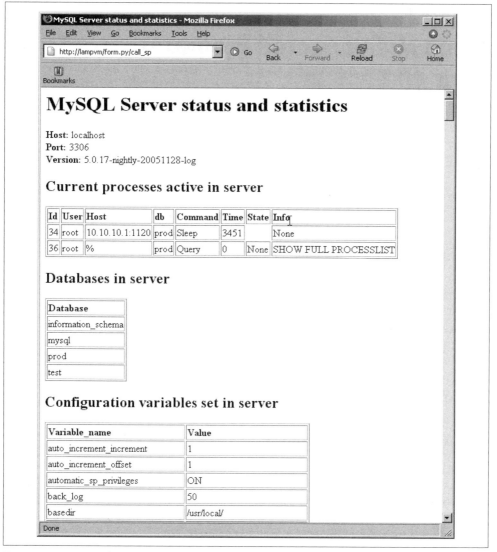

Figure 16-2. Output from our mod_python example

Conclusion

The Python MySQLdb extension contains all of the tools you need to interface with MySQL and MySQL stored procedures. Python is a pleasure to program, and it is a very viable alternative to other dynamic scripting languages such as PHP and Perl. Using mod_python (or CGI) allows us to easily implement dynamic web content in Python using MySQL as the backend.

## CHAPTER 17

Using MySQL Stored Programs with .NET

ADO.NET is Microsoft's database-independent, language-neutral data access interface included within the .NET framework. ADO.NET allows .NET languages such as C# and VB.NET to communicate with various data sources, primarily relational databases such as SQL Server, Oracle, and, of course, MySQL. MySQL provides an ADO-compliant driver—Connector/Net—that allows us to work with MySQL databases using the ADO.NET interfaces.

First, we'll start with a quick review of how we can use ADO.NET to process standard SQL statements against a MySQL database. Next, we'll examine the ADO.NET syntax for invoking stored programs, including handling input and output parameters and processing multiple result sets. Finally, we'll show how we can use a MySQL stored procedure as the basis for an ASP.NET web application.

Review of ADO.NET Basics

Before looking at how to invoke stored programs using ADO.NET, let's review how we perform operations in ADO.NET involving simple SQL statements. These operations form the foundation of stored program interactions. If you are already familiar with using ADO.NET with MySQL, you might want to skip forward to "Using Stored Programs in ADO.NET," later in this chapter.

Installing the Connector/Net Driver and Configuring Your IDE

To connect to MySQL from ADO.NET, we first need to download and install the Connector/Net provider from MySQL. We can download the Connector/Net driver from the MySQL web site at *http://dev.mysql.com/downloads/connector/net/*.

Once we have installed the Connector/Net driver, we are ready to write .NET programs to connect to MySQL. However, we must add a reference to the Connector/Net driver in our .NET application.

To do this in Visual Studio, select Project → Add Reference from the main menu, then select the Browse tab. We find the *MySQL.Data.dll* file on our system, usually located in a directory such as *C:\Program Files\MySQL\MySQL Connector Net <x.x.x>\bin\. NET <y.y>*; where *"x.x.x"* corresponds to the version of the Connector/Net driver (currently 1.0.7) and *"y.y"* corresponds to the version of .NET that we are using (usually 1.1 or 2.0). Figure 17-1 shows how we can configure Visual C# Visual Studio Express Edition to use the Connector/Net driver.

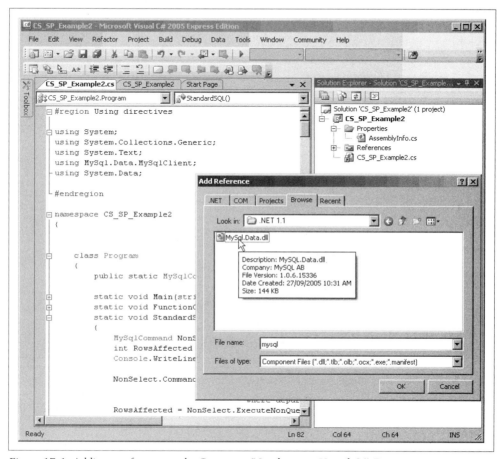

Figure 17-1. Adding a reference to the Connector/Net driver in Visual C# Express

Registering the Driver and Connecting to MySQL

To use the MySQL driver in your program code, we will normally first import the MySQL.Data.MySqlClient namespace so we don't have to fully qualify every reference to Connector/Net classes. In VB.NET, this means we would include Imports MySql. Data.MySqlClient as the first line of our VB.NET module. In C#, we would include a using `MySql.Data.MySqlClient;` statement within the `Using` directives region, as shown in Figure 17-2.

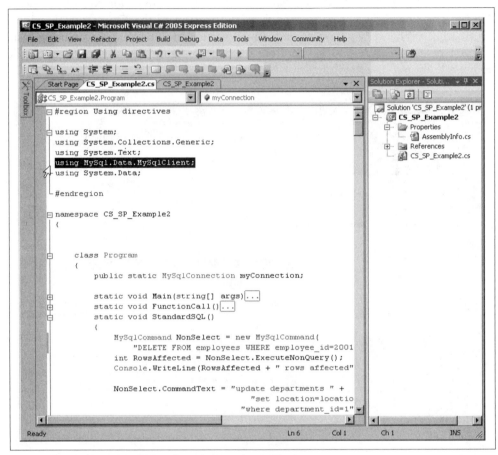

Figure 17-2. Adding the "using" clause in Visual C# Express

To establish a connection to MySQL we need to create a `MySQLConnection` object. The `Constructer` method for the `MySQLConnection` object accepts a string that defines the server, database, and connection credentials. This string consists of a set of name-value pairs separated by semicolons. For instance, the following string defines a connection to a server on the `localhost` at port 3306 and connects to database `prod` using the account `fred` and the password `freddy`:

```
Server=localhost;Port=3306;Database=prod;Username=fred;Password=freddy
```

Table 17-1 lists the most important keywords that you can provide for the `MySQLConnection` object; you can find a complete list in the Connector/Net documentation that ships with the driver.

Table 17-1. Some of the keyword values for the MySQLConnection

Keyword	Description
Host	Name of the host on which the MySQL server is located. This could be an IP address, hostname, or localhost.
Port	Port number upon which the MySQL server is listening.
Database	Name of the database for initial connection.
Username	MySQL username to use for the connection.
Password	Password for the MySQL account.

It would be unusual—and probably bad practice—to hardcode the MySQLConnection details in your program. More often, you will retrieve the keywords from command-line arguments or from a login dialog box.

Once the MySQLConnection object is initialized, we can establish the connection using the open( ) method. If the connection fails, a MySQLException will be thrown, so we need to enclose this call in a try block if we don't want to throw a non-handled exception (see "Handling Errors," later in this chapter). Example 17-1 shows us connecting to MySQL from within a VB.NET program, with the connection details specified as command-line arguments.

Example 17-1. Connecting to MySQL in VB.NET

```
Sub Main(ByVal CmdArgs( ) As String)

    Dim myHost As String = CmdArgs(0)
    Dim myUserId As String = CmdArgs(1)
    Dim myPassword As String = CmdArgs(2)
    Dim myDatabase As String = CmdArgs(3)

    Dim myConnectionString As String = "Database=" & myDatabase & _
        " ;Data Source=" & myHost & _
        ";User Id=" & myUserId & ";Password=" & myPassword


    Dim myConnection As New MySqlConnection(myConnectionString)

    Try
        myConnection.Open( )
        Console.WriteLine("Connection succeeded")
    Catch MyException As MySqlException
        Console.WriteLine("Connection error: MySQL code: " _
            & MyException.Number & " " & MyException.Message)
    End Try
```

Example 17-2 implements the same logic in C#.

Example 17-2. Connecting to MySQL in C#

```
static void Main(string[] args)
    {
        String myHost=args[0];
        String myUserId=args[1];
        String myPassword=args[2];
        String myDatabase=args[3];

        String myConnectionString = "Database=" + myDatabase +
            " ;Host=" + myHost +
            ";UserName=" + myUserId  + ";Password=" + myPassword;

        MySqlConnection myConnection;
        myConnection = new MySqlConnection( );
        myConnection.ConnectionString = myConnectionString;

        try {
            myConnection.Open( );
            Console.WriteLine("Connection succeded");
        }
        catch (MySqlException MyException)              {
            Console.WriteLine("Connection error: MySQL code: "+MyException.Number
                            +" "+ MyException.Message);
          }
```

Issuing a Non-SELECT Statement

It is fairly straightforward to execute a non-SELECT statement—such as UPDATE, INSERT, DELETE, or SET—in .NET. First, we create a new MySQLCommand object, passing it the SQL statement to be executed and the name of the active connection (these can also be specified using the properties of the MySqlCommand object at a later time).

The ExecuteNonQuery( ) method of the MySqlCommand executes a statement that returns no result sets. It returns the number of rows affected by the statement. Example 17-3 shows an example of this in C#.

Example 17-3. Executing a non-SELECT SQL statement in C#

```
 MySqlCommand NonSelect = new MySqlCommand(
        "DELETE FROM employees WHERE employee_id=2001", myConnection);
 int RowsAffected = NonSelect.ExecuteNonQuery( );
```

Example 17-4 shows the same logic in VB.NET.

Example 17-4. Executing a non-SELECT statement in VB.NET

```
Dim NonSelect As MySqlCommand
NonSelect = New MySqlCommand( _
        "DELETE FROM employees WHERE employee_id=2001", myConnection)
Dim RowsAffected As Int16
RowsAffected = NonSelect.ExecuteNonQuery( )
```

Reusing a Statement Object

We don't have to create a new statement object for every SQL statement we execute. By changing the `CommandText` property of the `MySqlCommand` object, we associate the object with a new SQL statement text, which we can submit to the database by calling the `ExecuteNonQuery()` method. Example 17-5 provides an example of this technique in C#.

Example 17-5. Reusing a MySqlCommand object in C#

```
MySqlCommand NonSelect = new MySqlCommand("set autocommit=0",myConnection);
int RowsAffected=NonSelect.ExecuteNonQuery();

NonSelect.CommandText = "update departments "+
                            "set location=location "+
                            "where department_id=1";
RowsAffected = NonSelect.ExecuteNonQuery();
Console.WriteLine(RowsAffected + " rows affected");
```

Using Parameters

A lot of the time we execute the same logical SQL statement with different values for the `WHERE` clause or some other variable part of the statement. It might seem simple to do this by manipulating the `CommandText` and "pasting it" in the variable portions. For instance, in Example 17-6 we generate a new unique SQL statement to update employees' salaries based on some values in arrays.

Example 17-6. "Paste" method of changing SQL parameters (not recommended)

```
For i = 1 To N
    NonSelect.CommandText = "UPDATE employees " + _
                            "  SET salary= " + EmployeeSal(i).ToString + _
                            " WHERE employee_id=" + EmployeeID(i).ToString
    NonSelect.ExecuteNonQuery()

Next
```

While this method will work—and is, in fact, a common technique—it is neither efficient nor safe. In particular, this style of coding cannot take advantage of MySQL server-side prepared statements, and it is vulnerable to SQL injection (a form of attack in which SQL syntax is inserted into parameters, leading to unintended SQL syntax being executed).

A far better way of performing this kind of iterative processing is to use the `Parameters` collection of the `MySqlCommand` object. Parameters are prefixed in the SQL text with the "?" character. You then use the `Parameter` methods of the `MySqlCommand` object to define the parameters and set their values, as shown in Example 17-7.

Example 17-7. Using parameters in VB.NET

```
1    Dim ParameterSQL As MySqlCommand
2    Dim SQLText As String
3    SQLText = "UPDATE employees " + _
4              "   SET salary= ?NewSal" + _
5              " WHERE employee_id= ?EmpID"
6    ParameterSQL = New MySqlCommand(SQLText, myConnection)
7
8    Dim EmpSal As MySqlParameter
9    EmpSal = ParameterSQL.Parameters.Add("?NewSal", MySqlDbType.Float)
10     Dim EmpId As MySqlParameter
11     EmpId = ParameterSQL.Parameters.Add("?EmpID", MySqlDbType.Int16)
12     Dim RowCount As Int16
13
14     For i = 1 To N
15         EmpSal.Value = EmployeeSal(i)
16         EmpId.Value = EmployeeID(i)
17         RowCount = ParameterSQL.ExecuteNonQuery()
18         Console.WriteLine(RowCount.ToString)
19     Next
```

Let's step through this example:

Line(s)	Explanation
3	Create the text for our SQL. The parameters in the SQL (?NewSal and ?EmpID) are prefixed by ? characters to distinguish them from normal MySQL identifiers.
6	Create the MySqlCommand object and associate it with our SQL text.
8-9	Declare a MySqlParameter object for the NewSal parameter on line 8, and on line 9, associate it with the MySqlCommand object. The name of the parameter provided to the Add() method should match exactly the name of the parameter in your SQL text. The second argument to Add() specifies the data type of the parameter.
10-11	Create a second parameter to represent the EmpID parameter.
14-19	Iterate through the EmployeeSal and EmployeeID arrays, which contain new salaries for specific employees.
15-16	Assign the appropriate values to the parameter objects. The values are taken from the EmployeeSal and EmployeeID arrays.
17	The ExecuteNonQuery() method executes the SQL with the parameters supplied.

Using parameters rather than hardcoded literals is highly recommended, especially since—as we will see later—we really must use parameters if we are going to invoke stored programs in .NET.

Example 17-8 shows the logic of Example 17-7 expressed in C#.NET.

Example 17-8. Using parameters in C#

```
String SQLText = "UPDATE employees " +
                 "   SET salary= ?NewSal" +
                 " WHERE employee_id= ?EmpID";
```

Example 17-8. Using parameters in C# (continued)

```
MySqlCommand ParameterSQL = new MySqlCommand(SQLText,myConnection);

MySqlParameter EmpSal  = ParameterSQL.Parameters.Add(
                              "?NewSal", MySqlDbType.Float);
MySqlParameter EmpId = ParameterSQL.Parameters.Add(
                              "?EmpID", MySqlDbType.Int16);

for(i=1;i<=N;i++)
   {
       EmpSal.Value = EmployeeSal[i];
       EmpId.Value = EmployeeID[i];
       RowCount = ParameterSQL.ExecuteNonQuery();
   }
```

Issuing a SELECT and Using a DataReader

MySQL supports a wide variety of methods of dealing with the output from a query. In this section, we will first review what is arguably the most straightforward of these methods: the DataReader.

A DataReader allows us to fetch rows from a result set in a manner similar to the fetching of rows from a stored program cursor. To create a MySqlDataReader object, we use the ExecuteReader( ) method of the MySqlCommand object. We iterate through the MySqlDataReader using the Read( ) method, and retrieve data values using GetInt32( ), GetString( ), and other data type–specific Get methods.

Example 17-9 is an example of using a MySqlDataReader in C#.

Example 17-9. Using a MySqlDataReader in C#

```
1   String SelectText = "SELECT department_id, department_name FROM departments";
2   MySqlCommand SelectStatement = new MySqlCommand(SelectText, myConnection);
3   MySqlDataReader SelectReader = SelectStatement.ExecuteReader();
4   while (SelectReader.Read())
5     {
6         Console.WriteLine(SelectReader.GetInt32(0) + "\t" +
7                           SelectReader.GetString(1));
8     }
9   SelectReader.Close();
```

Let us step through this example:

Line(s)	Explanation
2	Create a MySqlCommand object for a SELECT statement.
3	Use the ExecuteReader( ) method to create a MySqlDataReader object.
4-8	Loop through the rows returned by the SELECT statement using the Read( ) method of the MySqlDataReader.

Line(s)	Explanation
6	Use the GetInt32() and GetString() methods to retrieve the current values for the department_id and department_name columns. The argument for these methods is the numeric position of the column in the result set—starting with "0" as the first column.
9	Close the Reader. We should always do this since it releases database resources and is also a prerequisite for retrieving OUT parameters from stored procedures.

Example 17-10 shows the logic in Example 17-9 implemented in VB.NET.

Example 17-10. Using a MySqlDataReader in VB.NET

```
Dim SelectText As String
Dim SelectStatement As MySqlCommand
Dim SelectReader As MySqlDataReader
SelectText = "SELECT department_id, department_name FROM departments"
SelectStatement = New MySqlCommand(SelectText, myConnection)
SelectReader = SelectStatement.ExecuteReader()
While (SelectReader.Read())
    Console.WriteLine(SelectReader.GetInt32(0).ToString + _
            " " + SelectReader.GetString(1))
End While
SelectReader.Close()
```

Getting DataReader Metadata

The DataReader provides methods for retrieving information about the columns that will be returned in the Reader. This information is essential if we are going to process dynamic SQL—for instance, SQL that is entered at a terminal by an end user or generated on-the-fly by some other module in our program.

The FieldCount() method returns the number of columns in the DataReader's result set. GetFieldType() and GetName() return the name and data type of a column within the result set, where GetName(0) would return the name of the first column. Example 17-11 uses these methods to retrieve the names and data types of a query from within VB.NET and displays those to the console.

Example 17-11. Accessing DataReader metadata

```
SelectText = "SELECT * FROM departments"
SelectStatement = New MySqlCommand(SelectText, myConnection)
SelectReader = SelectStatement.ExecuteReader()
For i = 0 To SelectReader.FieldCount() - 1
    Console.WriteLine(SelectReader.GetName(i) + " " + _
                SelectReader.GetFieldType(i).ToString)
Next
```

DataSets

While DataReaders offer a convenient way to access query result sets, the ADO.NET DataSet class provides an alternative that is a little more complex, but that offers increased flexibility and functionality. In particular, because we can only ever have a single DataReader open simultaneously for a given connection, we are likely to use DataSets in most complex applications.

DataSets provide an in-memory, datasource-independent representation of data that can persist even when a connection is closed. DataSets offer a number of methods for handling data modification, including a mechanism for resynchronizing data when a closed connection is reopened.

In this section we will provide a simple example of using a DataSet to retrieve the outputs only from a simple SQL query.

A DataSet object contains a collection of tables, each of which includes a collection of columns and rows. We can access and manipulate the tables, columns, and rows in the DataSet using the DataTable, DataColumn, and DataRow objects.

A DataSet is associated with its data source through a DataAdapter object. In our case, we have to create a MySqlDataAdapator object to associate a DataSet with a MySqlCommand.

The general steps for processing a SQL query through a DataSet are as follows:

1. Create the MySqlCommand object.
2. Create a MySqlDataAdpator object and associate it with the MySQLCommand.
3. Create a DataSet object.
4. Use the MySqlDataAdapter object to populate the DataSet.
5. Use the DataTable, DataColumn, and DataRow objects to retrieve the contents of the DataSet.

Example 17-12 shows an example of populating and examining a DataSet object in C#.

Example 17-12. Populating a DataSet from a simple SQL statement in C#

```
1          String SqlText = "SELECT * FROM departments";
2          MySqlCommand SqlCmd = new MySqlCommand(SqlText, myConnection);
3
4          MySqlDataAdapter MyAdapter=new MySqlDataAdapter(SqlCmd);
5          DataSet MyDataSet=new DataSet();
6          int rows = MyAdapter.Fill(MyDataSet);
7
8          DataTable MyTable=MyDataSet.Tables[0];
9
10         //Write column headings
11         foreach(DataColumn MyColumn in MyTable.Columns)
12         {
13             Console.Write(MyColumn.Caption+"\t");
```

```
14              }
15              Console.WriteLine( );
16
17              //Write Column Rows
18              foreach(DataRow MyRow in MyTable.Rows)
19              {
20                  foreach(DataColumn MyColumn in MyTable.Columns)
21                  {
22                      Console.Write(MyRow[MyColumn]+"\t");
23                  }
24                  Console.WriteLine( );
25              }
```

Let's step through this example:

Line(s)	Explanation
1-2	Define a MySqlCommand object (SqlCmd) that will issue our query.
4	Create a new MySQLDataAdapator object and associate it with SqlCmd (our MySqlCommand object).
5	Create a new DataSet and, in line 6, we populate this data set with the output of the SELECT statement (via the MySqlDataAdapter).
8	Declare a DataTable (MyTable) that references the first table (index "0") in the DataSet MyDataSet. Remember that a DataSet can contain multiple tables, but in this case we know that we need only concern ourselves with the first and only DataTable in the DataSet.
11-15	Print the names of the columns in the DataTable. We do this by iterating through the Columns collection in the DataTable and printing the Caption property for each column.
18-25	Print out the data rows. We do this by iterating through the Rows collection in the DataTable. For each Row, we iterate through the Columns collection to print an individual column value. MyRow[MyColumn] represents the value of a specific column within a specific row.

Example 17-13 shows this logic in VB.NET.

Example 17-13. Populating a DataSet from a SELECT statement in VB.NET

```
Dim TabChr As Char = Microsoft.VisualBasic.Chr(9)
Dim SqlText As String = "SELECT * FROM departments"
Dim SqlCmd As MySqlCommand = New MySqlCommand(SqlText, myConnection)


Dim MyAdapter As MySqlDataAdapter = New MySqlDataAdapter(SqlCmd)

Dim MyDataSet As DataSet = New DataSet
Dim rows As Integer = MyAdapter.Fill(MyDataSet)

Dim MyTable As DataTable = MyDataSet.Tables(0)

For Each MyColumn As DataColumn In MyTable.Columns
    Console.Write(MyColumn.Caption + "" & TabChr & "")
Next
Console.WriteLine( )
For Each MyRow As DataRow In MyTable.Rows
```

```
        For Each MyColumn As DataColumn In MyTable.Columns
            Console.Write(MyRow(MyColumn).ToString + "" & TabChr & "")
        Next
        Console.WriteLine()
    Next
End Sub
```

As we will see later, using a DataSet is a good technique for stored procedures, which might return multiple result sets. However, for a single result set, we can populate the DataTable directly from the MySqlDataAdaptor() method, as shown in Example 17-14.

Example 17-14. Populating a DataTable directly from a MySqlDataAdapter( ) method

```
String SqlText = "SELECT * FROM departments";
MySqlCommand SqlCmd = new MySqlCommand(SqlText, myConnection);

MySqlDataAdapter MyAdapter = new MySqlDataAdapter(SqlCmd);
DataTable MyTable = new DataTable();

MyAdapter.Fill(MyTable);
```

Handling Errors

The Connector/Net methods will throw a MySqlException exception if the database returns an error with respect to any of our ADO.NET calls. Therefore, we will usually want to enclose our ADO.NET sections in a try/catch block to ensure that we do not generate an unhandled exception condition at runtime. Example 17-15 shows a simple example of using an exception handler in VB.NET.

Example 17-15. Error handling in VB.NET

```
Sub CreateDemoTables()
    Dim MySqlText As String
    MySqlText = "CREATE TABLE DEMO" & _
                " (MyInt INT," & _
                "    MyString VARCHAR(30)) "

    Dim CrDemoSQL As MySqlCommand

    Try
        CrDemoSQL = New MySqlCommand(MySqlText, myConnection)
        CrDemoSQL.ExecuteNonQuery()
    Catch MyException As MySqlException
        Console.WriteLine("Error creating demo tables:")
        Console.WriteLine(MyException.Number.ToString & ": " & _
                        MyException.Message)
        Console.WriteLine(MyException.StackTrace)
    End Try

End Sub
```

In this example, the SQL statement is executed within a Try block. If an error occurs, control is passed to the Catch block that creates a MySqlException object call "MyException". The Number property returns the MySQL error code; the Message property contains the MySQL error message. StackTrace generates a familiar .NET stack trace that can be useful during debugging (though not so useful for Auntie Edna or other end users).

Example 17-16 demonstrates the same exception handling in C#.

Example 17-16. Exception handling in C#

```
static void CreateDemoTables( )
{
    String MySqlText= "CREATE TABLE DEMO" +
                    "  (MyInt INT," +
                    "   MyString VARCHAR(30)) ";

    try
    {
        MySqlCommand CrDemoSQL=new MySqlCommand(MySqlText,myConnection);
        CrDemoSQL.ExecuteNonQuery( );
    }
    catch(MySqlException MyException)
    {
        Console.WriteLine("Error creating demo tables:");
        Console.WriteLine(MyException.Number +
                        ": " + MyException.Message);
        Console.WriteLine(MyException.StackTrace);
    }
}
```

Managing Transactions

You can execute the usual MySQL statements to manage your transactions in .NET programs, such as BEGIN TRANSACTION, COMMIT, and ROLLBACK. However, instead of using these statements, you may want to take advantage of the built-in transaction object to manage your transactions. Doing so may help make your code more readable and maintainable.

Connector/Net allows us to create a MySqlTransaction object that represents a transaction. Methods to the MySqlTransaction object allow us to commit and roll back our transaction, or to set the transaction isolation levels.

Example 17-17 shows an example of using these facilities in C#.

Example 17-17. Transaction management in C#

```
1  static void TferFunds(int FromAccount, int ToAccount, float TferAmount)
2  {
3      String TransSQL = "UPDATE account_balance " +
4                      "  SET balance=balance+?tfer_amount " +
5                      "WHERE account_id=?account_id";
```

Example 17-17. Transaction management in C# (continued)

```csharp
6      MySqlCommand TransCmd = new MySqlCommand(TransSQL, myConnection);
7      MySqlParameter P_tfer_amount = TransCmd.Parameters.Add("?tfer_amount",
8                                                     MySqlDbType.Float);
9      MySqlParameter P_account_id = TransCmd.Parameters.Add("?account_id",
10                                                    MySqlDbType.Int32);
11
12     MySqlTransaction myTransaction = myConnection.BeginTransaction( );
13     try
14       {
15         //Remove amount from from_account
16         P_tfer_amount.Value = TferAmount * -1;
17         P_account_id.Value = FromAccount;
18         TransCmd.ExecuteNonQuery( );
19         //Add amount to to_account;
20         P_tfer_amount.Value = TferAmount;
21         P_account_id.Value = ToAccount;
22         TransCmd.ExecuteNonQuery( );
23
24         myTransaction.Commit( );
25         Console.WriteLine("Transaction Succeeded");
26       }
27     catch (MySqlException TransException)
28       {
29         Console.WriteLine("Error in transaction: ");
30         Console.WriteLine(TransException.Message);
31         try
32           {
33               myTransaction.Rollback( );
34               Console.WriteLine("Transaction rollback");
35           }
36         catch (MySqlException RollbackException)
37           {
38               Console.WriteLine("Failed to rollback transaction:");
39               Console.WriteLine(RollbackException.Message);
40           }
41       }
42     }
```

The function is designed to transfer some money from one account to another. It is absolutely essential that both operations succeed or fail as a unit, and therefore they are enclosed within a transaction.

This is a relatively long example and ties in the use of parameters and exception handlers, so let us step through it line by line:

Line(s)	Explanation
3-9	Create a SQL UPDATE statement to adjust the account balance for a specific account. The statement includes parameters for the account ids and amounts, so we can reuse the statement to do both parts of the transfer and could also reuse it for subsequent transactions.
12	The BeginTransaction( ) method of the connection indicates the commencement of the transaction.

Line(s)	Explanation
13	Declare a `try`/`catch` block that will handle any errors that occur within our transaction.
15-22	Execute the transfer by placing the appropriate values into the account and amount parameters, and then executing the UPDATE statement twice— once to reduce the balance in the "from" account and once to increase the balance in the "to" account.
24	Commit the transaction. Note that this statement would be reached only if all of the previous statements succeed. If any of the previous ADO.NET statements raised an exception, control would be assumed by the code in the `catch` block.
27-41	This is the `catch` block that will be invoked if a SQL error occurs. It executes a ROLLBACK statement (line 33) to undo any parts of the transaction that may have successfully executed.
31-41	We've nested another `catch` block without the main error handler to catch any problems that occur when we execute the rollback. This might seem a bit paranoid, but it is possible that the errors that caused the statements to fail will also cause us to fail to execute a rollback (the server may have crashed, for instance).

Example 17-18 implements the same transaction logic in VB.NET.

Example 17-18. Transaction handling in VB.NET

```
Sub TferFunds(ByVal FromAccount As Integer, _
              ByVal ToAccount As Integer, _
              ByVal TferAmount As Single)

    Dim TransSQL As String = "UPDATE account_balance " + _
                        " SET balance=balance+?tfer_amount " + _
                        "WHERE account_id=?account_id"
    Dim TransCmd As MySqlCommand = New MySqlCommand(TransSQL, myConnection)
    Dim P_tfer_amount As MySqlParameter = _
        TransCmd.Parameters.Add("?tfer_amount", MySqlDbType.Float)
    Dim P_account_id As MySqlParameter = _
        TransCmd.Parameters.Add("?account_id", MySqlDbType.Int32)
    Dim myTransaction As MySqlTransaction = myConnection.BeginTransaction
    Try
        'Remove amount from FromAccount
        P_tfer_amount.Value = TferAmount * -1
        P_account_id.Value = FromAccount
        TransCmd.ExecuteNonQuery()
        'Add amount to ToAccount
        P_tfer_amount.Value = TferAmount
        P_account_id.Value = ToAccount
        TransCmd.ExecuteNonQuery()

        myTransaction.Commit()
        Console.WriteLine("Transaction Succeded")

    Catch TransException As MySqlException
        Console.WriteLine("Error in transaction: ")
        Console.WriteLine(TransException.Message)
        Try
            myTransaction.Rollback()
            Console.WriteLine("Transaction rollback")
```

Example 17-18. Transaction handling in VB.NET (continued)

```
        Catch RollbackException As MySqlException
            Console.WriteLine("Failed to rollback transaction:")
            Console.WriteLine(RollbackException.Message)
        End Try
    End Try
End Sub
```

Using Stored Programs in ADO.NET

Stored programs have always been an integral and important part of application development within SQL Server, and SQL Server support is a primary focus of the ADO.NET interfaces. Unlike some implementations of stored programs (Oracle's for instance), SQL Server's stored programs can directly return multiple result sets, which results in the ADO.NET interfaces providing very natural support for the MySQL implementation.

Calling a Simple Stored Procedure

Let's start with a very simple stored procedure. Example 17-19 shows a simple stored procedure that takes no parameters and returns no result sets.

Example 17-19. A simple stored procedure

```
CREATE PROCEDURE sp_simple()
BEGIN
 SET autocommit=0;
END;
```

Calling this stored procedure is only slightly more complex than calling a non-SELECT statement, as described in "Issuing a Non-SELECT Statement" earlier in this chapter. The procedure for calling this stored procedure differs in two small ways:

- The text for the SQL call contains only the stored procedure—the CALL statement is unnecessary, as are parentheses to represent the parameter list.
- The CommandType property of the MySqlCommand object should be set to CommandType.StoredProcedure.

Example 17-20 illustrates the process of calling the simple stored procedure from Example 17-19 in VB.NET. The name of the stored procedure is used to initialize the MySqlCommand object, and the CommandType for that object is set to CommandType. StoredProcedure. The stored procedure is then executed using the ExecuteNonQuery() method of the MySqlCommand object.

Example 17-20. Calling a simple stored procedure in VB.NET

```
        Dim SpSimple As MySqlCommand
        SpSimple = New MySqlCommand("sp_simple", myConnection)
```

Example 17-20. Calling a simple stored procedure in VB.NET (continued)

```
        SpSimple.CommandType = CommandType.StoredProcedure
        SpSimple.ExecuteNonQuery( )
```

Example 17-21 shows the same logic implemented in C#.

Example 17-21. Calling a simple stored procedure in C#

```
        MySqlCommand SpSimple;
        SpSimple = new MySqlCommand("sp_simple", myConnection);
        SpSimple.CommandType = CommandType.StoredProcedure;
        SpSimple.ExecuteNonQuery( );
```

Supplying Input Parameters

Earlier in this chapter we saw how to use the `Parameters` collection of the `MySqlCommand` class to specify parameters to simple SQL statements. The `Parameters` collection can be used to manipulate stored procedure parameters as well. In this section we'll look at specifying input parameters. Example 17-22 shows a simple stored procedure that takes a single input parameter.

Example 17-22. Stored procedure with an input parameter

```
CREATE PROCEDURE sp_simple_parameter(in_autocommit INT)
BEGIN
 SET autocommit=in_autocommit;
END;
```

To specify a value for this parameter, we can create a parameter object using the `Parameters.Add()` method of the `MySqlCommand` object. We can then use the `Values` property of the resulting object to set a value for the parameter prior to executing the procedure. Example 17-23 shows us doing just that in C#.

Example 17-23. Calling a stored procedure with an input parameter in C#

```
1   MySqlCommand SpCmd;
2   SpCmd = new MySqlCommand("sp_Simple_Parameter", myConnection);
3   SpCmd.CommandType = CommandType.StoredProcedure;
4   MySqlParameter Parm1 = SpCmd.Parameters.Add(
5                         "in_autocommit",MySqlDbType.Int32);
6
7   Parm1.Value = 0;
8
9   SpCmd.ExecuteNonQuery( );
```

In lines 1-3 we create the stored procedure definition. On line 4 we create a parameter object representing the first (and only) parameter to the stored procedure. On line 7 we assign a value to this parameter, and finally—on line 9—we execute the stored procedure.

Note that once the stored procedure (including its parameters) is defined, we can change the parameter value and re-execute the procedure as many times as we like. We'll see an example of this technique at the end of this chapter.

Example 17-24 shows how we can set the stored procedure parameter and execute the stored procedure in VB.NET.

Example 17-24. Calling a stored procedure with an input parameter in VB.NET

```
Dim SpCmd As MySqlCommand
SpCmd = New MySqlCommand("sp_Simple_Parameter", myConnection)
SpCmd.CommandType = CommandType.StoredProcedure
Dim Parm1 As MySqlParameter
Parm1 = SpCmd.Parameters.Add("in_autocommit", MySqlDbType.Int32)
Parm1.Value = 0
SpCmd.ExecuteNonQuery()
```

Using a DataReader with a Stored Program

Retrieving a single result set from a stored procedure can be achieved by using pretty much the same coding as we would use to obtain the results of a SELECT statement. Consider a stored procedure that returns only a single result set, as shown in Example 17-25.

Example 17-25. Stored procedure with a single result set

```
CREATE PROCEDURE Sp_one_result_set()
 SELECT department_id,department_name
   FROM departments;
```

To retrieve a result set from this stored procedure, we can use the ExecuteReader() method to return a DataReader object and then loop through the DataReader in the usual way. Example 17-26 shows how to do this in C#.

Example 17-26. Creating a DataReader from a stored procedure in C#

```
MySqlCommand SpCmd;
SpCmd = new MySqlCommand("sp_one_result_set", myConnection);
SpCmd.CommandType = CommandType.StoredProcedure;
MySqlDataReader MyReader=SpCmd.ExecuteReader();
while (MyReader.Read())
{
    Console.Write(MyReader.GetInt32(0)+"\t");
    Console.WriteLine(MyReader.GetString(1));
}
```

Example 17-27 shows how to create a DataReader from a stored procedure execution in VB.NET.

Example 17-27. Creating a DataReader from a stored procedure in VB.NET

```
Dim SpCmd As MySqlCommand
SpCmd = New MySqlCommand("sp_one_result_set", myConnection)
SpCmd.CommandType = CommandType.StoredProcedure
Dim MyReader As MySqlDataReader = SpCmd.ExecuteReader
While MyReader.Read
    Console.Write(MyReader.GetInt32(0).ToString + _
                    "" & Microsoft.VisualBasic.Chr(9) & "")
    Console.WriteLine(MyReader.GetString(1))
End While
MyReader.Close( )
```

Processing Multiple Result Sets in a DataReader

The DataReader class provides a method for processing multiple result sets: the DataReader method NextResult( ) will return true if there is an additional result set available from the SqlCommand and will move the DataReader to that result set.

To illustrate, let's retrieve the two result sets returned from the stored procedure in Example 17-28.

Example 17-28. Stored procedure returning two result sets

```
CREATE PROCEDURE sp_two_results( )
BEGIN
    SELECT location,address1,address2
      FROM locations;
    SELECT department_id,department_name
      FROM departments;
END;
```

We can process the second result set by calling the NextResult( ) method after finishing with the first result set, then reading the rows from the second result set. Example 17-29 illustrates this technique in VB.NET.

Example 17-29. Processing two result sets using a DataReader in VB.NET

```
Dim TabChr As Char = Microsoft.VisualBasic.Chr(9)
Dim SpCmd As MySqlCommand
SpCmd = New MySqlCommand("sp_two_results", myConnection)
SpCmd.CommandType = CommandType.StoredProcedure
Dim MyReader As MySqlDataReader = SpCmd.ExecuteReader
While MyReader.Read
    Console.Write(MyReader.GetString(0) + TabChr)
    Console.Write(MyReader.GetString(1))
    Console.WriteLine(MyReader.GetString(2))
End While
MyReader.NextResult( )
While MyReader.Read
    Console.Write(MyReader.GetInt32(0).ToString +TabChr)
    Console.WriteLine(MyReader.GetString(1))
End While
MyReader.Close( )
```

Using this technique is a bit cumbersome, especially if there is a large number of result sets. As we will see later on, writing code to dynamically process multiple result sets from a DataReader, or processing multiple result sets using the DataSet class, can often result in simpler and more robust code.

Dynamically Processing Result Sets

In the previous example, we knew exactly how many result sets to expect from the stored procedure and we knew in advance the number and types of columns to be returned from each. While this is a realistic scenario, we may often need to process a stored procedure where the number and types of result sets might change depending on the input parameters.

For instance, the stored procedure in Example 17-30 returns a different set of result sets depending on the characteristics of the employee whose identity is defined by the input employee_id parameter. If the employee is a sales representative, then three result sets are returned. Otherwise, only two result sets are returned. Furthermore, the structure of the second result set for a sales rep is different from the result set returned by a normal employee.

Example 17-30. Stored procedure that returns an unpredictable number of result sets

```
CREATE PROCEDURE sp_employee_report
    (in_emp_id decimal(8,0),
     OUT out_customer_count INT)
        READS SQL DATA

BEGIN

    SELECT employee_id,surname,firstname,date_of_birth,address1,address2,zipcode
      FROM employees
     WHERE employee_id=in_emp_id;

    SELECT department_id,department_name
      FROM departments
     WHERE department_id=
           (SELECT department_id
              FROM employees
             WHERE employee_id=in_emp_id);

    SELECT count(*)
      INTO out_customer_count
      FROM customers
     WHERE sales_rep_id=in_emp_id;

    IF out_customer_count=0 THEN
         SELECT 'Employee is not a current sales rep';
    ELSE
        SELECT customer_name,customer_status,contact_surname,contact_firstname
          FROM customers
```

```
              WHERE sales_rep_id=in_emp_id;

          SELECT customer_name,sum(sale_value) as "TOTAL SALES",
                 max(sale_value) as "MAX SALE"
            FROM sales JOIN customers USING (customer_id)
           WHERE customers.sales_rep_id=in_emp_id
           GROUP BY customer_name;
      END IF;

END$$;
```

To process this stored procedure, our code needs to:

- Loop through all of the result sets with no assumption as to how many there may be.
- Loop through the columns in each result set without knowing at compile time how many columns exist in each result set.

We can easily achieve the first objective simply by iterating through the result sets of a DataReader as long as the NextResult( ) call returns true.

We achieve the second objective by using the FieldCount property of the Reader and the GetName( ) and GetString( ) methods, which allow us to retrieve the name and value for each column, as shown in Example 17-31.

Example 17-31. Processing result sets dynamically with a DataReader

```
1   static void EmployeeReport(int EmployeeId)
2   {
3         MySqlCommand SpCmd = new MySqlCommand("sp_employee_report", myConnection);
4         SpCmd.CommandType = CommandType.StoredProcedure;
5         MySqlParameter Param_empid = SpCmd.Parameters.Add(
6                                     "in_emp_id", MySqlDbType.Int32);
7
8         Param_empid.Value = EmployeeId;
9         MySqlDataReader EmpReader=SpCmd.ExecuteReader( );
10
11        do
12        {
13            //Print Column Names
14            Console.WriteLine("-------------------------------------");
15            for (int i = 0; i < EmpReader.FieldCount; i++)
16            {
17                Console.Write(EmpReader.GetName(i)+"\t");
18            }
19            Console.WriteLine("\n-------------------------------------");
20            //Print out the row values
21            while (EmpReader.Read( ))
22            {
23                for (int i = 0; i < EmpReader.FieldCount; i++)
24                {
```

```
25                     Console.Write(EmpReader.GetString(i)+"\t");
26                 }
27                 Console.WriteLine( );
28             }
29         } while (EmpReader.NextResult( ));
30         EmpReader.Close( );
31     }
```

Let's step through this example:

Line(s)	Explanation
3-5	Define a MySqlCommand object to call the stored procedure. The object has a single parameter that corresponds to the EmployeeId argument passed to our routine on line 1.
8-9	Assign the value of the stored procedure parameter to the value of the input parameter and create a MySqlDataReader to process the result sets.
11-29	This loop will continue until a call to NextResult( ) returns false. In other words, it will continue until all of the result sets have been retrieved from the stored procedure.
15-18	Print out the names of the columns of the result set. FieldCount returns the number of columns; GetName(i) returns the name of a particular column.
21-28	Loop through each row in the result set.
23-26	Loop through each column in the current row. We use GetString(i) to retrieve the value of the current column. GetString will successfully retrieve values for most MySQL data types (numbers, dates, etc.), but if we need to retrieve the values into a more appropriate variable (perhaps we want to perform some calculations on a float, for instance), then we can use Get*Type*(i) to determine the appropriate method (GetFloat(i) for instance).
30	Close the DataReader having processed all of the rows in all of the result sets.

Example 17-32 shows Example 17-31 writen in VB.NET.

Example 17-32. Processing dynamic result sets using a DataReader in VB.NET

```
Sub EmployeeReport(ByVal EmployeeId As Integer)

        Dim i As Integer = 0
        Dim TabChr As Char = Microsoft.VisualBasic.Chr(9)
        Dim RetChr As Char = Microsoft.VisualBasic.Chr(10)
        Dim SpCmd As MySqlCommand
        SpCmd = New MySqlCommand("sp_employee_report", myConnection)
        SpCmd.CommandType = CommandType.StoredProcedure
        Dim Param_empid As MySqlParameter
        Param_empid = SpCmd.Parameters.Add("in_emp_id", MySqlDbType.Int32)
        Param_empid.Value = EmployeeId
        Dim EmpReader As MySqlDataReader = SpCmd.ExecuteReader
        Do
            Console.WriteLine("-------------------------------------")

            For i = 0 To EmpReader.FieldCount - 1
                Console.Write(EmpReader.GetName(i) + TabChr)
            Next
```

```
                Console.WriteLine(RetChr+ "---------------------------------")
                While EmpReader.Read( )

                    For i = 0 To EmpReader.FieldCount - 1
                        Console.Write(EmpReader.GetString(i) + TabChr)
                    Next
                    Console.WriteLine( )
                End While
            Loop While EmpReader.NextResult( )
            EmpReader.Close( )
        End Sub
```

Using DataSets with Stored Programs

DataSets offer an alternative to the DataReader class for retrieving result sets from stored procedures. We can store more than one result set into a single DataSet object, which allows us to easily process the multiple result sets that might be returned by a stored procedure.

A DataReader may be more convenient than a DataSet for processing a single result set where we know the column names and types in advance. However, when we are processing more than one result set, or when we don't know the structure of the result sets in advance, we find the DataSet more convenient.

Example 17-33 shows us dynamically processing multiple result sets from a stored procedure using a DataSet. We've used this stored procedure before: see Example 17-28.

Example 17-33. Dynamically processing multiple result sets using a DataSet in VB.NET

```
1       Dim TabChr As Char = Microsoft.VisualBasic.Chr(9)
2       Dim SpCmd As MySqlCommand
3       SpCmd = New MySqlCommand("sp_two_results", myConnection)
4       SpCmd.CommandType = CommandType.StoredProcedure
5
6       Dim MyAdapter As MySqlDataAdapter = New MySqlDataAdapter(SpCmd)
7       Dim SpDataSet As DataSet = New DataSet
8       MyAdapter.Fill(SpDataSet)
9
10      For Each SpTable As DataTable In SpDataSet.Tables
11          For Each SpCol As DataColumn In SpTable.Columns
12              Console.Write(SpCol.ToString( ) + TabChr)
13          Next
14          Console.WriteLine( )
15
16          For Each SpRow As DataRow In SpTable.Rows
17              For Each SpCol As DataColumn In SpTable.Columns
18                  Console.Write(SpRow(SpCol).ToString + TabChr)
```

```
19                Next
20                Console.WriteLine( )
21           Next
22      Next
```

You may want to review the section "DataSets" earlier in this chapter if you're not sure of the relationship between MySqlCommands, MySqlDataAdapters, and DataSets.

Let's look at how Example 17-33 works, line by line:

Line(s)	Explanation
2-4	Create a MySqlCommand object to represent our stored procedure call in the usual way.
6	Create a MySqlDataAdapter object and associate it with the MySqlCommand object.
7	Create a new DataSet object.
8	Populate the DataSet from our MySqlDataAdapter. Since MySqlDataApadapter is associated with the MySqlCommand for our stored procedure, this results in all of the results sets from the stored procedure being stored into the DataSet.
10	The DataSet will now contain one DataTable for each result set returned by the stored procedure. Here we iterate through these tables using the Tables collection of the DataSet object.
11-13	Iterate through the columns in the current DataTable using the Columns collection and print the column name.
16-21	Iterate through the DataRows in the current DataTable using the Rows collection of the DataTable object.
17-19	Iterate through the columns in the current DataRow and print the appropriate column value. SpRow(SpCol) represents a specific column value for a specific row.

Example 17-34 shows this logic implemented in C#.

Example 17-34. Dynamically processing result sets using a DataSet in C#

```
MySqlCommand SpCmd;
SpCmd = new MySqlCommand("sp_two_results", myConnection);
SpCmd.CommandType = CommandType.StoredProcedure;

MySqlDataAdapter MyAdapter = new MySqlDataAdapter(SpCmd);
MyAdapter.SelectCommand = SpCmd;
DataSet SpDataSet = new DataSet( );
MyAdapter.Fill(SpDataSet);

foreach (DataTable SpTable in SpDataSet.Tables)
{
    foreach (DataColumn SpCol in SpTable.Columns)
    {
        Console.Write(SpCol.ToString( ) + "\t");
    }
    Console.WriteLine( );

    foreach (DataRow SpRow in SpTable.Rows)
```

```
    {
        foreach (DataColumn SpCol in SpTable.Columns)
        {
            Console.Write(SpRow[SpCol] + "\t");
        }
        Console.WriteLine( );
    }
}
```

Retrieving Output Parameters

We've left the processing of output parameters until almost the end of this chapter, because obtaining the value of an output parameter (OUT or INOUT) is the *last* thing we should do when processing a stored program. In particular, we should make sure that we have retrieved *all* result sets from the stored procedure before trying to access the value of the output parameter. Before all the result sets are processed, the value of the parameter will be NULL, which could lead to subtle bugs—especially if there is a variable number of output parameters.

To use an output parameter in Connector/Net, we define the parameter as we would for an input parameter, but set the ParameterDirection property of the parameter to either Output or InputOutput.

Example 17-35 is an example of a stored procedure that contains an OUT parameter.

Example 17-35. Stored procedure with an OUT parameter

```
CREATE PROCEDURE sp_custsales
  (in_customer_id INT,
   OUT out_sales_total FLOAT)
BEGIN
    SELECT customer_name
      FROM customers
     WHERE customer_id=in_customer_id;

    SELECT sum(sale_value)
      INTO out_sales_total
      FROM sales
     WHERE customer_id=in_customer_id;

END;
```

In Example 17-36 we execute this stored procedure and retrieve the value of the output parameter. Prior to executing the stored procedure, we set the value of the Parameter.Direction property to ParameterDirection.Output. After we have processed all of the rows from the result set returned by the stored procedure, we can examine the parameter's Value property to see the value placed by the stored procedure into the OUT parameter.

Example 17-36. Processing a stored procedure with an OUT parameter in C#

```csharp
static void CustomerSales(int CustomerId)
{
    MySqlCommand SpCustSales;
    MySqlParameter PCustId,PSalesTotal;
    MySqlDataReader CustReader;

    SpCustSales = new MySqlCommand("sp_custsales", myConnection);
    SpCustSales.CommandType = CommandType.StoredProcedure;
    PCustId = SpCustSales.Parameters.Add(
                        "in_customer_id", MySqlDbType.Int32);
    PSalesTotal = SpCustSales.Parameters.Add(
                        "out_sales_total", MySqlDbType.Float);
    PSalesTotal.Direction = ParameterDirection.Output;

    PCustId.Value = CustomerId;
    CustReader=SpCustSales.ExecuteReader();
    while (CustReader.Read())
    {
        Console.WriteLine(CustReader.GetString(0));
    }
    CustReader.Close();
    Console.WriteLine(PSalesTotal.Value);

    Console.WriteLine("====");

}
```

Example 17-37 shows this logic coded in VB.NET.

Example 17-37. Processing an output parameter in VB.NET

```vbnet
Sub CustomerSales(ByVal CustomerId As Integer)

    Dim SpCustSales As MySqlCommand
    Dim PCustId As MySqlParameter
    Dim PSalesTotal As MySqlParameter
    Dim CustReader As MySqlDataReader

    SpCustSales = New MySqlCommand("sp_custsales", myConnection)
    SpCustSales.CommandType = CommandType.StoredProcedure
    PCustId = SpCustSales.Parameters.Add("in_customer_id", MySqlDbType.Int32)
    PSalesTotal = SpCustSales.Parameters.Add("out_sales_total", MySqlDbType.Float)
    PSalesTotal.Direction = ParameterDirection.Output

    PCustId.Value = CustomerId
    CustReader = SpCustSales.ExecuteReader()
    While CustReader.Read()
        Console.WriteLine(CustReader.GetString(0))
    End While
    CustReader.Close()
    Console.WriteLine(PSalesTotal.Value)

End Sub
```

Make sure you have processed all of the result sets returned from a stored procedure before attempting to access any output parameters.

Calling Stored Functions

In languages such as Perl or PHP, if we want to get the results of a stored function call, we simply embed it into a SELECT statement and retrieve the result of the function call as a single-row SELECT.

This technique is available to us in ADO.NET, but we also have the option of retrieving the result of a function call in a more direct fashion. We can call a function as we would a stored procedure that has no result sets, and we can retrieve the results of the function execution by associating a parameter with ParameterDirection set to ReturnValue.

For instance, consider the very simple stored function in Example 17-38, which returns a date formatted just the way we like it.

Example 17-38. Simple MySQL stored function

```
CREATE FUNCTION my_date( )
 RETURNS VARCHAR(50)
BEGIN
  RETURN(DATE_FORMAT(NOW( ),'%W, %D of %M, %Y'));
END$$
```

To call this directly in ADO.NET, we call the function as we would a stored procedure, but we create a special parameter to retrieve the function return value with the Direction property set to ReturnValue. Example 17-39 shows us processing our simple date function in C#.

Example 17-39. Processing a stored function in C#

```
MySqlCommand FCmd = new MySqlCommand("my_date", myConnection);
FCmd.CommandType = CommandType.StoredProcedure;
MySqlParameter rv = FCmd.Parameters.Add("rv", MySqlDbType.String);
rv.Direction = ParameterDirection.ReturnValue;
FCmd.ExecuteNonQuery( );
Console.WriteLine("return value=" + rv.Value);
```

Example 17-40 shows the same logic in VB.NET.

Example 17-40. Processing a stored function in VB.NET

```
Dim FCmd As MySqlCommand = New MySqlCommand("my_date", myConnection)
FCmd.CommandType = CommandType.StoredProcedure
Dim rv As MySqlParameter = FCmd.Parameters.Add("rv", MySqlDbType.String)
rv.Direction = ParameterDirection.ReturnValue
FCmd.ExecuteNonQuery( )
Console.WriteLine("return value=" + rv.Value)
```

Using Stored Programs in ASP.NET

In the final section of this chapter, let's put our newly acquired Connector/Net and stored program skills to work to create a simple ASP.NET application.

The stored procedure we will use is shown in Example 17-41. It takes as an (optional) argument a database name, and it reports on the objects within that database, along with a list of users currently connected to the server, server status variables, server configuration variables, and a list of databases contained within the server. It contains one OUT parameter that reports the server version.

Example 17-41. Stored procedure for our ASP.NET example

```
CREATE PROCEDURE sp_mysql_info
    (in_database VARCHAR(60),
     OUT server_version VARCHAR(100))
    READS SQL DATA
BEGIN

  DECLARE db_count INT;

  SELECT @@version
    INTO server_version;

  SELECT 'Current processes active in server' as table_header;
  SHOW full processlist;


  SELECT 'Databases in server' as table_header;

  SHOW databases;

  SELECT 'Configuration variables set in server' as table_header;
  SHOW global variables;
  SELECT 'Status variables in server' as table_header;
  SHOW global status;


  SELECT COUNT(*)
    INTO db_count
    FROM information_schema.schemata s
   WHERE schema_name=in_database;
  IF (db_count=1) THEN
    SELECT CONCAT('Tables in database ',in_database) as table_header;
    SELECT table_name
      FROM information_schema.tables
     WHERE table_schema=in_database;
  END IF;

END$$
```

The number and type of result sets is unpredictable, since a list of database objects is generated only if a database matching the stored procedure's first parameter is found on the server.

Prior to every major result set, the stored procedure generates a one-row "title" as a result set. This "title" result set is identified by the column title `table_header`.

First, we need to create an ASP.NET form to retrieve the information we need to connect to the MySQL server and to obtain the parameters we need to call the stored procedure.

Creating the input form in Visual Studio is fairly straightforward. We create `TextBox` controls to retrieve our input parameters, as shown in Figure 17-3.

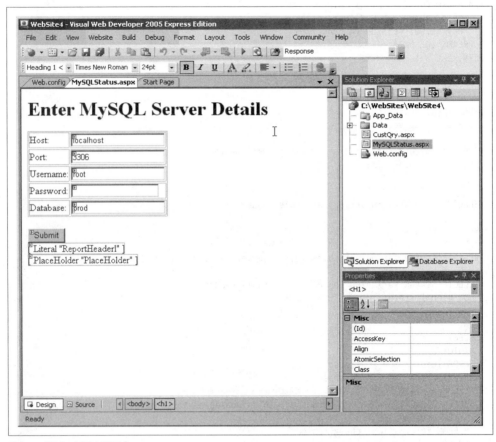

Figure 17-3. ASP.NET form

Notice that in addition to the standard `TextBox` controls, we also added `Literal` and `PlaceHolder` controls. These controls allow us to insert dynamic content when the stored procedure is executed.

Next, we add the code that controls the database interaction. All of our database interaction logic is contained within the method associated with the Submit button. This logic is shown in Example 17-42.

Example 17-42. Database access logic for our ASP.NET page

```
1    void FindButton_Click(object sender, EventArgs e)
2    {
3        //Arrays of grids and literals for our output.
4        System.Web.UI.WebControls.DataGrid[] DataGrids;
5        DataGrids = new System.Web.UI.WebControls.DataGrid[20];
6        System.Web.UI.WebControls.Literal[] Literals;
7        Literals = new System.Web.UI.WebControls.Literal[20];
8
9
10       String myConnectionString = "Database=" + tDatabase.Text +
11           " ;Host=" + tHost.Text +
12           ";UserName=" + tUsername.Text+ ";Password=" + tPassword.Text;
13
14
15       MySqlConnection myConnection = new MySqlConnection( );
16       myConnection.ConnectionString = myConnectionString;
17
18       try
19       {
20           myConnection.Open( );
21           MySqlCommand SpCmd = new MySqlCommand("sp_mysql_info", myConnection);
22           SpCmd.CommandType = CommandType.StoredProcedure;
23           MySqlParameter InDbParm = SpCmd.Parameters.Add(
24                       "in_database",MySqlDbType.String);
25           InDbParm.Value = tDatabase.Text;
26           MySqlParameter OutMyVersion = SpCmd.Parameters.Add(
27                       "server_version", MySqlDbType.String);
28           OutMyVersion.Direction = ParameterDirection.Output;
29
30           MySqlDataAdapter MyAdapter = new MySqlDataAdapter(SpCmd);
31           MyAdapter.SelectCommand = SpCmd;
32           DataSet SpDataSet = new DataSet( );
33           MyAdapter.Fill(SpDataSet);
34
35           ReportHeader1.Text = "<h1>MySQL Server status and statistics</h1>" +
36                   "<b>Host:</b>"+tHost.Text+"<br>"+
37                   " <b>Port:</b> "+tPort.Text+"<br>"+
38                   "<b>Version:</b>"+OutMyVersion.Value+"<br>";
39
40           int grid_no = 0;
41           int heading_no=0;
42           foreach (DataTable SpTable in SpDataSet.Tables) {
43               if (SpTable.Columns[0].ColumnName == "table_header")
44               {
45                   Literals[heading_no]=new Literal( );
46                   Literals[heading_no].Text="<h2>"+ SpTable.Rows[0][0]+"</h2>";
47                   PlaceHolder.Controls.Add(Literals[heading_no]);
```

Example 17-42. Database access logic for our ASP.NET page (continued)

```
48                      heading_no++;
49                  }
50              else
51              {
52                  DataGrids[grid_no] = new DataGrid( );
53                  DataGrids[grid_no].DataSource = SpTable;
54                  DataGrids[grid_no].DataBind( );
55                  DataGrids[grid_no].BorderWidth = 1;
56                  DataGrids[grid_no].HeaderStyle.BackColor =
57                          System.Drawing.Color.Silver;
58                  PlaceHolder.Controls.Add(DataGrids[grid_no]);
59                  grid_no++;
60              }
61          }
62
63
64
65      }
66      catch (MySqlException MyException)
67      {
68          Response.Write("Connection error: MySQL code: " + MyException.Number
69                          + " " + MyException.Message);
70      }
71
72
73  }
```

There is quite a bit of code in this example, but the basic principles are fairly simple:

- We connect to MySQL using the connection information given.

- We call the stored procedure, passing the database name as an input parameter.

- We cycle through the result sets in the stored procedure. If the result set is a one-line, one-column "title" for a subsequent result set, we store an HTML header into a literal control and add this to the Placeholder control we placed on the HTML form earlier.

- If the result set is not a "title" result set, we bind the result set to a DataGrid control and add that to the Placeholder.

- When all of the result sets have been processed, we retrieve the output parameter (MySQL version) and display this and other information in the Literal control we placed on the ASP.NET form earlier.

Let's examine this code in a bit more detail:

Line(s)	Explanation
4-7	Create an array of `DataGrid` and `Literal` controls. `DataGrid`s are data-bound controls similar to HTML tables. `Literal`s are controls in which we can insert regular HTML arguments. Later in the code, we will populate the controls in these arrays with data from the stored procedure output and insert the resulting controls into the `Placeholder` control on the ASPX page.
10-20	Construct a `MySqlConnection` string using the parameters provided in the input form and then establish a connection. The final connection call is embedded within a `try/catch` block so that we will handle any errors that might occur when attempting to connect.
21-28	Set up the stored procedure for execution. Both input and output parameters are defined.
30-31	Create a `MySqlDataAdpator` associated with the stored procedure.
23-33	Create a `DataSet`, and use the `MySqlDataAdapter` to populate the `DataSet`. This effectively executes the stored procedure and populates the `DataSet` with all the result sets from that stored procedure call.
35-38	Now that we have retrieved all of the result sets, we can access the value of the output parameter. Consequently, we can populate the `Literal` control with HTML to generate the first part of our report, which provides identity information for the MySQL server.
42-61	Generate the bulk of the report, which is based on the result sets generated from the stored procedure. This loop iterates through the `DataTables` contained within the `DataSet`.
43-49	If the first column within the table is called `table_header`, then this is a heading row, so we create a `Literal` containing an H2 HTML header containing the text of the row.
50-60	If the result set is not a heading, then we need to create an HTML table to represent the output. We use the ASP.NET `DataGrid` control, which is a data-bound table control. Line 53 attaches the `DataGrid` to the current `DataTable`. Lines 55-57 format the `DataGrid`. Finally on line 58 we add the `DataGrid` to the `PlaceHolder` control on the ASP.NET page.

Figure 17-4 shows some of the output generated by our ASP.NET application. The ASP.NET code can render virtually any output that might be returned by the stored procedure, so if we want to add a new set of output to the procedure, we do not need to modify the ASP.NET code.

Conclusion

In this chapter we looked at calling stored programs from within .NET code written in both C# and VB.NET.

Because of Microsoft's long history of stored procedures with SQL Server, support for stored programs in the ADO.NET interfaces is robust and feels very natural. There is no reason to avoid the use of stored programs in .NET applications, and no reason to avoid calling stored programs directly from .NET code.

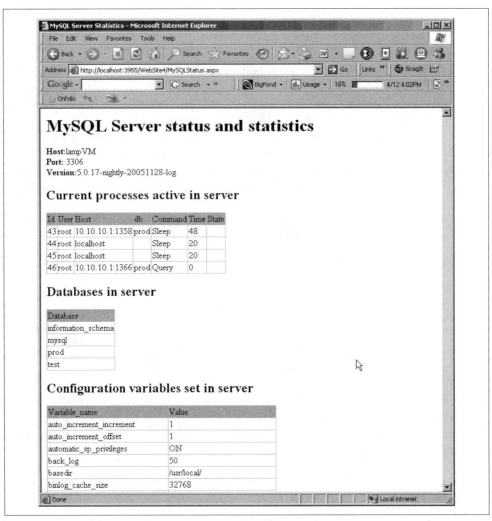

Figure 17-4. ASP.NET form in action

## PART IV

Optimizing Stored Programs

This final part of the book hopes to take you from "good" to "great." Getting programs to work correctly is hard enough: any program that works is probably a good program. A "great" program is one that performs efficiently, is robust and secure, and is easily maintained.

Stored procedures and functions raise a number of unique security concerns and opportunities: these are discussed in Chapter 18. Chapters 19 through 22 cover performance optimization of stored programs. Chapter 19 kicks off with a general discussion of performance tuning tools and techniques. The performance of your stored programs will be largely dependent on the performance of the SQL inside, so Chapters 20 and 21 provide guidelines for tuning SQL. Chapter 22 covers performance tuning of the stored program code itself.

Chapter 23 wraps up the book with a look at best practices in stored program development. These guidelines should help you write stored programs that are fast, secure, maintainable, and bug-free.

Chapter 18, *Stored Program Security*

Chapter 19, *Tuning Stored Programs and Their SQL*

Chapter 20, *Basic SQL Tuning*

Chapter 21, *Advanced SQL Tuning*

Chapter 22, *Optimizing Stored Program Code*

Chapter 23, *Best Practices in MySQL Stored Program Development*

Stored Program Security

Security has always been critical in the world of databases and stored programs that work with those databases. Yet database security has taken on heightened importance in the last decade, with the global reach of the Internet and the increasing tendency for the database to be the target of those trying to compromise application security. In this chapter we explore two different aspects of security as it pertains to MySQL stored programming:

- Controlling access to the execution and modification of stored programs themselves
- Using stored programs to secure the underlying data in MySQL databases

Stored programs—in particular, stored procedures—are subject to most of the security restrictions that apply to other database objects, such as tables, indexes, and views. Specific permissions are required before a user can create a stored program, and, similarly, specific permissions are needed in order to execute a program.

What sets the stored program security model apart from that of other database objects—and from other programming languages—is that stored programs may execute with the permissions of the user who *created* the stored program, rather than those of the user who is *executing* the stored program. This model allows users to execute operations via a stored program that they would not be privileged to execute using straight SQL.

This facility—sometimes called *definer rights* security—allows us to tighten our database security: we can ensure that a user gains access to tables only via stored program code that restricts the types of operations that can be performed on those tables and that can implement various business and data integrity rules. For instance, by establishing a stored program as the only mechanism available for certain table inserts or updates, we can ensure that all of these operations are logged, and we can prevent any invalid data entry from making its way into the table.

We can also create stored programs that execute with the privileges of the calling user, rather than those of the user who created the program. This mode of security is sometimes called *invoker rights* security, and it offers other advantages beyond those of definer rights, which we will explore in this chapter.

Before delving into the two execution modes available in MySQL, we will first examine the basic permissions needed to create, manage, and execute stored programs. Then we'll go into a detailed discussion of definer rights and invoker rights, and consider how these capabilities might be used in our applications. Finally, we will consider the use of stored programs to increase the general security of our MySQL server and, conversely, identify ways in which the use of stored programs can *reduce* overall security if developers are not careful.

Permissions Required for Stored Programs

MySQL 5.0 introduced a few new privileges to manage stored programs. These privileges are:

CREATE ROUTINE
> Allows a user to create new stored programs.

ALTER ROUTINE
> Allows a user to alter the security mode, SQL mode, or comment for an existing stored program.

EXECUTE
> Allows a user to execute a stored procedure or function.

With these distinct privileges available, we can very granularly decide what we want to allow individual developers to be able to do (as in "Sam can run program X, but not make any changes to it.").

Granting Privileges to Create a Stored Program

To give a user permission to create a stored procedure, function, or trigger, grant the CREATE ROUTINE privilege to that user using the GRANT statement. We can do this for a specific database or for all databases on the server. For example, the following GRANT statement gives the user sp_creator permission to create stored programs within the database mydatabase:

```
GRANT CREATE ROUTINE ON mydatabase.* TO sp_creator;
```

Granting Privileges to Modify a Stored Program

The ALTER ROUTINE privilege gives a user permission to change the security mode, SQL mode, or comment for a stored procedure or function. However, this privilege does not allow us to change the actual program code of a procedure. To change the program code, we must DROP and then CREATE a new program. In the following example, we change the security mode, sql_mode setting, and comment for a procedure:

```
ALTER PROCEDURE simple_stored_proc
    SQL SECURITY INVOKER
    READS SQL DATA
    COMMENT 'A simple stored procedure';
```

Granting Privileges to Execute a Stored Program

The EXECUTE privilege gives a user permission to execute a stored procedure or function. (For triggers, see Chapter 11.) EXECUTE privileges should be granted selectively, especially if the program is created with the "definer rights" security setting (see the section "The SQL SECURITY Clause" later in this chapter). The syntax for this form of the GRANT statement is:

```
GRANT EXECUTE [ON {PROCEDURE|FUNCTION}] database.program_name TO user
```

You can omit the ON PROCEDURE or ON FUNCTION clause if you are performing a wildcard grant, as in the following example:

```
GRANT EXECUTE ON mydatabase.* TO sp_creator;
```

If you are granting access to a specific program, you must specify ON PROCEDURE or ON FUNCTION explicitly; it is possible for a stored procedure and a stored function to have the same name, and it is unacceptable to issue an ambiguous security command. To grant the EXECUTE privilege on the procedure mydatabase.test1, issue the following statement:

```
GRANT EXECUTE ON PROCEDURE mydatabase.test1 TO sp_creator;
```

Execution Mode Options for Stored Programs

Stored program code differs from any other kind of code that might execute against the database in that it can have database privileges that are different from those of the account that executes the stored program. Normally, when we execute some SQL—whether it is inside the MySQL client, a PHP program, or whatever—the activities that the SQL will perform (read table X, update table Y, etc.) will be checked against the privileges that are associated with the database account to which we are connected. If our account lacks privilege to perform the activity, the SQL statement will fail with the appropriate error.

Stored programs can be defined to act in the same way, if the SQL SECURITY INVOKER clause is included in the CREATE PROCEDURE or CREATE FUNCTION statement used to create the program. However, if SQL SECURITY DEFINER (the default) is specified instead, then the stored program executes with the privilege of the account that *created* the stored program, rather than the account that is *executing* the stored program. Known as *definer rights,* this execution mode can be a very powerful way of restricting ad hoc table modifications and avoiding security breaches. Definer rights can also be a problem, however, if you are relying on traditional security privileges to secure your database.

Let's go through a quick example before we dig in more deeply. A user creates a procedure to execute a simple transaction, as shown in Example 18-1.

Example 18-1. Simple transaction using definer rights security

```
CREATE PROCEDURE tfer_funds
      (from_account INT, to_account INT,tfer_amount NUMERIC(10,2))
   SQL SECURITY DEFINER
BEGIN
   START TRANSACTION;

   UPDATE account_balance
     SET balance=balance-tfer_amount
   WHERE account_id=from_account;

   UPDATE account_balance
     SET balance=balance+tfer_amount
   WHERE account_id=to_account;

   INSERT into transaction_log
    (user_id, description)
    values(user( ), concat('Transfer of ',tfer_amount,' from ',
           from_account,' to ',to_account));

   COMMIT;
END;
```

We grant the EXECUTE privilege on this procedure to Fred, who has no other privileges to the account_balance table:

```
GRANT EXECUTE ON PROCEDURE prod.tfer_funds TO 'FRED'@'%';
```

Now, Fred would like to make some illicit changes to the account_balance table, but he is unable to do so directly:

```
C:\bin32>mysql -uFRED -pFRED -Dprod
Welcome to the MySQL monitor.  Commands end with ; or \g.
Your MySQL connection id is 7 to server version: 5.0.18-nightly-20051211-log

Type 'help;' or '\h' for help. Type '\c' to clear the buffer.

mysql> SELECT * FROM account_balance;
ERROR 1142 (42000): SELECT command denied to user 'FRED'@'localhost' for table
'account_balance'
mysql> INSERT INTO account_balance (account_id,balance) values(324,4000);
ERROR 1142 (42000): INSERT command denied to user 'FRED'@'localhost' for table
'account_balance'
mysql> ARGH!
    -> ;
ERROR 1064 (42000): You have an error in your SQL syntax; check the manual
that corresponds to your MySQL server version for the right syntax to use
near 'ARGH'!' at line 1
```

Fred can use the stored procedure to adjust balances (as shown in Figure 18-1), but by doing so he is required to take the money "from" somewhere and to create an incriminating row in the transaction_log table:

```
mysql> CALL tfer_funds(324,916,200);
Query OK, 0 rows affected (0.44 sec)

mysql> SELECT * FROM transaction_log WHERE user_id LIKE 'FRED%';
+---------------------+----------------+--------------------------------+
| txn_timestamp       | user_id        | description                    |
+---------------------+----------------+--------------------------------+
| 2005-04-14 11:23:45 | FRED@localhost | Transfer of 200 from 324 to 916 |
+---------------------+----------------+--------------------------------+
2 rows in set (0.00 sec)

mysql> ARGH!
    -> ;
ERROR 1064 (42000): You have an error in your SQL syntax; check the manual that
corresponds to your MySQL server version for the right syntax to use near ARGH!' at
line 1
```

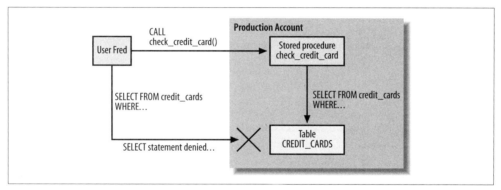

Figure 18-1. A definer rights stored program can execute SQL that the user does not have direct permission to execute

In short, using "definer rights" lets us grant permission to use the database only in ways that we clearly define through stored programs. If you like, you can think of such stored programs as an API to the database that we provide to users.

The down side of using stored programs in this way is that it makes it much harder to be certain how you have restricted access to certain objects. For instance, we can issue the following statement to try and make sure that Fred cannot look at account balances:

```
REVOKE SELECT ON prod.account_balance FROM 'FRED'@'%';
```

However, we would need to review all of the stored programs that Fred has access to before we could be 100% sure that he cannot perform any such activity.

If we want stored programs to succeed only if the user has sufficient privileges to execute the SQL statements that they contain, then we need to create an *invoker rights* program instead. Example 18-2 shows the tfer_funds stored procedure created with the SQL SECURITY INVOKER option specified.

Example 18-2. Invoker rights stored procedure

```
CREATE PROCEDURE tfer_funds
      (from_account INT, to_account INT,tfer_amount NUMERIC(10,2))
   SQL SECURITY INVOKER
BEGIN
   START TRANSACTION;

   UPDATE account_balance
      SET balance=balance-tfer_amount
    WHERE account_id=from_account;

   UPDATE account_balance
      SET balance=balance+tfer_amount
    WHERE account_id=to_account;

   INSERT into transaction_log
    (user_id, description)
    values(user( ), concat('Transfer of ',tfer_amount,' from ',
          from_account,' to ',to_account));

   COMMIT;
END;
```

Now if we want Fred to be able to execute this stored program, we will have to explicitly grant him access to the tables involved. Otherwise, he gets a security error when he executes the procedure:

```
mysql> CALL  tfer_funds(324,916,200);
ERROR 1142 (42000): UPDATE command denied to user 'FRED'@'localhost' for table
'account_balance'
```

Figure 18-2 illustrates these operations.

As well as arguably clarifying the relationship between users and table privileges, the use of the SQL SECURITY INVOKER option allows us to prevent certain security holes that can arise when stored programs execute dynamic SQL. A stored program that can execute dynamic SQL (see Chapter 5) and that runs with definer rights can represent a significant security risk; see the section "SQL Injection in Stored Programs" later in this chapter.

The SQL SECURITY Clause

The SQL SECURITY clause of the CREATE PROCEDURE and CREATE FUNCTION statements determines whether the program will operate with the privileges of the invoker or those of the definer. The syntax is straightforward:

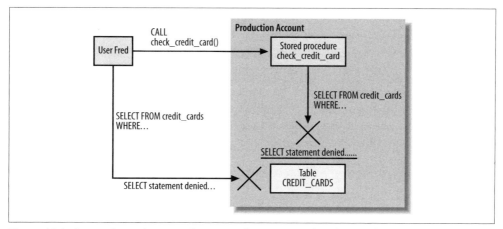

Figure 18-2. An invoker rights procedure can only issue SQL that the user has permission to execute

```
CREATE {PROCEDURE|FUNCTION} program_name (parameter_definitions)
    [ SQL SECURITY {INVOKER|DEFINER} ]
    stored_program_statements
```

If no SQL SECURITY clause appears, then the program is created with the SQL SECURITY DEFINER option.

The SQL SECURITY clause can be changed without having to re-create the stored procedure or function using the ALTER PROCEDURE or ALTER FUNCTION statement as follows:

```
ALTER {PROCEDURE|FUNCTION} program_name
    SQL SECURITY {INVOKER|DEFINER};
```

The SQL SECURITY clause applies only to procedures or functions; a related clause—DEFINER—can be applied to triggers if you want to change the execution privileges under which a trigger runs. See Chapter 11 for more details about this clause.

Using Definer Rights to Implement Security Policies

As we have already discussed, stored programs defined with the SQL SECURITY DEFINER clause can execute SQL statements that would normally not be available to the account executing the stored program. We can use this facility to provide extensive control over the way in which the user interacts with the database.

If we write our application without stored programs, then our front-end code (written in, say, PHP) interacts directly with the underlying MySQL tables. As a consequence, each MySQL account that will be used to run the application must be granted all of the permissions required by the application code.

Directly granting privileges to accounts, however, can lead to significant security problems. Users can take advantage of any client tool, including the MySQL command line, to connect to this account, thereby circumventing any security controls that might have been placed within the application logic.

Let's take a look at a scenario that demonstrates the security issues with a MySQL application that does not use stored programs. If an application performs operations on tables within the prod schema, we might create an account for that application and grant it rights to perform queries and DML on all of the tables in that schema:

```
GRANT SELECT, UPDATE, DELETE, INSERT ON prod.* TO myapp@'%'
```

The myapp account is now a highly privileged account—a hacker who got hold of the account password could delete any or all rows in any of the application tables, select any data (salaries, credit cards, etc.), and perform any number of malicious or dishonest activities.

On the other hand, in a scenario in which we use stored programs to control access to the database, we only need to grant EXECUTE permission on the programs that make up the application:

```
GRANT EXECUTE ON prod.* TO myapp@'%'
```

A user connecting to the myapp account can still get her work done, by calling the appropriate elements in the application—but that is precisely *all* that the user can do. If the capability is not implemented within the application, then it is not available to the user. This significantly reduces the exposure of the database to malicious users if the connection information for the myapp account is compromised.

For instance, our application might contain internal logic that prevents a user from accessing the salary information of employees unless the user is a senior-level manager or a member of the Payroll department. However, this application-level restriction can easily be circumvented if the user logs into the database using the MySQL Query Browser and issues SQL against the database.

By using a "definer rights" stored program, we can ensure that the user gains access to database tables only via code that we provide within the stored program. In that way, we can ensure that the security and integrity of our database is maintained, even if a user logs onto the database directly.

Example 18-3 shows a stored procedure that returns employee details. The stored procedure was created with the SQL SECURITY DEFINER clause, so anyone with the EXECUTE privilege on this procedure will be able to view the employee details, even if he or she doesn't have the SELECT privilege on this table.

The stored procedure checks the ID of the user who executes the procedure and compares this ID with information in the employees table. If the user executing the stored procedure is a senior-level manager or a member of the Payroll department, then the employee details are returned without modification. Otherwise, the employee details are returned with the salary details obscured.

Example 18-3. Procedure that restricts access to employee salary data

```
1  CREATE PROCEDURE sp_employee_list(in_department_id DECIMAL(8,0))
2      SQL SECURITY DEFINER READS SQL DATA
3  BEGIN
4      DECLARE l_user_name VARCHAR(30);
5      DECLARE l_not_found INT DEFAULT 0;
6      DECLARE l_department_name VARCHAR(30);
7      DECLARE l_manager_id INT;
8
9      DECLARE user_csr CURSOR FOR
10         SELECT d.department_name,e.manager_id
11           FROM departments d JOIN employees e USING(department_id)
12          WHERE db_user=l_user_name;
13
14     DECLARE CONTINUE HANDLER FOR NOT FOUND SET l_not_found=1;
15
16     /* Strip out the host from the user name */
17     SELECT  SUBSTR(USER(),1,INSTR(USER( ),'@')-1)
18      INTO l_user_name;
19
20     OPEN user_csr;
21     FETCH user_csr INTO l_department_name,l_manager_id;
22     CLOSE user_csr;
23
24     IF l_department_name='PAYROLL' OR l_manager_id IN (0,1) THEN
25         SELECT surname,firstname,salary
26           FROM employees
27            WHERE department_id=in_department_id
28            ORDER BY employee_id;
29     ELSE
30        /* Not authorized to see salary */
31        SELECT surname,firstname,'XXXXXXX' AS salary
32          FROM employees
33            WHERE department_id=in_department_id
34            ORDER BY employee_id;
35     END IF;
36
37 END;
```

Let's look at the key parts of this code:

Line(s)	Explanation
17	Retrieve the name of the account currently executing the stored procedure.
20-22	Retrieve the employee record with the matching ID.
24-28	If the corresponding user is in the Payroll department or is a first- or second-level manager, then we return the employee salary unmasked.
31-34	Otherwise, return the data with the salary details masked.

Fred is a software developer with our company who should not be able to see employee salary details. When he executes the stored procedure, the salary details are masked out, as shown in Example 18-4.

Example 18-4. Using a stored procedure to restrict access to sensitive information

```
C:\>mysql -ufred -pfred -Dprod
Welcome to the MySQL monitor.  Commands end with ; or \g.
Your MySQL connection id is 21 to server version: 5.0.18-nightly-20051211-log
Type 'help;' or '\h' for help. Type '\c' to clear the buffer.

mysql> CALL sp_employee_list(3);
+-------------+-----------+---------+
| surname     | firstname | salary  |
+-------------+-----------+---------+
| RAYMOND     | GOLDIE    | XXXXXXX |
| RACE        | ARLENA    | XXXXXXX |
| HAGAN       | LYNNA     | XXXXXXX |
| MARSTEN     | ALOYS     | XXXXXXX |
| FILBERT     | LEON      | XXXXXXX |
| RAM         | SANCHO    | XXXXXXX |
| SAVAGE      | SORAH     | XXXXXXX |
| FLOOD       | ULRIC     | XXXXXXX |
| INGOLD      | GUTHREY   | XXXXXXX |
| WARNER      | WORTH     | XXXXXXX |
| LEOPARD     | AUSTIN    | XXXXXXX |
| ROBBINETTE  | BRIAN     | XXXXXXX |
| REUTER      | LORIS     | XXXXXXX |
| MITCHELL    | HUGO      | XXXXXXX |
```

Fred is unable to select from the employees table directly, so there is no way for him to retrieve the employee salary data, as shown in Example 18-5.

Example 18-5. Direct access to the underlying tables is denied

```
mysql> SELECT * FROM employees;
ERROR 1142 (42000): SELECT command denied to user 'fred'@'localhost' for table
'employees'
```

Jane is a member of the Payroll department, so when she executes the procedure, she can see the salary details, as shown in Example 18-6.

Example 18-6. The stored procedure allows authorized users to view salary details

```
C:\>mysql -uJane -pJane  -Dprod
Welcome to the MySQL monitor.  Commands end with ; or \g.
Your MySQL connection id is 21 to server version: 5.0.18-nightly-20051211-log
```

Example 18-6. The stored procedure allows authorized users to view salary details (continued)

```
Type 'help;' or '\h' for help. Type '\c' to clear the buffer.

mysql> CALL sp_employee_list(3);
+-------------+-----------+--------+
| surname     | firstname | salary |
+-------------+-----------+--------+
| RAYMOND     | GOLDIE    | 53465  |
| RACE        | ARLENA    | 45733  |
| HAGAN       | LYNNA     | 85259  |
| MARSTEN     | ALOYS     | 49200  |
| FILBERT     | LEON      | 97467  |
| RAM         | SANCHO    | 58866  |
| SAVAGE      | SORAH     | 83897  |
| FLOOD       | ULRIC     | 84275  |
| INGOLD      | GUTHREY   | 60306  |
| WARNER      | WORTH     | 47473  |
```

Note that, like Fred, Jane may not directly access the employees table. Instead, she must call the sp_employee_list procedure when she wants to see the salaries for a department. If we move her to another department, she will automatically lose the ability to view these salary details.

We can also use definer rights programs to ensure that transactions applied to the database always conform to various business rules and regulatory compliance measures that we might have in place. Using a stored program to control all inserts into the sales table, for example, could be used to automate the maintenance of audit and summary tables. We saw an example of logging DML within a stored procedure in Example 18-2.

Stored Program or View?

It is sometimes possible to use a view rather than a stored program to implement some aspects of database security. For example, a user can select from a view even if he does not have access to the underlying tables, so with a view you can control which columns and rows a user can see.

Using CASE statements and WHERE clause conditions, it is often possible to create views that restrict access to only appropriate rows or—using updatable views—those that restrict modifications. For instance, the two views in Example 18-7 were designed to perform some of the security limitations provided by the stored procedure from Example 18-3.

Definer Rights in *N*-tier Applications

In the days when client/server applications ruled the earth, end users were often given individual database accounts, and they authenticated themselves to the application by connecting to the database. In modern web-based or *N*-tier applications, users typically authenticate with a middle-tier application or web server, and all users share a pool of common "proxy" database connections.

The definer rights stored program security model was first defined during the client/server era, and it largely reflects this idea that the end user might actually know her database username and password. Nevertheless, the definer rights model still has a valid role in a web-based environment, since it helps limit the exposure if the proxy account is compromised.

In a modern application that uses proxy accounts, access to the password for the proxy account will be carefully restricted. The proxy account should generally be used only by the application server. If a malicious user obtains the password to the proxy account, however, he could then have unrestricted access to the underlying database tables.

By using stored programs to mediate between the application server and the database, we can carefully limit the activities that the proxy account can undertake. We can also implement auditing, alarming, and logging to help us identify any malicious use of this account.

Of course, you should very carefully secure an application's proxy database account under any scenario. But if you are careful to limit that proxy account to execution of application stored programs, you will also limit the damage a malicious user can inflict in a compromised scenario.

Example 18-7. Using a view to implement security policies

```
CREATE VIEW current_user_details_view AS
        SELECT departments.department_name,employees.manager_id
          FROM employees join departments using (department_id)
         WHERE db_user=convert(SUBSTR(USER(),1,INSTR(USER( ),'@')-1) using latin1) ;

CREATE VIEW employees_view AS
     SELECT firstname,surname,salary,db_user,
       CASE  WHEN u.department_name='PAYROLL' OR u.manager_id IN (0,1) THEN
                    salary
            ELSE '0000000000'
       END CASE AS salary
  FROM employees e, current_user_details_view u ;
```

Using a view to implement these kinds of access restrictions is attractive, since the view implementation would allow the user more flexible query capabilities (aggregate functions, WHERE clause restrictions, etc.). On the other hand, as the security restrictions become more complex, it becomes increasingly difficult—and ultimately impossible—to create views to implement those restrictions. Finally, most organizations must ensure the integrity of transactions, and this cannot be encoded in view definitions.

Handling Invoker Rights Errors

When you create a stored program with invoker rights, you can be sure that the stored program will succeed only if the user executing the stored program has the necessary privileges. This means that you don't have to be particularly careful about who gets EXECUTE privileges to the program—the program will never let them do something that they didn't already have the privilege to do in native SQL. What this means, however, is that the program is now more likely to raise an exception at runtime, since we can't know in advance that the user has the required privileges.

The possibility of runtime security exceptions in invoker rights programs means that you will generally want to add handler logic to these programs. Consider the stored procedure shown in Example 18-8.

Example 18-8. Stored procedure using invoker rights

```
CREATE PROCEDURE sp_cust_list (in_sales_rep_id INT)
    SQL SECURITY INVOKER
BEGIN
    SELECT customer_id, customer_name
      FROM customers
     WHERE sales_rep_id=in_sales_rep_id;
END;
```

This stored procedure includes the SQL SECURITY INVOKER clause, so any user who invokes the stored procedure must have the SELECT privilege on the customers table. When Fred, who does not have this privilege, runs sp_cust_list, he will see the error message shown in Example 18-9.

Example 18-9. Invoker privileges can lead to unhandled security-violation errors

```
mysql> CALL sp_cust_list(14);
ERROR 1142 (42000): SELECT command denied to
   user 'fred'@'localhost' for table 'customers'
```

Under some circumstances, throwing an unhandled exception in this way might be sufficient. For many applications, however, it will be necessary to trap the error and provide better information and guidance to the user. Consider the revised implementation of the sp_cust_list procedure, shown in Example 18-10.

Example 18-10. Handling security violations with invoker rights procedures

```
CREATE PROCEDURE sp_cust_list2 (in_sales_rep_id INT)
    SQL SECURITY INVOKER
BEGIN
```

Example 18-10. Handling security violations with invoker rights procedures (continued)

```
    DECLARE denied INT DEFAULT 0;

    DECLARE command_denied CONDITION FOR 1142;
    DECLARE CONTINUE HANDLER FOR command_denied SET denied=1;

    SELECT customer_id, customer_name
      FROM customers
     WHERE sales_rep_id=14;

    IF denied =1 THEN
          SELECT 'You may not view customer data.'
              AS 'Permission Denied';
    END IF;
END;
```

Now when Fred runs this program, he is denied the ability to see the customer information, but at least gets a clearer explanation of the problem, as shown in Example 18-11.

Example 18-11. Handling security violations in a stored procedure

```
mysql> CALL sp_cust_list2(14);
+----------------------------------------------------------------------+
| Permission Denied                                                    |
+----------------------------------------------------------------------+
| You may not view customer data.                                      |
+----------------------------------------------------------------------+
1 row in set (0.00 sec)
```

Stored Programs and Code Injection

SQL injection is the name given to a particular form of security attack in applications that rely on dynamic SQL. With dynamic SQL, the SQL statement is constructed, parsed, and executed at runtime. If that statement is pieced together from one or more fragments of SQL syntax, a malicious user could *inject* unintended and unwanted code for execution within the dynamic SQL framework.

For an example of code injection, consider the PHP code shown in Example 18-12. This code requests a department ID from the user (line 7) and then builds up a SQL statement to retrieve the names of all employees in that department (lines 24-35).

See Chapter 13 for a detailed discussion of interfacing between PHP and MySQL.

Example 18-12. PHP code susceptible to SQL injection

```
1  <html>
2  <title>Employee Query</title>
3  <h1>Employee Query</h1>
4
5  <FORM ACTION="<?php echo $_SERVER['PHP_SELF']; ?>" METHOD=POST>
```

Example 18-12. PHP code susceptible to SQL injection (continued)

```
6   <p>Enter Department Id:
7   <input type="text" name="department" size="60">
8   <input type="submit" name="submit" value="submit"><p>
9   </form>
10
11  <?php
12  require_once "HTML/Table.php";
13
14
15  /*Check to see if user has hit submit*/
16  if (IsSet ($_POST['submit'])) {
17    $dbh = new mysqli($hostname, $username, $password, $database);
18
19    /* check connection */
20    if (mysqli_connect_errno()) {
21      printf("Connect failed: %s\n", mysqli_connect_error());
22      exit ();
23    }
24    $sql="SELECT employee_id,surname,firstname FROM employees".
25       "    WHERE department_id =".$_POST['department'];
26    print $sql;
27    if ($result_set = $dbh->query($sql)) {
28        $table =new HTML_Table('border=1');
29        $table->addRow(array('ID','Surname','Firstname'));
30        $table->setRowAttributes(0,array("bgcolor" => "silver"));
31
32      while ($row = $result_set->fetch_row()) {
33        $table->addRow(array($row[0],$row[1],$row[2]));
34      }
35      print $table->toHtml();
36    }
37    else {
38      printf("<p>Error retrieving stored procedure result set:%d (%s) %s\n",
39          mysqli_errno($dbh), mysqli_sqlstate($dbh), mysqli_error($dbh));
40    }
41
42
43  result_set->close();
44  $dbh->close();
45? >
46
47  </body></html>
```

Notice, however, that this program does not perform any validation of the user input; it is simply appended directly to the end of the SELECT statement. This careless method of construction allows a user to type in text that subverts the intention of the programmer, and—in this case—it causes the application to return data that was never intended. Figure 18-3 demonstrates this problem. The user enters UNION and SELECT clauses, and causes the application to return not just the names of employees for a specific department, but also the salaries of all employees in all departments.

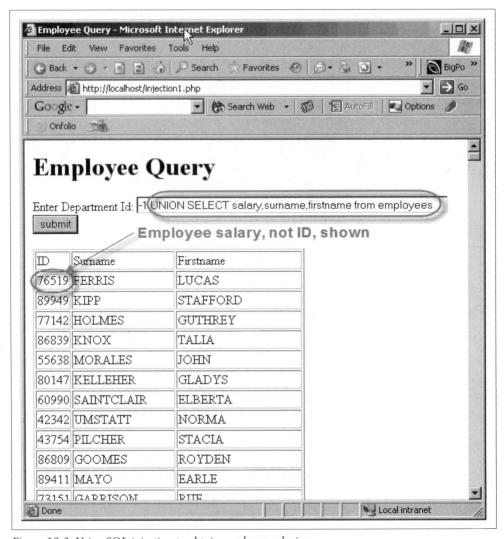

Figure 18-3. Using SQL injection to obtain employee salaries

The application intended to issue a SQL statement that looked something like this:

```
SELECT employee_id,surname,firstname
  FROM employees
 WHERE department_id =1;
```

However, by "injecting" SQL into the department_id, the application was tricked into running this SQL instead:

```
SELECT employee_id,surname,firstname
  FROM employees
 WHERE department_id =-1
 UNION
```

```
SELECT salary,surname,firstname
   FROM employees
```

Using this technique, it would be possible for a malicious user to "coerce" the application to display data from any tables to which it has access, even potentially including internal MySQL tables such as `mysql.user`.

Although it is distressingly easy to create an application that is vulnerable to SQL injection, it is, thankfully, not all that difficult to immunize an application from such an attack. Essentially, SQL injection becomes possible when the application fails to validate user input before inserting that text into a SQL statement. So the simplest solution is often to validate that input. For instance, in Example 18-13, we check that the user input represents a numeric value before inserting it into the SQL.

Example 18-13. Using simple validation to protect against SQL injection

```
$department=$_POST['department'];
if (is_numeric($department)) {

   $sql="SELECT employee_id,surname,firstname FROM employees".
     "    WHERE department_id = $department";
   if ($result_set = $dbh->query($sql)) {
```

Most of the APIs that support MySQL allow you to predefine parameters or "bind variables" to a SQL statement and to supply these just prior to execution of the SQL. These APIs will typically not allow the injection of SQL syntax into the resulting SQL and will often validate the data type of the user input. So, for instance, in Example 18-14, we use the `bind_param()` method of the `mysqli` PHP interface to accept only a numeric parameter. Even if the parameter were a string, it would be impossible to "inject" SQL syntax when using `mysqli` prepared SQL statements.

Example 18-14. Binding parameters to resist SQL injection

```
$sql="SELECT employee_id,surname,firstname FROM employees ".
   "    WHERE department_id = ? ";
$sth=$dbh->prepare($sql) or die($dbh->error);
$sth->bind_param("i",$department);
$sth->bind_result($employee_id,$surname,$firstname);
$sth->execute() or die ($dbh->error);
$table =new HTML_Table('border=1');
$table->addRow(array('ID','Surname','Firstname'));
$table->setRowAttributes(0,array("bgcolor" => "silver"));

 while ($sth->fetch()) {
    $table->addRow(array($employee_id,$surname,$firstname));
 }
```

Protecting Against SQL Injection with Stored Programs

MySQL stored programs provide yet another way to protect against SQL injection attacks. The CALL statement that is used to invoke stored programs cannot be modified by a UNION statement or other SQL syntax—it can only accept parameters to the stored program call. This makes a stored program call effectively immune to SQL injection—regardless of whether the application validates user input or uses parameter binding.

To illustrate, consider the short stored procedure in Example 18-15, which returns employee details for a specific department.

Example 18-15. Stored procedure to replace embedded SQL in PHP

```
CREATE PROCEDURE emps_in_dept(in_dept_id int)
      READS SQL DATA
BEGIN
   SELECT employee_id,firstname,surname
     FROM employees
    WHERE department_id=in_dept_id;
END;
```

We can use this stored procedure in our PHP program as the mechanism by which we retrieve our employee list, as shown in Example 18-16. This PHP code contains the same lack of input validation as our original example, and does not use parameter binding. Nevertheless, it is immune to SQL injection because the stored procedure can only accept a numeric input, and, additionally, the SQL statement within the stored procedure cannot be modified.

Example 18-16. Stored procedure calls are (usually) immune to SQL injection

```
$department = $_POST['department'];
$sql="CALL emps_in_dept( $department )";
if ($result_set = $dbh->query($sql)) {
  $table =new HTML_Table('border=1');
  $table->addRow(array('ID','Surname','Firstname'));
  $table->setRowAttributes(0,array("bgcolor" => "silver"));
  while ($row = $result_set->fetch_row()) {
    $table->addRow(array($row[0],$row[1],$row[2]));
  }
  print $table->toHtml();
```

 Although there are many ways of structuring application code to withstand a SQL injection attack, stored programs that do not contain prepared statements are immune to SQL statement injection, and an application that interacts with the database only through these stored programs will also be immune to SQL injection.

SQL Injection in Stored Programs

There is, unfortunately, one circumstance in which a stored program itself might be vulnerable to a SQL injection attack: when the stored program builds dynamic SQL using a PREPARE statement that includes values passed into the stored program as parameters.

We looked initially at prepared statements in Chapter 5: using prepared statements, we can build dynamic SQL that potentially includes strings provided as parameters to the stored program. These parameter strings might include SQL fragments and, hence, make the program susceptible to SQL injection.

Consider the stored procedure shown in Example 18-17; for reasons known only to the author, the stored procedure builds the SQL dynamically and executes it as a stored procedure. Strangely, the author also used a very long VARCHAR parameter even though department_id is a numeric column.

Example 18-17. Stored procedure susceptible to SQL injection

```
CREATE PROCEDURE `emps_in_dept2`(in_dept_id VARCHAR(1000))
BEGIN
  SET @sql=CONCAT(
      "SELECT employee_id,firstname,surname
         FROM employees
        WHERE department_id=",in_dept_id);
  PREPARE s1 FROM @sql;
  EXECUTE s1;
  DEALLOCATE PREPARE s1;
END;
```

This stored procedure is susceptible to exactly the same form of SQL injection attack as the PHP code shown in Example 18-12. For instance, we can extract employee details from the stored procedure by executing it as shown in Example 18-18.

Example 18-18. Injecting SQL into a stored procedure call

```
mysql> CALL emps_in_dept2("-1 UNION SELECT salary,surname,firstname
    FROM employees ");
+-------------+-----------+----------+
| employee_id | firstname | surname  |
+-------------+-----------+----------+
|      105402 | FERRIS    | LUCAS    |
|       89949 | KIPP      | STAFFORD |
|       77142 | HOLMES    | GUTHREY  |
|       86839 | KNOX      | TALIA    |
|       55638 | MORALES   | JOHN     |
```

If the PHP application relied on this stored procedure to retrieve department_ids, it would continue to be vulnerable to SQL injection attack.

SQL injection through stored programs can be serious, since stored programs that execute with definer rights can execute SQL not normally available to the user invoking the stored programs. Not only would the database be vulnerable to SQL injection attacks through a privileged account associated with a web application, but SQL could be injected by a nonprivileged user at the MySQL command line.

In this example, the use of dynamic SQL was unnecessary and arguably dangerous, since no validation of the input parameter was undertaken. In general, dynamic SQL inside of stored programs represents a significant security risk. We recommend the following policies to minimize your vulnerability:

- Use prepared statements inside of stored programs only when absolutely necessary.

- If you must use a prepared statement, and if that prepared statement includes strings provided as input parameters, make sure to validate that the strings are of the expected data type and length. For instance, in our previous example, had the input parameter been defined as an INTEGER, then the SQL injection would not be possible.

- Consider using invoker rights (SQL SECURITY INVOKER) when a stored program includes prepared statements. This limits your exposure, since the invoker will only be able to inject SQL that is within her security rights.

Conclusion

In this chapter we looked at the basic security permissions required for creating and executing stored programs and at how the SQL SECURITY clause affects the security context of an executing stored program.

By default—or if the SQL SECURITY DEFINER clause is specified—stored programs execute with the permissions of the account that *created* the stored program. This means that a database user can execute a stored program that can perform database operations not available to that user through normal SQL. You can use this feature to implement a scheme in which a user can manipulate the database through stored programs but has no privilege to manipulate the database through normal SQL. Restricting database access in this way through stored programs can improve database security, since you can ensure that table accesses are restricted to known routines that perform appropriate validation or logging. You can reduce your exposure should the database account involved be compromised.

If the SQL SECURITY INVOKER clause is specified, then the stored program will execute with the permissions of the account that is executing the stored program. In this case, an exception will be raised if the stored program attempts to execute a SQL statement that the invoker does not have permission to execute as native SQL.

Stored programs in MySQL 5.0 are implicitly resistant to SQL injection—unless they include dynamic SQL via prepared statements. We recommend that you exercise caution when using dynamic SQL in stored programs—take every precaution to ensure that the stored procedure or function is not vulnerable to malicious SQL injection. If prepared statements and dynamic SQL are necessary, then make sure to validate input parameters, and consider using the SQL SECURITY INVOKER mode to limit your exposure.

CHAPTER 19

Tuning Stored Programs and Their SQL

This chapter kicks off the set of chapters in this book that are concerned with optimizing the performance of your stored programs. Like any program, a stored program might be correct in all of its functional aspects, but still be considered a failure if it does not perform well. Performance tuning of MySQL stored programs is of particular importance because the stored program language is interpreted, and thus it does not benefit from the performance improvements that can be obtained by optimizing compilers such as the ones common in languages such as C and Java. (Strictly speaking, Java is also an interpreted language, but the Java JVM performs a number of sophisticated optimizations.) Stored programs also almost always involve significant database activity and therefore are quite likely to become a performance bottleneck for the application as a whole.

We believe that there are three main principles of stored program optimization:

Optimize SQL

> The SQL inside of a stored program must be optimized if the stored program has any chance of running efficiently. Untuned SQL statements can easily take hundreds or even thousands of times longer to return results than well-tuned SQL statements, so we therefore recommend tuning the SQL inside a stored program before tuning the stored program code itself. We'll look at SQL tuning in detail in the next few chapters.

Break up complex SQL

> Sometimes you can use stored programs to break up complex and hard-to-tune SQL statements into distinct, smaller statements that are easier to tune individually—both for the MySQL optimizer (the part of MySQL that determines how SQL should be executed) and for the programmer who is trying to tune the SQL. We'll look at these cases in Chapter 22.

Perform non-SQL optimization

> Finally, optimizations that are common and well known in other programming languages also apply to the MySQL stored program language. Loop structures, use of recursion, caching, and branching structures can all affect how fast the

SQL will run. We'll examine how to optimize the non-SQL stored program code in detail in Chapter 22.

In this chapter, we provide a brief overview of the way in which MySQL processes SQL statements, review the tuning tools at our disposal, and provide a brief overview of tuning. In subsequent chapters we will delve more deeply into the tuning of stored programs and the SQL statements they contain.

Why SQL Tuning Is So Important

It might be surprising to you that a book dedicated to stored programming has such extensive coverage of SQL tuning. The reason for this is simple: we regard SQL tuning as an essential skill for anyone writing MySQL stored programs. The simple fact is this:

> The vast majority of your stored program execution time is going to be spent executing SQL statements.

Furthermore, poorly tuned (or untuned) SQL can result in programs that are slower by orders of *magnitude* (e.g., thousands of times slower). Finally, untuned SQL almost never scales well as data volumes increase, so even if your program seems to run in a reasonable amount of time today, ignoring SQL statement tuning now can result in major problems later.

An Instructive Example

The following example demonstrates just how critical the role of SQL tuning is in overall system performance. An application executes a query (which might even be implemented within a stored program) that involves a simple join between two tables, as shown here:

```
SELECT sum(sale_value)
  FROM ta_10000 a,tb_10000 b
 WHERE a.sales_id=b.sales_id;
```

The tables grow in size with each day's accumulation of data. Initial performance is satisfactory, but within a few days performance is questionable, and within a week the application is virtually unusable. You are called in to examine the situation. When you examine the relationship between table size and elapsed time, you discover the relationship shown in Figure 19-1.

Not only is the performance of the query growing worse as the tables grow, but the rate of increase is itself accelerating. Extrapolating the performance trend, you predict that by the time the tables reach their estimated peak sizes of 1,000,000 rows each, the join will take more than 20 hours to complete!

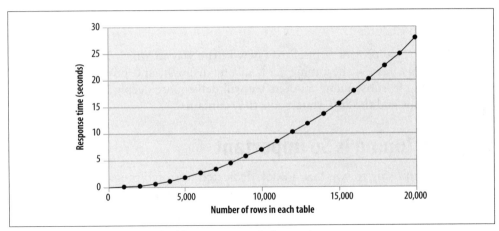

Figure 19-1. Response time and table row counts—before tuning

After examining the SQL statements involved in the application, the problem—and the solution—seems obvious. An index is needed to support the join, and you can create one with the following statement:

```
CREATE INDEX i_tb_1000 ON tb_1000 (sales_id)
```

Once the index is created, the performance trend adopts the profile shown in Figure 19-2.

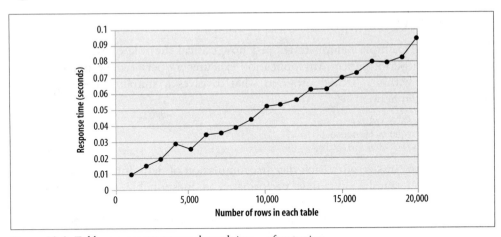

Figure 19-2. Table row counts versus elapsed time—after tuning

The performance improvement is remarkable—the elapsed time for the query has been reduced by more than 99%, and the SQL is more than 100 times faster. Furthermore, the SQL will now scale appropriately as the volumes of data in the tables increase.

No amount of server tuning, stored program tuning, or hardware upgrades could have obtained this improvement. Any such efforts would also have been ultimately futile, because the exponential degradation would eventually overwhelm any performance improvements gained by other measures. For these reasons, SQL tuning should *always* be performed before attempting any other optimization.

 SQL tuning is the most important aspect of overall MySQL tuning. Ensure that SQL is tuned before starting any other optimization exercises.

How MySQL Processes SQL

The following sections provide a brief overview of the parsing and caching steps that MySQL undertakes as it processes a SQL statement.

Parsing SQL

A SQL statement sent to the MySQL server must first be *parsed*. Parsing involves the following actions:

- Ensure that the SQL statement contains valid syntax.
- Check that that you have been granted appropriate access to the objects involved.
- Confirm that all required objects exist.
- Determine an execution plan for the SQL statement.

The *execution plan* represents MySQL's strategy for retrieving or modifying the data specified by the SQL statement. The *optimizer* is that part of the MySQL code that is responsible for making these decisions. Here are some of the questions that the optimizer needs to ask before it can come up with its plan:

- Is there a way to rewrite the SQL so that it will execute more efficiently?
- Are there any indexes available to retrieve the required data?
- Will using these indexes improve performance? If so, which of the possible indexes should be used?
- If multiple tables are to be processed, in what order should the tables be processed?

Compared to some of the major relational databases (Oracle, SQL Server, DB2), MySQL's optimizer might seem, at first glance, to be relatively simplistic. MySQL's optimizer is, however, extremely effective. You will only rarely need to rewrite a SQL statement to make it perform more efficiently—the optimizer will usually make the right decision. Since the optimizer cannot create "missing" indexes that might make your statement run faster, the most important thing you can do to assist the optimizer is to create a good set of supporting indexes on your tables.

Understanding how the optimizer makes its decisions will help you to make sound database design and SQL programming decisions. In the next two chapters, we will look at specific SQL tuning scenarios, explain how the optimizer deals with each of these scenarios, and discuss techniques for optimizing the SQL involved.

Caching

MySQL supports some in-memory structures (also known generally as *caches*), which can improve the performance of SQL statements.

Buffer pool and key cache

Almost every SQL statement needs to work with data from the database—either to return it to the calling program or to modify it as instructed by an INSERT, UPDATE, or DELETE statement. In many cases, however, MySQL can obtain this data without the overhead of disk I/O by retrieving the required data from one of a number of caches.

For MyISAM tables, MySQL relies on the operating system to cache the data contained in the individual files that make up the tables. All operating systems include read caches, and if you read from a MyISAM file more than once, there is a chance that the data will still be in the operating system cache when you try to read it a second time. You will usually have very little control over the size of the OS read cache, since it is normally managed by the operating system itself.

MyISAM does, however, have its own cache for index blocks. This is controlled by the startup parameter KEY_BUFFER_SIZE.

The InnoDB storage engine maintains a single cache for both index and table blocks. This is controlled by the parameter INNODB_BUFFER_POOL_SIZE.

Correctly sizing these two buffers can help reduce the amount of disk I/O required to satisfy the data requirements of your SQL statements. In general, you should allocate as much memory as possible to these caches. However, beware of allocating *too much* memory for the MyISAM key buffer—you might inadvertently starve the OS read buffer and reduce the amount of memory available for caching table data.

Table cache

The *table cache* maintains metadata about tables in memory and also contains the link to the storage handler's physical representation of the table. In MyISAM, these links are file descriptors pointing to the *.frm* files and the *.MYD* files. Each session that needs to access a table will require its own table cache entry. The default value of TABLE_CACHE (typically 256) is often too small for systems with large numbers of tables and/or high numbers of concurrent users.

Query cache

Before MySQL goes to the trouble of parsing a SQL statement, it will look in the *query cache* to see if it already has in memory a copy of the SQL statement and its result set. If it finds a match, it can return the result set directly from the query cache. This "shortcut" can greatly improve query performance. So what are the criteria for determining a match?

In order for MySQL to take advantage of a cached result set, the new SQL statement must match *exactly* the statement associated with the result set, including whitespace and comments. If the same logical statement is written more than once within an application, there is a very good chance that the statements will not be physically identical, thus negating a key performance enhancement.

In addition, if any table referred to in the statement is modified, then that statement and its result set will be flushed from the query cache. This behavior makes the query cache most useful for applications or tables that are read-intensive. If a table is being modified many times a second—as might be the case in an OLTP application—then it is unlikely that queries against that table are going to remain in cache long enough to be useful. Remember: any modification to the table will cause queries using that table to be flushed—even if the modification does not impact the rows returned by the query.

Some SQL statements cannot be cached at all—particularly if they contain a function that is not guaranteed to return the same result every time it is called. For instance, the CURDATE function will return a different value (the current date-time) every time it is called. So if you include a call to CURDATE in your query, it will not be cached.

The query cache will be most effective when at least some of the following are true:

- The SQL statements being cached are expensive to execute (they may require scans of big tables or sort operations).
- The result sets are relatively small (otherwise, the result set may not fit in the cache).
- The SQL statements are executed with some frequency (otherwise, the result set may be flushed from the cache before the SQL is re-executed).
- The underlying tables are rarely modified.

You can control the size of the cache with the SET GLOBAL query_cache_size=*size* statement.

You can view statistics about query cache usage with the SHOW STATUS LIKE 'qcache%'; statement.

Stored programs can benefit from the query cache. A stored program that returns a result set will be cached, and any subsequent execution of that program can be satisfied using the query cache. However, SQL statements within stored programs cannot currently be satisfied from the cache (we might imagine that when they execute within the database, they are executing "behind the cache").

Table statistics

Like most query optimizers, MySQL maintains statistics about table and index data so that it can use this additional information to formulate the most efficient execution plan.

You can view the statistics that MySQL keeps for a table with the SHOW TABLE STATUS statement. Example 19-1 shows an example of using this statement.

Example 19-1. Viewing table statistics

```
mysql> SHOW TABLE STATUS LIKE 'sales' \G
*************************** 1. row ***************************
           Name: sales
         Engine: InnoDB
        Version: 9
     Row_format: Fixed
           Rows: 2500137
 Avg_row_length: 114
    Data_length: 285016064
Max_data_length: 0
   Index_length: 0
      Data_free: 0
 Auto_increment: 2500001
    Create_time: 2004-12-28 10:47:35
    Update_time: NULL
     Check_time: NULL
      Collation: latin1_swedish_ci
       Checksum: NULL
 Create_options:
        Comment: InnoDB free: 1766400 kB
1 row in set (0.60 sec)
```

You can view the statistics that MySQL keeps for the indexes on a table with the SHOW INDEXES statement, as shown in Example 19-2.

Example 19-2. Viewing index statistics

```
mysql> SHOW INDEXES FROM sales \G
*************************** 1. row ***************************
        Table: sales
   Non_unique: 0
     Key_name: PRIMARY
 Seq_in_index: 1
  Column_name: SALES_ID
    Collation: A
  Cardinality: 2500137
     Sub_part: NULL
       Packed: NULL
         Null:
```

Example 19-2. Viewing index statistics (continued)

```
  Index_type: BTREE
     Comment:
1 row in set (0.18 sec)
```

The two most important columns in the output from these commands are Rows and Avg_row_length from SHOW TABLE STATUS and Cardinality from SHOW INDEXES. *Cardinality* reports the number of distinct rows in the index—this helps MySQL to determine how efficient the index will be in retrieving rows. Indexes that have a high cardinality-to-rows ratio are often called *selective* indexes.

These statistics are created by MySQL (or the storage engine) during certain operations such as bulk loads/deletes, index creation, and ALTER TABLE operations. You can request that MySQL update the statistics with the ANALYZE TABLE statement. If your database is subject to large fluctuations in data volumes, you may want to run ANALYZE TABLE periodically, but be aware that this statement places a read lock on the table, preventing concurrent update, and therefore should not be run during times of heavy concurrent updates activity.

The optimizer also obtains additional statistics at runtime by probing a table's indexes to determine the *relative* cardinality of an index against the query values requested. Through this analysis, the optimizer may determine that although an index has low overall cardinality, it is highly selective for the values provided in the query.

Suppose, for instance, that we have an index on gender ('male', 'female', 'unsure'). MySQL will ignore this index for a query that requests all males or all females, but will choose to use the index for a query of all those unsure of their gender. Since this group comprises only a small proportion of the rows, the index will, in this case, help MySQL locate the total result set quickly. We'll look in detail in the next chapter at how MySQL chooses indexes.

SQL Tuning Statements and Practices

MySQL provides several statements and utilities that assist with tuning SQL, and you need to be familiar with these resources. The statements and utilities are described in the following sections.

EXPLAIN Statement

The most important SQL tuning statement in the MySQL language is EXPLAIN. EXPLAIN exposes the execution plan that the optimizer will use to resolve a particular SQL statement. Without EXPLAIN, you are doomed to trial-and-error tuning.

EXPLAIN has a simple syntax:

```
EXPLAIN sql_text;
```

EXPLAIN returns a result set consisting of at least one row for each table referenced in the SQL. Additional rows might be returned to indicate how subqueries or derived tables are used in the query. Example 19-3 is a simple demonstration of an explain plan for a two-table join (we used the \G option to print the output with each column on a separate line).

Example 19-3. Example of EXPLAIN output

```
mysql> EXPLAIN SELECT customer_name
    ->    FROM employees join customers
    ->        ON(customers.sales_rep_id=employees.employee_id)
    ->  WHERE employees.surname='GRIGSBY'
    ->    AND employees.firstname='RAY' \G

*************************** 1. row ***************************
          id: 1
 select_type: SIMPLE
       table: employees¹
        type: ref
possible_keys: PRIMARY,i_employees_name³
         key: i_employees_name⁴
     key_len: 80
         ref: const,const
        rows: 1⁵
       Extra: Using where; Using index⁶
*************************** 2. row ***************************
          id: 1
 select_type: SIMPLE
       table: customers²
        type: ref
possible_keys: i_customers_sales_rep
         key: i_customers_sales_rep⁸
     key_len: 9
         ref: sqltune.employees.EMPLOYEE_ID⁷
        rows: 5558⁹
       Extra: Using where
2 rows in set (0.04 sec)
```

Let's take a look at the most important pieces of information from these plans. Numbers used in the explanation below correspond to superscripts in the EXPLAIN output above.

1. For joins, the order of the rows output by EXPLAIN corresponds to the join order, so the presence of the employees table in the first row indicates that employees was the first table in the join.

2. customers is the second table in the join.

3. MySQL had a choice between the primary key index and the i_employees_name index.

4. MySQL chose the i_employees_name index to retrieve rows from employees. This index was on (surname, firstname).

5. MySQL has determined that it will fetch only a single row in this stage of the query (e.g., it determined that there was only one `employees` row with that particular `surname+firstname` combination).

6. Because the columns in the `i_employees_name` index were the only `employees` columns included in the SQL, MySQL was able to satisfy this part of the query using the index alone—accessing rows in the table itself was unnecessary.

7. MySQL was required to find rows in the `customers` table that matched specific values of `employees.employee_id`.

8. MySQL used the `i_customers_sales_rep` index to retrieve these rows (this was an index on `customers.sales_rep_id`).

9. MySQL expected to retrieve about 5558 rows from `customers`. The value here refers to the number of rows that are expected to be processed each time this step is executed—which, in this case, is only once.

We'll look at a variety of `EXPLAIN` outputs for common query scenarios in the next few chapters. For now, the main thing to recognize and accept is that if you are going to be tuning SQL statements, you will need to get familiar with the `EXPLAIN` statement and learn how to interpret the `EXPLAIN` output.

 The `EXPLAIN` statement is the primary tool in your SQL tuning toolbox. You should become competent in the interpretation of `EXPLAIN` output.

EXPLAIN and Stored Programs

Unfortunately, there is no way to directly obtain `EXPLAIN` output for the SQL statements inside stored programs. `EXPLAIN` will generate an error if asked to explain a `CALL` statement or a stored program name.

We hope that this restriction will be relaxed in future releases. In the meantime, to tune the SQL in your stored programs, you need to work with the SQL outside of the stored program and only add it to the program when you are satisfied that it is optimized.

Details of the EXPLAIN Output

The output from the `EXPLAIN` statement consists of lines containing the following columns:

id

Identifies the individual `SELECT` statement within a SQL statement that contains multiple `SELECT` clauses. There will be multiple `SELECT` statements in SQL statements that contain subqueries, in-line views, or `UNION` operations. All rows in the `EXPLAIN` output that have the same ID will belong to the same `SELECT` statement.

select_type
>   This column identifies the type of the SELECT statement responsible for this step.
>   Table 19-1 lists the possible values.

Table 19-1. Possible values for the select_type column of the EXPLAIN statement output

select_type	Explanation
SIMPLE	A simple SELECT statement that does not involve either subqueries or UNIONs.
PRIMARY	If the SQL contains subqueries or UNIONs, PRIMARY indicates the outermost SQL. PRIMARY could be the SELECT statement that contains subqueries within it or the first SELECT in a UNION.
UNION	The second or subsequent SELECT statements contributing to a UNION operation.
UNION RESULT	The result set of a UNION operation.
SUBQUERY	A subquery that returns rows that are not "dependent" on the rows in the outer SELECT. In practice, this means that the subquery does not contain references to columns in other SELECT statements.
DEPENDENT SUBQUERY	A subquery whose results are dependent on the values in an outer SELECT. This is typical of EXISTS subqueries and of IN subqueries (which MySQL rewrites as EXISTS).
DEPENDENT UNION	The second or subsequent SELECT in a UNION that is dependent on rows from an outer SELECT.
DERIVED	SELECT that appears within a subquery within the FROM clause of another SQL.

table
>   Indicates the name of the table involved in this step. If the table is aliased within
>   the SQL statement, then the name of the alias rather than the name of the table
>   will be reported.

type
>   Indicates the method by which rows will be selected from the table involved.
>   Table 19-2 shows the possible values for the type column.

Table 19-2. Possible values for the type column of the EXPLAIN statement output

type	Explanation
all	All rows in the table concerned will be read. This occurs primarily when no suitable index exists to retrieve the rows, or when MySQL determines that a full scan of the table will be less expensive than an index lookup.
const	An index is used to retrieve all values from the table matching a constant value supplied in the WHERE clause.
eq_ref	An index is used to retrieve all rows from the table that match the rows supplied by a previous SELECT. eq_ref is typically seen in conjunction with a well-optimized, indexed join. eq_ref indicates that all parts of a unique or primary key index are used.
ref	Like eq_ref except that either only part of the index can be used or the index is not unique or primary.
ref_or_null	Like ref except that the condition also includes a search for null values.
index merge	Occurs when MySQL merges multiple indexes to retrieve the results.

type	Explanation
unique_ subquery	An index lookup is used to satisfy the result of a subquery.
range	An index is used to retrieve a range of values from the table. This occurs typically when >, <, or BETWEEN operators are involved.
index	A full scan of the index is undertaken to find the necessary rows.

possible_keys

> Lists all of the keys (indexes) that MySQL considered as having potential to resolve this step. If an index is listed here, but is not used to resolve the step, you can consider using optimizer hints to force or encourage the use of the index. If the index is not listed, then in all probability MySQL cannot use it.

key

> Indicates the key (index) that MySQL used to resolve the query.

key_len

> Shows the length of the columns in the index used to resolve the query. If there is more than one column in the index, key_len might indicate that only part of the index is used.

ref

> Shows which columns are used to select rows from the table. ref may list columns from other tables (join columns from other tables) or the word const if a constant value will be used (this constant value might have come from a WHERE clause literal, or might have been obtained earlier in the query execution).

rows

> Indicates the number of rows that MySQL estimates will be processed by this step.

Extra

> Contains additional information about the execution step. Possible values for Extra are shown in Table 19-3. Multiple values from this column may appear in the Extra column, separated by semicolons.

Table 19-3. Possible values for the extra column of the EXPLAIN statement output

Extra	Explanation
distinct	MySQL will stop searching for more rows after the first match is found.
not exists	Occurs in a LEFT JOIN when there is an additional WHERE clause condition that indicates that the WHERE clause condition will never be satisfied. A LEFT JOIN with an IS NULL condition will generate this output. This allows the optimizer to eliminate the table from further processing.
range checked for each record	There is no good general-purpose index to support a join. MySQL will determine on a row-by-row basis whether to use an index and/or which index to use.

Extra	Explanation
Using filesort	MySQL needs to return rows in order, and no index is available to support that ordering. MySQL will need to sort the rows and may need to write to disk during that sorting. Even if there is sufficient memory to avoid a disk sort, you will still see this tag if a sort is necessary.
Using index	This step could be resolved by reading an index alone. Typically, this occurs when all of the columns required to resolve the step are present in an index.
Using index for group-by	Same as Using index, but used to support a GROUP BY operation.
Using temporary	A temporary table is created to hold intermediate results. Often seen in conjunction with using filesort.
Using where	The results returned by this step are filtered to satisfy the WHERE clause condition.
Using sort_ union	Similar to using union except that the rows had to be sorted before the UNION could be performed, usually because range conditions are involved.
Using union	A form of index merge in which rows that appeared in any of the index scans are returned. Typically used to support WHERE clause conditions that include OR conditions.
Using intersect	A form of index merge in which only the rows appearing in all of the index scans are returned. Typically used to support WHERE clause conditions that include only AND conditions.

Extended EXPLAIN

An undocumented feature of the EXPLAIN statement can be used to reveal the rewrites that MySQL performs on a statement *prior* to execution.

If you issue the statement EXPLAIN EXTENDED *sql*, followed by SHOW WARNINGS, MySQL will print the SQL that it actually executes, including any rewrites applied to the SQL by the optimizer. For instance, in Example 19-4, we see how MySQL rewrites an IN subquery to an EXISTS subquery.

Example 19-4. Using EXPLAIN EXTENDED

```
mysql> EXPLAIN EXTENDED SELECT COUNT(*) FROM ta_5000 WHERE sales_id  IN (SELECT sales_id
FROM tb_5000)\G
*************************** 1. row ***************************
           id: 1
  select_type: PRIMARY
        table: ta_5000
         type: ALL
possible_keys: NULL
          key: NULL
      key_len: NULL
          ref: NULL
         rows: 5131
        Extra: Using where
*************************** 2. row ***************************
           id: 2
  select_type: DEPENDENT SUBQUERY
        table: tb_5000
```

Example 19-4. Using EXPLAIN EXTENDED (continued)

```
          type: ALL
possible_keys: NULL
           key: NULL
       key_len: NULL
           ref: NULL
          rows: 4985
         Extra: Using where
2 rows in set, 1 warning (0.04 sec)

mysql> SHOW WARNINGS \G
*************************** 1. row ***************************
  Level: Note
   Code: 1003
Message: select count(0) AS `count(*)` from `sqltune`.`ta_5000` where <in_optimizer>
(`sqltune`.`ta_5000`.`SALES_ID`,<exists>(select
1 AS `Not_used` from `sqltune`.`tb_5000` where (<cache>(`sqltune`.`ta_5000`.`SALES_ID`) =
`sqltune`.`tb_5000`.`SALES_ID`)))
1 row in set (0.05 sec)
```

Most of the time, MySQL rewrites are not particularly significant. However, if you are completely at a loss to understand MySQL's refusal to use an index or some other execution plan decision, examining the rewrite might be useful.

Optimizer Hints

Optimizer hints are instructions that you can embed in your SQL that do not change the meaning of the SQL, but rather instruct or suggest to the optimizer how you would like the SQL to be executed.

Most of the time, you will not need to add hints. In fact, hints can be dangerous because they limit the choices the optimizer has available, and if data in the tables change or if new indexes are added to the table, MySQL may be unable to adapt because of your hints. However, there definitely will be situations where you will discover that the optimizer has made a less than perfect decision and you will want to give the optimizer specific instructions.

Table 19-4 lists the commonly used optimizer hints. We will see examples of each of these hints in the next two chapters.

Table 19-4. MySQL optimizer hints

Hint	Where it appears	What it does
STRAIGHT_JOIN	After the SELECT clause	Forces the optimizer to join the tables in the order in which they appear in the FROM clause. Use this if you want to force tables to be joined in a particular order.
USE INDEX(*index* [,*index*...])	After a table name in the FROM clause	Instructs MySQL to only consider using the indexes listed. MySQL may choose to use none of the indexes if it calculates that using them would not be faster than scanning the entire table.

Table 19-4. MySQL optimizer hints (continued)

Hint	Where it appears	What it does
FORCE INDEX(`index` [,`index`...])	After a table name in the FROM clause	Instructs MySQL to use one of the indexes listed. This differs from USE INDEX in that MySQL is instructed not to perform a table scan of the data unless it is impossible to use any of the indexes listed.
IGNORE INDEX(`index` [,`index`...])	After a table name in the FROM clause	Instructs MySQL not to consider any of the listed indexes when working out the execution plan.

Measuring SQL and Stored Program Execution

When we execute a SQL statement from the MySQL command line, MySQL is kind enough to report on the elapsed time taken to execute the statement:

```
mysql> CALL TestProc1( );
Query OK, 0 rows affected (9.35 sec)
```

Elapsed time is a good first measurement of SQL or stored program performance, but there are lots of reasons why elapsed time might vary between runs that may have absolutely nothing to do with how well the SQL statement is optimized:

- Other users may be running jobs on the host while we execute our SQL statements; we will be contending with them for CPU, disk I/O, and locks.

- The number of physical I/Os necessary to execute our statement will vary depending on the amount of data cached in the operating system, the MyISAM key cache, the InnoDB buffer pool, and/or some other storage engine–specific cache.

For these reasons, it is sometimes better to obtain additional metrics to work out whether our tuning efforts are successful. Useful execution statistics can be obtained from the SHOW STATUS statement, although the level of detail will vary depending on our storage engine, with InnoDB currently offering the most comprehensive selection of statistics.

Generally, we will want to compare before and after variables for each statistic and—because the statistics are sometimes computed across all sessions using the MySQL server—ensure that our session has exclusive use of the server while the statement runs.

In Example 19-5, we calculate the number of logical and physical reads performed while counting the number of rows on the InnoDB-based sales table. Logical reads are the number of block requests from the InnoDB buffer pool, while physical reads reflect the number of blocks that actually had to be read from disk.

Example 19-5. Examining InnoDB execution statistics before and after SQL statement execution

```
mysql> /* Logical reads before execution*/
SHOW STATUS LIKE 'Innodb_buffer_pool_read_requests';
+--------------------------------+-------+
```

Example 19-5. Examining InnoDB execution statistics before and after SQL statement execution (continued)

```
| Variable_name                  | Value |
+--------------------------------+-------+
| Innodb_buffer_pool_read_requests | 598 |
+--------------------------------+-------+
1 row in set (0.01 sec)

mysql> /* Physical reads before execution*/
SHOW STATUS LIKE 'Innodb_data_reads';
+-------------------+-------+
| Variable_name     | Value |
+-------------------+-------+
| Innodb_data_reads | 79    |
+-------------------+-------+
1 row in set (0.01 sec)

mysql>
mysql> SELECT count(*) from sales;
+----------+
| count(*) |
+----------+
|  2500000 |
+----------+
1 row in set (27.67 sec)

mysql>
mysql> /* Logical reads after execution*/
SHOW STATUS LIKE 'Innodb_buffer_pool_read_requests';
+----------------------------------+--------+
| Variable_name                    | Value  |
+----------------------------------+--------+
| Innodb_buffer_pool_read_requests | 365177 |
+----------------------------------+--------+
1 row in set (0.46 sec)

mysql> /* Physical reads after execution*/
SHOW STATUS LIKE 'Innodb_data_reads';
+-------------------+-------+
| Variable_name     | Value |
+-------------------+-------+
| Innodb_data_reads | 17472 |
+-------------------+-------+
1 row in set (0.01 sec)
```

Subtracting the before values from the after values gives us a logical read count of 364,579 and a physical read count of 17,393. We also note the elapsed time of 27.67 seconds.

The next time we execute this query, we might see a lower physical read count and a lower elapsed time because the data we need is already in cache. However, we would not expect the logical read count to change unless the data in the table was changed.

This makes the logical read statistics (`Innodb_buffer_pool_read_requests`) arguably the most useful statistics for determining if our SQL tuning efforts have been successful.

Table 19-5 shows the `SHOW STATUS` variables that are most useful for measuring SQL execution performance.

Table 19-5. SHOW STATUS statistics that are useful when measuring SQL performance

SHOW STATUS statistic	Explanation
`Innodb_buffer_pool_ read_requests`	Number of requests from the InnoDB buffer pool. This statistic is sometimes called *logical reads* since it reflects the absolute number of data reads required to satisfy a query. This value will remain constant between runs provided that our data does not change. If we observe a reduction in this statistic, then we have almost certainly improved the performance of our query.
`Innodb_data_reads`	Number of blocks from disk that InnoDB had to read to execute the query. If the cache is empty, then this value will be equal to `Innodb_buffer_pool_read_requests`. If all of the required blocks are in the cache, then this statistic will be 0. Usually, the value will be somewhere in between. If two executions of the same SQL have different response times, we can look at this statistic to determine if the difference is because one execution required more physical I/O[a].
`Innodb_rows_read`	Number of rows read by InnoDB to satisfy the query. For some SQL statements, we may see excessive values for this statistic, which generally indicates that the SQL is inefficient (because it is accessing the same rows twice, or because it is accessing more rows than are required).
`Last_query_cost`	Optimizer's "cost" estimate for the last SQL executed. Unlike the other metrics, this statistic does not require us to have to calculate a delta value. Higher costs indicate that the optimizer thinks the SQL will take longer to run.
`Sort_rows`	Number of rows that had to be sorted.
`Sort_merge_passes`	Number of disk sort "merge runs" that had to be performed. The fewer merge runs, the faster the sort. Chapter 21 describes sort optimization in detail.

[a] For example, if we execute a new SQL statement twice, the second execution will usually have a lower elapsed time because the first execution brings the required blocks into the InnoDB buffer pool or the MyISAM key cache.

The Slow Query Log

One way to identify SQL statements or stored programs that may need tuning is to enable the MySQL *slow query log*. We can do this by adding the following lines to our MySQL initialization files:

```
log_slow_queries
long_query_time=N
```

This will cause MySQL to write any queries that exceed an elapsed time exceeding *N* seconds to a log file. The log file can be found in the MySQL data directory and is named `hostname-slow.log`. For each SQL statement identified, MySQL will print the SQL statement along with a few execution statistics, as shown in Example 19-6.

Example 19-6. Example of slow query log contents

```
Time                 Id Command     Argument
# Time: 050214 23:42:30
# User@Host: root[root] @ localhost [127.0.0.1]
# Query_time: 67  Lock_time: 0  Rows_sent: 1  Rows_examined: 101199
use sqltune;
select count(*) from customers where contact_surname not in (select surname from
employees);
```

The slow query log execution statistics are not particularly enlightening, and there is no EXPLAIN output, so we would normally paste the SQL into our MySQL client for further analysis.

Starting with MySQL 5.1.6, the slow query log can be directed to the database table mysql.slow_log. This allows us to more easily access the information from MySQL clients and gives us the power to analyze the information using SQL statements. We enable logging to this table by specifying log_output=TABLE in our initialization file.

About the Upcoming Examples

For every significant tuning principle in the following chapters, we have provided at least one benchmarked example to illustrate the performance gains that can be obtained. However, you should be aware of the following:

- Any example is just that—an example. Your real-life performance might not show the same improvements that we obtained in our tests, and indeed you might find that some of the techniques shown do not work for you at all. Differences in data volumes and distributions, the MySQL version, and the storage engine you are using—as well as many other factors—might result in significantly different outcomes. Nevertheless, the principles we outline are fairly general-purpose and should work for a wide range of applications and data types.

- All of our examples were done using MySQL 5.0 with either the InnoDB or MyISAM storage engine (with the InnoDB engine being our default). Many of the optimizations involved (index merges, for instance) appeared only in 5.0, and you will certainly see different results if you use a different storage engine such as HEAP or BDB.

- We looked only at "standard" SQL that is common to all of the storage engines. We felt that specialized operations—such as full text search or spatial queries—were beyond the scope of this book, since our intention is to provide a foundation in SQL tuning with respect to stored program development only.

We used a Perl program (MyTrace.pl) to perform our tests. This program can take a normal SQL file, such as you might submit to the MySQL command-line client, and it generates several varieties of performance reports that we used to display the execution plans and the performance characteristics of our examples.

We could have used the MySQL command line to do our tests, but we decided to develop this utility for a number of reasons:

- The EXPLAIN output is a bit awkward. When the output is printed one line per row, the output can become garbled when wrapped to the column length. If the output is printed one line per column (with the \G option), then the output appears very verbose. Either way, the output is hard to read. There is also no way to select which columns to display in the output.

- It's rather difficult to obtain the changed values from the SHOW STATUS statement that can reveal useful metrics such as logical or physical reads.

- For benchmarking purposes, we wanted to do things like averaging statistics over a number of executions, measuring statistics only on a second or subsequent execution so as to avoid discrepancies caused by caching of data.

- The utility was capable of generating comma-separated output that we could easily load into Excel to generate charts and perform analyses.

MyTrace.pl provides modified formats for EXPLAIN output and these formats are used throughout the next few chapters. We think you'll find this format easier to read and understand. For instance, whereas in the MySQL command-line client you might generate EXPLAIN output that looks like this:

```
mysql> EXPLAIN EXTENDED SELECT COUNT(*) FROM ta_5000
where sales_id  in (select sales_id from tb_5000)\G
*************************** 1. row ***************************
           id: 1
  select_type: PRIMARY
        table: ta_5000
         type: ALL
possible_keys: NULL
          key: NULL
      key_len: NULL
          ref: NULL
         rows: 5131
        Extra: Using where
*************************** 2. row ***************************
           id: 2
  select_type: DEPENDENT SUBQUERY
        table: tb_5000
         type: ALL
possible_keys: NULL
          key: NULL
      key_len: NULL
          ref: NULL
         rows: 4808
        Extra: Using where
2 rows in set, 1 warning (0.01 sec)
```

we would show the EXPLAIN in a more truncated format, as follows:

```
Short Explain
-------------
```

```
1       PRIMARY select(ALL) on ta_5000 using no key
            Using where
2       DEPENDENT SUBQUERY select(index_subquery) on tb_5000 using i_tb_5000
            Using index
```

or in a more extended format like this:

```
Explain plan
------------

ID=1    Table=a         Select type=SIMPLE      Access type=ALL     Rows=5158
        Key=            (Possible=                      )
        Ref=            Extra=
ID=1    Table=b         Select type=SIMPLE      Access type=ref     Rows=1
        Key=i_tb_5000   (Possible=i_tb_5000             )
        Ref=sqltune.a.SALES_ID      Extra=Using index
```

The output also includes timings for each stage of statement execution and details of any SHOW STATUS variables that changed during execution:

```
Phase       Elapsed (s)

Parse       0.0001
Exec        1.3808
Fetch       0.0001
-----------------
Total       1.3810

Statistic                                       Value
------------------------------------------------------------
Bytes_received                                  99
Bytes_sent                                      4862
Com_select                                      1
Handler_read_first                              1
Handler_read_key                                5003
Handler_read_rnd_next                           5001
Innodb_buffer_pool_pages_data                   57
Innodb_buffer_pool_pages_misc                   7
Innodb_buffer_pool_read_requests                15217
Innodb_buffer_pool_reads                        57
Innodb_data_read                                933888
Innodb_data_reads                               57
Innodb_pages_read                               57
Innodb_rows_read                                10000
Questions                                       2
Select_scan                                     1
Table_locks_immediate                           2
Uptime                                          3
```

You may find the MyTrace.pl utility useful. You can find documentation and download instructions for this utility at this book's web site.

Conclusion

There is nothing to be gained by trying to optimize a stored program without first optimizing the SQL statements that it contains. This chapter, therefore, intended to make you familiar with some basic principles of tuning MySQL stored programs and the SQL statements within those programs. With this knowledge, you will be able to better absorb the more specific tuning advice in the following chapters.

Remember that the performance of individual SQL statements can vary substantially, at least in part depending on whether the statement and/or the data it identifies resides in a MySQL memory cache. For this reason, you should be wary of basing your tuning efforts only on the elapsed time of SQL statements. Consider also calculating the number of logical reads required by your statements, as this will only decrease as efficiency improves. Unfortunately, at the time of writing, you can reliably obtain the logical read rate only from the InnoDB storage engine.

The EXPLAIN statement reveals how MySQL will execute a SQL statement. In order to effectively tune SQL, you need to become familiar with EXPLAIN and adept at interpreting its output.

Indexes exist primarily to improve query performance, so it's not surprising that creating a good set of indexes is the single most important thing you can do to obtain better SQL performance. In particular, you should support WHERE clause conditions and join conditions with appropriate indexes—this often means creating a concatenated ("composite" or multicolumn) index.

Basic SQL Tuning

In this chapter, we will tune of simple SQL statements that may be included in MySQL stored programs. In particular, we'll optimize two of the most often executed SQL operations: retrieving data from a single table and joining two or more tables. Topics include:

- How to determine when the use of an index is required to optimize a query
- How to construct the best indexes to support specific queries
- How MySQL chooses between available indexes, and how to direct MySQL to use a specific index if necessary
- How to avoid "suppressing" an index
- What to do when no index will suffice to optimize a query
- How MySQL processes joins between multiple tables
- How to create indexes that optimize table joins
- How to determine the optimal join order and how to force MySQL to use a particular join order

Chapter 21 builds on these fundamentals, optimizing more complex SQL operations.

Examples in this chapter are based on tables created using the InnoDB storage engine. Although the same MySQL optimizer is used for all storage engines, you may observe different behaviors in other storage engines because of differences in optimizer statistics and indexing approaches.

Tuning Table Access

When retrieving data from a table, MySQL can basically follow one of two paths to locating the relevant rows:

- Read every row in the table concerned (a *full table scan*), and return only those rows that match the WHERE clause criteria.
- Use an index to find a subset of rows, and return the rows that match the WHERE clause criteria.

Unless we need to retrieve a substantial proportion of the rows from a table, we probably want to use an index. It should not come as a big surprise, therefore, that much of this section will address creating the best indexes for our queries.

Index Lookup Versus Full Table Scan

A common mistake made by those new to SQL tuning is to assume that it is *always* better to use an index to retrieve data. Typically, an index lookup requires three or four logical reads for each row returned. If we only have to traverse the index tree a few times, then that will be quicker than reading every row in that table. However, traversing the index tree for a large number of rows in the table could easily turn out to be more expensive than simply reading every row directly from the table.

For this reason, we generally want to use an index only when retrieving a small proportion of the rows in the table. The exact break-even point will depend on your data, your indexes, and maybe even your server configuration, but we have found that a reasonable rule of thumb is to use an index when retrieving no more 5–10% of the rows in a table.

To illustrate this point, consider a scenario in which we are trying to generate sales totals over a particular period of time. To get sales totals for the previous week, for example, we might execute a statement such as the following:

```
SELECT SUM( s.sale_value ),COUNT(*)
  FROM sales s
 WHERE sale_date>date_sub(curdate( ),INTERVAL 1 WEEK);
```

Since we have sales data for many years, we would guess that an index on sales_date would be effective in optimizing this query—and we would be right.

On the other hand, suppose that we want to get the sales totals for the preceding year. The query would look like this:

```
SELECT SUM( s.sale_value ),COUNT(*)
  FROM sales s
 WHERE sale_date>date_sub(curdate( ),INTERVAL 1 YEAR);
```

It is not immediately obvious that an index-driven retrieval would result in the best query performance; it depends on the number of years of data in the table and the relative volume of data for the preceding year. Luckily, MySQL will, in most situations, make a good determination in such cases, provided that you have given MySQL a good set of indexes with which to work.

The MySQL optimizer predicts when to use an index based on the percentage of data from the table it expects to retrieve given our WHERE clause. The optimizer chooses to use the index for small intervals, while relying on a full table scan for large intervals. This basic algorithm works well when the volume of data is evenly distributed for the different indexed values. However, if the data is not evenly distributed, or if the statistics on table sizing are inaccurate, then the MySQL optimizer may make a less than perfect decision.

Figure 20-1 shows the elapsed time for retrieving various proportions of rows when forcing an index scan or a full table scan, or when allowing the MySQL optimizer to make that decision. In this example, MySQL switched from an index scan to a full table scan when the rows returned represented approximately 7% of the total. However, in this case, the index outperformed the table scan until about 17% of the rows were retrieved. So although MySQL made the correct decision in most cases, there were a few cases where forcing an index lookup would have improved performance.

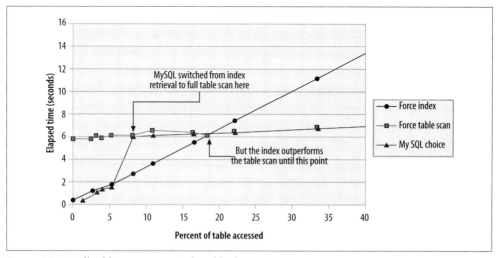

Figure 20-1. Full table scan versus indexed lookup

 As a very rough rule of thumb, you should not expect an index to improve performance unless you are retrieving less than 5–15% of the table data.

There are a number of circumstances in which MySQL might not pick the best possible index. One of these circumstances is when the data is "skewed." In the preceding example, sales were fairly evenly distributed over a five-year period. However, in the real world this is unlikely to be true—sales will be greater during certain periods (Christmas, perhaps) and we might hope that sales would increase over time. This "skewed" table data can make it harder for the MySQL optimizer to make the best decision.

If you think that your data may be skewed and that MySQL may choose a table scan or index inappropriately, you can use the USE INDEX, FORCE INDEX, or IGNORE INDEX optimizer hints, as appropriate, to force or suppress the index. Take care to only use these hints when absolutely necessary, as they can also prevent the MySQL optimizer from selecting the best plan if used inappropriately. These hints are explained in more detail later, in the section "Manually Choosing an Index."

It's also worth noting that it is sometimes possible to resolve a query using an index alone—provided that the index contains all of the columns from the table that are referenced in both the SELECT and WHERE clauses. In this case, the index can be used *in place of the table,* and can perform very efficiently, even when retrieving a very large proportion (or *all*) of the rows in the table. See the section "Covering indexes" later in this chapter for more details.

How MySQL Chooses Between Indexes

In the above examples, MySQL switched between an index and a full table scan as the number of rows to be retrieved increased. This is a pretty neat trick—just how did MySQL work this out?

When you send a SQL statement to the MySQL server, MySQL has to *parse* the statement, which involves all of the following: verify that the SQL syntax is correct; ensure that the user has the necessary authority to run the statement; and determine the exact nature of the data to be retrieved. As part of this process, MySQL determines if any of the indexes defined on the table would help optimize the query.

The MySQL optimizer has a general sense of the "selectivity" of an index—how many rows an average index lookup will return—and of the size of the table. The optimizer examines the index to work out how many rows will have to be used given the values in the WHERE clause and the range of values in the index. MySQL then calculates the relative overhead of using the index and compares this value to the overhead of scanning the full contents of the table.

For most queries, this simple but effective strategy allows MySQL to choose between a full table scan and an indexed lookup, or to choose between multiple candidate indexes.

Manually Choosing an Index

You can add *hints* to your SQL statement to influence how the optimizer will choose between various indexing options. You should only do this if you have determined that MySQL is not making the optimal decision on index utilization. These hints can appear after the table name within the FROM clause. The three hints are:

USE INDEX(*list_of_indexes*)
    Tells MySQL to consider only the indexes listed (i.e., to ignore all other indexes)

IGNORE INDEX(*list_of_indexes*)
    Tells MySQL to ignore any of the listed indexes when determining the execution plan

```
FORCE INDEX(list_of_indexes)
```
Tells MySQL to use one of the listed indexes even if it has determined that a full table scan would be more efficient

For instance, to force the use of an index named sales_i_date, we could write a query as follows:

```
SELECT SUM( s.sale_value ),count(*)
  FROM sales s FORCE INDEX(sales_i_date)
 WHERE sale_date>date_sub(curdate( ),INTERVAL 1 WEEK);
```

Prefixed ("Partial") Indexes

MySQL allows you to create an index based on the first few characters of a column. For instance, the following statement creates an index based on the first four bytes of the customer's address:

```
CREATE INDEX i_cust_name_l4 on customers(address1(4));
```

Partial indexes generally use less storage than "full" indexes, and in some cases may actually improve performance, since a smaller index is more likely to fit into the MySQL memory cache. However, we encourage you to create partial indexes with great care. A very short partial index may actually be worse than no index at all. For very long columns, the partial index might be as good as the full index—it all depends on how many bytes you need to read to get an exact match on the column concerned.

For instance, consider searching for a customer by address, as follows:

```
SELECT *
  FROM customers
 WHERE address1 = '1000 EXCEPTIONABLE STREET';
```

There might be plenty of customers that have an address starting with '1000'. Many fewer will have an address starting with '1000 E', and by the time we extend the search to '1000 EX', we might be matching only a single customer. As we extend the length of the partial index, it becomes more "selective" and more likely to match the performance of a full index.

Figure 20-2 shows the results of doing the above search for various prefix lengths. *For this data*, prefix lengths of 1 or 2 are worse than no index at all; a length of 3 is slightly better than no index; while lengths greater than 3 are quite effective. Once the length hits 6, no further increase in the length of the prefix increased the effectiveness of the index. Remember that the optimum length for your prefixed index depends entirely on the data item you are searching for—in this case, short prefixes did not work well because most addresses started with street numbers that were not very selective. For more selective data—surname for instance—prefixed indexes could be much more effective.

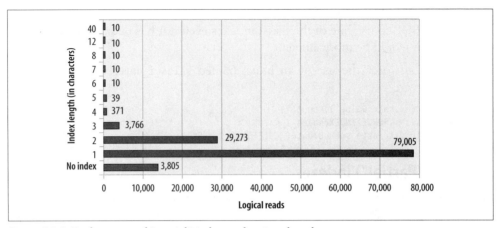

Figure 20-2. Performance of "partial" indexes of various lengths

Concatenated Indexes

A *concatenated index*—often called a *composite index*—is an index that is created on multiple columns. For instance, if we frequently retrieve customers by name and date of birth, we might create an index as follows:

```
CREATE INDEX i_customers_first_surname_dob ON
    customers(contact_surname, contact_firstname,date_of_birth);
```

There is very little chance that two customers would have the same first name, surname, and date of birth, so use of this index would almost always take us to a single, correct customer. If you find that you frequently need to query against the same set of multiple columns' values on a table, then a concatenated index based on those columns should help you optimize your queries.

 If a query references multiple columns from a single table in the WHERE clause, consider creating a concatenated (composite or multicolumn) index on those columns.

For instance, to optimize the following query, we should probably create a concatenated index on customer_id, product_id, and sales_rep_id:

```
SELECT count(*), SUM(quantity)
  FROM sales
 WHERE customer_id=77
   AND product_id=90
   AND sales_rep_id=61;
```

This index would be defined as follows:

```
CREATE INDEX I_sales_cust_prod_rep ON
    sales(customer_id,product_id,sales_rep_id);
```

We can use a concatenated index to resolve queries where only some of the columns in the index are specified, provided that at least one of the "leading" columns in the index is included.

For instance, if we create an index on (surname,firstname,date_of_birth), we can use that index to search on surname or on surname and firstname, but we cannot use it to search on date_of_birth. Given this flexibility, organize the columns in the index in an order that will support the widest range of queries. Remember that you can rarely afford to support all possible indexes because of the overhead indexes add to DML operations—so make sure you pick the most effective set of indexes.

 A concatenated index can support queries that provide a subset of the columns in the index, provided that none of the leading columns is omitted. Pick the order of your columns in the concatenated index carefully to support the widest possible range of queries.

Merging multiple indexes

While a concatenated index on all the columns in the WHERE clause will almost always provide the best performance, sometimes the sheer number of column combinations will prevent us from creating all of the desirable concatenated indexes.

For instance, consider the sales table in our sample database. We may want to support queries based on any combination of customer_id, product_id, and sales_rep_id—that would only require four indexes. Add another column and we would need at least six indexes. All of these indexes take up space in the database and—perhaps worse—slow down inserts, updates, and deletes. Whenever we insert or delete a row, we have to insert or delete the index entry as well. If we update an indexed column, we have to update the index as well.

If you can't create all of the necessary indexes, do not despair. MySQL 5.0 can merge multiple indexes quite effectively. So instead of creating a concatenated index on the three columns, we could create indexes on each of the columns concerned. MySQL will merge rows retrieved from each index to find only those rows matching all conditions.

Index merges can be identified by the index_merge access type in the EXPLAIN statement output. All the indexes being merged will be listed in the keys column, and the Extra column will include a Using intersect clause with the indexes being merged listed. Example 20-1 shows the EXPLAIN output for a query that performs an index merge.

Example 20-1. Example of an index merge

```
SELECT count(*), SUM(quantity)
  FROM sales
 WHERE customer_id=77
   AND product_id=90
```

Example 20-1. Example of an index merge (continued)

```
    AND sales_rep_id=61
```

```
Explain plan
-----------
```

```
ID=1   Table=sales   Select type=SIMPLE   Access type=index_merge   Rows=1
       Possible keys=i_sales_customer,i_sales_product,i_sales_rep
       Key=i_sales_rep,i_sales_customer,i_sales_product Length=9
       Ref=
       Extra=Using intersect(i_sales_rep, i_sales_customer,i_sales_product);
          Using where
```

Not all index merges are equal; just as indexes on different columns will have different performance characteristics (due to their *selectivity*), different combinations of merged indexes will yield the best result. Figure 20-3 shows the performance for the three possible single-column indexes created to support our example query, and shows the performance of each possible merge of two indexes. As you can see, the best result was obtained by merging the two most selective indexes.

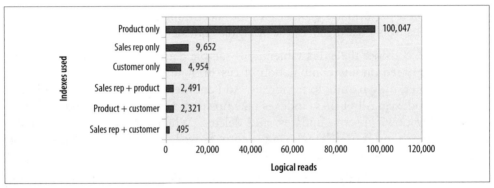

Figure 20-3. Comparison of various single-column indexes and index merge performance

Covering indexes

Creating a *covering index* is a very powerful technique for squeezing the last drop of performance from your indexes. If there are only a few columns in the SELECT clause that are not also in the WHERE clause, you can consider adding these columns to the index. MySQL will then be able to resolve the query using the index alone, avoiding the I/Os involved in retrieving the rows from the table. Such an index is sometimes called a covering index.

For our previous example, if we add the quantity column to the index, our query can be resolved from the index alone. In the EXPLAIN output, the Extra column will include the tag Using index to indicate that the step was resolved using only the index, as in Example 20-2.

Example 20-2. Using a covering index

```
SELECT count(*), SUM(quantity)
  FROM sales
 WHERE customer_id=77
   AND product_id=90
   AND sales_rep_id=61

Explain plan
------------

ID=1   Table=sales Select type=SIMPLE Access type=ref        Rows=1
    Possible keys=i_sales_cust_prod_rep_quant
    Key=i_sales_cust_prod_rep_quant     Length=27
    Ref=const,const,const
    Extra=Using index
```

For queries that retrieve only a single row, the savings gained by covering indexes are probably going to be hard to notice. However, when scanning multiple rows from a table, the cost savings add up rapidly. In fact, it is often quicker to use a covering index to return all the rows from a table than to perform a full table scan. Remember that for normal indexed retrieval, the (very rough) rule of thumb is that the index probably isn't worth using unless you are accessing maybe 10% of the rows in the table. However, a covering index might be appropriate even if all of the rows are being read.

> Covering indexes—which allow a query to be resolved from the index alone—can be efficient even if all or most of a table is being accessed.

Comparing the Different Indexing Approaches

Figure 20-4 summarizes the performance of the various options for resolving our sample query (retrieving sales totals for a specific sales rep, customer, and product). Even for this simple query, there is a wide range of indexing options; in fact, we did not try every possible indexing option. For example, we didn't try a concatenated index on product_id + sales_rep_id.

There are a several key lessons to be learned from these examples:

Not all index plans are equal
> Novice SQL programmers are often satisfied once they see that the EXPLAIN output shows that an index is being used. However, there is a *huge* difference between the performance provided by the "best" and the "worst" index (in this example, the worst index was more than 10,000 times more expensive than the best index!).

Concatenated indexes rule

The best possible index for any particular table access with more than one column in the WHERE clause will almost always be a concatenated index.

Think about over-indexing

If the SELECT list contains only a few columns beyond those in the WHERE clause, it is probably worth adding these to the index.

Remember that indexes come at a cost

Indexes are often essential to achieve decent query performance, but they will slow down every INSERT and DELETE and many UPDATE operations. You need to make sure that every index is "paying its way" by significantly improving query performance.

Rely on merge joins to avoid huge numbers of concatenated indexes

If you have to support a wide range of column combinations in the WHERE clause, create concatenated indexes to support the most common queries, and single-column indexes that can be merged to support less common combinations.

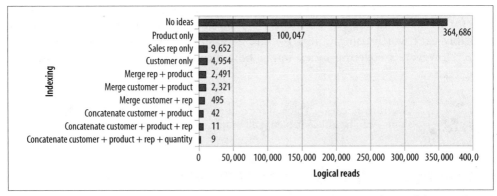

Figure 20-4. Comparison of different indexing techniques when retrieving sales total for specific product, customer, and sales rep

Avoiding Accidental Table Scans

There are a few circumstances in which MySQL might perform a full table scan even if a suitable index exists and perhaps even after you instruct MySQL to use an index with the FORCE INDEX hint. The three main reasons for such "accidental" table scans are:

- You modify an indexed column in the WHERE clause with a function or an operator.
- You are searching for a substring within an indexed column.
- You are using only some of the columns within a concatenated index, and the order of columns in the index does not support searching on the columns you have specified.

Let's look at each situation in the following sections.

Accidentally suppressing an index using a function

One of the most common causes for what might appear to be an inexplicable refusal by MySQL to use an index is some kind of manipulation of the query column.

For instance, let's suppose that we are trying to find all customers that are older than 55 (we might want to target them for a specific sales campaign). We have an index on date_of_birth and the index is certainly selective, but MySQL does not use the index, as shown in Example 20-3.

Example 20-3. Index suppressed by function on query column
```
SELECT *
  FROM customers
 WHERE (datediff(curdate( ),date_of_birth)/365.25) >55

Short Explain
-------------
1    SIMPLE select(ALL) on customers using no key
         Using where
```

The problem here is that by enclosing the date_of_birth column within the DATEDIFF function, we prevent MySQL from looking up values in the index. If we rewrite the query so that the functions are applied to the search value rather than the search column, we see that the index can be used, as shown in Example 20-4.

Example 20-4. Applying a function to the search value does not suppress the index
```
SELECT *
  FROM customers
 WHERE date_of_birth < date_sub(curdate( ),interval 55 year)

Short Explain
-------------
1    SIMPLE select(range) on customers using i_customer_dob
         Using where
```

> Avoid modifying search columns in the WHERE clause with functions or operators, as this could suppress an index lookup. Where possible, modify the search value instead.

Accidentally suppressing an index using a substring

Another way to suppress an index on a column is to search on a nonleading substring of the column. For instance, indexes can be used to find the leading segments of a column, as shown in Example 20-5.

Example 20-5. Indexes can be used to search for a leading portion of a string

```
SELECT *
  FROM customers
 WHERE customer_name like 'HEALTHCARE%'

Short Explain
-------------
1    SIMPLE select(range) on customers using i_customer_name
         Using where
```

But we can't use the index to find text strings in the middle of the column, as demonstrated in Example 20-6.

Example 20-6. Indexes can't be used to find nonleading substrings

```
SELECT * FROM customers WHERE customer_name LIKE '%BANK%'

Short Explain
-------------
1    SIMPLE select(ALL) on customers using no key
         Using where
```

 If you have text strings and need to search for words within those strings, you could consider using the MyISAM full-text search capability. Otherwise, be aware that you can only use indexes to find *leading* substrings within character columns.

Creating concatenated indexes with a poor column order

Another time we might experience an accidental table scan is when we expect a concatenated index to support the query, but we are not specifying one of the leading columns of the index. For instance, suppose that we created an index on customers as follows:

```
CREATE INDEX i_customer_contact
    ON customers(contact_firstname, contact_surname)
```

It might seem natural to create this index with firstname before surname, but that is usually a poor choice, since concatenated indexes can only be used if the leading columns appear in the query, and it is more common to search on surname alone than on firstname alone.

For instance, the index can support a query to find a customer by contact_firstname:

```
SELECT *
  FROM customers
 WHERE contact_firstname='DICK'

Short Explain
-------------
1    SIMPLE select(ref) on customers using i_customer_contact
         Using where
```

But MySQL cannot use the index if only contact_surname is specified:

```
SELECT *
  FROM customers
 WHERE contact_surname='RADFORD'

Short Explain
-------------
1    SIMPLE select(ALL) on customers using no key
         Using where
```

We probably should have created the index as (contact_surname,contact_firstname) if we need to support searching by surname only. If we want to support searching whenever either the surname *or* the firstname appears alone, then we will need an additional index.

 A concatenated index cannot be used to resolve a query unless the leading (first) column in the index appears in the WHERE clause.

Optimizing Necessary Table Scans

We don't necessarily want to avoid a full table scan at all cost. For instance, we might choose not to create an index to support a unique query that only runs once every month if that index would degrade UPDATE and INSERT statements that are being executed many times a second.

Furthermore, sometimes the nature of our queries leaves no alternative to performing a full table scan. For instance, consider an online book store that maintains a database of books in stock. One of the key tables might contain a row for each individual book, as shown in Figure 20-5.

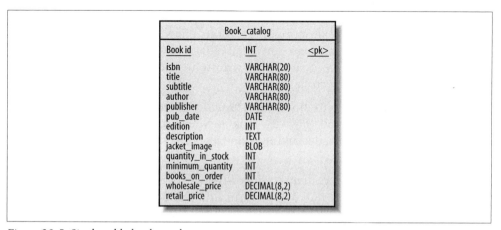

Figure 20-5. Single-table book catalog

Every day, an inventory report is run that summarizes inventory and outstanding orders. The core of the report is the SQL shown in Example 20-7.

Example 20-7. SQL for inventory report example

```
SELECT publisher,
       SUM(quantity_in_stock) on_hand_quantity,
       SUM(quantity_in_stock*wholesale_price) on_hand_value,
       SUM(books_on_order) books_on_order,
       SUM(books_on_order*wholesale_price) order_value
  FROM book_catalog
 GROUP BY publisher


Short Explain
-------------
1    SIMPLE select(ALL) on book_catalog using no key
         Using temporary; Using filesort
```

There is no WHERE clause to optimize with an index, so (we might think) there is no alternative to a full table scan. Nevertheless, the person who determines whether or not we get a raise this year strongly encourages us to improve the performance of the query. So what are we going to do?

If we must read every row in the table, then the path to improved performance is to decrease the size of that table. There are at least two ways of doing this:

- Move any large columns not referenced in the query to another table (provided that this doesn't degrade other critical queries).
- Create an index based on all of the columns referenced in the query. MySQL can then use the index alone to satisfy the query.

Let's consider splitting the table as a first option. We can see in Figure 20-5 that the book_catalog table contains both a BLOB column containing a picture of the book's cover and a TEXT column containing the publisher's description of the book. Both of these columns are large and do not appear in our query. Furthermore, it turns out that these columns are never accessed by a full table scan—the only time the description and cover picture are accessed is when a customer pulls up the details for a single book on the company's web site.

It therefore may make sense to move the BLOB and TEXT columns to a separate table. They can be quickly retrieved via index lookup when required, while their removal will make the main table smaller and quicker to scan. The new two-table schema is shown in Figure 20-6.

Removing the BLOB and TEXT columns reduced the size of the table by about 60% and more than halved the time required to perform a full table scan (see Figure 20-7).

Another option to consider when faced with a seemingly unavoidable full table scan is to create an index on the columns concerned and resolve the query with an index

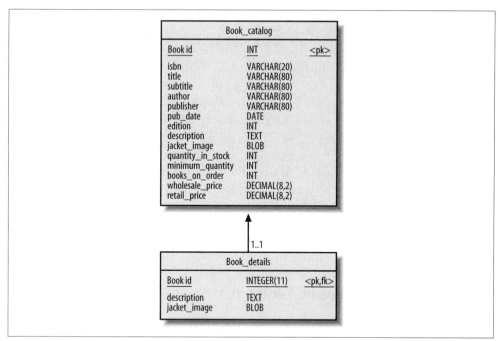

Figure 20-6. Two-column book schema

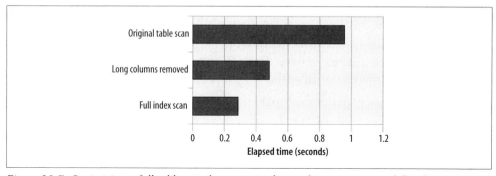

Figure 20-7. Optimizing a full table scan by removing long columns or using a full index scan

scan rather than a table scan. The index is likely to be smaller than the table. For our example report, we could create an index as follows:

```
CREATE INDEX i_book_inventory ON book_catalog
        (publisher,quantity_in_stock,wholesale_price,books_on_order)
```

The EXPLAIN output (which follows) shows that now only the index is used to resolve the query (as shown by the Using index note in the Extra column), and, as we can see in Figure 20-7, this results in even better performance than removing the large columns from the original table.

```
SELECT publisher,
       SUM(quantity_in_stock) on_hand_quantity,
```

```
      SUM(quantity_in_stock*wholesale_price) on_hand_value,
      SUM(books_on_order) books_on_order,
      SUM(books_on_order*wholesale_price) order_value
  FROM book_catalog
GROUP BY publisher

Short Explain
-------------
1    SIMPLE select(index) on book_catalog using i_book_inventory
        Using index
```

One of the reasons that the index performs so well in this case is that MySQL uses the index to optimize the GROUP BY clause. Previous examples all created and sorted temporary tables (shown by Using temporary;using filesort in the EXPLAIN output). Because the leading column of the index was publisher, and because this column is also the column to be sorted to support the GROUP BY clause, no sort was required. We'll discuss the topic of optimizing GROUP BY and ORDER BY using indexes in detail in the next chapter.

Using Merge or Partitioned Tables

Sometimes we are faced with queries that retrieve a proportion of the table that is too high to be optimized by an index, but that is still only a fraction of that table's total. For instance, we might want to optimize a query that retrieves sales data for a particular year. An index to support such a query might return too high a percentage of rows in the table and actually take longer than a full table scan.

One possible way to optimize this scenario is to create a separate table for each year's sales, so that we are able to retrieve data for a particular year from the particular table, thus avoiding the overhead of scanning all of our sales data.

Separate tables for each year would make application code fairly awkward; the programmer would need to know which table to use for a given query, and we would have to provide some way to retrieve data for all years when necessary. To avoid this problem, MyISAM offers *merge tables*. A MyISAM merge table is a logical table that comprises multiple real tables that are UNIONed together. You can insert into a merge table (provided that the INSERT_METHOD is not set to NO), and you can query from it as you would a normal table.

For instance, we could create separate sales tables for each year, as shown in Example 20-8.

Example 20-8. Creating MyISAM merge tables
```
CREATE TABLE SALES2000 TYPE=MYISAM AS
SELECT *
  FROM sales
 WHERE sale_date BETWEEN '2000-01-01' AND '2000-12-31';
```

Example 20-8. Creating MyISAM merge tables (continued)

```
CREATE TABLE SALES2001 TYPE=MYISAM AS
SELECT *
  FROM sales
 WHERE sale_date BETWEEN '2001-01-01' AND '2001-12-31';

 . . . Create other "year" tables . . .
CREATE TABLE all_sales
   (sales_id     INT(8)   NOT NULL PRIMARY KEY,
    . . . Other column definitions . . .
    Gst_flag     NUMERIC(8,0))
 TYPE=MERGE
 UNION=(sales_pre_2000,sales2001,sales2002,
        sales2003,sales2004,sales2005,sales2006)
 INSERT_METHOD=LAST ;
```

If we need to obtain sales data for a particular year, we can do so fairly quickly by accessing one of the merge table's constituents directly. For queries that span year boundaries, we can access the merge table itself. We also have the advantage of being able to purge old rows very quickly by rebuilding the merge table without the unwanted years and then dropping the old table.

However, you should bear in mind that when you access the merge table directly, you will experience an additional overhead as MySQL merges the individual tables into a logical whole. This means that scanning the merge table will take substantially longer than scanning a single table containing all of the necessary data.

In MySQL 5.1 (which is alpha as we finalize this chapter), we can create a partitioned table to provide a similar solution to merge tables, as well as to provide other management and performance advantages. Example 20-9 shows the syntax for creating a MySQL 5.1 partitioned table that is similar to the MyISAM merge table created in the previous example.

Example 20-9. Creating MySQL 5.1 partitioned tables

```
CREATE TABLE sales_partitioned (
   sales_id     INTEGER NOT NULL,
   customer_id  INTEGER NOT NULL,
   product_id   INTEGER NOT NULL,
   sale_date    DATE NOT NULL,
   quantity     INTEGER NOT NULL,
   sale_value   DECIMAL (8,0) NOT NULL
) ENGINE=InnoDB
PARTITION BY RANGE (YEAR(sale_date)) (
  PARTITION p_sales_pre2000 VALUES LESS THAN (2000),
  PARTITION p_sales_2000 VALUES LESS THAN (2001),
  PARTITION p_sales_2001 VALUES LESS THAN (2002),
  PARTITION p_sales_2002 VALUES LESS THAN (2003),
  PARTITION p_sales_2003 VALUES LESS THAN (2004),
  PARTITION p_sales_2004 VALUES LESS THAN (2005),
```

Example 20-9. Creating MySQL 5.1 partitioned tables (continued)

```
  PARTITION p_sales_2005 VALUES LESS THAN (2006),
  PARTITION p_sales_2006 VALUES LESS THAN (2007)
);
```

If we issue a query that requires data from only one of the partitions, MySQL will be able to eliminate unnecessary partitions from the scan, allowing us to rapidly retrieve information for an individual year. Partitioned tables offer a host of other performance advantages, such as rapid purging of stale data, parallel processing of large result sets, and easier distribution of I/O across multiple disk devices. Partitioning is one of the major new features of MySQL 5.1.

Tuning Joins

So far we have looked at tuning SQL queries against a single table only. Let's move on to tuning SQL queries that join rows from two or more tables.

How MySQL Joins Tables

MySQL currently joins tables using a fairly simple technique with a complicated-sounding name. The MySQL manual refers to the join algorithm as *single-sweep multi-join*. In essence, when MySQL joins two tables, it will read the rows from the first table and—for each row—search the second table for matching rows. Further details can be found in the *MySQL Internals Manual*; see *http://dev.mysql.com/doc/internals/en/index-merge-overview.html*.

Joins Without Indexes

The basic join algorithm is not very well suited to joining multiple tables unless there are indexes to support the join.* Performance might be adequate for very small tables, but as table sizes increase, the join overhead will increase rapidly. Even worse, the join overhead will increase almost exponentially.

Figure 20-8 shows how response time increases for nonindexed joins as the size of each table increases. This semi-exponential degradation is extremely undesirable: if we extrapolate the response time curve for larger tables, we predict that it would take 20 minutes to join two tables of 100,000 rows, 20 hours to join two tables with 1 million rows each, and *81 days* to join two tables of 10 million rows each! This is definitely not the way you want your applications to perform as your database grows in size.

---

* We are hoping to see a join algorithm that can perform adequately in the absence of indexes—the hash join algorithm—in MySQL 5.2.

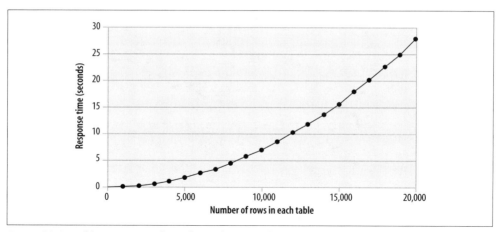

Figure 20-8. Table size versus elapsed time for nonindexed joins

Joins with Indexes

To get predictable and acceptable performance for our join, we need to create indexes to support the join. Generally, we will want to create concatenated indexes based on any columns in a table that might be used to join that table to another table. However, we don't need an index on the first (or "driving") table's columns; that is, if we are joining customers to sales, in that order, then our index needs to be on sales—we don't need an index on both tables.

Creating an index on the join column not only reduces execution time, but also prevents an exponential increase in response time as the tables grow in size. Figure 20-9 shows how the response time increases as the number of rows increases when there is an index to support the join. Not only is performance much better (about 0.1 second compared to more than 25 seconds for two tables of 20,000 rows), but the increase in response time is far more predictable. Extrapolating the response time for the indexed join, we can predict that joining two tables of 10 million rows each could be achieved in only 40 seconds—compared to 81 days for the nonindexed join.[*]

 Unless you are sure that the tables involved will always be very small, always create an index (concatenated, if appropriate) to support a join of one table to another.

---

[*] Joining two very large tables may involve other types of overhead, such as passing the data back to the client and fitting the tables in memory, but the overhead of actually performing the join with the index will be massively less than that of the unindexed join.

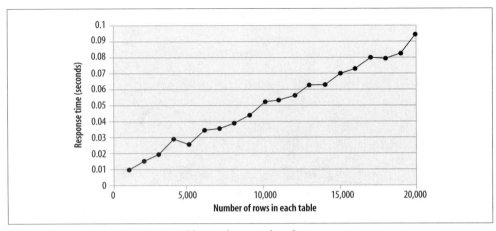

Figure 20-9. Response time versus table size for an indexed join

Join Order

By far, the most important factor in the optimization of MySQL joins is to ensure that each successive join is supported by an index. Beyond that, we should:

- Ensure that any rows to be eliminated by WHERE clause conditions are done so as early as possible in the join.
- Pick an optimal join order. A good rule of thumb is to join tables from smallest to largest.

Generally, the MySQL optimizer can be relied upon to pick a good join order. However, if we need to change the join order, we can use the STRAIGHT_JOIN hint to ensure that the tables are joined in the order in which they appear in the FROM clause. For instance, the following use of STRAIGHT_JOIN ensures that the join order is from the smallest table (ta_1000) to the largest (ta_5000):

```
SELECT STRAIGHT_JOIN count(*)
  FROM ta_1000 JOIN ta_2000 USING (sales_id)
  JOIN ta_3000 USING (sales_id)
  JOIN ta_4000 USING (sales_id)
  JOIN ta_5000 USING (sales_id);
```

Figure 20-10 shows the difference in elapsed time when joining tables in either ascending or descending order of table size. Joining from smallest to largest is about twice as fast as joining from largest to smallest.

 When determining a join order, tables with WHERE clauses that eliminate rows should be introduced to the join as early as possible. After that, try to join tables from smallest to largest.

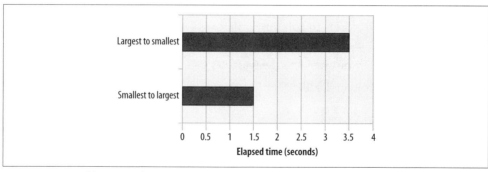

Figure 20-10. Table size and join order

A Simple Join Example

Based on our discussions so far, here is a summary of the most important rules for optimizing MySQL joins:

- Ensure that every join is supported by an index.
- Eliminate rows as early as possible in the join sequence.
- Join tables from smallest to largest.

Let's apply these rules to a simple example.

Consider the case in which we are listing all sales for a particular customer. The query looks like this:

```
SELECT SUM(sale_value)
  FROM sales JOIN customers
    ON (sales.customer_id=customers.customer_id)
 WHERE customer_name='LARSCOM INC'
```

With just the primary key indexes in place, the EXPLAIN output looks like this:

```
Short Explain
-------------
1    SIMPLE select(ALL) on sales using no key
1    SIMPLE select(eq_ref) on customers using PRIMARY
          Using where
```

This execution plan satisfies our first rule: an index (the primary key customer_id of customers) is used to join sales to customers.

However, our second rule—eliminating rows as early as possible in the join sequence—is violated: all of the sales rows are read first, even though only some of those sales (those for a particular customer) are needed. Furthermore, we are joining the larger table sales (2.5 million rows) to the smaller table customers (100,000 rows).

So, what we need to achieve is an efficient join from customers to sales. This means indexing the sales.customer_id column so that we can find sales for a particular customer. The following index should do the trick:

```
CREATE INDEX i_sales_customer ON sales(customer_id)
```

The execution plan now looks like this:

```
Short Explain
-------------
1    SIMPLE select(ALL) on customers using no key
         Using where
1    SIMPLE select(ref) on sales using i_sales_customer
         Using where
```

This is better, but we could improve matters further if we did not have to do the full scan on customers. Adding the following index will let us obtain the desired customer more efficiently:

```
CREATE INDEX i_customer_name ON customers(customer_name)
```

Once this is done, the execution plan looks like this:

```
Short Explain
-------------
1    SIMPLE select(ref) on customers using i_customer_name
         Using where; Using index
1    SIMPLE select(ref) on sales using i_sales_customer
         Using where
```

This is the optimal execution plan for this query. The desired customer is found quickly by the index, and then matching sales for that customer are found using the i_sales_customer index. Figure 20-11 shows the performance improvements gained by our optimizations.

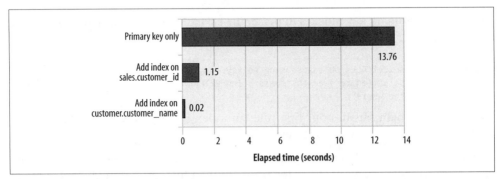

Figure 20-11. Optimization of a simple join

Conclusion

In this chapter we examined some of the basic principles for tuning simple SQL statements. Tuning SQL inside of MySQL stored programs is probably the single most important thing we can do to avoid poorly performing stored programs.

For SQL statements that retrieve a small proportion of the rows from a table (say, 5 to 15%), you will probably want to create indexes to obtain good performance. Here are some best practice guidelines for creating indexes:

- Create concatenated indexes that include all of the columns referenced in the WHERE clause.

- Consider adding additional columns that appear in the SELECT list to allow for an "index only" access path.

- Create concatenated indexes to support the widest possible range of queries—concatenated indexes can be used for queries that reference only a subset of the columns in the index, provided that the "leading" columns are in the WHERE clause. This means that you should put the most commonly used columns first in the index.

- If the number of concatenated indexes needed to support all possible queries is too large (say five or more), create single-column indexes on selective columns that MySQL can merge.

MySQL can join large tables effectively only if an index exists on the join columns for at least one of the tables being joined. To optimize basic joins:

- Create a concatenated index on all of the columns used to join the two tables.

- Make sure that any WHERE clause conditions are executed before the tables are joined. That is, the "driving table" should be the table that has the most selective condition in the WHERE clause. This will create the most efficient join.

- Provided that joins are supported by indexes and that WHERE clause conditions are processed in the first few tables to be joined, be aware that the best join order will be from smallest table to largest table.

CHAPTER 21

Advanced SQL Tuning

In the last chapter, we emphasized that high-performance stored programs require optimized SQL statements. We then reviewed the basic elements of SQL tuning—namely, how to optimize single-table accesses and simple joins. These operations form the building blocks for more complex SQL operations.

In this chapter, we will look at optimizing such SQL operations as:

- Subqueries using the IN and EXISTS operators
- "Anti-joins" using NOT IN or NOT EXISTS
- "Unamed" views in FROM clauses
- Named or permanent views
- DML statements (INSERT, UPDATE, and DELETE)

Tuning Subqueries

A *subquery* is a SQL statement that is embedded within the WHERE clause of another statement. For instance, Example 21-1 uses a subquery to determine the number of customers who are also employees.

Example 21-1. SELECT statement with a subquery

```
SELECT COUNT(*)
  FROM customers
 WHERE (contact_surname, contact_firstname,date_of_birth)
    IN (select surname,firstname,date_of_birth
          FROM employees)
```

We can identify the subquery through the DEPENDENT SUBQUERY tag in the Select type column of the EXPLAIN statement output, as shown here:

```
Explain plan
------------

ID=1    Table=customers      Select type=PRIMARY            Access type=ALL
        Rows=100459
        Key=                 (Possible=                              )
        Ref=                  Extra=Using where
ID=2    Table=employees      Select type=DEPENDENT SUBQUERY   Access type=ALL
        Rows=1889
        Key=                 (Possible=                              )
        Ref=                  Extra=Using where
```

The same query can also be rewritten as an EXISTS subquery, as in Example 21-2.

Example 21-2. SELECT statement with an EXISTS subquery

```
SELECT count(*)
  FROM customers
 WHERE EXISTS (SELECT 'anything'
                 FROM employees
                where surname=customers.contact_surname
                  AND firstname=customers.contact_firstname
                  AND date_of_birth=customers.date_of_birth)

Short Explain
-------------
1    PRIMARY select(ALL) on customers using no key
          Using where
2    DEPENDENT SUBQUERY select(ALL) on employees using no key
```

Note that the EXPLAIN output for the EXISTS subquery is identical to that of the IN subquery. This is because MySQL rewrites IN-based subqueries as EXISTS-based syntax before execution. The performance of subqueries will, therefore, be the same, regardless of whether you use the EXISTS or the IN operator.

Optimizing Subqueries

When MySQL executes a statement that contains a subquery in the WHERE clause, it will execute the subquery once for every row returned by the main or "outer" SQL statement. It therefore follows that the subquery had better execute very efficiently: it is potentially going to be executed many times. The most obvious way to make a subquery run fast is to ensure that it is supported by an index. Ideally, we should create a concatenated index that includes every column referenced within the subquery.

For our example query in the previous example, we should create an index on all the employees columns referenced in the subquery:

```
CREATE INDEX i_customers_name ON customers
  (contact_surname, contact_firstname, date_of_birth)
```

We can see from the following EXPLAIN output that MySQL makes use of the index to resolve the subquery. The output also includes the Using index clause, indicating that *only* the index is used—the most desirable execution plan for a subquery.

```
Short Explain
-------------
1    PRIMARY select(ALL) on employees using no key
         Using where
2    DEPENDENT SUBQUERY select(index_subquery) on customers
           using i_customers_name
         Using index; Using where
```

Figure 21-1 shows the relative performance of both the EXISTS and IN subqueries with and without an index.

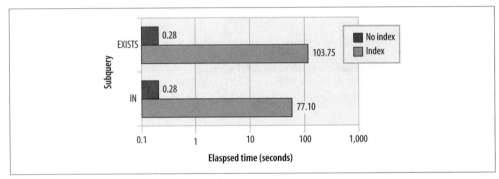

Figure 21-1. Subquery performance with and without an index

Not only will an indexed subquery outperform a nonindexed subquery, but the unindexed subquery will also degrade exponentially as the number of rows in each of the tables increases. (The response time will actually be proportional to the number of rows returned by the outer query times the number of rows accessed in the subquery.) Figure 21-2 shows this exponential degradation.

Subqueries should be optimized by creating an index on all of the columns referenced in the subquery. SQL statements containing subqueries that are not supported by an index can show exponential degradation as table row counts increase.

Rewriting a Subquery as a Join

Many subqueries can be rewritten as joins. For instance, our example subquery could have been expressed as a join, as shown in Example 21-3.

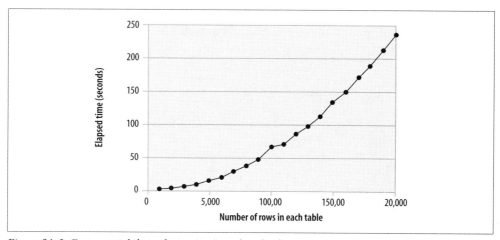

Figure 21-2. *Exponential degradation in nonindexed subqueries*

Example 21-3. *Subquery rewritten as a join*
```
SELECT count(*)
  FROM customers JOIN employees
    ON (employees.surname=customers.contact_surname
        AND employees.firstname=customers.contact_firstname
        AND employees.date_of_birth=customers.date_of_birth)
```

Subqueries sometimes result in queries that are easier to understand, and when the subquery is indexed, the performance of both types of subqueries and the join is virtually identical, although, as described in the previous section, EXISTS has a small advantage over IN. Figure 21-3 compares the three solutions for various sizes of tables.

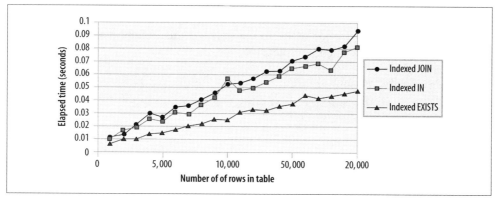

Figure 21-3. *IN, EXISTS, and JOIN solution scalability (indexed query)*

However, when no index exists to support the subquery or the join, then the join will outperform both IN and EXISTS subqueries. It will also degrade less rapidly as the number of rows to be processed increases. This is because of the MySQL join optimizations. Figure 21-4 shows the performance characteristics of the three solutions where no index exists.

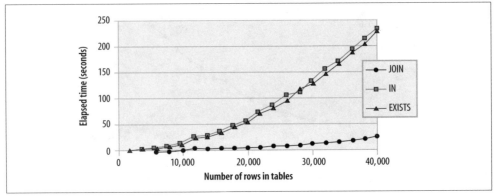

Figure 21-4. Comparison of nonindexed JOIN, IN, and EXISTS performance

 A join will usually outperform an equivalent SQL with a subquery—and will show superior scalability—if there is no index to support either the join or the subquery. If there are supporting indexes, the performance differences among the three solutions are negligible.

Using Subqueries in Complex Joins

Although a subquery, in general, will not outperform an equivalent join, there are occasions when you can use subqueries to obtain more favorable execution plans for complex joins—especially when index merge operations are concerned.

Let's look at an example. You have an application that from time to time is asked to report on the quantity of sales made to a particular customer by a particular sales rep. The SQL might look like Example 21-4.

Example 21-4. Complex join SQL

```
SELECT COUNT(*), SUM(sales.quantity), SUM(sales.sale_value)
  FROM sales
  JOIN customers ON (sales.customer_id=customers.customer_id)
  JOIN employees ON (sales.sales_rep_id=employees.employee_id)
  JOIN products  ON (sales.product_id=products.product_id)
 WHERE customers.customer_name='INVITRO INTERNATIONAL'
   AND employees.surname='GRIGSBY'
   AND employees.firstname='RAY'
   AND products.product_description='SLX';
```

We already have an index on the primary key columns for customers, employees, and products, so MySQL uses these indexes to join the appropriate rows from these tables to the sales table. In the process, it eliminates all of the rows except those that match the WHERE clause condition:

```
Short Explain
-------------
1     SIMPLE select(ALL) on sales using no key

1     SIMPLE select(eq_ref) on employees using PRIMARY
          Using where
1     SIMPLE select(eq_ref) on customers using PRIMARY
          Using where
1     SIMPLE select(eq_ref) on products using PRIMARY
          Using where
```

This turns out to be a fairly expensive query, because we have to perform a full scan of the large sales table. What we probably want to do is to retrieve the appropriate primary keys from products, customers, and employees using the WHERE clause conditions, and then look up those keys (quickly) in the sales table. To allow us to quickly find these primary keys, we would create the following indexes:

```
CREATE INDEX i_customer_name ON customers(customer_name);
CREATE INDEX i_product_description ON products(product_description);
CREATE INDEX i_employee_name ON employees(surname, firstname);
```

To enable a rapid sales table lookup, we would create the following index:

```
CREATE INDEX i_sales_cust_prod_rep ON sales(customer_id,product_id,sales_rep_id);
```

Once we do this, our execution plan looks like this:

```
Short Explain
-------------
1     SIMPLE select(ref) on customers using i_customer_name
          Using where; Using index
1     SIMPLE select(ref) on employees using i_employee_name
          Using where; Using index
1     SIMPLE select(ref) on products using i_product_description
          Using where; Using index
1     SIMPLE select(ref) on sales using i_sales_cust_prod_rep
          Using where
```

Each step is now based on an index lookup, and the sales lookup is optimized through a fast concatenated index. The execution time reduces from about 25 seconds (almost half a minute) to about 0.01 second (almost instantaneous).

 To optimize a join, create indexes to support all of the conditions in the WHERE clause and create concatenated indexes to support all of the join conditions.

As we noted in the previous chapter, we can't always create all of the concatenated indexes that we might need to support all possible queries on a table. In this case, we may want to perform an "index merge" of multiple single-column indexes. However, MySQL will not normally perform an index merge when optimizing a join.

In this case, to get an index merge join, we can try to rewrite the join using subqueries, as shown in Example 21-5.

Example 21-5. Complex join SQL rewritten to support index merge

```
SELECT COUNT(*), SUM(sales.quantity), SUM(sales.sale_value)
  FROM sales
 WHERE product_id= (SELECT product_id
                      FROM products
                     WHERE product_description='SLX')
   AND sales_rep_id=(SELECT employee_id
                       FROM employees
                      WHERE surname='GRIGSBY'
                        AND firstname='RAY')
   AND customer_id= (SELECT customer_id
                       FROM customers
                      WHERE customer_name='INVITRO INTERNATIONAL');
```

The EXPLAIN output shows that an index merge will now occur, as shown in Example 21-6.

Example 21-6. EXPLAIN output for an index merge SQL

```
Short Explain
-------------
1    PRIMARY select(index_merge) on sales using i_sales_rep,i_sales_cust
        Using intersect(i_sales_rep,i_sales_cust); Using where
4    SUBQUERY select(ref) on customers using i_customer_name

3    SUBQUERY select(ref) on employees using i_employee_name

2    SUBQUERY select(ref) on products using i_product_description
```

The performance of the index merge solution is about 0.025 second—slower than the concatenated index but still about 1,000 times faster than the initial join performance. This is an especially useful technique if you have a *STAR schema* (one very large table that contains the "facts," with foreign keys pointing to other, smaller "dimension" tables).

Figure 21-5 compares the performance of the three approaches. Although an index merge is not quite as efficient as a concatenated index, you can often satisfy a wider range of queries using an index merge, since this way you need only create indexes on each column, not concatenated indexes on every possible combination of columns.

 Rewriting a join with subqueries can improve join performance, especially if you need to perform an index merge join—consider this technique for STAR joins.

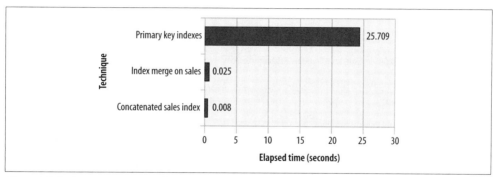

Figure 21-5. Optimizing a complex join with subqueries and index merge

Tuning "Anti-Joins" Using Subqueries

With an *anti-join*, we retrieve all rows from one table for which there is no matching row in another table. There are a number of ways of expressing anti-joins in MySQL.

Perhaps the most natural way of writing an anti-join is to express it as a NOT IN subquery. For instance, Example 21-7 returns all of the customers who are not employees.

Example 21-7. Example of an anti-join using NOT IN

```
SELECT count(*)
  FROM customers
 WHERE (contact_surname,contact_firstname, date_of_birth)
    NOT IN (SELECT surname,firstname, date_of_birth
              FROM employees)


Short Explain
-------------
1    PRIMARY select(ALL) on customers using no key
          Using where
2    DEPENDENT SUBQUERY select(ALL) on employees using no key
          Using where
```

Another way to express this query is to use a NOT EXISTS subquery. Just as MySQL will rewrite IN subqueries to use the EXISTS clause, so too will MySQL rewrite a NOT IN subquery as a NOT EXISTS. So, from MySQL's perspective, Example 21-7 and Example 21-8 are equivalent.

Example 21-8. Example of an anti-join using NOT EXISTS

```
SELECT count(*)
  FROM customers
 WHERE NOT EXISTS (SELECT *
                     FROM employees
                    WHERE surname=customers.contact_surname
                      AND firstname=customers.contact_firstname
                      AND date_of_birth=customers.date_of_birth)
```

Example 21-8. Example of an anti-join using NOT EXISTS (continued)

```
Short Explain
-------------
1    PRIMARY select(ALL) on customers using no key
          Using where
2    DEPENDENT SUBQUERY select(ALL) on employees using no key
          Using where
```

A third but somewhat less natural way to express this query is to use a LEFT JOIN. This is a join in which all rows from the first table are returned even if there is no matching row in the second table. NULLs are returned for columns from the second table that do not have a matching row.

In Example 21-9 we join customers to employees and return NULL values for all of the employees who are not also customers. We can use this characteristic to eliminate the customers who are not also employees by testing for a NULL in a normally NOT NULL customer column.

Example 21-9. Example of an anti-join using LEFT JOIN

```
SELECT count(*)
  FROM customers
      LEFT JOIN employees
        ON (customers.contact_surname=employees.surname
           and customers.contact_firstname=employees.firstname
           and customers.date_of_birth=employees.date_of_birth)
  WHERE employees.surname IS NULL

Short Explain
-------------
1    SIMPLE select(ALL) on customers using no key

1    SIMPLE select(ALL) on employees using no key
          Using where; Not exists
```

Optimizing an Anti-Join

The guidelines for optimizing anti-joins using subqueries or left joins are identical to the guidelines for optimizing normal subqueries or joins. Scalability and good performance will be achieved only if we create an index to optimize the subquery or the join. For the previous examples, this would mean creating an index on customer names as follows:[*]

```
CREATE INDEX i_customers_name ON employees(surname,firstname,date_of_birth);
```

---

[*] It might occur to you that creating an index on customers would produce a better join than the index on employees. However, LEFT JOINs can only be performed with the table that will return all rows as the first table in the join—this means that the join order can only be customers to employees, and therefore the index to support the join must be on employees.

Figure 21-6 shows the massive performance improvements that result when we create a supporting index for an anti-join.

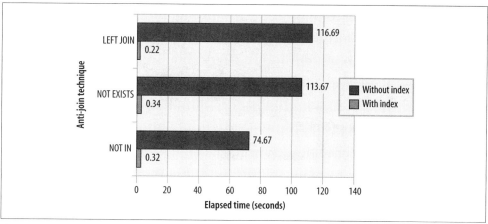

Figure 21-6. Comparison of anti-join techniques

Figure 21-6 also shows a substantial performance advantage for the NOT IN subquery over NOT EXISTS or LEFT JOIN when there is no index to support the anti-join. We noted earlier that MySQL rewrites the NOT IN-based statement to a NOT EXISTS, so it is at first surprising that there should be a performance difference. However, examination of the NOT IN rewrite reveals a number of undocumented compiler directives within the rewritten SQL that appear to give NOT IN a substantial performance advantage in the absence of an index.

Not only is the LEFT JOIN technique slower than NOT IN or NOT EXISTS, but it degrades much faster as the quantity of data to be processed increases. Figure 21-7 shows that the LEFT JOIN version of the anti-join degrades much more rapidly as the size of the tables being joined increases—this is the opposite of the effect shown for normal subqueries, where the join solution was found to be more scalable than the subquery solution (refer to Figure 21-3).

 To optimize an anti-join, create indexes to support the subquery or right hand table of a LEFT JOIN. If you cannot support the subquery with an index, use NOT IN in preference to NOT EXISTS or LEFT JOIN.

Tuning Subqueries in the FROM Clause

It is possible to include subqueries within the FROM clause of a SQL statement. Such subqueries are sometimes called *unnamed views*, *derived tables*, or *inline views*.

For instance, consider the query in Example 21-10, which retrieves a list of employees and department details for employees older than 55 years.

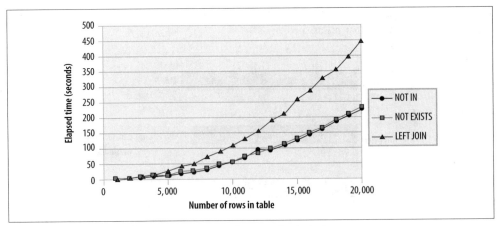

Figure 21-7. Scalability of various anti-join techniques (no index)

Example 21-10. Example SQL suitable for rewrite with an inline view

```
SELECT departments.department_name,employee_id,surname,firstname
  FROM departments
       JOIN employees
       USING (department_id)
 WHERE employees.date_of_birth<date_sub(curdate( ),interval 55 year)
```

```
Short Explain

1    SIMPLE select(range) on employees using i_employee_dob
         Using where
1    SIMPLE select(eq_ref) on departments using PRIMARY
         Using where
```

This query is well optimized—an index on date of birth finds the customers, and the primary key index is used to find the department name on the departments table. However, we could write this query using inline views in the FROM clause, as shown in Example 21-11.

Example 21-11. SQL rewritten with an inline view

```
SELECT departments.department_name,employee_id,surname,firstname
  FROM (SELECT * FROM departments ) departments
       JOIN (SELECT * FROM employees) employees
       USING (department_id)
 WHERE employees.date_of_birth<DATE_SUB(curdate( ), INTERVAL 55 YEAR)
```

```
Explain plan

1    PRIMARY select(ALL) on <derived2> using no key

1    PRIMARY select(ALL) on <derived3> using no key
         Using where
3    DERIVED select(ALL) on employees using no key

2    DERIVED select(ALL) on departments using no key
```

This execution plan is somewhat different from those we have looked at in previous examples, and it warrants some explanation. The first two steps indicate that a join was performed between two "derived" tables—our subqueries inside the FROM clause. The next two steps show how each of the derived tables was created. Note that the name of the table—<derived2>, for instance—indicates the ID of the step that created it. So we can see from the plan that <derived2> was created from a full table scan of departments.

Derived tables are effectively temporary tables created by executing the SQL inside the subquery. You can imagine that something like the following SQL is being executed to create the <derived2> table:

```
CREATE TEMPORARY TABLE derived2 AS
SELECT * FROM departments
```

Simply by using subqueries in the FROM clause, we have substantially weakened MySQL's chances of implementing an efficient join. MySQL must first execute the subqueries' statements to create the derived tables and then join those two derived tables. Derived tables have no indexes, so this particular rewrite could not take advantage of the indexes that were so effective in our original query (shown in Example 21-10). In this case, both the index to support the WHERE clause and the index supporting the join were unusable.

We could improve the query by moving the WHERE clause condition on employees into the subquery, as shown in Example 21-12.

Example 21-12. Rewritten SQL using an inline view

```
SELECT departments.department_name,employee_id,surname,firstname
  FROM (SELECT * FROM departments ) departments
  JOIN (SELECT * FROM employees
        WHERE employees.date_of_birth
              <DATE_SUB(curdate( ),INTERVAL 55 YEAR)) employees
 USING (department_id)

Explain plan
------------

1    PRIMARY select(system) on <derived3> using no key

1    PRIMARY select(ALL) on <derived2> using no key
        Using where
3    DERIVED select(range) on employees using i_employee_dob
        Using where
4    DERIVED select(ALL) on departments using no key
```

This plan at least allows us to use an index to find the relevant customers, but still prevents the use of an index to join those rows to the appropriate department.

In general, avoid using derived tables (subqueries in the FROM clause), because the resulting temporary tables have no indexes and cannot be effectively joined or searched. If you must use derived tables, try to move all WHERE clause conditions inside of the subqueries.

Using Views

A view can be thought of as a "stored query". A view definition essentially creates a named definition for a SQL statement that can then be referenced as a table in other SQL statements. For instance, we could create a view on the sales table that returns only sales for the year 2004, as shown in Example 21-13.

Example 21-13. View to return sales table data for 2004

```
CREATE OR REPLACE VIEW v_sales_2004
       (sales_id,customer_id,product_id,sale_date,
        quantity,sale_value,department_id,sales_rep_id,gst_flag) AS
SELECT sales_id,customer_id,product_id,sale_date,
       quantity,sale_value,department_id,sales_rep_id,gst_flag
  FROM sales
 WHERE sale_date BETWEEN '2004-01-01' AND '2004-12-31'
```

The CREATE VIEW syntax includes an ALGORITHM clause, which defines how the view will be processed at runtime:

```
CREATE [ALGORITHM = {UNDEFINED | MERGE | TEMPTABLE}] VIEW viewname
```

The view algorithm may be set to one of the following:

TEMPTABLE

> MySQL will process the view in very much the same way as a derived table—it will create a temporary table using the SQL associated with the view, and then use that temporary table wherever the view name is referenced in the original query.

MERGE

> MySQL will attempt to merge the view SQL into the original query in an efficient manner.

UNDEFINED

> Allows MySQL to choose the algorithm, which results in MySQL using the MERGE technique when possible.

Because the TEMPTABLE algorithm uses temporary tables—which will not have associated indexes—its performance will often be inferior to native SQL or to SQL that uses a view defined with the MERGE algorithm.

Consider the SQL query shown in Example 21-14; it uses the view definition from Example 21-13 and adds some additional WHERE clause conditions. The view WHERE clause, as well as the additional WHERE clauses in the SQL, is supported by the index i_sales_date_prod_cust, which includes the columns customer_id, product_id, and sale_date.

Example 21-14. SQL statement that references a view

```
SELECT  SUM(quantity),SUM(sale_value)
  FROM v_sales_2004_merge
 WHERE customer_id=1
   AND product_id=1;
```

This query could have been written in standard SQL, as shown in Example 21-15.

Example 21-15. Equivalent SQL statement without a view

```
SELECT SUM(quantity),SUM(sale_value)
  FROM sales
 WHERE sale_date BETWEEN '2004-01-01' and '2004-12-31'
   AND customer_id=1
   AND product_id=1
```

Alternately, we could have written the SQL using a derived table approach, as shown in Example 21-16.

Example 21-16. Equivalent SQL statement using derived tables

```
SELECT SUM(quantity),SUM(sale_value)
  from (SELECT *
          FROM sales
         WHERE sale_date BETWEEN '2004-01-01' AND '2004-12-31') sales
 WHERE customer_id=1
   AND product_id=1;
```

We now have four ways to resolve the query—using a MERGE algorithm view, using a TEMPTABLE view, using a derived table, and using a plain old SQL statement. So which approach will result in the best performance?

Based on our understanding of the TEMPTABLE and MERGE algorithms, we would predict that a MERGE view would behave very similarly to the plain old SQL statement, while the TEMPTABLE algorithm would behave similarly to the derived table approach. Furthermore, we would predict that neither the TEMPTABLE nor the derived table approach would be able to leverage our index on product_id, customer_id, and sale_date, and so both will be substantially slower.

Our predictions were confirmed. The SQLs that used the TEMPTABLE and the derived table approaches generated very similar EXPLAIN output, as shown in Example 21-17. In each case, MySQL performed a full scan of the sales table in order to create a temporary "derived" table containing data for 2004 only, and then performed a full scan of that derived table to retrieve rows for the appropriate product and customer.

Example 21-17. Execution plan for the derived table and TEMPTABLE view approaches

```
Short Explain
-------------
1    PRIMARY select(ALL) on <derived2> using no key
        Using where
2    DERIVED select(ALL) on sales using no key
        Using where
```

An `EXPLAIN EXTENDED` revealed that the `MERGE` view approach resulted in a rewrite against the sales table, as shown in Example 21-18.

Example 21-18. How MySQL rewrote the SQL to "merge" the view definition

```
SELECT sum(`prod`.`sales`.`QUANTITY`) AS `SUM(quantity)`,
        sum(`prod`.`sales`.`SALE_VALUE`) AS `SUM(sale_value)`
  FROM `prod`.`sales`
 WHERE ((`prod`.`sales`.`CUSTOMER_ID` = 1)
   AND (`prod`.`sales`.`PRODUCT_ID` = 1)
   AND (`prod`.`sales`.`SALE_DATE` between 20040101000000 and 20041231000000))

Short Explain
-------------
1    PRIMARY select(range) on sales using i_sales_cust_prod_date
        Using where
```

Figure 21-8 shows the performance of the four approaches. As expected, the `MERGE` view gave equivalent performance to native SQL and was superior to both the `TEMPTABLE` and the derived table approaches.

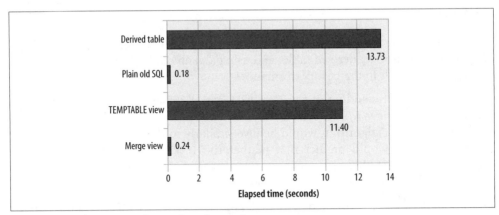

Figure 21-8. Comparison of view algorithm performance

Not all views can be resolved by a `MERGE` algorithm. In particular, views that include `GROUP BY` or other aggregate conditions (`DISTINCT`, `SUM`, etc.) must be resolved through a temporary table. It is also possible that in some cases the "merged" SQL generated by MySQL might be hard to optimize and that a temporary table approach might lead to better performance.

 Views created with the TEMPTABLE algorithm may be unable to take advantage of indexes that are available to views created with the MERGE algorithm. Avoid using views that employ the TEMPTABLE algorithm unless you find that the "merged" SQL cannot be effectively optimized.

Tuning ORDER and GROUP BY

GROUP BY, ORDER BY, and certain group functions (MAX, MIN, etc.) may require that data be sorted before being returned to the user. You can detect that a sort is required from the Using filesort tag in the Extra column of the EXPLAIN statement output, as shown in Example 21-19.

Example 21-19. Simple SQL that performs a sort

```
SELECT *
  FROM customers
 ORDER BY contact_surname, contact_firstname

Explain plan
------------

ID=1     Table=customers   Select type=SIMPLE  Access type=ALL
         Rows=101999
         Key=            (Possible=                          )
         Ref=              Extra=Using filesort
```

If there is sufficient memory, the sort can be performed without having to write intermediate results to disk. However, without sufficient memory, the overhead of the disk-based sort will often dominate the overall performance of the query.

There are two ways to avoid a disk-based sort:

- Create an index on the columns to be sorted. MySQL can then use the index to retrieve the rows in sorted order.
- Allocate more memory to the sort.

These approaches are described in the following sections.

Creating an Index to Avoid a Sort

If an index exists on the columns to be sorted, MySQL can use the index to avoid a sort. For instance, suppose that the following index exists:

```
CREATE INDEX i_customer_name ON customers(contact_surname, contact_firstname)
```

MYSQL can use that index to avoid the sort operation shown in Example 21-19. Example 21-20 shows the output when the index exists; note the absence of the Using filesort tag and that the i_customer_name index is used, even though there are no WHERE clause conditions that would suggest that the index was necessary.

Example 21-20. Using an index to avoid a sort

```
SELECT * from customers
 ORDER BY contact_surname, contact_firstname

Explain plan
------------

ID=1    Table=customers          Select type=SIMPLE
        Access type=index        Rows=101489
        Key=i_customer_name      (Possible=                    )
        Ref=                          Extra=
```

Reducing Sort Overhead by Increasing Sort Memory

When MySQL performs a sort, it first sorts rows within an area of memory defined by the parameter SORT_BUFFER_SIZE. If the memory is exhausted, it writes the contents of the buffer to disk and reads more data into the buffer. This process is continued until all the rows are processed; then, the contents of the disk files are merged and the sorted results are returned to the query. The larger the size of the sort buffer, the fewer the disk files that need to be created and then merged. If the sort buffer is large enough, then the sort can complete entirely in memory.

You can allocate more memory to the sort by issuing a SET SORT_BUFFER_SIZE statement. For instance, the following allocates 10,485,760 bytes (10M) to the sort:

```
SET SORT_BUFFER_SIZE=10485760;
```

You can determine the current value of SORT_BUFFER_SIZE by issuing the following statement:

```
SHOW VARIABLES LIKE 'sort_buffer_size';
```

As you allocate more memory to the sort, performance will initially improve up to the point at which the sort can complete within a single "merge run." After that point, adding more memory appears to have no effect, until the point at which the sort can complete entirely in memory. After this point, adding more memory will not further improve sort performance. Figure 21-9 shows where these two plateaus of improvement occurred for the example above. It also shows the effect of creating an index to avoid the sort altogether.

To find out how many sort merge runs were required to process our SQL, we can examine the value for the status variable SORT_MERGE_PASSES from the SHOW STATUS statement before and after our SQL executes.

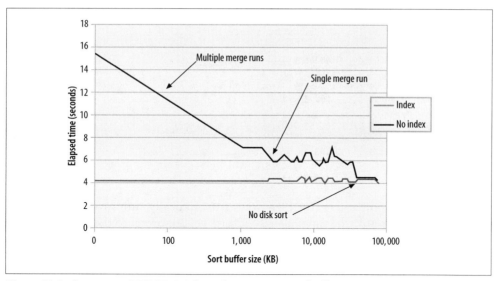

Figure 21-9. Optimizing ORDER BY through increasing sort buffer size or creating an index

> To optimize SQL that must perform a sort (ORDER BY, GROUP BY), con-
> sider increasing the value of SORT_BUFFER_SIZE or create an index on
> the columns being sorted.

Tuning DML (INSERT, UPDATE, DELETE)

The first principle for optimizing UPDATE, DELETE, and INSERT statements is to optimize any WHERE clause conditions used to find the rows to be manipulated or
inserted. The DELETE and UPDATE statements may contain WHERE clauses, and the
INSERT statement may contain SQL that defines the data to be inserted. Ensure that
these WHERE clauses are efficient—perhaps by creating appropriate concatenated
indexes.

The second principle for optimizing DML performance is to avoid creating *too many*
indexes. Whenever a row is inserted or deleted, updates must occur to every index
that exists against the table. These indexes exist to improve query performance, but
bear in mind that each index also results in overhead when the row is created or
deleted. For updates, only the indexes that reference the specific columns being modified need to be updated.

Batching Inserts

The MySQL language allows more than one row to be inserted in a single INSERT
operation. For instance, the statement in Example 21-21 inserts five rows into the
clickstream_log table in a single call.

Example 21-21. Batch INSERT statement

```
INSERT INTO clickstream_log (url,timestamp,source_ip)
values
  ('http://dev.mysql.com/downloads/mysql/5.0.html',
   '2005-02-10 11:46:23','192.168.34.87') ,
  ('http://dev.mysql.com/downloads/mysql/4.1.html',
   '2005-02-10 11:46:24','192.168.35.78'),
  ('http://dev.mysql.com',
  '2005-02-10 11:46:24','192.168.35.90'),
  ('http://www.mysql.com/bugs',
   '2005-02-10 11:46:25','192.168.36.07'),
  ('http://dev.mysql.com/downloads/mysql/5.1.html',
   '2005-02-10 11:46:25','192.168.36.12')
```

Batching INSERT operations in this way can radically improve performance. Figure 21-10 shows how the time taken to insert 10,000 rows into the table decreases as we increase the number of rows included within each INSERT statement. Inserting one row at a time, it took about 384 seconds to insert the rows. When inserting 100 rows at a time, we were able to add the same number of rows in only 7 seconds.

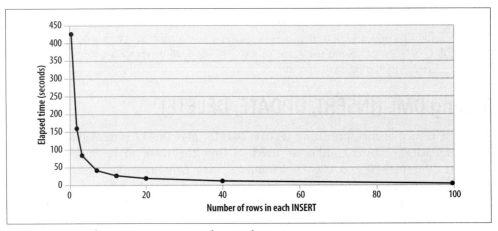

Figure 21-10. Performance improvement from multirow inserts

 Whenever possible, use MySQL's multirow insert feature to speed up the bulk loading of records.

Optimizing DML by Reducing Commit Frequency

If we are using a transactional storage engine—for instance, if our tables are using the InnoDB engine—we should make sure that we are committing changes to the database only when necessary. Excessive commits will degrade performance.

By default, MySQL will issue an implicit commit after every SQL statement. When a commit occurs, a storage engine like InnoDB will write a record to its transaction log on disk to ensure that the transaction is persistent (i.e., to ensure that the transaction will not be lost if MySQL or our program crashes). These transaction log writes involve a physical I/O to the disk and therefore always add to our response time.

We can prevent this automatic commit behavior by issuing the SET AUTOCOMMIT=0 statement and/or by issuing a START TRANSACTION statement before issuing our statements. We can then issue a COMMIT statement at regular intervals, reducing the number of writes to the transaction log that will be required. (Note, though, that MySQL will occasionally write to the transaction log anyway when memory buffers require flushing.)

Usually, the frequency with which we commit is driven by our application logic rather than by performance. For instance, if a user clicks a Save button in our application, he is going to expect that the information will be permanently saved to the database, and so we will be required to issue a COMMIT as a result. However, in batch applications, we can often choose to commit at relatively infrequent intervals. Reducing the commit frequency can have a huge effect on DML performance.

In Figure 21-11, we see how reducing the commit frequency affected the time taken to insert 10,000 rows into the database. At the default settings, it took about 850 seconds (about 14 minutes) to insert the 10,000 rows. If we commit only after every 100 rows have been inserted, the time taken is reduced to only 8 seconds.

In these tests, the InnoDB transaction log was on the same disk as the InnoDB tablespace files, which magnified the degradation caused by transaction log writes. Moving the transaction log to a dedicated disk can reduce—although not eliminate—the transaction log overhead.

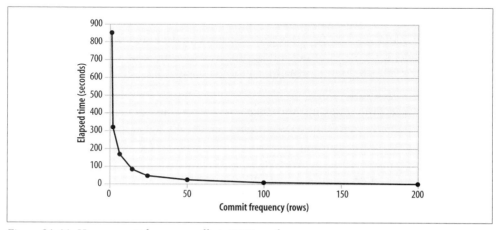

Figure 21-11. How commit frequency affects DML performance

When you are using a transactional storage engine (such as InnoDB) in situations where your application logic permits (batch applications, for instance), reducing the frequency at which you commit work can massively improve the performance of INSERTs, UPDATEs, and DELETEs.

We looked at how you can manipulate commit frequency in stored programs in Chapter 8.

Triggers and DML Performance

Because trigger code will be invoked for every row affected by the relevant DML operation, poorly performing triggers can have a very significant effect on DML performance. If our DML performance is a concern and there are triggers on the tables involved, we may want to determine the overhead of our triggers by measuring performance with and without the triggers.

We provide some more advice on trigger tuning in Chapter 22.

Conclusion

In this chapter, we looked at some more advanced SQL tuning scenarios.

We first looked at simple subqueries using the IN and EXISTS operators. As with joins and simple single-table queries, the most important factor in improving subquery performance is to create indexes that allow the subqueries to execute quickly. We also saw that when an appropriate index is not available, rewriting the subquery as a join can significantly improve performance.

The anti-join is a type of SQL operation that returns all rows from a table that do not have a matching row in a second table. These can be performed using NOT IN, NOT EXISTS, or LEFT JOIN operations. As with other subqueries, creating an index to support the subquery is the most important optimization. If no index exists to support the anti-join, then a NOT IN subquery will be more efficient than a NOT EXISTS or a LEFT JOIN.

We can also place subqueries in the FROM clause—these are sometimes referred to as *inline views, unnamed views,* or *derived tables*. Generally speaking, we should avoid this practice because the resulting "derived" tables will have no indexes and will perform poorly if they are joined to another table or if there are associated selection criteria in the WHERE clause. Named views are a much better option, since MySQL can "merge" the view definition into the calling query, which will allow the use of indexes if appropriate. However, views created with the TEMPTABLE option, or views that cannot take advantage of the MERGE algorithm (such as GROUP BY views), will exhibit similar performance to derived table queries.

When our SQL has an ORDER BY or GROUP BY condition, MySQL might need to sort the resulting data. We can tell if there has been a sort by the Using filesort tag in the Extra column of the EXPLAIN statement output. Large sorts can have a diabolical effect on our query performance, although we can improve performance by increasing the amount of memory available to the sort (by increasing SORT_BUFFER_SIZE). Alternately, we can create an index on the columns to be sorted. MySQL can then use that index to avoid the sort and thus improve performance.

We can achieve substantial improvements in performance by inserting multiple rows with each INSERT statement. If we are using a transactional storage engine such as InnoDB, we can improve the performance of any DML operations by reducing the frequency with which we commit data. However, we should never modify commit frequency at the expense of transactional integrity.

Most of our stored programs will perform only as well as the SQL that they contain. In the next chapter we will look at how to go the "last mile" by tuning the stored program code itself.

## CHAPTER 22

Optimizing Stored Program Code

In this chapter, we look at techniques for optimizing the stored program code itself.

As we have said before, the performance of a typical stored program will primarily depend on the performance of the SQL in that stored program. This is why we have devoted several chapters to showing how to tune MySQL SQL statements.

As with any language, however, it is possible to write inefficient code in the MySQL stored program language itself. So in this chapter, we're going to assume that we have tuned our stored program's SQL statements and are now ready to tune the stored program code.

Before we dig into tuning stored program code we will briefly review the performance characteristics of stored programs and look at the circumstances under which stored programs can improve application performance. For example, under certain circumstances, we can use a stored program *in place of* SQL statements that are difficult to optimize. Stored programs can also improve the performance of network-intensive operations. However, note that stored programs are not, in general, a good solution when we want to do mathematically intensive computation.

Performance Characteristics of Stored Programs

MySQL stored programs can often add to application functionality and developer efficiency, and there are certainly many cases where the use of a procedural language such as the MySQL stored program language can do things that a nonprocedural language like SQL cannot. There are also a number of reasons why a MySQL stored program approach may offer performance improvements over a traditional SQL approach:

It provides a procedural approach

> SQL is a declarative, nonprocedural language: this means that in SQL you don't specify how to retrieve data—you only specify the data that you want to retrieve (or change). It's up to MySQL itself—specifically, the MySQL query optimizer—to determine how to go about identifying the result set.

From time to time, we might have a very good idea about the most efficient way to retrieve the data, but find that the MySQL optimizer chooses another—less efficient—path.

When we think we know how the data should be retrieved but can't get the optimizer to play ball, we can sometimes use MySQL stored programs to force the desired approach.

It reduces client-server traffic

In a traditional SQL-based application, SQL statements and data flow back and forth between the client and the server. This traffic can cause delays even when both the client and the server programs are on the same machine. If the client and server are on different machines, then the overhead is even higher.

We can use MySQL stored programs to eliminate much of this overhead, particularly when we need to execute a series of related SQL statements. A succinct message is sent from the client to the server (the stored program execution request) and a minimal response is sent from the server to the client (perhaps only a return code). Furthermore, we can take advantage of database triggers to automatically execute statements in the database without any network interaction at all.

The resulting reduction in network traffic can significantly enhance performance.

It allows us to divide and conquer complex statements

As SQL statements become more complex, they also get harder and harder to fully optimize, both for the MySQL optimizer and for the programmer. We have all seen (and some of us have written) massive SQL statements with multiple subqueries, UNION operations, and complex joins. Tuning these "monster" SQL statements can be next to impossible for both humans and software optimizers.

It's often a winning strategy to break these massive SQL statements into smaller individual statements and optimize each individually. For instance, subqueries could be run outside of the SQL statement and the results forwarded to subsequent steps as query parameters or through temporary tables.

Having said that, we don't want to give you the impression that we think you should rewrite all of your non-trivial SQL statements in MySQL stored programs. In fact, it is usually the case that if you can express your needs in "straight" SQL, that will be the most efficient approach. And do remember that complex arithmetic computations will usually be slower in a stored program than in an equivalent SQL statement.

How Fast Is the Stored Program Language?

It would be terribly unfair of us to expect the first release of the MySQL stored program language to be blisteringly fast. After all, languages such as Perl and PHP have been the subject of tweaking and optimization for about a decade, while the latest generation of programming languages—.NET and Java—have been the subject of a shorter but more intensive optimization process by some of the biggest software companies in the world. So right from the start, we expected that the MySQL stored program language would lag in comparison with the other languages commonly used in the MySQL world.

Still, we felt it was important to get a sense of the raw performance of the language. So we put together a number of test scripts. First off, we wanted to see how quickly the stored program language could crunch numbers. Stored programs generally do not perform computationally expensive operations, but—given that you sometimes have a choice between various application tiers when performing some computationally intensive task—it's worth knowing if the stored program language is up to the job.

To test basic compute performance, we wrote a stored program that determines the number of prime numbers less than a given input number. (We're sure that some of you will know better algorithms, but remember that the point is to compare languages, not to calculate prime numbers in the most efficient manner possible.) The stored program is shown in Example 22-1.

Example 22-1. Stored program to find prime numbers

```
CREATE PROCEDURE sp_nprimes(p_num int)
BEGIN
    DECLARE i INT;
    DECLARE j INT;
    DECLARE nprimes INT;
    DECLARE  isprime INT;

    SET i=2;
    SET nprimes=0;

    main_loop:
    WHILE (i<p_num) do
        SET isprime=1;
        SET j=2;
        divisor_loop:
        WHILE (j<i) DO
            IF (MOD(i,j)=0) THEN
                SET isprime=0;
                LEAVE divisor_loop;
            END IF;
            SET j=j+1;
        END WHILE ;
        IF (isprime=1) THEN
            SET nprimes=nprimes+1;
        END IF;
        SET i=i+1;
    END WHILE;
    SELECT CONCAT(nprimes,' prime numbers less than ',p_num);
END;
```

We implemented this algorithm in a variety of languages—C, Java, VB.NET, Perl, PHP, and PL/SQL (the Oracle stored program language). For instance, the Oracle implementation of the procedure is shown in Example 22-2; as you can see, while some of the language constructs differ, the algorithms are identical.

Example 22-2. Oracle implementation of the prime number procedure

```
PROCEDURE N_PRIMES
   ( p_num NUMBER)
   IS

   i INT;
   j INT;
   nprimes INT;
   isprime INT;

BEGIN

   i:=2;
   nprimes:=0;

   <<main_loop>>
   WHILE (i<p_num) LOOP
       isprime:=1;
       j:=2;
       <<divisor_loop>>
       WHILE (j<i) LOOP
           IF (MOD(i,j)=0) THEN
               isprime:=0;
               EXIT divisor_loop;
           END IF;
           j:=j+1;
       END LOOP ;
       IF (isprime=1) THEN
           nprimes:=nprimes+1;
       END IF;
       i:=i+1;
   END LOOP;
   dbms_output.put_line(nprimes||' prime numbers less than '||p_num);
END;
```

We executed each program multiple times to seek the number of prime numbers less than 8000. The results are shown in Figure 22-1. We ran these tests on the same machine and did our best to minimize any interference from other running programs and, in every other way, to keep the playing field level. Nevertheless, for this computationally intensive trial, MySQL performed poorly compared with other languages—twice as slow as an Oracle stored procedure, five times slower than PHP or Perl, and dozens of times slower than Java, .NET, or C. Remember that Oracle in particular has been optimizing its stored procedure language for over a decade now; in comparison with the initial releases of PL/SQL, the MySQL stored program language is a speed demon!

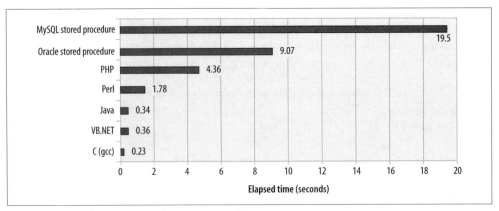

Figure 22-1. Finding prime numbers in various languages

We are confident that the MySQL stored program language will become more efficient in future releases, but for now we recommend that you avoid using this language for mathematically intensive operations.

> The MySQL stored program language is relatively slow when it comes to performing arithmetic calculations. Avoid using stored programs to perform number crunching.

Reducing Network Traffic with Stored Programs

If the previous section left you feeling less than enthusiastic about stored program performance, this section should cheer you right up. Although stored programs aren't particularly zippy when it comes to number crunching, you don't normally write stored programs that simply perform math—stored programs almost always process data from the database. In these circumstances, the difference between stored program and (for instance) Java performance is usually minimal—unless network overhead is a big factor. When a program is required to process large numbers of rows from the database, a stored program can substantially outperform programs written in client languages, because it does not have to wait for rows to be transferred across the network—the stored program runs inside the database.

Consider the stored program shown in Example 22-3; this stored program retrieves all sales rows for the past five months and generates some statistical measurements (mean and standard deviation) against those rows.

Example 22-3. Stored program to generate statistics

```
CREATE PROCEDURE sales_summary()
    READS SQL DATA
BEGIN
```

Example 22-3. Stored program to generate statistics (continued)

```
        DECLARE SumSales    FLOAT DEFAULT 0;
        DECLARE SumSquares  FLOAT DEFAULT 0;
        DECLARE NValues     INT   DEFAULT 0;
        DECLARE SaleValue   FLOAT DEFAULT 0;
        DECLARE Mean        FLOAT;
        DECLARE StdDev      FLOAT;

        DECLARE last_sale INT DEFAULT 0;

        DECLARE sale_csr CURSOR FOR
         SELECT sale_value FROM SALES s
          WHERE sale_date >date_sub(curdate( ),INTERVAL 6 MONTH);

        DECLARE CONTINUE HANDLER FOR NOT FOUND SET last_sale=1;

        OPEN sale_csr;
        sale_loop: LOOP
            FETCH sale_csr INTO SaleValue;
            IF last_sale=1 THEN LEAVE sale_loop; END IF;

            SET NValues=NValues+1;
            SET SumSales=SumSales+SaleValue;
                SET SumSquares=SumSquares+POWER(SaleValue,2);

        END LOOP sale_loop;
        CLOSE sale_csr;

        SET StdDev = SQRT((SumSquares - (POWER(SumSales,2) / NValues)) / NValues);
        SET Mean = SumSales / NValues;

        SELECT CONCAT('Mean=',Mean,' StdDev=',StdDev);

END
```

Example 22-4 shows the same logic implemented in a Java program.

Example 22-4. Java program to generate sales statistics

```java
import java.sql.*;
import java.math.*;

public class SalesSummary {

    public static void main(String[] args)
        throws ClassNotFoundException, InstantiationException,
                IllegalAccessException  {
        String Username=args[0];
        String Password=args[1];
        String Hostname=args[2];
        String Database=args[3];
        String Port=args[4];
```

Example 22-4. Java program to generate sales statistics (continued)

```java
        float SumSales,SumSquares,SaleValue,StdDev,Mean;
        int    NValues=0;

    SumSales=SumSquares=0;

    try
    {
        Class.forName("com.mysql.jdbc.Driver").newInstance( );
        String ConnString=
          "jdbc:mysql://"+Hostname+":"+Port+
                "/"+Database+"?user="+Username+"&password="+Password;
        Connection MyConnect = DriverManager.getConnection(ConnString);

        String sql="select sale_value from SALES s" +
                    " where sale_date >date_sub(curdate( ),interval 6 month)";

        Statement s1=MyConnect.createStatement( );
        ResultSet rs1=s1.executeQuery(sql);
        while (rs1.next( ))
        {
            SaleValue = rs1.getFloat(1);
            NValues = NValues + 1;
            SumSales = SumSales + SaleValue;
            SumSquares = SumSquares + SaleValue*SaleValue;
        }
        rs1.close( );

        Mean=SumSales/NValues;
        StdDev = (float) Math.sqrt((((SumSquares -
                    ((SumSales*SumSales) / NValues)) / NValues));

        System.out.println("Mean="+Mean+" StdDev="+StdDev+" N="+NValues);

    }
    catch(SQLException Ex)           {
            System.out.println(Ex.getErrorCode()+" "+Ex.getMessage( ));
            Ex.printStackTrace( );}

  }
}
```

As we saw earlier in this chapter, Java is much, much faster than the MySQL stored program language when it comes to performing calculations. Therefore, we expect that the Java program would be faster in this case as well. In fact, when we run the Java program on the same host as the relevant MySQL server, the Java program is faster—though not by much: the Java program completed in about 22 seconds while the stored program took about 26 seconds (see Figure 22-2). Although Java is faster than the stored program when it comes to performing the arithmetic calculations needed, the bulk of the time is spent retrieving rows from the database, and so the difference is not very noticeable.

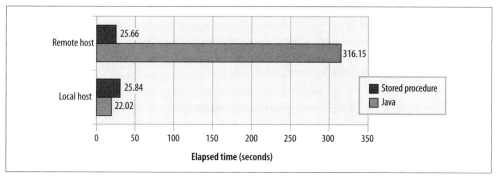

Figure 22-2. Java versus stored program performance across the network

However, when we invoke each program from a remote host across a network with relatively high latency, we see that while the stored program execution time stays the same, the Java program takes *much* longer to execute (increasing from 22 seconds to 5 minutes). The Java program has to fetch each row from the database across the network, and these network round-trips dominate the overall execution time. The lesson is clear: if your program causes a large amount of network traffic, such as those that fetch or change a large number of rows across the network, a stored program can outperform a program written in a client language such as Java or PHP.

 Stored programs do not incur the network overhead of languages such as PHP or Java. If network overhead is an issue, then using a stored program can be an effective optimization.

Stored Programs as an Alternative to Expensive SQL

Sometimes we can use a stored program to perform query or DML operations that perform badly in standard SQL. This usually happens when the "pure" SQL statement becomes overly complex because of limitations in the SQL syntax or when the MySQL optimizer isn't able to come up with a sensible plan for your SQL query. In this section we offer two scenarios in which a stored program can be expected to outperform a SQL statement that executes the same logical steps.

Avoid Self-Joins with Procedural Logic

One situation in which a stored program might offer a better solution is where you are forced to construct a query that joins a table to itself in order to filter for the required rows. For instance, in Example 22-5, we issue a SQL statement that retrieves the most valuable order for each customer over the past few months.

Example 22-5. Finding the maximum sale for each customer

```sql
SELECT s.customer_id,s.product_id,s.quantity, s.sale_value
  FROM sales s, (SELECT customer_id,max(sale_value) max_sale_value
                  FROM sales
                GROUP BY customer_id) t
 WHERE t.customer_id=s.customer_id
   AND t.max_sale_value=s.sale_value
   AND s.sale_date>date_sub(currdate(),interval 6 month);
```

This is an expensive SQL statement, partially because we first need to create a temporary table to hold the customer ID and maximum sale value and then join that back to the sales table to find the full details for each of those rows.

MySQL doesn't provide SQL syntax that would allow us to return this data without an expensive self-join. However, we can use a stored program to retrieve the data in a single pass through the sales table. Example 22-6 shows a stored program that stores maximum sales for each customer into a temporary table (max_sales_by_ customer) from which we can later select the results.

Example 22-6. Stored program to return maximum sales for each customer over the last 6 months

```
1    CREATE PROCEDURE sp_max_sale_by_cust()
2        MODIFIES SQL DATA
3    BEGIN
4        DECLARE last_sale INT DEFAULT 0;
5        DECLARE l_last_customer_id INT DEFAULT -1;
6        DECLARE l_customer_id INT;
7        DECLARE l_product_id INT;
8        DECLARE l_quantity INT;
9        DECLARE l_sale_value DECIMAL(8,2);
10       DECLARE counter INT DEFAULT 0;
11
12       DECLARE sales_csr CURSOR FOR
13           SELECT customer_id,product_id,quantity, sale_value
14             FROM sales
15            WHERE sale_date>date_sub(currdate(),interval 6 month)
16            ORDER BY customer_id,sale_value DESC;
17
18       DECLARE CONTINUE HANDLER FOR NOT FOUND SET last_sale=1;
19
20       OPEN sales_csr;
21       sales_loop: LOOP
22           FETCH sales_csr INTO l_customer_id,l_product_id,l_quantity,l_sale_value;
23           IF (last_sale=1) THEN
24               LEAVE sales_loop;
25           END IF;
26
27           IF l_customer_id <> l_last_customer_id THEN
28               /* This is a new customer so first row will be max sale*/
29               INSERT INTO max_sales_by_customer
30                   (customer_id,product_id,quantity,sale_value)
```

Example 22-6. Stored program to return maximum sales for each customer over the last 6 months (continued)

```
31                        VALUES(l_customer_id,l_product_id,l_quantity,l_sale_value);
32          END IF;
33
34          SET l_last_customer_id=l_customer_id;
35
36    END LOOP;
37
38    END;
```

Let's look at the most significant lines in this program:

Line(s)	Explanation
12	Declare a cursor that will return sales for the past 6 months ordered by `customer_id` and then by descending `sale_value`.
27-32	Check to see whether we have encountered a new `customer_id`. The first row for any given customer will be the maximum sale for that customer, so we insert that row into a temporary table (line 30).

The stored program is significantly faster than the standard SQL solution. Figure 22-3 shows the elapsed time for the two solutions.

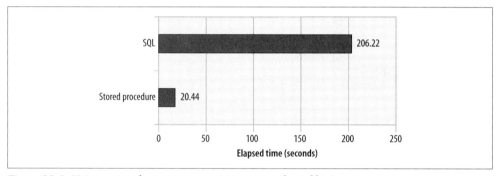

Figure 22-3. Using a stored program to optimize a complex self-join

Optimize Correlated Updates

A correlated update is an UPDATE statement that contains a correlated subquery in the SET clause and/or WHERE clause. Correlated updates are often good candidates for optimization through procedural execution. In Example 22-7 we have an UPDATE statement that updates all customers who are also employees, and assigns the employee's manager as their sales representative.

Example 22-7. Correlated UPDATE statement

```
UPDATE customers c
   SET sales_rep_id =
       (SELECT manager_id
          FROM employees
              WHERE surname = c.contact_surname
```

Example 22-7. Correlated UPDATE statement (continued)

```
        AND firstname = c.contact_firstname
        AND date_of_birth = c.date_of_birth)
WHERE (contact_surname,
      contact_firstname,
      date_of_birth) IN
  (SELECT surname, firstname, date_of_birth
    FROM employees and );
```

Note that the UPDATE statement needs to access the employees table twice: once to identify customers who are employees and again to find the manager's identifier for those employees.

Example 22-8 offers a stored program that provides an alternative to the correlated update. The stored program identifies those customers who are also employees using a cursor. For each of the customers retrieved by the cursor, an UPDATE is issued.

Example 22-8. Stored program alternative to the correlated update

```
CREATE PROCEDURE sp_correlated_update( )
    MODIFIES SQL DATA
BEGIN
    DECLARE last_customer INT DEFAULT 0;
    DECLARE l_customer_id INT ;
    DECLARE l_manager_id  INT;

    DECLARE cust_csr CURSOR FOR
          select c.customer_id,e.manager_id
            from customers c,
                 employees e
          where e.surname=c.contact_surname
            and e.firstname=c.contact_firstname
            and e.date_of_birth=c.date_of_birth;

    DECLARE CONTINUE HANDLER FOR NOT FOUND SET last_customer=1;

    OPEN cust_csr;
    cust_loop: LOOP
          FETCH cust_csr INTO l_customer_id,l_manager_id;
          IF (last_customer=1) THEN
              LEAVE cust_loop;
          END IF;
          UPDATE customers
        SET sales_rep_id=l_manager_id
      WHERE customer_id=l_customer_id;
    END LOOP;

END;
```

Because the stored program does not have to do two separate accesses of the customers table, it is significantly faster than the standard SQL. Figure 22-4 compares the performance of the two approaches.

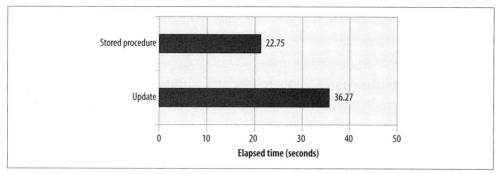

Figure 22-4. Performance of a correlated update and stored program alternative

Optimizing Loops

In the remainder of this chapter we will look at techniques for the optimization of stored program code that does *not* involve SQL statements, starting with the optimization of loops.

Because the statements executed within a loop can be executed many times, optimizing loop processing is a basic step when optimizing the performance of a program written in any language. The MySQL stored program language is no exception.

Move Unnecessary Statements Out of a Loop

The first principle of optimizing a loop is to move calculations out of the loop that don't belong inside the loop (these are known as *loop-invariant statements*, since they do not vary with each execution of the loop body). Although such a step might seem obvious, it's surprising how often a program will perform calculations over and over within a loop that could have been performed just once before the start of loop execution.

For instance, consider the stored program in Example 22-9. This loop is actually fairly inefficient, but at first glance it's not easy to spot where the problem is. Fundamentally, the problem with this stored program is that it calculates the square root of the i variable for every value of the j variable. Although there are only 1,000 different values of i, the stored program calculates this square root five *million* times.

Example 22-9. A poorly constructed loop

```
WHILE (i<=1000) DO
    SET j=1;
    WHILE (j<=5000) DO
        SET rooti=sqrt(i);
        SET rootj=sqrt(j);
        SET sumroot=sumroot+rooti+rootj;
        SET j=j+1;
```

Example 22-9. A poorly constructed loop (continued)

```
        END WHILE;
        SET i=i+1;
    END WHILE;
```

By moving the calculation of the square root of i outside of the loop—as shown in Example 22-10—we substantially reduce the overhead of this loop.

Example 22-10. Moving unnecessary calculations out of a loop

```
    WHILE (i<=1000) DO
        SET rooti=sqrt(i);
        SET j=1;
        WHILE (j<=5000) DO
            SET rootj=sqrt(j);
            SET sumroot=sumroot+rootj+rooti;
            SET j=j+1;
        END WHILE;
        SET i=i+1;
    END WHILE;
```

Figure 22-5 shows the performance improvements achieved from moving the calculation of the square root of the i variable outside of the inner loop.

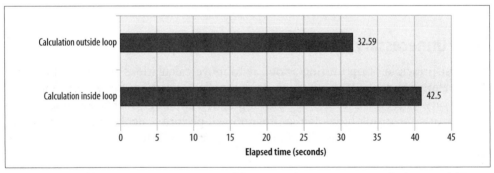

Figure 22-5. Performance improvements gained from removing unnecessary calculations within a loop

 Ensure that all statements within a loop truly belong within the loop. Move any loop-invariant statements outside of the loop.

Use LEAVE or CONTINUE to Avoid Needless Processing

Just as it is important to remove all unnecessary processing from a loop, it is equally important to leave the loop when you are finished. Again, this seems obvious, but it is easy to write a fully functional loop that performs unnecessary iterations. When you look at your code, it's not always that obvious that the loop is inefficient.

Consider the loop shown in Example 22-11: this is a variation on the loop used in Example 22-1 to count prime numbers. This loop is functionally correct, but inefficient. On line 2 we cycle through all numbers less than the given number looking for divisors. If we find a divisor (line 4), we know that the number is not a prime number. However, in Example 22-11, we continue to check each number even though we have already found the first divisor. This is unnecessary, since once we find even a single divisor, we know that the number is not prime—there is no need to look for further divisors.

Example 22-11. Loop that iterates unnecessarily

```
1        divisor_loop:
2        WHILE (j<i) do  /* Look for a divisor */
3
4            IF (MOD(i,j)=0) THEN
5                SET isprime=0;   /* This number is not prime*/
6            END IF;
7            SET j=j+1;
8        END WHILE ;
```

Example 22-12 shows the same loop, but with a LEAVE statement added that terminates the loop once a divisor is found.

Example 22-12. Loop with a LEAVE statement to avoid unnecessary iterations

```
        divisor_loop:
        WHILE (j<i) do  /* Look for a divisor */

            IF (MOD(i,j)=0) THEN
                SET isprime=0;   /* This number is not prime*/
                LEAVE divisor_loop; /* No need to keep checking*/
            END IF;
            SET j=j+1;
        END WHILE ;
```

Although the LEAVE statement terminates the loop and reduces the elapsed time for the stored procedure, it may decrease readability of the code because the loop now has two sections that determine if the loop continues—the WHILE clause condition and the LEAVE statement. Constructing a loop with multiple exit points makes the code harder to understand and maintain.

It would be equally valid in this case to modify the WHILE clause so that the loop ceases its repetitions once it has determined that the number is not a prime, as shown in Example 22-13.

Example 22-13. Modifying the WHILE condition to avoid unnecessary iterations

```
        divisor_loop:
        WHILE (j<i AND isprime=1) do  /* Look for a divisor */

            IF (MOD(i,j)=0) then
```

```
            SET isprime=0;    /* This number is not prime*/
        END IF;
        SET j=j+1;
    END WHILE ;
```

Figure 22-6 shows the improvements gained in our prime number search when we add the LEAVE statement or modify the WHILE clause. Modifying the WHILE clause leads to a comparable performance increase without reducing the readability of the loop.

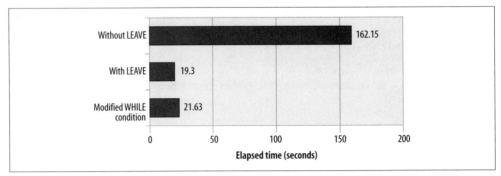

Figure 22-6. Effect of using LEAVE or modifying WHILE clause to avoid unnecessary iterations

Make sure that your loops terminate when all of the work has been done, either by ensuring that the loop continuation expression is comprehensive or—if necessary—by using a LEAVE statement to terminate when appropriate.

IF and CASE Statements

Another category of statement that is highly amenable to code optimization is the conditional statement category—IF and CASE statements. This is especially true if these statements are called repetitively within a loop. The essence of optimizing conditional statements like IF and CASE is to reduce the number of comparisons that are performed. You can do this by:

- Testing for the more likely matches earlier in the IF or CASE statement
- Stopping the comparison process as early as possible

Test for the Most Likely Conditions First

When constructing IF and CASE statements, try to minimize the number of comparisons that these statements are likely to make by testing for the most likely scenarios first. For instance, consider the IF statement shown in Example 22-14. This statement maintains counts of various percentages. Assuming that the input data is evenly distributed, the first IF condition (percentage>95) will match about once in every 20 executions. On the other hand, the final condition will match in three out of four executions. So this means that for 75% of the cases, all four comparisons will need to be evaluated.

Example 22-14. Poorly constructed IF statement

```
IF (percentage>95) THEN
    SET Above95=Above95+1;
ELSEIF (percentage >=90) THEN
    SET Range90to95=Range90to95+1;
ELSEIF (percentage >=75) THEN
    SET Range75to89=Range75to89+1;
ELSE
    SET LessThan75=LessThan75+1;
END IF;
```

Example 22-15 shows a more efficiently formed IF statement. In this variation, the first condition will evaluate as true in the majority of executions and no further comparisons will be necessary.

Example 22-15. Optimized IF statement

```
IF (percentage<75) THEN
    SET LessThan75=LessThan75+1;
ELSEIF (percentage >=75 AND percentage<90) THEN
    SET Range75to89=Range75to89+1;
ELSEIF (percentage >=90 and percentage <=95) THEN
    SET Range90to95=Range90to95+1;
ELSE
    SET Above95=Above95+1;
END IF;
```

Figure 22-7 shows the performance improvement gained by reordering the IF statement so that the most commonly satisfied condition is evaluated first.

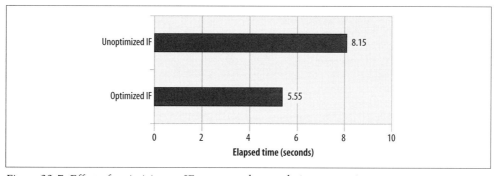

Figure 22-7. Effect of optimizing an IF statement by reordering comparisons

If an IF statement is to be executed repeatedly, placing the most commonly satisfied condition earlier in the IF structure may optimize performance.

Avoid Unnecessary Comparisons

Sometimes an IF or CASE statement will be constructed that has some kind of common condition in each comparison clause. For instance, in Example 22-16, each of the expressions in the IF statement includes an employee_status='U' condition. Even if the employee_status is not equal to "U", each of these comparisons will need to be evaluated—adding some processing overhead.

Example 22-16. IF statement with common condition in each expression

```
IF (employee_status='U' AND employee_salary>150000) THEN
    SET categoryA=categoryA+1;
ELSEIF (employee_status='U' AND employee_salary>100000) THEN
    SET categoryB=categoryB+1;
ELSEIF (employee_status='U' AND employee_salary<50000) THEN
    SET categoryC=categoryC+1;
ELSEIF (employee_status='U') THEN
    SET categoryD=categoryD+1;
END IF;
```

Example 22-17 shows a more optimized IF structure. In this example, the employee_status is checked first and then—only if employee_status='U'—are the additional comparisons are evaluated. Figure 22-8 demonstrates the optimization.

Example 22-17. Nested IF statement to avoid redundant comparisons

```
IF (employee_status='U') THEN
    IF (employee_salary>150000) THEN
        SET categoryA=categoryA+1;
    ELSEIF (employee_salary>100000) THEN
        SET categoryB=categoryB+1;
    ELSEIF (employee_salary<50000) THEN
        SET categoryC=categoryC+1;
    ELSE
        SET categoryD=categoryD+1;
    END IF;
END IF;
```

To be honest, under most circumstances, tuning IF statements will not greatly improve the performance of your code. The overhead of SQL processing will usually dominate overall execution time. Consequently, we suggest that when it comes to conditional statements, you should prioritize writing readable and maintainable code. If a particular IF statement becomes a bottleneck, then you should consider a rewrite that will improve performance even at the expense of maintainability.

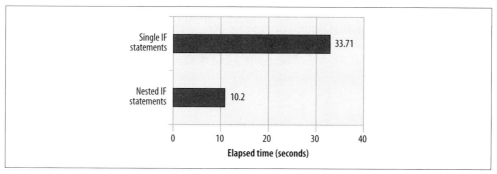

Figure 22-8. Effect of nesting an IF statement to eliminate redundant comparisons

 If your IF or CASE statement contains compound expressions with redundant comparisons, consider nesting multiple IF or CASE statements to avoid redundant processing.

CASE Versus IF

We wondered if there was any performance difference between a CASE statement and an equivalent IF statement. We thought that CASE might be more optimal for comparing a variable against a range of set values, so we speculated that this statement:

```
CASE customer_code
    WHEN 1 THEN
        SET process_flag=7;
    WHEN 2 THEN
        SET process_flag=9;
    WHEN 3 THEN
        SET process_flag=2;
    ELSE
        SET process_flag=0;
END CASE;
```

might be more efficient than the equivalent IF statement:

```
IF customer_code= 1 THEN
    SET process_flag=7;
ELSEIF customer_code= 2 THEN
    SET process_flag=9;
ELSEIF customer_code=3 THEN
    SET process_flag=2;
ELSE
    SET process_flag=0;
END IF;
```

In fact, the opposite turned out to be true. The IF statement is roughly 15% faster than the equivalent CASE statement—presumably this is the result of a more efficient internal algorithm for IF in the MySQL code.

As noted earlier, we advise you to structure your stored program's statements primarily for readability and maintainability, since it is almost always the elapsed time of SQL statements that dominates performance. However, if performance is critical, you may want to make a habit of using IF statements rather than CASE statements in your code.

Recursion

A *recursive routine* is one that invokes itself. Recursive routines often offer elegant solutions to complex programming problems, but they also tend to consume large amounts of memory. They are also likely to be less efficient and less scalable than implementations based on iterative execution.

Most recursive algorithms can be reformulated using nonrecursive techniques involving iteration. Where possible, we should give preference to the more efficient iterative algorithm.

For example, in Example 22-18, the stored procedure uses recursion to calculate the Nth element of the *Fibonacci* sequence, in which each element in the sequence is the sum of the previous two numbers.

Example 22-18. Recursive implementation of the Fibonacci algorithm

```
CREATE PROCEDURE rec_fib(n INT,OUT out_fib INT)
BEGIN
  DECLARE n_1 INT;
  DECLARE n_2 INT;

  IF (n=0) THEN
    SET out_fib=0;
  ELSEIF (n=1) then
    SET out_fib=1;
  ELSE
    CALL rec_fib(n-1,n_1);
    CALL rec_fib(n-2,n_2);
    SET out_fib=(n_1 + n_2);
  END IF;
END
```

Example 22-19 shows a nonrecursive implementation that returns the Nth element of the Fibonacci sequence.

Example 22-19. Nonrecursive implementation of the Fibonacci sequence

```
CREATE PROCEDURE nonrec_fib(n INT,OUT out_fib INT)
BEGIN
  DECLARE m INT default 0;
  DECLARE k INT DEFAULT 1;
  DECLARE i INT;
  DECLARE tmp INT;
```

```
  SET m=0;
  SET k=1;
  SET i=1;

  WHILE (i<=n) DO
    SET tmp=m+k;
    SET m=k;
    SET k=tmp;
    SET i=i+1;
  END WHILE;
  SET out_fib=m;
END
```

Figure 22-9 compares the relative performance of the recursive and nonrecursive implementations. Not only is the recursive algorithm less efficient for almost any given input value, it also degrades rapidly as the number of recursions increases (which is, in turn, dependent on which element of the Fibonacci sequence is requested). As well as being inherently a less efficient algorithm, each recursion requires MySQL to create the context for a new stored program (or function) invocation. As a result, recursive algorithms tend to waste memory as well as being slower than their iterative alternatives.

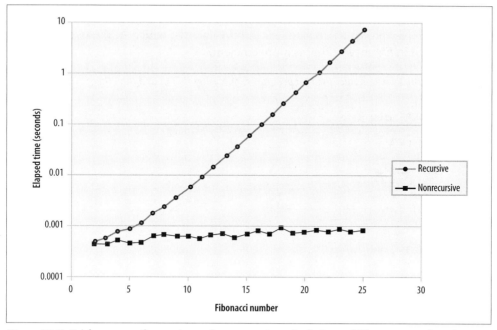

Figure 22-9. Performance of recursive and nonrecursive calculations of Fibonacci numbers (note logarithmic scale)

The maximum recursion depth—the number of times a procedure can call itself—is controlled by the MySQL configuration parameter max_sp_recursion_depth. The default value of 0 disables all recursive procedures. A procedure that attempts to recurse beyond the value of max_sp_recursion_depth will encounter a runtime error:

```
mysql> CALL rec_fib(10,@x);
ERROR 1456 (HY000): Recursive limit 0 (as set by the max_sp_recursion_depth variable)
was exceeded for routine rec_fib
```

Recursion in stored functions is not allowed. An attempt to recurse in a function will always generate a runtime error:

```
mysql> SELECT rec_fib(10);
ERROR 1424 (HY000): Recursive stored functions and triggers are not allowed.
```

 Recursive solutions rarely perform as efficiently as their nonrecursive alternatives.

Cursors

When you need to retrieve only a single row from a SELECT statement, using the INTO clause is far easier than declaring, opening, fetching from, and closing a cursor. But does the INTO clause generate some additional work for MySQL or could the INTO clause be more efficient than a cursor? In other words, which of the two stored programs shown in Example 22-20 is more efficient?

Example 22-20. Two equivalent stored programs, one using INTO and the other using a cursor

```
CREATE PROCEDURE using_into
      ( p_customer_id INT,OUT p_customer_name VARCHAR(30))
    READS SQL DATA
BEGIN
        SELECT customer_name
          INTO p_customer_name
          FROM customers
         WHERE customer_id=p_customer_id;
END;

CREATE PROCEDURE using_cursor
    (p_customer_id INT,OUT  p_customer_name VARCHAR(30))
    READS SQL DATA
BEGIN

    DECLARE cust_csr CURSOR FOR
        SELECT customer_name
          FROM customers
         WHERE customer_id=p_customer_id;
```

Example 22-20. Two equivalent stored programs, one using INTO and the other using a cursor (continued)

```
    OPEN cust_csr;
    FETCH cust_csr INTO p_customer_name;
    CLOSE cust_csr;

END;
```

Certainly, it is simpler to code an `INTO` statement than to code `DECLARE`, `OPEN`, `FETCH`, and `CLOSE` statements, and we will probably only bother to do this—when we know that the SQL returns only one row—if there is a specific performance advantage. As it turns out, there is actually a slight performance penalty for using an explicit cursor. Figure 22-10 shows the relative performance of each of the stored programs in Example 22-20—over 11,000 executions, the `INTO`-based stored program was approximately 15% faster than the stored program that used an explicit cursor.

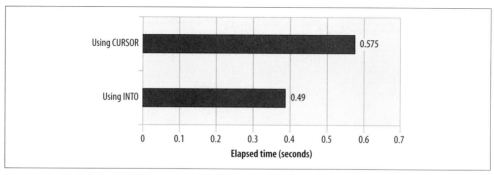

Figure 22-10. Relative performance of INTO versus CURSOR fetch

 If you know that a SQL statement will return only one row, then a `SELECT ... INTO` statement will be slightly faster than declaring, opening, and fetching from a cursor.

Trigger Overhead

Every database trigger is associated with a specific DML operation (`INSERT`, `UPDATE`, or `DELETE`) on a specific table—the trigger code will execute whenever that DML operation occurs on that table. Furthermore, all MySQL 5.0 triggers are of the `FOR EACH ROW` type, which means that the trigger code will execute once for each row affected by the DML operation. Given that a single DML operation might potentially affect thousands of rows, should we be concerned that our triggers might have a negative effect on DML performance? Absolutely!

For all of the reasons outlined previously, triggers can significantly increase the amount of time taken to execute DML operations and can have a detrimental effect on overall application performance if trigger overhead is not carefully managed.

The overhead of a trigger itself is significant, though not unmanageable. For instance, consider the trigger shown in Example 22-21; this trivial trigger serves no purpose, but it allows us to measure the overhead of a trigger that does virtually nothing.

Example 22-21. "Trivial" trigger

```
CREATE TRIGGER sales_bi_trg
  BEFORE INSERT ON sales
  FOR EACH ROW
  SET @x=NEW.sale_value;
```

When we implemented this trivial trigger, the time taken to insert 100,000 sales rows increased from 8.84 seconds to 12.9 seconds—an increase of about 45%. So even the simplest of triggers adds a significant—though bearable—overhead.

But what about a complex trigger? In Chapter 11, we created a set of triggers to maintain a sales summary table. One of the triggers we created is the BEFORE INSERT trigger, shown in Example 22-22.

Example 22-22. A more complex trigger

```
CREATE TRIGGER sales_bi_trg
  BEFORE INSERT ON sales
  FOR EACH ROW
BEGIN
  DECLARE row_count INTEGER;

  SELECT COUNT(*)
    INTO row_count
    FROM customer_sales_totals
   WHERE customer_id=NEW.customer_id;

  IF row_count > 0 THEN
    UPDATE customer_sales_totals
       SET sale_value=sale_value+NEW.sale_value
     WHERE customer_id=NEW.customer_id;
  ELSE
    INSERT INTO customer_sales_totals
       (customer_id,sale_value)
      VALUES(NEW.customer_id,NEW.sale_value);
  END IF;

END
```

This trigger checks to see if there is an existing row for the customer in the summary table and, if there is, updates that row; otherwise, it adds a new row. Since we are performing a single additional update or insert for every row inserted, we do expect an increase in our INSERT overhead. However, we might not expect that the time taken to insert 10,000 rows increases from 0.722 second to 64.36 seconds—almost 100 times more!

The problem with our trigger is obvious on reflection. The SQL that checks for a matching row is not supported by an index, so for every row inserted into sales, we are performing a full scan of customer_sales_totals. This is not a huge table, but these scans are performed for every row inserted, so the overhead adds up rapidly. Furthermore, the UPDATE statement is also not supported by an index, so a second scan of the customer_sales_totals table is performed to support the UPDATE.

The solution is to create an index on customer_sales_totals.customer_id, as shown in Example 22-23.

Example 22-23. Index to support our trigger

```
CREATE UNIQUE INDEX customer_sales_totals_cust_id
   ON customer_sales_totals(customer_id)
```

Once the index is created, the performance improves: time to insert 10,000 rows is reduced to about 4.26 seconds, which—although much slower than the performance we achieved without a trigger—is certainly more acceptable than 64 seconds. Performance variations are shown in Figure 22-11.

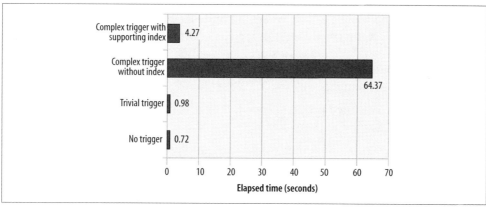

Figure 22-11. Trigger performance variations

The lesson here is this: since the trigger code will execute once for every row affected by a DML statement, the trigger can easily become the most significant factor in DML performance. Code inside the trigger body needs to be as lightweight as possible and—in particular—any SQL statements in the trigger should be supported by indexes whenever possible.

Conclusion

In this chapter we looked at the particular performance characteristics of stored programs and offered advice about when to use stored program logic in place of "straight" SQL and how to optimize the algorithms we write in the MySQL stored program language.

As we have emphasized repeatedly, the performance of most stored programs will depend primarily on the performance of the SQL statements found within the stored program. Before optimizing stored program statements, make sure that all of the SQL statements are fully optimized.

The MySQL stored program language is currently slower than most alternative procedural languages—such as Java and PHP—when it comes to number crunching. In general, we are better off implementing computationally expensive code in one of these other languages.

Stored programs can, however, really shine from a performance standpoint when a relatively small output is calculated from a large number of database rows. This is because other languages must transfer these rows across the network, while stored program execution occurs inside the database, minimizing network traffic.

Sometimes stored programs can also be used as an alternative to hard-to-optimize SQL. This will typically be true when the SQL language forces we to repetitively fetch the same data, or when the SQL logic is enormously complex and we need to "divide and conquer." However, a stored program solution will typically take more programming investment than a SQL equivalent, so we must be sure that we are obtaining the improvements we expect.

The optimization of stored program code follows the same general principles that are true for other languages. In particular:

- Optimize loop processing: ensure that no unnecessary statements occur within a loop; exit the loop as soon as you are logically able to do so.
- Reduce the number of comparisons by testing for the most likely match first, and nest IF or CASE statements when necessary to eliminate unnecessary comparisons.
- Avoid recursive procedures.

Because MySQL triggers execute once for each row affected by a DML statement, the effect of any unoptimized statements in a trigger will be magnified during bulk DML operations. Trigger code needs to be very carefully optimized—expensive SQL statements have no place in triggers.

## CHAPTER 23

Best Practices in MySQL Stored Program Development

The objective of this chapter is to provide concrete, immediately applicable, quickly located advice that will assist you in writing code that is readable, maintainable, and efficient.

It might seem odd that we have written a "best practices" chapter for a language that is still in its first major release. Aren't "best practices" supposed to be determined and documented after years of trial and error, sweat, and heartache? Absolutely. Those are, in fact, precisely the kinds of best practices you will find in this chapter.

We spent more than a year between the first alpha release of MySQL 5.0 in late 2004 and the most recent production release in early 2006, learning the hard way about what works and does not work in MySQL stored programs. Beyond that, while stored programs might be new to MySQL, they have been around in other databases for years—and both of us have plenty of experience (altogether over two decades' worth) to draw from—with MySQL, Oracle, and SQL Server. Most of the lessons learned in developing stored programs in other languages apply directly to MySQL.

We will start off with some general-purpose guidance that is intended to assist with software development in any language, then move on to guidelines specifically crafted for the MySQL stored program language. If you find yourself reading these and saying "Well, sure, *of course* that is what you are supposed to do!" then we congratulate you and hope that you not only *know* about these best practices, but also apply them as you write your code!

The Development Process

To do your job well, you need to be aware of, and to follow, both "little" best practices—tips focused on particular coding techniques—and "big" best practices. This section offers some suggestions on the big picture: how to write your code as part of a high-quality development process.

In other words, if you (or your methodology) don't follow some form of the best practices in this section, you are less likely to produce high-quality, successful software.

DEV-01: Set standards and guidelines before writing any code

These standards and guidelines might include many or all of the best practices described in this book. Of course, you need to make your own decisions about what is most important and practical in your own particular environment.

Key areas of development for which you should proactively set standards are:

- *Selection of development tools*: You should avoid relying on the MySQL command-line client to compile, execute, and test code, and avoid relying on a basic editor like Notepad or vi to write the code. MySQL AB and other software companies offer a multitude of tools (with a wide range of functionality and price) that will help you to dramatically improve your development environment. Decide on the tools to be used by all members of the development group.

- *How SQL is written in stored programs:* The SQL in your application can be the Achilles' heel of your code base. If you aren't careful about how you place SQL statements in your stored program code, you'll end up with applications that are difficult to optimize, debug, and manage over time.

- *An exception-handling architecture*: Users have a hard time understanding how to use an application correctly, and developers have an even harder time debugging and fixing an application if errors are handled inconsistently (or not at all). Use a consistent approach to handling runtime errors using exceptions.

- *Processes for code review and testing:* There are some basic tenets of programming that must not be ignored. You should never put code into production without first having it reviewed by one or more other developers, and performing tests on both the individual programs in your application and the overall application.

Benefits

By setting clear standards and guidelines for at least the areas we listed above (tools, SQL, error handling, and code review and testing), you ensure a foundation that will allow you to be productive and to produce code of reasonable quality. We offer detailed advice on most of these areas later in the chapter.

Challenges

The deadline pressures of most applications mitigate against taking the time up front to establish standards, even though we all know that such standards are likely to save time down the line.

DEV-02: Ask for help after 30 minutes on a problem

Following this simple piece of advice might have more impact on the quality of your code (and your productivity) than anything else in this book!

How many times have you stared at the screen for hours, trying this and that in a vain attempt to fix a problem in your code? Finally, exhausted and desperate, you call over your cubicle wall: "Hey, Melinda (or Jose or Farik or Lakshmi), could you come over here and look at this?" When Melinda reaches your cube she sees in an instant what you, after hours, still could not see (and she doesn't even know MySQL all that well!). Gosh, it's like magic!

Except it's not magic and it's not mysterious at all. Remember: humans write software, so an understanding of human psychology is crucial to setting up processes that encourage quality software. We humans like to get things right, like to solve our own problems, and do not like to admit that we *don't* know what is going on. Consequently, we tend to want to hide our ignorance and difficulties. This tendency leads to many wasted hours, high levels of frustration, and, usually, nasty, spaghetti code.

Team leaders and development managers need to cultivate an environment in which we are encouraged to admit what we do not know, and ask for help earlier rather than later. Ignorance isn't a problem unless it is hidden from view. And by asking for help, you validate the knowledge and experience of others, building the overall self-esteem and confidence of the team.

There is a good chance that if you have already spent 30 minutes fruitlessly analyzing your code, two more hours will not get you any further along to a solution. So get in the habit of sharing your difficulty with a coworker (preferably an assigned "buddy," so the line of communication between the two of you is officially acknowledged and doesn't represent in any way an acknowledgement of some sort of failure).

Example

Programmers are a proud and noble people. We don't like to ask for help; we like to bury our nose in our screen and create. So the biggest challenge to getting people to ask for help is to change behaviors. Here are some suggestions:

- The team leader must set the example. When we have the privilege to manage a team of developers, we go out of our way to ask each and every person on that team for help on one issue or another. If you are a coach to other teams of developers, identify the programmer who is respected by all others for her expertise. Then convince *her* to seek out the advice of others. Once the leader (formal or informal) shows that it is OK to admit ignorance, everyone else will gladly join in.

- Post reminders in work areas, perhaps even individual cubicles, such as "STUCK? ASK FOR HELP" and "IT'S OK NOT TO KNOW EVERYTHING." We need to be reminded about things that don't come naturally to us.

Benefits

Problems in code are identified and solved more rapidly. Fewer hours are wasted in a futile hunt for bugs.

Knowledge about the application and about the underlying software technology is shared more evenly across the development team.

Challenges

The main challenge to successful implementation of this best practice is psychological: don't be afraid to admit you don't know something or are having trouble figuring something out.

Resources

Peopleware: Productive Projects and Teams, by Tom DeMarco and Timothy Lister (Dorset House). This is a fantastic book that combines deep experience in project management with humor and common sense.

DEV-03: Walk through each other's code

Software is written to be executed by a machine. These machines are very, very fast, but they aren't terribly smart. They simply do what they are told, following the instructions of the software we write, as well as the many other layers of software that control the CPU, storage, memory, etc.

It is extremely important, therefore, that we make sure the code we write does the right thing. Our computers can't tell us if we missed the mark ("garbage in, garbage out" or, unfortunately, "garbage in, gospel out"). The usual way we validate code is by running that code and checking the outcomes (well, actually, in most cases we have our *users* run the code and let us know about failures). Such tests are, of course, crucial and must be made. But they aren't enough.

It is certainly possible that our tests aren't comprehensive and leave errors undetected. It is also conceivable that the *way* in which our code was written produces the correct results in very undesirable ways. For instance, the code might work "by accident" (two errors cancel themselves out).

A crucial complement to formal testing of code is a formalized process of code review or walk-through. Code review involves having other developers actually read and review your source code. This review process can take many different forms, including:

- *The buddy system:* Each programmer is assigned another programmer to be ready at any time to look at his buddy's code and to offer feedback.
- *Formal code walk-throughs:* On a regular basis (and certainly as a "gate" before any program moves to production status), a developer presents or "walks through" her code before a group of programmers.
- *Pair programming:* No one codes alone! Whenever you write software, you do it in pairs, where one person handles the tactical work (thinks about the specific code to be written and does the typing), while the second person takes the strategic role (keeps an eye on the overall architecture, looks out for possible bugs, and generally critiques— always constructively). Pair programming is an integral part of Extreme Programming. However, note that reports from the field are mixed with regard to pair programming—there are some indications that it relies too heavily on an intimate relationship between members of a pair that is rarely achieved.

Benefits

Overall quality of code increases dramatically. The architecture of the application tends to be sounder, and the number of bugs in production code goes way down. A further advantage is that of staff education—not just awareness of the project, but also an increase in technological proficiency due to the synergistic effect of working together.

Challenges

The development manager or team leader must take the initiative to set up the code review process and must give developers the time (and training) to do it right. Also, code review seems to be the first casualty of deadline crunch. Further, a new project involving MySQL stored programs might not have the language expertise available on the team to do complete, meaningful walk-throughs.

Resources

- *Handbook of Walkthroughs, Inspections, and Technical Reviews*, by Daniel Freedman and Gerald M. Weinberg (Dorset House). Now in its third edition, this book uses a question-and-answer format to show you exactly how to implement reviews for all sorts of product and software development.
- *Extreme Programming Explained*, by Kent Beck (Addison Wesley). The first book on Extreme Programming offers many insights into pair programming.
- *Extreme Programming Refactored,* by Matt Stephens and Doug Rosenberg (APress). An often funny critical examination of Extreme Programming that argues against (in particular) pair programming.

DEV-04: Use independent testers for functional sign-off

Individual developers should and must be responsible for defining and executing unit tests on the programs they write. Developers should not, on the other hand, be responsible for overall functional testing of their applications. There are several reasons for this:

- We don't own the requirements. We don't decide when and if the system works properly. Our users or customers have this responsibility. They need to be intimately connected with, and drive, the functional tests.
- Whenever we test our code, we follow the "pathways to success" without ever knowing it. In other words, the mindset we had when we wrote the code is the same mindset we have when testing the code. Other people, other eyes, need to run the software in complete ignorance of those pathways. It is no wonder that unit testing was so successful and yet integration testing has such problems.

To improve the quality of code that is handed over to customers for testing, your team leader or development manager should:

- Work with the customer to define the set of tests that must be run successfully before an application is considered to be ready for production.
- Establish a distinct testing group—either a devoted Quality Assurance organization or simply a bunch of developers who haven't written any of the software to be tested.

This extra layer of testing, based on the customer's own requirements and performed before the handoff to customers for their "sign off" test, will greatly improve code quality and customer confidence in the development team.

Example

We spend several days building a really slick application in PHP (or VB.NET or Java or...). It allows users to manage data in a few different tables, request reports, and so on. We then devote most of a day to running the application through its paces. We click here, click there, enter good data, enter bad data, find a bunch of bugs, fix them, and finally hand it over to our main customer, Johanna. We feel confident in our application. We can no longer break it.

Imagine how crushed we feel (and we bet you *can* imagine it, because undoubtedly the same thing has happened to you) when Johanna sits down in front of the computer, starts up the application, and in no more than three clicks of the mouse causes an error window to pop up on the screen. The look she sends our way ("Why are you wasting my time?") is not rewarding.

There is no way for us to convince Johanna that we really, truly did spend hours testing the application. Why should she believe such a thing?

Benefits

Quality of code handed to users for testing is higher, which means the end result moved to production is of correspondingly higher quality.

Customer confidence in the development organization remains high. This confidence—and the respect that comes with it—makes it easier for developers to negotiate with customers over the time-versus-quality dilemma so many of us face in software development.

Challenges

Many small development groups can't afford (i.e., can't convince management to spend the money) to staff a separate QA organization. At a minimum, you must make sure that customers have defined a clear set of tests. Then distribute the functional testing load to the developers so that they do not test their own code.

Resources

http://www.well.com/~vision/sqa.html: A gathering place for references related to the theory and practice of Software Quality Assurance. This site is growing to include information on Standards and Development Procedures, Product Evaluation and Process Monitoring, Configuration Management Monitoring, the role of SQA in the Product Development Cycle, and Automated Testing Tools.

DEV-05: Use source controlled files to maintain the "reference" copy of your stored routines

Source code control systems (SCCSs) allow us to keep copies of major revisions of our program source code, allowing us to roll back an application's source code to an earlier point in time or to examine the source code in use with an earlier version of the application (which might still be in use somewhere). Virtually all professional software developers could—or at least should—employ an SCCS to store their application code.

Unfortunately, developers often fail to source control the DDL code to create database objects and often neglect to include stored program code in the SCCS. To some extent, the ability to extract the source code for a stored program from the database encourages us to edit a stored program "in place"—even when we would never dream of editing PHP code "in place" (e.g., directly editing the .php files in the Apache document directory).

If your stored programs are part of an application, then the source program code is just as much a part of the application source code as code written in other languages such as PHP or Java. You should therefore keep the "reference" copy of your stored program code in your version control system (such as CVS, ClearCase, BitKeeper, etc.). This means saving your stored program code as a text file and performing explicit check-in and check-out from your version control system.

Think of that text file as the original source code for your procedure. Applying the source code to the MySQL server is analogous to compiling that source as a binary. Extracting it from a server for editing is equivalent to decompiling a binary and is usually *not* how you obtain a copy of the source for editing. Instead, you should perform an explicit check-out of the source code from the SCCS, edit it in the MySQL Query Browser or other tool, and then apply it to a test database for unit testing. Later you can deploy the source code for the stored program to a production database by running a script that executes it inside of the MySQL command-line client.

Coding Style and Conventions

Software developers are a very privileged bunch. We don't have to work in dangerous environments, and our jobs aren't physically taxing (though carpal tunnel syndrome is always a threat). We are paid to think about things, and then to write down our thoughts in the form of code. This code is then used and maintained by others, sometimes for decades. Now just think of your code as a form of poetry and rejoice in your fortunate circumstances!

Given this situation, we all have a responsibility to write code that can be easily understood and maintained (and, c'mon, let's admit our secret desires, *admired*) by developers who follow in our footsteps.

 Steve McConnell's *http://www.construx.com* site, along with his book, *Code Complete* (Microsoft Press), offers checklists on coding style, naming conventions and rules, and module definitions.

STYL-01: Adopt a consistent, readable format that is easy to maintain

Your code should have a "signature," a style that is consistent (all your programs look the same), readable (anyone can pick up your code and make sense of it), and maintainable (a minor change in the code shouldn't require 15 minutes of reformatting).

Ideally, everyone in your organization would adopt a similar style, so that everyone can easily understand everyone else's code. This can be tricky, as programmers sometimes take a dogmatic approach to such issues as size of indentation and use of whitespace. However, research and experience confirm that the benefit of adopting a similar style is not so much that any one standard confers a significant benefit over another, but rather that the use of a consistent standard throughout an organization improves efficiency and reduces maintenance costs.

STYL-02: Adopt logical, consistent naming conventions for modules and data structures

Adopt and promote standard ways to define names of program elements. Choose a level of "formality" of naming conventions based on your needs. If, for example, you have a team of two developers working on a small code base, you can probably get away with naming conventions that don't go far beyond "use meaningful names." If you are building a massive application involving dozens of developers, you probably need to define more comprehensive rules.

Here are some general recommendations for conventions:

- *Identify the scope of a variable in its name:* A global variable can be prefaced with v_ , for example.

- *Use a prefix or suffix to identify the types of structures being defined:* Consider, for example, declarations of cursors. A standard approach to declaring such a structure is *<name>*_csr. Cursors are quite different from variables; you should be able to identify the difference with a glance.

- *Use a readable format for your names:* Since the stored program language isn't case sensitive, the "camel notation" (as in minBalanceRequired), for example, is probably not a good choice for constructing names. Instead, use separators such as _ (underscore) to improve readability (as in min_balance_required). While MySQL allows names to be extremely long (compared with other databases and/or languages), keep them short, as well as readable.

- *Consider portability:* If you ever want to port your code to an alternate RDBMS (perish the thought!) you should consider adopting a naming convention that will work across RDBMS types. You can find a summary of the conventions for the "other" databases at *http://www.dbazine.com/db2/db2-disarticles/gulutzan5.*

It isn't possible to provide a comprehensive list of naming conventions in this book. The particular conventions you choose, furthermore, aren't nearly as important as the fact that you set some standard for naming conventions.

STYL-03: Self-document using block and loop labels

While block and loop labels are often necessary to allow for variable scoping or as targets for LEAVE or ITERATE statements, they can also be a big help in improving the readability of code.

Use a label directly in front of loops and nested blocks:

- To name that portion of code and thereby self-document what it's doing
- So that you can repeat that name with the END statement of that block or loop
- To provide a target for a LEAVE or ITERATE statement

This recommendation is especially important when you have multiple nestings of loops (and possibly inconsistent indentation), as in the following:

```
WHILE condition DO
    some code
    WHILE condition DO
        some code
    END WHILE;
    some code
END WHILE;
```

Example

In this example we use labels for a block and two nested loops, and then apply them in the appropriate END statements. We can now easily see *which* loop and block are ending, no matter how badly the code is indented!

```
CREATE PROCEDURE display_book_usage( )
  READS SQL DATA
BEGIN
   DECLARE v_month INT;
   DECLARE v_x   INT;
   DECLARE yearly_analysis_csr CURSOR FOR SELECT ...;
   DECLARE monthly_analysis_csr CURSOR FOR SELECT ...;

   OPEN yearly_analysis_csr;
   yearly_analysis:
   LOOP
     FETCH yearly_analysis_csr INTO v_month;
     OPEN monthly_analysis_csr;
     monthly_analysis:
     LOOP
       FETCH monthly_analysis_csr INTO v_x;
... Lots of monthly analysis code ...
END LOOP monthly_analysis;
...Lots of yearly analysis code
END LOOP yearly_analysis;
```

Benefits

If you use labels, it's much easier to read your code, especially if it contains loops and nested blocks that have long bodies (i.e., the loop starts on page 2 and ends on page 7, with three other loops inside that outer loop—not that we recommend this!).

STYL-04: Express complex expressions unambiguously using parentheses

The rules of operator precedence in the MySQL stored program language follow the commonly accepted precedence of algebraic operators. The rules of precedence often make many parentheses unnecessary. When an uncommon combination of operators occurs, however, it may be helpful to add parentheses even when the precedence rules apply.

The rules of evaluation do specify left-to-right evaluation for operators that have the same precedence level. However, this is the most commonly overlooked rule of evaluation when checking expressions for correctness.

Many developers apply a consistent rule for improved readability in this area: always use parentheses around every Boolean expression, including IF, ELSEIF, and WHILE statements, as well as variable assignments, regardless of the simplicity of the expressions. So, rather than:

```
IF min_balance < 1000 THEN ...
```

you instead write:

```
IF ( min_balance < 1000 ) THEN ...
```

Example

You might not want a standard that requires you to always use parentheses, but in some situations, parentheses are all but required for readability. Consider the following expression:

```
5 + Y**3 MOD 10
```

MySQL will not be the least bit confused by this statement; it will apply its unambiguous rules and come up with an answer. Developers, however, may not have such an easy time of it. You are better off writing that same line of code as follows:

```
5 + ((Y ** 3) MOD 10)
```

Benefits

Everyone, including the author of the code, can more easily understand the logic and intent (which is crucial for maintenance) of complex expressions.

STYL-05: Use vertical code alignment to emphasize vertical relationships

A common code formatting technique is *vertical alignment*. Here is an example in a SQL WHERE clause:

```
WHERE  COM.company_id      = SAL.company_id
   AND COM.company_type_cd = TYP.company_type_cd
   AND TYP.company_type_cd = CFG.company_type_cd
   AND COM.region_cd       = REG.region_cd
   AND REG.status          = RST.status;
```

You should use vertical alignment only when the elements that are lined up vertically have a relationship with each other that you want to express. In the WHERE clause shown here, however, there is no relationship between the right sides of the various expressions. The relationship is between the left and right sides of each individual expression. This is, therefore, a misuse of vertical alignment.

Example

Developers often (and justifiably) use vertical alignment with program parameter lists, as in:

```
CREATE PROCEDURE maximize_profits
   (
   IN      advertising_budget   NUMERIC(12,2),
   INOUT   bribery_budget       NUMERIC(12,2),
   IN      merge_and_purge_on   DATE ,
   OUT     obscene_bonus        NUMERIC(12,2))
```

Vertical alignment allows you to easily see the different parameter modes and data types.

Vertical alignment is also handy when declaring many variables, as in:

```
CREATE PROCEDURE genAPI( )
      DETERMINISTIC
BEGIN
   DECLARE c_table       CHAR(5)  DEFAULT 'TABLE';
   DECLARE c_column      CHAR(6)  DEFAULT 'COLUMN';
   DECLARE c_genpky      CHAR(6)  DEFAULT 'GENPKY';
   DECLARE c_genpkyonly  CHAR(10) DEFAULT 'GENPKYONLY';
   DECLARE c_sequence    CHAR(7)  DEFAULT 'SEQNAME';
   DECLARE c_pkygenproc  CHAR(10) DEFAULT 'PKYGENPROC';
   DECLARE c_pkygenfunc  CHAR(10) DEFAULT 'PKYGENFUNC';
   DECLARE c_usingxmn    CHAR(8)  DEFAULT 'USINGXMN';
   DECLARE c_fromod2k    CHAR(8)  DEFAULT 'FROMOD2K';
```

In this case, we want to be able to scan the list of values to make sure they are unique. I can also easily compare lengths of strings with the CHAR declarations, avoiding nuisance truncation exceptions on initialization.

Benefits

Careful and appropriate use of vertical alignment enhances readability. Used inappropriately, however, vertical alignment actually makes it harder to see what is really going on in your code.

Challenges

Vertical alignment is a "high maintenance" format. Add a new, long variable name, and you find yourself reformatting 20 other lines of code to match.

STYL-06: Comment tersely with value-added information

The best way to explain what your code is doing is to let that code speak for itself. You can take advantage of many self-documentation techniques, including:

- Use meaningful variable, procedure, and function names.
- Use the language construct that best reflects the code you are writing (choose the right kind of loop for your logic, label loops and BEGIN-END blocks, etc.).

Whenever you find yourself adding a comment to your code, first consider whether it is possible to modify the code itself to express your comment. Good reasons to add comments include:

- Program headers, explanations of workarounds, patches, operating-system dependencies, and other "exceptional" circumstances
- Complex or opaque logic

Example

Let's follow a trail of unnecessarily commented code to self-documenting code. We start with:

```
-- If the first properties element is N...
IF properties1 = 'N'
```

Yikes! Our line of code was incomprehensible and our comment simply repeated the code using the English language, rather than the stored program language. No added value, no real assistance, yet not at all uncommon. The least we can do is use the comment to "translate" from computer-talk to business requirement:

```
-- If the customer is not eligible for a discount...
IF properties1 = 'N'
```

That's better, but we have created a redundancy: if our requirement ever changes, We have to change the comment *and* the code. Why not change the names of our variables and literals so that the code explains itself?

```
IF customer_discount_flag = const_ineligible
```

Much better! Now we no longer need a comment. Our remaining concern with this line of code is that it "exposes" a business rule; it shows how (at this moment in time) we determine whether a customer is eligible for a discount. Business rules are notorious for changing over time—and for being referenced in multiple places throughout our application. So our best bet is to hide the rule behind a self-documenting function call:

```
IF NOT eligible_for_discount (customer_id)
```

Variables

The MySQL stored program language is technically a *strongly typed* language in the sense that before you can work with a variable, you must first declare it. And when you declare it, you specify its type and, optionally, an initial or default value. Be aware, however, when not in "strict" mode (sql_mode contains neither STRICT_TRANS_TABLES nor STRICT_ALL_TABLES), MySQL will generate warnings only when you violate a variable's type or storage limits.

We strongly urge you, therefore, to take special care with declaring your variables.

DAT-01: Use a consistent and meaningful variable naming style

All of us have a distinct variable naming style, often based on the conventions of our first programming language. In the very early days of programming, programmers were required to keep variable names short so as to reduce memory overhead. Various programming languages impose additional restrictions on the programmer: case-sensitivity, maximum lengths, and allowable characters, for instance.

However programmers might differ as regards the "one true style" that is optimal for a particular language, almost every programmer would agree that, above all, variable names should be *meaningful*, and whatever style might be employed, it should be employed *consistently* throughout your programs.

Meaningful variable names are those that clearly articulate the data that the variable holds. It's as simple as that. Avoid variable names that contain confusing or ambiguous abbreviations, and certainly avoid meaningless variable names such as v1, v2, etc.

Beyond being meaningful, conventions can help us understand the scope, data type, or some other property of our variables. In MySQL stored programs, we could use a convention that allows us to:

- Determine the data type of a variable from its name.
- Distinguish table column names from local variables or parameters.
- Identify the type of data held in the variables: data from a cursor, intermediate data, bits of SQL for a dynamic SQL, etc.

We believe that most of the above items are matters of personal preference and that, while arguments can be made for and against any or all of these styles, you can write high-quality code regardless of the style you adopt. We feel that the following recommendations, however, should be followed:

- You should generally identify local variables with a prefix or a suffix, especially if they are used to receive values from cursors. Creating local variables with the same name as a column returned by a cursor is dangerous.
- Because variable names are case insensitive, "camel" notation—in which capitalization is used to separate "words" within a variable name—is possibly inappropriate since isNull and isnull will reference the same variable.

Example

If you're not sold on the value of meaningful variable names, try to work out what this assignment statement is doing:

```
SET ns=gs-tx+bn-fd;
```

Now try one with meaningful variable names:

```
SET net_salary=gross_salary-tax+bonus-fund401k;
```

DAT-02: Avoid overriding variable declarations within "inner" blocks

It is possible to declare a variable inside an inner block that has the same name as a variable in the enclosing block. Nevertheless—though legal—this practice can be extremely confusing.

For instance, in the following example the v_counter variable is declared both within the inner block and within the outer block:

```
DECLARE  v_counter INT DEFAULT 1;

    . . . Lots of code . . .

  inr_blk: BEGIN
    DECLARE v_counter INT DEFAULT 2;

    . . . Lots of code . . .

    SET v_counter=v_counter+1;

  END inr_blk;
```

There are two undesirable consequences to this practice:

*   Someone reading the code might be confused as to which variable is being updated.
*   It is not possible in the inner block to modify the value of a variable in the outer block. The SQL:2003 specification allows us to prefix a variable name with its block label, but this isn't supported in MySQL yet.

It's much better to ensure that every variable declared in a stored program has a unique name, regardless of its block scope.

DAT-03: Replace complex expressions with functions

A Boolean function evaluates to one of three values: TRUE (1), FALSE (0), or NULL. You can use Boolean functions to hide complex expressions; the result is code that is virtually as readable as "straight" English—or whatever language you use to communicate with other human beings.

Example

Consider this code:

```
    SELECT salary, status, hire_date
      INTO v_total_sal, v_emp_status,  v_hire_date
      FROM employees
     WHERE employee_id=in_employee_id;

    IF (v_total_sal BETWEEN 10000 AND 50000)
       AND  v_emp_status  = 'N'
       AND DATEDIFF(NOW( ), v_hire_date)>  365
    THEN
       CALL give_raise (in_employee_id);
    END IF;
```

Wow, that's hard to understand! It would be much easier if the code looked like this:

```
IF eligible_for_raise(in_employee_id) THEN
   CALL give_raise(in_employee_id);
END IF;
```

Benefits

It will be much easier for anyone to read your code; you can literally *read* it. If you then need to understand how the Boolean expression is computed, you can look "under the covers."

This is a technique that can be applied (with care) to existing "spaghetti code." As you go into a program to fix or enhance it, look for opportunities to simplify and shorten executable sections by shifting complexity to other functions or procedures.

Challenges

Before you modify existing code, make sure you have solid unit test scripts in place so you can quickly verify that your changes haven't introduced bugs into the program.

DAT-04: Remove unused variables and code

You should go through your programs and remove any part of your code that is no longer used. This is a relatively straightforward process for variables and named constants. Simply execute searches for a variable's name in that variable's scope. If you find that the only place it appears is in its declaration, delete the declaration and, by doing so, delete one more potential question mark from your code.

There is never a better time to review all the steps you took, and to understand the reasons you took them, than immediately upon completion of your program. If you wait, you will find it particularly difficult to remember those parts of the program that were needed at one point but were rendered unnecessary in the end. "Dead zones" in your code become sources of deep insecurity for maintenance programmers.

Example

The following block of code has several dead zones that could cause a variety of problems. Can you find them all?

```
CREATE PROCEDURE weekly_check (
   in_isbn   VARCHAR(20),
   in_author VARCHAR(60)
)

BEGIN
   DECLARE  v_count INT;
   DECLARE  v_counter INT;
   DECLARE  v_available INT;
   DECLARE  v_new_location INT DEFAULT 1056;
   DECLARE  v_published_date DATE DEFAULT NOW();

   SET  v_published_date=book_published_date(in_isbn);
```

```
        IF DATE_SUB(NOW( ), INTERVAL 60 DAY) > v_published_date THEN
            CALL review_usage( );
        ELSEIF DATE_SUB(NOW( ), INTERVAL 24 DAY) > v_published_date
        THEN
            CALL check_availability (in_isbn, v_available, v_count);
          IF v_available
            AND /* Turn off due to Req A12.6 */ FALSE
          THEN
             CALL transfer_book (in_isbn, v_count - 1, v_new_location);
          END IF;
        -- Check for reserves
        -- CALL analyze_requests (isbn_in);
        END IF;
    END$$
```

Here are a few potential dead spots:

- The in_author parameter is declared but never used. It doesn't even have a default value, so you have to pass in an ignored value.
- v_counter is declared but not used.
- v_published_date is assigned a default value of NOW( ), which is immediately overridden by the call to book_published_date.
- The call to transfer_book has been turned off with the addition of AND FALSE.
- The call to analyze_requests has been commented out.

Benefits

It's much easier to maintain, debug, and enhance code that doesn't have "dead zones."

Challenges

There are sometimes valid reasons for keeping dead code in place. You may want to turn off code temporarily. Also, you may need to comment out some logic but still show that this action was done and explain why. In such cases, make sure that you include the necessary documentation in the code. Even better, use problem-tracking or bug-reporting software to keep a comprehensive history of any changes made to code.

DAT-05: Don't assume that the result of an expression is TRUE or FALSE; it could be NULL

Three-valued logic—the logic that includes NULLs—is an essential part of the relational database model. However, the tendency of humans to think in terms of two-valued logic—an expression is either TRUE or FALSE—can lead to serious logic bugs.

For instance, consider the following logic, which is intended to retire employees older than 65 years and older, and keep those younger than 65 years:

```
    IF v_date_of_birth > DATE_SUB(NOW( ), INTERVAL 65 YEAR)  THEN
        CALL keep_employee( v_employee_id);
    ELSE
        CALL retire_employee( v_employee_id);
    END IF;
```

This logic seems valid from a two-valued logic perspective, but what if v_date_of_birth is NULL? If the date of birth is NULL, then the date comparison will return NULL, rather than TRUE or FALSE. Consequently, the ELSE condition will be executed and we will retire an employee, although in fact we have no idea how old the employee is.

NULL values can be handled in a couple of ways:

- Explicitly check that a value is NOT NULL before attempting a comparison.
- Explicitly check each condition: don't assume that an expression that is not TRUE, is necessarily FALSE.

If we are worried about the date of birth being NULL in the above example, we might recode it as follows:

```
SET  v_age_in_years=DATEDIFF(NOW( ), v_date_of_birth)/365.25;

IF  v_age_in_years > 65 THEN
   CALL retire_employee( v_employee_id);
ELSEIF  v_age_in_years <= 65 THEN
   CALL keep_employee( v_employee_id);
ELSE
   CALL invalid_dob_error( v_employee_id);
END IF;
```

DAT-06: Employ "user" variables for global data sparingly

A *global variable* is a data structure that can be referenced outside the scope or block in which it's declared. In MySQL, we can use "user" variables—which can be recognized by being prefixed with @—to set values that are available to any program within the current session.

In the following procedure, for example, we store the number of customers into the user variable @customer_count:

```
CREATE PROCEDURE sp_customer_count( )

   SELECT COUNT(*)
      INTO @customer_count
      FROM customers;
```

Other procedures can examine the @customer_count and make decisions without having to recalculate the value. For instance, in this procedure we use the session variable in our setup logic:

```
CREATE PROCEDURE sp_crm_setup ( )

BEGIN
   IF @customer_count IS NULL THEN
     CALL sp_customer_count( );
   END IF;

   IF @customer_count > 1000 THEN
           . . . Logic for larger enterprises . . ..
```

There is no doubt that the use of global variables can create easy solutions for difficult problems. However, the modern consensus is that global variables create their own problems and that these problems generally overwhelm any of the advantages they might confer.

Global variables defeat modularity and hinder code reuse, because any module that uses a global variable becomes dependent on some other module that creates or initializes the global variable. In the case of MySQL user variables—which don't require a formal declaration—there is also the chance that two programmers might create identical "global" variables of the same name, thus causing subtle bugs that might occur only when modules are called in a certain order.

References

Code Complete, by Steve McConnell (Microsoft Press) contains an excellent discussion on the pros and cons of global variables.

DAT-07: Create stored programs in strict mode to avoid invalid data assignments

Stored program type checking is very dependent on the setting of the sql_mode configuration variable. If a program is created when the sql_mode variable includes one of the "strict" settings (STRICT_TRANS_TABLES or STRICT_ALL_TABLES), then the program will reject invalid variable assignments with an error. If neither of the strict modes is in effect, then the stored program will generate a warning when invalid data assignments occur, but will continue execution.

For instance, in the following program, we accidentally declared a variable as CHAR(1) instead of INT:

```
CREATE PROCEDURE TenPlusTen( )
BEGIN
  DECLARE a INTEGER DEFAULT 10;
  DECLARE b CHAR(1) DEFAULT 10;
  DECLARE c INTEGER;
  SET  c=a+b;
  SELECT c ;
END;
```

If created in "non-strict" mode, this program generates a warning, but continues execution and returns the wrong result (10+10=11?):

```
mysql> CALL TenPlusTen( );
+------+
| c    |
+------+
|   11 |
+------+
1 row in set (0.00 sec)

Query OK, 0 rows affected, 1 warning (0.01 sec)

mysql> SHOW WARNINGS;
+---------+------+----------------------------------------+
| Level   | Code | Message                                |
```

```
+---------+------+----------------------------------------+
| Warning | 1265 | Data truncated for column 'B' at row 1 |
+---------+------+----------------------------------------+
1 row in set (0.00 sec)
```

If created in strict mode, the program generates an error during execution, which is clearly better than returning the wrong result:

```
mysql> CALL TenPlusTen( );
ERROR 1406 (22001): Data too long for column 'b' at row 1
```

Non-strict stored program behavior can lead to unexpected and subtle bugs, and we recommend that you use strict mode when creating your stored programs. To enable strict mode, assign one of STRICT_TRANS_TABLES or STRICT_ALL_TABLES to your sql_mode variable:

```
SET sql_mode='STRICT_TRANS_TABLES';
```

Remember, it is the sql_mode that was in effect *when the program is created* that determines program behavior.

Conditional Logic

Follow the best practices in this section when you are using IF or CASE statements in stored programs.

IF-01: Use ELSEIF with mutually exclusive clauses

When you need to write conditional logic that has several mutually exclusive clauses (in other words, if one clause is TRUE, no other clause evaluates to TRUE), use the ELSEIF construct:

```
IF condA THEN
   ...
ELSEIF condB THEN
   ...
ELSEIF condN THEN
   ...
ELSE
   ...
END IF;
```

Example

At first glance, the following statement makes sense, but on closer examination, it's a mess:

```
CREATE PROCEDURE process_lineitem(line_in INT)
BEGIN

   IF line_in = 1 THEN
      CALL process_line1( );
   END IF;
   IF line_in = 2 THEN
      CALL process_line2( );
   END IF;
```

```
...
    IF line_in = 2045 THEN
        CALL process_line2045();
    END IF;

END$$
```

Every IF statement is executed and each condition is evaluated. You should rewrite such logic as follows:

```
CREATE PROCEDURE process_lineitem(line_in INT)
BEGIN

    IF line_in = 1 THEN
        CALL process_line1();
    ELSEIF line_in = 2 THEN
        CALL process_line2();
    /*... */
    ELSEIF line_in = 2045 THEN
        CALL process_line2045();
    END IF;

END$$
```

Benefits

This structure clearly expresses the underlying "reality" of your business logic: if one condition is TRUE, no others can be TRUE.

ELSEIF offers the most efficient implementation for processing mutually exclusive clauses. When one clause evaluates to TRUE, all subsequent clauses are ignored.

IF-02: Use IF...ELSEIF only to test a single, simple condition

The real world is very complicated; the software we write is supposed to map those complexities into applications. The result is that we often end up needing to deal with convoluted logical expressions.

You should write your IF statements in such a way as to keep them as straightforward and understandable as possible. For example, expressions are often more readable and understandable when they are stated in a positive form. Consequently, you are probably better off avoiding the NOT operator in conditional expressions.

Example

It's not at all uncommon to write or maintain code that is structured like this:

```
IF condA AND NOT (condB OR condC) THEN
    CALL proc1;
ELSEIF condA AND (condB OR condC) THEN
    CALL proc2;
ELSEIF NOT condA AND condD THEN
    CALL proc3;
END IF;
```

It's also fairly common to get a headache trying to make sense of all of that. You can often reduce the trauma by trading off the simplicity of the IF statement itself (one level of IF and ELSEIF conditions) for the simplicity of clauses within multiple levels:

```
IF condA THEN
   IF (condB OR condC)    THEN
     CALL  proc2;
   ELSE
     CALL  proc1;
   END IF;
ELSEIF condD THEN
   CALL proc3
END IF;
```

Don't forget, by the way, to take into account the possibility of your expressions evaluating to NULL. This can throw a monkey wrench into your conditional processing.

Benefits

Following this best practice will make your code easier to read and maintain.

Breaking an expression into smaller pieces can aid maintainability; if and when the logic changes, you can change one IF clause without affecting the logic of others.

Challenges

Multiple levels of nested IF statements can also decrease readability. You need to strive for a workable balance.

IF-03: Make sure that a CASE statement is inclusive, or construct a handler to catch any unmatched cases

If none of the CASE statements match as the input condition, CASE will raise MySQL error 1339 (Case not found for CASE statement). You should either construct an error handler to ignore this error, or ensure that the exception never occurs by including an ELSE clause in every CASE statement (the easier solution).

Example

In the following example, the CASE statement will fail if the customer status is not one of 'PLATINUM', 'GOLD', 'SILVER', or 'BRONZE':

```
CASE customer_status
    WHEN 'PLATINUM' THEN
        CALL apply_discount(sale_id,20); /* 20% discount */

    WHEN 'GOLD' THEN
        CALL apply_discount(sale_id,15); /* 15% discount */

    WHEN 'SILVER' THEN
        CALL apply_discount(sale_id,10); /* 10% discount */
```

```
             WHEN 'BRONZE' THEN
                    CALL apply_discount(sale_id,5); /* 5% discount*/
        END CASE;
```

Here we add an ELSE clause to avoid the error. Since we don't have anything for the ELSE clause to do, we use a dummy SET statement.

```
        CASE customer_status
            WHEN 'PLATINUM' THEN
                    CALL apply_discount(sale_id,20); /* 20% discount */
            WHEN 'GOLD' THEN
                    CALL apply_discount(sale_id,15); /* 15% discount */
            WHEN 'SILVER' THEN
                    CALL apply_discount(sale_id,10); /* 10% discount */
            WHEN 'BRONZE' THEN
                    CALL apply_discount(sale_id,5); /* 5% discount */
            ELSE
                    SET dummy=dummy;
        END CASE;
```

In this alternative solution, we construct a handler to allow the error to be ignored:

```
        DECLARE not_found INT DEFAULT 0;
        DECLARE no_matching_case CONDITION  FOR 1339;
        DECLARE CONTINUE HANDLER FOR no_matching_case SET not_found=1
        CASE
          WHEN (sale_value>200) THEN
            CALL free_shipping(sale_id);
            CASE customer_status
              WHEN 'PLATINUM' THEN
                CALL apply_discount(sale_id,20);
              WHEN 'GOLD' THEN
                CALL apply_discount(sale_id,15);
              WHEN 'SILVER' THEN
                CALL apply_discount(sale_id,10);
              WHEN 'BRONZE' THEN
                CALL apply_discount(sale_id,5);
            END CASE;
        END CASE;
```

See Chapter 5 for more details.

IF-04: Use CASE and IF consistently

Any conditional statement that can be expressed as an IF statement can also be expressed as a CASE statement—and vice versa. While you might heatedly debate the relative benefits of each over a few beers after work, it's fairly clear that you can write high-quality code no matter which statement you employ.

However, randomly alternating between the two statements does not lead to high-quality code. It's harder to compare the logic of two routines if—for instance—one expresses its branching logic with the CASE statement while the other uses IF. So try not to mix IF and CASE arbitrarily within your programs.

Loop Processing

Follow the best practices in this section when you are performing iterative processing in stored programs using the various looping controls: LOOP, WHILE, and REPEAT.

LOOP-01: Make sure the loop will terminate

One of the most annoying and potentially disruptive bugs that can be created in any language is the inadvertent infinite loop.

Making sure that a loop will terminate requires that you simulate all possible paths through the loop and assure yourself that the loop will always encounter an exit condition. If the loop does not terminate, it will likely consume excessive CPU and/or memory resources until it is manually terminated by the system administrator. In a worst-case scenario, the MySQL server itself may be terminated.

Example

The following stored procedure calculates the number of prime numbers less than the supplied input parameter. It's part of a larger routine that we plan to put in action when we're next contacted by extraterrestrial intelligences that announce their presence by broadcasting prime numbers at planet Earth.

```
CREATE PROCEDURE check_for_primes(in_limit INT)
BEGIN
  DECLARE i INT DEFAULT 2;
  DECLARE j INT DEFAULT 1;
  DECLARE n_primes INT DEFAULT 0;
  DECLARE is_prime INT DEFAULT 0;

  REPEAT

    -- See if i is a prime number
    SET j=2;
    SET is_prime=1;
    divisors: WHILE(j< i) DO
      IF MOD(i,j)=0 THEN
         SET is_prime=0;
         LEAVE divisors;
      END IF;
      SET j=j+1;
    END WHILE;

    IF is_prime THEN
      SET n_primes=n_primes+1;
    END IF;

    -- Move onto the next number
    IF (MOD(i,2)=0) THEN
      SET i=i+1;
    ELSE
      -- Next number is even, no need
```

```
      -- to check for it as a prime
      SET i=i+2;
    END IF;

  UNTIL (i=in_limit) END REPEAT;

  SELECT CONCAT(n_primes,' prime numbers <= ',in_limit);

END$$
```

Unfortunately, this routine has a bug that will lead to an infinite loop if the input number is even. A clever programmer altered the loop increment value so that even numbers—which can never be prime—were skipped as the loop incremented. Unfortunately, the UNTIL loop contains an equality check, i=in_limit, that will never be satisfied if the input parameter is even, and hence the loop will never terminate.

This bug could have been detected or averted in a number of ways:

- Walk-through of the program's algorithm
- Testing of the routine with a variety of inputs (including, of course, even numbers)
- Adoption of a defensive programming philosophy that could have led to the inclusion of a more robust i>in_limit condition in the UNTIL clause

LOOP-02: Make the termination conditions of a loop obvious

Loop logic is easier to determine if all the control logic is in one place, either in the WHILE or UNTIL clauses or in a LEAVE statement within the loop. It's particularly confusing to include a RETURN statement within a loop.

To that end, we suggest that you avoid LEAVE or RETURN statements within WHILE or REPEAT UNTIL loops.

Example

In the following example, borrowed from the prime number routine in the preceding section, a WHILE loop contains a LEAVE clause—there are two ways for the loop to terminate, and this makes the code harder to analyze and trace:

```
SET j=2;
SET is_prime=1;
divisors: WHILE(j< i) DO
  IF MOD(i,j)=0 THEN
    SET is_prime=0;
    LEAVE divisors;
  END IF;
  SET j=j+1;
END WHILE;
```

One way to improve the readability of the loop would be to move all of the termination logic into the WHILE clause:

```
SET j=2;
SET is_prime=1;
divisors: WHILE(j< i AND is_prime=1) DO
```

```
   IF MOD(i,j)=0 THEN
      SET is_prime=0;
   END IF;
   SET j=j+1;
END WHILE;
```

Alternatively, we could employ a simple loop and place all termination logic within the loop.

LOOP-03: Use a single LEAVE in simple loops

This best practice is another variation on "one way in, one way out." It suggests that, whenever possible, you consolidate all exit logic in your simple loop to a single LEAVE statement.

Example

Here is another variant on our prime counting loop. It contains some new logic to handle the special cases of 1 and 2 (1 is not prime; 2 is prime).

```
SET j=2;
SET is_prime=1;
divisors: LOOP
  IF (j=1) THEN
    SET is_prime=0;
    LEAVE divisors;
  END IF;

  IF (j=2) THEN
    SET is_prime=1;
    LEAVE divisors;
  END IF;

  IF MOD(i,j)=0 THEN
    SET is_prime=0;
  END IF;

  SET j=j+1;
  IF (is_prime=0 OR j>=i ) THEN
    LEAVE divisors;
  END IF;

END LOOP divisors;
```

The multiple LEAVE statements make it difficult for us to work out which segments of the code are actually executed for any given number. A rewrite that relies on a single LEAVE looks like this:

```
SET j=2;
SET is_prime=1;
divisors: LOOP

  IF (i=1) THEN
    SET is_prime=0;
```

```
    ELSEIF (i=2) THEN
      SET is_prime=1;

    ELSEIF MOD(i,j)=0 THEN
      SET is_prime=0;
      SELECT i,'is divisible by',j;

    END IF;


    IF (i=2 OR is_prime=0 OR j+1>=i ) THEN
      LEAVE divisors;
    END IF;

    SET j=j+1;

  END LOOP divisors;
```

Now we have a single place in the code where we make the decision to leave the loop, and, consequently, our code is more readable and robust.

LOOP-04: Use a simple loop to avoid redundant code required by a WHILE or REPEAT UNTIL loop

This guideline is particularly relevant when you are writing cursor loops.

The structure of MySQL cursors, and the necessity of setting an indicator variable to detect the end of the cursor, means that you usually want to execute the cursor loop at least once. You will then continue executing the loop until the indicator variable changes.

This sounds like a perfect opportunity to apply the REPEAT UNTIL loop. So as you start to create the program, you create a structure that looks like this:

```
DECLARE dept_csr CURSOR FOR
     SELECT department_name
       FROM departments;

DECLARE CONTINUE HANDLER FOR NOT FOUND SET no_more_departments=1;

OPEN dept_csr;
REPEAT
    FETCH dept_csr INTO  v_department_name;
UNTIL (no_more_departments) END REPEAT;

CLOSE dept_csr;
SET no_more_departments=0;
```

Of course, you always want to do something with the data fetched from a cursor, but you need to make sure that you don't try to process data after the last row has been returned. So in order to keep the REPEAT loop, you create an IF structure to enclose your processing:

```
DECLARE dept_csr CURSOR FOR
 SELECT department_name
   FROM departments;
```

```
DECLARE CONTINUE HANDLER FOR NOT FOUND SET no_more_departments=1;

    OPEN dept_csr;
    REPEAT
        FETCH dept_csr INTO  v_department_name;
            IF (no_more_departments=0) THEN
            SET v_count= v_count+1;
            END IF;
    UNTIL (no_more_departments) END REPEAT;

        CLOSE dept_csr;
      SET no_more_departments=0;
```

The problem with this solution is that you now have redundant tests to determine if you have reached the end of the cursor. If you change the CONTINUE handler, you will have to change your code in two places.

The code would be simpler and more maintainable if the test were conducted only once:

```
    DECLARE CONTINUE HANDLER FOR NOT FOUND SET no_more_departments=1;

    OPEN dept_csr;
    dept_loop: LOOP
        FETCH dept_csr INTO  v_department_name;
        IF (no_more_departments)  THEN
          LEAVE dept_loop;
        END IF;
        SET  v_count= v_count+1;

    END LOOP;
    CLOSE dept_csr;
    SET no_more_departments=0;
```

Exception Handling

Even if you write such amazing code that it contains no errors and never acts inappropriately, your users might still *use* your program incorrectly. The result? Situations that cause programs to fail. MySQL provides *exceptions* to help you catch and handle error conditions.

EXC-01: Handle exceptions that cannot be avoided but can be anticipated

If you are writing a program in which you can predict that a certain error will occur, you should include a handler in your code for that error, allowing for a graceful and informative failure.

Example

This recommendation is easily demonstrated with a simple, single-row lookup cursor. An error that often occurs is No data to FETCH, which indicates that the cursor didn't identify any rows. Consider the following function that returns the name of a department for its ID:

```
CREATE FUNCTION department_name(in_dept_id INT) RETURNS VARCHAR(30)
  READS SQL DATA
BEGIN
  DECLARE  v_dept_name VARCHAR(30);

  DECLARE dept_csr CURSOR FOR
  SELECT department_name
    FROM departments
   WHERE department_id=in_dept_id;

   OPEN dept_csr;
   FETCH dept_csr INTO  v_dept_name;
   CLOSE dept_csr;

  RETURN  v_dept_name;
END;
```

As currently coded, this function will raise the No data to FETCH error if an invalid department ID is passed in.

```
mysql> SELECT department_name(1);
+--------------------+
| department_name(1) |
+--------------------+
| DUPLIN             |
+--------------------+
1 row in set (0.00 sec)

mysql> SELECT department_name(60);
ERROR 1329 (02000): No data to FETCH
```

That may be fine for some scenarios, but in this particular case, we simply want to return a special string (No such Department). The program that calls department_name can then decide for itself if it wants or needs to raise an error or simply proceed. In this case, the solution is to add a simple CONTINUE handler:

```
CREATE FUNCTION department_name(in_dept_id INT) RETURNS VARCHAR(30)
  READS SQL DATA
BEGIN
  DECLARE  v_dept_name VARCHAR(30);

  DECLARE dept_csr CURSOR FOR
  SELECT department_name
    FROM departments
   WHERE department_id=in_dept_id;

  DECLARE CONTINUE HANDLER FOR NOT FOUND
          SET  v_dept_name='No such Department';

  OPEN dept_csr;
  FETCH dept_csr INTO  v_dept_name;
  CLOSE dept_csr;

  RETURN  v_dept_name;
END;
```

EXC-02: Use named conditions to improve code readability

Any MySQL programmer worth her salt knows all the MySQL error codes by heart, right? Wrong!

Exception handlers defined against MySQL error codes might work, but they will almost never be easy to read.

The best way to improve the readability of your exception handling routines is to define a named condition for every MySQL error code that you might be anticipating. So instead of the following declaration:

```
DECLARE CONTINUE HANDLER FOR 1216 mysql_statements;
```

you should use the following, more readable *pair* of declarations:

```
DECLARE foreign_key_error CONDITION FOR 1216;

DECLARE CONTINUE HANDLER FOR foreign_key_error mysql_statements;
```

EXC-03: Be consistent in your use of SQLSTATE and MySQL error codes in exception handlers

You often have the choice between a MySQL error code and an ANSI-standard SQLSTATE code when creating your exception handler. Be as consistent as possible in your choice between the two. In some cases, an explicit SQLSTATE code might not be available for the error you are trying to catch, and you will want to use a MySQL error code. Unless portability is your primary concern—and in reality, this will rarely be the case—we recommend that you use MySQL error codes exclusively in your stored programs.

EXC-04: Avoid global SQLEXCEPTION handlers until MySQL implements SIGNAL and SQLCODE features

In the initial 5.0 release of MySQL, it is not possible to access the MySQL error code or SQLSTATE code that caused a handler to be invoked. You also can't raise your own exceptions (the SIGNAL/RESIGNAL statements are not yet supported). What this means is that unless your handler is very specific, you won't know exactly why it was raised. Furthermore, you won't have a reliable mechanism for propagating the exception to the calling program.

Under normal circumstances, it can be very helpful to implement a general-purpose exception handler. This handler would acquire all kinds of handy information about the current state. If, however, you are unable to determine the error that was raised, this kind of general-purpose handler is of little use, and it can even cause a *loss* of useful information. For instance, in the following example, a general-purpose hander is invoked but cannot report accurately the reason it fired:

```
DECLARE CONTINUE HANDLER FOR SQLEXCEPTION
BEGIN
    SET  v_status=-1;
    SET  v_message='Some sort of error detected somewhere in the application';
END;
```

Given these restrictions, it is best not to create general SQLEXCEPTION handlers. Rather, you should handle only specific, foreseeable errors, and let the calling program handle any unexpected errors.

SQL in Stored Programs

One area in which the MySQL stored program language really shines is the ease with which you can include SQL inside of stored program code (this was, after all, one of the key motivations for the introduction of this functionality in MySQL). While you might occasionally write stored programs without any SQL, it would be almost completely pointless to use stored programs if it weren't for their ability to issue SQL.

Best practices related to SQL inside of MySQL stored programs are, therefore, among the most important in this chapter.

SQL-01: Start a transaction explicitly with the START TRANSACTION statement

Although MySQL will automatically initiate a transaction on your behalf when you issue DML statements, you should issue an explicit START TRANSACTION statement in your program to mark the beginning of your transaction.

It's possible that your stored program might be run within a server in which autocommit is set to TRUE, and by issuing an explicit START TRANSACTION statement you ensure that autocommit does not remain enabled during your transaction. START TRANSACTION also aids readability by clearly delineating the scope of your transactional code.

SQL-02: Don't leave transactions "dangling"

Once you start a transaction, you should take responsibility for completing the transaction. Since transactions lock rows and potentially block other transactions, you need to ensure that transactions do not persist indefinitely. Generally, you should place the START TRANSACTION and COMMIT or ROLLBACK statements in the same stored program. This program may also call other programs, and you need to make sure that these called programs do not contain transactional code.

There are some exceptions to this recommendation. In particular, modular design might prompt you to break down a transaction into separate modules and control the overall transaction state from a master procedure.

SQL-03: Avoid use of savepoints—they can obscure program logic and reduce program efficiency

Savepoints allow you to define a point within a transaction to which you can roll back without losing all of the changes made by the transaction. In essence, a savepoint facilitates the "partial rollback" of a transaction.

Indiscriminate use of savepoints can lead to inefficient and hard-to-maintain code. This is because when you roll back to a savepoint, your program flow is harder to follow, and you have almost by definition wasted system resources by issuing DML that you later aborted.

Quite often, you will find that instead of rolling back to a savepoint, you can simply issue a SELECT statement to validate an operation prior to actually issuing the DML. This technique was demonstrated in Chapter 8.

A valid use of a savepoint is within a stored program that you are using to execute a "nested" transaction without affecting the status of a transaction that may be in progress in the calling program. The "nested" program creates a savepoint and rolls back to that savepoint if any errors occur. In this way the procedure could be safely called by a program that has an open transaction, since any rollback issued in the nested program would affect only statements issued in that program.

SQL-04: Use an appropriate locking strategy

There are two major patterns in transaction management: the *optimistic* locking strategy and the *pessimistic* locking strategy.

The pessimistic locking strategy assumes that concurrent updates are quite likely. To prevent this, the transaction locks rows as they are read. Other transactions that want to update the row must wait until the pessimistic transaction ends.

The optimistic locking strategy assumes that in the period of time between a user reading and then updating a row, it is unlikely that another user will attempt to update that same row. Of course, optimism in and of itself is not sufficient; when following this locking strategy, the program should check to ensure that the row has not been updated, immediately prior to the update. If the row has been updated, then the transaction is aborted.

Each locking strategy is based on assumptions regarding the behavior of other transactions or application users. Each has different implications for the duration of any locks acquired during the transaction and the possibility that a transaction will be aborted. Make sure that you weigh carefully the implications of the two strategies and pick the approach that best suits your application.

SQL-05: Keep transactions small

The larger the transaction, the more likely it is that the transaction will lock rows needed by another transaction, and the greater the chance that a deadlock might occur. Transactions should therefore usually be no larger than is absolutely necessary.

SQL-06: Always reset the NOT FOUND variable after completing a cursor loop

You should usually terminate a cursor loop when a CONTINUE handler for the NOT FOUND condition fires and modifies the value of a status variable. For instance, in the following fragment, the CONTINUE handler sets the v_last_row_fetched variable to 1, and we test this value after each FETCH call:

```
DECLARE CONTINUE HANDLER FOR NOT FOUND SET  v_last_row_fetched=1;

OPEN cursor1;
cursor_loop:LOOP
    FETCH cursor1 INTO  v_customer_name, v_contact_surname, v_contact_firstname;
    IF  v_last_row_fetched=1 THEN
        LEAVE cursor_loop;
    END IF;
    -- Do something with the row fetched.
END LOOP cursor_loop;
CLOSE cursor1;
SET  v_last_row_fetched=0;
```

It is important to reset this status value to 0 after the cursor loop terminates; otherwise, subsequent or nested cursor loops may terminate prematurely.

The following code incorrectly fetches employees for only a single department, because after the first cursor loop, the status variable continues to indicate that the last row has been fetched:

```
DECLARE CONTINUE HANDLER FOR NOT FOUND
    SET  v_not_found=1;

SET  v_dept_id=1;
WHILE( v_dept_id<=10) DO
  OPEN dept_emp_csr;
  emp_loop:LOOP
    FETCH dept_emp_csr INTO  v_employee_id;
    IF  v_not_found THEN
      LEAVE emp_loop;
    END IF;
    CALL process_employee( v_employee_id);
  END LOOP;
  CLOSE dept_emp_csr;

  SET  v_dept_id= v_dept_id+1;
END WHILE;
```

SQL-07: Use SELECT FOR UPDATE when retrieving rows for later update

Use the SELECT FOR UPDATE statement to request that locks be placed on all rows identified by the query. You should do this whenever you expect to change some or all of those rows, and you don't want another session to change them out from under you. Any other session trying to update the rows, or lock the rows (perhaps using FOR UPDATE), will have to wait.

Example

Here we are processing a special bonus payment for needy employees. We issue the FOR UPDATE clause so that the rows concerned are locked until our transaction completes:

```
CREATE PROCEDURE needy_bonus( )
BEGIN
  DECLARE  v_employee_id INT;
  DECLARE  v_salary      NUMERIC(8,2);
  DECLARE  v_last_emp    INT DEFAULT 0;

  DECLARE emp_csr CURSOR FOR
   SELECT employee_id,salary
     FROM employees
    WHERE salary <45000
      FOR UPDATE;

  DECLARE CONTINUE HANDLER FOR NOT FOUND SET  v_last_emp=1;

  START TRANSACTION;
    OPEN emp_csr;
    emp_loop:LOOP
      FETCH emp_csr INTO  v_employee_id, v_salary;
      IF  v_last_emp THEN
        LEAVE emp_loop;
      END IF;
      CALL grant_raise( v_employee_id, v_salary);
    END LOOP emp_loop;
    CLOSE emp_csr;
    SET  v_last_emp=0;

  COMMIT;

END;
```

You can also use the LOCK IN SHARE MODE clause to lock the rows against update but continue to allow reads.

SQL-08: Avoid including SQL in functions that may be used in SQL

You are free to include SQL statements within stored functions (with the exception of SQL statements that return result sets to the calling program). You should, however, be very wary of doing so if you think that your stored function might itself be called inside a SQL statement.

When you use a function that contains SQL in a SQL statement, you are effectively "nesting" two SQL statements. For every row returned by the "outer" SQL, you will have to execute the "inner" SQL. Such nested SQL statements can exhibit extremely unpredictable or undesirable performance.

For instance, consider the simple stored function below:

```
CREATE FUNCTION cust_contact_name (in_customer_id INT)
  RETURNS VARCHAR(100)
  READS SQL DATA
```

```
BEGIN
  DECLARE  v_contact_name VARCHAR(100);

  SELECT CONCAT(contact_firstname,' ',contact_surname)
    INTO  v_contact_name
    FROM customers
  WHERE customer_id=in_customer_id ;

  RETURN( v_contact_name);

END$
```

It contains an efficient query, but nevertheless, if we include it in a query against the customers table as follows:

```
SELECT cust_contact_name(customer_id) FROM customers
```

our execution time is about five times greater than if we performed the same operation within the SQL itself:

```
SELECT CONCAT(contact_firstname,' ', contact_surname) FROM customers
```

The situation becomes even worse if the SQL inside the function is not completely optimized. In Chapter 10 we provide an example in which the use of a stored function inside a SQL statement lengthens execution time by a factor of 300!

Dynamic SQL

"Dynamic" means that the SQL statement that you execute is constructed, parsed, and compiled at runtime, not at the time the code is compiled. Dynamic SQL offers a tremendous amount of flexibility—but also complexity and more than a little risk.

In the MySQL stored program language, you can process dynamic SQL by using the MySQL prepared statement feature. You can create a prepared statement with the PREPARE statement, supplying the SQL text in a session variable. The SQL can then be executed with the EXECUTE statement.

DYN-01: Bind, do not concatenate, variable values into dynamic SQL strings

When you bind a variable value into a dynamic SQL string, you can insert a "placeholder" into the string. This allows MySQL to parse a "generic" version of that SQL statement, which can be used over and over again, regardless of the actual value of the variable, without repeated parsing.

This technique also makes your code more resistant to SQL injection attacks (see Chapter 18), since the value supplied to placeholders cannot include SQL fragments.

Example

Here's an example of binding with the PREPARE and EXECUTE statements. This program updates any numeric column in the specified table, based on the supplied name:

```
CREATE PROCEDURE update_anything
  (in_table     VARCHAR(60),
   in_where_col VARCHAR(60),
   in_set_col   VARCHAR(60),
   in_where_val VARCHAR(60),
   in_set_val   VARCHAR(60))
BEGIN

  SET @dyn_sql=CONCAT(
      'UPDATE ' , in_table ,
        ' SET ' , in_set_col, ' = ?
      WHERE ' , in_where_col, ' = ?');

  PREPARE s1 FROM @dyn_sql;
  SET @where_val=in_where_val;
  SET @set_val=in_set_val;
  EXECUTE s1 USING @where_val,@set_val;
  DEALLOCATE PREPARE s1;

END$$
```

If you want to update the salary of employee #1 to $100,000, you might call this stored procedure as follows:

```
CALL update_anything_g('employees','employee_id','salary',100000,1)
```

The dynamic SQL generated will look like this:

```
'UPDATE employees SET salary = ? WHERE employee_id = ?'
```

The ? characters indicate placeholders that will be replaced with the values for salary and employee_id. Those values are provided in the USING clause of the EXECUTE statement. Attempts to "inject" SQL into these values will fail (although injection into the table or column name parameters is still possible—we'll address that in the next best practice).

DYN-02: Carefully validate any parameter values that might be used to construct dynamic SQL

Whenever you create a dynamic SQL statement based on parameters to a procedure or user inputs, you should always guard carefully against SQL injection (see Chapter 18). SQL injection allows the user to provide fragments of SQL as parameters to your stored programs, potentially subverting the resulting dynamic SQL.

Therefore, you should always carefully validate the inputs to your stored programs if they contribute to your dynamic SQL.

In the previous example, we prevented SQL injection through the careful use of place-holders. Variable binding could not, however, address the potential vulnerability of concatenating in the names of tables and columns.

In the modified version below, we perform a SQL query to confirm that the parameter inputs do, in fact, represent valid table and column names. Once we validate the inputs, we then construct and execute the dynamic SQL:

```
CREATE PROCEDURE update_anything_2
  (in_table     VARCHAR(60),
```

```
    in_where_col VARCHAR(60),
    in_set_col   VARCHAR(60),
    in_where_val VARCHAR(60),
    in_set_val   VARCHAR(60))
BEGIN

  DECLARE  v_count INT;

  SELECT COUNT(*)
    INTO  v_count
    FROM information_schema.columns
   WHERE table_name=in_table
     AND column_name IN (in_set_col,in_where_col);

  IF ( v_count <2 ) THEN
     SELECT 'Invalid table or column names provided';
  ELSE
     SET @dyn_sql=CONCAT(
       'UPDATE ' , in_table ,
         ' SET ' ,in_set_col, ' = ?
          WHERE ' , in_where_col, ' = ?');

  SELECT @dyn_sql;
  PREPARE s1 FROM @dyn_sql;
  SET @where_val=in_where_val;
  SET @set_val=in_set_val;
  EXECUTE s1 USING @where_val,@set_val;
  DEALLOCATE PREPARE s1;
 END IF;

END;
```

DYN-03: Consider the invoker rights method for stored code that executes dynamic SQL

The *definer rights model*—in which stored programs execute with the permissions of the creator rather than the invoker—generally confers significant security advantages, since you can allow access to database objects only under the controlled conditions implemented in your stored programs.

However, in the case of stored programs that contain dynamic SQL, the definer rights model can create security concerns, since these programs can conceivably be vulnerable to SQL injection, as described in Chapter 18. Since the creator of the stored program is almost always a highly privileged user, the implications of SQL injection into a definer rights procedure is potentially very serious indeed.

Whenever you create a stored program that processes a dynamic SQL statement, you should consider defining the program with the *invoker rights model*. Do this by adding the following clause to the program header:

```
SQL SECURITY INVOKER
```

This clause ensures that the dynamic SQL string is parsed under the authority of the account currently running the program.

Without the SQL SECURITY INVOKER clause, the stored program will execute with the privileges of the user that created the stored program. Since—by definition—you don't know exactly the full text of the dynamic SQL to be executed, you almost always want the SQL to be rejected if the user does not have sufficient privileges.

Using the alternative *definer rights model* also magnifies the potential vulnerabilities created should your stored program be susceptible to SQL injection.

Example

In the previous examples, we created a stored program that would update the value of any column in any table. Since we omitted the SQL SECURITY clause, a user can use the stored program to update tables to which she wouldn't normally have access. We didn't intend that!

So we should have defined the stored program with invoker rights, as follows:

```
CREATE PROCEDURE update_anything_2
  (in_table     VARCHAR(60),
   in_where_col VARCHAR(60),
   in_set_col   VARCHAR(60),
   in_where_val VARCHAR(60),
   in_set_val   VARCHAR(60))
   SQL SECURITY INVOKER
BEGIN
. . . .
```

Program Construction

There are as many ways to write and structure a program as there are programmers—or so it sometimes seems. We offer suggestions on how to structure your programs and how best to design parameter lists that we have found effective.

PRG-01: Encapsulate business rules and formulas behind accurately named functions

This might be one of the most important best practices you will ever read—and, we hope, follow. There is only one aspect of every software project that never changes: the fact that everything always changes. Business requirements, data structures, user interfaces: all of these things change and change frequently. Your job as a programmer is to write code that adapts easily to these changes.

So whenever you need to express a business rule (such as, "Is this string a valid ISBN?"), put it inside a subroutine that hides the individual steps (which might change) and returns the results (if any).

And whenever you need a formula (such as, "the total fine for an overdue book is the number of days overdue times $.50"), express that formula inside its own function.

Example

Suppose that you must be at least 10 years old to borrow books from the library. This is a simple formula and very unlikely to change. We set about building the application by creating the following logic:

```
IF  v_dob > DATE_SUB(now( ), INTERVAL 10 YEAR) THEN
  SELECT 'Borrower must be at least 10 yrs old';
ELSE
  INSERT INTO borrower
    (firstname,surname,date_of_birth)
  VALUES( v_firstname, v_surname, v_dob);
END IF;
```

Later, while building a batch-processing script that checks and loads over 10,000 borrower applications, we include the following check in the program:

```
load_data:BEGIN
  IF DATEDIFF(now( ), v_dob)/365 < 10 THEN
    select ('Borrower  is not ten years old.');
  ELSE
    . . . load data . . .
  END IF;
END load_data;
```

And so on from there. We are left, unfortunately, with a real job on our hands when we get a memo that says: "In order to support a new city-wide initiative to increase literacy, the minimum age for a library card has been changed from 10 to 8." And then, of course and by the way, there is the minor bug we introduced into our second construction of the rule (we forgot about leap years).

If only we had created a simple function the first time we needed to calculate minimum valid age! It would be something like this:

```
CREATE FUNCTION borrower_old_enough (in_dob DATE)
  RETURNS INT
  NO SQL
BEGIN
  DECLARE  v_retval INT DEFAULT 0;
  IF (in_dob < DATE_SUB(NOW( ), INTERVAL 10 YEAR)) THEN
    SET  v_retval=1;
  ELSE
    SET  v_retval=0;
  END IF;
  RETURN( v_retval);
END;
```

And this function copes correctly with a NULL input, for which we forgot to check in those other programs. We can correct the age calculation logic in one place and easily change the minimum age from 10 to 8:

Benefits

You can update business rules and formulas in your code about as quickly and as often as users change that which was supposedly "cast in stone." Developers apply those rules consistently throughout the application base, since they are simply calling a program.

Your code is much easier to understand, since developers don't have to wade through complex logic to understand which business rule is being implemented.

Challenges

It's mostly a matter of discipline and advance planning. Before you start building your application, create a set of programs to hold business rules and formulas for distinct areas of functionality. Make sure that the names of the programs clearly identify their purpose. Then promote and use them rigorously throughout the development organization.

PRG-02: Standardize module structure using function and procedure templates

Once you adopt a set of guidelines for how developers should write procedures and functions, you need to help those developers follow their best practices. The bottom line is that guidelines will be followed if you make it easier to follow them than to ignore them.

For module standards, you can use either of the following approaches:

- Create a static template file that contains the generic logical structure for a procedure and/or function. Developers then copy that file to their own file, "de-genericize" the template by performing search-and-replace operations on placeholder strings with their own specific values (such as table names), and modify it from there.

- Use a program (one that you've written or a commercially available tool) that generates the code you want. This approach can be more flexible and can save you time, depending on how sophisticated a generator you use/create.

Example

Here's a simple function template that reinforces the single RETURN recommendation and encourages a standard header.

```
CREATE FUNCTION f_<name>
   (IN in_<parm> <datatype>)
      RETURNS <datatype>
      DETERMINISTIC
BEGIN
   /*
   || STANDARD COPYRIGHT STATEMENT HERE
   || Author:
   ||   File:
   ||
   || Modification history:
   */

   DECLARE retval <datatype> DEFAULT <value>
   -- Put your code here

   RETURN retval;

END
```

Some third-party products (Toad for MySQL, for instance) allow you to define such a template and have it automatically applied to new stored programs.

Benefits

The quality of each individual program is higher, since it's more likely to conform to best practices.

Programs are more consistent across the team and therefore easier to maintain and enhance.

PRG-03: Limit execution section sizes to a single page (50-60 lines) using modularization

Sure, you're laughing out loud. You write code for the real world. It's really complicated. Only 50 or 60 lines? You're lucky if your programs are less than 500 lines! Well, it's not a matter of complexity; it's more an issue of how you handle that complexity.

If your executable sections go on for hundreds of lines, with a loop starting on page 2 and ending on page 6, and so on, you will have a hard time "grasping the whole" and following the logic of the program.

An alternative is to use step-wise refinement (a.k.a. "top down decomposition"): don't dive into all the details immediately. Instead, start with a general description (written in actual code, mind you) of what your program is supposed to do. Then implement all subprogram calls in that description following the same method.

The result is that at any given level of refinement, you can take in and easily comprehend the full underlying logic at that level. This technique is also referred to as "divide and conquer."

Example

Consider the following procedure. The entire program might be hundreds of lines long, but the main body of assign_workload (starting with BEGIN /*main*/) is only 24 lines long. Not only that, you can read it pretty much as an exciting novel: "For every telesales rep, if that person's case load is less than his department's average, assign the next open case to that person and schedule the next appointment for that case" (well, maybe not *that* exciting).

```
CREATE PROCEDURE assign_workload( )
BEGIN /*main*/
  DECLARE  v_last_row INT DEFAULT 0;
  DECLARE  v_case_id, v_telesales_id, v_department_id  INT;

  DECLARE telesales_cur CURSOR FOR
    SELECT telesales_id,department_id FROM telesales;

  DECLARE CONTINUE HANDLER FOR NOT FOUND SET  v_last_row=1;

  OPEN telesales_cur;
  ts_loop:LOOP
    FETCH telesales_cur INTO  v_telesales_id, v_department_id;
    IF  v_last_row THEN LEAVE ts_loop; END IF;
```

```
      IF analysis_caseload( v_telesales_id)<
         analysis_avg_cases( v_department_id) THEN

         SET  v_case_id=assign_next_open_case( v_telesales_id);
         CALL schedule_case( v_case_id);
      END IF;
   END LOOP;
   CLOSE telesales_cur;
   SET  v_last_row=0;

  END$$
```

Benefits

You can implement complicated functionality with a minimum number of bugs by using step-wise refinement. A developer can understand and maintain a program with confidence if he can read and grasp the logic of the code.

Challenges

You have to be disciplined about holding off writing the low-level implementation of functionality. Instead, come up with accurate, descriptive names for procedures and functions that contain the implementations themselves.

Resources

http://www.construx.com: Contains lots of good advice on writing modular code.

PRG-04: Avoid side-effects in your programs

Build lots of individual programs. Design each program so that it has a single, clearly defined purpose. That purpose should, of course, be expressed in the program's name, as well as in the program header.

Avoid throwing extraneous functionality inside a program. Such statements are called *side-effects* and can cause lots of problems for people using your code—which means your code won't get used, except perhaps as source for a cut-and-paste session (or—in hardcopy form—for kindling).

Example

Here's a program that by name and "core" functionality displays information about all books published within a certain date range:

```
CREATE PROCEDURE book_details (
  in_start_date DATE,
  in_end_date   DATE)
BEGIN
  DECLARE  v_title, v_author VARCHAR(60);
  DECLARE  v_last_book,  v_book_id INT DEFAULT 0;

  DECLARE book_cur CURSOR FOR
```

```
      SELECT book_id,title,author
        FROM books
       WHERE date_published BETWEEN in_start_date
                   AND in_end_date;

   OPEN book_cur;
   book_loop:LOOP
     FETCH book_cur INTO  v_book_id, v_title, v_author;
     IF  v_last_book THEN LEAVE book_loop; END IF;

     CALL details_show( v_title, v_author);
     CALL update_borrow_history ( v_book_id);
   END LOOP;
 END$$
```

Notice, however, that it also updates the borrowing history for that book. Now, it might well be that at this point in time the display_book_info procedure is called only when the borrowing history also needs to be updated, justifying to some extent the way this program is written.

However, regardless of current requirements, the name of the program is clearly misleading; there is no way to know that display_book_info also updates borrowing history. This is a hidden side-effect, and one that can cause serious problems over time.

Benefits

Your code can be used with greater confidence, since it does only what it says (via its name, for the most part) it's going to do. Developers will call and combine single-purpose programs as needed to get their jobs done.

PRG-05: Avoid deep nesting of conditionals and loops

Many studies have confirmed that excessive nesting of IF, CASE, or LOOP structures leads to code that is difficult to understand. More than two or three levels of nesting is probably undesirable.

Consider the following logic:

```
IF  v_state='CA' THEN
    IF  v_quantity > 100 THEN
      IF  v_customer_status='A' THEN
        IF  v_product_code='X' THEN
           SET  v_discount=.04;
        ELSEIF  v_product_code='Y' THEN
           SET  v_discount=.04;
        ELSE
           SET  v_discount=.01;
        END IF;
      ELSE
        SET  v_discount=0;
      END IF;
    ELSEIF  v_quantity > 50 THEN
      SET  v_discount=.1;
    . . . More logic . . .
    END IF;
```

It's fairly difficult to determine which set of conditions is applied to any particular discount. For instance, consider the highlighted line above—it takes a bit of puzzling to work out which states, quantities, and so on are associated with this discount: and that is with the vast majority of the logic removed. There are a few possible solutions to this deep nesting:

- *Including multiple conditions in each IF or ELSEIF clause:* For instance, we might test for a specific combination of state, quantity, and status on the one line.
- *Removing parts of the logic to separate subroutines:* For instance, we might create separate subroutines that calculate discounts for each state.
- *Creating a data-driven solution:* For instance, in the above example it would probably be preferable to create a table that includes the discount for each combination of values.

PRG-06: Limit functions to a single RETURN statement in the executable section

A good general rule to follow as you write your stored programs is: "one way in and one way out." In other words, there should be just one way to enter or call a program (there is; you don't have any choice in this matter). And there should be one way out, one exit path from a program (or loop) on successful termination. By following this rule, you end up with code that is much easier to trace, debug, and maintain.

For a function, this means you should think of the executable section as a funnel; all the lines of code narrow down to the last executable statement:

```
RETURN return value;
```

Example

Here's a simple function that relies on multiple RETURNs:

```
CREATE FUNCTION status_desc (in_cd CHAR(1))
  RETURNS VARCHAR(20)

    DETERMINISTIC
BEGIN

  IF in_cd = 'C' THEN
     RETURN 'CLOSED';
  ELSEIF in_cd = 'O' THEN
     RETURN 'OPEN';
  ELSEIF in_cd = 'I' THEN
     RETURN 'INACTIVE';
  END IF;
END;
```

At first glance, this function looks very reasonable. Yet this function has a deep flaw, due to the reliance upon separate RETURNs: if you don't pass in "C", "O", or "I" for the cd_in argument, the function raises:

```
mysql> SELECT status_desc('A');
ERROR 1321 (2F005): FUNCTION status_desc ended without RETURN
```

Here's a rewrite that relies upon a single RETURN at the end of the function:

```
CREATE FUNCTION status_desc (in_cd CHAR(1))
  RETURNS VARCHAR(20)

    DETERMINISTIC
BEGIN
  DECLARE  v_status VARCHAR(20) ;
  IF in_cd = 'C' THEN
     SET  v_status='CLOSED';
  ELSEIF in_cd = 'O' THEN
     SET  v_status='OPEN';
  ELSEIF in_cd = 'I' THEN
     SET  v_status='INACTIVE';
  END IF;
  RETURN  v_status;
END$$
```

This program also safely and correctly returns NULL if the program doesn't receive a value of "C", "O", or "I", unlike the first implementation.

Benefits

You're less likely to write a function that raises the exception ERROR 1321 (2F005): FUNCTION %s ended without RETURN—a nasty and embarrassing error.

A single RETURN function is easier to trace and debug, since you don't have to worry about multiple exit pathways from the function.

PRG-07: Use stored programs to implement code common to multiple triggers

Because you often need to create both an UPDATE and an INSERT trigger to maintain a derived or denormalized column, you might find yourself replicating the same logic in each trigger. For instance, in a previous example we created BEFORE UPDATE and BEFORE INSERT triggers to calculate free shipping and discount rate. If the logic is nontrivial, you should implement the logic in a stored procedure or function and call that routine from your trigger.

Example

Imagine that we are trying to automate the maintenance of a superannuation (18K plan) for our employees. We might create a trigger as follows to automate this processing upon insertion of a new employee row:

```
CREATE TRIGGER employees_bu
    BEFORE UPDATE
    ON employees
     FOR EACH ROW
  BEGIN
    DECLARE  v_18k_contrib NUMERIC(4,2);

    IF NEW.salary <20000 THEN
      SET NEW.contrib_18k=0;
```

```
      ELSEIF NEW.salary <40000 THEN
        SET NEW.contrib_18k=NEW.salary*.015;
      ELSEIF NEW.salary<55000 THEN
        SET NEW.contrib_18k=NEW.salary*.02;
      ELSE
        SET NEW.contrib_18k=NEW.salary*.025;
      END IF;
    END$$
```

But we need to ensure that this column is maintained when we create a new employee row.
Instead of performing a copy-and-paste into a BEFORE INSERT trigger, we should locate this
logic in a stored function as follows:

```
    CREATE FUNCTION emp18k_contrib(in_salary NUMERIC(10,2))
      RETURNS INT
        DETERMINISTIC
    BEGIN
      DECLARE  v_contrib NUMERIC(10,2);
      IF  in_salary <20000 THEN
        SET  v_contrib=0;
      ELSEIF in_salary <40000 THEN
        SET  v_contrib=in_salary*.015;
      ELSEIF in_salary<55000 THEN
        SET  v_contrib=in_salary*.02;
      ELSE
        SET  v_contrib=in_salary*.025;
      END IF;

      RETURN( v_contrib);
    END;
```

Now we can use that function in both the INSERT and the UPDATE triggers. If the logic
changes, we can modify the logic in one place and can therefore eliminate the risk of any
inconsistency between inserted and updated rows.

```
    DROP TRIGGER employees_bu$$

    CREATE TRIGGER employees_bu
        BEFORE UPDATE
        ON employees
         FOR EACH ROW
      BEGIN
        SET NEW.contrib_18k=emp18k_contrib(NEW.salary);
      END;
```

Performance

Most of the best practices outlined so far concentrate on the maintainability and correctness of our stored programs. The following practices concentrate on the performance of stored programs.

PER-01: Concentrate on tuning SQL to improve stored program performance

There are many ways to improve stored program performance, but none of these are likely to have much effect if the SQL within the stored program is inefficient.

Most stored programs contain SQL, and for almost all of those stored programs, the SQL makes up the vast majority of stored program elapsed time. Attempts to tune the stored program by other means (loop tuning, for instance) should only be attempted once the SQL in the stored program has been tuned.

PER-02: Carefully create the best set of indexes for your application

The primary purpose of indexes is to allow MySQL to rapidly retrieve the information you need. Just as the index in this book allows you to find some information without having to read the entire book, an index allows MySQL to get rows from the table without reading the entire table.

Determining the optimal set of indexes for your application is, therefore, probably the single most important step you can take to optimize MySQL stored program performance. In general, you should create indexes that support WHERE clause conditions and joins. You should also create multicolumn (concatenated) indexes, so that a single index can support all of the columns in the WHERE clause or all of the columns required to join two tables.

You should create indexes to support joins, since without an appropriate index, joins will degrade rapidly as the row counts in the involved tables increase.

PER-03: Avoid accidental table scans

One of the most common causes of poor application performance is the "accidental" full table scan. An accidental table scan occurs when the nature of the query, or the expectations of the programmer, suggests that the query will be satisfied using an index, but instead a full table scan is performed.

Accidental table scans can occur under the following circumstances:

- The index that you believe supports the query does not exist.
- You have an index that includes the columns in the query, but you don't include the foremost, "leading" columns in your query.
- You suppress an index by enclosing the column concerned with a function or an expression.
- You specify a nonleading substring as the search condition. For instance, you try to find all employees whose name ends in "STONE" (WHERE name LIKE '%STONE').

Most accidental table scans can be resolved by creating a new index or rewording the SQL so that the index is not suppressed. See Chapters 20 and 21 for more details.

PER-04: Optimize necessary table scans

Using an index to retrieve rows from a table is worthwhile only when you are retrieving a relatively small subset of rows from the table. Over a certain proportion of the table (say 5-20%), it is more efficient to read every row from the table. However, it is still possible to optimize these "necessary" table scans. For instance:

- You can move long, infrequently accessed columns to a secondary table.
- You can create an index on all of the columns required for the query. MySQL can then scan the entire index to resolve the query. Since the index will normally be smaller than the table, it ought to be quicker to scan the index.

These techniques are discussed in detail in Chapter 21.

PER-05: Avoid using stored programs for computationally expensive routines

Like most stored program implementations, MySQL stored programs are optimized for database access, not computational speed. If you have a choice, place your most computationally expensive routines in client or middle-tier code. For instance, you might want to implement your most expensive calculations in PHP or Java rather than in stored programs.

PER-06: Move loop invariant expressions outside of loops

Whenever you set out to tune your stored programs (having completed your SQL optimization), you should first take a look at your loops. Any inefficiency inside a loop's body will be magnified by the multiple executions of that code.

A common mistake is to put execute code within the body of a loop that has the same result with each iteration of the loop. When you identify such a scenario, extract the static code, assign the outcomes of that code to one or more variables in advance of the loop, and then reference those variables inside the loop.

Example

At first glance, this loop block seems sensible enough, but in reality it is quite inefficient:

```
WHILE (i<=1000) do
    SET j=1;
    WHILE (j<=1000) do
      SET counter=counter+1;
      SET sumroot=sumroot+sqrt(i)+sqrt(j);
      SET j=j+1;
    END WHILE;
    SET i=i+1;
END WHILE;
```

This code contains two loops: we calculate the square root of i inside of the inner loop, even though it only changes for each iteration of the outer loop. Consequently, we calculate the square root 1,000,000 times, even though we have only 1,000 distinct values.

Here's the optimized version of that same code:

```
WHILE (i<=@i) do
      SET rooti=sqrt(i);
      SET counter=counter+1;
      SET j=1;
      WHILE (j<=@j) do
        SET sumroot=sumroot+rooti+sqrt(j);
        SET j=j+1;
      END WHILE;
      SET i=i+1;
   END WHILE;
```

A small change, but one that will have a massive effect on performance.

PER-07: Optimize conditional structures

The performance of IF and CASE statements is highly dependent on the number of comparisons that the statement must execute. The number of comparisons can be optimized in two ways:

- By placing the comparisons that are most frequently true earliest in the set of comparisons, you reduce the number of comparisons that must be executed.
- If any comparison is repeated in multiple expressions within the CASE or IF statement, you can extract that comparison and "nest" multiple CASE or IF statements. The inner comparisons need only be executed when the outer comparison evaluates to TRUE.

PER-08: Structure IF and CASE statements so more likely expressions appear earliest in the list

When MySQL processes a CASE or an IF statement, it works through every ELSEIF or WHEN condition in the statement until if finds a condition that returns TRUE. If you place the condition that is most likely to evaluate to TRUE at the beginning of your conditional statement, you will improve the overall efficiency of your program.

Your primary concern, however, should be the readability of your IF and CASE statement. Don't worry about reorganizing the clauses of your IF and CASE statements unless you have identified them as a bottleneck in application performance.

Example

In this example the most likely condition is tested last:

```
IF (percentage>95) THEN
    SET Above95=Above95+1;
ELSEIF (percentage >=90) THEN
    SET Range90to95=Range90to95+1;
ELSEIF (percentage >=75) THEN
    SET Range75to89=Range75to89+1;
ELSE
    SET LessThan75=LessThan75+1;
END IF;
```

To optimize the statement, we can reword it so that in most cases, only one comparison is necessary:

```
IF (percentage<75) THEN
    SET LessThan75=LessThan75+1;
ELSEIF (percentage >=75 AND percentage<90) THEN
    SET Range75to89=Range75to89+1;
ELSEIF (percentage >=90 and percentage <=95) THEN
    SET Range90to95=Range90to95+1;
ELSE
    SET Above95=Above95+1;
END IF;
```

Conclusion

In this final chapter, we've attempted to enumerate coding practices that will result in efficient, robust, and easily maintainable stored programs. These practices are based on lessons learned in various development environments—including Oracle and SQL Server stored procedures—as well as from our experiences with the MySQL stored program language. We hope that you find these practices worthy of consideration. We do not, however, hope or expect that you will automatically adopt every recommendation. As always, you should exercise your judgment, tempered by your unique understanding of your own specific requirements, before adopting any standard, recommendation, or practice.

Index

Symbols

/* */ (multi-line comments), 60
( ) (parentheses), applying to
        expressions, 542
- - (single-line comments), 60
+ (addition) operator, 61
& (AND) operator, 62, 64
/ (division) operator, 61
= (is equal to) operator, 62
> (is greater than) operator, 62
< (is less than) operator, 62
<– (is less than or equal to) operator, 62
<>,!= (is not equal to) operator, 62
% (modulus) operator, 61
* (multiplication) operator, 61
<=> (null safe equal) operator, 62
| (OR) operator, 63, 64
; (semicolons) in code, 165
<< (shifts bits to left) operator, 64
>> (shifts bits to right) operator, 64
- (subtraction) operator, 61
˜ (NOT or invert bits) operator, 64

A

ABS function, 218
abstraction, stored programs, 265
access, 140
    column values, 369
    DataReader metadata, 394
    locks
        deadlocks, 193
        timeouts, 196
    restricting, 430

result sets, DataSets, 395–397
    SQLSTATE code, 140
    tables
        direct, 430
        SQL tuning, 463–480
ACID (atomic, consistent, isolated,
        durable), 179
ACOS function, 223
actions, triggering, 250
ADDDATE function, 232
adding dummy ELSE clauses, 91
addition (+) operator, 61
ADDTIME function, 223
ADO.NET
    applying, 401–412
    calling, 391
    dynamic result sets, 405–408
    error handling, 154, 397
    input parameters, 402
    multiple result sets, 404
    output parameters, retrieving, 410–412
    overview of, 386–401
    stored functions, calling, 412
    stored programs
        calling, 401
        DataReader, 403
        DataSets, 408–410
        input parameters, 402
    transaction management, 398–401
    (see also .NET)
AFTER clause triggers, 251
algorithms
    Fibonacci, 526
    MERGE, 498
    TEMPFILE, 498

We'd like to hear your suggestions for improving our indexes. Send email to *index@oreilly.com*.

external files, maintaining stored programs in, 167
Extra column in EXPLAIN statement, 453
EXTRACT function, 228

F

FALSE, IF statements, 83
FETCH statements, cursors, 102
fetchall( ) method, 368
fetch_field( ) method, 288
fetching
    multiple result sets, 288
    single rows from cursors, 103
fetchmany( ) method, 369
fetch_object( ) method, 278, 284
fetchone( ) method, 368
fetch_row( ) method, 279
fetchrow_array method, 349
fetchrow_arrayref method, 349
fetchrow_hashref method, 349
Feuerstein, Steven, 13
Fibonacci sequences, 526
FIELD function, 217
FieldCount( ) method, 394
files, maintaining in external, 167
finder method (EJB), 331
FLOOR function, 219
flow of control, statements, 82–93
flow of execution, stored statements, 30
FORCE INDEX hint, 467, 472
<form> tag, 383
FORMAT numeric function, 219
formatting
    CASE statements, 580
    connections, MySQLdb extensions, 365
    cursors, 101–112
    exceptions, SIGNAL statements, 141
    IF statements, 85, 580
    indexes, 467, 578
        avoiding sorts, 501
    stored functions, 238–242
    stored programs, 159–166
    temporary tables, 117
    triggers, 249–251
forms, ASP.NET, 414
FOUND error handler, 33
fragmentation, logic, 269
FROM clauses, subqueries, 495–500
FROM_DAYS function, 233
full table scans, 463, 464

functions
  built-in, 64–68, 205–237
    ABS, 218
    ACOS, 223
    ADDDATE, 232
    ADDTIME, 223
    ASCII, 206
    ASIN, 223
    ATAN, 223
    BENCHMARK, 233
    BIN, 218
    BINARY, 216
    BIT_LENGTH, 216
    CEILING, 218
    CHAR, 207
    CHARACTER_LENGTH, 216
    CHAR_LENGTH, 216
    CHARSET, 208
    COALESCE, 234
    COMPRESS, 216
    CONCAT, 208–210
    CONCAT_WS, 210
    CONV, 219
    CONVERT_TZ, 223
    COT, 223
    CRC32, 223
    CURDATE, 232
    CURRENT_DATE, 224
    CURRENT_TIME, 224
    CURRENT_TIMESTAMP, 224
    CURRENT_USER, 234
    CURTIME, 232
    DATABASE, 234
    DATE, 224
    DATE_ADD, 224
    DATEDIFF, 227
    DATE_FORMAT, 225
    DATE_SUB, 226
    DAY, 225, 228
    DAY_HOUR, 225
    DAY_MINUTE, 225
    DAYNAME, 228
    DAYOFMONTH, 232
    DAYOFWEEK, 228
    DAYOFYEAR, 228
    DAY_SECOND, 225
    DECODE, 217
    DEGREES, 223
    ELT, 217
    ENCODE, 217
    ENCRYPT, 217

functions
  built-in *(continued)*
    VERSION, 236
    WEEK, 231
    WEEKDAY, 232
    WEEKOFYEAR, 233
    YEAR, 225, 232
    YEARWEEK, 232
    CREATE FUNCTION statement, 21,
      171, 238
    encapsulating, 569
    expressions, replacing, 546
    html_table, 384
    IF statements, 67
    indexes, suppressing, 473
    limiting, 575
    mathematical, 65
    SET statements, 67
    stored, 4, 6, 9
      ADO.NET, 412
      applying, 244–248
      best practices, 565
      calling, 242–244, 273
      creating, 238–242
      SQL statements in, 242
    UDFs, 244

G

generating statistics, 513
getColumnMeta( ) method, 295
getErrorCode( ) method, 152, 317
GetFieldType( ) method, 394
GETFORMAT function, 229
GetInt32( ) method, 393
GET_LOCK function, 234
getMessage( ) method, 152, 317
GetName( ) method, 394
getNamedQuery( ) method, 335
getSQLState( ) method, 152
getStackTrace( ) method, 317
GetString( ) method, 393
global variables, 549
  user variables, applying as, 59
GRANT statement, 423
GROUP BY clause, 501–502
grouping code segments, 78

H

handling, 398
  dynamic result sets, Perl, 356
  exceptions
    best practices, 559–562
    MySQLdb extensions, 366
  invoker rights security, 433
  multiple result sets, 299
    Perl, 355
  output parameters, 287, 302
  output variables, Perl, 357
  transactions, JDBC, 315
  (see also error handling)
Harrison, Guy, 13
HEX function, 219
Hibernate, stored procedures, 332–337
hints
  FORCE INDEX, 467, 472
  IGNORE INDEX, 466
  manually choosing an index, 466
  optimizer, 455, 465
  USE INDEX, 466
history of MySQL, 5–7
hostnames, Perl, 346
HOUR function, 225, 233
HOUR_MINUTE function, 225
HOUR_SECOND function, 225
HTML (Hypertext Markup Language), 381
html_table function, 384
Hypertext Markup Language (see HTML)

I

id column in EXPLAIN statement, 451
IDE (Integrated Development Environment)
  ADO.NET, configuring, 386
  configuring, 310
IF statements, 8, 82–88
  CASE statements, comparing, 92
  formatting, 580
  functions, 67
  optimizing, 522–526
  tuning, 524
IFNULL function, 235
IF-THEN-ELSE statements, 85, 86
IGNORE INDEX hint, 466
implementing
  logging, 253
  security policies, 427–431
IN attribute, 53
IN operator, 62
IN parameter, 28

J

J2EE applications, 323–332
Java, 261, 310–342
  CallableStatement interface, 317
  calling, 273
  connections, 310
  EJBs, 328–332
  error handling, 152, 316
  Hibernate, 332–337
    queries, 335
    support, 333
  IDE, configuring, 310
  input parameters, 319
  non-SELECT statement, 312
  objects, loading, 333
  OUT variables, 319
  output parameter values, 322
  overhead, 512
  persistence, 336
  prepared statements, 313
  procedures, executing, 320
  result sets, 321
    metadata, 313
    retrieving, 312
  servlets, 324–328
  Spring, 337–342
  statistics, generating, 513
  transactions, handling, 315
  type checking, 73
JBoss, xiii
JDBC (Java Database Connectivity)
  error handling, 152
  overview of, 310–317
  stored functions, 244
  stored programs, applying, 317–323
joins
  anti-joins, tuning, 493–496
  example of, 483
  with indexes, 481
  without indexes, 480
  ordering, 482
  overhead, 480
  self-joins, avoiding, 515
  single-sweep multi-joins, 480
  SQL tuning, 480–484
  subqueries
    applying in complex, 490
    rewriting as, 488
  tables, 480

K

key caches, 446
key column in EXPLAIN statement, 453
KEY_BUFFER_SIZE parameter, 446
key_len column in EXPLAIN statement, 453
keywords
  language SQL, 170
  MySQLConnection object, 388
  SQL SECURITY
    {DEFINER|INVOKER}, 171
Kline, Kevin, 14
Krukenberg, Michael, 14

L

labels, 541
  blocks, 79
  exiting, 81
LAMJ (Linux-Apache-MySQL-JBoss), xiii
LAMP (Linux-Apache-MySQL-PHP/Perl/
  Python), xiii, 275
LANGUAGE SQL keyword, 170
languages
  built-in functions, 64–68
  data types, 68–71
  expressions, 64
  Java, 261, 310–342
  literals, 51–60
  .NET, 261, 386–418
  operators, 60
    bitwise, 63
    comparison, 61
    logical, 62–63
    mathematical, 61
  Perl, 261, 343–363
  PHP, 261, 275–308
  PL/SQL, 7
  Python, 261, 364-385
  SQL, 7
  stored programs
    applying, 4
  strict mode, 72–76
  Transact SQL, 7
  variables, 49–51
  (see also specific languages)
Larsson, Allan, 5
last row conditions, error handling, 128–129
LAST_DAY function, 233
LCASE function, 212
LEAST function, 219

triggers, 4, 6, 12
    actions, 250
    applying, 251–256
    check constraint, 254
    column values, 250
    CREATE TRIGGER statement, 21
    creating, 249–251
    data, validating, 254–256
    DML performance, 506
    indexes, 531
    multiple, 576
    overhead, 256, 529
    tutorial, 43–45
    (see also stored programs)
TRIM function, 216
troubleshooting
    stored procedures, 32
    stored programs, 10
TRUE, IF statements, 83
truth tables
    AND operator, 62
    OR operator, 63
    XOR operator, 63
try blocks, 370
tuning (SQL), 443, 578
    anti-joins, 493–496
    DML, 503–506
    examples of, 459–461
    FROM clause, 495–500
    GROUP BY clause, 501–502
    IF statements, 524
    joins, 480–484
    ORDER clause, 501–502
    statements, 449–459
    stored programs, 508
    subqueries, 486–493
    table access, 463–480
    (see also optimizing)
tutorials
    stored functions, 41–43
    stored procedures, 20
        calling stored programs, 38–39
        conditional execution, 30
        creating procedures, 21–23
        creating procedures using MySQL
            Query Browsers, 20–25
        database interactions, 33
        error handling, 32
        loops, 31
        parameters, 27–29

PHP, calling from, 45
    SELECT INTO syntax, 33–37
    variables, 25, 27
    triggers, 43–45
types
    of built-in functions, 64–68
    of columns in EXPLAIN statement, 452
    of comments, 60
    of condition handlers, 130
    of cursor loops, 105–108
    of data types, 68–71
    of expressions, 64
    of literals, 51
    of loops, 31
    of stored programs, 4

U

UCASE function, 216
UDFs (user-defined functions), 244
unbounded SELECT statements,
        applying, 112–118
UNCOMPRESS function, 218
UNCOMPRESSED_LENGTH function, 217
UNHEX function, 218
Unireg, 5
Unix, xiii
    installing DBD::mysql drivers, 344
unnamed views, 495
UNTIL loops, 95
UPDATE statements
    correlated updates, optimizing, 517
    embedding, 38
updating
    Hibernate, 337
    SELECT FOR UPDATE statement, 564
UPPER function, 218
USE INDEX hint, 466
USER function, 236
user variables, 57
user-defined functions (see UDFs)
utilities, MyTrace.pl, 461
UUID function, 236

V

validating
    code injection, binding parameters, 437
    correct behavior, 76
    data (with triggers), 254–256
    parameter values, 567

values
- columns
  - accessing, 369
  - triggers, 250
- literals, 51–60
- NULL, 50
- output parameters, retrieving, 322
- parameters, validating, 567
- triggers, setting, 45
- variables, 49–51
  - assigning, 52
  - binding, 566
- (see also NULL values)

variables, 25, 27
- best practices, 544–551
- bind, Perl, 348
- creating, 50
- declaring, 51
- deleting, 547
- dynamic typing (in PHP), 74
- global, 549
- languages, 49–51
- naming, 52, 545
- OUT, registering, 319
- output, Perl, 357
- overloading, 80
- overriding, 80, 546
- scope, controlling, 78
- SELECT INTO syntax, 33–37
- stored procedures, defining cursors, 102
- user, 57
- values
  - assigning, 52
  - binding, 566

VB.NET
- connecting to MySQL, 389
- DataReader, applying, 394
- DataSets, populating, 396
- dynamic result sets, 407
- error handling, 155, 397
- multiple result sets, 405
- output parameters, 410
- parameters, applying, 391

stored functions, 412
stored procedures
- calling, 401
- calling input parameters, 403
- DataReader, 403
- transaction management, 400
VERSION function, 236
vertical code alignment, 542
viewing
- index statistics, 448
- stored procedures, 430
- stored programs, 431
- table statistics, 448
views
- applying, 498
- referencing, 499

W

walkthroughs, code, 536
Wall, Larry, 343
web sites, resources, xiii
WEEK function, 231
WEEKDAY function, 232
WEEKOFYEAR function, 233
WHILE loops, 8, 96
WHILE-END WHILE loops, 107
Widenius, Michael "Monty", 5
Williams, Hugh, Lane, David, 13
Windows, installing DBD::mysql
    drivers, 345

X

XOR operator, 63

Y

YEAR function, 225, 232
YEARWEEK function, 232

Z

Zawodny, Jeremy, 14

About the Authors

Guy Harrison has worked with relational databases for more than 15 years as a developer, administrator, and performance expert. He is the author of many articles for database technical journals, as well as *Oracle SQL High Performance Tuning* (Prentice Hall, 1997, 2000) and *Oracle Desk Reference* (Prentice Hall, 2000). He is the Chief Architect of Database Solutions at Quest Software, where he was the originator of the popular Spotlight database diagnostic product line, including Spotlight on MySQL and Spotlight on Oracle. Guy lives in Melbourne, Australia with his wife Jenni; children Christopher, Kate, Michael, and William; one dog; and no cats.

Steven Feuerstein is the author or coauthor of *Oracle PL/SQL Programming*, *Oracle PL/SQL Best Practices*, *Oracle PL/SQL for DBAs*, *Oracle PL/SQL Developer's Workbook*, *Oracle Built-in Packages*, and several pocket reference books (all from O'Reilly Media). Steven has been developing software since 1980. He spent five years with Oracle (1987–1992) and now serves as a Senior Technology Advisor to Quest Software. His products include utPLSQL (an open source unit-testing framework for PL/SQL) and Qnxo (active mentoring software that helps to generate, reuse, and test code; *http://www.qnxo.com*). He has won numerous awards for his writing and trainings, offers a PL/SQL portal at *http://www.oracleplsqlprogramming.com*, and can be reached via email at *steven@stevenfeuerstein.com*. He lives in Chicago with his wife, Veva, and three cats. Two sons, Eli and Chris, orbit nearby.

Colophon

The animal on the cover of *MySQL Stored Procedure Programming* is a middle spotted woodpecker (*Dendrocopos medius*). Often mistaken for the more common great spotted woodpecker, the middle spotted woodpecker is distinguished by its smaller size and bright red crown. The bird can be found high among the trees in the deciduous forests of Europe and southwest Asia. Preferring oaks, hornbeams, and elms, the woodpecker tends to stay in the same area once it finds a patchwork of these trees. Despite their non-migratory nature, middle spotted woodpeckers are constantly on the move, making them difficult to spot and a rare treat for birdwatchers.

The cover image is from *Wood's Animate Creation*. The cover font is Adobe ITC Garamond. The text font is Linotype Birka; the heading font is Adobe Myriad Condensed; and the code font is LucasFont's TheSans Mono Condensed.

Better than e-books

Buy *MySQL Stored Procedure Programming* and
access the digital edition FREE on Safari for 45 days.

Go to www.oreilly.com/go/safarienabled
and type in coupon code Q3A2-Y3AC-TCQB-B3B7-87DV

Search
thousands of
top tech books

Download
whole chapters

Cut and Paste
code examples

Find
answers fast

Search Safari! The premier electronic reference
library for programmers and IT professionals.

Related Titles from O'Reilly

Oracle PL/SQL

Learning Oracle PL/SQL

Oracle PL/SQL Best Practices

Oracle PL/SQL for DBAs

Oracle PL/SQL Language Pocket Reference, *3rd Edition*

Oracle PL/SQL Programming, *4th Edition*

Oracle Books for DBAs

Oracle DBA Checklists Pocket Reference

Oracle DBA Pocket Guide

Oracle RMAN Pocket Reference

Unix for Oracle DBAs Pocket Reference

Oracle SQL and SQL Plus

Mastering Oracle SQL, *2nd Edition*

Oracle SQL Plus: The Definitive Guide, *2nd Edition*

Oracle SQL Tuning Pocket Reference

Oracle SQL*Plus Pocket Reference, *3rd Edition*

Oracle

Building Oracle XML Applications

Optimizing Oracle Performance

Oracle Application Server 10*g* Essentials

Oracle Essentials: Oracle Database 10*g*, *3rd Edition*

Oracle in a Nutshell

Oracle Regular Expressions Pocket Reference

Perl for Oracle DBAs

SQL Cookbook

SQL in a Nutshell, *2nd Edition*

SQL Pocket Guide

TOAD Pocket Reference for Oracle, *2nd Edition*

O'REILLY®

Our books are available at most retail and online bookstores.

To order direct: 1-800-998-9938 • *order@oreilly.com* • *www.oreilly.com*

Online editions of most O'Reilly titles are available by subscription at *safari.oreilly.com*